P9-DEQ-912

STATISTICAL QUALITY CONTROL

Strategies and Tools for Continual Improvement

JOHANNES LEDOLTER
CLAUDE W. BURRILL
University of Iowa

JOHN WILEY & SONS, INC.
New York • Chichester • Weinheim • Brisbane • Singapore • Toronto

To our spouses, Lea and Shew Hui, and our children, Thomas, Jeffrey, and Thomas.

ACQUISITIONS EDITOR Brad Wiley II
MARKETING MANAGER Leslie Hines
DESIGNER Karin Kincheloe
FREELANCE PRODUCTION MANAGER Jeanine Furino
ILLUSTRATION EDITOR Sigmund Malinowski
ELECTRONIC ILLUSTRATIONS Wellington
OUTSIDE PRODUCTION SERVICES Susan Reiland

This book was set in Helvetica by TechBooks and printed and bound by Quebecor Printing/Fairfield. The cover was printed by Phoenix Color Corporation.

This book is printed on acid-free paper. ♾

The paper in this book was manufactured by a mill whose forest management programs include sustained yield harvesting of its timberlands. Sustained yield harvesting principles ensure that the numbers of trees cut each year does not exceed the amount of new growth.

ISBN 0-471-18378-4

Printed in the United States of America

10 9 8 7 6 5 4 3 2 1

AUTHORS

Johannes Ledolter is a Professor at the University of Iowa in the Department of Statistics and Actuarial Science and the Department of Management Sciences, and a Professor at the Wirtschaftsuniversität Vienna, Austria. He received a Ph.D. in Statistics from the University of Wisconsin-Madison in 1975. Professor Ledolter held visiting positions at the University of Wisconsin, Princeton University, and Yale University. His area of research centers around time series analysis and forecasting, statistical methods for quality improvement, and applications of statistics in business and engineering. He has coauthored the books *Statistical Methods for Forecasting*, published by Wiley in 1983, and *Applied Statistics for Engineers and Physical Scientists*, published by Macmillan (Prentice Hall) in 1992. He and Dr. Burrill are coauthors of the book *Achieving Quality Through Continual Improvement*, published by Wiley in 1999. Professor Ledolter is a Fellow of the American Statistical Association, and an Elected Member of the International Statistical Institute.

Dr. Claude W. Burrill is a consultant on quality and project management. He is an Adjunct Professor in the School of Business at the University of Iowa. He received a Ph.D. in Mathematics from the University of Iowa in 1952, and an honorary doctorate from William Patterson College of New Jersey in 1979. His experience includes a year as a Fulbright Scholar at the University of Manchester, UK, ten years as a member of the New York University Graduate Center at Bell Labs, and ten years as a member of the IBM Systems Research Institute. He has held visiting faculty appointments at Columbia University, Dartmouth College, and the National University of Singapore, and has lectured and consulted internationally. He has authored or coauthored eight books on a variety of topics, including mathematics, probability, computer modeling, quality, and project management. He and Professor Ledolter are coauthors of the book *Achieving Quality Through Continual Improvement*, published by Wiley in 1999.

PREFACE

This is a book on problem-solving tools and their use in quality improvement. The book is appropriate as a text for use in colleges, primarily for undergraduate and graduate-level courses on quality. These courses are typically taught in Industrial Engineering programs, Departments of Statistics, and Schools of Business and Management. This text is also appropriate for use in two-year colleges, as well as for in-house company training courses on quality.

Courses on quality are generally taught in two different ways: "technique-oriented" courses, which emphasize the statistical tools, and "management-oriented" courses, which stress the managerial side of quality. This book is intended as a main text for a technique-oriented course. However, it is also useful in a managerial-type course on quality, as it serves as a useful primer and reference book on problem-solving tools.

Problem-solving skills are important for improving quality. This text provides the reader with a general and widely applicable problem-solving strategy. It covers a variety of "nonstatistical" problem-solving tools, which are neglected in most statistically oriented texts on quality. Furthermore, it discusses techniques that are useful when problems are solved by groups or teams of people. This discussion is important since most problem solving takes place within an organizational framework; in addition to the technical aspects, there is a human side to problem solving that cannot be neglected. This book shows how the success of problem solving is influenced by the style of management and the type of management–employee interaction.

This book gives a comprehensive treatment of statistical tools for problem solving and quality improvement. Our discussion starts from elementary principles of data analysis. No prior background in statistics is needed; only minimal mathematics background is required. The coverage is self-contained, and concepts and techniques are presented in a logical sequence. This text is not intended to be a "cookbook"; the emphasis of this book is on understanding and on laying the foundation for further continual learning.

The book provides a solid introduction to commonly used probability distributions, including the binomial, Poisson, and normal distributions, and it illustrates their importance in the quality arena. An introduction to surveys and sampling is given, and it is shown how methods of statistical inference can be used to generalize sample findings. The text covers sample inspection plans, statistical process control, control charts, and capability indexes. It provides an extensive discussion of the statistical design of experiments; this discussion starts from basic principles, and proceeds to the analysis of factorial and fractional factorial designs. The book also contains a chapter on Taguchi methods, illustrating their main features with examples that can be easily understood. Furthermore, the text includes a comprehensive chapter on regression.

Appropriate exercises are included in each chapter, and many references for further reading are listed. Each major section of the book concludes with the assignment of several projects. The aim of these end-of-section projects is to show, by example, how quantitative analysis can contribute to the solution of problems. Problem-solving techniques and statistical analysis are most meaningful when you have personal experience with their use.

Several large data sets are analyzed or assigned as exercises and projects. To save you the work of entering the data, we have stored data files on the Wiley web site given below. The computer files are in ASCII format. Files start with a brief description of the variables, and then list the observations. The first four symbols of each file name indicate the chapter or the project in which these data are first used; the next four symbols provide an abbreviated informative title.

There are many books that can be used in a course on the tools for quality improvement, and one may ask why one should prefer this text over all others. We believe that this book stands out for several reasons:

1. Discussion of nonstatistical problem solving tools found in Chapters 2–5 covers the organizational aspects of general or team-based problem solving techniques—topics not usually found in other statistical quality control books.

2. Thorough coverage of statistical quality control, with emphasis on the understanding of concepts and their practical use in solving quality problems. Coverage of sample inspection plans, control charts, and capability indexes includes a careful discussion of the differences between statistical control and capability.

3. Extensive discussion of design of experiments for process improvement, from basic principles through the analysis of factorial and fractional factorial designs, concludes with a chapter on Taguchi methods.

4. The large collection of exercises for each chapter is supported by Problem Solving Projects at the end of each of the five sections of the text. Several of the exercises and projects involve the analysis of large, case-oriented data sets. An ASCII version of all data sets from the text can be found on the Wiley Web Site at www.wiley.com/college/ledolter/qualitytools.

We hope you will find our book useful. If you have any comments or suggestions that could help us improve this book, please let us know. You can reach us through the Department of Statistics and Actuarial Science at the University of Iowa, Iowa City, IA 52242, or through e-mail at ledolter@stat.uiowa.edu.

A note to instructors: There may be more material in this book than can be covered comfortably in a one-semester or, especially, a one-quarter course. How much can be covered and which chapters should be emphasized or omitted will depend on the background of your students. Chapters 1 through 14 can be covered if your students have had no prior background in statistics. In fact, we have done this at the University of Iowa in our statistics modules for MBA students (in ten weeks) and for Executive MBA students (in eight weeks, without Chapter 14). If your students have had some introduction to statistics and if they are familiar with the material in Chapters 6 through 10, then the course can focus on Chapters 1 through 5 (problem solving) and Chapters 11 through 17 (sample inspection, statistical process control, design of experiments, and regression).

Supplements

Instructor's Solutions Manual. Provides extensive solutions for end-of-chapter exercises and end-of-section problems.

Data Disk. Contains all data sets from the text. Files are in ASCII format and are included with the Instructor's Solutions Manual available only upon request to adopting instructors. The files can also be found on the Wiley Web Site at www.wiley.com/college/ledolter/qualitytools.

Acknowledgments

We greatly appreciate the writings and teaching of people from whom we learned. Learning is incremental, and we could not have written this book without being able to stand on the shoulders of the books that came before us. A most heartfelt "thank you" goes to George Box, who was the catalyst and who triggered my (Ledolter's) desire to learn more about statistics. By watching a true master problem solver, I learned more about statistics during George's weekly "Monday Night Beer Seminars" than at any other course I have ever taken. Thank you, George!

We thank the various professional societies, companies, and publishers who have given permission to reproduce their materials in our text. Permission credit is acknowledged at appropriate places in the book. We also acknowledge the comments of our students at the University of Iowa and at Yale University who were exposed to previous versions of this material. Your feedback helped us greatly in improving this manuscript.

We would also like to thank the following people for their many constructive comments during the development of this book: Michael Adams (University of Alabama), Bala Balasubramanian (California Polytechnic State University), Milton Chen (San Diego University), Amanda Chou (University of Texas at San Antonio), Charles Cwiek (University of Tennessee), Steve Hillmer (University of Kansas), Bob Hogg (University of Iowa), Stu Hunter (Princeton University), Marie Klugman (Drake University), Mike Longnecker (Texas A&M University), David Lopez (Central Michigan University), Douglas Pollock (NORTEL), Victor Prybutok (University of North Texas), Elizabeth Rose (University of Southern California), Diane Schaub (University of Florida), D.G. Vandenberghe (University of Regina, SK).

We would like to express our thanks and appreciation to our editor, Brad Wiley, and his efficient staff. Brad was always here for us. He helped us along by providing insightful reviews at just the right times; and he always seemed to sense when encouragement was needed.

Finally, we would like to thank our families for their understanding and their assistance in making this book a reality. Writing a book is a time-consuming and daunting process. By providing the push "to finally get it done," and by giving us the time needed to actually do it, our families made this book happen.

CONTENTS

SECTION 3
PROCESS STABILIZATION: MAKING PROCESSES PREDICTABLE 303

SECTION 4
IMPROVEMENT THROUGH DESIGNED EXPERIMENTS 397

SECTION 5
OTHER USEFUL STATISTICAL TECHNIQUES 475

SECTION 1

QUALITY PROBLEMS AND PROBLEM-SOLVING STRATEGIES

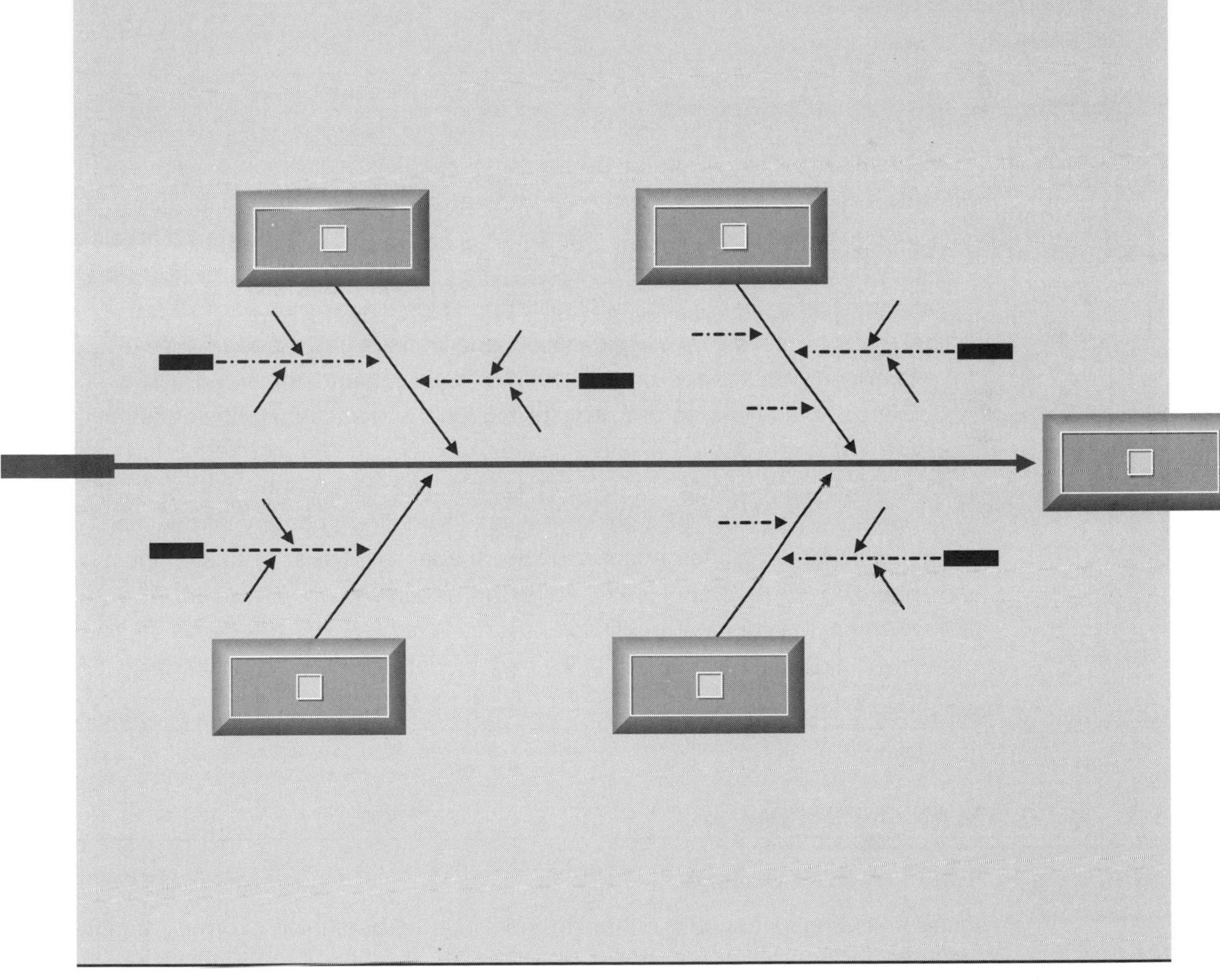

CHAPTER 1

INTRODUCTION AND OUTLINE OF THE BOOK

In this introductory chapter we summarize the objectives that we pursue with this text. The aim of this book is to provide the reader with an effective set of tools that he or she can use in problem solving, especially in problems that relate to quality and quality improvement issues. We start this chapter by giving a brief introduction to the area of quality. Quality and its continual improvement are critical to the success of any organization, and workers and managers must have familiarity with the appropriate tools for achieving and improving quality.

Our book emphasizes problem-solving tools and says very little about the managerial aspects of quality. Nevertheless, we need the subsequent brief introduction to the concept of quality to describe the background in which these tools operate. The following section gives only a very rudimentary introduction to quality. If you want to learn more about management issues of quality, then you should consult our other book, *Achieving Quality through Continual Improvement*, which is also published by John Wiley & Sons, 1999. This second book gives a detailed discussion of the managerial aspects of quality and covers the organizational and tactical issues of implementing quality.

1.1 QUALITY: AN OVERVIEW

1.1.1 A Brief History

Quality has been a concern of humankind since the beginning of time. Throughout history, the wealthy and powerful sponsored artisans who produced quality products for them. Over time, various guilds were formed to promote professionalism and standards for quality.

The industrial revolution made goods available to the masses, but introduced a basic change in commerce by separating the workers who made products from the customers who received them. This depersonalization of production introduced the need for producers to evolve new means to monitor and control the quality of their products. Originally, the focus was on *quality control*, that is, on inspection to identify faulty products and prevent their being shipped to customers. In the early part of this century, this inspection approach to quality was augmented with the employment of *statistical process control* (SPC), also known as *statistical quality control* (SQC), a concept developed by W. A. Shewhart of Bell Labs. SPC comprises a set of techniques for monitoring a production process to determine if it is stable over time and capable of producing quality products. It shifts the focus of attention from the product to the process that is used to make the product. SPC was widely practiced by U.S. industry during World War II, and it is credited by many observers as playing a key role in bringing about the defeat of Japan.

In the period following World War II, U.S. manufacturers enjoyed a huge pent-up demand for their products. They could sell whatever they produced, so their emphasis was on quantity of production, not product quality. Many of the wartime quality lessons were forgotten by manufacturers, and consumers did not seem to care because jobs were plentiful, wages were good, and if something broke, one could always replace it. The United States developed into a "throwaway" society—one bought a product, soon discovered that it failed to perform satisfactorily, threw it away, and bought another.

Postwar Japan faced an entirely different situation. With food and shelter scarce and their factories in ruins, Japan assessed and corrected the causes of their failure. Product quality was one area where America had definitely outperformed Japan, so they attempted to correct this situation. They soon mastered the inspection and SPC quality concepts, and went on to invent their own quality improvement techniques. By the 1970s, they had achieved world leadership in quality.

Today, some Western firms have closed the quality gap with Japan, and a few of them have managed to surpass their Japanese competitors. But much of the Western World still is playing catch-up with Japan in the quality arena. The aim of this book is to provide you with knowledge that you can use to help organizations improve the quality of their products.

1.1.2 Quality in Goods, Services, and Information Products

There are various formal definitions of quality; one is the definition of the *International Organization for Standardization* (ISO):

> ***Quality*** *is the totality of features and characteristics of a product or service that bear on its ability to satisfy stated or implied needs.*

As this definition implies, quality is an attribute of a product. A product is a quality product if it meets all the requirements established for it; that is, it is a defect-free product. In other words, *quality* means meeting requirements.

The pioneers of the quality movement—Walter A. Shewhart, W. Edwards Deming, Joseph M. Juran, Philip B. Crosby, and Kaoru Ishikawa—all were physical scientists or engineers. The focus of their quality efforts was on *goods*—manufactured or constructed products—and their approach to quality improvement leaned heavily on the use of statistical methods. More recently, the focus of quality efforts has been expanded to include *services*—the performance of labor for the benefit of another. This expansion has placed a greater emphasis on human factors and their impact on product quality.

Service is a broad category, including food services, health care, cleaning and building services, transportation, education, finance, government, and so on. Service accounts for about two-thirds of the jobs in an industrial economy; even in manufacturing, about two-thirds of the jobs are in service areas such as design, finance, advertising, and sales (*The Economist*, May 6, 1995, p. 15).

The traditional view of the economy in terms of goods and services tends to obscure what people in America really do for a living. About 60 percent of U.S. employment is in two categories—(1) managerial and professional specialty, and (2) technical, sales, and administrative support—both white-collar jobs (*Bureau of Labor Statistics*, U.S. Department of Labor Employment; 1993 counts). Most of these employees do not deal with physical objects, such as nuts and bolts; instead they deal with sales slips, correspondence, reports, checks, and the like. Thus, at least half the people in this country are *information workers*—some estimates place the number as high as 70 percent. In industries such as banking and insurance, the number is almost 100 percent. What these people deal with are *information products*. Quality products for information workers means instructions that are clear and complete, documents that are correct, checks in the right amount, and so on.

Quality in the office is every bit as important as quality on the factory floor. To appreciate this, think about what takes place when a customer buys a "widget" from a manufacturing company: A salesperson obtains and documents an order; components and supplies are ordered; incoming goods are stockpiled and listed in inventory; a production order is written, causing a worker to build the widget; the widget is built and sent to the customer with a shipping slip and an invoice; the customer pays, and appropriate transactions are made in the accounting system; checks are issued to the worker for his or her effort and to the people providing supplies, heat, light, and space; and, finally, the government gets tax reports and a check for part of the profit. This is a very much abbreviated list of activities and products, but notice that for each physical product (components, supplies, widgets, and so on) there are many information products (orders, inventory records, production orders, accounting statements, check, bills, reports, and so on). To provide proper service to the customer, *all* products—goods, services, and information—must be quality products.

1.1.3 Processes and Quality

The starting point in understanding how to achieve quality is to examine how products come into being. A product is the output of a *production process* (or simply a *process*), which is a logically related collection of actions or operations that produce results, called the *outputs* of the process. A process must be supplied with necessary ingredients, and those are the *inputs* to the process. For a manufacturing process, the inputs include parts and components, and the outputs include the finished products as well as scrap. For a service process, inputs may include a package and delivery instructions, and the output may be a delivered package. For an information product, inputs may be a class assignment and source materials, and the output a term paper. In all cases, the process involves some arrangement of equipment, tools, methods, procedures, and instructions for converting appropriate inputs into the desired product (and ancillary outputs, such as scrap). The quality of a product depends heavily on the production process that is used to produce it. If you want to produce quality widgets, then you must have an effective widget-producing process. If you want to produce quality cars, then you must have an effective assembly line. A major cause of poor products is the failure to build effective production processes.

Every production process can be thought of as consisting of four stages: analyze, design, build, test. *Analyze* involves learning what customers want and expressing these "wants" as a set of customer requirements. *Design* means establishing the requirements for a product that will meet the customer requirements. *Build* means actually building the product. *Test* involves checking to learn whether the product meets the customer requirements that were established for it. Each of these four subprocesses must be carried out properly to have a product that meets customer requirements. *Quality control* is an important component, especially in the fourth step of the production process. Here we confirm that the product meets the requirements that were established for it. If the product does, it is judged to be a *quality product*.

1.1.4 Management and Quality

Our focus in this book is on the *tools* that can be used to improve quality. But tools are only one part of the total effort required to achieve quality. Because management has ultimate control of all resources in an organization, it also has ultimate responsibility for the quality of all products. To make its views on quality known, management must establish a *quality policy* in which it states the organization's commitment to quality and establishes general guidelines for supporting that policy. Management must then support the quality policy by properly managing work, workers, work processes, and the work environment. There is an extensive literature on each of these topics. You should consult our other book for information on these issues.

1.1.5 ISO 9000 and Quality

For years, many organizations have strived for quality because they were convinced it was good business practice—it increased the demand for their products and reduced the cost of production. But others were not always convinced that costs would decrease so their quality initiatives were half-hearted. Now, however, many of these reluctant organizations are pushing for quality because of an initiative of the *International Organization for Standardization*, commonly referred to as ISO.

ISO was founded in 1946 to establish a series of international standards for products and production processes. Currently over 90 countries are members, including the United States and all of its major trading partners. In 1987, the organization published the ISO 9000 series of generic standards for quality management and quality assurance. These standards apply to companies of every size and to all industrial sectors—goods, services, and information. Various extensions of the original ISO 9000 standards have been introduced since 1987; ISO 14000, a new environmental management systems standard, was added in 1996.

The ISO 9000 standards provide guidance for suppliers who want to implement effective quality systems. Also, they can be used by customers to evaluate the adequacy of a supplier's quality system. To avoid the need for each customer to check each supplier, a system of *registration* has been established. A group of registrars has been accredited by ISO to audit quality systems of suppliers and certify those suppliers that are in compliance with a specific standard of the ISO series. A customer can then ask a supplier to become registered as a precondition to placing an order with that supplier. Registration gives the customer an assurance that the supplier has an effective quality system in place; this increases the likelihood that the supplier will provide quality products. In the past, suppliers were motivated to establish quality systems by the carrot of increased customer satisfaction. Today, many suppliers are motivated by the stick of ISO 9000—if they don't register, then they may not be able to sell to some potential customers.

1.1.6 Achieving Quality

There are two basic strategies for achieving quality: *prevention* and *improvement*. One strategy is to prevent quality problems by having a good understanding of customer requirements, by designing, building, and documenting production processes capable of producing the required products, and by using well-trained, highly motivated process operators who consistently do first-class work. Some organizations do a very good job on all of these tasks, which helps them avoid quality problems. However, many times companies will fall far short of this ideal, and they need to employ an equally important second strategy, namely, to practice continual process improvement.

Quality improvement efforts are designed to make a production process less likely to produce defective products. Examples of typical improvement efforts are:

Document a process in an attempt to make it more consistent; train operators to improve their job performance; collect and analyze defect information to determine the causes of product defects; make process changes to remove the causes of product defects; redesign the product to make its production less error-prone. The aim of this book is to present techniques and tools that aid such quality improvement efforts.

1.2 OUTLINE OF THIS BOOK

1.2.1 Quality Problems and Problem-Solving Strategies

This is a book on problem-solving tools and their use in quality improvement. Problem-solving skills are important for achieving and improving quality. Above all, one needs to have a general strategy for solving problems, and one must know techniques that help to *find*, *prioritize*, and *solve problems*. Useful systematic techniques for detecting and prioritizing problems are discussed in *Chapter 2*. Flowcharts and Pareto diagrams are explained. Flowcharts are important tools for visualizing the sequence of events in a process and they can help locate problems and unneeded complexity. Pareto diagrams are useful tools for prioritizing problems by focusing one's attention on the most commonplace problems.

A general four-step problem-solving strategy and a collection of simple but helpful problem-solving techniques are given in *Chapter 3*. Different ways of approaching the solutions to problems are explored. Cause-analysis and Ishikawa cause-and-effect diagrams are explained; these diagrams represent useful graphical displays of possible causes and their interrelationships.

Team-based approaches to problem solving are vital, as more and more problems are solved in groups. In order to solve problems within a team structure, we must have procedures for sharing and assessing information. *Chapter 4* of this book emphasizes the benefits of team-based approaches to problem solving, and discusses brainstorming, the nominal group technique, and the Delphi method—three useful techniques for the structured exchange of information.

Problem solving usually takes place within an organizational framework, and certainly not in a vacuum that is devoid of human interaction. In addition to the technical aspects, there is a human side to problem solving that cannot be neglected. The reward system and leadership, in particular, have a major influence on the creation as well as the solution of problems. These issues are explored in *Chapter 5*. We discuss how the success of problem solving is influenced by the style of management and the type of management-employee interaction.

1.2.2 Management Based on Facts: The Importance of Data and Data Analysis

We need to understand how data helps us solve problems. The *collection* and the *analysis* of relevant data through appropriate statistical techniques are important components of any problem-solving strategy. Solutions to problems must be based on facts, and management decisions must be supported by data. One must understand how to obtain the relevant data and one must know how to analyze the resulting information. Basic statistical concepts and techniques must be understood. This book gives a comprehensive treatment of the statistical tools that are essential for problem solving and quality improvement.

In *Chapter 6* we discuss measurements, their importance for problem solving and their impact on quality. We describe the measurement process through several simple illustrative examples, emphasizing the fact that measurements themselves are outcomes of a (measurement) process. We talk about variability among observations, distinguishing between the variability that comes from the underlying process that generates the observations and the variability that comes from the measurement system itself.

Chapter 7 describes the basic statistical tools for the effective display and summary of information. Several useful graphical displays of data are introduced. Time-sequence plots are useful if observations are collected sequentially in time. Such displays can reveal trends and shifts that may be related to process changes, unusual observations that may be related to special events, and seasonal or cyclical behavior. The overall variability of measurement data is effectively displayed through dot diagrams, histograms, and stem-and-leaf displays. These graphs show the extent of the variability, the shape of the distribution, as well as typical values of the measurements. Recommendations for producing good, informative graphical displays are reviewed.

Numerical summary statistics of the information are discussed. Measures of location such as the average and the median of a set of observations, and measures of variability such as the range and the standard deviation are considered.

The variability among measurements is usually the outcome of several causes. For example, defect rates taken during day and night shifts may be different, or fill weights in a bottling operation may be influenced by the particular nozzle of the filling machine. We emphasize the importance of stratifying the data into meaningful groups; stratification can reveal whether these groupings do in fact have an impact on the measurements.

Often we collect data on more than one variable. For example, we collect data on the strength of certain steel flats, but also have information on what happened during their production. The strength of steel flats may be affected by the time that billets spend in the reheat furnace and also by the furnace temperature. Scatter plots are used to describe, graphically, the relationships among variables. Correlation coefficients are used to express the association numerically.

Measurements vary, hence one needs tools to model their variability. For example, one may want to calculate the probability that a measurement exhibiting certain variability exceeds a certain threshold value, or the probability that the measurement falls within given specification limits. In *Chapter 8*, we model the variability in measurements through probability distributions. We introduce important probability distributions such as the binomial and the Poisson distributions for discrete random variables, and the uniform and the normal distributions for continuous random variables. We carry out basic probability calculations with these distributions. For example, under a normal distribution assumption it is quite easy to calculate the proportion of items that exceed a certain threshold or the proportion of items that fall within certain specifications.

In many situations we collect information on a relatively small sample, but want to extrapolate the results of the sample to the population from which the sample was taken. For example, we may sample 50 bread loaves from among the 10,000 loaves that were baked in our bakery today and find that the average weight of these 50 loaves is 1.05 pounds. We may also calculate the standard deviation from these 50 measurements so that we know something about the variability among weights of individual loaves. What do the results of this particular sample imply about the mean weight of today's production? Provided that we selected these 50 loaves from our daily production of 10,000 loaves in some "fair" manner, one can argue that the sample average 1.05 pounds is the best estimate of the mean weight of all 10,000 loaves. In fact, we can say more as we can attach a confidence (or reliability) coefficient to this estimate.

One needs to understand how to obtain fair and representative samples. It clearly isn't enough to just pick the first 50 loaves that come off the assembly line during the early morning hours because this wouldn't give every loaf the same chance of being in the sample. *Chapter 9* is on sample surveys. We talk about general principles for constructing good surveys. We discuss the most important probability sample survey plans, including simple random sampling and stratified random sampling, and we show how to carry out such sample surveys in practice.

We also discuss the various errors that are involved in sample surveys. There are the *sampling errors*, which arise because of the probability sampling scheme. The weights of the 10,000 bread loaves vary. While the overall mean may be 1.065 pounds, it could easily happen that the 50 loaves that we sample result in an average weight of 1.05 pounds. If you took yet another sample of 50 loaves, its average weight may be 1.07 pounds. For probability sampling schemes the sampling error can be quantified. The statistical theory in Chapter 10 shows us how to put bounds on the sampling error. However, there are also *nonsampling errors*, which are usually much harder to quantify. Several people may be involved in the sampling and they may measure things differently; measurement procedures may be unclear; computational errors in summarizing the results may have crept in; the selection may not have been totally random; and so on.

Chapter 10 gives an introduction to methods of statistical inference where one uses the results from random samples to make statements about characteristics of the population. Many times the sample information is summarized in terms of an average. The Central Limit Effect tells us about the variability of such averages if the averages come from random samples. The Central Limit Effect implies that the distribution of averages is well approximated by a normal distribution. This fact helps us in judging the statistical relevance of sample results. In Chapter 10 we discuss confidence intervals and explain how such intervals can be used to assess whether a certain hypothesis about the population is justified by the sample data. For example, the confidence interval for the mean weight of all 10,000 bread loaves baked may extend from 1.03 to 1.07 pounds, implying that we are reasonably confident that the true mean weight (that is, the mean weight of all 10,000 loaves) is somewhere in this range. On the basis of this sample evidence one could safely reject someone's claim that the mean weight is 1.00 pound. We also discuss predictions and prediction intervals, which are important for making inferences about future values of a process.

Chapter 11 introduces several sample inspection plans that are still widely used in quality assurance. There the decision whether a certain lot is accepted or not is based on the results of a small sample from that lot. We discuss the properties of various sample inspection plans, including the errors that arise with such plans. One can make two types of errors: One can reject a good lot, and one can fail to reject a bad lot. One needs to balance the probabilities of making these two types of errors. Our discussion of sampling inspection plans includes single, double, and sequential sampling plans, as well as commonly used Military Standard sampling inspection plans.

1.2.3 Process Stabilization: Making Processes Predictable

Processes are usually affected by a multitude of factors; these, in turn, introduce variability into the process results. An important question is whether the variation among process results is stable, or consistent over time. A process whose variability is stable over time is referred to as being *in statistical control*. Then a constant-chance system is operating, which makes the process predictable over time.

Control charts are used to monitor the stability of processes over time. Small samples of measurements on the process are taken at periodic intervals and the results (in particular, the sample average, the sample range or standard deviation, or the proportion of defects) are entered on control charts. The control limits on these charts tell us whether the sample results are consistent with a constant chance system. If the sample statistics exceed the limits on these charts, then this is taken as an indication that a "special event" must have taken place that altered the behavior of the process. Causes for such special events must be uncovered and, if found, prevented from occurring in the future. For example, a switch to a new supplier, a sudden change in operating conditions, or a new employee with insufficient training—any of these could be the underlying reason why a sample average is unusually high (or low), or why the variability in the sample is unusually large (or small). It is important that such special events are detected as soon as possible and that they are prevented in the future. We assume here that the special effect has a negative impact. Of course, if the impact is positive, then one must try to retain this condition. *Chapter 12* discusses statistical process control, common and special causes of variation, and several commonly used control charts. These include x-bar charts for monitoring the level of a process; range and standard deviation charts for monitoring its variability; p-charts for monitoring the proportion of defectives; c-charts for monitoring the number of defects; and x-charts for modeling individual observations.

A process is called *capable* if its products satisfy the required specifications. The specifications are usually expressed in terms of a target value that should be attained, and lower and upper specification limits that prescribe the range of values that are considered acceptable to the customer. Several commonly used measures, also called capability indexes, are discussed in *Chapter 13*; among them are the C_p and C_{pk} capability indexes.

Process capability is different from process stability, and the differences are explained in detail. Processes may be stable (and hence predictable, and in statistical control), but they may fail to satisfy the required specifications. In other words, the process may be consistent, but consistently bad. On the other hand, processes may be capable of meeting the specifications, but not in statistical control. This, too, is an undesirable situation because there is no assurance that an unpredictable process will stay capable in the future. Of course, one would like processes that are both capable and in statistical control.

Chapter 13 includes a discussion of Pre-Control charts. These are charts for assessing the capability over time. Similar to control charts, these charts track measurements over time. However, the warning limits on these charts are determined not by the natural variability of the process, but by the specification limits. A discussion of the usefulness and the limitations of this approach is included.

1.2.4 Improvement through Designed Experiments

To solve quality problems, one needs timely and relevant information on how variables interact. Experimentation through a sequence of well-planned experiments provides valuable information. Prior to experimentation one may have a long list of factors that could conceivably have an impact on the response. For example, a brainstorming session may have resulted in a fairly long list of possible factors. However, one does not always know which of the identified factors are relevant and how the settings (or levels) of the relevant factors affect the response. One needs to collect meaningful information. By changing the factor levels and by observing the impact of these changes on the variable of interest, one can learn much about the relationships among the response and the influencing factors. Whenever one has a long list of possible factors to investigate, it is important to have a "road map" for carrying out these experiments. This road map is the *design of the experiment*. Changing factors here and there, without reliance on a carefully thought-out plan, is inefficient. Such an approach would require lots of experiments, and in the end it may never get us to the desired solutions.

General principles of good statistical design of experiments are discussed in *Chapter 14*. These principles involve randomization, blocking, replication, and the sequential arrangement of experiments.

When carrying out experiments to learn about the effects of certain controlled factors (that is, factors that can be changed on purpose), one must be keenly aware that results can also be affected by "nuisance" factors that are not controlled during the course of the experiment. Quite often, one doesn't even know what these nuisance factors are or how they enter into the experiment. For illustration, consider an experiment that attempts to compare the impact of two training methods by exposing different groups of employees to the two methods and studying whether the type of training affects certain test scores. One must find a "fair" way to partition the work force into two comparable groups. It certainly would be bad to have responsible workers in one training method and the rest in the other; such an arrangement could bias the comparison because responsible workers might score higher on any test. *Randomization*, where the participants in method 1 (and method 2) are selected at random, provides a fair way. Such randomization is essential, as quite often we don't even know which employee characteristics could have an impact on the comparison. Of course, if we knew of such a characteristic, then we could consider this factor explicitly in our design. Assume, for example, that "problem-solving skill" is that important factor and suppose that we can measure it reliably. Then we can divide the workers into groups with "low" and "high" problem-solving skills. We could *block* the experiment on this particular factor and carry out the randomization within each group. The "low" problem-solving skill group would be divided at random into two subgroups. One of the subgroups would be exposed to method 1; the other to method 2. The same is done with the "high" group. This design would not only tell us whether there is a difference in effectiveness, but also confirm whether the effectiveness varies with the level of problem-solving ability.

Variation in experimental results is a fact of life. It arises because of the many uncontrolled and uncontrollable factors that influence the process. By *replicating* (repeating) the experiment, one guards against interpreting too much from the result of a single run.

Learning is an *iterative process*. Each time we look at the results of an experiment we obtain further information which allows us to focus our investigation even better. Because of this fact, one should always carry out investigations in the form of a sequence of small experiments. Experiments cost money and normally one operates within a certain fixed budget. If all resources are used up in one giant experiment, then there is no opportunity to put the resulting knowledge to use and to ask further, more focused, questions. Hence it is bad idea to exhaust one's budget with a single massive experiment. It is much better to conduct a sequence of smaller experiments. Each time we finish one of these smaller experiments, we will have learned something and be able to design the next experiment even better.

In Chapter 14, we also illustrate that a very poor approach to experimentation is a strategy of changing only one factor at a time while the remaining factors are held fixed. We show that factors must be *changed together* if one hopes to learn about their joint effects.

Chapter 15 discusses the analysis of comparative experiments. The data from such experiments provides information as to whether one method, or the level of one factor, is better than the others. Factorial experiments are discussed in great detail, especially two-level factorial experiments. For instance, one might investigate the effects on a response of three factors where each factor is studied at two levels, a low level and a high level. In a factorial experiment, we study all possible factor-level combinations. Hence for three factors our factorial experiment consists of $2^3 = 8$ runs. One of these is the run where all three factors are at their low levels; one is where all three factors are at their high levels; one is where the first and second factors are at their low levels and the third one at the high level, and so on. We show how the analysis of the resulting data can tell us much about the effects of these factors, either through the main effects or their interactions.

A disadvantage of factorial designs is the large number of necessary runs whenever the number of factors is large. Take the situation where you study seven factors. The factorial experiment consists of $2^7 = 128$ runs. Usually it is not economically feasible to carry out that many runs. However, one can economize on the number of runs by considering certain well-chosen fractions of the 128 runs. Such fractional factorial designs are discussed in this chapter. It turns out that a design with just eight runs (that is, 1/16 of the 128 runs) is quite capable of isolating the main effects of the seven factors.

Chapter 16 discusses Taguchi design methods for product and process development. Genichi Taguchi, a Japanese engineer, has had a significant impact on experimentation in Japanese industry, and his ideas have found significant acclaim in the United States. Taguchi's major contributions are (1) his adoption of a loss-function approach to deviations from target, (2) his emphasis of making products robust to uncontrolled environmental conditions, and (3) his use of alternative designs and alternative methods of analysis for his experiments. Taguchi was one of the first to realize that every deviation from the target results in a loss, even though the part may still be within the current required specifications. To state it quite simply: Being away from the target by any amount is not as good as being right on the target! Taguchi also recognized that products are used under various conditions; and very often under conditions that are far from optimal. It is important to design products that are insensitive (that is, robust) to environmental conditions that are not being controlled. Taguchi advocates the use of certain orthogonal array designs for his experiments. He distinguishes between controllable factors (those that can be changed and controlled) and noise factors (those that we have to live with). He selects the levels of the controllable factors so that the variability due to the noise variables is as small as possible, while bringing the process levels close to the target. He achieves this by considering various signal-to-noise ratios. Several examples are given to illustrate his approach.

1.2.5 Other Useful Statistical Techniques

Chapter 17 gives an introduction to regression modeling. There we relate a response variable functionally to one or more explanatory variables. Tool wear on a lathe may be the response variable; speed and the type of the tool may be the explanatory variables. The knowledge of the functional relationship among the variables allows us to predict the value of the response for given values of the explanatory variables. If the response variable is related to a single explanatory variable and if, furthermore, the relationship is linear, then one talks about simple linear regression, or "straight-line fitting." We show how to estimate the coefficients of the linear equation and how to judge the "fit" of the model. The general situation where the response variable is related to several explanatory variables is also discussed. In empirical model building it is important to know which explanatory variables to consider and which functional relationship to entertain. Practical guidelines for which model and which variables to select are given and illustrated by several examples.

This was a very brief outline of the material you will learn in this book. The discussion in this book is kept at a basic level; many examples and exercises are included to illustrate the concepts and to help you apply these tools. We also provide references to many other texts and papers that can be used for additional reading and further study. We hope that you will enjoy our presentation, and we welcome your suggestions for its improvement.

1.3 EXERCISES

1.1 Skim the book *Quality Planning and Analysis*, by J. M. Juran and F. M. Gryna (McGraw-Hill, 1993). According to the authors, what were the two major forces following World War II that had a profound impact on quality?

1.2 Ask several people who have *not* studied about quality to define quality. Comment on the results you obtain.

1.3 Scan some recent magazines or newspapers and find examples of quality problems with **(a)** a good, **(b)** a service, and **(c)** an information product.

1.4 In *Quality Is Free* (McGraw-Hill, 1979), Philip Crosby lists several of what he calls erroneous assumptions about quality, including:

(a) Quality means goodness,

(b) Quality is intangible, therefore it cannot be measured,

(c) Quality problems are caused by workers,

(d) Quality is the responsibility of the quality department.

Discuss each; if possible, give examples to support Crosby's view.

1.5 It was said of the original Model T car produced by the Ford Motor Company, "You can have any color you want as long as it is black." Comment on the quality of the Model T as it related to this fact.

1.6 List your requirements for:

(a) A pair of shoes,

(b) A software data processing program,

(c) A course on quality,

(d) A meal in the student cafeteria,

(c) A meal at an upscale restaurant.

1.7 Give several examples of processes operated by a restaurant.

1.8 Give several examples of processes operated by an educational institution.

1.9 What are the four stages of a production process (analyze, design, build, test) as they apply to:

(a) Writing a term paper,

(b) Taking an examination,

(c) Washing a car by hand,

(d) Washing a car at a car-wash facility,

(e) Playing a game of football.

1.10 Give several examples of achieving quality through **(a)** prevention, **(b)** process improvement, and **(c)** product improvement.

1.11 For a recent assignment that required a written report from you, critique **(a)** the requirements that were explicitly stated, and **(b)** the requirements that were "understood," but not explicitly stated. For instance, speculate on what would result if your report were written in Malay.

1.4 REFERENCES

Burrill, C. W., and J. Ledolter. *Achieving Quality through Continual Improvement.* New York: Wiley, 1999.

Crosby, P. B. *Quality Is Free.* New York: McGraw-Hill, 1979.

Juran, J. M., and F. M. Gryna. *Quality Planning and Analysis.* New York: McGraw-Hill, 1993.

CHAPTER 2

DETECTING AND PRIORITIZING PROBLEMS

2.1 INTRODUCTION

- Why were sales off in the Springfield branch last month?
- What is causing our employee turnover rate to increase?
- Why was productivity on the Baker line so much higher than average?
- What procedure should we use to handle the new reporting requirement?
- What caused this product to be defective?
- Should our company open an overseas office?
- How do we cope with the problem of insufficient parking spaces?

These are typical of the questions facing managers and professionals in most organizations—questions describing problems or opportunities facing the organization. It is up to managers and professionals to handle these questions. To do so, they must gather information, analyze it, and devise a scheme for addressing the situation confronting them. The success of the organization depends to a large extent on how well they perform this task.

Unfortunately, many people are not very good at solving problems. They have trouble getting started; they get problems, causes, and actions intertwined; and they jump to conclusions before examining all alternatives. In short, they do not follow a *systematic approach*. And that is not surprising because, although they have been given problems to solve all their lives, rarely have they been taught a problem-solving procedure. They are expected to pick it up naturally.

Most managers and professionals are knowledge workers; the raw material with which they work is information. One of their major tasks in the organization can be viewed as the effective use of information to solve problems. This means they should be very familiar with procedures and techniques for problem solving, and they should study these topics just as they study other topics connected with their profession. That's where this book comes in. It presents a problem-solving strategy, as well as techniques that managers and professionals can learn to use in solving the problems facing them. The basic content of the book is about problem solving in general. Special emphasis, however, is placed on problems that relate to quality because that is such a vital area for all organizations.

A *problem* is a gap between what is and what should be. Stated another way, it is a gap between actual and target, product characteristics and product specifications, or process capability and required tolerances. It can also be a gap between what we know and what we want to know, or between what we have and what we want. *Problem solving* is the process of finding a way to convert what is into what should be.

Usually the gap between what is and what should be is a "negative" gap in that we want to improve something, remove some obstacle, or remove some unwanted condition. But a problem can also be a "positive" gap—an opportunity—in that we might want to understand why something is much better than expected, presumably to use that knowledge to make similar improvements elsewhere. In our terminology, then, an opportunity is simply a "nice" problem.

Quality improvement activities are a fertile source of quality problems. One is continually trying to find ways to move a production process from its present capability to the point where it produces defect-free products—to move it from what is to what should be. Rarely is there one, simple, giant step from present reality to the desired state; progress is usually made slowly, a step at a time. In effect, quality improvement usually means solving lots of small problems, no one of which is terribly significant, but that taken together have a tremendous impact. Problems typically involve these activities: finding defects; finding a way to fix a defect; finding and removing all similar defects from the product; finding the cause of a defect; finding a way to remove the cause of a defect; finding better ways to specify product requirements; finding new, innovative processes. In facing such problems, the procedures and techniques of this book can be applied.

2.2 THE NEED FOR A PROBLEM-SOLVING STRATEGY

You can't be sure what goes on in a person's mind when he or she is solving a problem; you can't be sure whether people used an efficient problem-solving procedure or not. But you can be sure what happens when a group goes to work on a problem because you can watch and listen to their deliberations. The behavior you are likely to witness is this:

- Without a clear understanding of the problem, the group waffles in its search of a solution.
- With no analysis to speak of, the group jumps to conclusions.
- Instead of searching for a solution, the group's time is spent on justifying a preselected course of action.
- No attempt is made at concentrating on the most important aspects of the problem, and undue time is spent on trivial details.
- The group confuses problems, causes, and solutions.
- With no orderly approach, the group cycles back and forth between problem definition and analysis.

With no clear procedure to steer them, a problem-solving group wastes considerable time and frequently arrives at a poor decision. Often group members come away from the experience feeling frustrated and complaining of "another useless meeting." To avoid such behavior and to prevent wasted effort, there is a need for a *standardized procedure* for tackling problems; a procedure that can be learned and routinely applied. This procedure must include techniques for *recognizing problems*, methods for *prioritizing problems*, and methods for *solving problems*. The ideas behind recognizing, prioritizing, and solving problems provide managers and professionals with a basic approach to handling problems, one that can be adapted to a wide variety of specific problems. These issues are addressed in this and the next chapter.

Many benefits accrue from having standard procedures for solving problems. Above all, you should get better solutions to your problems: By forcing concentration on problem definition, you will have a better understanding of the problem; there is less chance of solving the wrong problem or only part of the problem. More directed analysis of the problem should result in increased alternatives, thereby increasing the chance of getting a good solution. The examination of more alternatives decreases the chance of getting a solution that later must be changed through another problem-solving session. A standard approach promotes "right-the-first-time" problem solving, decreasing the chance of making an error in the process.

People find personal benefits, as well: A standard procedure for solving problems saves "reinventing the wheel" each time a new problem arises. A procedure can be learned; it allows people to gain a new skill. By following a procedure, people can assess their own performance and make self-improvements; people can't learn to do better if they don't know how well they are doing in the first place. If aware of what they are doing while problem solving, people are more productive and they save time. Once learned through practice, a procedure helps people through emergency situations when efficiency is essential. A procedure can be taught to others, thereby making the entire work group more effective.

Of course, procedures for performing tasks are not universal panaceas. They are not a substitute for knowledge and the ability to think. But a problem-solving procedure can help make your efforts more effective.

2.3 RECOGNIZING PROBLEMS

We have said that a problem is a gap between what is and what should be. But, in fact, for us to be concerned about the problem, some other conditions must fall in place. First, we have to be aware of the gap. Second, even if we recognize a gap, it must be serious enough for us to view it as a problem. Finally, even if we recognize a gap and consider it to be serious, we don't usually recognize it as a problem unless we have some intention to do something about it. Our concern, then, is *recognized gaps* between what is and what should be that we have some *intention of closing*. Where do such problems come from? Where and how do we find them?

There are many sources of problems. For convenience, we group these sources into three categories:

- **Unexpected (or spontaneous) problems.** These are problems that just show up. You don't go looking for them, they come looking for you.
- **Detected problems.** These are problems that show up through some kind of routine examination or detection process.
- **Acknowledged problems.** These are problems that you realize when you consciously set out to think about and list your problems.

These three categories might not cover all problems, but they cover the major sources.

2.4 UNEXPECTED PROBLEMS

Unexpected problems are those that arise without warning in the normal course of events. Suddenly you become aware that something is not right or something is needed. You become angry, anxious, frightened, or frustrated about a situation. Or you realize that something is possible; there is some opportunity to be exploited or some difficulty that should be removed. Or, your organization faces an unsatisfactory situation that could bring embarrassment, poor performance, or calamity. For example:

- You try to start the car and find it won't even turn over.
- Your teacher announces that a term paper is due next Friday.
- Your boss offers you a promotion to a job located in another city.

- You learn that productivity is low and turnover is excessive.
- The latest quarterly report shows unacceptable performance.
- An audit shows lax adherence to standards causing serious quality problems.
- Productivity on the night shift is 30 percent higher than on the day shift.

All of these can be viewed as problems. In most cases, you must take some action to turn what is into what should be: repair a product, build a new product, make a decision, or find the cause of some defect. We put the last problem on the list to emphasize that sometimes the gap you perceive is a "good" gap; here the problem is to discover the cause of the superior performance so you can replicate it elsewhere. With all problems, good or bad, you will do a better job of handling them if you use a systematic approach.

2.5 DETECTED PROBLEMS

There is little for you to do about collecting unexpected problems; they just happen. *Detected problems*, on the other hand, are those found through some systematic examination of a product conducted with the intent of detecting problems if they exist. Examples of such detection procedures are:

- An examination of a student in an academic institution
- The examination of a patient by a doctor
- The examination of a car for defects
- The examination of company books by an auditor
- The examination of plant security by management
- The review of a play by a critic

What we are calling detected problems arise as a result of some detection procedure that is specifically designed to review a product against the requirements for the product. A problem amounts to an observation that the product is not as it should be; in other words, it has a defect. Detected problems are defects that are uncovered through the exercise of some examination activity.

Most processes contain steps at which products are examined to see that they meet requirements; this is known as *quality control.* Failure to meet requirements is usually regarded as a problem. Often quality control activities are associated with the review of products in an industrial setting. However, the above examples of examinations show that quality control is a pervasive activity.

To detect problems, one must have a specific product that is to be examined and a detection procedure for examining that product. A detection procedure can have any of several names: an inspection, examination, review, audit, investigation, and so on. No matter what the name, however, a detection procedure has three steps:

Step 1: Study product requirements
Step 2: Examine the product
Step 3: Document detected defects

We shall refer to this as the ***SED procedure: Study, Examine, Document***. Let us explore each of these steps.

Step 1: Study Product Requirements The first step of SED is to understand the requirements for the product. What attributes or functions should the product possess? For each attribute or function, what standards are to be met? For each such standard, how is the product to be measured to verify that the standard is met?

Frequently, product standards are not specified well enough for these three questions to be answered clearly. This, of course, is a problem, but it is not a product problem of the type you are attempting to discover by using the SED procedure. Instead, it is a unexpected problem—poorly specified requirements—stumbled upon while checking to learn if the product meets requirements.

Step 2: Examine the Product Once requirements are understood, the second step is to examine the product to ascertain if all requirements are met. The product is examined against each requirement; there are two basic ways that this can be done: *Operate* the product, or *observe* the product.

Some products can be operated. A car can be driven, a computer program can be run, a play can be performed. For such products, one way to examine the product against requirements is to operate it. Examination by operation goes under many names: test drive, test run, unit test, system test, acceptance test, burn in, dry run, dress rehersal, and so on.

Most products cannot be examined by being operated, or it is impractical to do so. Operation cannot be used to verify all requirements; for example, the appearance of a car cannot be checked by running it. Also, it is not practical to examine the plan for building a building by constructing it, that is, by building a practice building. Most products must be examined through observation. The procedure of observing the product goes under many names: desk check, peer review, inspection, walkthrough, phase review, audit, and so on. Observation might be by an individual or by a group. However done, it amounts to a systematic inspection of the product to verify that each requirement is met.

Step 3: Document Detected Defects The third step of SED is to document all problems discovered in Step 2. Documentation, recording the defect in some permanent medium, needs to be stressed because memory is fleeting; what is not written down is likely to be forgotten. Remember the problem of the King in *Through the Looking-Glass and What Alice Found There* (Lewis Carroll; Macmillan, 1871):

> *"The horror of that moment," the King went on, "I shall never, never forget!"*
> *"You will, though," the Queen said, "if you don't make a memorandum of it."*

Documentation should include all information that is likely to be needed for subsequent handling of any problem that is discovered—this includes information that might be used to improve the production process to prevent a similar product problem in the future. What is actually documented, of course, depends on what is to be done with the product. In some cases, defective products simply are scrapped, so a count and description of the defect may be all that is required. In other cases, defective products are repaired; then it might be necessary to record additional information needed to make the repair. In any event, defect data will help guide attempts to improve the process. Part of the design of an SED procedure is the careful analysis of what information needs to be collected in Step 3 and the design of appropriate forms and procedures to ease the collection of that information.

Detection is widely practiced. Every process contains quality control points at which products are examined against requirements. In manufacturing, for example, requirements for a product are reviewed, and then the product design itself is examined. A prototype may be built and tested, and the actual production is inspected for its conformance to the requirements. In the development of an information system, an individual programmer will first desk-check a module of code, and then perform a unit test. Later, that module is examined as part of an integration test, and later still as part of a system test or a final test.

2.6 ACKNOWLEDGED PROBLEMS

Aside from unexpected and detected problems, there is a third source. Some problems are discovered by a conscious attempt to discover them, not through examining a product for defects, but by directly searching for problems. These are found in the course of answering questions such as: "What problems do we have?" "What potential problems will we have if we attempt to install a certain new piece of equipment or a new procedure?" "What are the side-effects of this drug?" The problems one discovers generally are not new; they have been there all the time. All that the conscious attempt at discovery does is to acknowledge in an open way what has existed all along.

Structured group activities, such as brainstorming and processes involving the nominal group technique, can be used to generate lists of problems; these activities are discussed in Chapter 4. What these techniques tend to bring out are problems that people have been aware of, perhaps for some time, but that no one has bothered to report in a formal way. One reason for consciously searching for problems is to openly acknowledge them with the aim of doing something about them.

2.7 FLOWCHARTS: USEFUL TOOLS FOR DETECTING PROBLEMS

A *flowchart* is a useful tool for mapping the time-sequence of events in a process. A flowchart shows the chronological steps that an operation follows; it displays the order in which work steps are performed and the logic governing their order of performance. Flowcharts can be used both to design a process and to document a process.

Various symbols are used to denote the elements in a flowchart. Boxes or rectangles are used to represent tasks or work activities; circles or ovals are used to denote beginning and ending points. Diamonds are used to show points in the process where decisions must be taken, for example, the decision "if it is under 100 pounds, do this; otherwise, do that." Arrows show the chronological flow of the process; an arrow from step A to step B indicates that step A must be completed before step B can be started. Other constructs can be used to represent inputs and outputs, documents, special operations, and flow conditions. As the following examples will show, there are many variations of flowcharts; the best way to display the chronological flow of a process will depend on the particular problem under study.

Flowcharts have many uses. They provide a visual display of processes and help us to understand the sequence of events. They document current knowledge about processes, and they can aid in identifying complexity and potential problem areas. Their use helps to identify data-gathering areas and stimulates ideas for process improvement. And they are an important tool for communication and training about processes.

A flowchart can provide a very general picture of the process, outlining the general process flow; or it can be very specific, showing each individual step within an operation. The amount of detail provided depends on one's objective. Sometimes it is enough to just understand the basic outline of a process; at other times, one needs a detailed understanding to help in identifying problem areas in the process.

If the flowchart maps the *process as it actually is* (and not as it should be), then it can help us locate problem areas such as unneeded complexity, redundancies, and unnecessary loops. Such a flowchart helps us identify improvement opportunities, and its use can lead to simplification and standardization of the process.

We don't mean to imply, however, that a flowchart *automatically* will contain all the inefficiencies and redundancies that are actually part of the system. Most of the time, the first attempt to flowchart a process produces a "the way things should be" flowchart rather than "the way things are." It usually takes some effort to get people to draw in all the absurd things that actually go on in their processes. Only if one is successful in getting people to draw "the way things really are" will the flowchart reveal problems in the system.

EXAMPLE 1

Our first example traces the steps that are involved in a cash sale (Figure 2.1). This example is adapted from J. A. Swift, *Introduction to Modern Statistical Quality Control and Management* (Delray Beach, FL: St. Lucie Press, 1995). This flowchart reveals a major problem. We can see that a nonoperating cash register causes serious delays, resulting in lost sales and customers. Waiting in front of a nonoperating cash register for more than five minutes will drive even your most loyal customer away! It is important to establish contingency plans for the event that the cash register is out of operation. ■

EXAMPLE 2

The example in Figure 2.2 (page 26), taken from the U.S. Navy, charts the chronological steps in the dental appointment procedure at the San Diego Naval Dental Center. This example is included in *The Memory Jogger II*, written by Michael Brassard and Diane Ritter (published by GOAL/QPC in 1994), which is a very useful pocket guide of tools for continuous improvement and effective planning. This particular flowchart documents the present appointment scheduling procedure. It indicates that the process is fairly efficient, as it keeps track of people who don't show up for appointments. If one were dissatisfied with certain aspects of the present scheduling procedure, then this flowchart would help highlight inefficiencies of the process. ■

EXAMPLE 3

Promotion and tenure are important decisions at every university. The University of Iowa has developed detailed procedures that give everyone involved in the process fair notice and equal treatment. These procedures ensure uniformity across departments and colleges and provide quality control of the review of scholarship, thus minimizing the risks of denying promotion to qualified candidates or awarding

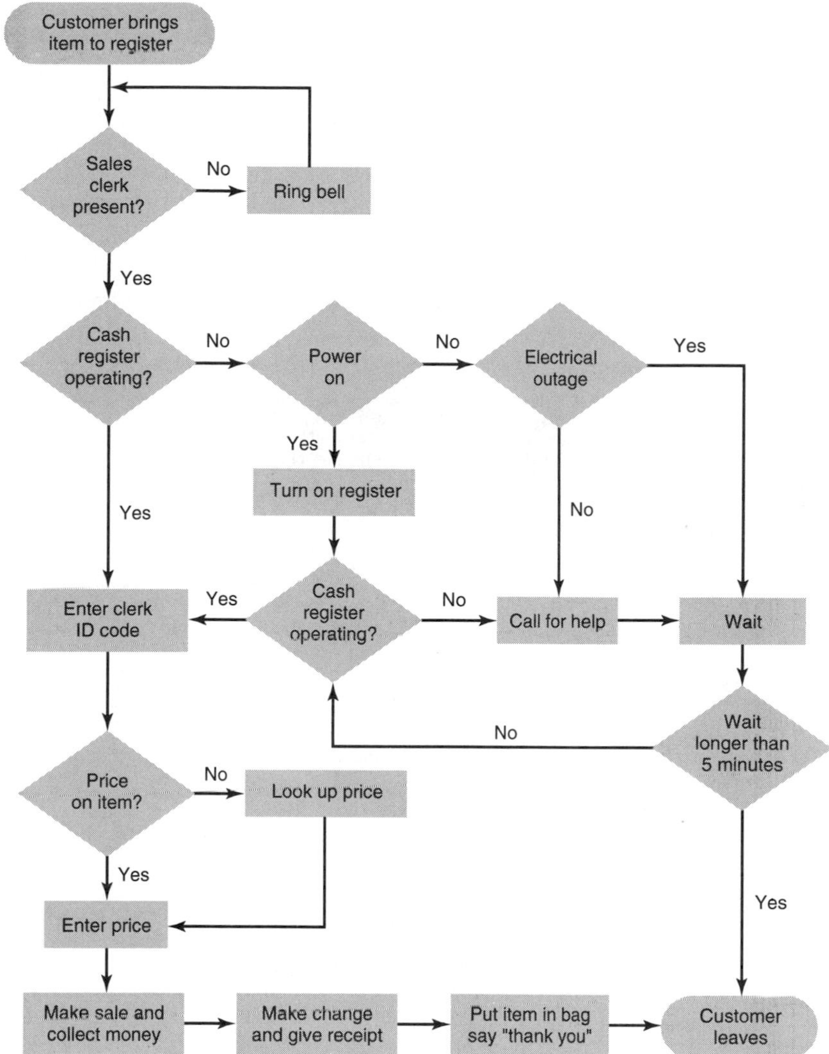

FIGURE 2.1 Flowchart of a cash sale.

promotion to candidates who lack some of the required qualifications. Figure 2.3 (page 27) shows the sequential development of the promotion record through various decision makers. This flowchart shows, for example, that the procedures establish a significant faculty role in the evaluation of the candidate's dossier. The Faculty Review Committee (the departmental faculty committee appointed to compile an initial written report on the candidate's work) and the Departmental Consulting Group (the members of a candidate's department who are eligible to participate in the decision-making process) provide reports to the Departmental

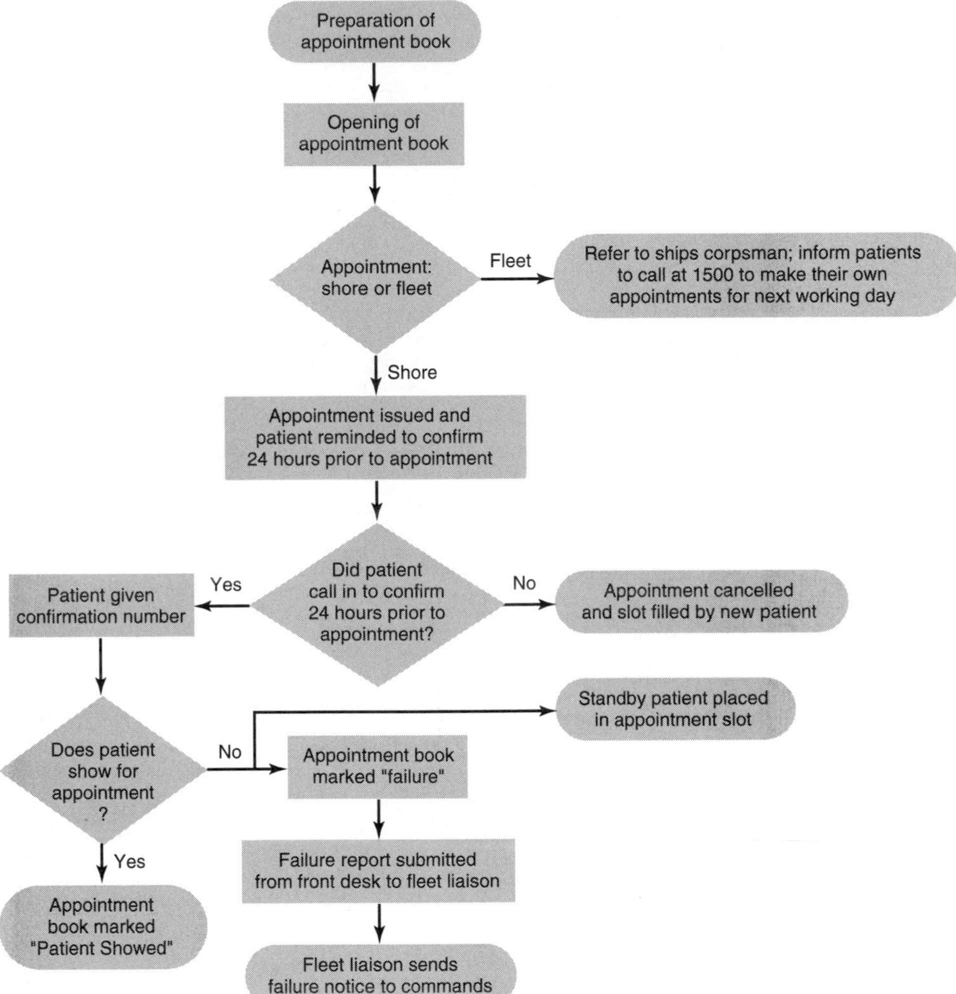

FIGURE 2.2 Flowchart of a patient appointment procedure.

Executive Officer (DEO). The procedures create a presumption that, ordinarily, these activities are independent of the DEO. The chart also documents very clearly that each candidate is provided access and input into the decision-making process at a number of separate points. ■

Another good use of flowcharts is to ask people to draw the *process as it should be*. A "the way things should be" flowchart can reveal whether the process can actually be implemented and whether unforeseen negative side effects are present.

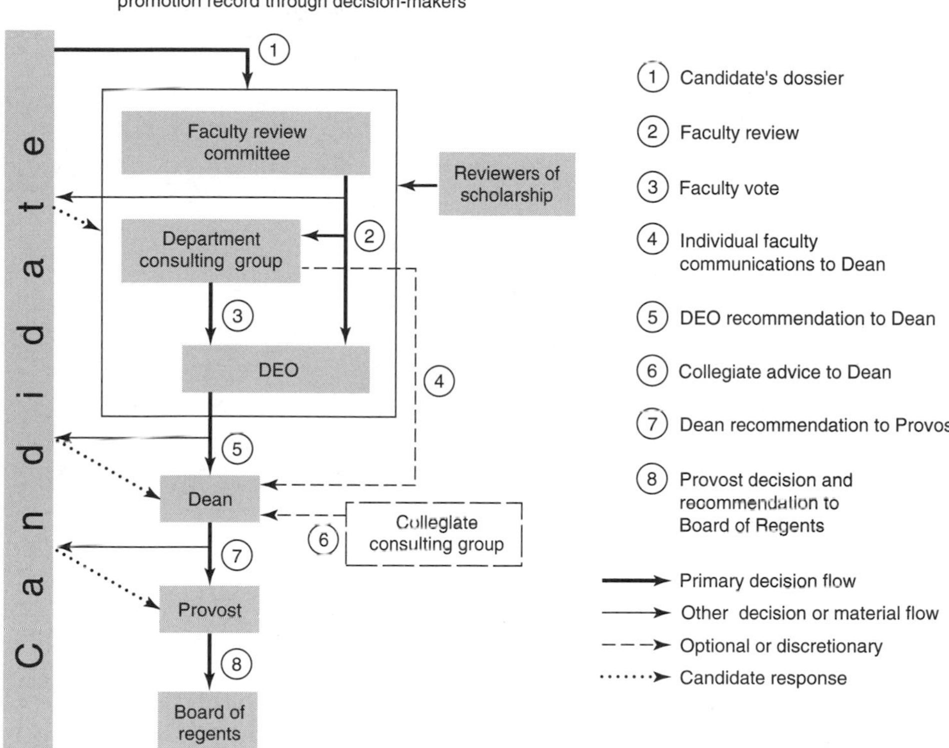

FIGURE 2.3 Sequential development of the promotion records through decision makers.

EXAMPLE 4

The next example, taken from the book *Fourth Generation Management* by Brian L. Joiner (New York: McGraw-Hill, 1994, p. 17), illustrates this point. Joiner attributes this example to Tim Fuller. An assembly operation was supposed to work as follows: Get a kit of components consisting of parts A, B, and C; put them together; move the assembled product to the stock area. (Note that in a realistic assembly process, the assembled product will consist of many parts, say 100 or so.) The flow diagram at the top of Figure 2.4 (page 28) shows how the assembly is supposed to work. However, the kits were not always complete; quite often a single part was missing. In that case, employees would use what parts they had to construct a partial assembly, log the information into a computer database, and store the partially completed assembly on a shelf. When the missing part arrived, an employee would go to the computer, find a partial assembly that was missing that part, retrieve it from the shelf, and complete the assembly. The work process that was actually used is documented in the flowchart at the bottom of Figure 2.4. The broken line on that diagram separates the "real work," which are the steps necessary

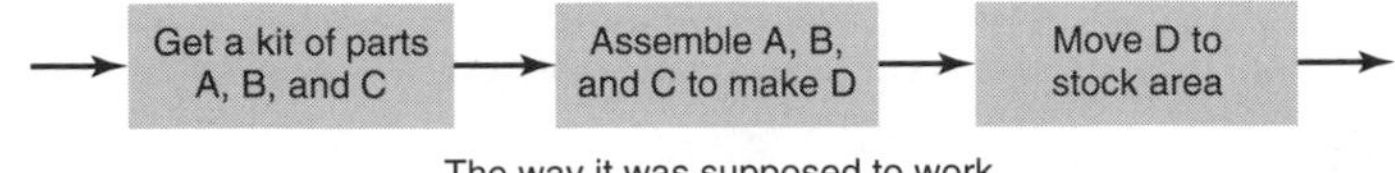

The way it was supposed to work

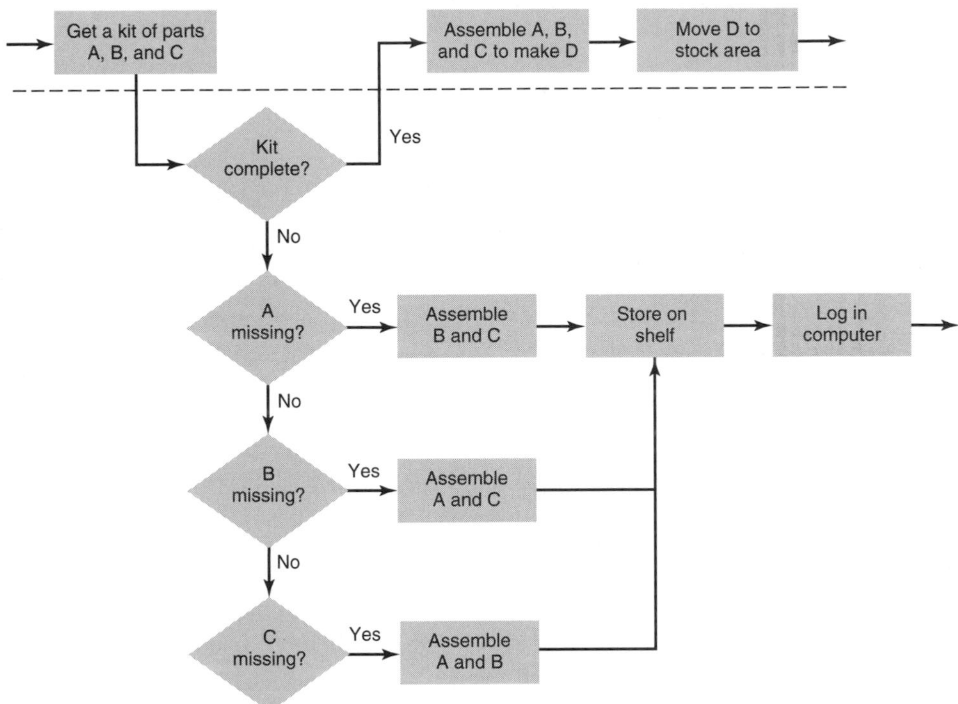

The way it actually worked

FIGURE 2.4 Flowcharts of an assembly operation. The top segment of the chart shows the idealized assembly operation; the bottom segment displays the actual operation.

when everything works perfectly, from the "added complexity," which is introduced because parts sometimes are missing. The work below the broken line represents the steps that could be avoided if all kits were complete. ■

EXAMPLE 5

An example of a flowchart that is particularly relevant to the topics discussed in this text is shown in Figure 2.5. We have taken this flowchart from the book *Defect Prevention: Use of Simple Statistical Tools*, by Victor Kane (New York: Marcel Dekker, 1989, p. 541). This flowchart documents the process of finding and implementing solutions to problems; Kane calls this "problem analysis."

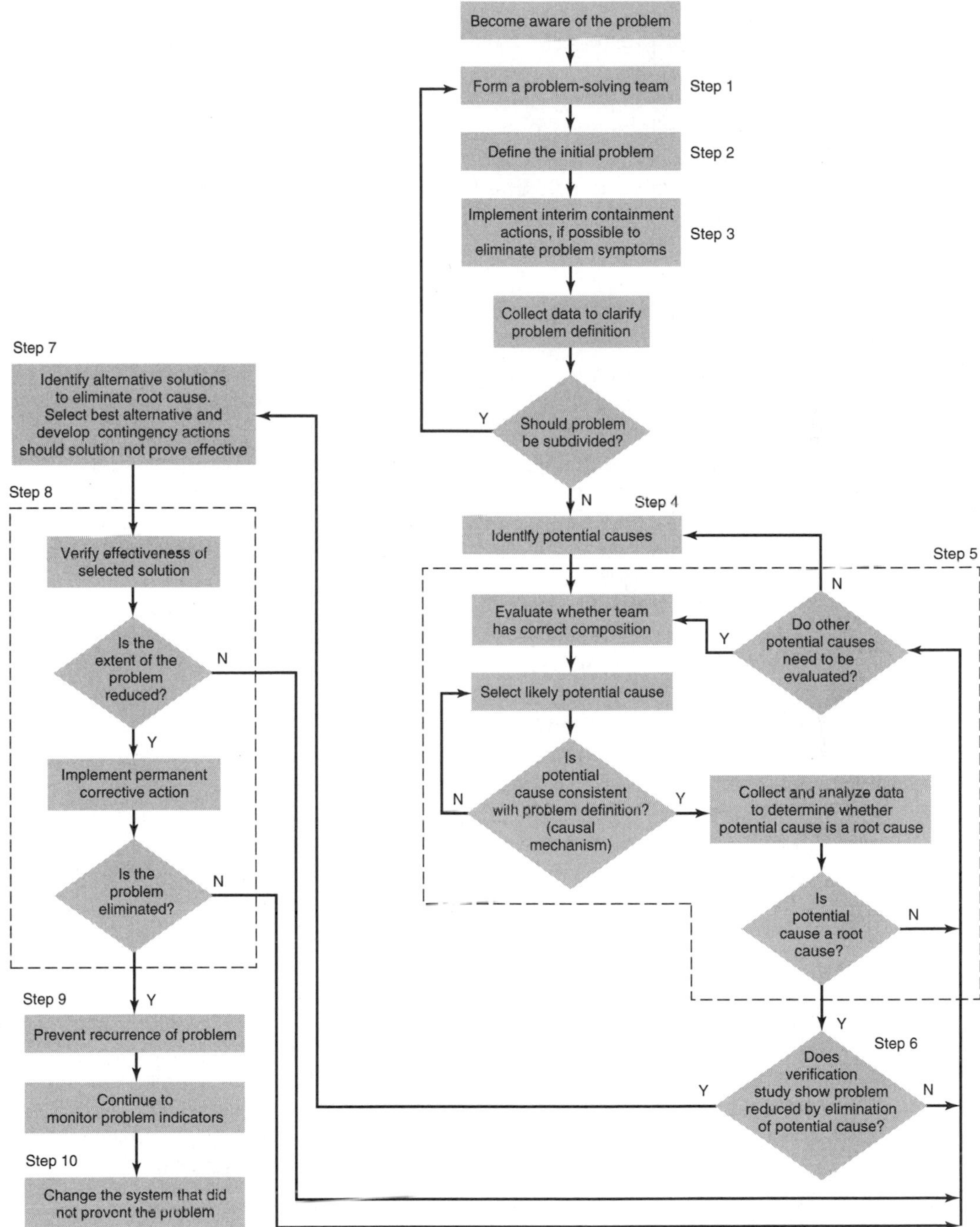

FIGURE 2.5 Flowchart: Finding and implementing problem solutions.

The process starts with problem awareness, problem definition, and the implementation of preliminary containment actions. Potential causes are then identified and studies are carried out to determine whether potential causes are in fact root causes. A solution is adopted, and it is verified whether the adopted solution is effective in correcting the problem. Steps must then be taken to prevent the recurrence of the problem. Problem indicators must be monitored, and the process that allowed the problem to arise in the first place must be changed. ■

2.8 PRIORITIZING PROBLEMS

Most organizations have an immense number of problems but only limited resources to tackle them. That in a nutshell is why it is necessary to identify all your problems and rank them in the order you intend to address them.

In concept, establishing priorities is simple. One starts with a list of all problems and a set of criteria by which to judge their importance. Each problem is graded against the criteria, and these grades determine the rank. There are really only two questions to explore: What criteria should be established for problems, and how is the grading done?

There is no shortage of criteria by which to judge problems. Whatever criteria are used, they are bound to lead to conflicting judgments: Some problems will score high against some criteria and low against others. Furthermore, different criteria are likely to be used in different parts of an organization. Upper management of an organization tends to have a broad view and a focus on basic issues affecting the organization. Their criteria for selecting problems, therefore, might cover such *business issues* as the potential for quality improvement, the potential for improving economic performance, the support of organizational goals, the attainment of political goals, or the support of social goals. People in an operational capacity have a more immediate view of problem situations. They are likely to focus on criteria more directly related to *operational issues*, such as the urgency of the problem, the impact of the problem, the trend of the problem, and the visibility of the problem. People having responsibility for coping with problems tend to focus more directly on the problem-solving process. They are likely to be more concerned with *implementation issues*, such as technology issues, the capability of the organization, the ease of finding and implementing solutions, the resistance to change, and the required deadlines for solution. Finally, there are questions that any evaluator might ask: What's in it for me? Will solving the problem increase my position? Is it an interesting, new problem; will it be a challenge? Will I gain new skills from solving it? Will it be fun? Problems are judged by people, and *personal criteria* inevitably have an influence on the judgments that are made.

Of course, not everyone will be rigid and stick to the typical classes of criteria we described. A top official might well be concerned about some details of solving

TABLE 2.1 Example of a Scorecard for Ranking Problems

	Score	Weight	Score × Weight
Capability to solve	10	0.30	3.00
Ease of solution	5	0.15	0.75
Resistance to change	3	0.35	1.05
Professional growth	4	0.20	0.80
Total weighted score			5.60

the problem, and an implementer about the impact on organizational goals. We offered a classification of these criteria simply to help you think about them. Nor have we exhausted all the criteria people use. A problem might be selected for attention simply because a top manager says, "Do it." It might be selected because it has been a tradition to handle such problems and the organization is equipped to do it. Or it might be selected simply because it happens to be on top of the stack of problems at the right time—strictly by chance.

The difficulty of ranking problems stems from the fact that problems are usually judged against several criteria. Measures are made against each criterion, and the fundamental problem is to reduce multiple measures to a single number. Two basic approaches are taken to solve this fundamental problem; we shall refer to these approaches as *scoring* and *voting*.

Scoring is a process of assigning a grade to each problem, where the grade of one problem is independent of the assessment of the others. Problems then are ranked by scores. Scores can be assigned to problems directly based on individual judgment. For example, people doing the ranking can be told: "Rate this problem from 1 to 10, where 10 means very important and 1 means very unimportant." Alternatively, scores can be assigned by more elaborate procedures making use of a scorecard, such as the one in Table 2.1. In this table, four criteria for evaluating a problem are listed in the first column. The relative importance of these four criteria is indicated by the weights assigned to them, as shown in column 3. The weights are usually expressed such that their sum equals 1. The higher the weight, the more important the criterion. Both the criteria and weights assigned to them are taken as given by the people who are to do the scoring. Each problem is then scored against each criterion, being assigned a score from 1 to 10, where 1 indicates an unfavorable score and 10 a favorable one. For example, a score of 10 for resistance to change would indicate little resistance; a score of 10 for professional growth would indicate much potential. As shown in Table 2.1, scores for individual criteria are multiplied by the corresponding weights; then these figures are added to obtain the total score for the problem. Problems are then ranked by these total scores. The use of weights to reflect the relative value of criteria allows additional flexibility over a system that treats all criteria equally.

Whether it leads to a better ranking of problems depends, of course, on how well the weights are chosen.

In assigning scores to problems, it is not necessary to make a comparative analysis of problems. It is a technique that can be used on problems that come in a few at a time, not all together in one bundle. Also, it is a technique that is useful when the number of problems is so large that a comparison among problems is not feasible.

The second approach to ranking problems is voting. *Voting* is a process of making comparative assessments among problems to select the most important ones. It is a process of casting a ballot for the best candidates.

Voting can be, and often is, done by a simple show of hands. "How many think this is the most important problem?" is sufficient in most small groups. However, to avoid pressure, voting can be done secretly in writing. Alternatively, elaborate procedures for proportional voting can be used. For example, people can be told to select the five most important problems of a group, order them in importance, and assign a 5 to the most important, a 4 to the next most important, and so on. This is the method used in the nominal group technique; see Chapter 4.

Use of voting requires that all problems be judged relative to one another, and this means that they must all be judged at the same time. Voting requires that all problems are considered together; the technique cannot be used if problems come in a few at a time.

However done, the final ordering of problems becomes the priority list for solving problems. How many problems can be tackled is, of course, a function of the resources available. The priority list serves two purposes. It can be matched against available resources to determine the problems that will be worked on. And, if the remaining untackled problems are severe enough, the priority list can be used to bolster an argument for more resources.

Before attempting to rank problems, you should examine them to determine whether you are judging the correct thing. What passes for a problem sometimes is really a cluster of related problems. Keeping the cluster together makes it appear to be more important than would be the case if each of the related problems were judged separately. You might want to split clusters of problems into constituent components in order to assess their relative importance more correctly.

But you should also be careful of splintering problems. Several problems classified as distinct may, in fact, be instances of a general problem. A usual example of this is in the area of maintenance. Individual maintenance problems are usually small; but taken together, they can represent a significant expenditure of resource. Anyone who has ever owned an old car is aware of this phenomenon. By clustering maintenance problems according to some natural grouping, one might discover that what seemed to be an inconsequential problem is, in fact, a significant one. The moral in this discussion about defining the problem is this: What you decide to group together and call a problem will be an important factor in determining the rank that gets assigned to it.

The rank assigned to a problem and how it is ranked also depends to some extent on who does the grading. Individuals who are required to grade problems do so very informally. They use their judgment to sort out the important problems, then use more judgment to pick the most important. Judgments by a small team sometimes are based on the opinions of one or two strong members, but more often are made by vote. A simple show of hands is used to answer most questions. Committees make judgments in a variety of ways. Some simply vote by show of hands. Some hold secret ballots. Some are governed by formal procedures, such as Robert's Rules of Order. Some committees use elaborate scoring devices to rate problems, others simply allow members to vote their own judgments.

2.9 PARETO DIAGRAMS: USEFUL TOOLS FOR PRIORITIZING PROBLEMS

Usually, data is available on how frequently various categories of problems have occurred in operating a production process. For instance, in the production of optical lenses, summary statistics usually are available on the number of lenses that are chipped, scratched, cloudy, of unequal color, of wrong dimensions, and any "other" causes. Or, in a survey of owners of a certain window air conditioning unit, complaints might be classified as due to excessive noise, unacceptable vibration, high energy consumption, poor final finish, excessive condensation, and so on. Or, a survey of tourists on their intention to return to an area they have just visited might categorize tourist concerns according to high expense, lack of attractions, unfriendliness of service, lack of modern hotels, poor roads, problems of crime, and so on. A simple tabulation of the survey results will provide the frequencies of the dominant reasons (dominant categories) for their reluctance to return.

Data on the frequencies of quality problems can be used to direct one's efforts to the most troublesome problem(s). One graph that can be used for this purpose is the *Pareto diagram*, named after the Italian economist Vilfredo Pareto. It is basically a graph of the frequencies of the various categories of quality problems, where the categories are arranged according to the frequency of their occurrence. The data class with the most members is listed first, the second largest class is second, and so on.

A feature of the Pareto diagram is that it highlights the most frequent problems. Quite often it turns out that a few categories are responsible for most of the problems. A Pareto diagram is a useful tool for separating the "vital few" problems from the "trivial many." The "80/20 rule," which says that usually about 80 percent of the quality problems can be attributed to only 20 percent of the categories of unacceptable performance, is a good rule of thumb. This rule applies in many situations. It applies to customer complaints (most of the time 80 percent of the complaints arise from 20 percent of the customers), warranty and repair costs, and product defects (80 percent of manufacturing defects arise from 20 percent of the processing stages). It applies to machine downtime, material/time utilization, injury types (80 percent of the injuries originate from only 20 percent of the operations), energy use, clerical errors, and sales (80 percent of the sales originate from 20 percent of the customers).

Use of Pareto diagrams is promoted as a standard tool for quality improvement efforts. If you want to improve quality, you should eliminate your most common problems (that is, the vital few), and not those that occur only occasionally. Even if you fix a rare problem, the resulting impact will be small. Reducing the incidence of a frequently occurring problem by one-half (that is, cutting a large bar in a Pareto diagram in half) yields a much greater improvement that a 50 percent reduction in a small bar. A Pareto diagram helps to focus improvement efforts. It channels them into a direction where the actions will have the largest impact.

In constructing a Pareto diagram, one must make certain that the categories are meaningful and the "other" category is not too large. For example, instead of a classification according to reject codes, it might be better to arrange the information according to the components that cause the reject. Or, instead of listing individual defects, it might be better to summarize the information according to the operations that generate the defects.

If one knows the cost that is associated with each category, then one can construct a Pareto diagram that is based on the total costs of the errors in each category rather than their frequencies. A Pareto diagram organized according to total cost allows you to identify and attack first the categories with the highest cost. Note that a Pareto diagram based on total cost does not necessarily point to the same "vital few" problems as those identified by a chart based on frequencies of occurrence.

The Pareto diagram is a very simple and useful tool. However, one should be aware of its limitations. It might be deceptive to base a Pareto diagram on information collected over a very short time period, especially if the process is unstable, because the information might not be reliable. One must collect defect information over a representative time interval. Also, one must select the criterion for ranking the categories wisely; the number of occurrences might not be the most meaningful measure, especially if the costs of the various causes of defects are widely different. In this case, it is better to base the Pareto diagram on total cost.

EXAMPLE 1

During the spring semester 1994, one of the authors taught an introductory statistics course to a group of 100 students. About six weeks through the semester he handed out the questionnaire given in Table 2.2.

Sixty-two students returned the questionnaire; this is not a particularly good response rate, as there were 100 students in the course. Of the 62 responses, 41 (or $100(41/62) = 66$ percent) indicated that they had no difficulties understanding

TABLE 2.2 Questionnaire to Assess Student Perceptions of the Course, and Frequencies of Problems Mentioned

SPRING 1994—Statistical Methods II—2/23/1994

1. Do you have difficulties understanding the material covered in this course?

   NO YES

2. If your answer is YES, please go on. Circle the top two reasons that prevent you from learning the material in this course.

   Instructor generally not prepared
   Instructor not accessible outside of class
   Poor teaching assistants
   Book and Minitab handbook difficult to understand
   Computer software for statistical analysis
   Uncomfortable lecture room
   Your failure to keep up with readings and homework
   Any other reason—please specify

Frequencies of Problems Mentioned

2	Instructor generally not prepared
0	Instructor not accessible outside of class
5	Poor teaching assistants
11	Book and Minitab handbook difficult to understand
5	Computer software for statistical analysis
3	Uncomfortable lecture room
9	Your failure to keep up with readings and homework
2	No interest in the course
2	Too few examples
3	Difficult nature of the subject
42	Total number of mentioned difficulties

the material. Twenty-one of the respondents, or 100(21/62) = 34 percent, said that they had difficulties. In addition to the seven reasons for their difficulties in understanding statistics listed on the questionnaire, students mentioned several others: (i) no interest in the subject; (ii) too few examples; (iii) difficult nature of the subject. The frequencies with which the various difficulties were mentioned are also given in Table 2.2.

The particular ordering of these categories in Table 2.2 and their associated frequencies is arbitrary. However, in quality applications it makes sense to rank the causes according to decreasing frequencies of their occurrences. We start with the most common cause ("Book and Minitab difficult to understand"). The frequencies, the relative frequencies (which are obtained by dividing the frequencies by the sum of all frequencies), and the relative cumulative frequencies are all given in

TABLE 2.3 Frequency Distribution of Problems Mentioned

(Categories are ordered from the most common to the least common)

	Frequency	Relative frequency	Cumulative relative frequency
Book and Minitab difficult to understand	11	26.2	26.2
Failure to keep up with readings and homework	9	21.4	47.6
Poor teaching assistants	5	11.9	59.5
Computer software for statistical analysis	5	11.9	71.4
Uncomfortable lecture room	3	7.1	78.5
Difficult nature of the subject	3	7.1	85.6
No interest in the course	2	4.8	90.4
Too few examples	2	4.8	95.2
Instructor generally not prepared	2	4.8	100.0
Instructor not accessible outside of class	0	0.0	100.0
	42	100.0	

Table 2.3. For example, dividing the frequency "11" for book/Minitab difficulties by 42, leads to 0.262 or 26.2 percent. 26.2 percent of all difficulties are due to the course materials. The second most prevalent reason has to do with students' failure to keep up with the material. This reason accounts for 21.4 percent of all difficulties. Together these top two reasons account for 47.6 percent.

Figure 2.6 displays the information in Table 2.3 in the form of a Pareto diagram. Categories are listed on the horizontal axis, while frequencies are shown on the vertical axis. The scale on the left-hand side of the vertical axis refers to relative frequencies, while the scale on the right-hand side refers to cumulative relative frequencies. From this graph it is easy to locate, for example, the two most common causes of defects (difficulties with the reading materials and students' failure to keep up) and the proportion of defects that are due to these two leading causes (which is 47.6 percent). In our example, problems related to the text and problems related to students' failure to keep up are by far the most frequent ones. These two together are responsible for about 50 percent of the problems. ■

EXAMPLE 2

In Figure 2.7 we show two Pareto diagrams for defects in a lens coating operation. The diagram on the left shows the daily frequencies under the original process. Poorly coated lenses account for 45 of the 110 defects; scarred lenses contribute another 30 defects. Together, these two categories account for 68 percent of all

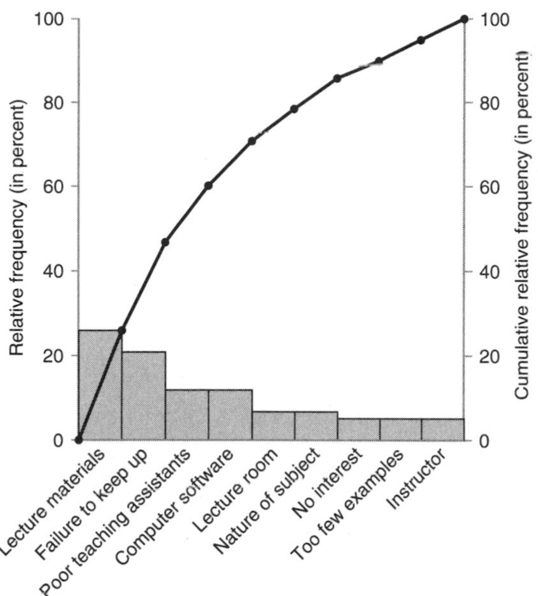

FIGURE 2.6 A Pareto diagram: Causes of difficulties understanding the course material.

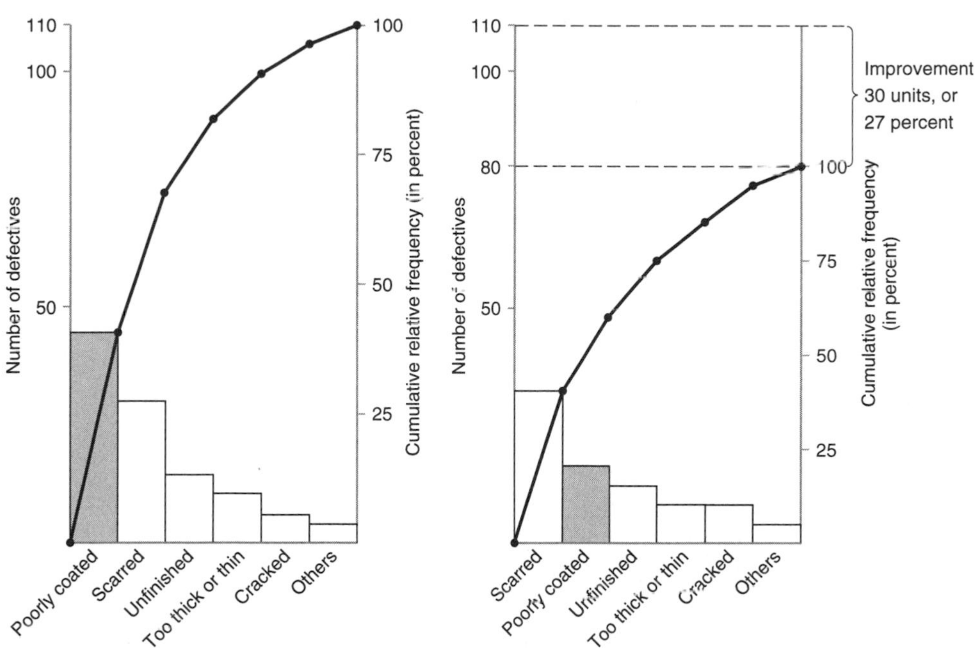

FIGURE 2.7 Pareto diagrams for lens coating defects.

defects. It is easy to see this from the cumulative frequency scale on the right-hand side of the diagram.

New procedures were adopted to prevent the poor coating of lenses. The Pareto chart on the right side of Figure 2.7 shows daily defect frequencies for the improved process. We notice a reduction in the total number of defects from 110 to 80—a 27 percent decrease. Furthermore, the frequency of poorly coated lenses is cut by more than half. ■

2.10 EXERCISES

2.1 Give examples of unexpected problems, detected problems, and acknowledged problems. Discuss the contexts in which they arise.

2.2 Select a consumer product of your choice. Discuss how a consumer would detect problems.

2.3 Discuss how you would detect problems associated with a service—for example, the delivery of health care or the service quality in a restaurant.

2.4 Construct a flowchart of a process you are familiar with. For example, construct a flowchart of the appointment procedure in a doctor's office. Or, construct a flowchart of baking a frosted cake, a flowchart of your weekday morning routine going to school or work, or a flowchart of changing the oil in your car. Or, make a flowchart of the telephone answering process at a major mail-order company that sells (and services) computers.

2.5 Family medical guides, such as the *American Medical Association Family Medical Guide* (Random House, 1987), provide "Self-Diagnosis Symptom Charts" for common ailments. These are basically flowcharts of the decision process that is used to arrive at a self-diagnosis for a given ailment. Draw the chart for "Chest Pains" and the chart for "Painful Ankles."

2.6 Consider problems that are associated with poor instruction of college courses. Form a group of fellow students and prioritize the problems. Discuss the criteria and explain the ranking.

2.7 Assume that as a city manager you want to create a better image of your community. Prioritize the problems of your city, carefully discussing the criteria and the ranking procedure that are used in your investigation.

2.8 Ask fellow students in your class about the various reasons that prevented them from obtaining better grades. Construct a Pareto chart.

2.9 Select a functional area of your educational institution that you are familiar with (e.g., your cafeteria), generate a list of problems that you perceive in that area, and rank the problems in order of importance.

2.10 Interview an employee of some organization to learn about the processes they operate. In particular, attempt to learn about problems that everyone is familiar with, but nevertheless remain unsolved. For each such problem, attempt to learn why the problem remains unsolved.

2.11 Read and discuss the paper by M. Benjamin and J. G. Shaw, "Harnessing the Power of the Pareto Principle," in *Quality Progress*, September 1993 (Vol. 26), 103–107.

2.12 The *World Almanac* contains data on Personal Consumption Expenditures in the United States for a number of selected categories. For example, the 1995 *Almanac* provides personal consumption expenditures in 1993 (and other years) for eleven categories, ranging from Food & Tobacco to Religious & Welfare Activities. Use such data from a recent copy of the *World Almanac* and construct a Pareto diagram of U.S. Personal Expenditures employing the categories in your copy.

2.11 REFERENCES

Benjamin, M., and J. G. Shaw. "Harnessing the Power of the Pareto Principle," *Quality Progress*, September 1993 (Vol. 26), 103–107.

Brassard, M., and D. Ritter. *The Memory Jogger II.* Methuen, MA: GOAL/QPC, 1994.

Carroll, Lewis. *Through the Looking-Glass and What Alice Found There.* New York: Macmillan, 1871.

Joiner, B. L. *Fourth Generation Management.* New York: McGraw-Hill, 1994.

Kane, V. E. *Defect Prevention: Use of Simple Statistical Tools.* New York: Marcel Dekker, 1989.

Swift, J. A. *Introduction to Modern Statistical Quality Control and Management.* Delray Beach, FL: St. Lucie Press, 1995.

CHAPTER 3

PROBLEM-SOLVING STRATEGIES

In this chapter we describe strategies for solving problems. When you look at this, we hope you will say: "That's simple and obvious—just plain common sense." We hope you will say that because, in our opinion, that is the test of a good procedure: Something that people recognize as being natural—something they can learn, remember, and use effectively.

3.1 IDEA: A GENERAL PROBLEM-SOLVING PROCEDURE

IDEA is a four-step problem-solving procedure. The acronym is derived from the first letters of the four steps, which are:

Step 1: Inspect the problem
Step 2: Devise a strategy for solving it
Step 3: Execute the strategy
Step 4: Affirm the solution

We use the acronym IDEA because it should help you to remember the steps: *Inspect, Devise, Execute*, and *Affirm*. We shall discuss each of these steps in detail; but first, some general comments about using this or any other procedure.

A procedure is intended as an aid in performing a task; IDEA is intended as an aid in solving problems. For it to serve in this capacity it must be understood thoroughly. And it must be practiced because true understanding comes with use, both with failures and successes. You should get to the point where you can apply IDEA with natural ease, understanding through trial and error how it should be adjusted to various situations.

Unfortunately, there are people who insist on applying a procedure rigidly, often doing so blindly and without understanding. They follow the words and rules, but not the intent of the procedure. An attempt to use IDEA in this fashion might be better than using no procedure, but certainly it will not give you maximum benefit. You should use IDEA as a guide, not a straightjacket; you should learn how to make adjustments to accommodate the various kinds of problems that you encounter.

3.2 THE FOUR COMPONENTS OF THE IDEA APPROACH

3.2.1 Step 1. Inspect the Problem

The first step of IDEA is to inspect the problem carefully from all angles. After all, it is foolish to attempt to solve a problem you do not understand. Yet precisely this behavior is common because a frequent failing in problem solving is to forget to look carefully at the problem. People jump right into working on the problem before it is well understood. You will find the IDEA procedure of great value even if all it ever does is force you to investigate a problem before rushing into its solution.

The following material is a guide to some specific points you might address. This guide is *not* meant as a comprehensive checklist, but as a list of suggestions.

1. Attempt to describe the problem precisely:
   - How is this a problem? What is and what should be?
   - Look at both sides of the issue. What is wrong? What is right? What is distinctive about the problem?
   - Ask what, when, where, why, how, who, and to what extent?
   - Attempt to see connections. Relate details to other details.
   - Examine present conditions, symptoms, and underlying causes.
   - Ask if there is more than one problem. Decompose complex problems into simpler subproblems.
2. Examine the criteria for solution. Try to understand exactly what is required:
   - What is required, what should be? What condition should exist?
   - What are the objectives and priorities? Are these the same for everyone? If not, who wants what?
   - What are the constraints: financial, political, technical, and so on?

- Are all constraints real, or are they imagined or self-imposed by the problem solvers?
- Is it possible to satisfy the conditions? Does a solution exist?

3. Ask what has been done so far to solve the problem:
   - What steps were taken? What were the outcomes of these efforts?
4. Analyze all available data on the problem:
   - Look at *all* data. Don't assume some of it is meaningless.
   - What additional data is needed to define the problem? For example, should there be more experiments or test cases? If more data is required, who has it or can get it?
   - Are there contradictions in the data? For example, does a problem happen only under certain conditions?
   - Can the data be trusted? Was it collected under conditions suggesting that it might not be reliable or representative?
   - Does the time-order in which the data was collected give a clue?
5. Document the problem:
   - Don't assume you will remember; write it down. You might be interrupted and forced to resume problem-solving later.
   - Prepare documentation so other people can tell what it means. Label and date documents, show sources of information.

EXAMPLE

To illustrate Step 1, assume that you have been given the problem of establishing a quality improvement effort in your organization. Before starting on this task, there is much you would need to learn: What was the reason for the request? Is quality improvement truly the goal, or is it just to say we have such an effort underway? What would be the benefits of such an effort? Who would benefit? What would be the problems? Who would be impacted negatively? Where is resistance likely to arise? What results are expected? When are they expected? What resources are available? What attempts have been made in the past to improve quality? What were the outcomes of those efforts? Obviously, this is but a small sample of the questions that need to be asked in order to understand the problem before attempting to find a strategy for solving it. ■

3.2.2 Step 2. Devise a Strategy

The second step of IDEA is to find a strategy for getting from what is to what should be. This means determining a scheme for getting from the existing to the desired state. This can be a long and tortuous step because, for all but the simplest of problems, a strategy is likely to emerge gradually. The step will be finished when you have an outline of what must be done to solve the problem.

There are two major activities in Step 2: One activity is to *generate strategies*; the other is to *select the best strategy*. These two activities should be performed separately. First, efforts should be made to generate as many strategies as possible. This is accomplished by conducting a wide-open search for ideas. Every effort should be made to find new ideas and to avoid restricting or focusing the search. During this search, no attempt should be made to evaluate strategies or judge them because the evaluation process tends to restrict the flow of ideas. After ideas are generated, they are examined and judged.

The process of generating strategies brings a divergence in thought about the problem. The evaluation of strategies brings convergence back to the problem, a narrowing of attention to those ideas that seem best. For a problem of any complexity, this cycling between divergence and convergence is likely to be repeated many times during Step 2. On each cycle, further insight is gained about a feasible strategy for solving the problem; and based on this further insight, the next cycle typically brings more progress toward the goal.

Generating Strategies Generating strategies for solving the problem means identifying as many ideas as possible without any regard to their suitability. You never know, a crazy, far-out idea just might trigger another thought that turns out to be the best way to handle the problem. Useful techniques for generating ideas include *Escape from Conventional Thinking, Analogy*, and *Cause Analysis* (all discussed in this chapter); *Brainstorming* and the *Nominal Group Technique*, two structured group activities discussed in the next chapter; and *Data Analysis Techniques*, covered in Sections II through V of this book.

Faced with several techniques, the natural question is: Which is the best one to use? Some people have a favorite that they tend to use in all situations. Other people tend to try a variety of techniques on a problem, on the theory that if you try everything, something should work. A more reasonable approach seems to be to match the technique to the problem and the group solving it. There is no magic formula for making such a match; a reasonable approach, however, is for the group to become familiar with all the techniques and make a group decision as to which technique to apply in a particular situation. As a matter of fact, we have imposed our judgment to some extent by limiting the techniques that we have included in this book. However, the few we have included here will serve most purposes in solving problems related to quality.

Selecting the Best Strategy Selecting the best among a collection of strategies is a matter of evaluating each strategy. Each strategy is evaluated against the criteria for solution of the problem, and the best strategy is identified. A check is made that the identified strategy does not have any adverse side effects.

If you are lucky, a single best strategy will emerge; but, of course, difficulties can arise. If an identified strategy has adverse side effects, it might be necessary to discard it in favor of a somewhat less desirable strategy. There could be many strategies that tie for best, and then it will be necessary to find additional criteria to use in selecting the best. It may be that no strategy is satisfactory, but that a satisfactory one can be fashioned by combining two or more ideas. And it may be that nothing emerges that is satisfactory, which means going back to redefine the problem or repeating Step 2.

EXAMPLE *(continued)*

Let us look further at the problem of establishing a quality improvement effort in your organization. Suppose you have inspected the problem and feel fairly comfortable with what is required. The question now is: What strategy will accomplish the objective? You think of several ways this could be done:

1. You could have a companywide effort kicked off with a "Pledge Day" in which everyone is asked to commit to quality. Then local units could build programs with your help.
2. You can settle on the total information systems (IS) area, install quality there, then move to other parts of the organization. In the typical business much information is processed manually, but a growing amount of information flows through computers at some stage. The IS area is the field that involves computerized information processes.
3. You can start with some local efforts, then build on those successes.

Of course, these are mere skeletons of the strategies you might evolve, and they do little more than suggest the wide range of options available. The three given above look at the size and organizational setting of the initial effort. There are also questions of what activities to engage in, what organizational structure to establish for a quality function, what outside support will be required in the form of consultants and classes, and so on. Having generated strategies, you must next evaluate them. Of the three just listed, you might reject strategy 1 as being too shallow; waving banners and hoping for the best is not too practical. You might reject strategy 3 because a bottom-up approach seldom works; upper management must be committed and involved or the program will never get off the ground. You might consider strategy 2 as an alternative to be explored further; it may not be ideal to start with IS only because that area interacts with every other area. But if IS management is solidly behind the program and has sufficient clout with top management to gain their solid support and involvement, then it might work. At least, it is a strategy worth exploring. ■

3.2.3 Step 3. Execute the Strategy

The third step in IDEA is to execute the strategy developed in Step 2. This is an easier step than Step 2. It calls for two major activities:

1. Build an action plan.
2. Implement the action plan.

The strategy devised in Step 2 is a general outline of what is needed to solve the problem. Now it is necessary to examine the details of the strategy and build a step-by-step plan for executing it. Carrying out the strategy is a *project*; essentially what is needed, then, is a *project plan*.

If executing the strategy requires extensive effort, then you should consult a reference on project planning to learn what to do; for example, H. Kerzner, *Project Management: A Systems Approach to Planning, Scheduling, and Controlling* (3rd edition; New York: Van Nostrand Reinhold, 1989); or J. R. Meredith, *Project Management: A Managerial Approach* (3rd edition; New York: Wiley, 1995). If your project will take only a short period of time, then you can probably handle the plan relatively informally. Simply list the activities to be performed, assign each to a responsible person, and give them a date by which to be finished.

We wish to make a few general comments on projects. Build your work assignments on the basis of completed work products. That is, don't give someone the job of "building half the training package"—no one knows what that means. Take the trouble to decide what half consists of, then make a specific assignment, such as, "produce the material needed to teach these four topics." Be sure to give each person a specific set of activities to accomplish and a schedule for when their work outputs should be completed. When you plan, don't forget all the support activities and systems you will need: clerical services, machine time, printing services, as well as places to work. Don't be surprised if support services take as much effort and attention as all the rest of the project. And be wary of the trap that your entire project is driven by time deadlines to the detriment of quality. Try to make reasonable estimates of the time needed to perform tasks (get help from the people who actually have to do them); starting your project with a reasonable schedule is essential, otherwise you will be pressed for time and quality will suffer. When your initial plan is in place, have some knowledgeable people review it to see if they can spot potential problems. If some are identified, try to find ways to avoid or minimize them.

If you have a good action plan, implementing it should be routine. You can control the project simply by keeping track of when people complete their assignments. If you have given relatively short work assignments (and you should), then it is sufficient just to know when the job is done. This method of control saves asking people to estimate when they will complete a task—a particularly useless activity because nobody knows how to estimate well.

If the project gets off schedule, then replan. If you find yourself getting behind the original schedule, admit it to yourself. Don't pretend that "next week we'll catch up"; that's the sure way to miss the final deadline. Face up to problems that arise and attempt to solve them; if necessary, get more resources or ask people to put in extra time. Better to do that early and get back on schedule than to ignore a problem and have a crash effort at the end.

EXAMPLE *(continued)*

For our continuing example of installing quality improvement, suppose you decided to start the improvement program in IS. Your strategy calls for the appointment of a Quality Assurance Manager who will: provide basic education in quality to IS professionals, IS management, and the senior managers to whom IS reports; and develop a quality improvement plan covering the next two years. Included in that plan will be two specific projects, namely, building a prototyping facility and building a testing facility, both to be used by the entire IS department. To help you, you have hired an outside consulting firm to conduct the education and to act as coach in guiding you through your first year in the new assignment. Plans for these activities should include specific dates for courses, for the delivery of the various versions of the quality improvement plan, and for major milestones on the two special projects. ■

3.2.4 Step 4. Affirm the Solution

The last step of IDEA is to affirm that the problem is solved—and that no new problems have been created! Look at the solution; review and discuss it among the people involved. In particular, ask:

- Was the goal reached? Is the problem solved? Are all criteria met?
- Are there any adverse impacts that must be handled?
- Have all people been notified who are involved in making the change or who are impacted by it?
- Does the solution suggest any new problems that should be tackled? In particular, can the solution be installed elsewhere to solve a related problem in the organization?

If what you have accomplished is important enough, publicize your success. That might sound like tooting your own horn, but it is important to do. For one thing, it gives the people involved in solving the problem the recognition they deserve for a job well done. For another, it calls attention to the fact that something was done about a problem. That can be an inspiration for others in the organization to make similar efforts. Done with taste, publicity is important to the organization.

EXAMPLE *(continued)*

For our continuing example of installing quality improvement, affirmation that a solution was in place undoubtedly would not wait until the entire project was finished. Instead, as with any large project, affirmation would be made as each major piece of the solution was installed. For each class, each version of the quality improvement plan, and each milestone of the two major activities, affirmation would be made that the installed solution met the relevant criteria. Also, it is highly likely that additional problems would be recognized on a regular basis and added to the problem pending list. Chances are that the scheme sketched in the example would be a very successful means of starting the improvement effort. ■

3.3 IMPLEMENTING A PROBLEM-SOLVING STRATEGY

So far we have discussed problem solving strictly from the procedural side. Now let us look at some of the human factors involved and some of the experiences you can expect to have in a typical problem-solving session.

Success at problem solving requires *determination.* A good procedure is of little help if the problem solver does not have the will to succeed. There are ups and downs in solving most problems. Unless you have the determination to stick it out during the low points, you will never go through to success. A procedure such as IDEA is a help: Knowing where you are in the problem-solving process helps with your resolve to carry on when things look dark and hope is waning.

A related, but different, factor is *involvement* with the problem. This means eating and sleeping with the problem—becoming so familiar with it that you dream about it. Involvement helps to conjure up ideas that have long been dormant in your mind, and helps you to make connections that otherwise would not be made.

Problem-solving involves *speculation.* The heart of solving a problem is getting a good idea. No one can tell you how to do that. But you can be advised to let your mind run free; think of all sorts of things that on closer inspection might just work.

Another useful notion is *deferment.* Don't be too quick to jump to conclusions. Don't jump right into problem-solving mode before you inspect the problem carefully. Don't start evaluating an idea as soon as it occurs to you. Follow IDEA; it has deferment built in.

Finally, *take a break* from the problem. We spoke of involvement just a few lines above. Involvement is one thing, but working on a problem when you are stale is another. When you reach an impasse, turn to something else—preferably something quite different so you really have a break. When you take a break from a problem, try to make it at a natural point, some place where you have completed an activity and are ready to start on something new.

Let us look at some of the things that might transpire as you apply IDEA to a problem. Step 2 of IDEA, Devise a Strategy, is the most creative, hence the least procedural step; this is the step we want to discuss a bit further.

A common question during Step 2 is "Where do I start?" That is easy: You start with the problem statement. From Step 1 you should understand clearly what is wanted and what the conditions are. So concentrate on the problem. Examine it as a whole, and ignore details and special cases that only confuse in the beginning. Try to grasp the essence of the problem and keep it in your mind; in that way you will stimulate your memory to recall relevant facts and ideas that might be useful. When useful but partial ideas occur, use them to stimulate other ideas that might take you a step further toward the goal. Don't expect the entire answer to spring full blown from your mind; be thankful for any progress you make. If nothing comes, try restating the problem or attacking it from another angle. Or sleep on it and see what turns up tomorrow.

You can't solve problems without knowing something. You need knowledge, some subject matter with which to work. Good ideas are based on past experience and formerly acquired knowledge. Part of what you must do is bring these past experiences to mind. Then you must combine ideas and attempt to adapt them to the problem under investigation. These two activities—searching for ideas and organizing them—go on together.

As you progress toward the solution, your view of the problem must change—lack of change would indicate that you had made no progress. As you progress, you gain insight into the problem. This insight allows you to see connections and potential solutions that you could not grasp before; and this, in turn, leads to further insight. As your understanding deepens, you gain a better feeling for the problem's structure and basic nature. Step by step you progress—in an iterative fashion—to a full solution of the problem.

Once in a while the slow step-by-step march toward a solution is interrupted by a sudden bright idea—a sudden flash that brings an abrupt change of outlook. And once in a while what you think is a sudden bright idea turns out on closer inspection to be flawed. But inspiration does come occasionally; when it does you will find there are few experiences that can top it. But in order to be safe, don't rely on inspiration, rely on perspiration.

3.4 SOLVING PROBLEMS: ESCAPE FROM CONVENTIONAL THINKING

At times one just can't make progress in solving a problem. One keeps thinking the same thoughts over and over, but new ideas just won't come. What is needed is an *escape from conventional ways of approaching the problem*; one needs new attitudes and new ways of thinking. The purpose of this section is to suggest several techniques for bringing this about. What we shall present are new ways to view a problem and new ways to attack it.

3.4.1 The Problem Statement

The place to start developing a new way of attacking the problem is with the problem itself. One must take a careful look at the way the problem is currently being viewed. Often hidden assumptions are being made, and these bind people and constrain their ability to solve the problem. For example, one may have instructed teams that they should write certain information on a card that is to be exchanged with another team. The written instructions carefully state what must be included on the card, but do *not* state that nothing else can be added. Most teams, however, make the *tacit* assumption that nothing can be put on the card other than the required material; consequently they unilaterally prevent themselves from passing information that would be to their advantage.

Success in solving a problem depends on choosing the right way to view it. In the late 1970s, American car manufacturers were complacent about the threat of competition from Japan because they felt that the Japanese faced an insurmountable problem: American manufacturers all had extensive dealer networks to provide service and repairs for their cars; there was no way that the Japanese could duplicate the American service networks without expending much time and resources. But the Japanese viewed the problem differently and found an innovative solution: They simply produced cars with so few defects that the service network was not that essential.

To learn the right view, you must vary the way you look at the problem. Variation of the problem tends to bring new ideas; and these new ideas, in turn, change the way you view the problem. Thus problem variation and problem solution are intertwined. Variation of the problem can be achieved by changing the problem concept, the problem vantage, or the problem-solving technique. Let's look at each of these.

3.4.2 The Problem Concept

To get a fresh approach, one might attempt to change the concept of the problem. If the altered problem can be solved, then the solution usually can be adjusted to fit the original problem. Some ideas for altering the problem concept are these:

Rephrase the problem. This is really not a change of concept, but a change in the way the original problem is stated. By taking a different point of view, adding more detail, deleting some of the detail, changing the tone of the statement, or some other modification of the original problem statement, it may be possible to stimulate the problem solvers into a new way of thinking.

Expand the problem. Sometimes a larger problem is easier to solve than is a smaller problem. Instead of trying to justify the cost of attending a particular class, focus on justifying education in the organization. Instead of trying to find a way to handle paper flow in one office, ask how to do it for the division. Instead of designing a system for a certain volume of business, ask how the system should function for ten times that volume. Expanding the problem frequently allows people to consider solutions that don't occur when the smaller problem is being considered.

Contract the problem. Sometimes a smaller problem is easier to solve than a larger one. Instead of handling the complaints of all customers, consider what to do for just the few most frequent complaints. Instead of trying to automate an entire factory, consider the problem of automating one or two key stations. Contracting the problem can allow people to escape from an overwhelming situation to one that they can handle. Having solved the smaller problem, they then have more experience with which to tackle the larger, original problem.

Consider a parallel problem. An important technique in problem solving is to replace the real problem with one that is similar, but more familiar. This is the technique of using an analogy to solve a problem. Because it is such an important technique, it is discussed in some detail in the next section.

Change the parameters or boundaries of the problem. Instead of solving the problem for this location, consider the problem as if it were for another plant or another country. Instead of looking at the problem today, consider what it will be like in five years' time. Instead of considering the problem for Departments A and B, consider it for Departments A and C. Changes in the parameters or boundaries can bring a changed perspective and can loosen some of the hidden assumptions that constrain the problem solvers.

Split the problem into two problems. The problem of getting increased sales might be split into the problems of increasing sales to large accounts and to small accounts. Or it could be divided into a problem of designing products and selling products, or into a problem of Eastern Division and Western Division. Even an arbitrary split can jog people's thoughts by giving a new perspective.

Combine the problem with another seemingly unrelated problem. The problem of improving employee morale might be combined with the problem of how to do long-range planning. Or it might be combined with the problem of increasing sales. As with all these suggestions, the object of combining dissimilar problems is to break the old, ineffective approach to the problem and stimulate new ideas.

Decompose and recombine. This technique can be viewed as a joining of the two previous techniques: splitting a problem into parts, then combining the parts in some new way. The basic idea is to focus on details, thereby breaking the problem into parts; then to recombine the parts into a whole. Each such recombination gives a different view of the problem. The problem might be to put a man on the moon. This problem could be divided into a very large number of pieces, each piece calling for a specific accomplishment. These pieces could be combined based on responsibility, or based on how soon the pieces must be accomplished, or based on the skill and technical knowledge needed to accomplish them.

3.4.3 The Problem Vantage

Another way to generate new ideas is to change the vantage point of the problem solver. This can be done in several ways:

Problem perspective. The problem solver comes from a particular background and naturally tends to view the problem from the perspective of that background. One way to get new ideas is to view the problem from someone else's perspective. If the problem is building a house, it can be viewed from the perspective of the contractor who builds it, the potential occupant, the bank that finances it, the neighbors who will surround, and so on. The problem solver can get new ideas by looking at the problem from the these different vantage points.

Level of attention. For any problem, one can look at the big picture or the nitty-gritty details. If you have been concentrating on details, step back and look at the big picture. Look at the forest rather than the trees. Conversely, if you have been looking at the big picture, focus on some of the details. This will bring reality to your overall view and prevent wasting time on solutions that are impractical. Also, it will help you to see the big picture differently if later you switch back to that vantage.

Point of entry. Many problems have a natural order to them where there is a sequence of things to be determined. The natural tendency is to start at the beginning and try to settle each piece before going on to the next. An alternative approach is to start somewhere in the middle and try to cope with that portion on the assumption that earlier bits have been worked out satisfactorily. This can allow progress to be made, and it can break the problem of not knowing how to get started. For example, suppose that the problem is to decide whether or not to start a company. The first step, settling legal and tax questions involved with incorporating, involves many difficult decisions and requires much time and thought. But instead of getting stuck on these issues, one might assume that they can be worked out and proceed to address questions about sales and marketing.

Direction of solution. Instead of starting with the first thing to be done and working through in sequence, one might start working on a problem with the last thing to be done and work toward the first. This reversal of direction is another way of overcoming the problem of getting started. If the problem is to build and sell a product, one might start with questions about how the product will be delivered and serviced, then deal with marketing, manufacturing, and development in that order.

3.4.4 The Problem-Solving Technique

For any problem, there are some problem-solving techniques that seem more appropriate than others. A problem solver generally applies an appropriate technique, but the trouble is he tends to stick to that technique even past the point where useful results are being generated. A more effective approach might be to try some other technique to discover if it will yield additional useful ideas. Some techniques that might be tried are these:

Extract a pattern. Through data analysis it is sometimes possible to extract patterns, and this information can help to provide solutions to the problem at hand. For example, suppose that the problem is to reduce the number of defects. An analysis of information on defects (displayed in a Pareto chart) might point out the major causes of the problem and might make it possible to make significant inroads on solving the problem.

Analogy. Earlier we suggested that an analogy can be used to generate a new problem statement. Similarly, an analogy can be used to generate a solution to a given problem. This important technique is discussed in the next section.

Cause-and-effect analysis. For some problems it is appropriate to trace chains of cause and effect in an attempt to solve the problem. Cause-and-effect analysis is discussed in Section 3.6 of this chapter.

Think opposite. To gain insight into the problem, it is often useful to "think opposite" about the problem. Traditionally we have brought the workers to the parts, but what happens if we bring the parts to the workers? Henry Ford answered this by building the production line. Traditionally we have brought the crops to the consumers, but what happens if we bring the consumers to the crops? We now have farms where the consumers pay a fee and gather their own produce. Traditionally the worker has gone to the office, but what happens if we bring the office to the worker? Modern communication and computing have made this technically feasible, but it remains to be seen if several practical problems can be solved to make this a reality for a significant part of the office work force. Thinking opposite is an effective tool for generating revolutionary solutions to problems, and for that reason it is a strong contender as an alternative technique for attacking any problem.

Retrace steps. For some problems, a careful retracing of steps will generate a solution. If I've mislaid my glasses, a good way to find them is to retrace my steps from the time I last remember having them. If the car will start for you but not for me, a good way to learn how to start it is for me to watch very carefully as you start it and to compare that with what I do. If something went wrong in a meeting, a step-by-step investigation might indicate what the problem was. If a project went wrong, a careful retracing of events may suggest the cause.

Reduce to another problem. Sometimes the easy way to solve a problem is to show that it can be transformed into a problem for which there is already a solution. For instance, suppose that visitors are coming to inspect our new facility; what we'll do is give them a brief orientation, have lunch with them, and then give them the same tour we gave the last group. Suppose we need to design a special one-week course on statistical process control; what we'll do is use the relevant modules from our regular course offerings. In all these cases, the problem becomes minor because we have reduced major portions of it to something we know how to handle.

3.4.5 Additional Hints

At times, problems almost seem to solve themselves. For example, it is a common experience for a person to start explaining a problem to another, but then to stop abruptly because the solution has suddenly become clear to the presenter. What may seem to be a stroke of insight usually amounts to nothing more than seeing the problem clearly for the first time—a view gained from the need to understand the problem well enough to explain it to another. Along the same lines but less common is the sudden solution of a problem being triggered by the act of writing it down in an organized way.

Problem solution is sometimes inhibited by the tendency of problem solvers to view things as binary. An idea is either good or bad. A suggestion is either useful or not. Generally it is more helpful to judge ideas and suggestions on a scale from zero to ten where zero is bad and ten is good. If looked at in this manner, most ideas and suggestions will fall somewhere in the middle. Then the natural questions are: What is there in the idea that is useful? What are the concerns that keep it from being judged as good? Can those concerns be eliminated? By judging ideas and suggestions on a spectrum instead of in a binary fashion, it is possible to salvage the parts that are useful and to build even better ideas on those parts.

Problem solving is hard work; and as with any kind of hard work, you can't keep at it too long. When you get stuck on a problem, switch to another problem; then after a while, switch back. That's what we did in writing this book. When we couldn't think of a good example to illustrate a point, we put in a few asterisks and a note to remind ourselves that something was missing, then went on to the next part. Eventually we went back and replaced all the asterisks with appropriate text. If we had not done that, we would have wasted a lot of time trying to complete each passage before starting the next.

3.5 SOLVING PROBLEMS: UTILIZING ANALOGY

An important technique for solving a problem is to relate it to another, more familiar problem, and to use information about the new problem to solve the original one. One of the most impressive examples of this technique is that discovered by René Descartes in the seventeenth century. By introducing a so-called *Cartesian coordinate system*, Descartes devised a means of translating any geometric problem into an algebraic problem. Thus, to solve a problem in geometry, one translates it into a problem in algebra, solves the algebra problem, then translates this result into a solution to the original problem. This technique is extremely helpful because algebraic problems are usually more easily solved than the corresponding geometric problems.

For nonmathematical situations, one is not likely to find a complete one-to-one correspondence between problems. Instead, one looks for a problem that bears a close resemblance to the one in hand and tries to use that resemblance to advantage. This concept is explored in this section.

An *analogy* is a similarity or likeness between two things. Analogies are expressed in statements of comparison, such as, "This organization is like the army." By exploiting the analogy, characteristics of the analogue ("the army" in this example) might suggest characteristics to be found in the original thing ("this organization").

Use of analogy pervades our thinking and language. We use analogues from the level of simple metaphors to mathematical homomorphisms. We use analogies in everyday speech and for artistic expression. Analogies help to give us understanding and interesting ways to express our thoughts. They also provide insight into problems, which is our interest here.

An analogy is rarely an absolute similarity. To be useful, the analogy should show close resemblances in the areas relevant to the issue being addressed. Also, differences should be irrelevant to the issue and such that they can be safely ignored. Resemblances of a functional kind are likely to be fundamental and useful, whereas resemblances that are quantitative often are not. For example, the above analogy between "this organization" and "the army" might be useful if the similarity is in their mode of organization, operation, treatment of individuals, or some other way in which the two organizations function. If, however, the resemblance is simply that the two organizations have approximately the same number of people, then the analogy is probably not too useful.

Analogies are used primarily when devising a strategy. But they also can be used to suggest a better understanding of the problem, and to guide the execution of a strategy. That is, an analogy can be used to understand a problem, generate an idea of what to do, and guide how to do it. Before attempting to use an analogy, the assumption is that there is a problem to be solved. Let us refer to this problem as the *basic problem* to be solved. Use of an analogy to solve a basic problem really involves three steps:

Step 1: Find an analogue of the original situation and map the basic problem onto an analogous problem.

Step 2: Solve the analogous problem.

Step 3: Use the insight from solving the analogous problem to solve the basic problem.

We shall explore each of these subsidiary problems in turn.

Step 1: One must think of an object, process, system, situation, or some other thing that can serve as a useful analogue to the context in which the basic problem is embedded. Once a promising analogue is discovered, it must be developed and refined to make the similarities more pronounced. Particular attention should be paid to functional similarities between the original problem context and the analogue.

Often the hardest part of using an analogy to solve a problem is to think of a good analogue. But, fortunately, one need not always start from scratch. Most basic problems are not brand new; they probably resemble problems that have been faced by others. Examining what others have done and scanning the literature will frequently suggest potential analogues. And once a good analogue is discovered, it can be reused for a succession of related problems.

As an example of establishing an analogy, consider the basic problem of building a good system for producing computer software.

The key idea is that we are to build something, so one might think of other things that are built; the concept of building a house comes to mind. So we might say that the analogue of building computer software is to build a house. But that analogy can be sharpened. Computer software products tend to be quite distinctive, whereas some people build houses based on one of a few set patterns. To sharpen the analogy, we might consider only that part of the construction business that deals with custom houses. More reflection might suggest that the task of building a house is too small to be compared with the software produced by the organization we are considering. Perhaps a better analogue of building computer software is the building of a large office building. If this analogy seems to fit well enough, we can stop here and go on to exploit the analogy.

Of course, finding a good system for building computer software is not a new problem; it has been faced by countless organizations over several decades. Nor is the analogue of building a house new; it is a standard device for understanding the building process and explaining the construction of computer software to nonspecialists.

Step 2: The second problem, solving the analogous problem, should be very simple, otherwise you do not have a useful analogue. The *point* of an analogue is to use something familiar to gain insight into the basic problem. If you don't understand the analogous problem, you are not gaining on the basic problem, so you better look for another analogy. To ensure that the problem of solving the analogous problem is very simple, you should select analogies with these properties:

The analogue should be *concrete*. It should be specific rather than abstract, so that solutions to the analogous problem are specific.

The analogue should be *familiar to the problem solver*. Don't compare building computer software with building a ship if you know nothing about the ship-building industry. Building a house is a good analogue because most people are familiar with the process and know roughly how house-building problems are solved.

The analogue should *not be too close to the basic problem context*. Comparing the building of software with the process of enhancing software (adding additional functions) is not too useful; if you don't understand how to do one, you aren't likely to understand how to do the other because the processes are quite similar.

Step 3: Having a solution to an analogous problem does not guarantee a solution to the basic problem. Because an analogy is never perfect, all that can be translated from the analogue to the original situation is a suggestion and guideline for tackling the basic problem. But with this direction, tackling the basic problem should be easier. If not, seek another analogy or attempt another method of problem solution.

3.6 CAUSE ANALYSIS: FINDING CAUSES OF PROBLEMS

"What was the cause of this defect?" "What will help us produce better products?" "What change in our process will result in a lower error rate?" These questions all have the same intent; they ask for the *cause of an effect*. The effect may be a desirable one, such as better products, or an undesirable effect one would like to eliminate, such as a defect in a product. This section is about finding causes by using a general approach called *cause-and-effect analysis*.

A *cause* is that which produces an effect or a result. We see an effect, and we want to know what caused it. Usually we don't know for certain what the cause was. Unless we actually observe the cause in operation, we can only speculate about what happened. The best we can do is to use all the available evidence to make a reasonable judgment as to the cause.

In searching for the cause of an effect, we start by looking for likely candidates. A *possible cause* is one which could cause an effect or a result. For any effect there are always many possible causes. For example, the failure of a car to start could be caused by having no gas, a dead battery, the gear shift in the wrong position, or many other conditions. A search for the cause of an effect starts by listing all possible causes.

The next step is to ask: What most likely caused the effect? A *most likely cause* or a *probable cause* is the possible cause that best explains the observed effect. The task, then, is to sift through all possible causes, weigh available evidence, and determine which possible cause most nearly explains the effects that were observed.

In searching for the cause of a problem, be certain it is a single problem, not a collection of problems. With a multiple problem, each of the constituent subproblems could have a separate cause, and it might be impossible to find any of them without splitting the problem into logical pieces.

Specify a problem completely before starting a cause analysis. Much of your analysis will amount to the elimination of possible causes from further consideration. The more carefully the problem is stated, the easier it will be to find discrepancies or distinctions that will make such elimination possible. With a thorough knowledge of the problem, you will be able to spot clues proving that certain possible causes just could not have produced the observed effect. Without knowing the problem thoroughly, you will waste much time searching for additional evidence as you examine each possible cause.

Don't mix the search for possible causes with the search for the most likely cause. They are different activities requiring different approaches. The search for possible causes is a divergent process, looking for new information about the problem. The search for the most likely cause is a convergent process in which that information is sifted and narrowed down.

Don't mix cause determination with the elimination of cause. These are two separate problems: finding the cause of an effect, and finding a way to eliminate that cause. The second problem can be addressed only after the first has been solved. Some people try to mix the two; they find what might be the probable cause and start to eliminate it before they are certain it is the right one. Then they discover they really don't have the probable cause, so they go back to cause analysis. Mixing the two problems and switching back and forth wastes time and leaves a good chance that the real cause may never be discovered.

A cause may, in turn, be a problem. It is quite usual to encounter a chain of causes and effects as you search for the cause of some problem. The beginning of the chain is called the *root cause* of the effect—the basic cause behind the observed result.

3.6.1 Generating Possible Causes

The search for the most likely cause of an effect begins with the search for possible causes. This is a divergent process; the object is to generate as many ideas as possible about the cause of an event, knowing that this must be sifted later to converge on the most likely cause. Possible causes can be generated in several ways; we shall look at three.

Top-down generation of causes. One way to generate possible causes is to start with the effect and systematically work toward the cause by asking over and over: Why? We shall call this the *top-down* generation of causes; it is also referred to as *dispersion analysis* or *why-why analysis*.

With the top-down method, one starts with the effect and asks: Why did this effect happen? What caused it? Usually there will be several primary reasons that come to mind. About each of these one repeats the question, asking why each of these happened. By repeating this process as often as seems fruitful, one generates a collection of possible causes.

The top-down approach usually results in a large number of possible causes. Moreover, these are automatically classified into categories and subcategories by the generation process; the answers to a "why question" always form a subcategory of possible causes of the initial effect.

Bottom-up generation of causes. One of the problems with top-down generation of causes is that the first step, answering why the given effect happened, molds the entire analysis. Only the causes identified in the first step are explored further in subsequent steps. More generally, the answers given at any one step determine and limit the area that will be explored on subsequent steps. A bad first step—for example, initial answers that are too specific—may limit the subsequent analysis so as to make it ineffective.

The problems of top-down generation of causes can be eliminated by attacking the problem generating ideas without any restriction. We shall refer to this as the *bottom-up* approach to finding possible causes. With the bottom-up approach, the idea is to generate ideas for causes by whatever means are available. Two popular methods for generating ideas are brainstorming and the nominal group technique. They are discussed in the next chapter.

The bottom-up approach results in a very large number of possible causes, typically more than will be discovered by the top-down approach. Moreover, because the search is not directed, all kinds of causes can be discovered. A problem with this approach, however, is that possible causes flow freely; therefore they appear in random sequence. It is necessary to analyze them and classify them into fewer categories.

Process phases generation of causes. Usually the effect being analyzed is associated with a process. For example, one might be interested in determining the cause of a defective product produced by a particular manufacturing process. In such cases, it seems natural to look for causes by examining the phases of the process one at a time. We shall refer to this as the *process phases* approach to finding possible causes. This approach to generating causes can also be viewed as a combination of the first two approaches: The first step is to ask "why" the effect, the answer being the process phases. Then the next step is to examine the process phases free-form. Concentration on possible cause by process phase forces a structure on responses that corresponds with the traditional way the process is viewed and organized. This is an advantage in that there is usually an established organizational structure for dealing with the causes. But the structure forced on the responses may also be a disadvantage in that it precludes a fresh point of view, which might provide additional insight into the problem area.

3.6.2 Possible Causes for Difficult Problems

For some problems there are so many possible causes that it is not feasible to list them all. Then one uses the problem statement to guide the search toward the causes that have the highest probability of being the probable cause. An example of this is provided by the search for the cause of the Challenger space shuttle accident. The Challenger space shuttle was launched from Cape Kennedy on January 28, 1986. It exploded seconds into the launch, leading to lost lives and a serious setback to the space program. It would be possible to identify literally thousands, perhaps millions, of possible causes for the accident. Instead of attempting to build an exhaustive list, investigators took clues from the problem. Two characteristics about the ill-fated flight seemed particularly significant: (1) temperatures during the launch were unusually low, and (2) final pictures of the craft showed gas escaping from the side, which should not have happened. These two clues caused investigators to concentrate their attention on possible causes that might have been influenced by the temperature and were near the site where trouble most likely developed. In effect, instead of asking the question "What caused the accident?", they narrowed the search by solving the more specific question "What could be influenced by temperature and cause the escape of gas on the side of the craft?" Finally, it was found that certain "O-rings" were at fault.

It is common practice to screen out possible causes that are remote. One does this even for simple problems. In attempting to explain a defect, one might think of the latest quarterly earnings of the company as a causal factor. Low earnings might have caused a change in the budget that caused the cancellation of a class, and not attending that class might have denied a worker the information needed to avoid the defect. But such a remote cause generally would not be listed in any serious attempt at finding the cause of a defect.

The search for possible causes must always be governed by common sense. One must strike a balance between listing everything under the sun, including wild, unproductive ideas, and being "overly practical" and overlooking good ideas in the process.

3.6.3 Cause-and-Effect Diagrams

A useful way to display a collection of possible causes and to show relationships among them is with the so-called *cause-and-effect diagram*. This diagram is also called a *fishbone diagram* because of its shape, or an *Ishikawa diagram* in honor of Kaoru Ishikawa, who developed the concept (*Guide to Quality Control*, 1982).

To construct a cause-and-effect diagram, first find all possible causes of an effect, classify them into about 4 to 8 categories, and into subcategories where appropriate. Draw a horizontal arrow pointing to a box at the right end, which is labeled with the effect under consideration. For each category, draw a line slanting into the horizontal arrow so that the resulting pattern resembles the skeleton of a fish; label each slanting line with the name of a major category. Then draw horizontal arrows into each slanting line to represent the subcategories within the labeled major category. If it is useful to further divide a subcategory, the causes affecting it can be represented by slanting arrows toward the horizontal line that characterizes each subcategory. This process can be repeated indefinitely, but usually two or three levels of classification are sufficient. A generic cause-and-effect diagram is shown in Figure 3.1.

A good cause-and-effect diagram shows several major categories with many causes and subcategories attached to each. A diagram with a severe imbalance among categories, with one having many causes and subcategories and the others having hardly any, is a poor diagram. Another poor diagram is one with a dozen categories, none of which has any branching members.

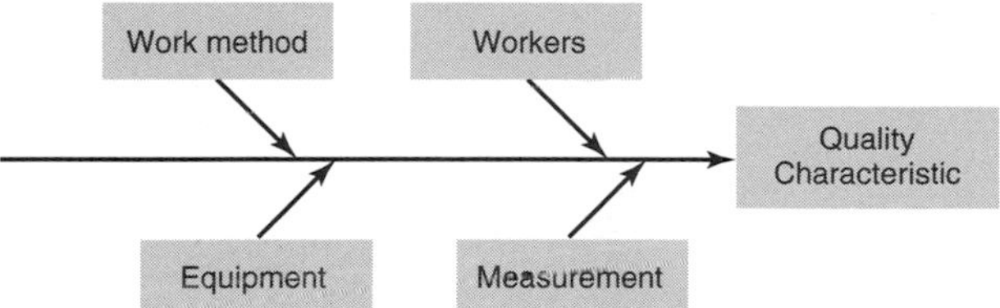

FIGURE 3.1 A generic Ishikawa cause-and-effect diagram.

One can distinguish two types of cause-and-effect diagrams: *flow diagrams* and *process diagrams*. Our generic cause-and-effect diagram in Figure 3.1 is a process diagram as it shows the causes that affect the overall process.

The flow version of a cause-and-effect diagram documents causes as they relate to each stage of the process flow. The first step in drawing a flow cause-and-effect diagram is to prepare a flow diagram of the process; this is valuable in itself because defining how work is accomplished usually is the first step in solving a problem. The second step is to list the factors that affect the process at each stage. A disadvantage of the flow cause-and-effect diagram is that it may be quite difficult to construct a diagram for a long, complicated process. Also, the same potential causes might appear in several stages. Ishikawa illustrates a flow cause-and-effect diagram in the context of steel pipe scars. There the process starts by transforming the raw materials into pipes, which are then corrected and planed. After that, pipes are water-pressure tested, remaining beads are removed, and the finished pipes are inspected. Twigs pointing to each stage represent the various factors that are thought to have an effect on that particular stage of the process.

We asked a group of IS professionals to tell us about the factors that influence the quality of a software system during the four stages: requirements determination, design, build, and test and install. The resulting flow cause-and-effect diagram is shown in Figure 3.2.

There are many advantages to using cause-and-effect diagrams. Cause-and-effect diagrams provide a method of identifying and organizing potential causes of a problem. Making a cause-and-effect diagram helps you understand the problem. The discipline of categorizing data and displaying it graphically helps you see interconnections among causes that are not as clearly evident from a simple list.

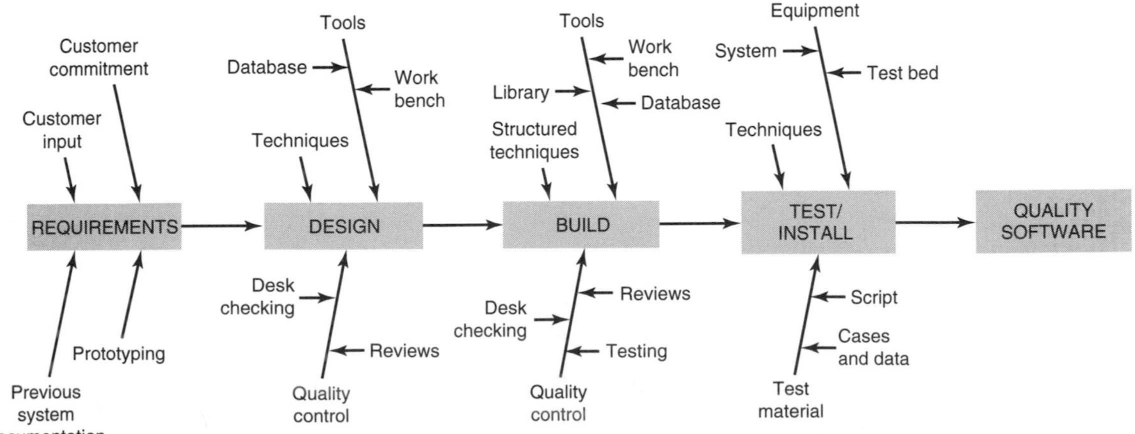

FIGURE 3.2 A flow cause-and-effect diagram: Quality of a software system.

A cause-and-effect diagram is a focus around which to gather data about a problem. It suggests what additional data is needed and how data might be interrelated. A cause-and-effect diagram is a focus for discussion. It can be used to direct attention or to encourage a systematic discussion of causes. A cause-and-effect diagram is an educational tool. A good diagram of a process is an excellent tool for training people about the process. Cause-and-effect diagrams of major processes can be posted on the bulletin board to encourage employees to understand the processes. Most people find it easier to grasp information and concepts if they are presented pictorially or graphically. A cause-and-effect diagram, much like a graph, is a very effective communication tool.

A cause-and-effect diagram helps you solve problems. By providing a better understanding of the problem, supporting the collection of necessary data, and assisting the problem-solving process, these diagrams definitely contribute to the solution of problems.

Cause-and-effect diagrams can be applied widely. Our concern is with their use in solving quality problems, but the tool can be used in many other contexts. For instance, it can be used to describe interconnecting activities in a production process, the sequence of assembling parts of a complex product, or the flow of information in an organization.

3.6.4 Two Examples of Cause-and-Effect Diagrams

When dealing with processes and operations, we are constantly faced with problems: The variability in a certain quality characteristic of our product may be too large, the depletion of carbon on a steel flat may be too high, the product dimensions may vary too much, there may be too many errors in certain operations, it may take students too long to graduate with a bachelor's degree, and so on. What are the reasons for these problems? Where does the variability come from? Problems and excessive variability are often due to variation in raw materials (input variables), variation in the process and shifts in the work method, variation in the tools, machinery, and equipment, and sometimes they are due to measurement variability. The cause-and-effect diagrams for the following two examples are process diagrams as they display factors that affect the overall process. Our displays start with four main branches: work steps (or process), workers, equipment (and materials), and measurement. Other texts use a larger number of main branches, such as machines, people, methods, materials, environment, and measurements.

EXAMPLE 1: *Production of Steel Flats*

Consider the production of steel flats. The raw material for the steel flats are steel billets, which are massive square bars of molten steel. Steel billets are produced in the company's melt shop by melting down a mixture of scrap metal and alloys. Steel billets are then sent through the rolling mill. First they enter a reheat furnace where they are heated up to the required high temperature. Then the red-hot

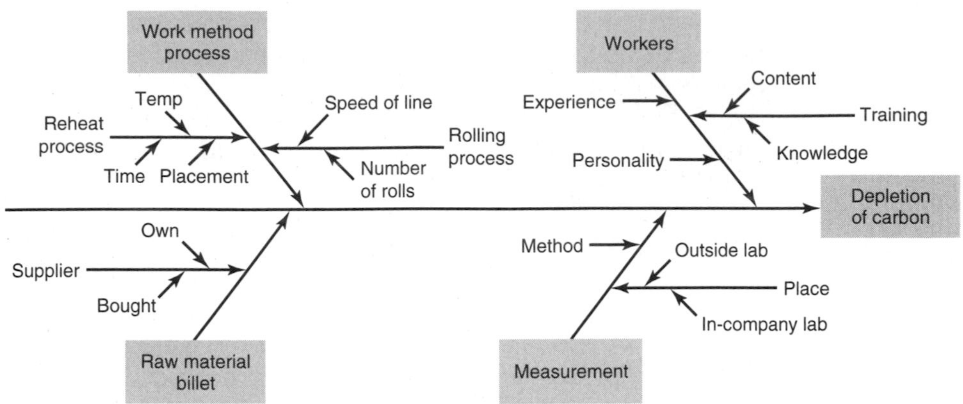

FIGURE 3.3 Cause-and-effect diagram: Depletion of carbon.

billets are sent through a sequence of rolls which reduce their size to the required dimensions. A cause-and-effect diagram that addresses the depletion of carbon is given in Figure 3.3.

The depletion of carbon is an important quality characteristic, as too much depletion weakens the steel. The determination of the depletion of carbon in itself is not easy. It involves polishing a small area of the steel flat and determining the depletion of carbon through a visual inspection under the microscope. The measurement process itself is a source of the variability in the quality characteristic; thus a main branch points from "*measurement*" to the quality characteristic. More than a single method of measuring may be in use; thus a smaller twig extends from (measurement) "method" to the main "measurement" branch. Furthermore, the measurement may depend on where the measurement is carried out. This particular steel plant uses both an in-house laboratory and an independent lab. Thus a small twig extends from "place" to the main "measurement" branch. "*Raw material*" also plays an important role. In our example, the raw material is the billet. Thus there is a main branch from "raw material" to the quality characteristic. The supplier of the raw material may be important. In our plant the supplier is either our own melt shop, or an outside supplier. Thus a twig extends from "supplier" to the main branch that comes from raw material. The "*work method*" is another main branch in our diagram. A very critical component in the work method is the reheat process; thus a twig goes from "reheat furnace" to the main branch representing the work method. The reheat process, in turn, depends on the length of exposure ("time") and the "temperature" in the furnace. In addition, it may depend on the particular "placement" of the billet within the reheat furnace. The "rolling mill" is another main component of the work method. It, in turn, is affected by the "speed of the line" and the "number of size reductions" (rolls), represented by the smaller twigs. "*Workers*" are another critical component in the operation. A smaller twig connects "training" to this main branch. Training, itself, can focus on "content" as well as "knowledge." Twigs also lead from "personality" and "experience," as these may be two important factors. ■

EXAMPLE 2: *Graduation Rates*

Each state, and the state of Iowa is no exception, has a strong interest in the academic progress of students enrolled at its state universities. How many of the entering freshman students fail to graduate, and among those that graduate how many take longer than four years? Many parties (in particular, the legislature and concerned parents) believe that graduation rates are too low and the time until graduation is too long.

Let us first look at data on graduation rates. A recent study ("Persistence at the State Universities: A Study of the Fall 1985 Entering Class of Undergraduate Students who Enrolled at the University of Northern Iowa, Iowa State University, and the University of Iowa") followed the progress of the fall 1985 freshman class. Of the fall 1985 freshmen who entered directly from high school, 54 percent at the University of Northern Iowa, 62 percent at Iowa State University, and 60 percent at the University of Iowa received a bachelor's degree by the end of the 1991 summer session. An additional 5 percent of students from the University of Northern Iowa, 2 percent from Iowa State University, and 2 percent from the University of Iowa received a bachelor's degree at one of the other Iowa Regents' institutions. In addition, 3 percent of the study population at the University of Northern Iowa, 4 percent at Iowa State University, and 5 percent at the University of Iowa were still enrolled during the spring or summer of 1991 and assumed to be making progress toward a degree. Thus, the proportions of "persisting" students (that is, those who by the end of this study in 1991 had received a bachelor's degree from one of the Iowa Regents' institutions or were still enrolled) were 62 percent for those who first enrolled at the University of Northern Iowa, 68 percent at Iowa State University, and 67 percent for the University of Iowa.

The study also showed that of the entering freshmen who earned their degrees during the time period of this study (that is, during six years), 56 percent at the University of Northern Iowa completed their degree in four years or less; the proportion was 38 percent for Iowa State University and 50 percent for the University of Iowa. Women at all three Iowa Regents' institutions were more likely to complete their degree within four years of their first enrollment.

While these numbers may be lower than desired, the *persistence* at Iowa Regents' institutions compare favorably to the 48.9 percent 6-year persistence proportion that is reported in a study for the Institute of Independent Colleges and Universities. The data suggests that, indeed, it generally takes longer than four years to get an undergraduate degree at an Iowa Regents' institution.

What factors affect the drop-out rates and the time until graduation? In August of 1989, the firm of Peat Marwick submitted a report to the Iowa Board of Regents,

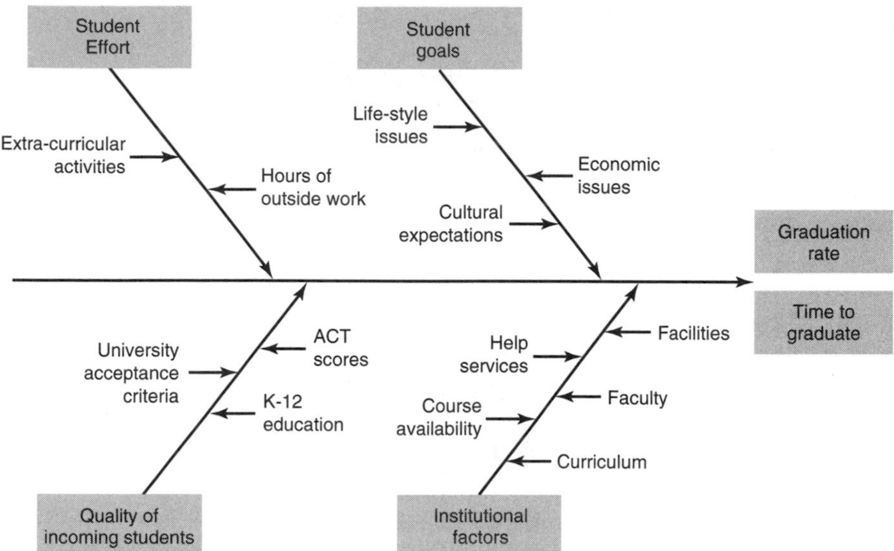

FIGURE 3.4 Ishikawa cause-and-effect diagram: Graduation rate and time to graduate.

titled "Length of Time to Complete an Undergraduate Degree." The authors of that report conclude that although institutional factors are marginally responsible for extended degree completion time frames (in particular, curricula with little flexibility and difficulties in access to courses), extrainstitutional factors and personal factors are significantly responsible for extended degree completion time frames.

A cause-and-effect diagram that sheds some light on possible causes for drop-out rates and extended degree completion time frames is given in Figure 3.4.

"*Student effort*" is certainly one important factor that affects success. Student effort is affected by outside activities a student is engaged in. Outside activities include work (number of hours per week holding a job), which in turn is influenced by economic conditions such as the availability of financial aid. Outside activities also include university-encouraged extracurricular activities (such as athletics, student government, etc.), as well as the attractions of college life that compete for time.

It should be mentioned that extending the completion time for graduation may also benefit the student. Opportunities for internships and cooperative experiences, multiple majors, international programs, professional endorsements and licenses may extend the time, but they will also broaden the educational experience.

"*Student goals*" will also play a role. Students may not register for a sufficient number of courses and they may drop courses. "Economic issues" such as rising education costs and reduced access to financial aid must be underscored as having considerable impact on how students spend their time during their undergraduate years. Students have little control over tuition and educational costs. "Life-style issues," that is, how students adjust their move from a protective home environment to college life, also may have a large impact. "Cultural expectations" with respect to the degree completion time frames may also affect the personal reasons.

Graduation rates and time to completion also depend on the raw material or "*quality of incoming students*." The quality of incoming students depends on the university's acceptance criteria (which, for example, specify that students from the state of Iowa must be in the top 50 percent of their graduating high school class, or their ACT scores must exceed a certain cutoff). The quality also depends on the level of preparedness of incoming freshmen, which in turn is affected by their previous K–12 education.

"*Institutional factors*" certainly play a role. A "curriculum" with little flexibility could be a cause, as this will make it more difficult to complete the program in the usual time. "Course availability" is probably another major reason why the graduation of some students is delayed. If, for example, juniors cannot get into the right courses, they may lack the prerequisites for their senior year courses. "Faculty" is another important component. Their teaching abilities and their mentoring qualities may make a difference whether students drop out. University "help services" (including programs for students with disabilities, help sessions for students with study problems, etc.) may also have an effect on the retention of students. "Facilities" (such as study spaces in libraries, computer labs for computer work) may also be of importance. ■

3.6.5 Finding Most Likely Causes

Given a collection of possible causes of an event, the next question is to determine the most likely cause (or most likely causes). This is a convergent process, calling for the analysis of a large amount of information and narrowing it down to the best explanation.

The search for the most likely cause amounts to the elimination of all possible causes but one. As we stressed earlier, this process depends on a thorough knowledge of the problem. It is important to gather as much information about the problem as you can before starting your search for the most likely cause. It is not easy to get information about a problem. People are reluctant to admit facts that might ultimately show that they helped cause the problem. To avoid stone walls, you must emphasize that the purpose of your investigation is to fix a problem, not to fix blame.

As you search for the most likely cause, one cause may stand out with very little analysis. This is particularly true if the analysis is being made by someone who is familiar with the problem area. For example, a professional programmer looking for the cause of an error in her own work will often be able to identify the cause simply by tracing the code. But even when the probable cause seems obvious, you must be careful. It is very common for programmers to jump to the conclusion that the first anomaly they encounter is the probable cause, only to find on closer inspection that they were mistaken.

When the most likely cause is not obvious, one must go about disproving possible causes. Sometimes a group of possible causes can be analyzed together, sometimes they must be taken one at a time. To show that a possible cause cannot be the real cause of the effect, it is necessary to find some distinction that the possible cause cannot explain. A possible cause of a mix-up over the scheduling of a meeting might be that the notice of the meeting was incorrect. But if some people understood the meeting date correctly while others did not, the notice could not have been wrong. The distinction in this case is that some got the message correctly, some incorrectly; a possible cause, such as the same faulty notice to all, that fails to explain this distinction can be ruled out.

For some problems, the search for the most likely cause is a search for some change that could have produced the effect. Suppose, for example, that a production process has been working properly for some time; then all at once it starts to produce defective products. The natural question would be: "What has changed? What changed the process from satisfactory to unsatisfactory?" Frequently a key to analyzing this problem is to discover what changes took place at or about the time that the problem arose. Unfortunately, for many quality problems, the search for the most likely cause cannot be done by an analysis of change because the processes involved were not working properly in the first place.

Aside from suggesting that you look for distinctions that cannot be explained, there is no general rule that can be given for eliminating possible causes from consideration. One first attempts to reduce the full set of possible causes to a few most likely candidates. Then one keeps eliminating these until satisfied that the most likely cause is discovered. If not, the only thing to do is go back for a better understanding of the problem and try again.

During this process, your attitude must be a willingness to disprove possible causes. Sometimes this is difficult, particularly if one has a pet theory about what the problem is. But a careful, unbiased assessment of each possible cause is what is needed.

Once you feel confident that you have identified the most likely cause, you need to test it thoroughly. Does it explain all the conditions of the problem? All the distinctions? If you are satisfied that it does, there is one more test: Does it seem reasonably logical and intuitive? If not, you should be wary. A theory can explain all the facts, and still be suspect. Note that we are saying you should be suspicious, not that you should reject an idea simply because your intuition is against it. In the early days of flying, the low-powered planes sometimes lost flying speed and went into tailspins. Attempts by pilots to raise the plane's nose and pull out of the spin usually failed, and crashes ensued. Finally, someone got the idea to push the *nose down.* Seemingly this would simply hasten the crash. It did cause the plane to fall faster, but this meant regaining sufficient air speed for the pilot to maneuver the plane. And the pilot could pull the plane out of the dive before it crashed. This example shows you shouldn't simply discard a counterintuitive idea; who knows, it might just help you out of a tailspin.

3.7 THE SHEWHART/DEMING WHEEL

In this chapter we have outlined a detailed structured approach that will help you solve quality problems, and by solving problems you will improve the quality of your processes. There are several other widely used quality improvement strategies. The *Shewhart wheel*, which is also known as the *Deming wheel* or *Deming cycle*, is perhaps the best-known approach (Figure 3.5). This idea originated with Walter A. Shewhart in the late 1930s and it has been popularized by W. Edwards Deming, who introduced this idea to the Japanese in the early 1950s. For the history on the Shewhart/Deming wheel, you should refer to the book by W. Edwards Deming, *Out of the Crisis*, published by the Massachusetts Institute of Technology in 1986. This book has much to say about quality and its improvement. It should be read by all students of quality.

The Shewhart/Deming cycle is also known as the *PDCA cycle*: P stands for *Plan*, D stands for *Do*, C stands for *Check*, and A stands for *Act*. The PDCA cycle represents a series of activities that are pursued to improve a process. The initial step in any effort to accomplish a goal is to recognize the improvement opportunity. This begins with the study of the current situation and a plan for improvement. The *Plan step* consists of planning a change or a test with the aim of improvement. Processes are identified and problems are defined at this stage; goals and priorities are determined, and possible causes of problems are listed.

Once the plan has been finalized, it is implemented. The *Do step* executes the planned change. Initially changes are often implemented on a small scale. After the modifications are implemented, a check is made to see whether they have brought about the anticipated improvement. The *Check* (or study) *step* is concerned with observing results, summarizing data, and analyzing and evaluating the effects of the actual change against expected or planned outcomes. The Check step involves studying the results to understand what has been learned. Finally, one takes action on the results. The *Act step* consists of adopting the change if it has been successful, and abandoning changes that haven't worked. When the experiment has been successful, a final action such as the elimination of causes or the standardization of the process is taken to ensure that the new methods introduced will be practiced continually for sustained improvement.

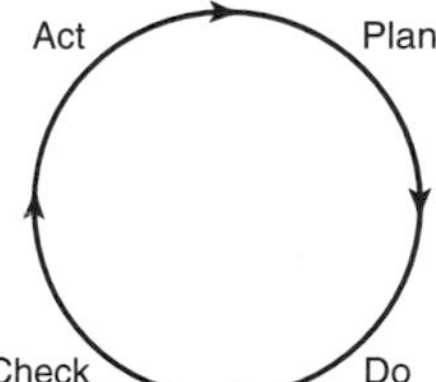

FIGURE 3.5 The Shewhart/Deming wheel.

The Shewhart/Deming cycle represents a model for a never-ending cycle of experimentation that structures all quality improvement efforts. At the end of each cycle future improvements are planned and the PDCA cycle is repeated. Gains that have been achieved so far are held and the process is repeated to achieve breakthroughs to even higher performance levels. The Shewhart/Deming cycle is usually depicted as a wheel in order to emphasize that there really is no beginning and no end to the quality improvement process. It is a continual and iterative process.

3.8 EXERCISES

3.1 The game of *nim* involves two players and fifteen objects, which we shall call sticks, arranged in three piles. One pile has three sticks, another has five sticks, and the third has seven sticks. Taking turns, each player selects a pile and removes one or more sticks from that pile. During a turn, a player can take as many sticks from a pile as he wants—including all remaining sticks—but must take at least one. During a turn, it is not allowed to remove sticks from more than one pile. There is no constraint on which pile a player draws from; he can draw from one pile on one turn and from the same or a different pile on the next turn. The object of the game is *not* to pick up the last stick.

The problem facing a player is to devise a strategy for winning the game. The problem is complicated by the fact that a player might be the first or the second to start play. *We suggest you try to solve the problem before reading on.*

This game provides a good illustration of some of the problem-solving techniques we have described. Players usually attempt to solve the problem by focusing on initial moves; they ask, "What is the best opening move to make?" We shall describe a solution that involves thinking opposite (focusing on the end of the game) and reducing the problem to a collection of other problems. To solve the problem, we shall switch our vantage from a strategy for winning to one of making our opponent face a losing situation.

Near the end of a game, suppose that your opponent faces a situation with one stick in each of three piles. Then he cannot win, for he must take one stick from any pile, you will then take one stick from another pile, and he is left taking the last stick. Thus one strategy for winning is to play the game so as to make your opponent face this 1-1-1 situation.

Next, suppose your opponent faces a situation with one pile empty and two sticks in each of the other piles; a 0-2-2 situation. Then your opponent cannot win. If he takes a single stick from one pile, you take two from the other pile, and he is left facing a single stick. If he takes both sticks from one pile, you take a single stick from the other pile, and he loses. Thus 0-2-2 is a losing position for your opponent to face.

In much the same way, your opponent will lose if he faces a 0-3-3 situation. If he takes a single stick from a pile, you take a single stick from the other, and he is left with a 0-2-2 losing position. If he takes two sticks from a pile, you take all from the other, and he loses. If he takes all from a pile, you take two from the other, and he loses.

You can prove in much the same way that 0-4-4 and 0-5-5 are losing situations for your opponent. We leave it to you to prove that 1-2-3 is also a losing situation for your opponent. Also, we leave it to you to build on the results established so far, and analyze the game back to the opening position.

3.2 Select a few quality problems which personally interest you. For example,

(a) Low college graduation rates
(b) Uneven quality of the coffee served in the cafeteria
(c) Long waiting times in your doctor's office
(d) Teen smoking
(e) Unsatisfactory U.S. trade balance
(f) Your own basketball free-throw percentage: low average and high variability
(g) Unacceptable personal academic progress
(h) Poor teaching at your university
(i) Variability in your own job performance
(j) Traffic congestion in front of toll booths on a busy interstate
(k) Too many students skipping lectures in the introductory statistics course

Discuss how IDEA, the four-step problem-solving procedure presented in this chapter, can be applied for each of the selected problems. Outline the four steps in sufficient detail. Use the techniques in this chapter to find the possible causes for the listed problems. Organize the information in cause-and-effect diagrams.

3.3 Select two problems from those listed in Exercise 3.2. For each of these, restate the problem in one or more ways with the aim of escaping from conventional thinking about the problem.

3.4 Select two problems from those listed in Exercise 3.2. For each of these, view the problem from a different vantage point with the aim of escaping from conventional thinking about the problem.

3.5 Describe the principles that *you* are using to solve problems. Relate them to the material that you learned in this chapter.

3.6 A good way to use analogy effectively is to practice making up comparisons. Try to think of analogies for various things, such as:

(a) Building computer software
(b) Software development process
(c) Removing defects from an information system
(d) Changing the software development process
(e) Auditor
(f) Relationship between manager and employee
(g) Quality control function in your company
(h) Booking airplane seats
(i) Teamwork

3.7 The following papers include examples of cause-and-effect diagrams. Read and comment.

(a) Q. R. Skrabec, "Process Diagnostics: Seven Steps for Problem Solving," in *Quality Progress*, November 1986 (Vol. 19), 40–44.

(b) R. Hoexter and M. Julien, "Legal Eagles Become Quality Hawks," in *Quality Progress*, January 1994 (Vol. 27), 31–33.

3.8 Read and discuss the paper by S. C. Hillmer, "A Problem-Solving Approach to Teaching Business Statistics," in *The American Statistician*, Vol. 50 (1996), 249–256. Relate the ideas in this paper to our discussion in the previous two chapters.

3.9 For the top two ranking problems discovered in Exercise 2.9 of Chapter 2, attempt to restate the problem concept or problem vantage.

3.10 In many educational institutions, the Athletic Department does a much better job of teaching teamwork than does the Business School. What can a Business School learn about teaching teamwork by examining the analogy of an athletic team?

3.9 REFERENCES

Deming, W. Edwards. *Out of the Crisis*. Cambridge, MA: Massachusetts Institute of Technology, Center for Advanced Engineering Study, 1986.

Hillmer, S. C. "A Problem-Solving Approach to Teaching Business Statistics," *The American Statistician*, Vol. 50 (1996), 249–256.

Hoexter, R., and M. Julien. "Legal Eagles Become Quality Hawks," *Quality Progress*, January 1994 (Vol. 27), 31–33.

Ishikawa, K. *Guide to Quality Control*, 2nd edition. Tokyo: Asian Productivity Organization, 1982.

Kerzner, H. *Project Management: A Systems Approach to Planning, Scheduling, and Controlling*, 3rd edition. New York: Van Nostrand Reinhold, 1989.

Meredith, J. R. *Project Management: A Managerial Approach*, 3rd edition. New York: Wiley, 1995.

Skrabec, Q. R. "Process Diagnostics: Seven Steps for Problem Solving," *Quality Progress*, November 1986 (Vol. 19), 40–44.

CHAPTER 4

GROUP-BASED PROBLEM SOLVING

Often the most effective way to solve a problem is to have only one person work on it. But if a problem is ambiguous, if knowledge about the problem is widely distributed, or if the implementation of a solution requires acceptance or action by a group, the best approach to the problem may be to have a group solve it. If problems are solved by groups, then *group-dynamics* plays an important role.

4.1 FACILITATING PROBLEM SOLVING BY GROUPS

Use of a group is based on several premises:

- Creativity is present in everyone.
- People are willing, even anxious to contribute; they want to offer ideas and advice about problems relating to their job.
- The more people who generate ideas, the better the solution is likely to be.
- People find group problem solving a rewarding activity; they like to be part of an achieving team.

Not everyone believes in these premises. Some hold a view that people are lazy, unimaginative, don't want to contribute, work only because they have to, and must be checked every step of the way to see that they do a job properly. Others believe that a group can never accomplish anything, and to illustrate their view they may cite the old joke about a camel being a horse designed by a committee. Still others say that the quantity of ideas is unrelated to the quality of the final recommendation.

For people to find reward in a group problem-solving effort, the effort must be successful; and for success, there are several prerequisites. Certainly the group must have knowledge of the problem area. Moreover, it is helpful if group members come from different backgrounds because different views of the problem are an asset. The group must also know how to work together as a team. Group members must be able to communicate effectively, which means being able to listen as well as speak. They must respect one another and know how to build on the team's strengths, rather than highlight its weaknesses. And, of course, group members must understand the methods and procedures appropriate to the problem-solving process.

Problem solving by a group should be just that—a group effort. However, quite often participation is not equal. The group is dominated by some members, causing others to withdraw from active participation. Dominance sometimes comes from a participant's status; presence of a high-ranking person or an acknowledged expert can cause others to remain quiet. Dominance sometimes stems from personal characteristics; a forceful, talkative individual can so dominate a discussion that more reserved individuals withdraw. Another difficulty with group problem solving is known as *discounting*. Members discount or downplay aspects of the activity. They discount problems, suggesting they are trivial or unimportant. They discount the context of problems, forgetting that a solution is not satisfactory if it doesn't fit into the special circumstances surrounding a problem. They discount the ability of the group to solve the problem, saying that the problem is too hard and the group too inexperienced or lacking in authority. And a very common tendency is for people to discount themselves. Discounting is a negative approach; successful problem solving requires a positive, "can do" approach.

4.1.1 The Importance of the Group Leader

Effective groups usually operate under the leadership of one individual. This person might be appointed as leader by someone with authority over the group or might be elected to that position by the group. If a leader is not formally appointed, one usually tends to emerge naturally as the group begins to operate.

A group leader should be people-oriented. He should be able to view the problem-solving process from the team's perspective and understand the motives and expectations of the members. He must be able to draw people out so they will take an active part in the process, expressing their ideas and making constructive comments about the ideas of others. A good leader listens carefully to all comments and takes pains to see that every member is involved. He recognizes contributions and dampens attempts to discount any aspect of the problem-solving process. A good leader does not manipulate people and does not compete with group members. He is sure of his ability and doesn't need to prove it to the team.

But being people-oriented is not enough; a good leader must also know how to run a successful meeting. He must have a clear agenda in mind. The leader should understand that there are three goals for a problem-solving meeting:

- For the meeting to be effective in discovering the best solution to the problem being considered,
- For the meeting to be rewarding to individual participants by bringing them satisfaction and professional growth, and
- For the meeting to be rewarding to the organization by improving the ability of the team to work together effectively.

During a meeting, the leader functions as a facilitator. His task is to maintain a comfortable atmosphere, one that promotes problem solving. At times he must promote communication, which he does by suggesting answers to questions, paraphrasing points, or suggesting a completely different approach to a problem. The leader must manage conflict. He must recognize that a certain amount of conflict is healthy and can aid in the problem-solving process, but he must also understand the danger of letting a conflict get out of hand. Being a good leader is not an easy task. As with most activities, one gets better at it with practice.

4.1.2 Activities of a Group Problem-Solving Session

Several things should be done to increase the likelihood of a problem-solving session being successful. Usually the leader is responsible to see that these actions take place.

Before a Session As with any situation, people are more comfortable in a problem-solving session if they understand what they are getting into. The following points must be made clear to them:

- **The problem.** The group should understand the problem, its context, and its importance.
- **The process.** People should understand they will be involved in a group process. The process should be explained; people should be told what help or training they will receive as part of the process.
- **The group.** People should understand enough about fellow group members to appreciate the expertise represented. People should understand the roles they are to play and the roles of others.
- **The leader.** The group should understand the position of the leader, his expertise with the problem area, and his experience in conducting group sessions.

During a Session At all times, members should be kept informed so that their expectations are not disappointed. They should understand what they are doing, what they are about to do, and why they are taking these actions. At the beginning of each stage of the session, the procedure and any special instructions for that stage should be reviewed. No member should have any doubt about the role he or she is to perform or how to perform it.

During the session the physical and psychological atmosphere should be conducive to problem solving. Group problem-solving sessions are meant to be team efforts, the idea being to exploit the strength that a team can bring to bear on the problem. At all times during the session, team-building activities should be encouraged.

After a Session One of the best ways to give group problem-solving a bad name is to fail to inform people about the outcome of a session in which they have participated. After devoting a great deal of time and effort to solving a problem, participants deserve some report about the activity. They would like to know who received their suggestions, how they were received, and what actions will be taken.

To be successful, a session must be rewarding to the individuals as well as to the organization. Members should get part of their reward from the session itself; they should find it stimulating, a chance to "stretch" and an assist to their professional growth. But members should also get recognition from the group leader and their own management for their contribution. Sometimes the way this comes about is by the leader publicizing the group's accomplishments. Sessions that are part of a quality improvement effort frequently are publicized as part of the general attempt to promote quality.

4.1.3 Importance of Communication

Group problem solving is largely an exercise in communication. The leader must communicate the problem to the team members. Members must present their views and convince others to accept them. The leader must facilitate productive communication, avoiding conflict and domination of the session by a few. And the results of a session must be presented so as to persuade others to accept them. With the process so dependent on it, communication should be understood by the team, and especially by the team leader.

Peter Drucker, in his 1970 book *Technology, Management, and Society* (pp. 4–12), calls attention to some basic facts about communication:

- **Communication is perception.** A message is transmitted by a sender to a receiver. The important thing is not what is sent, but what is perceived by the receiver. If the sender transmits "green" but the receiver perceives "red," then to the receiver the message *is* "red" and she will react accordingly.
- **Communication is expectations.** The receiver perceives what she expects to perceive. If the receiver expects to hear "green," then that is what will be heard unless the sender makes a special effort to highlight the unexpected message.

- **Communication is involvement.** The purpose of a message is to involve the receiver. It is an attempt to convince her of something or get her to do something. Communication always makes a demand on the recipient.

Because the receiver hears what she expects to hear and because communication makes demands that the receiver might prefer not to face, failures to get a message across are commonplace. We have all witnessed exchanges where it was clear that, despite repeated attempts, the sender and receiver were on different wavelengths. In a group session, unremitting effort must be made to see that the message received is the message sent. Each group member has a responsibility to make communication effective.

To understand the content of some messages, one must realize that communication is both verbal and nonverbal. *Verbal communication* refers to what is said—the spoken message. *Nonverbal communication* refers to signals accompanying the verbal message such as behavior, emotions, or patterns of communication. How something is said often is as important as what is said. A look of doubt accompanying a statement that a certain point is understood is a nonverbal clue; perhaps the understanding is not complete. An appearance of a group member who is perspiring and nervous may say something about the degree of conviction the member has about a statement being put forward. A restless group can be a nonverbal clue that the problem-solving session is in trouble and likely to be unsuccessful.

4.1.4 Benefits of Group-Based Problem Solving

Many organizations recognize the benefits that are derived from shared experience in decisions, and they are seeking ways to encourage employee participation in decision making. Group problem solving is one technique that can advance these organizational goals. A successful session gives individuals a chance to make a meaningful contribution by solving a problem that is related to their job. This rewarding experience increases their enthusiasm and sense of responsibility to the organization. The organization gains directly through an increased ability to recognize and cope with problems. It gains indirectly through improved communication and an increased level of trust among team members. Ties are built among different parts of the organization or different levels depending on where the members are from. But to reap such benefits, the session must be successful; paying attention to human factors is one way to increase the probability of success.

4.2 PROBLEM-SOLVING GROUPS

Through the years, various techniques have been used to organize workers to improve quality and productivity. We shall examine two such techniques, quality circles and self-directed work teams, then cite some examples of improvements made by quality improvement teams.

4.2.1 Quality Circles

Quality circles (also called quality control circles) were devised in Japan in the 1960s as a means of helping workers improve quality. A *quality circle* is a group of about 4 to 10 employees performing similar work who meet regularly to solve problems related to quality. A quality circle generally is taught a methodology for problem solving, and it is supplied with such resources as a meeting place, supplies, and organizational data about problems. A circle can propose solutions to quality problems, but usually it does not have the authority to install process improvements.

It wasn't until about 1980 that the quality circle concept was widely publicized in the United States. By 1982 quality circles were springing up everywhere, then the movement fizzled as rapidly as it grew. A major reason for the failure of circles was that they were not installed as a part of a comprehensive quality movement. They were an isolated action, not part of the basic authority structure.

In retrospect, the real importance of the quality circle movement in the United States was that it opened the eyes of management to the value of worker participation in activities that previously had been the domain of management. This paved the way for the acceptance of self-directed work teams, which we discuss next.

4.2.2 Self-Directed Work Teams

A *self-directed work team* (SDWT) is a highly trained group of employees who are fully responsible for producing a set of work products. The group usually consists of from 6 to 18 people who work together as a team, not "for" someone. Such teams have more resources, better access to information, greater decision-making authority, a wider range of cross-functional skills within the team, and more resources than traditionally are assigned to workers. Companies who have formed such teams include Xerox, General Motors, Federal Express, Aid Association for Lutherans, and Shenandoah Life. For a detailed discussion of such teams, we refer you to the 1990 book *Self-Directed Work Teams*, by Jack D. Orsburn, Linda Moran, Ed Musselwhite, and John H. Zenger.

Because the SDWT has total responsibility for their area, they develop a better understanding of their processes than do traditional operators and managers. For an SDWT, quality improvement becomes part of the job and a matter of professional pride. In fact, improved quality and improved productivity are the two most commonly cited reasons for implementing SDWTs, according to a 1991 study in *Quality Progress* (March 1991, "News," p. 15).

4.2.3 Quality Improvement Teams

Project-by-project improvement is a successful technique for achieving quality. This involves forming a project team to address a specific quality problem; the team is disbanded when a solution has been found and installed. A project team formed to address a quality problem sometimes is referred to as a *quality improvement team*.

A team consists of a project manager, project secretary, and about two to six additional team members. All team members should have knowledge of the problem area and the ability to work with others. Sometimes it is useful to have people from different functional areas so as to broaden the knowledge base of the team.

The duty of the project leader is to steer the team. This requires knowing how to manage a project and skill in getting people to work together as a team. The secretary handles all project documentation—agendas, minutes, and reports.

A project typically consists of four steps: Examine the problem to understand it thoroughly, analyze its cause, devise and install a remedy, and institute controls to prevent reoccurrence.

At a Teamwork '91 forum, Xerox showcased quality improvements made by more than 200 teams (*Quality Progress*, Feb. 1992, p. 14). Among those featured were the following:

- Eight service technicians developed a new repair procedure that reduced copier downtime in the Dallas/Fort Worth area, saving the company about $9,000 annually.
- By expanding the recycling and reuse of parts from unusable equipment, a management team reduced waste and will save the company $70 million over a four- to five-year period.
- Twenty-six employees devised ways to help the company respond to the needs of hearing-impaired employees.

4.3 GROUP-BASED PROBLEM-SOLVING TOOLS: FACILITATING THE EXCHANGE OF IDEAS

Organizations recognize the benefits that can be gained from teamwork and by adopting a group-based approach to problem solving. Team-based problem-solving techniques tap the creativities and experiences of numerous people coming from different backgrounds. In the next three sections in this chapter we discuss three team-based problem-solving tools: brainstorming, the nominal group technique, and the Delphi method. These techniques are examples of *structured* group activities that facilitate a controlled exchange of information.

4.4 BRAINSTORMING

Brainstorming is a structured problem-solving technique designed to generate ideas and produce group consensus on their relative importance. The technique was developed by Alex Osborn in the late 1930s (Osborn, 1957). Brainstorming is one of the best known and most widely used *group idea-generation methods*. Countless variations of the idea have been developed.

A brainstorming session is governed by four rules, which participants must understand. The *first rule* is to postpone evaluation of ideas. This rule promotes the principle of deferred judgment. There is to be no discussion of an idea's value or practicality during the brainstorming session; such discussion is to take place at a later evaluation session. Deferring judgment is what makes a brainstorming session different from a typical problem-solving meeting, and it is the most important of the four rules.

The *second rule* is that any and all ideas are welcome. "Freewheeling" is encouraged; participants should suggest any idea that comes to mind. One's imagination should be allowed to run wild.

The *third rule* is that the more ideas, the better. The more ideas, the better the chance of finding a successful solution to the problem. Experience shows that the best ideas seldom are the initial ones; the best ideas flow as more and more ideas are presented.

The *fourth rule* is that "piggybacking" is encouraged. Participants are encouraged to piggyback or build on the ideas of others. Combinations and variations of ideas are welcomed; in fact, they are given priority over new, unrelated ideas.

4.4.1 Participants

A brainstorming exercise requires a leader, six to eight group members to generate ideas, and a recording secretary. There must also be a team to evaluate ideas. The task of the leader is to prepare for the brainstorming session, conduct it, and conduct the evaluation session that follows. The task of group members is to generate ideas relating to the problem under consideration. The task of the evaluation team is to classify ideas and judge which are best. The evaluation team might be the same as the idea-generating group or it might consist of different people. The task of the recording secretary is to make a numbered, written list of all ideas generated during the session.

The leader of a brainstorming session must have the ability to conduct a meeting and be firm enough to see that the group follows the rules. At the same time, the leader must have the ability to maintain a relaxed, friendly atmosphere so as to encourage members to participate and produce the maximum number of ideas. The leader must also have knowledge and experience with the brainstorming process and the problem under consideration.

It is helpful if one or two group members are familiar with the brainstorming process, but most need not be. Members should, however, have knowledge and experience in the area covered by the problem under consideration. If possible, members should have diverse backgrounds so that many different points of view are brought to bear on the problem. Group members should be of nearly equal status to prevent a situation where high-status members dominate the session.

There are different schools of thought about the evaluation team. Some hold that members should be drawn from the idea-generating group because they are familiar with the ideas generated. Others believe that the evaluation team should represent the problem "owner" (that is, the person bringing the problem), because such people are more familiar with the problem setting. However chosen, members of the evaluation team must be familiar with the problem area and know the general criteria by which a potential solution to the problem should be judged. It is sometimes recommended that an evaluation team consist of five members because such a group is large enough to represent different points of view and, being an odd number, can avoid tied votes.

The recording secretary should be someone who grasps ideas quickly and can write them quickly and legibly.

4.4.2 Problem Statement

A good problem for a brainstorming session is one that is capable of eliciting a large number of ideas. It should be a problem for which new, unusual, and different approaches are welcome. It should be a relatively important problem, because a brainstorming session requires time commitments from several very able people.

Brainstorming is not suitable as a tool for evaluating an idea that has already been generated. Thus it might be used to generate ideas for a new product, but it would not be used to evaluate a new product, where the idea is already formed. It might, however, be suitable for determining the use to which a new product could be put.

Brainstorming is designed to elicit ideas on a specific problem. Complex problems should be broken into simple ones, and separate sessions should be conducted on each of these. Thus the problem, "What can we do about unemployment?," is too general for brainstorming to offer much help. The problem, "What can we do for the people we must lay off in this plant?," is specific enough for brainstorming to be considered as a way to generate useful ideas.

4.4.3 Brainstorming Process

The brainstorming process consists of the following five steps:

Step 1: Prepare for session
Step 2: Orient group
Step 3: Generate ideas
Step 4: Evaluate ideas
Step 5: Follow up

Step 1: Prepare for Session The first step of a brainstorming session is for the leader to make preparations for the session. The leader should prepare a statement of the problem and give it to group members sufficiently far in advance so that they become familiar with it and have time to think about solutions prior to attending the session. The purpose of this step is to create an environment that is conducive to the generation of ideas. The specific duties of the leader are:

1. Write an appropriate problem statement.
2. Make meeting arrangements and obtain the needed supplies.
3. Arrange with group members. Members should be selected and their agreement to participate obtained. With this invitation, the leader should send each member a statement of the problem to be addressed, information about the background of the problem, examples of possible solutions to the problem, and the four rules for a brainstorming session.
4. Arrange with evaluators. Evaluators must be selected if group members are not to perform that activity.

Step 2: Orient Group The second step of a brainstorming session is for the leader to convene the group and hold a warm-up session. The purpose of this session is to develop a team spirit among the members and to give them practice in creative thinking and building on ideas. This step proceeds as follows:

1. The session starts with introductions.
2. The leader proposes activities to warm up the group. This may involve a group discussion on creativity that is followed by a brief creativity exercise ("What helps creativity? hinders it? How many uses can you find for a book on solving quality problems?"). Or, it may focus on problem redefinition ("Can you think of an analogy? What happens if you think opposite? Suppose you think of the problem as an opportunity, what then?"). Or, it may involve an exercise in piggybacking ("You can use a book on solving quality problems to swat flies. Try to build on that idea.")
3. The leader concludes this step with a practice brainstorming session. The four rules, the brainstorming procedure, and the roles of participants are explained. A practice problem is brainstormed, after which questions about the brainstorming session are discussed. The entire step should take between 30 and 60 minutes.

The warm-up session is very important and should not be omitted. It is an opportunity to brush up on the procedure and to practice techniques for generating ideas. The leader must make the group realize that the warm-up is an important part of the session as a whole, not just to break the ice.

Step 3: Generate Ideas The third step is the idea-generation session. The purpose of the session is to generate as many ideas as possible. This step proceeds as follows:

1. The leader starts the session by stating the problem and providing any clarification that is required. The leader then establishes a goal for the number of ideas to be generated in the session.
2. The leader acts as moderator for the session. Group members are asked to raise hands whenever they have an idea to suggest, and the group leader recognizes people one at a time. As ideas are stated, they are listed on flipchart paper by the recording secretary and numbered sequentially.
3. If a slump in activity develops, the leader must decide how to cope with it. A period of silence might be allowed to continue, or it might be broken by a suggestion designed to stimulate additional ideas.
4. When the group appears to be running out of ideas, the leader halts the session. If the group members are not to do the evaluation, the leader thanks the members for their participation and states that the results of the evaluation session will be communicated to them. The total time for Step 3 should be 30 minutes to an hour.

Stating an ambitious goal for the total number of ideas has a stimulating effect on the group. In response to a particular question in a classroom setting, groups without a goal generally produced under 30 ideas. We have found that with a stated goal of at least 100 ideas, identical groups produced as many 120 ideas and averaged about twice the number of ideas as the group without a goal.

During an active period, the group can generate five to six ideas a minute. This production can keep the recording secretary very busy. As flipchart pages are filled, they should be torn off and posted around the room with masking tape. All ideas should be posted where they will be visible throughout the session. This allows members to become familiar with the ideas and encourages piggy-backing.

One sign of an experienced leader is his or her ability to deal with periods of silence. Sometimes these should be allowed to run their natural course; silence gives people an opportunity to let their minds wander and can result in new directions. At times, silence means exhaustion, and some form of stimulation is needed to jog the group. Several techniques can be used for this: The leader can ask an open-ended question, share his or her own ideas with the group, suggest changing or building on an idea or two already presented, or encourage members to give the wildest idea they can imagine. Alternatively, group members can be asked to work independently and silently generate ideas, then these can be read aloud or can be passed to another who is asked to build on them. Such special "trigger" exercises, however, should not be allowed to run for more than 10 or 15 minutes before resuming the standard brainstorming format.

Step 4: Evaluate Ideas The next step of a brainstorming exercise is to classify the ideas presented into categories and to select those that are judged best. This step proceeds as follows:

1. The leader assembles the evaluation team. If necessary, people who were not part of the idea-generating team are informed about the results of the preceding session.
2. The evaluation team is asked to classify the ideas into 5 to 10 categories, focus on the categories that have the most potential, and start thinking about which ideas are best.
3. The leader comments on the criteria for judging ideas, then asks the group, as a team, to select the best ideas. They are to do this in any way that they wish.
4. This step is completed when the evaluation team reports the classified ideas and its list of the best ideas. Step 4 should take about 30 minutes to an hour.

A key to the success of the evaluation session is for the evaluation team to be knowledgeable about the criteria for judging the worth of an idea. This can be achieved by having the problem owner discuss the criteria with the group.

Step 5: Follow Up After the brainstorming session, several actions must be taken:

1. Results of the evaluation session are conveyed to all participants. Thus, all participants are given a list of all ideas generated and an assessment of which ideas are the best.
2. The evaluation report is transmitted to the problem owner for implementation.
3. A mechanism and contact are established to allow members to transmit ideas that occur after the session. The problem owner or a designee is a likely contact person.

4.4.4 Evaluation of Brainstorming

Brainstorming is an effective procedure for generating a large number of ideas and reaching group consensus on their importance in a relatively short time. With a properly chosen group, ideas can be obtained from various disciplines and levels within the organization.

Brainstorming is a good tool for building teams and developing interactive problem-solving skills. Most people who participate in brainstorming sessions find it a satisfying experience. For many, it results in a changed attitude toward idea generation; they become more open to new ideas and more willing to suspend judgment after a brainstorming experience.

The chief drawback of brainstorming is that the process is much more structured and requires a much more qualified leader than most people realize. As a consequence, it is likely that brainstorming is frequently done improperly. At the extreme, people talk about "brainstorming a problem" when all they mean is that they will think about it. Because of misapplication and so many variants of the basic procedure, it can be difficult to get a group to conduct a proper session.

Even if a session is well conducted, brainstorming has some inherent limitations. The technique is limited to simple problems; it can only be used for an intermediate step in the solution of a complicated problem. By failing to provide an incubation period for digesting ideas, brainstorming may not bring out ideas that require deeper thought.

4.5 THE NOMINAL GROUP TECHNIQUE

The *nominal group technique* (NGT) is a structured problem-solving technique designed to generate ideas and produce group consensus on their relative importance. The technique was developed by Andre Delbecq and Andrew Van de Ven in 1968 (Delbecq, Van de Ven, and Gustafson, 1975).

The word "nominal" suggests that the participants are a group in name only—something like the nominal group of all people in the United States over six feet tall. Participants don't interact; if the group does meet, the proceedings follow a prescribed format that calls for written recording followed by verbal discussion of all ideas generated. This format provides anonymity for the generation of ideas, but identification for discussion and defense. This mix of privacy and openness of the NGT technique helps promote an equality of participation among group members.

4.5.1 NGT and Brainstorming

Research reveals that individuals generate more ideas when they work in groups than they do when working alone. This result does not seem surprising; one can speculate that people see themselves in competition and try harder than they do without that spur. But research reveals another fact. People who are brought into a group but are not allowed to communicate generate more ideas than do groups where people are allowed to discuss, exchange information, debate, or otherwise communicate. That is, nominal groups (groups in name only, or noninteracting groups) generate more ideas than interactive groups! One can only speculate as to the reason, but one hypothesis certainly is that many people do not like to talk in a formal setting, and so their ideas go unheralded. This finding about nominal and interactive groups suggests that, in general, the NGT might yield more ideas than brainstorming. Aside from generating ideas, however, if one is interested in team building and establishing esprit de corps, then brainstorming might produce better results than NGT.

4.5.2 Preparation

The NGT session requires a leader and from five to eight group members. The task of the leader is to prepare for the session and to conduct it. The task of group members is to generate ideas and to rank those ideas according to their importance.

The leader must also be familiar with the NGT process. Group members need no prior knowledge of the NGT process, but they should be experts in the area covered by the problem under consideration. If possible, members should be drawn from different professions, functional areas, and organizational ranks so that many different points of view are brought to bear on the problem. A group member's background doesn't matter; what matters is that the member is an expert in the problem area.

Before an NGT session, the leader should write an appropriate, provocative problem statement. This statement should stand on its own, requiring no elaboration during the session. The statement should be written at the top of worksheets that are given to the members during the session. The leader must also make the appropriate meeting arrangements and arrange the participation of group members.

4.5.3 The NGT Process

The NGT process consists of the following four steps:

Step 1: Generate ideas silently
Step 2: Record ideas
Step 3: Discuss ideas
Step 4: Rank ideas

Step 1: Generate Ideas Silently The leader gives each member a written statement of the problem. Working individually and silently, each member creates a list of ideas. The purpose of this step is to allow members time to react to the problem and to generate a large number of ideas. The first step proceeds as follows:

1. The session starts with introductions. Positions and job titles should be downplayed to prevent job status from interfering with the session.
2. The leader outlines the process. The purpose of the session and the four steps of the process are described.
3. The leader starts Step 1 by giving each member a written statement of the problem. The leader then reads the problem statement, making certain that it is clear but resisting requests to elaborate or explain the statement. No examples are given or any other information that might influence or direct members' responses.

4. The leader describes the kind of responses that are desired: Any and all ideas are welcome, whatever comes to mind. Ideas should be expressed in short, written phrases suitable for posting on a flipchart. Elaborations or arguments for ideas should be omitted.
5. Group members then silently write down their ideas without discussion. The leader discourages talking or any other distracting activity.
6. The leader stops the step when it appears that people have finished writing. Step 1 should take about 30 minutes.

The format of the Step 1 session offers many benefits. It allows adequate time for people to absorb the question and record their responses. It encourages people to work as they see others working. By preventing communication, thinking becomes divergent, particularly if members are chosen from different backgrounds and have different views of the problem. Moreover, without communication the group is not dominated by vocal or high-status members.

Step 2: Record Ideas The second step is for members to share their ideas about the problem. Ideas are reported to the leader round-robin and are posted around the room. Ideas are recorded in members' own words, so as to avoid changing the interpretation. At this stage, ideas are not discussed; that comes later. This step proceeds as follows:

1. The leader opens by clarifying the procedure and the goals of the step. Members are encouraged to continue to think of ideas and to piggyback or build on the ideas of others.
2. The leader asks the first member for one idea. This idea is written on a flipchart in front of the group just as the person states it. Ideas are numbered sequentially as they are recorded.
3. The leader asks for variations of the idea just presented and records them before going on.
4. The leader goes to the next member for one idea, then asks for variations of it. Duplicate ideas are discarded. If the person passes, the leader goes to the next.
5. The leader continues round-robin until all members have shared as many ideas as they wish.
6. When all ideas are recorded, Step 2 ends. The entire Step 2 should take about 30 to 35 minutes.

Care should be taken that ideas are written legibly and that they are numbered sequentially (these numbers will be used subsequently for identification). As flipchart pages are filled, they should be posted around the room where they will be visible throughout the session. This allows members to become familiar with the ideas.

The leader must give continual encouragement for new ideas because frequently people mistakenly think that idea generation should only take place during the first step. The leader must also enforce the rule that there is no discussion of ideas at this step; members must be reminded that discussion comes later.

By the end of the second step, a large number of conflicting ideas are in front of the group, offering many views on the problem. Having ideas in writing avoids their loss; moreover, it increases the group's ability to deal with all the ideas presented.

The format of the second step allows members to present ideas on an equal footing. As before, the step cannot be dominated by a few people. It also encourages the formation of group cohesion because by the second or third round each member is an involved participant.

Step 3: Discuss Ideas The purpose of this step is to clarify the ideas presented in Step 2. Taking each idea in turn, the leader asks for questions or comments. The member who presented the idea explains the meaning, importance, and logic behind it. Others are encouraged to join in the discussion, either to ask questions or to help with the clarification. During this process, the leader encourages members to treat clarification as a group responsibility. Step 3 proceeds as follows:

1. The leader starts by clarifying the goal and the procedure to be followed.
2. Stepping through the ideas one at a time, the leader invites discussion about the idea.
3. Under the leader's guidance and encouragement, members clarify the idea. This is done by examining the meaning of words, logic and thoughts behind the idea, examples, and anything else that can shed light on the idea.
4. The step terminates when all ideas have been examined. Step 3 should take about 30 minutes.

The leader should encourage members to have an egoless attitude and to treat the clarification process as a group activity. The leader must prevent the discussion from turning into an argument and should attempt to give all ideas equal emphasis.

Step 4: Rank Ideas In this step the group judges the relative importance of the ideas that have been presented. Each participant selects the five best ideas and ranks them. These judgments are then tallied to obtain group consensus. Step 4 proceeds as follows:

1. The leader starts by clarifying the goal and procedure for this step.
2. The leader asks each member to select the five best ideas that have been presented. Participants record their five best ideas on 3×5 cards, one idea to a card. They are instructed to put the phrase for the idea in the center of the card and the identifying number of the idea in the upper-left corner. Members are to work independently.

3. The leader asks each participant to rank order their five selected ideas, with the best idea given a score of 5 points, the second best 4 points, and so on. The scores for the ideas are to be recorded on the respective cards in the lower-right-hand corner. It is important that scoring be done individually and anonymously to prevent social pressure from distorting the ranking process.
4. The leader collects all cards, shuffles them to conceal identities, records the scores, and tallies them. Recording and tallying are done in front of the group so they automatically learn the group consensus about the importance of the ideas.
5. The session terminates at this point unless the leader decides that a clearer consensus is needed. In order to gain a clearer consensus, the leader may decide to extend the session by adding two steps, consisting of a discussion of the vote with subsequent reranking of the ideas. Step 4 should take about 15 minutes.

After the session is completed, all ideas and tallies should be collected by the leader. A letter should be sent to each member confirming the results obtained in the session and thanking them for their participation.

4.5.4 Evaluation of NGT

The NGT is an effective procedure for generating ideas and reaching group consensus on their importance in a relatively short time. It is an easy process to run, and group members need no prior training to participate effectively. The format of the process promotes equality of participation; vocal and high-status members are less likely to dominate than they are in more openly participative procedures. Participants in NGT sessions usually leave with a sense of accomplishment and satisfaction.

NGT has a drawback in requiring a trained leader to conduct the session, although the level of training is similar to that required by many other group techniques. Also, NGT might be an inappropriate technique to use when the aim is team building or the development of interactive problem-solving skills.

4.6 THE DELPHI METHOD

The Delphi method, which is named after the ancient oracle of Apollo in Greece, is a method for the controlled exchange of information within a group. It provides a formal, structured procedure for the exchange of opinion, and is frequently used to *obtain estimates*. The method allows for feedback of information among group members. It allows individuals an opportunity to assess group views and to make their opinions known to the group. And it also provides anonymity for individuals.

This makes it different from brainstorming, which allows no anonymity, and the nominal group technique, which allows limited anonymity for individuals.

The method was developed at the Rand Corporation in the early 1950s. It was noted that there is a vast difference in our society between the way we treat facts and the way we treat opinions. The former are widely available in libraries, books, and magazines. But prior to the work of the Rand group, very little had been done to catalogue opinions, and there was no formal technique for their exchange.

Since its conception, thousands of Delphi studies have been conducted by government and business. The method is now a standard tool to be considered whenever a consensus of experts is sought on a subject. The method has been used for planning, budgeting, and market research, and for gathering estimates of current and historical data that are not otherwise available. Several large-scale Delphi experiments have been conducted to forecast on topics of general interest, and the results of the studies have been widely used.

When other methods of estimation fail, the Delphi method should be considered as a way to obtain data. It can be used to estimate such items as duration, resource requirements, risk, costs, and benefits. The method can also be used to estimate aspects of products, such as utilization rates, useful life, acceptability, quality, and operational costs.

4.6.1 The Delphi Group

A participating group and a person to serve as a monitor are needed to conduct a Delphi experiment. The group should consist of experts on the topic under discussion—people who by training, experience, or position are qualified to have an opinion on the subject. At the same time, the group should be diverse.

The panel of experts must be committed to the study and must take its job seriously. They must be prepared to devote sufficient time and thought. A panel should consist of at least ten people, as with fewer it is difficult to generate a meaningful exchange of ideas. Members can and should be drawn from the parts of the organization that are concerned about the problem under consideration. If it is difficult to select the required number of people, additional panel members can be drawn from parent organizations, trade groups, consultants, and others who are familiar with the type of problem to be considered.

A Delphi group need not be assembled in one location to conduct a session because all communication is done in writing. If the group is widely scattered or if meetings are difficult to schedule, it is quite possible to conduct the experiment by conventional mail or by e-mail.

The monitor is in charge of the experiment. She selects the panel and establishes the wording of the questions to be considered. She makes physical arrangements for the experiment and conducts it. If the group needs instruction, she introduces them to the Delphi technique, perhaps by making a practice run. During the experiment, she gathers and tabulates statistics, monitors responses that are generated, and presents appropriate information to the group. She communicates the final outcome of the experiment to the group.

The job of the monitor is difficult because it is easy to bias results. One common reason for the failure of experiments is that the monitor imposes a view on the group, perhaps by subtle, unconscious actions or statements. The monitor has to maintain strict neutrality throughout the experiment.

4.6.2 Overview of the Method

There are many variations on the procedure. We shall describe one procedure that is relatively simple, but useful.

The questions posed to a Delphi group should require a quantitative answer—a duration, a cost, or some other number. Many questions involving estimates naturally lend themselves to quantitative answers. With a little practice, some that don't can be revised to meet this requirement. For example, a question may be posed so as to require rating the importance of a topic on a scale from 1 to 10. Or a question may require assessing the probability of an event.

A Delphi experiment is conducted in four rounds. Each round calls for a response from each group member. Each response contains an answer to the question, and it might also contain supporting reasons, as described below. The answer to the question is a number, which will be referred to as an *estimate* because of the nature of the question being asked. Responses are anonymous, and to achieve this the responses are made in writing. No names are affixed to the responses, and it is important that group members not look at each other's answers. At the end of each round, the monitor provides the group with certain information, which will be detailed later.

Before describing the four rounds in detail, we shall explain some statistical terms that will be used. Additional discussion of these concepts is given in Chapter 7. Suppose that the responses to a question are arranged in order from the smallest to the largest. The smallest response is also called the *minimum* response, and the largest the *maximum*. The *first quartile* is the response such that 25% of the responses are equal to it or are less, and 75% are equal to it or are greater. The *second quartile* or *median* response is such that 50% are equal to it or are less, and 50% are equal to it or are greater. In other words, the second quartile or median is the "middlemost" response. The *third quartile* is the response such that 75% are equal to it or are less, and 25% are equal to it or are greater. Finally, the *interquartile range* is the range from the first quartile to the third quartile. It is a range that contains the middle one-half of the responses.

How do we obtain a quartile? Arrange the responses in order from the smallest to the largest. Count up one-fourth of the responses from the lower end—that gives you the first quartile. Then count up one-half of the responses from the lower end—this is the second quartile. Then count up three-fourths of the responses—this gives you the third quartile.

To illustrate these concepts, suppose that there are 15 responses to a question as follows:

4, 6, 9, 5, 8, 2, 7, 3, 9, 6, 6, 8, 2, 5, 1

The first step is to order or rank them:

1, 2, 2, 3, 4, 5, 5, 6, 6, 6, 7, 8, 8, 9, 9

One-fourth of 15 is 4 (after rounding), and the fourth response in order is 3. Thus the first quartile is 3. In a similar way the second quartile is 6, and the third is 8. The interquartile range extends from 3 to 8.

Another statistical term used is the *mode*; this is the response that is given most frequently. In the example above, the mode is 6 because there are three responses of 6 and no other response is more frequent. (Note: If another response of 8 were added to the above example, the collection of responses would be *bimodal* with modes at 6 and 8.)

4.6.3 The Delphi Process

A round-by-round description of the Delphi process is as follows.

Round 1: The monitor poses a question that requires a numerical answer, which will be referred to as an estimate. Participants respond to the question in writing. The responses are gathered by the monitor, tabulated, and analyzed. The monitor then gives the group the following information: minimum response, maximum response, the first, second, and third quartiles, the interquartile range, and the mode(s).

Round 2: The monitor asks each participant to provide a new response (estimate) to the question. This new estimate can be the same as the one the participant made in Round 1 or it can be different. No one will know which it is except the participant—the system has no memory. After making the new estimate, the participant must compare it with the interquartile range presented to the group at the end of Round 1. If the new estimate is *outside* the interquartile range, the participant is to write a brief statement of his reason for his estimate.

The monitor then collects a response from each participant. These responses consist of (1) the new estimate and (2) a reason for holding an extreme view *if* the new estimate is outside the Round 1 interquartile range.

The monitor tabulates the new estimates exactly as in Round 1 and presents to the group the same kind of summary information as in Round 1—namely, the minimum, maximum, first, second, and third quartiles, interquartile range, and the mode(s), all computed from the Round 2 estimates. In addition, she presents to the group the reasons for extreme views. She does that without revealing the identity of the writers.

Round 3: The monitor asks each participant to make a new estimate. Each participant compares the new estimate with the interquartile range given at the end of Round 2. If the new estimate is *inside* the range, the participant must state why the arguments for the extreme views given at the close of Round 2 did not convince him. This resembles Round 2, except that reasons are now given for an estimate falling *inside* the interquartile range.

The monitor collects all responses. She tabulates the new estimates and gives the group the same type of summary information as in Rounds 1 and 2. After editing the written reasons, the monitor presents them to the group.

Round 4: The monitor asks for a new estimate; no reasons need to be given. The new estimates are tabulated and summary statistics are presented to the group in the same manner as was done in the three previous rounds.

The estimates of Round 4 are the final results of the experiment. The median from this last round is taken as the central group view on the question. The interquartile range gives some idea of the range in which the actual answer might be found. In addition, this range gives some indication as to the degree of consensus among the group on the question. The greater the spread, the less the consensus and the greater the risk associated with the median estimate.

4.6.4 Additional Comments

The question often arises as to whether it would be advantageous to continue a Delphi experiment beyond four rounds. This seems not to be worthwhile. Four rounds provide opportunity for extreme and central views to be aired, and additional rounds generally produce little new information. As a result, estimates generally do not change much if the experiment is continued past four rounds.

Teaching a group how to perform a Delphi experiment is best accomplished by holding a practice session conducted by two individuals. One explains the Delphi process and plays the role of the monitor in the practice session. The other assists by collecting and editing responses, calculating the summary statistics required at the end of each round, sorting responses for extreme views, and so on. Conducting a session with two people avoids awkward periods of silence while the calculations and other administrative chores are being done.

During an experiment, the monitor is often asked to clarify the question being considered. This should *not* be done. Part of the experiment involves bringing out differences in the interpretation of the question, and an experienced group will add clarifying comments to the reasons they submit in Rounds 2 and 3. For instance, they might make such comments as: "I interpret 'most' to mean 50%, therefore . . . ," "I assume 'most companies' means most *domestic* companies . . . ," "I assume the question only refers to large projects, say more than 25 person-years of effort, therefore . . . ."

From the comments that arise during the Delphi experiment, the monitor can determine just how much confusion the question generates. If it appears necessary, the question can be reformulated and a new experiment can be conducted. If trouble is anticipated with a question, it might even be worthwhile to run a small experiment to pretest the question before conducting the major experiment.

In training a new group in the Delphi method, it is a good idea to ask a factual question whose answer can be verified. If everyone in the group is familiar with John, then "How old is John?" is a good beginning question—provided John is not sensitive about his age. The advantage of a factual question is that the group can compare their estimate with the actual answer and thereby gain confidence in the technique.

A simple Delphi experiment can be conducted in an hour or less. At the other extreme, an experiment can extend over several weeks or several months. The time schedule will depend partly on the physical location of the participants and partly on the amount of thought and work they are expected to put into the project. Explanations or reasons can be brief, or they can be important studies in their own right. The major cost of a Delphi experiment is the time of the participants.

In using the Delphi method, it is important to remember that it does not give a 20-20 view into the future. Its use and the interpretation of results should be viewed as something of an art rather than as an exact science. If a better method of estimating is available, then of course it should be used; but even then, a Delphi estimate can be used to corroborate that estimate. A member of a company who uses the Delphi method extensively once remarked, "Our estimates aren't perfect, but they're a whole lot less wrong than they used to be."

4.7 EXERCISES

4.1 Brian Joiner and Peter Scholtes (*The Team Handbook: How to Use Teams to Improve Quality*, Madison, WI: Joiner and Associates, 1988) have written an excellent book on how to work in teams. Read this book and discuss their ideas and techniques.

4.2 Look at past issues of *Quality Progress* and locate articles on quality circles. Discuss these articles.

4.3 Summarize the benefits of quality circles and discuss possible drawbacks.

4.4 How would you train quality circles? What problem-solving tools should they know?

4.5 Discuss the advantages of group-based problem-solving techniques over those that are carried out by individuals.

4.6 Form appropriate groups and use the brainstorming technique to generate ideas about the topics listed below. Carefully discuss and document your procedures.

(a) Difficulties that prevent college undergraduates from graduating in four years

(b) Improving your MBA program

(c) Improving communication between faculty and students

(d) Improving teaching effectiveness

(e) Finding ways to increase the proportion of minority students

4.7 Select those questions that you have not addressed in Exercise 4.6. Use the NGT technique to generate ideas and reach a group consensus on their importance.

4.8 Conduct Delphi experiments to estimate:

(a) The proportion of female tenured or tenure-track faculty members at your University

(b) The total annual faculty payroll at your Business School

(c) The age of your instructor

Carefully describe your procedure. Compare your estimate with the actual figure (which can be determined in these exercises).

4.9 Consult the literature (for example, the *Harvard Business Review, Quality Progress*, as well as other publications) for recent articles on the topics covered in this chapter. Discuss these papers in your own words.

4.8 REFERENCES

Delbecq, A. L., A. H. Van de Ven, and D. H. Gustafson. *Group Techniques for Program Planning*. Glenview, IL: Scott, Foresman, 1975.

Drucker, P. F. *Technology, Management, and Society*. New York: Harper and Row, 1970.

Joiner, B. L., and P. R. Scholtes. *The Team Handbook: How to Use Teams to Improve Quality*. Madison, WI: Joiner and Associates, 1988.

Orsburn, J. D., L. Moran, E. Musselwhite, and J. H. Zenger. *Self-Directed Work Teams*. Homewood, IL.: Business One Irwin, 1990.

Osborn, A. F. *Applied Imagination: Principles and Procedures of Creative Thinking*. New York: Scribner, 1957.

CHAPTER 5

THE REWARD STRUCTURE: THE HUMAN SIDE OF PROBLEM SOLVING

Discussions of problem solving, such as are presented in this book, tend to dwell on methods and procedures: the tools and techniques for generating ideas, and how to evaluate and install them. The people side of problem-solving tends to be neglected; yet, how people interact and respond is crucial to the success of the effort. In this chapter, we shall discuss aspects of the human side of problem solving. Human issues cannot be ignored. Questions of motivation, expectations, support, and reward must be considered. If you are a professional whose education has been almost exclusively on technical subjects, then for you this may be among the most important chapters of this book.

Organizations tend to get the behavior from people that they reward. People are rational. When they observe that certain behavior is rewarded, then that is how they behave. Or, if they find that way too unpleasant, they move to another job. The phrase "you get what you pay for" is usually applied to consumer products, but it applies to employee behavior, too.

Rewards come in many forms: salary, monetary fringe benefits, a corner office, an imposing title, or other formal benefits. Rewards can also be less formal: being turned to for advice, remembered by name, part of a winning team, or simply being thanked for a job well done. Often the day-to-day informal rewards have more influence on behavior and performance of people than do formal benefits.

The reward system influences the problems of an organization in two ways. The reward system influences the creation of problems, and the reward system influences the solution of problems. Let's take a look at some of these influences.

5.1 REWARD AND PROBLEM CREATION

If you want to keep out of the problem-solving business, then you must avoid as many problems as you can. To do so, here are five simple actions you should take regularly:

5.1.1 Action 1: Reward Purposeful Action, Not Fire Fighting

A good way to avoid additional problems is to reward purposeful action, not "fire fighting."

Ron is a project manager in the IS department of a Fortune 500 company. He is highly regarded by management as a troubleshooter. Whenever a project gets in serious trouble (as commonly happens in his organization), Ron is called in to set things right. And he does; his years of experience in fire fighting have taught him all the tricks he needs to turn bad situations around. Ron is one of the highest paid members of his department and is admired by most of the young project managers, who are trying hard to master Ron's skill. Of course, for Ron to have become a good fire fighter, he had to have fires on which to practice. But that was never a problem; fires were plentiful in Ron's early years because his projects usually got into trouble. But doesn't that happen to everyone?

Many people find fire fighting exciting. On the other hand, a well-run project or department is a dull place. There are no exciting catastrophes, no people running around or frantically shouting on the phone. Just quiet efficiency. In fact, a well-run organization doesn't attract much attention, and the people in it can easily be overlooked.

It is extremely common for organizations to reward people who solve problems without asking who *caused* the problem. Do this regularly and you are sure to have plenty of problems to solve.

5.1.2 Action 2: Reward Producing Quality Products, Not Meeting Deadlines

You are asking for problems if you consistently reward people who meet deadlines at the expense of creating quality products.

Susan is a marketing representative for a multinational corporation. She was accustomed to having an annual quota, and knew that meeting it was important to her long-term success in the organization. With a whole year to work her quota, however, she always met it. Recently, her industry experienced a downturn and the corporation's profits came under severe pressure. So that the company could manage affairs more closely, Susan and other marketing reps were required to meet quarterly quotas; as before, failure to meet quota would damage their career prospects. Marketing people found it difficult to "make their numbers" under the quarterly quota system because their customers didn't make snap decisions about the big-ticket items their firm sold. One quarter Susan needed a particular order to meet her quota, but the customer was debating about signing it. Susan was quite confident the order would be signed, but she couldn't be certain. After much agonizing, she decided to submit the order even though it was unsigned. After all, if the customer finally signed it, there would be no problem. If he didn't, there would be a big mess—the order would have to be backed out of the system, delivery schedules would have to be modified, and so on. And, of course, Susan's career would suffer seriously when it was discovered that she had purposely lied. But if she didn't submit the false order, she would not make the quarterly quota and her career would suffer immediately. In effect, the only hope she had to avoid a personal problem was to lie and hope for the best.

Susan's situation was extreme. Usually pressure to meet deadlines can be handled without making it so obvious that corners are being cut. This happens all the time with the development of products and information systems. Deadlines for such systems are based on estimates that are notoriously poor and, therefore, extremely difficult to meet in an honest way. A deadline, however, can always be met by skimping on documentation, omitting a few of the tests, or providing less than the full function required. Chances are that most of these omissions will not be noticed immediately, and they can always be rectified while maintenance changes are made, which usually is as soon as the system is delivered. Moreover, if any serious problem does develop, most likely it will be difficult to trace the problem to the corner-cutting needed to meet the deadline. And by the time it is traced, the project personnel most likely will be on some other job. So who cares? Just meet the deadline somehow, and don't worry about the problems it creates.

5.1.3 Action 3: Reward Cooperation, Not Internal Competition

Internal competition is another rich source of problems; to avoid them, reward cooperation instead of internal competition.

In 1969, on the last day of the Johnson administration, the U.S. Justice Department slapped an antitrust suit on IBM, threatening to split the giant computer maker into several pieces. While defending itself vigorously, IBM also prepared for the worst. As it appeared to the outside world, they embarked on a conscious effort to structure the company into divisions that, if forced by the government, could be split apart and would become formidable organizations in their own right. To prepare for such a split, these divisions developed separate product lines; soon they were competing among themselves in various segments of the marketplace. This competition certainly led to an inefficient mode of operation and it inconvenienced customers, but the establishment of competing divisions probably was the correct strategic decision at that time. In 1982, after wasting untold millions of IBM's and taxpayers' dollars, the government finally withdrew its suit. But the internal competition IBM fostered as a precautionary measure left the company with an inappropriate organizational structure and incompatible product lines. Problems stemming from the forced internal competition plagued the company for years.

As the IBM story illustrates, internal competition is destructive at the divisional level; it also creates problems at the individual level. At quarterly meetings held by one company, it was customary to single out three or four individuals for special recognition. Each of these was given a modest cash prize—about the price of a dinner for two at an expensive restaurant. The most frequently heard comment after such a meeting was: "I don't see why an award went to X; it should really have gone to Y, who did much more for the organization." Of course, many making such comments felt: "It should really have gone to me," but obviously they could not say that. Judging from the tone of the discussion, the awards fostered resentment in most people and a resolve not to help someone else because it really meant hurting yourself.

Competition is the name of the game in the marketplace. "Friendly" competition is appropriate within the organization. But when destructive competition is fostered, whether by the reward system or some unusual situation as in the case of IBM, it results in problems.

5.1.4 Action 4: Reward Contribution, Not Busywork

Still more problems will arise if you reward people for keeping busy rather than for making a contribution.

When Ruth became head of the administrative group serving a large department of professional workers, the work was getting done somehow. Much of it, however, was conducted informally following ad hoc procedures. Requests made of the administrative staff by the professionals often were handled without being cleared by management; as a result it usually was not possible to account for the way the administrative people spent their time and to document the contribution being made by them to the organization. To correct this lax situation, Ruth directed the staff to standardize and document all administrative procedures. She installed a formal system for requesting administrative services and had her people log the time actually spent on various tasks. To keep everyone informed, she sent messages to the professionals on an almost daily basis describing the latest changes in administrative procedures. This additional work burdened the administrative staff, of course, and soon more people were required; within a year it was necessary to add a layer of management between Ruth and the staff to keep her span of control reasonable.

After about two years on the job, Ruth had everything ship-shape. All procedures were formalized and she could report to upper management exactly how many requests of various kinds her group was handling, how many bulletins they distributed, and other measures of productivity. Because of her impressive record, Ruth was promoted to head the administrative staff of an important division of the company. The professionals in the department were not at all sorry to see her go. Because of the red tape she imposed, most professionals stopped using the administrative staff for support, preferring to do their own typing, copying, and other clerical tasks. Ruth had managed to keep her staff busy—indeed, to enlarge it—but her contribution to the business was negative: Partially she had turned the professionals into clericals.

Rewarding people for keeping busy, rather than making a contribution, is a sure way to create problems. Yet it happens all the time, often occurring in the name of productivity. Very often, the productivity measures used by organizations have more to do with how busy people are than with the contribution being made. The same is true of the "informal" measures of productivity: How many people do you know who measure their personal contribution by how many phone calls they make or how many meetings they attend? People should be measured and rewarded on the products they produce, not by the activities they perform in producing the products. They should be rewarded for results, not actions.

5.1.5 Action 5: Reward Good Management, Not Political Activity

A rich source of problems is to reward the office politicians while overlooking good managers.

This error is very hard to document because everybody must engage in a certain amount of political activity. How much is too much? Also, a good politician conducts most of his political business in private; much of his effort would be ineffective were it done publicly. How do you document what goes on in private? Every office is full of rumors about political activity: Mary got the promotion because she helped her boss by knifing a potential rival; Alan gets what he wants because he has something on his manager; Ed got the support of Joe by promising to make him Sales Manager. In some offices, politics is the major topic of office gossip. The accepted "truth" is that rewards go to the politicians, not the workers. The view is that it doesn't matter what you know, it's who you know. So why work? Just find a way to win favor with someone who has clout.

Decisions should be based on what is right, not who is right. This rule gets distorted, however, when politics becomes the major concern of decision makers. Then good management loses, and problems multiply.

5.2 REWARD AND PROBLEM SOLUTION

Not only will an improper reward system cause problems, it also can inhibit their solution. These are some of the actions organizations can take to make their problem-solving process more effective:

5.2.1 Action 6: Reward Process Improvement, Not Quick Fixes

One way to make problem solving more effective is to reward process improvement, not quick fixes.

Tom is manager of the IS Department of a large U.S. corporation. Like most companies in the United States, his organization spends more time on maintaining (correcting and enhancing) existing software than on creating new. Tom is very concerned about his maintenance backlog and continually presses his group to keep it low. Consequently, they spend as little time on each maintenance request as possible, doing only the work required. Even when they spot a situation where an ounce of prevention—say, a slight restructuring of the code—might save a pound of repair in the future, they won't do it. By making maintenance changes quickly, they manage to keep their maintenance backlog under control. Their approach, however, does nothing to reduce the number of maintenance requests, so they are not gaining on their problem.

An emphasis on quick fixes inhibits people from taking preventive actions that can stave off future problems. It tends to focus concern on the repair of a defective product and to divert it from the repair of the *process* that allowed the defect to happen. This is precisely the wrong focus from a long-term view because fixing the process prevents problems in the future.

5.2.2 Action 7: Reward Reasonable Risk, Not Safe Solutions

Another way to make problem solving more effective is to reward people for taking reasonable risks, not for simply playing it safe.

When Ed started working in the Purchasing Department, he couldn't understand why the company dealt with a particular supplier, even though it was a well-known firm. Each time he placed an order with them, it got fouled up in some way, leaving Ed with a problem to correct. Moreover, their prices were not all that great either; a friend of his in purchasing with another company had told him of a supplier who was more dependable and generally cheaper than the firm they were using. So Ed went to his boss, Joe, with the proposal that they dump the well-known supplier and start using the new group. To Ed's surprise, Joe turned down the suggestion without hesitation. When pressed hard by Ed for a reason, this is what Joe finally said. Years ago when Joe was new to purchasing, there was a similar situation. The boss at that time dropped a well-known supplier and started using another firm about which he had heard very favorable reports, and which gave much better prices. Their initial experience with the new firm was excellent, and all signs seemed to vindicate their having made the change. Then, on a crucial, large order, the new firm messed up completely, causing problems that were heard all the way up to the executive office. The company lost an important customer over the situation; and in an ensuing witch hunt, the boss of purchasing lost his job. Even though many years had passed since the episode, Joe was making very certain that the same thing didn't happen to him.

Solving problems means making a change, and with change there is *always* a risk. But there is also a risk in doing nothing. Part of finding an appropriate solution to a problem is balancing risk against reward. People must be encouraged to take reasonable risks, otherwise no one will innovate and problem causes will never be addressed. The reward system in some organizations, however, gives employees the impression that to err is human, but to forgive is not company policy.

5.2.3 Action 8: Reward Creativity, Not Conformity

You can make problem solving more effective by rewarding creativity rather than conformity and preserving the status quo.

Tina was elated when she was offered a staff position as Manager of Quality Assurance for a chain of hotels, even though she was manager in name only because no one reported to her. She viewed the promotion as a sign that management was pleased with her performance. Moreover, she could offer many suggestions for improving quality that ultimately would save the hotel a lot of money. She started meeting with people, making presentations, and generally promoting quality. Tina took great pains to make people understand that quality was everybody's job; she was merely there to support and assist. And she minded the political side of her job, too, carefully cultivating the right people.

After six months on the new job, Tina had to admit to herself that things weren't going too well. She couldn't point to one solid achievement; moreover, a disturbing pattern was developing. Each time she suggested something to the professionals, she heard: "It won't work here." "We tried that before, and it didn't work." "We would like to, but management (or the customers, or the government) won't let us." And from managers she heard: "That would take too long." "That's a great idea, but we don't have the resources for it." "The professionals wouldn't like that idea, and I can't just cram it down their throats." "Later—we're too busy just now." By the end of a year, she had enough. Far from being rewarded for her attempts to create change, she felt frustrated and unappreciated. Finally she quit her job, and the company lost a very capable employee.

Solving a problem means causing a change—the whole *point* is to change what is to what should be. It calls for creativity, not just maintaining the status quo. If your organization rewards conformity and discourages change, then forget about trying to solve problems. It won't work.

5.2.4 Action 9: Reward Reasoned Action, Not Overplanning

Still another way to handle problems effectively is to reward reasoned actions, not "paralysis by analysis."

As the Quality Control Manager in the IS Department of a manufacturing company, Tom was charged with the task of installing a standard methodology for developing new applications. Not that the company didn't have such a methodology; the problem was that they had six of them, one in each of six development centers spread over the United States. These six methodologies were incompatible; moreover they were not used regularly. The Vice President was convinced the company would benefit from a single methodology, regularly applied; it was the Vice President who was behind Tom's project.

Tom knew he had a tough job. His position did not allow him to develop a methodology and mandate its acceptance; and even if it had, he felt the only way to gain acceptance for a new methodology was to involve each of the six sites in building it. This would require careful planning and coordination of a joint effort.

To achieve consensus, Tom formed a task force, which started to have regular monthly meetings to develop the new methodology. Progress was slow; each site argued for adoption of its own process and resisted incompatible suggestions from the others. Each proposal required careful analysis to determine its likely impact, then it went through a series of modifications in an attempt to overcome objections. Task force meetings, which were started in the spring, dragged through the summer vacation period, then into the fall. Tom felt the task force needed better guidance, so he brought in a consultant as advisor; this had the impact of taking the group back to the beginning.

By spring of the next year, the task force had a draft methodology and started circulating it to the six sites for their reaction. Comments on the draft were collected at open forum meetings; as they had expected, there was no shortage of objections, counterproposals, and suggestions for change. So the task force went back into sessions in an attempt to meet the criticisms. By this time, three task force members had completely lost interest in their project and had managed to get replaced; several months were needed to bring their replacements up to speed. Then, in effect, the replacements started raising objections that the old group had aired a year earlier but were fresh to the new members. Gradually, people took less and less interest in meetings; attendance dwindled, and soon meetings were being skipped. The last meeting of the task force was held two and one-half years after the first; after that the project simply died. By that time, Tom had become heavily involved in several other projects, so his management didn't seem to care that the methodology did not materialize. The Vice President, fortunately, seemed to have forgotten about the project entirely. And, of course, no one knew how much it cost the company to have incompatible methodologies, let alone the cost of the unsuccessful task force.

You can analyze a problem to death, as did Tom. Effective problem solving requires planning and action to carry out the plan.

5.2.5 Action 10: Reward Learning from Others, Not Reinvention

"Reinventing the wheel" is a favorite activity in many organizations. In solving problems, try to avoid costly reinvention by learning from others.

The Boston facility of a manufacturing plant developed a very effective method for improving the quality of one of their important processes. Over a two-year period, they honed their method until they had worked out all major procedural difficulties and management issues. They were proud of their accomplishment and were eager to share their method with other company facilities. Top management was also eager for this to happen because the Boston method, as it had come to be known, could be credited with measurable improvements in quality.

At the suggestion of top management, a group from the Chicago facility went to Boston for a one-week briefing on the Boston method. They returned to Chicago with the intent to install it there, but somehow that never happened. The people in Chicago complained that the Boston method didn't quite fit in with the Chicago process and the procedures weren't quite right for the Chicago style of management. So, with the encouragement of local management, the Chicago people ignored the Boston method and, at considerable expense, developed their own Chicago method.

Now the company has two methods, for which they paid double development costs and incur double maintenance expenses. Furthermore, to an outsider the two methods are difficult to distinguish. The "NIH (Not Invented Here) complex" is alive and well in most large organizations. Encourage that, and you will waste resources that might have been used to solve other problems.

5.3 EXERCISES

5.1 We have limited our discussion to ten major actions involving the reward system. What additional actions can you add to our list?

5.2 What do you see wrong with the reward system in your organization, or at your school?

5.3 Read and discuss the paper, "On the Folly of Rewarding 'A' While Hoping for 'B'," by Steve Kerr in the *Academy of Management Journal* (1975, pp. 769–783). This paper illustrates how some reward systems pay off for one behavior, even though the rewarder dearly hopes for another. Moreover, many systems reward behavior that the rewarder is actually attempting to discourage, while the desired behavior is not being rewarded at all. Give several examples of this type of behavior. Discuss some of the reasons why systems reward behavior A, while hoping for behavior B. Apply this discussion to the following situations:

(a) You are a candidate for a seat on your local school board. At a town meeting, all candidates have been invited to speak. To increase your chance of being elected, should you speak in generalities about "the best education for our children" or should you discuss the impact that hiring better qualified teachers will have on property taxes?

(b) Your health plan requires you to pay 50% of all doctor bills. You have just moved into a new community and are deciding whether your family should go to Dr. A, who has a reputation for not taking any chances and prescribing medicine for almost any ailment, and Dr. B, who is viewed as conservative and only prescribes medicine when convinced it is necessary. Which doctor would you select?

(c) You are a professor at a university and want to provide students with excellent instruction. Like most others, however, your university rewards professors based on research and publication, not on teaching effectiveness. Should your energy be spent on improving your teaching ability or on research?

(d) You are the Head of Administration in a teaching hospital that is part of a state university. Many of the patients treated in the hospital are indigent and do not have medical insurance to pay for their care. Should you adjust charges so that people with medical insurance cover their fair fees plus an additional amount to cover fees that cannot be collected from the indigent?

(e) A very hard-working student went to his teacher and asked, "Why should Mary get a higher grade than I do, simply because she's smarter than I am?" As the teacher, how should you respond? Defend or attack the award system implicit in the example.

(f) Discuss situations (other than those in the text or examples) where a system rewards behavior A while hoping for behavior B.

5.4 One can think of many reasons why systems reward behavior A while hoping for B. Overemphasis on "objective" criteria is one of them; for example, it is always easier to measure and reward work attendance than active productive participation. Overemphasis on highly visible behavior is another possible cause. It is easier to measure the number of publications and the number of baskets scored than good teaching and one's contribution to a team effort. Give other examples of overemphasis on "objective criteria" or "highly visible behavior" as a reason for rewarding behavior A while hoping for B.

5.5 Your "significant other" is a very poor driver, and several times has nearly caused a serious accident. Should you remain silent and hope for the best, or point out mistakes and possibly sour your relationship?

5.6 Your professor has assigned you to a team that is to accomplish a project for a class. Each member of the team will be assigned the same grade, and the grade will count heavily toward your grade for the semester. What is your opinion of this method of grading (giving a reward)?

5.7 The primary goal of an orphanage is to place children in good homes. Often, however, the budget and the prestige of such institutions are determined by their size. How do these two factors impact the adoption process?

5.8 Read "The Theory and Practice of Employee Recognition" by Brooks Carder and James D. Clark (*Quality Progress*, December 1992, p. 25). List and briefly summarize the nine "facets of recognition" given by the authors.

5.9 Read *Gain Sharing* (pp. 184–188) in *Self-Directed Work Teams*, by J. D. Orsburn, L. Moran, E. Musselwhite, and J. H. Zenger.

(a) What is your view of this reward system as it relates to product quality?

(b) In the same book, read *Pay for Skill (Knowledge)* (pp. 188–192), and answer the same question.

5.4 REFERENCES

Carder, B., and J. D. Clark. "The Theory and Practice of Employee Recognition," *Quality Progress*, December 1992 (Vol. 25), p. 25.

Kerr, Steve. "On the Folly of Rewarding 'A' While Hoping for 'B'," *Academy of Management Journal*, 1975, pp. 769–783.

Orsburn, J. D., L. Moran, E. Musselwhite, and J. H. Zenger. *Self-Directed Work Teams*. Homewood, IL: Business One Irwin, 1990.

PROJECTS FOR SECTION 1

We believe that the most effective way to learn problem solving and statistics is to be actively engaged in doing it. For this reason we conclude this and all following sections of this book with the assignment of projects. These projects can be solved with the concepts and techniques that are covered in the chapters of the section in which they are assigned. Each project is motivated by a question that needs to be answered; the answers to these problems and the techniques that are used for their analysis flow quite naturally from the question asked. The aim of the projects is to show, by example, how quantitative analysis can contribute to the solution of the problem. The scope of these end-of-section projects is larger than that of the exercises at the end of each chapter. The projects require more discussion and analysis, and they ask for a brief report to communicate the findings. We recommend that these projects be undertaken by groups of students so that students can share the work as well as their talents.

In addition to these projects we recommend that other projects be undertaken in which you identify the problem, design a study, and collect, analyze, and interpret the results. Problem-solving techniques and statistical analysis are most meaningful when you have personal experience with their use. For ideas on how to use projects effectively, you may want to consult the paper "Projects in Introductory Statistics Courses," by Johannes Ledolter, *The American Statistician*, Vol. 49, 1995, 364–367.

PROJECT 1 ABLE CORPORATION INFORMATION SYSTEMS DEPARTMENT

At 5 o'clock on Friday, when most people had left work, George Howe sat in his office and contemplated his first week on the job as Director of Information Systems Quality at Able Corporation. Able manufactured auto parts, which were sold mainly to independent repair facilities. During his job interviews with the President, Nan Baker, and the Director of Quality, Charlie Fox, it had been stressed how important his job was and how critical quality data was to the organization. Yet in each meeting with a department head during the past week, he heard only about how much trouble they had with their information systems and how incompetent his predecessor had been.

George also had made a cursory inspection of the documentation in the IS area. On Tuesday, he requested a copy of the organization's project development methodology, but it wasn't until Thursday that one was supplied to him; he was told it had taken some time to get it "ship shape." A quick review showed him it was a fairly standard methodology, but it was incomplete and needed some tuning to clarify some steps and responsibilities. He also attempted to review the error and repair record of one of their major IS systems. However, he was told by the people responsible for it that they were very busy making changes and corrections, but they would try to gather the information and get back to him as soon as possible.

On Wednesday, George spent some time in the Operations Department, which is responsible for running the computer and doing the batch processing of major systems, such as the payroll system. He learned that when a batch program abends (abnormally terminates), the problem frequently is that the people submitting the job have made an error in the job control language (JCL) that directs the computer operation. He also learned that some of the more experienced operators know enough about JCL to correct the problem without bothering to notify the person who submitted the job. They keep no record of such corrections and don't bother to notify the person submitting it, so the errant behavior persists.

On Thursday, George had lunch with the Sales Manager; this was his initial step in lunching periodically with his customers. At that time, he learned that the order entry system was plagued with problems. A later look at the records in his department verified that this was correct, but the records were not complete enough to ascertain the real problems with the system. In later conversations with the people who maintained the marketing system, he was told that the sales personnel didn't enter the data properly, were forever making changes in the system, and "wouldn't follow the rules." But there was no clear record to indicate just what were the problems, how frequently they occurred, or how the situation might be corrected.

In a conversation on Friday morning with the head of Personnel, he learned that the Personnel Department was fed up with how slowly IS reacted to requests for service, so on their own they had developed several PC-based programs to assist them and had imported others from cooperating customers. Since these programs were resident on the mainframe computer and run over a communications network, George asked about data security and the problem of importing viruses into the computer network. He was told, however, that people in Personnel were careful and the probability of that happening was insignificant.

As George looked back on the week, he asked himself if it was such a good idea to leave Mighty Corporation and join a small company such as Able. He realized there was a great risk that he might fail, but he also saw that there was a great opportunity to make real improvements. Moreover, there was a chance for advancement because Charlie was nearing the retirement age. Where, however, should he start?

Questions

1. There may be many reasons for dissatisfaction with IS service at Able Corporation. How would you classify the reasons and how would you obtain information on their importance?

2. Clearly the project development methodology is not being used regularly. Construct a cause-and-effect diagram to investigate why the developmental methodology is not being used.
3. What data should be collected about the problems with the order-entry system, and how could this information be used to improve the quality of the system?
4. Documentation of processes seems to be a problem. What might be some of the causes of this problem?
5. The relationship between IS and the Sales Department is poor. Discuss the benefits of forming a joint Sales/IS team to address this issue.
6. What other problems do you see with Able Corporation's information systems? Where would some of the tools discussed in Section I fit in to address these problems? Think about JCL training, change procedures, and security of PC systems.
7. List several critical actions that George should undertake as soon as possible.

PROJECT 2 ACME ELECTRONICS

Acme Electronics is a small manufacturer of television sets and a supplier of electronic components. They are located on the East Coast and operate mainly in a six-state region. Acme always has prided itself on its service and fast response to customers, so the President, Dave Borum, was shocked when he learned that a major customer was dissatisfied with the quality of their components and stated they would not place another order with Acme "until they get their act together."

A phone call to the customer did little to soothe him or change his mind. But his parting words did make a deep impression on Dave: "You'd better get your quality act together or you'll be out of business."

Dave wasted no time in hiring a Director of Quality, Rod Larson. With Rod's help, Dave then established a Quality Council consisting of Dave, Rod, all department heads, and the head of the employee union. At their initial meeting a week later, the Council reviewed the situation and agreed that Rod would draft a Quality Policy and a quality improvement plan for discussion at their next meeting, which was to be held in one week's time. Meanwhile, they would all do some outside reading about how to improve product quality.

At their meeting a week later, several ideas were proposed for a quality policy. After some discussion it was agreed that "Our business is quality" set the right tone. After more discussion, it was decided that what they meant by "quality" was producing what you were supposed to produce—that is, meeting requirements. It was agreed that the failure to meet a requirement was a *defect*—a quality product is one that is defect-free. With this definition, each department could measure their quality by measuring their defect rates.

Next, Rod discussed his plan for improving quality at Acme. First, they would inform all employees that Acme was establishing a new direction and making quality a major goal of the organization. In a special Quality Day meeting, employees would be introduced to the new emphasis, told the part they were to play in the effort, and asked to sign a pledge that they would strive to produce quality products. Soon after that, all employees would be given training on the importance of doing things right the first time. Working together, managers and workers would establish measures of quality and goals for quality improvement. Also, there would be a program to recognize individuals who made a significant contribution to quality.

Quality Day was very successful. To mark the event, the families of employees were invited, and the ice cream was a big hit with the children. Because of its size, the event was held outdoors and the weather cooperated beautifully. Everyone had a good time; and everything went without a hitch except that the banner with "Our business is quality" blew down in the middle of Rod's speech. The success of the kick-off could be measured by the favorable comments one could hear the next day in the hallways and company cafeteria.

Dave was pleased with the success of Quality Day. This convinced him that Rod was a good choice, and that Rod could be trusted to handle quality while he got back to running the business. For his part, Rod was busy working with managers to establish departmental measures of quality and quality recognition programs.

Managers soon came to realize that one way to be popular with Dave Borum was for their department to have a reputation for quality. And this could be done by being generous in assessing quality accomplishments. So gradually there was an increase in recognition awards even though the general level of quality remained more or less constant.

Several months after Quality Day, Dave was again shocked to learn that another major customer was dropping Acme as a supplier because of the quality of their products. "How can that be? We've got a quality program in place!" What could Rod Larson say?

Questions

1. Critique the quality program initiated by Rod Larson. What are its strong points? What are its weak points?
2. Compare and contrast Rod Larson's quality program with that offered by Philip Crosby as described in *Quality Is Free* (McGraw-Hill, 1979).
3. Critique Rod Larson's quality program against the three interrelated factors required for corporate revitalization as discussed in "Why Change Programs Don't Produce Change," by Michael Beer, Russell A. Eisenstat, and Bert Spector (*Harvard Business Review*, November–December, 1990, p. 158).
4. As part of Acme's manufacturing process, television sets are examined to see that they meet all requirements. Currently, little use is made of the inspection

data. If you were a consultant to Rod Larson, what suggestions would you make concerning the analysis of this defect information?

In your investigation, you discovered that many defects are due to faulty tubes. What steps would you take to address this problem? Note that some tubes are manufactured by Acme, while others are purchased from an outside supplier.

What data would you collect to assist you in your improvement efforts? Note that the manufacture of television sets is by assembly. What tools could you use to understand the assembly process?

5. Under the current management system, most decisions concerning the manufacture of TV sets are made by management. Discuss the pros and cons of introducing self-directed work teams as an alternative model for managing the work effort.

6. What steps should Rod take to institute an effective quality improvement program? Which tools discussed in Section 1 might come into play?

References for Projects for Section 1

Beer, Michael, Russell A. Eisenstat, and Bert Spector. "Why Change Programs Don't Produce Change," *Harvard Business Review*, November–December, 1990, p. 158.

Crosby, Philip. *Quality Is Free*, New York: McGraw-Hill, 1979.

Ledolter, Johannes. "Projects in Introductory Statistics Courses," *The American Statistician*, Vol. 49, 1995, 364–367.

SECTION 2

MANAGEMENT BASED ON FACTS: THE IMPORTANCE OF DATA AND DATA ANALYSIS

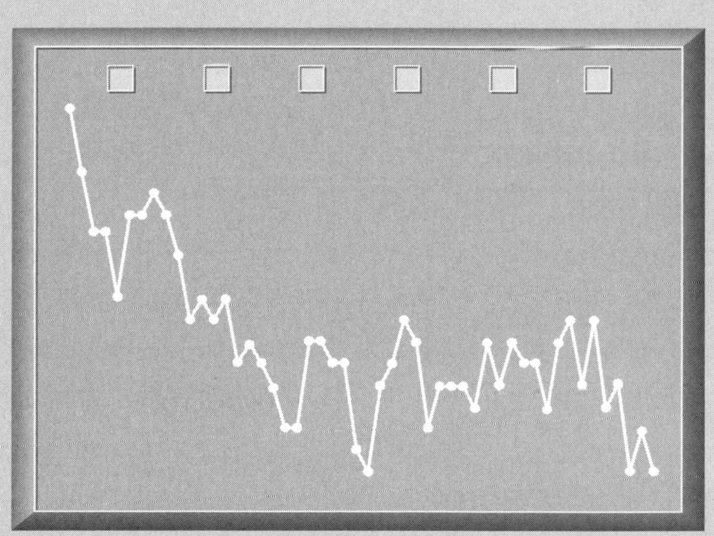

CHAPTER 6

MEASUREMENTS AND THEIR IMPORTANCE FOR QUALITY

6.1 MEASUREMENTS AND THE MEASUREMENT PROCESS: AN INTRODUCTION

Quality assessment and quality improvement require evaluations, asking questions such as:

How satisfied are our customers? What do customers expect from our products? Are our services done well?

How good are our products? Do they meet the requirements? Are we meeting the standards consistently?

How good are our processes? How are processes affected if we make certain changes? How do we know whether a certain change has worked?

How reliable are our measurements?

Which processes perform best?

The answers to these questions require information. This information is obtained through measurements on processes and products, which can be goods, services, or information products.

What is involved in taking measurements? Let us start our discussion with four simple examples. These examples illustrate several important concepts about the *measurement process* and the output of that process, the *measurement*.

6.1.1 Example 1

"Our carpenter uses an ordinary tape measure to measure the length of our kitchen table in inches. He fixes the beginning of the tape measure at one end of the table, stretches the tape to the other side, and takes a reading. He finds that the length of our table is 40 1/4 inches."

What is involved in this simple statement? We are interested in an attribute of *our* kitchen table. We are only interested in this one particular table. We are interested in the length of the table. A standard tape measure is used to obtain data on the length of the table. The measurement is taken by our carpenter. The measurement procedure is described in detail: The tape measure is fixed at one end of the table, it is stretched out to the other end of the table, and a reading is taken. The unit of measurement is the inch (if we wanted the measurement in centimeters, we could always multiply the result by 2.54). The length of the table is 40 1/4 inches.

6.1.2 Example 2

"My son, who is in the second grade, measures the length of an extra-large egg as 6.21 cm."

Here we are interested in the length of an extra-large egg. The situation is not as clear as in the previous case, where we measured the length of a specific item. It is not apparent which extra-large egg he measured. Extra-large eggs are not uniform in size, and there is variation in length from one egg to another. The one egg my son measured is the one he took from our refrigerator, out of a carton that we selected in the supermarket from among many cartons of extra-large eggs.

Little is said on how he has measured the length of this egg. The procedure is not fully explained. His procedure was to use a simple caliper with a metric scale. He was somewhat frustrated as it was difficult for him to line up the egg exactly. He, in fact, told me that he could vary the length somewhat by changing the angle of the alignment. He selected the measurement which corresponded to the alignment which he thought was "just right."

6.1.3 Example 3

"Quality inspectors measure the hardness of today's production of steel billets. Twenty measurements were taken. The twenty measurements yielded (in units of Brinell hardness): 212, 197, 207, ..."

We are told that "quality inspectors" take the measurements. In fact, there are three of them: Joe, Mary, and Bob. Since they may differ in the way they take the measurements, it is always advisable to keep track of who has measured.

They take measurements on "today's production." A typical day's production may amount to 100 billets and they have measured twenty of them. It is not obvious which twenty were selected. More should be said about this. If we want a fair assessment of today's production, then one should select from the 100 billets *at random*. That is, each billet should have the same chance of being selected. (We will say much more on sampling and random sampling in Chapter 9.) Of course, if we want the hardness of the worst-looking billets, then we should measure the twenty worst-looking ones. It depends on what one wants to measure.

Little is said about "how" hardness is actually measured. Step-by-step procedures for measuring hardness should be written out and followed by all inspectors. Sticking to well-documented procedures reduces the variation. If different inspectors use different procedures, then the measurements may not be comparable. In this particular example, hardness was measured by dropping a 3000-kilogram load on the surface and measuring the depth of the indentation. A chart was then used to convert the magnitude of the indentation to Brinell hardness numbers.

6.1.4 Example 4

"A survey of first-time buyers of a certain 1993-model luxury car shows that after one year 56 percent of all respondents are satisfied with the quality of their cars. The survey also shows that the median family income of the surveyed first-time buyers is $90,000."

Where do these numbers come from? Every buyer of our 1993 luxury car was sent a questionnaire on customer satisfaction. Of the 21,000 questionnaires that were sent out, 3,251 were returned. The response rate for this survey was $(100)(3{,}251/21{,}000) = 15.5$ percent. One question of the survey was: "How satisfied are you with the quality of the purchased car?" Responses were recorded on a scale of 1 through 5, with 1 meaning extremely unhappy, 2 somewhat unhappy, 3 neutral, 4 somewhat satisfied, and 5 extremely satisfied. The number of people who selected categories 4 and 5 represented 56 percent of the responses. Furthermore, an analysis of family incomes indicated a median income of $90,000, implying that half of the 3,251 respondents had incomes in excess of $90,000, while half of them had incomes less than that value.

The response rate for this questionnaire is rather low. One should explore why 85 percent of first-time buyers did not bother to respond. Is it because they felt neutral about their purchased product, or is it because they were so dissatisfied that they didn't bother to respond? We don't know. One needs to follow up on the nonrespondents and check whether the satisfaction among the respondents and nonrespondents is the same. However, such follow-up analyses are only possible if one has kept track of who has responded. The company should certainly increase their efforts to improve the response rate. Perhaps customers need additional incentives to respond. Perhaps the company should replace their mail survey with a telephone survey.

These four examples illustrate that measurements are not just numbers. *Measurements are outcomes of a measurement process* that is subject to many inputs such as measurement instruments, measurement procedures, and the actions of people who carry out the measurement. Measurement instruments have an impact on the actual measurement. Not all calipers are identical, not all tape measures are the same, and not all people interpret "somewhat satisfied" in the same way. Measurement procedures have an impact, resulting in variation from one measurement to the next. When measuring the length of an egg, one is not always consistent in lining up the egg in the same way. When determining hardness of steel by measuring the indentation of a steel ball, one may not always follow the procedures exactly. Measurement procedures may also be poorly described or documented, and this may introduce even more variability. Different people may be involved in taking measurements. Not everyone will measure an identical item in exactly the same way. Since measurements may depend on who has carried out the measurement, it is always a good idea to keep track of who has measured what.

6.1.5 Statistical Terminology

Statistical terminology, such as the accuracy, bias, precision, repeatability, reproducibility, and stability of measurements, is widely used and needs to be explained. The *American Society for Testing and Materials* (ASTM), an organization concerned with all aspects of measurements, uses the following definitions. *Accuracy* of a measurement refers to the closeness of the measurement to the true or actual value of the quantity that is being measured. Of course, very few measurements are perfect and there is always measurement error, also referred to as measurement noise. The *bias* of a measurement refers to the systematic over- or underestimation of the quantity that is being measured. The bias may be introduced by an incorrect calibration of the measurement instrument. For example, the use of an incorrectly calibrated measurement tape may underestimate the actual length of our kitchen table by 1/4 inch. Or, our survey procedure of assessing the level of satisfaction of car buyers may overestimate the satisfaction by 15 percentage points. In addition to the systematic component to the measurement error, there is also a random or unpredictable component. *Precision* is the ability of the measurement system to give repeated measurements that are close together. For precise measurements the random error of the measurement system is kept small.

The accuracy of the measurement system looks at both the bias (the systematic part of the measurement error) and the precision (the random component of the measurement error). Inaccuracy can result from either a bias or a lack of precision. Although accuracy is usually of greatest overall concern, one should examine the bias and the precision components separately to identify the most likely component.

The terms repeatability and reproducibility are similar, and they address the precision of the measurement system. *Repeatability* addresses the question of how well repeated measurements that are carried out by the same person agree among themselves. *Reproducibility* addresses the question how well repeated measurements that are carried out by different individuals or laboratories agree with each other. Reproducibility includes the random errors that are made by each individual in repeating the measurement as well as the variability from one subject to the other.

Stability of a measurement system addresses the issue whether the properties of the measurement system change with time. There may be trends or cyclical patterns over time due to such factors as operator fatigue and measurement tool wear.

6.1.6 Importance of Clear Operational Definitions

The purpose of an operational definition is to convey meaning that will be precisely the same to different individuals and that will stay stable over time. An *operational definition* defines a characteristic of an object or an event, not just by descriptive adjectives, but through a set of operations and a process by which the characteristic can be measured and evaluated. Operational definitions are characterized by specific criteria that are to be applied to objects or events, and by specific tests or measurement procedures.

For example, an operational definition replaces a loosely specified plan of action to do something when it is "too hot" with an exact rule that specifies action if the temperature is higher than 80 degrees Fahrenheit. An operational definition replaces a vague statement about an "item being acceptable" with detailed criteria for specified product characteristics, and by stipulating a well-defined and well-described procedure to measure the characteristics.

An operational definition puts communicable meaning into a concept. Adjectives such as "acceptable" products coming off the assembly line, "clean" dishes in a restaurant, items of "bright red" color, or "unacceptable" pollution in the environment have no communicable meaning until they are expressed in operational terms; and this requires a sampling strategy, a testing protocol, and a comparison with specified criteria. An operational definition must have the same meaning for everyone.

Clarity of operational definitions is essential. W. Edwards Deming, in his 1986 book, *Out of the Crisis*, talks at great length about the importance of clear operational definitions and he provides several illustrations. On page 288 he tries to answer the question: "What does it mean to have a label on a blanket that says 50 percent wool?" One possible operational definition may be as follows:

> *Cut ten round swatches, each one centimeter in diameter, from the blanket. Use a random mechanism to decide where to locate these swatches. Hand these pieces to the chemist for testing. Ask the chemist to follow certain prescribed rules and to record the percentage of wool by weight for each of the ten swatches. Compute the average of these ten numbers. Conclude that the blanket meets the specification (50 percent wool) if the sample satisfies the criteria that: (i) the average percentage is equal to or larger than 50 percent,*

and (ii) the difference between the largest and smallest measurement is not more than two percent. Otherwise, conclude that it fails the specification.

Another possible operational definition of "50 percent wool" is one that requires that the top half of the blanket is all cotton, while the bottom half of it is all wool. Note that neither operational definition is right or wrong. The point that Deming makes is that it is important to specify exactly what one means, as this precludes misunderstandings.

6.1.7 Other Things to Realize about Measurements

1. The act of studying a problem may alter the nature of the studied problem in a fundamental way. This is known as the *Heisenberg uncertainty principle.* It is true that important things should be measured. However, things that are measured may take on an importance by the very fact that they are being measured. This result is also known as the "halo effect" or the "Hawthorne effect," found by Mayo and Roethlisberger in the Hawthorne works of Western Electric in Cicero, IL (Roethlisberger and Dickson, 1939).
2. Any measure can be manipulated. Social factors, especially fear, are powerful forces that can distort measurements. What do you think would happen to measurements on defect rates if the rumor circulates that the company will close its doors if the defect rate reaches 10 percent? What a powerful temptation to falsify measurements if your job is on the line. Why do you think that there are so few measurements just outside the acceptable level? If in doubt, inspectors will "round" doubtful measurements so that they fall just inside the acceptable range. Sometimes this is done to protect fellow workers; sometimes it is done because inspectors themselves doubt their measurement procedures and tools. What will happen to your measurements if you are told to ship the products by all means?

   This discussion makes two important points: It is very important who controls the measurement process. Furthermore, if the company wants accurate information, then it should make every effort to reduce fear.
3. Data and information are not the same. Data becomes information if it is *relevant* for solving the question that is being studied. If the data is not relevant, then even the largest data set does not provide useful information; you may have lots of measurements, but they may contain very little information that allows you to solve the particular question at hand. For example, repeated measurements that are collected by the same person provide little information about the reproducibility of the measurement system. The most extensive data set collected at one particular time period is not informative if your objective is to assess changes over time. "Soft" measurements on the right variable are better than "hard" accurate data on the wrong one. Precise data on the wrong variable does not help us solve the problem at hand.

Accounting data, for example, is very precise. However, quite often it is not very useful to get a handle on the cost of quality.

Usually there is a limited budget for obtaining relevant data, and one must think about the problem of how to maximize the information content of the collected data. Imagine studying the output of a chemical process that is influenced, in some ways unknown to you, by many different input factors. You want to learn about the relationships by carrying out a sequence of experiments where you observe the process under different sets of input conditions. You can change input factors around haphazardly, but you will soon realize that without a roadmap for experimentation you may have to run a large number of experiments before reaching a definite conclusion. After "wandering around" aimlessly by trial and error, you will agree that it is much better to have a good experimental plan as such a plan will allow you to reach a conclusion with fewer experiments. In other words, there is more information in the data that you get from a carefully designed experiment. (Detailed discussion of the statistical design of experiments is given in Chapters 14 through 16.)

6.2 PROCESSES AND MEASUREMENTS: PROCESS VARIABILITY AND MEASUREMENT VARIABILITY

Measurements are taken on products. The products may be goods, services, or information. We may measure the dimensions and hardness of steel flats, the diameter of holes cut into metal, the quality of service at a fast-food restaurant, the amount of air pollution in Los Angeles, the customer satisfaction for certain cars, and the failure times of a certain critical component.

While measurements are taken on products, the measurements give us important information on the underlying process that is generating these products. We measure products to study and improve processes, not just to fix the products before they are shipped to a customer. Processes generate results and measurements on these results lead to data.

Simply stated, a *process* is a sequence of steps that are carried out to achieve a certain goal or result. A process transforms inputs, such as raw materials or vendor-supplied goods, into outputs, such as finished steel flats in a steel factory or hamburgers at a fast-food establishment. It is important that one understands the technical steps that are involved in this transformation (such as methods, machinery, and tools), as well as the human-factor and managerial aspects (such as people, environment, and information). Understanding the process is essential if one wants to improve it. It is also a fact that process conditions will not stay the same all the time, resulting in variability of the output. We refer to the variability that comes from changes in the process as *process variability.*

Let us illustrate these concepts—process, process variability, measurement variability—with the following three examples.

6.2.1 Example 1: Making the Morning Coffee

Making coffee in the morning involves filling the coffee machine (in this case an automatic drip coffee machine) with water, grinding the coffee beans in an electric grinder, putting the ground coffee in the filter bag, turning on the coffeemaker, and waiting until the coffee has gone through the filter. The result is several cups of (hopefully excellent) coffee (Figure 6.1).

We are interested in the "quality" of the brewed coffee. Here I define quality very personally, meaning how the coffee tastes to me. I have a five-point scale for rating the quality: 1, or lowest, through 5, or highest.

Each morning I use this scale to rate my coffee. Looking at my ratings over the last month, I notice that the results vary somewhat from one day to the next. On some days the coffee tastes better than on others. Why?

1. First, there is variability in my data because of measurement error. We call this the *measurement variability*, or the *measurement noise*. It is often difficult to distinguish between a "3" and a "4" rating, and an identical cup of coffee sipped on two different occasions may lead to different quality ratings. The measurement error may be caused by many factors. It may be influenced by the way I feel in the morning; if I stayed up late the night before, that first cup of coffee may taste just a little bit better.

   What would happen if, in addition to me, someone else (for example, my wife) would test the coffee? Her assessment wouldn't always agree with mine, and the measurement error would now also include person-to-person variability.
2. Second, there is variability that comes from the process. We call this *process variability*. It is important to understand the process, because this will be the key to understanding the sources of this variability. The amount of water in my drip coffeemaker may not always be the same. The quality of the water may vary from day to day. The amount of coffee that is put in the filter may not always be the same; if you were to watch me make coffee in the morning you would see that I am not always consistent. The coffee beans are not always the same. Even if the beans are from the same company, there is variability from one package to the next. The beans ground one day may have been sitting around in an open bag, while on the next

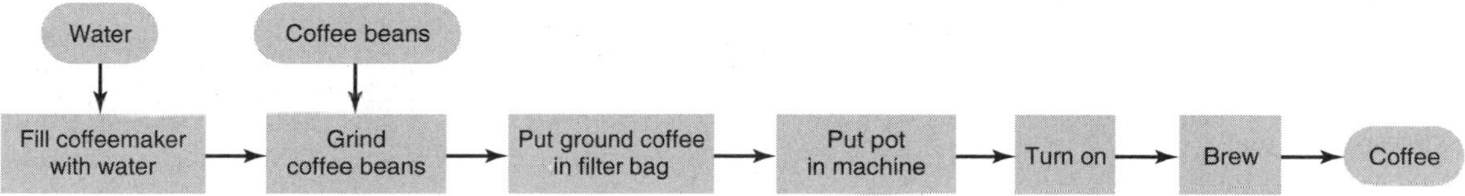

FIGURE 6.1 A simple diagram that describes the chronological steps in the process of brewing coffee.

day they come from a fresh package. The equipment used may not always be clean, and that also could affect the quality of the coffee. The hard water deposits could make a difference. The instruction manual says that the coffeemaker should be cleaned regularly with vinegar; my coffeemaker rarely gets cleaned.

6.2.2 Example 2: Manufacturing Steel Flats

Consider the manufacture of steel flats of certain dimensions (Figure 6.2). The small steel mill that one of us studied during a consulting assignment includes a meltshop where scrap metal is melted into 5.25 by 5.25 inch billets, 20 feet long. Depending on the type of steel, various alloys are added to the mixture. Billets are drawn from that mixture, then cooled off and stored on the lot for inventory. At a later time, the billets are taken to a reheat furnace, where they are heated to a predetermined temperature for a prescribed period of time. Then the billets are sent through a sequence of size reductions, which reduce the billet to steel flats of the required size. These flats are then cut to obtain flats of the required length. During shiftovers to new sizes, operators have to change the sequence of rolls for the required size reductions. Steel flats are the final output of this process.

Steel flats are sampled from the process and various measurements are taken on the final product. Measurements are taken on dimensions, steel hardness, surface conditions such as smoothness, and percent depletion of carbon content. Steel hardness and depletion of carbon are good indicators of the strength of the steel; the loss of too much carbon deteriorates the steel.

Measuring the depletion of carbon is not easy and is subject to considerable *measurement variability*. The measurement process involves polishing a small area of the steel, viewing the polished surface through a microscope, and looking for the presence of certain characteristics. You can imagine that identical pieces of steel could easily lead to different measurements on depletion of carbon.

Process variability is also present. There are many sources for process variability. It arises, in part, because of variation among time and temperature in the reheat furnace. Since it is not always possible to keep time and temperature of the reheat furnace at the same fixed level, variability is introduced into the manufactured product. Furthermore, the reheat furnace holds many billets and the location of the billet within the furnace affects the depletion of carbon. Also, the scrap metal

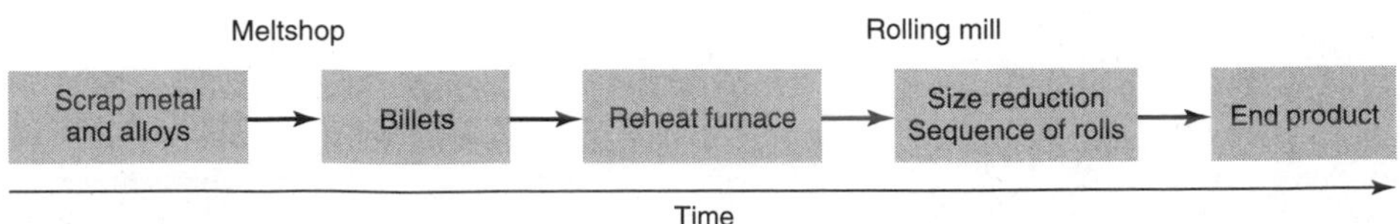

FIGURE 6.2 A simple diagram that describes the manufacture of steel flats.

that goes into each billet has variability which, in turn, affects the variability of the final product.

6.2.3 Example 3: Service Quality at a Mail-Order Company

As a third example, let us consider the *service quality* of a certain computer mail-order company that relies heavily on telephone communication for its sales and its technical support. One measure of service quality is the waiting time until customers are connected to the appropriate service person. Customers may inquire about shipping and billing problems (customer services) or may call about technical issues or questions (tech support). As did many other companies, this particular (unnamed) firm installed a very elaborate automatic telephone answering system which directs calls to the appropriate customer service person. A very frequent problem with such systems is the length of time the customer has to wait until the call is answered by the appropriate person, especially during busy periods. I still remember my secretary's comment when I asked her to check the status of an order: "I just waited on the phone for more than thirty minutes."

This particular company was very concerned about its response time, and for a month they kept track of the waiting times for each incoming call. They noticed great variation among waiting times from one call to the next. Why? In this particular example we probably can ignore the measurement variability. It is probably safe to assume that the technology to measure waiting time is fairly accurate. However, there is one aspect of the measurement process that deserves mention. There is a problem of how to assign waiting times to customers who hang up before they are connected. What is the waiting time if a customer hangs up after 30 minutes, before being connected? The waiting time is certainly larger than 30 minutes, but by how much? Let us ignore this aspect in this discussion. Statisticians call such "truncated" data *censored*.

The process variability accounts for virtually all the variability among waiting times. Where does this process variability come from? It basically comes from the amount of staffing (the supply of operators) and the number and time of arrival of incoming calls (demand for service). It may also depend on the quality of the operators; for example, weekday and weekend staff may not be the same. Fatigue factors such as the number of hours on the job may also come into play. Furthermore, variability may arise because of the characteristics of incoming calls; the ratio of customer service calls to technical support calls may have an influence, and so on.

6.3 IMPORTANCE OF MEASUREMENTS FOR QUALITY

Evaluation and control of products and processes are two closely related concepts; both of them depend on reliable and timely measurements. What cannot be measured cannot be controlled.

Measuring is an essential activity in quality improvement. Quality control and quality improvement, however, are not unique in depending on measurements. All managerial actions aimed at directing events (such as time, cost and profit control, employee evaluation, competitive analysis) depend on measurements. We depend on data. However, often we don't know how to obtain the *relevant data* and we are not sure how to analyze the resulting information. As a consequence, we don't always use data when we make decisions. Bill Hunter described the situation very well, when he remarked that "next to people, data are the most underutilized resource available to management." (Hunter, 1986.)

Several examples of quality measurements are listed below. Here the examples are organized according to functional areas.

Customer: Customer opinions (for example, after purchasing a car); Teacher evaluations by students; Patterns of customer reorders; Returns of merchandise; Customer complaints (on customer hot-line).

Marketing Sales/Service: Number of errors in filling out dealer orders; Number of customer complaints by categories; Time of transit of parts to customer; Waiting time for ordered products.

Engineering: Time to process engineering changes; Number of change requests; Number of engineering design changes; Failure time of product.

Manufacturing: Downtime as a percentage of availability; Amount of scrap or rework; Level of inventory; Outgoing quality level.

Administrative: Time to process travel expense reports; Number of errors in personnel files; Number of retyped letters; Time spent correcting billing errors; Wasted time due to system problems; Time to submit semester grades in college.

Management: Time spent on fire fighting and troubleshooting; Time wasted because of unclear directives; Time spent on correcting poor plans, directives, and reports; Employee turnover rates.

Organizationwide: Number of accidents and associated loss; Percent of overtime; Wasted person-hours due to system problems; Training and educating employees; Warranty and replacement cost; Employee absentee times.

Competition: Product quality; Process effectiveness; Customer perceptions of their products.

6.4 DATA COLLECTION AND DATA SOURCES

How do we obtain the needed information? We need to plan a system for data collection and we need to establish a database. Data may come from our customers (who actually use our products and services) or from the processes that generate the products and services.

6.4.1 Measuring Customer Satisfaction

How can you get information on how your customers view your products and services? How do you learn quickly about product failures and flaws? Early craftsmen learned about customer satisfaction from the customers; but times have changed considerably, removing most company employees from direct involvement with the customers. Today it is important to have a good system that tracks levels of customer satisfaction and that provides timely information on product failures.

Car companies, for example, receive failure information on their products from several sources:

1. Warranty reports
2. Summary problem reports from each of their regional managers throughout the country
3. Individual problem reports from dealer service operations
4. Special investigations

Companies such as Sears & Roebuck use early warning surveys on new products. Service calls for targeted new products are handled routinely, but additional follow-up is carried out to permit analysis of significant problems and their causes. Special check lists are used for customer follow-up.

Companies such as IBM and Xerox survey a proportion of their customer base each month. But in addition to their own customers they survey owners of competitive products. This provides valuable information on the products of the competition.

Companies use information from independent (third-party) laboratories such as Consumers Union or the J.D. Power survey of car quality (Figure 6.3, page 124).

6.4.2 Customer Surveys

Customer surveys play an important role. How should one design a system that leads to meaningful and timely assessment of customer satisfaction? The following principles should be kept in mind when designing a customer survey:

1. If *sampling* of customers is involved (as compared to a 100 percent census where every customer is asked), the sampling should be done according to a probability sample. (We will have more to say on this topic in Chapter 9, where we give a detailed discussion of probability sampling, including simple random sampling and stratified sampling.) Sampling a mix of long-term customers and new buyers usually proves most useful.
2. Telephone surveys usually provide the best all-around method of collecting data from customers. Mail surveys usually get more response from those who feel strongly and who take the trouble to respond. Typically customers

Lexus leads results of car quality survey

DETROIT (AP) — Japanese cars again dominate the annual J.D. Power survey of new car quality, and even the highest-ranking American-built car — the Geo Prizm, at No. 4 — is in part a Japanese product.

Toyota's Lexus luxury cars took the first three spots in the rankings released Thursday by J.D. Power and Associates, a marketing information company. The Japanese carmaker's LS400 was No. 1, followed by the GS300 and SC300–400 models.

Next was the Geo Prizm, a compact sedan made in California.

It was followed by the Acura Legend (made by Honda), Infiniti J30 (made by Nissan), Mercury Grand Marquis, Toyota Camry, Toyota Tercel, Lexus ES300 and Lincoln Town Car.

The J.D. Power Initial Quality Studies were based on questionnaires answered by about 32,000 car buyers and 12,000 truck buyers who registered new 1994 vehicles in November and December last year. Owners were asked about their vehicles during the first 90 days of ownership.

The survey found that the average quality of 1994 cars, measured in terms of the number of defects reported by owners in the first three months, dropped almost 3 percent from 1993.

FIGURE 6.3 Newspaper clipping about the J.D. Power survey of car quality.

will answer on the phone, but they tend not to write unless they are very dissatisfied. Occasionally a very satisfied customer will write; however, the proportion of satisfied customers that respond is usually much smaller than that of dissatisfied clients.

3. The survey should have a dual purpose of providing both a performance measurement and a diagnostic tool. It is not very helpful just to know that there is a problem, without having some leads on how to fix it.
4. Track customers' repurchase intent and willingness to recommend your company to another person.
5. Include in the customer survey the entire array of product and service attributes that determine customer satisfaction and purchase behavior.
6. The survey should include an avenue for identifying any customer-specific problems.
7. Competitive quality and customer-satisfaction benchmarks should be used to establish your company's relative quality position in the market.
8. The assessment of customer satisfaction should be continual in nature, providing information at periodic points in time (such as every three or six months). The information should be timely.
9. Survey results should be put to work at once and all the time. Use the results to make improvements. There is little point to conduct a survey and then not act on its findings.

6.4.3 Measuring Conformance of Products

One of the most basic objectives of quality control is to assess whether a product satisfies the required specifications. Specifications are usually expressed in terms of a target value and specification limits. Physical measurements on such characteristics as length and width of steel flats, fill weight of toothpaste tubes, hardness and tensile strength of steel alloys, and pH values of solutions are obtained routinely. These measurements are then compared to the required standards or specifications.

Today's business requires that products are measured for conformance. In some cases companies measure each item before they ship it to a customer. For example, each individual John Deere tractor is thoroughly tested before it is delivered to the dealer. Other products, in particular if they are inexpensive and produced in large lots, are subject to sample inspection.

6.4.4 Measurements for Process Monitoring

Production processes must be well tuned in the sense that they are consistent in turning out similar (and acceptable) products. *Quality points* must be inserted at the appropriate points in the process. A quality point can be at the very end of the process and amount to an inspection of the final product, or it can be at any other intermediate position in the process at which relevant information can be obtained. The stability of production processes needs to be checked on a regular basis, as such checks give us information whether one should intervene in the process. One typically takes small samples at specified periods (say every 30 minutes, every hour, or every shift), takes measurements on these items, and displays the resulting information on charts. Chapter 12 on process control and control charts discusses in detail how such observations are best displayed and analyzed.

6.4.5 Measurements for Problem Solving

In order to improve processes, we must identify the problems, find root causes for their occurrence, and prevent these causes from recurring again. This is like detective work and it requires people with problem-solving skills. The initial chapters of this book presented an effective problem-solving strategy.

Good problem solving is mostly common sense, but it can be learned. Different people have different abilities; a few exceptional individuals are truly master problem solvers, just as there are a few outstanding painters. It may not be possible to teach everyone to be a world-class painter (or problem solver), but people can be taught to paint (or problem-solve). A combination of good study materials on applicable techniques (as provided in this book), case studies (which describe the problem-solving strategy in action), and graduated project assignments (from simple to more elaborate ones, carried out by individuals or teams) is a good way of teaching people how to solve problems.

Before we can solve the problem, we need to know that there is a problem. We need a good problem (defect) reporting system. Problems must be prioritized and ranked in terms of their importance, and one must focus on solving the problem(s) whose solution leads to the greatest benefit.

A list of possible root causes for the problem under study must also be established, and data must be collected to confirm or refute the validity of the various hypothesized causes. Experimentation with the process by changing several of the normal operating conditions according to well-thought-out plans is important. Obtaining and evaluating the appropriate data plays a big role in problem solving!

6.4.6 Measuring Service Quality

How do we measure the quality of a service that we provide? The evaluation of conformance to service standards is somewhat different from the industrial techniques of inspecting and testing. In the case of service operations, we can only inspect the evidence of past transactions or check the readiness for future transactions (as indicated by the conditions of premises, the available equipment and goods, and the skills and knowledge of the staff). This is a reason why service quality control systems are often more process-oriented than output-oriented.

While we sometimes can observe service operations in progress, the very act of observation may affect the performance of the service and may intrude on the privacy of the customer. This is different from the inspection of products. If interactions with customers are carried out over the telephone, then there are ways of recording randomly selected conversations without being too intrusive. Most financial transactions, order information, and interaction with government agencies (such as the IRS) are conducted over the phone. More and more companies and agencies have started to record these conversations, so that they can check the quality and accuracy of the given information and, if it is found unacceptable, take corrective action.

Customer feedback is still the most important part of the service quality control system, since it represents a real evaluation of the output. However, the evaluations can be made only after the service has been performed, and only by customers willing to provide them, as opposed to product inspections that are made on statistically determined samples of output.

Customer surveys play an important role in providing feedback on what the customer wants. You have seen questionnaires in restaurants, car rental agencies, hotel rooms, and even hospitals. In Figure 6.4, we include one very simple form that comes from Einstein's Cafe at the St. Louis Science Center. It includes five categories that are to be rated from 1 (poor) through 5 (very good), room for comments, and the date of the visit. The date may turn out to provide important information as it allows us to search for causes for bad service. Perhaps the service varies according to the day of the week or with the staffing of the restaurant.

One problem with cards like this, even if they are very nicely composed and printed, is that most customers do not bother filling them out unless they are

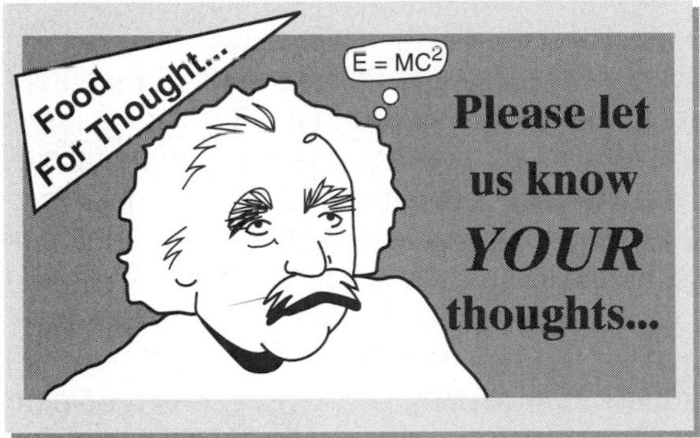

Einstein's Cafe

Your Comments, Please

Please rate our restaurant from 5 to 1.

	Very Good				Poor
Atmosphere	5	4	3	2	1
Cleanliness	5	4	3	2	1
Food	5	4	3	2	1
Service	5	4	3	2	1
Value	5	4	3	2	1

__________ Date

23¢ of every dollar goes toward exhibit development and Science Center operations.

St. Louis Science Center

THANK YOU FOR YOUR COMMENTS...

We'd appreciate hearing your additional comments and suggestions.

We want to please you–and can do a better job if we have your help. If we're not doing something right–let us know–we'll try to improve.

We're glad to get compliments, too. We'll be sure to share them with our staff!

____

____

____

(Optional)

Name ____________________

Address ____________________

City __________ State _____ Zip ______

Phone ____________________

Please drop this card in Einstein's comment box.
Additional comments can be addressed to:

Einstein's Cafe
St. Louis Science Center
5050 Oakland Ave.
St. Louis, MO 63110

Printed on recycled paper

FIGURE 6.4 Questionnaire evaluating food and service at Einstein's Cafe at the St. Louis Science Center.

very dissatisfied. With most service-oriented businesses, such as restaurants, this is a problem as you don't have a list of your customers. If you want to assess the quality of hotels, you are in a better position as you have the addresses and telephone numbers of the people who used your services. You could conduct a telephone survey to get more accurate information. Many hospitals have patient representatives who will talk to patients when they leave the hospital about the service they received.

Another difference between service and product quality assessment is that service customers usually don't purchase services in quantity lots. They stay for a few nights at a hotel, they may call the IRS for forms or information once a year, and they may go to a three-star restaurant once in their whole life.

Quality control activities for service operations may be required at times or in places where supervision and control personnel cannot be present. Work may be performed at the customer's home, or in a large number of outlets. For example, your insurance agent may visit you at your home, and your company may deliver tax advice at a thousand different offices. A frequent approach to quality control in such situations is to develop highly detailed operating procedures and to limit the discretion left to local personnel. For example, the service (and also the product) at any fast-food franchise restaurant is fairly uniform. A large arsenal of quality control tools ranging from inspections to test kitchens, detailed job descriptions, and written procedures for food production provide this uniformity.

The service quality assurance system is somewhat different from manufacturing quality control. It uses market research techniques in the forms of surveys to assess customer satisfaction and it uses human resource techniques to create a climate that fosters good interaction with customers. Quality managers in service organizations are less apt to deal with sophisticated statistical techniques and more apt to deal with evasive data such as the emotional content of customer complaints or the degree of empathy shown by an employee. Interestingly enough, many manufacturers are finding that they have a sizable part of their total business tied up in the service of the products they produce. The John Deere tractor that was delivered earlier needs to be serviced by field engineers working together with dealers and farmers.

6.5 EXERCISES

6.1 Take a dozen extra-large eggs and number them 1 through 12. Measure the length of each egg. You should measure the eggs in random order. Discuss why. (You can achieve a random order by putting twelve slips of paper, with numbers 1 through 12, into a jar, and by drawing consecutive slips from this jar. If the slip with "5" is drawn first, then the first egg to be measured is number 5.) Most likely, your twelve measurements will vary. Discuss the sources for the variability.

Take another round of measurements. That is, select another random order and measure the same 12 eggs a second time. Make sure that your measurements in the second round are not affected by those of the first round. Why is this important? (If you carry out this problem as part of a team, you may think about splitting tasks: One of you could be responsible for the randomization and record keeping, while the other takes the measurements.)

At the end of this procedure you will have collected two measurements on each egg. Assess the measurement variability. What can you say about the process variability? Use graphs to make your points.

6.2 Count the number of raisins in several trial-size boxes of raisins. Is there variability in the number of raisins? If so, discuss why.

6.3 Consider the time it takes you to drive (walk) to work (or school). Discuss the sources of variability.

6.4 Consider the variability among your free throw percentages. Think about the process that you use in making a free throw. Discuss the factors that affect the variability.

6.5 Student evaluations are used as a measure of teaching effectiveness. Discuss why evaluations by different students of the same instructor in the same course are not all the same.

6.6 You are the manager of the local fast-food restaurant, and you want to know whether your products and your service satisfy (or even "delight") your customers. What data should you collect, and how should you go about collecting the information? Discuss.

6.7 You are the plant manager in charge of manufacturing and bottling a certain brand of hair shampoo. What data do you need in carrying out your job?

6.8 Flowcharts were discussed in Chapter 2. Discuss how these charts can bring out unnecessary process complexity. Discuss how these charts can help you identify the sources of process variation.

6.9 (Possible group project) Contact several companies in your area. Select a manufacturing company, a service company such as a restaurant or a doctor's office, and a company that deals with information products. Find out what data they collect and how they use the data in running their business. For example, you may want to ask the following questions:

- How much of the collected information is used for inspection? How much is used for process monitoring? How much is used for problem solving and process improvement?
- Do the companies rely on surveys? If they do, how do they sample? Do the companies rely on sample inspection, or on total inspection?
- Who is collecting the information and how is the information stored and processed?
- How much of the data collection is mandated by customers?
- Ask the companies about any problems they see with their data collection. Do they believe that they collect too much or too little data, or the "wrong" data? Is the collected data useful to them, or is data collected primarily to satisfy customers downstream?
- Ask companies whether they believe that the collected data is accurate, or whether they suspect some tampering by those who collect the information.
- Ask about the variability in the collected information (for example, product dimensions in the case of a manufacturing company; waiting times in a doctor's office; errors in filling out reports in the case of a company that primarily deals with the processing of information). Assess whether companies have a good idea about the variability and where it comes from.

Write a report on your findings.

6.10 In this chapter we discussed accuracy, bias, and precision of measurements. Illustrate these concepts with simple diagrams that display the measurements as dots around a specified target.

6.6 REFERENCES

Deming, W. Edwards. *Out of the Crisis.* Cambridge, MA: MIT Center for Advanced Engineering Study, 1986.

Hunter, W. G. "Managing Our Way to Economic Success: Two Untapped Resources." University of Wisconsin Center for Quality and Productivity Improvement, Report No. 4, February 1986.

Roethlisberger, F. J., and W. Dickson. *Management and the Worker.* Cambridge, MA: Harvard University Press, 1939.

CHAPTER 7

ANALYSIS OF INFORMATION: GRAPHICAL DISPLAYS AND NUMERICAL SUMMARIES

In the previous chapter we discussed the need for obtaining relevant information through measurements on products and processes. In this chapter we introduce simple but highly effective graphical methods for the analysis of measurements, and we discuss ways of summarizing the information through summary statistics.

7.1 CONTINUOUS AND CATEGORICAL DATA

Measurements on dimensions such as the length of an egg, the weight of a quarter-pound hamburger, the length, width, and gauge of a steel flat, and the tensile strength of a steel billet lead to what we call *continuous measurements*. Continuous measurements are measurements that can take on any value (of course, always within certain intervals). For example, the weight of a quarter-pound hamburger patty could be a value within 0.20 and 0.30 pound; we certainly would hope for a value that is close to the target, 0.25 pound! Due to rounding we may ignore differences beyond the third decimal digit; that is, we would record 0.254 for any measurement between 0.2535 and 0.2544. The weight of the contents of a 16-ounce box of Wheaties is another example of a continuous measurement; the weight could be any value within a certain interval (say, between 15 and 17 ounces).

Categorical measurements represent the other commonly encountered type of data. For example, products may be divided into defective and good products, and we may code this information by 1 (defective) and 0 (good). Similarly, we may describe the quality of a steel surface as "smooth," "slightly scratched," or "rough."

The questionnaire of first-time car buyers in the previous chapter measured customer satisfaction on a five-point scale, from 1 representing extreme dissatisfaction to 5 representing total satisfaction. We call the resulting data *ordered categorical*, as there is an order to the different categories. Similarly, we may collect data on family income from a survey question where "1" represents income below $40,000, "2" income between $40,000 and $60,000, "3" income between $60,000 and $80,000, "4" income between $80,000 and $120,000, and "5" income exceeding $120,000. Again, income is an ordered categorical variable.

We may collect data on family status (1 for single, 2 for married, 3 for widowed, 4 for divorced), or ethnicity (1 for white, 2 for black, 3 for Hispanic, and 4 for others). These are examples of *unordered categorical* measurements, as there is no natural ordering among the categories. We could have ordered the categories for family status or ethnicity in any other way.

It is often the case that continuous measurements are taken, but the measurements are subsequently transformed into categorical data. For example, the target value for the gauge of a steel flat may be 0.25 inch, with lower and upper specification limits of 0.235 and 0.265 inch, respectively. A quality inspector checking the dimensions of a certain steel flat records a gauge of 0.234. The steel flat is coded as defective, as its dimension is outside the specification limits. The item is given a "1" for being defective. It should be kept in mind that such an approach will throw away valuable information. A good item with gauge 0.236 (which is barely within the specification limits) is certainly worse than a good item that is right on the target value 0.25. Similarly, a defective item (with gauge 0.234) is bad, but is certainly better than a defective item with gauge 0.220. Categorizing continuous data leads to a loss of information. We don't want to be just within the specification limits; we want to be right on target! In quality applications it is common to refer to the coded categorical data as *attribute data* (it characterizes attributes of the items—good or bad); continuous data is also referred to as *variables* data.

7.2 TIME SEQUENCE DISPLAYS OF MEASUREMENTS COLLECTED OVER TIME

In a time sequence display we plot the measurements against time, or the order in which measurements are collected. In order to emphasize the time series nature of the observations, it is common to display the observations as dots and to connect successive observations. Since time order is a common feature of so many of our measurements, it is important to construct and study such displays. Just think about observations that arise from process control. There we take consecutive small samples of observations each hour, or each half hour, depending on the particular application. The first thing we want to do with data of that sort is to plot it against time. Time sequence plots will tell us about unusual observations, trends or runs in the data, cycles, periods of increased variability, and unusual time patterns such as low measurements followed by high ones, and high measurements followed by low ones.

7.2.1 Example 1: Dimensions of Steel Flats

A steel company produces industrial steel flats which are used for kick plates on catwalks and brackets on telephone poles. The required dimensions are 4 inches (width) by 0.25 inch (center gauge). The lower and upper specification limits for width are 3.97 and 4.03 inches, respectively. The specification limits for center gauge are 0.235 and 0.265.

Samples from our production were taken over a period of two days. The width and the gauge of 95 selected flats, as well as the time at which they were taken, are given in Table 7.1.

Time order could be important in this application. The measurements were taken at approximately half-hour intervals. One would like to check whether there are trends in the data. Do the width (or the gauge) measurements drift over time? Does the variability change over time? Are the dimensions of items produced during the day shift different from those produced during the night shift? Questions such as these can be answered easily from a time sequence plot.

The time sequence plots in Figure 7.1 (page 134) show no strong trends in the data. It appears that each series varies around a fixed level, and the variation seems to be stable and not to be shifting over time. We recognize a few unusual observations; in particular, the third (3.968) and the 33rd (3.969) measurement on width, and the eighth measurement (0.273) on gauge.

7.2.2 Example 2: Tool Wear

As another example we consider data on the dimensions of holes that are cut into gear blanks. The gear blanks are used in the manufacture of large farm tractors. The cutting operation starts by placing a cutting tool into a tool holder and cutting successive holes of specified dimensions without moving the location of the cutting tool. Cuts are made until the operator decides that the tool has to be changed. Deviations from the target bore size on successive cutting operations are given below. Results for five cutting tools are listed in Table 7.2 (page 135). The deviations are given in 10^{-5} inch. Time sequence plots for the first three tools are given in Figure 7.2 (page 136). In order to facilitate easy comparisons among tools, we have made these plots on the same scales.

TABLE 7.1 Width and Gauge Measurements on 95 Steel Flats

Time	Width	Gauge	Date	Time	Width	Gauge	Date
16.10	3.990	.256	May 19, 1990	12.00	3.988	.242	
16.21	3.993	.252		1.15	4.000	.262	
16.27	3.968	.257		1.20	4.004	.252	
16.32	3.993	.250		1.25	3.998	.247	
17.00	3.998	.248		1.35	3.992	.248	
17.30	4.002	.247		2.00	3.992	.250	
18.00	3.994	.247		2.35	3.989	.248	
18.51	3.990	.273		15.00	3.992	.244	
18.57	3.989	.257		15.15	3.995	.247	
19.00	3.990	.252		15.30	3.992	.249	
19.35	3.988	.257		16.00	3.992	.247	
20.00	3.985	.254		16.30	3.989	.247	
20.30	3.996	.253		17.00	3.998	.246	
21.00	3.994	.245		17.30	3.997	.246	
21.30	3.988	.250		18.00	3.991	.246	
22.00	3.987	.249		18.30	3.993	.246	
22.30	3.988	.249		19.12	4.002	.251	
23.00	3.988	.249		19.50	3.994	.248	
23.30	3.986	.251		20.00	3.997	.245	
24.00	3.984	.250		20.30	3.994	.246	
0.30	3.984	.239	May 20, 1990	21.00	3.991	.248	
1.00	4.000	.246		21.30	3.988	.250	
1.15	4.012	.249		22.00	3.987	.248	
1.30	4.012	.246		22.30	3.989	.245	
2.00	4.003	.248		23.00	3.997	.245	
2.30	3.994	.252		23.40	3.990	.250	
3.00	3.994	.250		24.00	3.991	.248	
3.30	3.990	.247		0.45	4.006	.248	May 21, 1990
4.00	3.994	.249		1.00	4.006	.249	
4.30	3.989	.249		1.40	4.000	.251	
5.00	4.000	.249		2.00	4.021	.246	
5.30	3.994	.246		2.30	3.998	.250	
7.05	3.969	.253		3.10	3.990	.254	
7.10	3.997	.250		3.30	3.990	.246	
7.15	3.996	.249		4.00	3.990	.245	
7.20	3.992	.250		4.30	3.994	.250	
7.30	4.002	.250		5.00	3.993	.249	
8.00	3.999	.250		5.30	3.990	.246	
8.05	4.000	.249		6.00	4.006	.249	
8.20	4.005	.248		6.30	4.009	.249	
8.30	4.003	.251		7.00	4.009	.249	
9.20	4.009	.250		7.30	4.005	.250	
9.30	3.995	.244		8.30	4.006	.252	
9.50	3.989	.249		8.35	4.000	.249	
10.00	3.990	.244		8.40	3.998	.247	
10.30	3.990	.243		9.00	3.996	.247	
11.00	3.991	.245		9.30	3.995	.246	
11.30	3.987	.245					

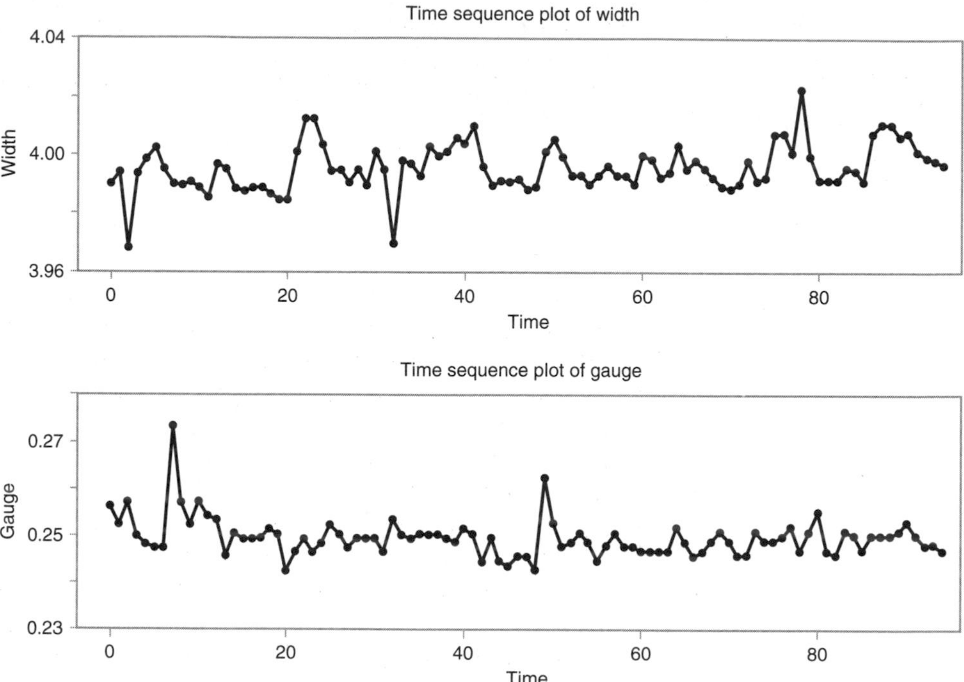

FIGURE 7.1 Time sequence plots of 95 time-ordered measurements on width and gauge.

It is obvious from these graphs that time trends are present. This is because of tool wear. The operator is aware of this fact. For this reason, he starts by cutting slightly larger, but still acceptable, holes. This explains the initially positive deviations from the target. As the tool wears, the holes become smaller and at a certain point in time the deviation from the target becomes unacceptable. When this point is reached, the operator stops and changes the tool. Note that not all three tools wear exactly the same; the trends in Figure 7.2 vary somewhat from one tool to the next.

It was decided to compensate for tool wear by adjusting the cutting position. A simple feedback control algorithm was used to change the position of the cutting tool. If the deviation was close to zero, no adjustment was made and the tool position was kept the same. However, if the deviation (in absolute value) was larger than a certain amount, then the position of the tool was adjusted by a fraction of the previous deviation. The feedback algorithm was implemented with tools 4 and 5. The time-sequence plots in Figure 7.3 (page 137) show that the feedback control algorithm has, in fact, removed the trend component. Furthermore, the graphs show that (1) the tools can be used much longer and (2) the extent of the deviations from the target bore size is reduced (more discussion on this point is given in Section 7.7).

TABLE 7.2 Deviations from Target Bore Size

				Tool 1 (without adjustment)					
15	0	10	5	5	10	−10	15	15	0
5	−5	−25	−15	−15	−15	−20	−15	−10	5
−20	−40								
				Tool 2 (without adjustment)					
70	75	70	65	65	50	55	40	35	10
10	10	20	−5	0	35	45	15	20	20
−10	−10	−5	−15	15	−15	−20	5	−15	−10
				Tool 3 (without adjustment)					
70	55	40	40	25	45	45	50	45	35
20	25	20	25	10	15	10	5	−5	−5
15	15	10	10	−10	−15	5	10	20	15
−5	5	5	5	0	15	5	15	10	10
0	15	20	5	20	0	5	−15	−5	−15
				Tool 4 (with feedback control)					
7.5	0	−2.5	−10	17.5	7.5	17.5	7.5	7.5	−2.5
−2.5	12.5	−10.0	2.5	−7.5	5.0	−7.5	2.5	−5.0	−7.5
−10	−5	7.5	7.5	7.5	7.5	7.5	5	17.5	−17.5
7.5	5	7.5	0	7.5	0	7.5	−2.5	7.5	7.5
7.5	5	7.5	7.5	−2.5	7.5	7.5	5	7.5	5
7.5	20	0	−2.5	0	0	0	2.5	5	0
20	0	2.5	−5	−7.5	−12.5	0	10	−2.5	−7.5
				Tool 5 (with feedback control)					
10	10	5	0	−15	5	15	−5	0	0
0	−10	−10	10	5	10	10	5	−5	10
5	0	0	0	−5	−10	−10	20	5	5
0	5	10	10	0	5	5	5	5	−5
0	−5	−5	5	0	−10	−15	10	10	10
5	10	0	0	10	5	5	20	−5	0
−5	−5	−15	10	0	10	−5	5	5	10
−5	5	5	10	0	0	−5	0	10	5
10	15	10	5	15	10	10	10	5	0
5	0	5	10	−15	20	10	−5	5	0
−10	−10	15	−10	5	0	−5	10	5	0
−5	5	5	−10	10	5	10	10	10	5
0	5	10	10	5	0	10	10	5	0
5	10	10	5						

Read across. Subsequent metal cutting operations with five different tools. A feedback algorithm is used to adjust tools 4 and 5. Deviations are in 0.00001 inch.
SOURCE: Data taken from Hogg and Ledolter, *Applied Statistics for Engineers and Physical Scientists*, 2nd edition, New York, Macmillan, 1992.

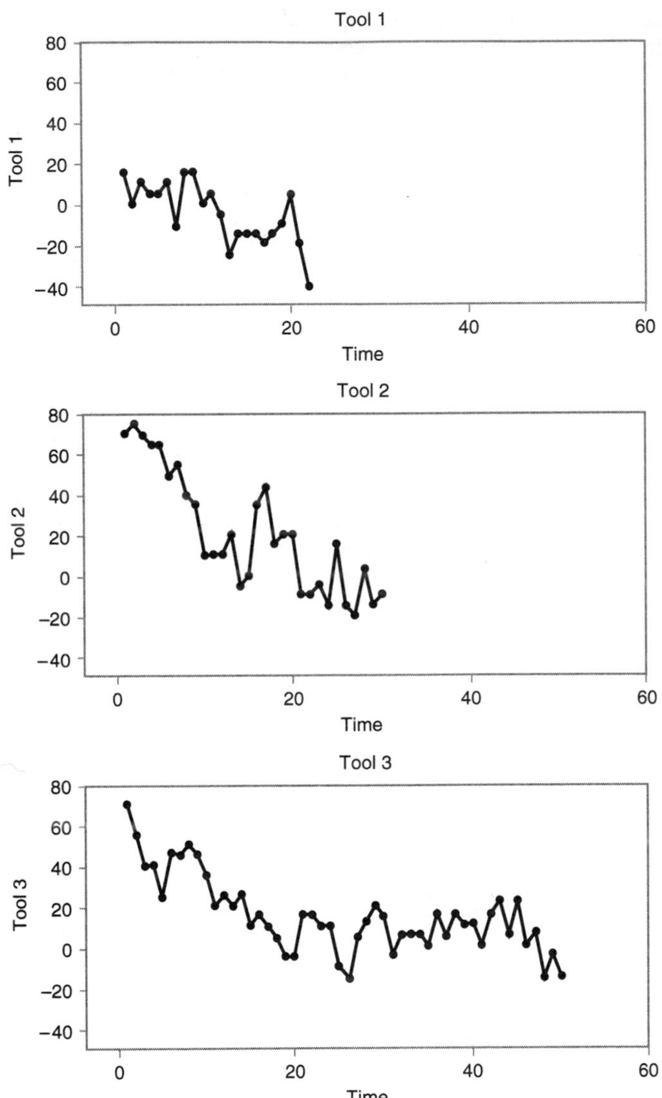

FIGURE 7.2 Time sequence plots of successive deviations from the target bore size: Tools 1 through 3.

7.3 DISPLAYING THE VARIABILITY IN DATA: DOT DIAGRAMS, HISTOGRAMS, STEM-AND-LEAF DISPLAYS, AND DIGIDOT PLOTS

The time-sequence plots for width and gauge of the 95 steel flats in Figure 7.1 do not indicate time trends. There is no evidence that time has an effect on the measurements; the variation in the process appears stable over time.

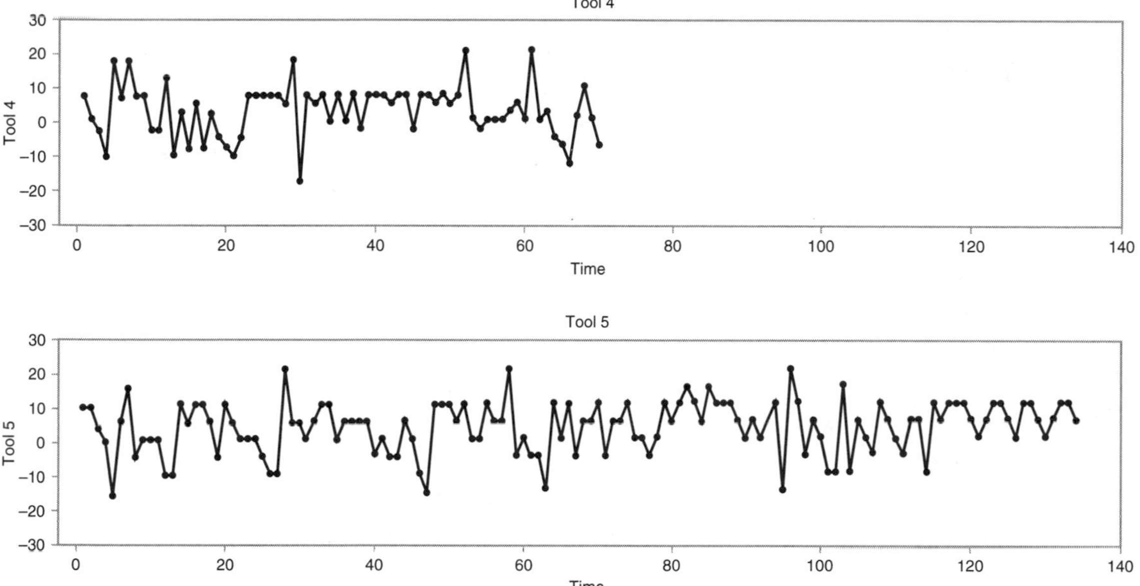

FIGURE 7.3 Time sequence plots for successive deviations from the target bore size: Tools 4 and 5.

What is the variability in the process? How can we describe this variability? In this section we introduce dot diagrams, histograms, and stem-and-leaf displays. These are simple, yet very useful, graphical displays of the variability among measurements.

7.3.1 Dot Diagrams

In a *dot diagram* each measurement is represented on a horizontal line by a dot that indicates its magnitude. For small data sets such diagrams are easily drawn by pencil and paper. For larger data sets one can use one of the many available statistics software packages to create these displays.

Dot diagrams for the 95 measurements on width and gauge are given in Figure 7.4 (page 138). The observation 3.990 (the first width measurement) is plotted as the point right above the tick mark at 3.99. Note that there are 11 measurements with that particular value; there are 11 dots stacked above the value 3.99. The dot diagram shows many facets of the data set and is much more informative than the listing of the data in Table 7.1. We see that the largest observation is 4.021, and that the smallest observation is 3.968. The two smallest observations are outside the specification limits 3.97 and 4.03. We also notice that the process is slightly off-target; more than 50 percent of the width measurements are below the target value 4.00.

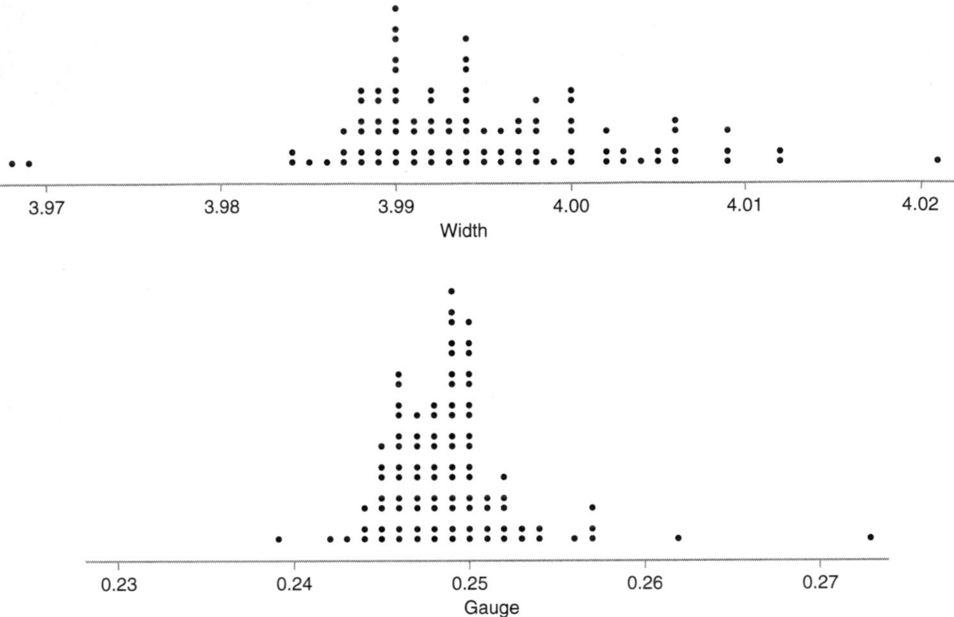

FIGURE 7.4 Dot diagrams of width and gauge measurements. Each of the 95 measurements is represented by a dot.

The gauge measurements are also slightly off-target. More than half of the measurements are below the target value 0.25. One measurement (0.273) is beyond the specification limits 0.235 and 0.265.

A dot diagram gives a very detailed graphical description of the information. Since the numerical value of each observation can be inferred from such a graph, no precision is lost. For large data sets, however, the dot diagram tends to be somewhat too detailed and one prefers a larger degree of summarization (or smoothing) of the information. Histograms, discussed in the next subsection, do exactly that.

7.3.2 Histograms

In a histogram we divide the range of our observations into nonoverlapping intervals, usually of equal length. A typical rule takes the square root of the number of observations as the number of intervals. For the 95 observations in our data set on width and gauge of steel flats, this rule leads us to consider about 10 intervals (also called groups or classes).

Width measurements vary from a minimum measurement of 3.968 to a maximum of 4.021. Here we select eleven nonoverlapping intervals with interval width 0.005. Every data point has to be covered by one of these intervals. The interval width is obtained by dividing the range of the observations by the number of intervals. In this example, the range is 4.021 − 3.968 = 0.053, and division by 11 leads to the interval width 0.005. The first interval goes from 3.9675 to 3.9725, with midpoint 3.970; it covers the smallest observation. The second interval goes from 3.9725 to 3.9775, with midpoint 3.975; the third from 3.9775 to 3.9825 with midpoint 3.980; and so on, until the last one that goes from 4.0175 to 4.0225, with midpoint 4.020; the last interval covers the largest observation. We then count the number of observations that fall into the various intervals. For example, the observation 3.975 falls within the second interval. Note that the boundaries of these intervals have four significant digits, which is one more than the significant digits in the observations. Thus there is no ambiguity as to the interval in which an observation falls. If boundaries are selected such that an observation can fall right on the boundary, then one needs to specify a rule about the allocation. The common convention is that an observation that falls exactly on one of the class boundaries is allocated to the class that has this value as the lower boundary.

The number of observations that fall into each of these classes are called the *absolute frequencies* and they are denoted by $f_1, f_2, \ldots, f_k$, where k is the number of classes. In our case $k = 11$; $f_1 = 2$, $f_2 = 0, \ldots, f_5 = 33$, $f_6 = 23$, and $f_{11} = 1$. The absolute frequencies of the various classes sum up to the total number of observations; in this case $n = 95$. One can also calculate the *relative frequencies*, $f_1/n, \ldots, f_k/n$. For example, $f_1/n = 2/95 = 0.021$ and $f_5/n = 33/95 = 0.347$. The sum of the relative frequencies gives one. The frequencies for the 11 selected intervals are given in Table 7.3. The *cumulative relative frequencies* are given in the last column. They are obtained by accumulating the relative frequencies. For example, the value 0.442 in the fifth row indicates that 44.2 percent of the width measurements are smaller than 3.9925.

TABLE 7.3 Intervals and Frequencies for the 95 Width Measurements

Interval	Midpoint	Freq	Rel freq	Cum rel freq
[3.9675, 3.9725)	3.970	2	0.021	0.021
[3.9725, 3.9775)	3.975	0	0.0	0.021
[3.9775, 3.9825)	3.980	0	0.0	0.021
[3.9825, 3.9875)	3.985	7	0.074	0.095
[3.9875, 3.9925)	3.990	33	0.347	0.442
[3.9925, 3.9975)	3.995	23	0.242	0.684
[3.9975, 4.0025)	4.000	15	0.158	0.842
[4.0025, 4.0075)	4.005	9	0.095	0.937
[4.0075, 4.0125)	4.010	5	0.053	0.990
[4.0125, 4.0175)	4.015	0	0.000	0.990
[4.0175, 4.0225)	4.020	1	0.010	1.000

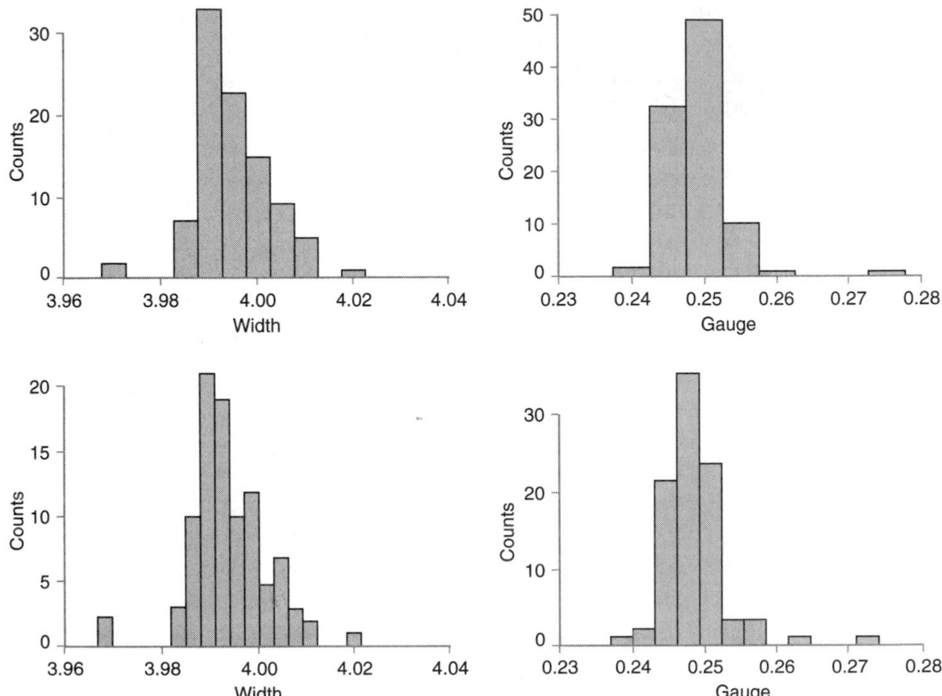

FIGURE 7.5 Histograms of the 95 width and gauge measurements. The histograms on top use interval width 0.005 and correspond to the frequency tallies in Tables 7.3 and 7.4. The two histograms on the bottom use interval width 0.003.

A histogram is a picture of these frequencies. We call it a *frequency histogram* if we display the frequencies. We call it a *relative frequency histogram* if we display the relative frequencies. Switching from absolute frequencies to relative frequencies does not affect the shape of the graph; the only difference in the two displays is in the labeling of the y-axis. The frequency histogram for the width measurements is given in the upper-left corner of Figure 7.5.

The table of frequencies for the 95 gauge measurements is given in Table 7.4. The observations range from the smallest observation 0.239 to the largest observation 0.273. Our histogram uses eight intervals, the first one going from 0.2375 to 0.2425, with midpoint 0.240, to the last one going from 0.2725 to 0.2775, with midpoint 0.275. The corresponding histogram is shown in the upper-right corner of Figure 7.5.

The visual appearance of a histogram will change if one selects a different set of intervals. The interval width controls the smoothing of the information and determines how much detail is shown by the histogram. You can see this by comparing the histograms for width and gauge in the top panel of Figure 7.5 (here we use interval width 0.005) with the two histograms on the bottom panel

TABLE 7.4 Intervals and Frequencies for the 95 Gauge Measurements

Interval	Midpoint	Freq	Rel freq	Cum rel freq
[0.2375, 0.2425)	0.240	2	0.021	0.021
[0.2425, 0.2475)	0.245	32	0.337	0.358
[0.2475, 0.2525)	0.250	51	0.537	0.895
[0.2525, 0.2575)	0.255	8	0.085	0.980
[0.2575, 0.2625)	0.260	1	0.010	0.990
[0.2625, 0.2675)	0.265	0	0.0	0.990
[0.2675, 0.2725)	0.270	0	0.0	0.990
[0.2725, 0.2775)	0.275	1	0.010	1.000

(where we use interval width 0.003). More detail is shown on the graphs in the lower panel. However, it is not always true that an extra level of detail provides more information. The extra precision may be just noise that is better smoothed out by taking wider intervals. Note that the scales on the horizontal axes for the two width histograms are the same. So are the ones for the two gauge histograms. This is important if one wants to compare the two versions of the histograms.

A Comment: When constructing histograms of continuous data one must decide on the number of intervals, as well as on the midpoint of the first interval. Computer software packages usually have "automatic" (and usually quite good) procedures which make this decision for you, but also include options that allow you to make your own selection if necessary.

Histograms for categorical data are constructed alike. They are even easier to construct than the ones for continuous data, as it is not necessary to make any decisions on how to group the data; for categorical data the categories are already given. An example of a histogram (or bar chart) of a categorical variable was given in Chapter 2, when we discussed the Pareto diagram. We should mention that there are other ways of displaying frequency distributions of categorical data. The *pie chart*, for example, displays the frequencies in the form of a "pie" in which the area of each segment is proportional to the frequency of that category.

7.3.3 Stem-and-Leaf Displays

Another way to display the information is to construct stem-and-leaf displays. These displays were recommended by John Tukey (1977), who has written extensively on issues of exploratory data analysis. He has developed several innovative techniques for displaying data, and the stem-and-leaf display is just one of them.

Each measurement is represented by a *stem* and a *leaf.* Take the number 3.968, for example. Its stem is 396, and its leaf is given by the last digit 8. The leaf

Stem-and-leaf of width $N = 95$
Leaf unit = 0.001
396 | 8 = 3.968

Count	Stem	Leaves
2	396	89
2	397	
2	397	
4	398	44
21	398	56777888888999999
(34)	399	0000000000011112222222333344444444444
40	399	5556667777888889
24	400	000000222334
12	400	556666999
3	401	22
1	401	
1	402	1

FIGURE 7.6 Stem-and-leaf display: 95 width measurements.

unit is 0.001, which tells us that the number that is represented by this stem and leaf is 3.968. The number 3.985 is represented by stem 398, leaf 5, and leaf unit 0.001. The number 4.021 is represented by stem 402 and leaf 1.

In a stem-and-leaf display we display the different stems in a column, with one number placed on top of the other. Next to the stem (to the right of it) we display the leaf of each number. We carefully align the leaves, one next to the other. Doing that will create a histogram, but none of the original data will be lost. The stem-and-leaf display constructs the distribution of a variable with the numbers themselves. The idea of making every graphical element effective was behind the design of the stem-and-leaf plot. John Tukey writes: "If we are going to make a mark, it may as well be a meaningful one. The simplest—and most useful—meaningful mark is a digit."

In the example of the width measurements we create seven stems: 396, 397, . . . , 402. If we feel that the resolution of this display is too coarse (as there are only seven stems), then we can divide each stem into two. The first stem stands for leaves from 0 to 4, while the second accommodates leaves 5 through 9. This leads to the stem-and-leaf display in Figure 7.6; it uses a total of 12 stems. Note that the leaves in this display are already ordered within each stem. We call this an *ordered stem-and-leaf display*.

The number "34" in parentheses in row 6 of the first column (the column of counts) represents the frequency of the stem which contains the median of the data set. (The median is defined in Section 7.5; it is the middle value in a data set after ordering the observations from the smallest to the largest.) There are 34 observations in the interval from 3.990 to 3.994. The other numbers in the

Stem-and-leaf of gauge $N = 95$
Leaf Unit = 0.001
23 | 9 = 0.239

Count	Stem	Leaves
1	23	9
1	24	
3	24	23
13	24	4445555555
34	24	666666666666777777777
(27)	24	888888888899999999999999999
34	25	0000000000000001111
15	25	2222233
8	25	44
6	25	6777
2	25	
2	26	
2	26	2
1	26	
1	26	
1	26	
1	27	
1	27	3

FIGURE 7.7 Stem-and-leaf display: 95 gauge measurements.

first column are cumulative frequencies. For example, the number 21 in the fifth row indicates that there are 21 measurements at or below 3.989. The numbers in the rows that follow the one that contains the median represent the numbers of observations with stems equal to or larger than the indicated value. For example, the 12 in the ninth row indicates that 12 observations are larger than or equal to 4.005.

The stem-and-leaf display for the gauge measurements is given in Figure 7.7. Note that here we have divided each stem into five groups. The first one is for leaves 0 and 1, the second for leaves 2 and 3, and so on. Dividing the stems this way stretches the axis and leads to higher resolution. If stems were chosen as 23, 24, 25, 26, and 27, resulting in only five groups, the height of the picture would appear too contracted.

7.3.4 Digidot Plots

The time sequence plot and the stem-and-leaf display can be combined to show both the movement of a sequence over time as well as its variability. J.S. Hunter (1988, p. 54) coined the term *digidot plot* for such a display (digidot, because

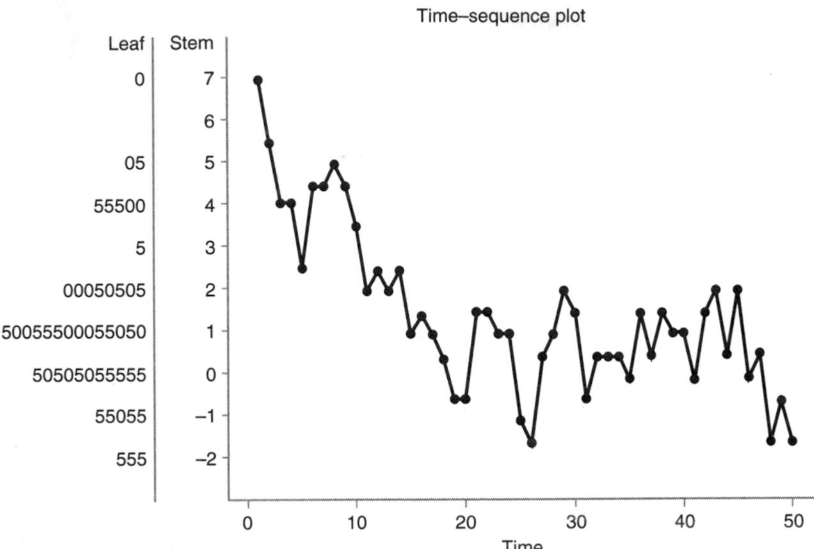

FIGURE 7.8 Digidot plot: Deviations from target bore size for tool 3.

the time-sequence observations are shown as connected *dots* and because the *digits* of the numbers are displayed in the left-hand margin in form of a stem-and-leaf display). We illustrate the digidot plot with the successive deviations from the target bore size from cutting tool 3 (see Table 7.2). Measurements range from −15 to 70. The first digit becomes the stem (leading to stems from −1 to 7), and the second digit becomes the leaf; for example, the number 70 is represented by stem 7 and leaf 0. The digidot plot in Figure 7.8 shows both the trend in the time-sequence and the variability in the measurements. We notice that much of the variability can be explained by the time trend.

7.4 ADDITIONAL EXAMPLES OF DATA DISPLAYS: SKEWED AND BIMODAL DISTRIBUTIONS

The histograms for the dimensions on width and gauge of steel flats in Figure 7.5 (1) have pronounced single peaks and (2) look more or less symmetric. The class with the largest frequency (for width, it is the class that goes from 3.9875 to 3.9925) is also called the *modal class*, and the midpoint of this interval (for width, it is 3.990) is then called the *mode* of the distribution. The observations in the histogram for width (and also for gauge) vary around a single mode and the number of observations below the mode equals (more or less) the number of observations above the mode. We say that such a histogram is *unimodal* and *symmetric*.

Many histograms and distributions are unimodal and symmetric. However, not all of them are, as the following examples show.

7.4.1 Example 1: Carbon Monoxide Emissions

R.D. Snee and C.G. Pfeifer (1983, pp. 488–511) analyze the carbon monoxide emissions of 794 cars. The data given in Table 7.5 is already grouped in intervals of length 24 grams per mile.

The histogram for this data set is given in Figure 7.9 (page 146). We notice that the distribution has one mode, but that it is not symmetric. The right tail of the distribution is much longer than the left tail. We call such a distribution *skewed to the right*.

TABLE 7.5 Carbon Monoxide Emissions of 794 Cars

Interval	Midpoint	Frequency
0–24	12	13
24–48	36	98
48–72	60	161
72–96	84	189
96–120	108	148
120–144	132	85
144–168	156	45
168–192	180	30
192–216	204	10
216–240	228	5
240–264	252	5
264–288	276	1
288–312	300	2
312–336	324	1
336–360	348	1

An observation that falls exactly on one of the class boundaries is allocated to the class that has this value as its lower boundary.

7.4.2 Example 2: Human Mortality Data

Actuaries study human mortality. Looking at birth and death records of large cohorts of people, actuaries can describe the distribution of human length of life (just as engineers know much about the failure times of technical components).

Table 7.6 (page 146) displays the number of deaths for given age groups of five years. The histogram of this information is given in Figure 7.10. Apart from the

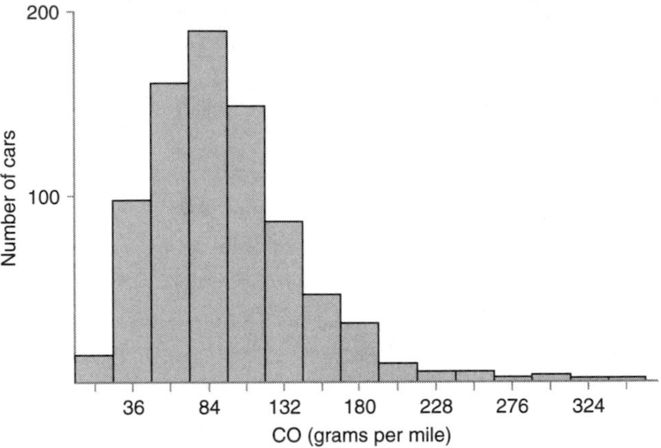

FIGURE 7.9 Histogram of carbon monoxide emissions.

TABLE 7.6 Number of Deaths for Given Age Groups

Age group	Number of deaths (in 1000s)
0–5	39.3
5–10	12.0
10–15	9.5
15–20	10.8
20–25	12.3
25–30	14.6
30–35	18.1
35–40	23.2
40–45	30.8
45–50	41.7
50–55	56.7
55–60	76.4
60–65	99.9
65–70	123.3
70–75	138.6
75–80	134.2
80–85	103.6
85–90	56.6
90–95	18.6
95–100	3.0

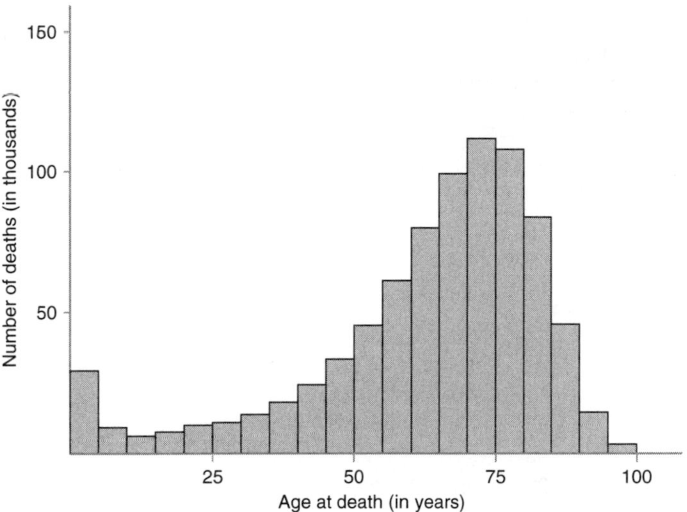

FIGURE 7.10 Histogram of human length of life.

somewhat larger frequency for the first age group (0 to 5 years), the distribution looks unimodal. However, it is not symmetric; in this case the left tail is longer than the right tail. We call such a distribution *skewed to the left*. The unusually high frequency for the first group is due to infant mortality.

7.4.3 Example 3: Thickness of Ears of Paint Cans

Ron D. Snee (1983, pp. 76–88) has measured the thickness of the ears of paint cans. Ears of paint cans are the tabs that secure the lids of large paint cans. At periodic intervals, five paint cans were taken from a hopper that collected the production from two different machines. The results of 30 samples are given in Table 7.7 (page 148); observations listed are measurements in inches times 1000.

We use the 150 observations to construct a histogram with 14 classes. The result in Figure 7.11 (page 149) shows a distribution with two modes; we call this a *bimodal* distribution.

It is not too difficult to guess why there are two distinct modes. The production comes from two machines and the product dimensions vary from one machine to the other. The thickness of items produced by the first machine varies around 30, while the thickness from the second machine varies around 35. Now this is just a good guess as no records on the origin of the paint cans were kept. In order to confirm this theory one should keep track of where the items came from.

Bimodal (or multimodal) distributions come up in practice. For example, in filling operations (of let's say toothpaste tubes or detergent containers) the filling operation may involve 16 different nozzles and the mean fill weights of the 16

TABLE 7.7 Thickness of Ears of Paint Cans

Thickness				
29	36	39	34	34
29	29	28	32	31
34	34	39	38	37
35	37	33	38	41
30	29	31	38	29
34	31	37	39	36
30	35	33	40	36
28	28	31	34	30
32	36	38	38	35
35	30	37	35	31
35	30	35	38	35
38	34	35	35	31
34	35	33	30	34
40	35	34	33	35
34	35	38	35	30
35	30	35	29	37
40	31	38	35	31
35	36	30	33	32
35	34	35	30	36
35	35	31	38	36
32	36	36	32	36
36	37	32	34	34
29	34	33	37	35
36	36	35	37	37
36	30	35	33	31
35	30	29	38	35
35	36	30	34	36
35	30	36	29	35
38	36	35	31	31
30	34	40	28	30

(In 10^{-3} inch): 150 observations.

nozzles may differ somewhat. A batch of parts exhibiting a multimodal distribution is usually an indication that we are dealing with a mixture of parts coming from different machines or processes.

A bimodal distribution also arises if you make a histogram of the weights of the students in this class. Why? The reason is that there are males and females

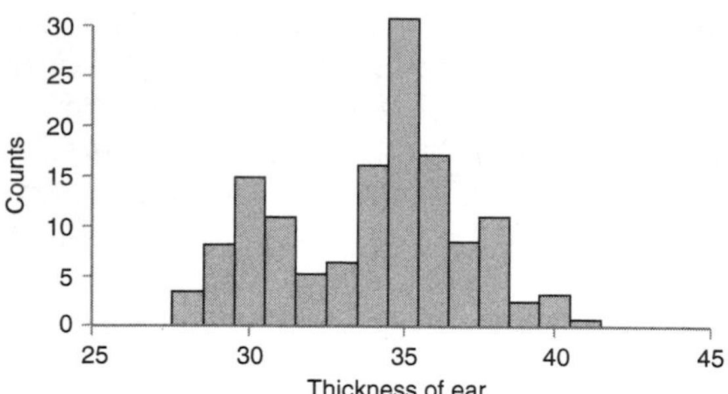

FIGURE 7.11 Histogram of thickness of ears of paint cans (in 0.001 inch).

in this class and each group has its own distribution, with the mean weight for females smaller than that for males.

7.5 NUMERICAL SUMMARY STATISTICS

In the previous sections we displayed measurements graphically, using time sequence plots, dot diagrams, histograms, and stem-and-leaf displays. In this section we are discussing commonly used summary statistics.

7.5.1 Median and Percentiles

The *median* of a set of observations, say $x_1, x_2, \ldots, x_n$, is the observation with the middle rank. Half of the observations are smaller than the median, while half of them are larger. We obtain the median by (1) ordering the observations from the smallest one (that is the observation with rank 1) to the largest one (that is the observation with rank n), and by (2) selecting the median as the observation with rank $(n + 1)/2$.

For $n = 5$ observations (say the first five observations on gauge in Table 7.1: 0.256, 0.252, 0.257, 0.250, 0.248), we first order the five observations from the smallest observation to the largest: 0.248, 0.250, 0.252, 0.256, 0.257, and take as the median the observation with rank $(n + 1)/2 = 3$. The median is 0.252 inch. Two observations are smaller than that value, and two observations are larger.

For $n = 6$ observations (say the first 6 observations on gauge), we order the observations to obtain 0.247, 0.248, 0.250, 0.252, 0.256, 0.257. The median is the observation with rank $(n + 1)/2 = 3.5$. Since 3.5 is not an integer number, we average the observations with rank 3 and 4, respectively. This gives the median $(0.250 + 0.252)/2 = 0.251$. Half of the observations (3 observations) are below, and half of them (3 observations) are above that value.

With $n = 95$ observations we look for the observation with rank $96/2 = 48$. For width, the median is 3.994. The ordered stem-and-leaf display in Figure 7.6, with its

cumulative frequencies in the left column, helps us to quickly locate the observation with rank 48. The observation with rank 48 has stem 3.99, the observation with rank 22 is 3.990, and moving through the ordered leaves in this particular stem we find that the observation with rank 48 is 3.994. For gauge, the median is 0.249.

The median is also called the 50th percentile. We can obtain other *percentiles* just as easily; for example, the 20th percentile, the 75th percentile, or, more general, the $(100p)$th percentile where p is a number between 0 and 1. The $(100p)$th percentile is obtained by arranging the observations from the smallest to the largest, and selecting for the $(100p)$th percentile the observation with rank $(n+1)p$. Again, if this is not an integer, we can average the observations with the closest ranks. This definition assures that $100p$ percent of the observations are below that value, and $100(1-p)$ percent are above that value.

As an example let us calculate the 80th percentile of the 95 gauge measurements. Since $(95 + 1)(0.80) = 76.8$, we average the observations with rank 76 and rank 77. (Note that some computer programs take a weighted average; since 76.8 is closer to 77, they give more weight to the observation with rank 77 and less to the observation with rank 76.) The observations are located quickly from the stem-and-leaf display in Figure 7.7. The observation with rank 76 is given by 0.250; the observation with rank 77 is 0.251. Thus the 80th percentile is given by $(0.250 + 0.251)/2 = 0.2505$ inch.

The 25th percentile is also called the first quartile, as 25 percent of the observations are below that value. The 75th percentile is called the third quartile. For the 95 observations in our example the first quartile (that is, the observation with rank $(96)(0.25) = 24$) is 3.99 inches for width and 0.246 inch for gauge. The third quartile (which is the observation with rank 72) is 4.00 inches for width and 0.25 inch for gauge. This says that 75 percent of the data on width is less than 4 inches; 75 percent of the gauge measurements are smaller than 0.25 inch.

7.5.2 Mean (Arithmetic Average)

The *mean* of a set of n observations $x_1, x_2, \ldots, x_n$ is the arithmetic average of these observations,

$$\bar{x} = [x_1 + x_2 + \cdots + x_n]/n.$$

We designate it with the same symbol as the observations, but with a bar placed over it. We also call it the *average*, implicitly implying that we consider the arithmetic average. The average is a good measure for the center of a set of observations, especially for distributions that are nearly symmetric. The average is easy to calculate. For example, the averages of the 95 observations on width and gauge are

$\bar{x}$ (width) $= 3.9947$ inches

$\bar{x}$ (gauge) $= 0.2489$ inch

Average or Median—Which Measure Should One Use?

1. The average can be sensitive to unusual observations. Unusual observations are called *outliers* (or mavericks). For example, misrecording the first width measurement 3.99 as 4.99 changes the average of the 95 observations from 3.9947 to 4.005. This is a very large change, considering that the resulting average is now larger than the third quartile. You can check that in this case the median is not affected at all by changing this single observation. In general, the median could change somewhat if one observation is increased by a very large amount; this happens if the original rank of the changed observation is less than $(n + 1)/2$ and if the associated change in the ranks of the observations makes a difference in calculating the median. However, any changes in the median are usually very small.

   In order to guard against the influence of unusual observations (outliers), one can also calculate a *trimmed mean*. For example, in a 5 percent trimmed mean, one omits the largest 5 percent and the smallest 5 percent of the observations, and calculates the mean of the remaining 90 percent of the observations. The trimmed mean is useful if one deals with large data sets where there is a good possibility that some of the measurements have been entered incorrectly. In our case, with $n = 95$, this amounts to omitting the smallest 5 and the largest 5 observations. The 5 percent trimmed means are 3.9946 for width and 0.2486 for gauge. In this example, where we have no outliers to speak of, the trimmed means are virtually the same as the means.

2. For symmetric distributions the mean and the median are the same. (Of course, with data where we don't have exact symmetry, the mean and the median cannot be expected to be exactly the same; however, they should be close.) It is for skewed distributions that there are differences. For example, for a distribution with a long right tail (such as the distribution of losses from natural disasters, the distribution of carbon monoxide emissions in Section 7.4, and most income distributions) the average will be larger than the median. For example, the average income is "pulled up" by the high incomes in the right tail. In this particular situation, the median income, which divides incomes into a lower 50 and an upper 50 percent, is going to be smaller than the mean. For distributions with long left tails (such as the distribution of age at death in Section 7.4), the opposite is true. There the median is larger than the average.

   If the distribution is not symmetric, then it depends on the particular contextual question whether one should prefer the median or the mean. For example, the buyer of a single light bulb may be more interested in the median life length; half of the bulbs he could have bought will burn out before the median and half of them will last longer. On the other hand, a buyer of millions of light bulbs for a large chain of supermarkets may be more interested in the mean life length. From this average the buyer can infer the total lifetime he will get from his purchase.

7.5.3 Measures of Variability

Our discussion of the mean and the median has focused on the location of the distribution. But what about variation? *Variability*, also called variation or dispersion, is present everywhere! Next, we discuss the most commonly used measures of variation: the range, the interquartile range, and the standard deviation.

Range: The range is the difference between the largest and the smallest observation. That is,

$$\text{Range} = x_{\max} - x_{\min}.$$

The range tells us about the extent of the variability. It is very easy to calculate and is used in statistical process control (range charts are discussed in Chapter 12). However, one problem with this particular measure of variation is that the range is quite sensitive to extreme observations. Just one small or large observation can change its value greatly. The range for the width measurements is $4.021 - 3.968 = 0.053$ inch. For gauge, the range is $0.273 - 0.239 = 0.034$ inch.

Interquartile Range: The interquartile range is a more "robust" measure of variability. It is defined as the difference between the third and the first quartiles:

$$\text{Interquartile Range} = \text{IR} = Q_3 - Q_1.$$

The interquartile range describes the extent of the middle 50 percent of the data. The interquartile ranges for our 95 observations are $\text{IR(width)} = 4.00 - 3.99 = 0.01$ inch, and $\text{IR(gauge)} = 0.250 - 0.246 = 0.004$ inch.

Standard Deviation: The standard deviation is by far the most commonly used measure of variation. The standard deviation measures the "average distance" of the observations from the mean. It is defined as

$$s = \sqrt{[(x_1 - \bar{x})^2 + (x_2 - \bar{x})^2 + \cdots + (x_n - \bar{x})^2]/(n-1)} = \sqrt{\left[\sum (x_i - \bar{x})^2\right] \Big/ (n-1)}.$$

The summation symbol $\sum$ is used as a short-cut notation; it indicates that the squared deviations $(x_i - \bar{x})^2$, for $i = 1, 2, \ldots, n$, are added up. The standard deviation is obtained by summing the squared distances of the observations from their mean, taking an "average" by dividing by $n - 1$, and calculating the square root to get back to the original measurement units.

We said that we calculate an average, but then we divide by $n - 1$, instead of n. Why? Several theoretical explanations can be given of why it is better to divide by $n - 1$ than by n. One of them is as follows: Since the n deviations from the mean always add to zero, we know that the last deviation from the mean, $x_n - \bar{x}$, is the negative of the sum of the first $(n - 1)$ deviations. Since only $n - 1$ "independent" components go into the calculation of the standard deviation, there is justification to divide by $n-1$. Let it suffice to say that division by n or $n-1$ usually won't make a difference, provided of course that n is reasonably large. Dividing by 94 instead of 95 will make no appreciable difference.

The above expression for s shows that a standard deviation can never be negative: A sum of squares, and the square root of a sum of squares, cannot be negative.

The definition shows that the unit of the standard deviation s is the same as the unit of the observations. If the observations x are measured in inches, then the standard deviation s is in inches. If x is measured in kilograms, then the standard deviation is expressed in kilograms. You can see this fact from the definition. Take x as width in inches; hence the mean width and deviations from the mean width are also expressed in inches. The squared deviation is in (inches)^2, and so is the sum and the average of the squared deviations. In order to get to s, we take the square root of a quantity that is expressed in (inches)^2. Hence, the standard deviation is expressed in inches.

Let us take the first five observations on width: 3.990, 3.993, 3.968, 3.993, 3.998. The mean is $\bar{x} = 3.9884$ inches. The standard deviation is

$$s = \sqrt{[(3.990-3.9884)^2+(3.993-3.9884)^2+(3.968-3.9884)^2+(3.993-3.9884)^2+(3.998-3.9884)^2]/(5-1)}$$
$$= 0.01176.$$

For the complete data set of 95 observations the standard deviations are given by $s(\text{width}) = 0.0080$ inch, and $s(\text{gauge}) = 0.0042$ inch.

The equation for the standard deviation also shows that the only way that s can be zero is if all observations are identical. In other words, $s = 0$ implies that there is no variability among the measurements.

The standard deviation has another property that is very useful for its interpretation. It turns out that the interval $(\bar{x} - s, \bar{x} + s)$ usually covers about 2/3 of the observations. The interval $(\bar{x} - 2s, \bar{x} + 2s)$ usually covers about 95 percent of the observations, and the interval $(\bar{x} - 3s, \bar{x} + 3s)$ covers virtually all observations. This remarkable result holds, approximately, for most symmetric distributions that are encountered in practice. It works best for bell-shaped distributions; more on that in the next chapter when we discuss the normal distribution. This property is very useful. If one knows that the average width is 3.9947 inches and the standard deviation is 0.008 inch, then one also knows that about 68 percent of the observations are within the interval from (3.9867 and 4.0027). In fact, you can check that 74 observations on width, or 100(74/95) = 77.9 percent, are within that interval; this is not too far from the expected 68 percent. Furthermore, about 95 percent of the observations should be within the interval (3.9787 and 4.0107). You can check that actually 90 observations, or 94.7 percent, are within that interval. Table 7.8 (page 154) lists the summary statistics for the 95 measurements on width and gauge of steel flats.

TABLE 7.8 Summary Statistics for the 95 Measurements on Width and Gauge

	n	Mean	Median	Trimmed mean	StdDev	Min	Max	Q1	Q3
Width	95	3.9947	3.9940	3.9946	0.0080	3.9680	4.0210	3.990	4.000
Gauge	95	0.2489	0.2490	0.2486	0.0042	0.2390	0.2730	0.246	0.250

7.5.4 Coefficient of Variation

The average expresses the level of the observations and the standard deviation characterizes the variability. In certain situations it is meaningful to consider the *coefficient of variation* (CV), which expresses the standard deviation as a percentage of the average:

$$\text{CV} = 100(s/\bar{x}).$$

Consider, for example, the 95 measurements on width with average $\bar{x} = 3.9947$ and standard deviation $s = 0.008$. The coefficient of variation $CV = 100(0.008/3.9947) = 0.20$ implies that the standard deviation amounts to 0.20 percent of the average level.

The coefficient of variation is a special case of what is called a *signal-to-noise ratio*. Signal-to-noise ratios combine the signal in observations (commonly measured by the average) and the noise (commonly measured by the standard deviation) into a single measurement, usually in the form of a ratio. A frequently used signal-to-noise ratio considers the logarithm of the squared ratio of the average and the standard deviation:

$$\text{SN-Ratio} = 10\log_{10}[(\bar{x}/s)^2].$$

Simple algebra shows that this particular signal-to-noise ratio is linearly related to the coefficient of variation; that is, SN-Ratio $= 40 - 20\log_{10}(\text{CV})$. A more thorough discussion of signal-to-noise ratios is given in Chapter 16.

7.5.5 A Note on Statistical Computing

You probably appreciate by now that the "hand-calculation" of an average and especially a standard deviation from 95 observations is a pretty cumbersome task. Fortunately, computer programs for carrying out these calculations are readily available. *Statistical computing* is concerned with the efficient and accurate calculation of summary statistics. The standard deviation is a good example to illustrate the ideas behind good statistical computing. Our earlier definition of the standard deviation s is quite informative, as it tells us what s stands for. However, it is not the best definition for computation, especially if the data set is large. This is because rounding is involved in the calculation of the average, and this rounding gets introduced into every one of the squared deviations from the average. The rounding errors can add up, especially if the data set is large. The following equivalent definition of s is much better suited for calculation:

$$s = \sqrt{\left[\sum (x_i^2) - \left(\sum x_i\right)^2 / n\right] / (n-1)}.$$

In this expression the division and hence all rounding takes place at the very end. In Exercise 7.14 we ask you to show the equivalence of the two definitions for the standard deviation.

7.6 BOX PLOTS: GRAPHICAL DISPLAYS OF PERCENTILES

Box plots summarize the distribution of a data set through a limited number of percentiles. The line in the middle of the box represents the median of the distribution. The lower and the upper ends of the box are the lower and the upper quartiles. The distance between these two values represents the interquartile range, which is a measure of the spread of the distribution. The box contains the middle 50 percent of the data. If the box is small, then the data is tightly packed around the median. The lines extending outward from the box are called the whiskers of the box plot; they characterize the tails of the distribution. In small data sets they extend to the extreme values. In larger data sets the whiskers extend to the 10th and the 90th percentile, or the 5th and the 95th percentile. If this is done, then the extreme values are usually displayed as unconnected dots. Different programs have various ways of calculating the ends of the whiskers. John Tukey (1977), who studied such displays in great detail, obtains the endpoints of the whiskers by adding 1.5 times the interquartile range to the upper quartile, and subtracting 1.5 times the interquartile range from the lower quartile. This is the convention that is used by most statistics packages.

Box plots can be aligned either horizontally or vertically. In Figure 7.12 we display the box plot for the 95 width measurements horizontally. The quartiles are given by $Q_1 = 3.990$, $Q_2 = 3.994$, and $Q_3 = 4.000$; the interquartile range multiplied by 1.5 amounts to $(4.000 - 3.990)(1.5) = 0.015$, and the whiskers on the

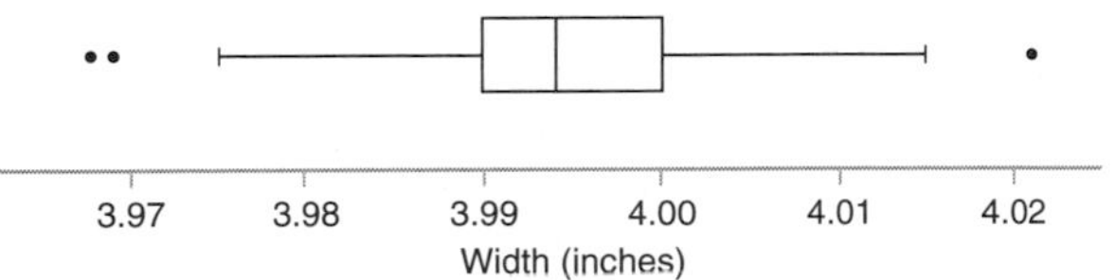

FIGURE 7.12 Box plot of width measurements. The quartiles are given by 3.990, 3.994, and 4.000, respectively. The whiskers extend to 3.975 and 4.015.

box plot extend to 3.975 and 4.015. The three observations outside the whiskers (3.968, 3.969, and 4.021) are represented by unconnected dots.

7.7 THE IMPORTANCE OF STRATIFICATION

By now you are probably convinced that there is variability among observations. The next step is to find out where this variability comes from. Can we "explain" part of the variability through factors that we know have changed, or were deliberately changed during the observation period? For example, does the feedback control in Section 7.2, which aims to compensate for tool wear, have an impact on the variability among the deviations from the target? We actually have measurements under feedback control, as well as under the uncontrolled situation. Is the variability of the deviations affected by the control, or is it the same? We ought to find out whether it makes a difference! One way to compare different groups is through good graphical displays and well-chosen summary statistics. We call this *stratification*.

Stratification is very important as it brings out relationships among variables that otherwise would go unnoticed. Unfortunately, the correct stratification factors for resolving a problem are often not known at the outset. Hence, one should keep track of and record all factors that change while collecting the data. This information may turn out to be very helpful at a later analysis stage. One should use good comparative graphical procedures to bring out the differences among groups. The following two examples show that histograms (or dot diagrams), drawn on the same scale, are very useful for bringing out similarities and differences.

7.7.1 Example 1: Lead Concentrations

Afternoon four-hour lead concentrations, in micrograms per cubic meter, were recorded next to the San Diego Freeway in Los Angeles during the fall seasons of 1976 and 1977. Table 7.9 lists the weekday (Monday through Friday) concentrations; the weekend concentrations are not given here, as different weekday/weekend traffic patterns cause differences among weekday and weekend lead concentrations.

We are interested in a comparison of the 1976 and 1977 data. Is there a difference between the 1976 and the 1977 measurements? If so, how do they differ? In order to detect differences between the 1976 and 1977 data we display the data on two dot diagrams, separately for the two years, but drawn on the same scale. Similarly, we could display the data through two box plots, one for each year. We also calculate, for each year separately, the relevant summary statistics including the mean and the standard deviation.

The dot diagrams in Figure 7.13, as well as the summary statistics in Table 7.10 (page 158), show that the 1977 observations tend to be higher than the ones for 1976. Initially this was very surprising to us as we expected the opposite to happen. Lead-free gasoline was introduced in the mid-seventies and in 1977 more cars used lead-free gasoline than in 1976. Since virtually all lead roadside

TABLE 7.9 Daily Afternoon Weekday Lead Concentrations at the San Diego Freeway in Los Angeles

				Fall 1976					
6.7	5.4	5.2	6.0	8.7	6.0	6.4	8.3	5.3	5.9
7.6	5.0	6.9	6.8	4.9	6.3	5.0	6.0	7.2	8.0
8.1	7.2	10.9	9.2	8.6	6.2	6.1	6.5	7.8	6.2
8.5	6.4	8.1	2.1	6.1	6.5	7.9	15.1	9.5	10.6
8.4	8.3	5.9	6.0	6.4	3.9	9.9	7.6	6.8	8.6
8.5	11.2	7.0	7.1	6.0	9.0	10.1	8.0	6.8	7.3
9.7	9.3	3.2	6.4						
				Fall 1977					
9.5	10.7	8.3	9.8	9.1	9.4	9.6	11.9	9.5	12.6
10.5	8.9	11.4	12.0	12.4	9.9	10.9	12.3	11.0	9.2
9.3	9.3	10.5	9.4	9.4	8.2	10.4	9.3	8.7	9.8
9.1	2.9	9.8	5.7	8.2	8.1	8.8	9.7	8.1	8.8
10.3	8.6	10.2	9.4	14.8	9.9	9.3	8.2	9.9	11.6
8.7	5.0	9.9	6.3	6.5	10.2	8.8	8.0	8.7	8.9
6.8	6.6	7.3	16.7						

(In micrograms/cubic meter.)
SOURCE: Data taken from Hogg and Ledolter, *Applied Statistics for Engineers and Physical Scientists*, 2nd edition, New York, Macmillan, 1992.

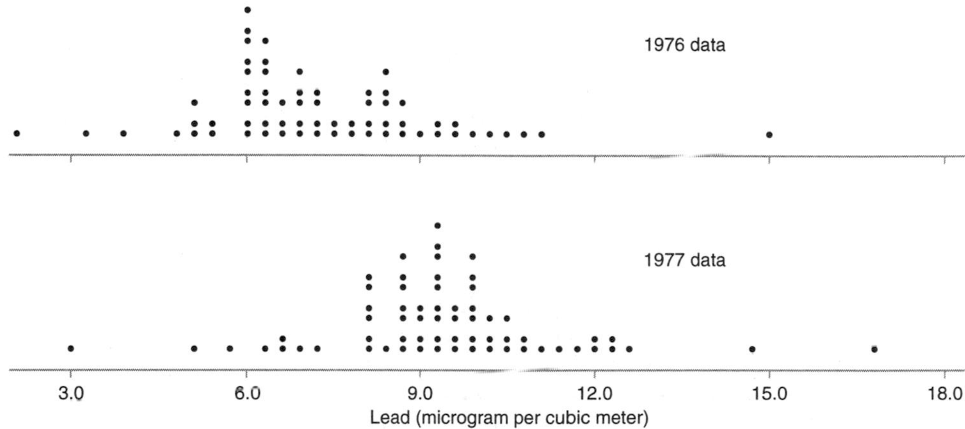

FIGURE 7.13 Dot diagrams of the 1976 and 1977 lead concentrations (in micrograms per cubic meter).

TABLE 7.10 Summary Statistics of 1976 and 1977 Lead Concentrations

	n	Mean	Median	Trimmed Mean	StdDev	Q1	Q3
1976	64	7.457	7.200	7.423	2.109	6.200	8.525
1977	64	9.422	9.400	9.402	2.081	8.625	10.275

(In micrograms/cubic meter.)

deposits come from automobile emissions, we expected the 1977 lead measurements to be lower than the ones for 1976. Why did we see a different result? The reason had to do with a traffic flow change that took place between 1976 and 1977 (see the paper by Ledolter and Tiao, 1979). In 1976 the freeway consisted of four lanes in each direction. In 1977 an additional fifth lane was added to the northbound direction. This change increased the traffic speed, which, in turn, increased the lead emissions.

7.7.2 Example 2: Diameter Deviations

We continue our analysis of the data in Table 7.2, which lists successive deviations from the target diameter for five different tools. Experiments for the first three tools are carried out without any control. A feedback controller is used in the experiments with the last two tools. Dot diagrams (or histograms), all made on the same scale to facilitate easy comparison, show that the variability among bore size deviations for the controlled runs is considerably smaller than that for the uncontrolled situation. Much of the variability in the uncontrolled situation comes from the trend component (tool wear), which is removed by the feedback control mechanism. (Exercise 7.6 at the end of this chapter asks you to draw these dot diagrams.)

Table 7.11 lists the means and standard deviations of the deviations from these five runs. The results show that the feedback control has reduced the

TABLE 7.11 Summary Statistics for Deviations from Target: Experiments with Five Tools

	n	Mean	StdDev
Tool 1	22	−4.77	14.84
Tool 2	30	20.83	29.86
Tool 3	50	14.80	18.73
Tool 4	70	2.79	7.64
Tool 5	134	3.28	7.44

standard deviations by more than 50 percent. In addition, the average deviations from the two controlled runs are closer to zero.

7.8 ASSOCIATIONS AMONG VARIABLES

7.8.1 Scatter Diagrams

A scatter diagram (or scatter plot) is a plot of one variable against another. Assume we observe two characteristics on each item; for example, width y and gauge x. Then we can display the pairs of measurements in the form of a scatter plot, where width is plotted on the y (the vertical) axis and gauge on the x (horizontal) axis. Of course, one could switch the y and x axes, and flip the graph about the 45 degree line. A scatter plot helps us see how measurements on one variable are related to measurements on the other.

EXAMPLE 1

The scatter diagram in Figure 7.14 displays information on the performance of certain "O-rings" during launches of NASA space shuttles. The figure graphs the number of distressed O-rings during a launch against the temperature at launch. The number of O-ring failures can be determined after the space shuttle's return to earth. Looking at that graph, it is fairly obvious that the temperature at the launch has something to do with the failures of these O-rings. For launches during cold temperature conditions, the chance of failure goes up. On January 28, 1986 it was 31 degrees when the space shuttle Challenger was launched from Florida. It was a terrible mistake. The space shuttle disintegrated shortly after launch, leading to lost lives, billions of dollars in damage, and a severe setback to the space program. ■

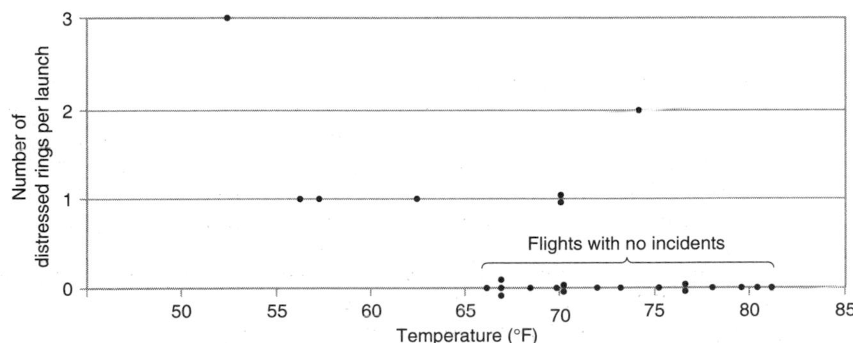

FIGURE 7.14 Scatter plot of number of O-ring failures against launch temperature.

EXAMPLE 2

Consider the width and gauge measurements on the 95 sampled steel flats. One may wonder whether there is a relationship between the width and the gauge measurements. Could it be that a particularly wide steel flat also has a larger-than-average gauge? Or, could it be that a particularly wide steel flat is thinner than others? The scatter plot of width against gauge is shown in Figure 7.15. It appears that width and gauge are pretty much unrelated. ■

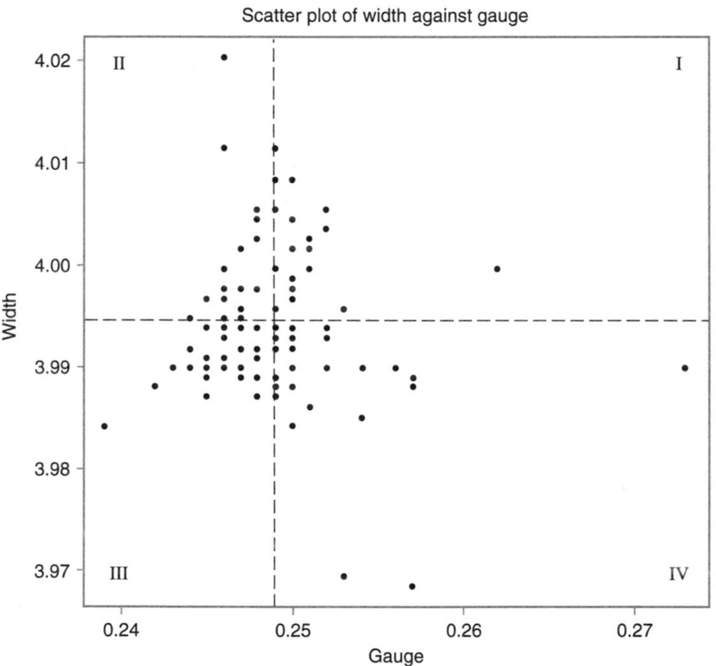

FIGURE 7.15 Scatter plot of width against gauge: 95 steel flats. Horizontal and vertical lines are drawn at the width and gauge averages.

7.8.2 A Simple Nonparametric Measure of the Strength of a Relationship

How can one capture certain characteristics of a graph, in particular the strength of an association between two variables, with a single summary statistic? Here is an easy and instructive method. First, calculate the averages for the two variables. In our case, the averages are 3.9947 for width, and 0.2489 for gauge. Lines representing the averages are added to the scatter plot in Figure 7.15. These lines divide the scatter plot into four quadrants. Note that we could have used medians to create the four quadrants. However, in our example means and medians are fairly similar, and so it makes little difference whether we use one or the other.

TABLE 7.12 Critical Values L for Assessing Whether Association Is Present

n	L	n	L	n	L	n	L
15	3	40	13	65	24	90	35
20	5	45	15	70	26	95	37
25	7	50	17	75	28		
30	9	55	19	80	30		
35	11	60	21	85	32		

The critical values are obtained from the sign test under a 5 percent significance level.
SOURCE: K. Ishikawa, *Guide to Quality Control,* 2nd edition, Tokyo: Asian Productivity Organization, 1982.

Quadrant I represents cases that are larger than average on both variables; quadrant III represents cases that are smaller than average on both variables. Quadrant II includes cases that are larger than average on the y-variable in the scatter plot of y against x, and smaller than average on the x-variable. Quadrant IV represents cases that are smaller than average on the y variable and larger than average on the x variable. One then counts the number of observations in each of the four quadrants. If there is no association, then the numbers of observations in each of the four quadrants should be fairly similar.

Let a be the sum of the counts in quadrants II and IV, and let b be the sum of the counts in quadrants I and III. A positive association is indicated if a is particularly small relative to the number of pairs of observations; say smaller than L (where L depends on the total number of cases, $n = a + b$). On the other hand, if b is small (smaller than L) a negative association is indicated. If a and b are similar (and hence neither a nor b is small), then there is no association.

How small should "small" be, before we conclude that there is evidence of an association? Table 7.12 lists the critical values L; they depend on the total number of cases. In our example, the counts are 22, 18, 26, and 29 for quadrants I through IV, respectively. These counts are fairly similar and one can conclude, even without a table of critical values, that there is no association between these two variables. Following the above rule we would calculate $a = 18 + 29 = 47$ and $b = 22 + 26 = 48$. For $n = 95$, the critical value from Table 7.12 is $L = 37$. Neither a nor b is smaller than 37. Hence we conclude that there is neither a positive nor a negative association. We conclude that there is no association between the two dimensions.

7.8.3 The Correlation Coefficient

The correlation coefficient is a frequently used measure of a (linear) association. Instead of counting the number of cases in each of the four quadrants, one calculates, for each pair of observations (x_i, y_i), the product $[(x_i - \bar{x})/s_x][(y_i - \bar{y})/s_y]$. Here $\bar{x}$ and $\bar{y}$ are the averages, and s_x and s_y are the respective standard deviations. The above product is positive for cases in quadrants I and III, and negative in quadrants II and IV. Also note that the two quantities that are multiplied together are standardized; the division of $(x_i - \bar{x})$ and $(y_i - \bar{y})$ by their respective standard deviation gives these deviations unit dimensions; in other words, it makes them dimensionless. The *correlation coefficient* is given by

$$r = \frac{1}{n-1} \sum_{i=1}^{n} \frac{(x_i - \bar{x})}{s_x} \frac{(y_i - \bar{y})}{s_y}$$

where the summation symbol indicates that we add up these n products. The division by $n - 1$ results in an "average" of these n product terms.

The correlation coefficient has several very useful properties.

1. The correlation coefficient is always between -1 and $+1$.
2. The *sign* of the correlation coefficient tells us about the direction of the association. A positive value indicates a positive (or direct) association; if one variable is larger than average, then the other variable also tends to be larger than average. A negative value indicates negative (or indirect) association; if one variable is larger than average, then the other tends to be smaller than average.
3. The *absolute value* of the correlation coefficient indicates the strength of the association. The correlation coefficient $r = +1$ implies that all points (x_i, y_i) lie exactly on a straight line with a positive slope. The correlation coefficient $r = -1$ implies that all points lie exactly on a straight line with negative slope. The further away the correlation coefficient is from -1 or $+1$, the weaker the linear association. A correlation coefficient $r = 0$ means that there is no linear association between the two variables.

The correlation coefficient measures only the *linear association*. You can understand this fact by considering the situation where the observations lie, equally spaced, on a circle of a certain fixed radius. Such a situation reflects a perfectly deterministic, but nonlinear, relationship. However, the numbers of observations in the four quadrants of the scatter plot of y against x are the same; and the (linear) correlation coefficient is zero.

This is a limitation of the correlation coefficient, and it suggests the following approach. In addition to calculating the correlation coefficient, we recommend that you always supplement it by a scatter plot of the data. The scatter plot includes more information, as it is not always possible to characterize a scatter diagram by just a single number. The scatter plot can tell us whether the relationship between the two variables is more complicated than a linear association. Nonlinearity may be present.

Note that for the correlation coefficient it does not matter which variable is selected as the x or the y variable. The variables enter the correlation coefficient through their product, and the order does not matter. The correlation between width and gauge is the same as the correlation between gauge and width.

The correlation coefficient for the 95 measurements on width and gauge is -0.103. It is close to zero, indicating that there is little association between these two measurements. It confirms the conclusion that we had formed earlier by looking at the scatter plot in Figure 7.15.

The calculation of the correlation coefficient is a standard feature of all statistics packages, and hence there is little need to calculate this coefficient by hand. Our definition of the correlation coefficient facilitates its interpretation. However, better ways for calculating the correlation coefficient r are available and statistical packages make use of an equivalent definition that is better suited for computation. One can show that an equivalent expression for the correlation coefficient is given by

$$r = \frac{\sum x_i y_i - \frac{(\sum x_i)(\sum y_i)}{n}}{\sqrt{\sum (x_i^2) - \frac{(\sum x_i)^2}{n}}\sqrt{\sum (y_i^2) - \frac{(\sum y_i)^2}{n}}}.$$

(See Exercise 7.15 for a proof.) This particular definition reduces the number of rounding operations.

7.8.4 Correlation and Causation

The fact that two variables are correlated does not necessarily mean that a cause-and-effect relationship exists between them. The fact that y tends to be larger than average whenever x is larger than average cannot be interpreted as revealing that increases in x "cause" y to rise. Beware of the effects of the "lurking" variable. Two variables may appear heavily correlated, but this correlation is not because of a direct link between these variables. There may be a third variable that affects either variable; we call this third variable the lurking variable. As an example, take one variable that increases with time and another that decreases with time. Then a scatter plot of the first variable against the second will show a strong relationship; convince yourself that the association is negative. Here "time" is the lurking variable. The association between the two variables does not imply that there is a causal relationship.

One can use many other examples to show that correlation and causation should not be confused. One study, for example, showed that the consumption of alcohol is positively correlated with teachers' salaries; the higher the salaries, the greater the consumption of alcohol. But it isn't that teachers rush out to cash in their latest pay rise at the nearest bar; rather it seems that underlying economic conditions affect both variables. During good times, people spend more on alcohol as well as on teachers.

As another example, consider plotting the annual number of births in post–World War II Europe against the annual number of storks. A scatter diagram with annual data for the period from 1950 to 1980 reveals a strong positive relationship between these two variables. Despite the strong positive correlation, no adult would take this as a proof for a causal link. The relationship arises because both the number of storks and the number of births are affected by a dramatic rise in the living standard. The rapid economic development after World War II affected people's decision to have children, and at the same time it influenced the living and breeding areas for storks.

7.8.5 Another Word of Caution

In correlation studies one should be aware of one other pitfall. The range of the variables that are being related may be very narrow, and with such limited-range data it may not be possible to obtain strong relationships. In fact, over a narrow range it often looks like there is no relationship at all. But if one could observe the variables over a wider range, relationships would become evident. As an example, consider the relationship between high school and college grade point averages for students enrolled at your university. Obtain the relevant data from the registrar's office and convince yourself that the correlation between these two variables is rather weak. Why is the correlation so low? One reason for this fact is that students accepted to your institution have fairly similar academic backgrounds. Your university probably does not admit many students with poor high school GPAs. The range of one of your variables is quite narrow, and as a result the correlation coefficient is rather low.

7.9 THE ANALYSIS OF CATEGORICAL DATA

Histograms, dot diagrams, stem-and-leaf displays, and summary statistics such as averages and standard deviations are appropriate for describing continuous measurement data. But how should one proceed if the information is categorical in nature? Consider, for example, the information that we collected on our students in a recent statistics course for off-campus MBA students at the University of Iowa.

In addition to questions on personal characteristics, such as their height and weight, we asked our students about their gender and the number of biological children. Students in the off-campus MBA program have full-time jobs and they are older than traditional college students. Gender represents an unordered categorical variable. The number of children represents a discrete variable and, because of its limited range, we treat it as an ordered categorical variable with outcomes $0, 1, 2, \ldots$. It turned out that no student in our class had more than five children.

The tools for summarizing categorical data are *tallies* and *tables*. Consider the tallies in Table 7.13 on gender and on the number of children. These tallies show the frequencies as well as the proportions relative to the total number. For the

TABLE 7.13 Frequency Tallies for Gender and for the Number of Biological Children

	Frequencies	
Gender	Count	Proportion
Female	14	25.9
Male	40	74.1
Total	54	100.0

	Frequencies	
Number of children	Count	Proportion
0	30	55.6
1	9	16.7
2	10	18.5
3	4	7.4
4	0	0.0
5	1	1.8
Total	54	100.0

	Frequencies	
Number of children	Count	Proportion
0	30	55.5
1	9	16.7
2 or more	15	27.8
Total	54	100.0

SOURCE: Data taken from the STUDENT.DAT file.

subsequent analysis we have collapsed the table that represents the information on the number of children, and we have combined the categories for 2, 3, 4, and 5 children into a new class called "2 or more."

The information in tallies can be displayed graphically through *bar charts*, where heights of the bars are proportional to frequencies, or *pie charts*, where areas of the pie segments are proportional to frequencies.

Tallies and bar and pie charts display the information in a single categorical variable. The simultaneous information in two categorical variables can be

TABLE 7.14 Two-Way Tables According to Gender and Number of Children

Frequencies

Gender	Number of children 0	1	2 or more	Total
Female	11	2	1	14
Male	19	7	14	40
Total	30	9	15	54

Frequencies, expressed as row proportions

Gender	Number of children 0	1	2 or more	Total
Female	78.6	14.3	7.1	100.0
Male	47.5	17.5	35.0	100.0
Total	55.5	16.7	27.8	100.0

Average weight (counts in parentheses)

Gender	Number of children 0	1	2 or more	Total
Female	138.8	157.5	130.0	140.9
	(11)	(2)	(1)	(14)
Male	176.3	196.7	198.6	187.7
	(19)	(7)	(14)	(40)
Total	162.5	188.0	194.1	175.5
	(30)	(9)	(15)	(54)

SOURCE: Data taken from the STUDENT.DAT file.

displayed through *tables*. For example, Table 7.14 shows a two-way table that displays the frequencies when we classify our students simultaneously according to gender and the number of children. We have seven male students with exactly one child. The margins of the table display the summary counts for each one of the two variables. We have 54 students in total, and 40 of them are males. The frequencies in a two-way table can also be expressed as percentages—either as a percentage of the grand total, a percentage of the row total, or a percentage of the column total. Here we express the frequencies as row percentages. We learn that among males 47.5 percent have no children, 17.5 percent have one child, and 35 percent have 2 or more children. For females the proportions are 78.6, 14.3, and 7.1 percent, respectively. Across each row, these proportions add up to 100 percent. We notice that the row proportions vary according to gender; males tend to have more children than females. It could be that professional women are delaying the decision to have children. For a graphical display we can use a bar chart with number of children representing the categories on the horizontal axis and frequencies displayed as bars along the vertical axis. In order to show the differences between males and females we can arrange the male/female bars right next to each other.

In addition to displaying the frequencies in two-way tables, we can add the information from additional variables; these variables can represent continuous measurement data such as the weight or the height of the student. For example, we can calculate—for each of the cells in the cross-classification according to gender and number of children—summary statistics on the variable weight. In other words, we stratify our analysis of weight with respect to two categorical variables. This is shown in the last entry in Table 7.14, where we list the average weights; we have also included the number of observations in each of the cells, as averages that come from very few observations may not be that reliable. A case in point is the average weight for females with 2 or more children; we had only one woman with 2 or more children. It seems that for both males and females weight increases with the number of children. We can speculate about the reasons; it could be that with children one has less time for physical exercise.

7.10 ISHIKAWA'S SEVEN BASIC TOOLS

A wide spectrum of statistical techniques can be applied to the solution of quality problems. Experience shows that a surprisingly small set of basic tools will solve a large proportion of problems. This is fortunate, as it implies that the more elaborate statistical tools can be left to specialists. It is important, however, that everyone involved in problem solving, from the line worker to the manager, understands the most basic tools.

Kauro Ishikawa (1982) refers to these tools as the *Seven Basic Tools*. They are: time sequence plots and control charts, histograms, Pareto diagrams, scatter diagrams and correlation, cause-and-effect diagrams, check sheets, and basic sampling inspection plans. We have discussed most of these techniques in this chapter. Pareto diagrams were covered in Chapter 2, and cause-and-effect diagrams were discussed in Chapter 3. An introduction to sampling inspection techniques will be given in Chapter 11, and control charts, a special version of time-sequence plots, will be addressed in Chapter 12. A discussion of check sheets is included in this section.

7.10.1 Check Sheets

Check sheets are forms used for organizing and displaying data as it is collected. Assume that you want to collect data on possible defects on a certain final product. You could tell your employees to "just go out and obtain the data." However, an instruction like this may be too vague and the employees may have difficulties obtaining the right data. Also, if several people collect the data, then there may be a problem with consistency, or lack thereof; each worker may use a somewhat different classification scheme. Hence systematic data-gathering devices are clearly preferable. A *preprinted check sheet* that lists the types of possible defects, like the one given in Table 7.15, makes the data collection much easier. It enforces consistency from one worker to the next, and from one time period to the other. Furthermore, by just looking at the tallies one immediately gets a summary of the data that has been collected thus far. Check sheets must be clear and simple with instructions on who collects the data and how the data should be included on these sheets.

Check sheets can be used to help workers keep track of the dimensions of a product, and hence the capability of the process. The example in Table 7.16 uses the first 45 measurements on the width of the steel flats. The completed check sheet gives a pictorial view of what the production has been like up to this point in time. Check sheets help with the data collection, and at the same time they can result in a useful graphical display of the information.

Another illustration of check sheets is the "personal quality check list" given in Table 7.17. The quality check list is a preprinted form to keep track of weekly (or daily) personal shortcomings. Simple tally strokes can be made for the defects throughout the week, and at the end of the week the numbers can be added up. With this check list one can keep track of one's shortcomings and learn whether certain problems come up repeatedly. The number of shortcomings can be totaled for each week; a plot of the total number of shortcomings against time (week) can show whether there is improvement over time.

TABLE 7.15 Defect Check Sheet

Type of defect	Tally	Counts
Surface scratches	~~////~~ ~~////~~ //	12
Cracks	~~////~~ //	7
Unacceptable shape	~~////~~ ~~////~~ ~~////~~ /	16
Incomplete assembly	//	2
Others	///	3
Total		40

TABLE 7.16 Process Capability Check Sheet for the Width of Steel Flats

Frequency
15
10
5

3.9675 3.9725 3.9775 3.9825 3.9875 3.9925 3.9975 4.0025 4.0075 4.0125 4.0175
3.9725 3.9775 3.9825 3.9875 3.9925 3.9975 4.0025 4.0075 4.0125 4.0175 4.0225

Width (in inches)

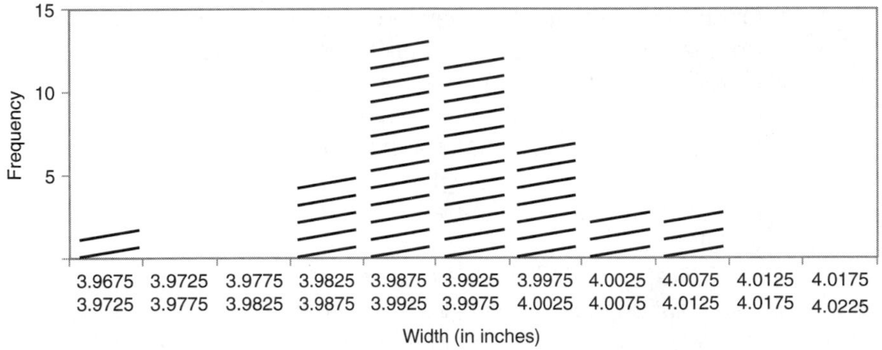

We use the first 45 measurements on the width of steel flats in Table 7.1. The specification limits are given by 3.97 and 4.03.

TABLE 7.17 A Personal Quality Check Sheet

Categories	Week 1	Week 2	Week 3
On time for meeting	2	1	
Search for something misplaced	5	3	
Return phone call same or next day	4	3	
Respond to letters within two days	0	4	
Referee paper within one month	2	1	
Exercise every day	5	2	
Read to children every other day	3	0	
Make someone smile each day	2	4	
Fewer than 3 cups of coffee/day	3	3	
No more than one dessert everyday	1	3	
At least two pieces of fruit/day	1	2	
Total	31	26	

7.11 THE VISUALIZATION OF DATA: FURTHER COMMENTS

William S. Cleveland, in the preface to his book, *Visualizing Data* (1993), writes:

> *Visualization is critical to data analysis. It provides a front line of attack, revealing intricate structure in data that cannot be absorbed in any other way. We discover unimagined effects, and we challenge imagined ones.*

A picture may be worth a thousand words. Graphs, charts, and diagrams are very important instruments for reasoning about quantitative information. Often the most effective way to describe, explore, and summarize a set of numbers is through pictures of these numbers. Pictures force us to notice what we never expected to see. Well-designed graphs are essential for analyzing and communicating statistical information; they are useful for data analysis, when the analyst wants to study data, and for data communication, when the analyst wants to communicate data to others. Graphical displays can provide valuable insight into the structure of data and they can reveal interesting relationships among variables.

Graphical methods are useful at all stages of the statistical analysis. Data visualization tools need to be integrated into the data analysis. Cleveland argues that relying exclusively on numerical statistical methods without appropriate data visualization is a crippling data analysis strategy that can lead to incorrect and missed conclusions. Graphical information, in combination with prior knowledge of the subject under investigation, becomes a powerful tool. Graphical presentations supplement and assist in the interpretation of formal statistical inference procedures.

Graphing data is an iterative and often experimental process. The only limitation to the development and use of graphics is the creativity of the data analyst.

There are many variations of the graphical displays that we have presented in this chapter and there are many more techniques that we haven't even mentioned. We recommend that you study the book by John W. Tukey, *Exploratory Data Analysis*, the books by William S. Cleveland, *Visualizing Data* and *The Elements of Graphing Data*, and the books by Edward R. Tufte, *The Visual Display of Quantitative Information* and *Envisioning Information*. You should also look at recent issues of *Chance*, a magazine of the American Statistical Association (published by Springer). The focus of our discussion in this chapter was on univariate displays (histograms and stem-and-leaf displays, where we display the distribution of a single variable) and on bivariate displays (scatter plots, which display relationships between two variables). Cleveland and Tufte show how to display more than two variables. They discuss, in great detail and in much clarity and beauty, how to analyze multivariate data structures that involve three and more variables and that include variables such as time and space. This is very important as data sets are nearly always multivariate. With three variables one can stratify the scatter plot of two variables with respect to the values of the third variable. This works especially well if the third variable is categorical. For example, imagine a scatter plot of tool wear against cutting speed. You may have data on two different tools: a standard tool and one that is reinforced with a certain alloy. It is quite informative to construct two separate scatter plots, or to overlay the two scatter plots using different symbols or colors for the two types of tools.

Tufte (1983; 1990) pays great attention to the design of statistical graphics; his writings are concerned with both the design and the statistics. Tufte views excellence in graphics as the well-designed, truthful presentation of interesting data; for him it is a matter of substance, of statistics, and of design. Graphical excellence involves communicating complex ideas with clarity, precision, and efficiency. In Tufte's view, graphical excellence is what gives the viewer the greatest number of ideas in the shortest time, with the least ink, and in the smallest place.

Graphs need to be effective. Cleveland and Tufte have much to say about the principles of good graph construction, and their books are full of practical advice. Let us list some of the important principles behind good graphical displays: Make the data stand out, and avoid superfluity. Above all else show the data, and avoid unneeded "chart junk." Use visually prominent graphical elements to show the data. Do not overdo the number of tick marks; tick marks should point to the outside. Do not use so many data labels in the interior of the graph that they interfere with the quantitative data. Add reference grids if you want to draw attention to certain values. Visual perception is affected by proportions and scale. Choose appropriate scales. Use the logarithmic scale if you want to bring out changes. For ready comparisons, use the same scale when comparing data from different groups or panels. Be aware of the effect of the "zero"; the way the zero is located on a graph may change your perception of the data. Tufte asserts that graphs should tend toward the horizontal; graphs should be greater in width than in height.

When a graph is made, quantitative and categorical information is encoded by the display method, and then the information is visually decoded. The visual perception is the vital link. Graphs need to be truthful to the data and one must be concerned about graphical integrity. Tufte's 1983 book includes many well-selected examples of misleading graphical displays. An important principle in graph construction is that the representation of the numbers as physically displayed on the graph should be proportional to the numerical quantities represented. A common way to distort the truth is to deviate from that principle. A pie chart where the depicted areas are not proportional to the frequencies that are being represented is one example of a misleading representation. Displaying the magnitude of numbers by squares where the length of a square is proportional to the number is another example of a deceptive display. Assume that one number is twice as large as the other; then the larger square would be four times the size of the smaller one. Incorrect and nonuniform scales and unclear labeling are further sources for creating impressions that are not truthful to the data. Cutting off the bottom part of bars in a comparative bar chart creates a wrong impression. Assume, for example, that we encountered 50 problems in one process, and 60 in the other. Representing this information in the form of a bar chart where the heights of the respective bars are graphed on a scale from 0 to 60 will look quite different than a display where the bars are plotted on a scale from 40 to 60. The perception from the second display is that the number of problems has doubled, even though problems went up by only 20 percent. Quoting data out of context is another common trick to distort the truth. Assume that a change in the process has led to a onetime reduction in the number of defectives. Displaying just this onetime change, without displaying all the other changes that occur during the normal operation of the process, would be quite misleading. Just focusing on one part of the data set while leaving out all others distorts the truth.

Most graphs can be carried out by pencil and paper as long as one understands the general principles of good graphing. In today's computer age virtually all statistical software packages and spreadsheet programs include many different options for graphical displays. Computers have certainly changed the way we carry out the graphics; however, they have not affected the goals of such analysis. While modern spreadsheet software makes it quite easy to produce graphics, not all of the displays they create are good. For example, a rather substandard histogram function can be found in EXCEL, the Microsoft spreadsheet program. First, it displays histograms of continuous measurement data in the form of a frequency bar chart where the bars are separated and do not touch; this gives the wrong impression that one deals with discrete data. Second, the choice of the intervals in EXCEL histograms (bins, as they are called in EXCEL) is often rather poor; the endpoints of the intervals usually employ too many significant digits. Third, EXCEL mislabels the midpoints of the intervals, as it uses for the midpoint the value of the upper endpoint of the interval. Furthermore, it has great difficulties labeling the tick marks on the horizontal axis. Of course, an expert in EXCEL can get around these difficulties by using special tricks and options; the chart wizard within EXCEL provides a very general graphical interface. However, it is unlikely that most EXCEL users have the background to make these adjustments.

The graphs that are produced by commonly used spreadsheet programs are quite cute, but they are not always meaningful. Here is one example. When comparing two or more groups with respect to a certain response, one can use a bar chart with the heights of the bars representing the responses. As a simple example, imagine displaying the success rates of several different teaching methods. Spreadsheets often add a false (nonexistent) third dimension and represent the two-dimensional bars as three-dimensional columns. This extra dimension does nothing to help you interpret the quantitative information. On the contrary, it makes it more difficult to make the relevant comparisons. It is easy to be dazzled by a display, especially if it is rendered with color or depth. However, the success of a graphical display should be based solely on the amount we learn about the phenomenon under study. "Chart junk," as Tufte calls it, must be avoided; unneeded cute ornamental hatching and false perspectives should be left off. Color can be an aid, but it can also be used to no purpose.

For a marvelous and comprehensive discussion on how to display information, we recommend the books by Cleveland, Tufte, and Tukey, which are listed in the references to this chapter.

7.12 EXERCISES

7.1 Consider the data on compressive strength of concrete blocks in units of 100 lb per square inch. (The data is taken from R.V. Hogg and J. Ledolter, 1992.)

49.2	53.9	50.0	44.5	42.2	42.3	32.3	31.3	60.9	47.5
43.5	37.9	41.1	57.6	40.2	45.3	51.7	52.3	45.7	53.7
51.0	45.7	45.9	50.0	32.5	67.2	55.1	59.6	48.6	50.3
45.1	46.8	47.4	38.3	41.5	44.0	62.2	62.9	56.3	35.8
38.3	33.5	48.5	47.4	49.6	41.3	55.2	52.1	34.3	31.6
38.2	46.0	47.0	41.2	39.8	48.4	49.2	32.8	47.9	43.3
49.3	54.5	54.1	44.5	46.2	44.4	45.1	41.5	43.4	39.1
39.1	41.6	43.1	43.7	48.8	37.2	33.6	28.7	33.8	37.4
43.5	44.2	53.0	45.1	51.9	50.6	48.5	39.0	47.3	48.8

Use the first 10 observations (first row). Obtain a dot diagram and calculate the mean, median, and standard deviation.

Use all 90 data and construct a histogram and a stem-and-leaf display of the information. Calculate summary statistics, including the mean, median, interquartile range, and the standard deviation. Use a computer program to carry out the calculations.

What number characterizes the center of the distribution? Give the interval that contains the central 50 percent of the data. Give an interval that contains approximately 95 percent of the distribution.

7.2 Fifty ordinary household light bulbs were purchased and their length of life (in hours) was determined.

443	1124	602	992	1485	1834	514	552	1047	716
446	1372	450	729	113	840	731	773	77	1490
473	679	402	1574	4015	1347	559	120	774	806
467	240	626	367	1033	1089	968	2243	728	936
241	296	1494	574	467	662	641	1023	941	446

Construct a histogram and comment on its shape. Calculate the mean and the median and comment on why they are different. Calculate the 90th percentile and interpret its meaning. Obtain the standard deviation.

On the box of these light bulbs it was claimed that the average length of life for bulbs of this type is 1,200 hours. Do your data indicate otherwise? If you find otherwise, speculate on the reasons for this difference (relatively small sample; perhaps different experimental protocol, etc.).

7.3 Joe, the janitor at our new business school, installed brand new light bulbs in the offices of the economics faculty. He kept track of burned out bulbs and the times when he had to replace them. After 12 months he had to replace 25 of the 30 bulbs. The length of life (in weeks) for the 25 bulbs is given below:

33	19	11	22	22	15	37	5	7
10	38	19	46	20	23	50	30	22
10	15	37	15	22	40	22		

Obtain a dot diagram and calculate the mean, median, and the standard deviation from the 25 observations. Calculate the 90th percentile. Discuss possible sources for the observed variability.

We would like to obtain the mean and the median life length of all 30 observations. However, by the end of the 12 months, five bulbs had not yet burned out. Can you calculate the mean of the 30 observations without waiting until the five remaining bulbs fail? If not, what can you say about this mean? Can you calculate the median of the 30 observations without waiting until the five remaining bulbs fail? What about the 90th percentile?

7.4 The data given below are hours to failure of 40 motors with a new Class-H insulation run at 190, 220, 240 and 260 degrees (Celsius). For each test temperature, the 10 motors were periodically examined for insulation failure. The given failure time is midway between the inspection time when the failure was found and the time of the previous inspection. (See Nelson, 1990, p. 115.)

Hours to Failure

190 C	220 C	240 C	260 C
7228	1764	1175	600
7228	2436	1175	744
7228	2436	1521	744
8448	2436	1569	744
9167	2436	1617	912
9167	2436	1665	1128
9167	3108	1665	1320
9167	3108	1713	1464
10511	3108	1761	1608
10511	3108	1953	1896

Display the information in form of dot diagrams, drawn on the same scale. Calculate the median failure time for each of the four temperatures.

The original test purpose was to estimate the median life of this particular type of insulation at a design temperature of 180 degrees. A median of 20,000 hours was desired. Do you think that this goal can be reached?

7.5 At the end of the semester students complete an evaluation of the course that they just took. Here is the form that is used in the Department of Statistics at the University of Iowa. We have also listed the results for one of our large undergraduate statistics courses. A total of 309 students completed the report. Students can check as many items as they want.

23	1.	No changes should be made
17	2.	Speed up the pace of the course
105	3.	Slow down the pace of the course
10	4.	Decrease the amount of discussion and class participation
100	5.	Increase the amount of discussion and class participation
86	6.	Reduce the amount of required work

(*continues*)

32	7.	Increase the amount of required work
141	8.	Make better use or more frequent use of examples
151	9.	Clarify the direction and purpose of the course
112	10.	Provide better or more frequent evaluations of students' progress
25	11.	Present or allow more than one viewpoint on controversial topics
24	12.	Broaden the scope of the course
49	13.	Narrow the scope of the course
57	14.	Be more available to students outside of class
62	15.	Be more receptive to students' viewpoints
28	16.	Correct distracting mannerisms or speech habits

Analyze the information and write a short report to the department summarizing your suggestions for improving the course. In addition, comment on possible ways of improving the questionnaire.

7.6 Compare the five tools in Table 7.2 with regard to their deviations from the target bore size. Construct five dot diagrams and draw them on the same scale. Comment on your findings.

7.7 In order to make the introductory statistics course more relevant, one of us (Ledolter) collected data on the background and the opinions of students in this class. During the first lecture the following questionnaire was handed out to each attending student; 324 students returned the questionnaire. The collected data was used throughout the semester to illustrate statistical ideas and methods. It was hoped that the data collected on the class would be seen as more relevant than textbook examples.

The responses of 324 students are given in the file *SURVEY.DAT*, which can be found on the accompanying data disk. Use the data to construct histograms of categorical variables (such as student standing, type of living arrangement, drug use, drinking habits) and continuous variables (such as college GPA, high school GPA, ACT score, number of hours studying on an average day). Construct and comment on scatter plots of college GPA against high school GPA and ACT scores. Stratify the scatter plots with respect to gender (that is, construct two scatter plots, one for males and one for females).

The questionnaire is given below:

22S:008 - - - SPRING 1994 - - - LEDOLTER

GENDER: male female

HEIGHT (in feet and inches):

WEIGHT (in pounds):

AGE (in years):

BACKGROUND: White, not of Hispanic origin
Black/Afro-American
Latino or Hispanic
American Indian/Alaskan Native
Asian or Pacific Islander
Other

CURRENT COLLEGE GPA:

CURRENT STANDING: freshman sophomore junior senior other

(*continues*)

ACT SCORE:
HIGH SCHOOL GPA:
STUDENT-ATHLETE ON SCHOLARSHIP: no yes
WEEKLY NUMBER OF HOURS SPENT ON A PAYING JOB:
NUMBER OF HOURS STUDYING ON AN AVERAGE DAY (OUTSIDE CLASS):
LIVING ARRANGEMENT: dorm Greek-system
apartment at home with family
SMOKING: yes no
DRUG USE: never
moderate (once a week)
heavy (more than once a week)
DRINKING: no
moderate (up to 3 drinks/week)
heavy (more than 3 drinks/week)
TELEVISION EXPOSURE (hours per *day*):
INTEREST IN LEARNING ABOUT STATISTICS: none somewhat yes
YOUR PERCEPTION OF THE "QUALITY" OF 22S:008: good average bad
YOUR ATTITUDE TOWARD MATHEMATICS:
on a scale from 0 to 100, with 0 representing an extreme dislike of math, and 100 a love for math
PRIOR EXPOSURE TO COMPUTERS AND FAMILIARITY WITH WORDPROCESSING:
no experience some lots of experience

7.8 Find examples of noncausal correlations.

7.9 (Group project) Look up the last 24 monthly average temperatures for the community you live in. Furthermore, obtain data on your energy consumption (that is, your gas and electricity usage). Relate your monthly energy consumption to monthly average temperature. Use the techniques that you learned in this chapter (in particular, scatter plots and correlation coefficients).

You may keep the following things in mind: Monthly average low and monthly average high temperatures may be available. Which variables should you use? Your electric company may have data on monthly degree cooling (heating) days. Could this information be used? Assuming that you have air conditioning, you are using energy for both heating and cooling. Why does this matter?

7.10 (Group project) Use recent issues of *Consumer Reports* to obtain information on the fuel efficiency of automobiles. Relate a car's fuel efficiency to characteristics of the car that you believe to have an effect on fuel efficiency. What about the weight of the car? Make scatter plots, calculate correlation coefficients, and interpret.

7.11 (Group project) Salary data for your university may be public information and may be available in the library. Look up the salaries of the professors in your business school. Business schools are usually divided into several departments, such as accounting, finance, economics, marketing, management sciences, and management organizations. Compare the salaries across departments. How do you explain the variability between departments, and how can you explain the variability within departments?

Obtain additional information that can help you explain the variability in salaries. For each professor, obtain data on the number of years since the faculty member's terminal degree (usually a Ph.D.). Plot salary against the time since getting a Ph.D., and interpret your findings. The time since Ph.D. will explain some of the variability, but considerable variability will be left. What else could affect the variability among salaries? Investigate and summarize your conclusions.

7.12 Your library should have at least one book by W.S. Cleveland and one by Edward R. Tufte. Read and discuss. Summarize their principles for excellence in graph construction and for achieving graphical integrity.

Read and discuss the following two articles in the summer 1996 (Vol. 9, No. 3) issue of *Chance*, a magazine of the American Statistical Association (published by Springer): R.A. Reese, "Graphical Literacy," pp. 23–28, and H. Wainer, "Visual Revelations: Scaling the Heights (and Widths)," pp. 43–49.

7.13 (Group project) Collect data of your choice. Analyze the data, using the statistical techniques that we studied in this chapter.

7.14 Show that $\sum(x_i - \bar{x})^2 = \sum(x_i^2) - (\sum x_i)^2/n$. This shows the equivalence of the two definitions for the standard deviation s.

7.15 Consider the correlation coefficient r as it is defined in Section 7.8. Use the definition of the standard deviation in Section 7.5 and show that the correlation coefficient can be written as

$$r = a/[\sqrt{bc}]$$

where $a = \sum x_i y_i - [(\sum x_i)(\sum y_i)/n]$, $b = \sum(x_i^2) - [(\sum x_i)^2/n]$, and $c = \sum(y_i^2) - [(\sum y_i)^2/n]$.

7.16 The file *STUDENT.DAT* contains information on 54 students in an off-campus MBA statistics course at the University of Iowa. The following variables are recorded: height (in inches), weight (in pounds); gender (male/female), and the number of biological children.

(a) Display the distribution of height, weight, and number of children. Consider dot diagrams, histograms, stem-and-leaf displays, and box plots. Summarize the information numerically by calculating averages, medians, and standard deviations.

(b) Stratify by gender and repeat your analysis in (a) for each of the two groups. Display the dot diagrams on the same scale.

(c) Construct a scatter diagram of weight (on the vertical axis) against height (on the horizontal axis). Calculate the correlation coefficient.

(d) Identify the points in the scatter plot in (c) according to gender. Calculate the correlation coefficient between weight and height, for each gender group separately.

(e) Recreate the two-way tables in Table 7.14.

7.17 The data set given below lists the annual 1996 salary (in \$1000) and the educational background for a sample of 25 employees at a large Iowa manufacturing company. Educational background is measured by the number of years of formal schooling (12 refers to a high school graduate; 16 refers to a college graduate; 17 through 20 refer to college degree plus the number of years of graduate work).

Educ	Salary	Educ	Salary
16	32.3	17	29.4
12	23.7	16	25.4
12	19.5	13	21.3
16	27.8	12	17.6
18	33.0	12	13.3
15	29.0	19	44.8
11	13.7	16	30.7
12	12.1	17	34.5
11	9.8	16	27.3
20	37.7	12	14.8
15	26.3	16	21.7
16	22.0	16	33.8
16	27.0		

Construct a scatter diagram of salary against educational achievement. Calculate the correlation coefficient.

7.18 The following data was collected from a local charity donation drive. Phone solicitors called from a list of local phone numbers. If the phone was answered and the phone solicitor was able to finish her or his 45-second speech about the charity, then the length of the call and the amount of the donation were recorded.

Min	Amount	Min	Amount	Min	Amount
1	0	6	100	1	0
4	5	5	0	9	0
1	5	5	0	14	85
1	0	2	0	1	5
3	0	1	0	3	5
9	50	6	0	1	0
1	5	4	10	1	5
5	75	4	5	1	0
1	5	1	0	1	80
2	0	5	5	3	20
4	0	5	0		
3	0	1	10		
1	0	5	0		
5	0	1	40		
1	90	1	5		
4	0	3	0		
1	0	1	0		
1	10	7	10		
1	0	2	75		
2	75	2	0		

Analyze the information. For both variables obtain dot diagrams and summary statistics (including average, median, mode, and standard deviation). Interpret the information. Construct a scatter plot of the amount of the donation against the time spent on the phone. Calculate the correlation coefficient and interpret the result.

7.19 The operations department of a custom injection molding company uses the utilization percentage of a machine as a predictor of profitability. Data on machine utilization and pretax profit over the last 25 months is listed below.

(a) Discuss whether machine utilization is a good indicator of profit. Make the appropriate graphs and calculate the appropriate statistics.

(b) Plot the observations over time. Do you see any trend patterns in the utilization rates?

Month	Utilization	Pretax profit
1	62	35,456
2	68	90,069
3	76	130,324
4	68	20,146
5	65	23,795
6	73	34,543
7	81	81,972
8	74	155,130
9	81	121,336
10	83	117,927
11	85	191,035
12	53	8,870
13	56	24,834
14	48	17,084
15	43	−7,492
16	42	−72,002
17	40	−5,351
18	41	−52,004
19	40	−96,571
20	47	−57,306
21	47	22,722
22	35	−45,865
23	33	10,926
24	56	−85,845
25	50	13,890

A negative value on profit means a loss.

7.20 In the process of manufacturing baby diaper backsheets, a key dimension is the flat width of the sheet of film. Width measurements (in inches) on 42 diaper backsheets are given below. Obtain the histogram and the summary statistics for the data.

Specification requirements for this process call for a target value of 13.8 inches, with lower and upper specification limits of 13.75 and 13.85 inches, respectively. Does your process satisfy the requirements?

Width (in inches)	
13.8125	13.7701
13.8435	13.8010
13.7810	13.8000
13.8015	13.8014
13.7950	13.7950
13.7900	13.7920
13.8564	13.7980
13.7999	13.8050
13.7800	13.8100
13.7950	13.8100
13.8012	13.8200
13.8004	13.8050
13.8100	13.8050
13.8010	13.8110
13.7994	13.8240
13.7840	13.8140
13.8900	13.8500
13.8400	13.8210
13.8410	13.7950
13.7520	13.7850
13.8000	13.8400

7.21 The money manager of a fixed-income mutual fund known as the "Liquid Gold Fund" has a five-year track record. The manager decides to compare the performance of her fund against that of an established index portfolio of similar credit risk. Quarterly returns over this five-year period for both the Liquid Gold Fund and the index portfolio are given below.

(a) For each portfolio obtain a time sequence plot of the 20 time-ordered measurements. Comment and discuss issues of trend and seasonality.

(b) For each portfolio calculate the mean, the median, and the standard deviation of the 20 measurements.

(c) Make a scatter plot of quarterly returns of the Liquid Gold Fund against the quarterly returns of the index portfolio. Calculate the correlation coefficient.

(d) How successful do you think the money manager will be in marketing her Liquid Gold Fund to potential investors?

Liquid Gold Fund Quarterly Returns (In Percent)

Year 1	1.98	3.51	4.52	5.12
Year 2	−1.01	3.79	3.86	0.68
Year 3	1.80	0.21	3.48	0.35
Year 4	−1.82	−1.47	0.77	−0.25
Year 5	5.51	5.35	1.03	3.75

Index Portfolio Quarterly Returns (In Percent)

Year 1	3.26	1.88	5.02	4.45
Year 2	−0.21	4.23	3.08	1.32
Year 3	3.93	2.28	1.15	1.34
Year 4	−1.65	−0.50	0.97	0.82
Year 5	5.12	5.21	2.22	3.33

7.22 Quarterly percent changes in stock price indices across four countries for the period from 1980 through 1989 are given below.

(a) For each country make a time-sequence plot of the 40 time-ordered observations. Make these plots on the same scale.

(b) For each country calculate the mean, median, and standard deviation of the quarterly percentage changes. Compare the four countries with respect to their average returns and return variability.

(c) Obtain pairwise scatter plots of quarterly returns of one country against the other. Some computer packages will display a scatter plot matrix containing all pairwise scatter plots.

(d) Calculate all possible pairwise correlation coefficients.

Stock Price Change (In Percent)

Year	Qu	US	Japan	Germany	UK
1980	1	22.81	11.80	−2.78	13.75
	2	−9.92	1.64	−2.79	2.14
	3	59.29	8.56	7.64	43.50
	4	35.07	14.77	−9.47	19.62
1981	1	−6.73	13.47	−10.51	−5.87
	2	1.80	37.24	27.39	37.95
	3	−23.32	19.42	4.66	−6.80
	4	−13.71	−18.52	−23.42	−19.01
1982	1	−27.22	2.39	3.67	33.03
	2	0.00	−11.52	0.00	19.78
	3	0.42	−11.16	−11.31	18.53
	4	79.92	26.55	22.45	49.47
1983	1	34.54	20.19	45.67	16.03
	2	40.88	26.90	73.14	34.23
	3	8.54	25.21	16.43	10.59
	4	0.00	12.42	23.82	−1.64
1984	1	−12.68	51.47	13.27	41.67
	2	−8.93	20.38	−10.48	15.14
	3	12.18	−11.31	−11.04	−8.22
	4	6.79	31.59	31.28	44.26
1985	1	27.60	43.15	37.74	44.19
	2	13.59	14.51	36.13	7.99

(*continues*)

(continued)

Year	Qu	US	Japan	Germany	UK
1985	3	8.67	12.85	35.93	−4.34
	4	19.04	0.56	75.22	32.36
1986	1	43.22	25.79	53.68	37.27
	2	41.88	69.02	0.44	39.94
	3	−2.41	59.31	−16.98	−5.06
	4	6.26	0.52	18.04	5.65
1987	1	67.16	76.54	−39.34	74.22
	2	30.46	85.40	17.03	53.54
	3	38.74	−11.27	33.92	36.42
	4	−85.33	−31.01	−93.65	−88.23
1988	1	5.39	15.26	−47.19	−3.29
	2	10.34	40.45	22.51	8.34
	3	2.45	−1.48	30.95	7.27
	4	12.45	9.02	29.85	−5.83
1989	1	24.15	41.03	24.31	42.50
	2	28.71	7.54	21.60	24.40
	3	34.64	17.00	34.78	34.50
	4	3.40	24.43	3.14	−21.00

7.23 From a data set of the weights (in pounds) of $n = 54$ students we have calculated the following summary statistics:

Mean: $\bar{x} = 160$ pounds

Standard deviation: $s = 18.5$ pounds

We decide to express weight in kilograms. Note that weight in kg, y, is related to weight in lb, x, as follows: $y = x/2.2$. What are the mean and the standard deviation of weight, expressed in kilograms?

Mean: $\bar{y} =$ ______ kg

Standard deviation: $s =$ ______ kg

Hint: Look at the definitions of the mean and the standard deviation. What happens to the mean and the standard deviation if you replace each measurement by bx_i, where b is a known constant (in our example $b = 1/2.2$)?

7.24 True/False: The distance from the first quartile to the median is always the same as the distance from the median to the third quartile. Support your answer.

7.25 You are given the following five pairs of observations:

y	*x*
2	6
3	8
3	10
1	5
0	3

Determine the correlation coefficient r, just by looking at the scatter diagram of the data.
(a) $r = -0.75$ **(c)** $r = 0.00$ **(e)** None of these
(b) $r = 1.25$ **(d)** $r = 1.00$

7.26 Use the table below to answer the following questions. The numbers that you see are frequencies, expressed as a percentage of the total.
For Owner: 1 = sole proprietorship, 2 = partnership, 3 = corporation
For Size: 1 = small, 2 = medium, 3 = large

Rows: Owner Columns: Size

	1	2	3	All
1	31.80	6.90	0.77	39.47
2	6.13	2.30	1.53	9.46
3	15.33	16.09	19.16	50.57
All	53.26	25.29	21.46	100.00

(a) What percentage of the restaurants in the survey were small partnerships?
(b) What percentage of the restaurants in the survey were large?
(c) Of the large restaurants, what percentage were corporate owned?

7.27 Read and summarize the paper "Using Personal Checklists to Facilitate TQM," by Harry V. Roberts in *Quality Progress* (June 1993, pp. 51–56). Discuss the personal check lists of Sergesketter and Roberts. Construct your own personal check list.

7.13 REFERENCES

Cleveland, W. S. *Visualizing Data* (Revised Edition). Summit, NJ: Hobart Press, 1993.

Cleveland, W. S. *The Elements of Graphing Data*. Summit, NJ: Hobart Press, 1994.

Hogg, R. V. and J. Ledolter. *Applied Statistics for Engineers and Physical Scientists*, 2nd edition. New York: Macmillan, 1992.

Hunter, J. S. "The Digidot Plot," *The American Statistician*, Vol. 42, 1988, 54.

Ishikawa, K. *Guide to Quality Control*, 2nd edition. Tokyo: Asian Productivity Organization, 1982 (available through UNIPUB, New York).

Ledolter, J. and G. C. Tiao. "Statistical Methods for Ambient Air Pollutants with Special Reference to the Los Angeles Catalyst Study (LACS) Data," *Environmental Science and Technology*, Vol. 13, 1979, 1233–1240.

Nelson, W. *Accelerated Testing: Statistical Models, Test Plans, and Data Analyses*. New York: Wiley, 1990.

Reese, R. A. "Graphical Literacy," *Chance*, Vol. 9, 1996, No. 3, 23–28.

Roberts, H. V. "Using Personal Checklists to Facilitate TQM," *Quality Progress*, June 1993, 51–56.

Snee, R. D. "Graphical Analysis of Process Variation Studies," *Journal of Quality Technology*, Vol. 15, 1983, 76–88.

Snee, R. D. and C. G. Pfeifer. "Graphical Representation of Data," in *Encyclopedia of*

Statistical Sciences, S. Kotz and N. L. Johnson, editors, Vol. 3. New York: Wiley, 1983, 488–511.

Tufte, Edward R. *The Visual Display of Quantitative Information*. Cheshire, CT: Graphics Press, 1983.

Tufte, Edward R. *Envisioning Information*. Cheshire, CT: Graphics Press, 1990.

Tukey, John W. *Exploratory Data Analysis*. Reading, MA: Addison Wesley, 1977.

Wainer, H. "Visual Revelations: Scaling the Heights (and Widths)," *Chance*, Vol. 9, 1996, No. 3, 43–49.

CHAPTER 8

MODELING VARIABILITY AND UNCERTAINTY: AN INTRODUCTION TO PROBABILITY DISTRIBUTIONS

8.1 UNDERSTANDING AND MODELING UNCERTAINTY

Measurements on products and processes vary. Methods for describing the variability in data were given in the previous chapters. In this chapter we discuss how to model *uncertainty*. We discuss discrete and continuous random variables, and we describe the probability distributions that govern their behavior.

Describing and modeling variability is important, but it is usually not enough. What is also needed is a good, and as W. Edwards Deming says, "profound" understanding of the nature of variation. It is often argued that a central problem with management is management's failure to understand uncertainty and the information in variation. The uncertainty must be considered and incorporated into the analysis when making decisions about people and processes. Let us illustrate the role of uncertainty in decision making with a few examples.

Illustration 1 Often there is a temptation to assign cause to certain occurrences even though none is justified by the data. Deming's *red bead experiment* is a useful exercise to illustrate this point (see W.E. Deming, *Out of the Crisis*, p. 346). The experiment proceeds as follows. You are given a large jar with many beads where 90 percent of the beads are white and 10 percent of the beads are red. Think of this jar of beads as a production process; a red bead represents a defective item and a white bead represents an acceptable item. On average, this process produces 10 percent defectives. In order to simulate outcomes from this process, participants in this exercise take repeated samples of 50 beads. Joe, the first participant, walks up to the jar, takes the paddle and selects 50 beads. He finds three defective beads among the 50; his defect rate is 6 percent. Joe gets some praise since "he has done well," better than the 10 percent average. The next person, Mary, takes a full paddle and finds two red beads among the 50; her defect rate is 4 percent. Because her defect rate is "considerably smaller" than the 10 percent average, she gets promoted to line supervisor. John, the next participant, steps up to the jar, takes his 50 beads and finds 8 defectives, or 16 percent. Because of this "poor performance" he gets scolded and his salary is cut.

This simple experiment illustrates that it is all too easy to blame workers for faults that belong to the system. Management in this example doesn't realize that it is the process that generates defectives. The numbers of defectives vary because of the process, and not because of the people. The workers in our exercise have no influence on the process; the outcomes are governed by the random draws from the jar of beads. Of course, there are instances where a defect arises because of errors and inattentiveness of the worker, but most people argue that these cases are rare. Most of the variability and many of the defects come from the system, and management shouldn't blame the worker if the worker is not responsible for the system. Joseph M. Juran, a respected authority on aspects of quality, argues that 85 percent of the problems are management controllable, while only 15 percent are controllable by the operator. Deming, on page 315 of his book *Out of the Crisis*, goes even further, arguing that 94 percent of the problems belong to the system and are responsibility of management, and only 6 percent are due to the operator. Management shouldn't waste its time trying to find reasons why Mary did well and John did poorly. Time is better spent fixing the process and lowering the overall defect level of the process.

Illustration 2 We need a methodology that allows us to decide whether a specific result is unusual or extraordinary. If a process is stable over time and if a process produces on average 10 percent defectives, then it would be highly unusual to observe 15 defectives in a sample of 50 items. For a process with a defect rate of 10 percent, the chance (or probability) of observing 15 defectives or more in a sample of size 50 is virtually zero. On the other hand, it would not be that unusual to observe seven defectives or more. The discussion of probability distributions in this chapter shows us how to make these calculations. It teaches us about the natural variability in processes and provides guidelines when the information should be considered unusual.

Illustration 3 Observations vary; because of the variability some observations are below average, and some are above. How can we calculate the chance that a measurement exceeds a certain value, or the chance that a measurement will be within a certain given interval? For example, take a toothpaste-filling process which puts on average 12.5 ounces of toothpaste in a tube; assume that the standard deviation among individual fill weights amounts to 0.2 ounce. The advertised fill weight of the tubes is 12 ounces. What is the chance that we underfill the tubes? The discussion of probability distributions in this chapter will give us the answers to such questions.

Illustration 4 It happens quite often that whenever a rookie has had a particularly good first year, his performance slips during the second. We can call this the "sophomore jinx." How do you explain this phenomenon? Is it that our rookie has rested on his laurels?

Not necessarily; we all know that the rookie of the year in baseball doesn't win the title with an average or below-average year. His performance is probably in the upper tail of the batting distribution curve that reflects his performance throughout his career. Assume that it is the 95th percentile. This means that in the second year he has only a 5 percent chance to improve his performance. Thus it is very likely that his performance in the second year is going to be poorer than that in his first.

Illustration 5 Sales have been higher than average for each of the last two quarters. The manager concludes that the company is "on a roll." This reasoning may not be correct. Simple calculations show that for a stable symmetric process (that is, a process which does not change from one period to the next and which generates observations above or below the process average with equal probabilities) the chance of being above average twice in a row is 0.25. Thus it is quite likely that the process hasn't changed at all. What about if sales were above average for four quarters in a row? Then, the evidence is somewhat stronger, but there is still a 6.25 percent chance that we can get such a result from a process that hasn't changed at all.

8.2 DISCRETE RANDOM VARIABLES AND DISCRETE DISTRIBUTIONS

8.2.1 Random Variables and Probability Distributions

Random variables are variables whose outcomes are uncertain. Realizations of random variables cannot be predicted with certainty before the activity that leads to this variable is performed. For example, prior to actually measuring the width of a steel flat, we are uncertain as to the value of the measurement. Prior to getting on the road to commute to work, we are uncertain about the commuting time. Prior to carrying out a sample inspection, we are uncertain about the number of defectives in the sample that we selected.

A random variable that can take on distinct values only, is called a *discrete* random variable. For example, the activity may be the inspection of an item, and the variable of interest may be the number of flaws on a produced item. We denote the random variable, number of flaws, by uppercase X; its possible outcomes are (lowercase) $x = 0$ (no flaw), $x = 1$ (exactly one flaw), $x = 2$ (exactly two flaws), and so on. Our convention is to use uppercase letters for random variables and lowercase letters for their possible outcomes. Or, consider X, the outcome of a quality inspection in which the item is classified as good ($x = 0$) or defective ($x = 1$). Or, consider rolling a die and the random variable X, the number of spots on the upside of the die; here the possible outcomes are $x = 1, 2, 3, 4, 5, 6$. Or, consider X, the number of defective items in a sample of five items; here, the outcome can be 0 (that is, no defective), 1 (exactly one defective), 2, 3, 4, or 5.

We use distributions to quantify uncertainty. The *distribution of a discrete random variable* consists of (1) the collection of all possible outcomes and (2) their associated probabilities.

EXAMPLE 1

The probability (or chance) of producing a good item is 0.98, while the probability of producing a defective item is 0.02. That is, $P(\text{item is good}) = P(X = 0) = 0.98$ and $P(\text{item is defective}) = P(X = 1) = 0.02$. ■

Probabilities are always nonnegative numbers. Furthermore, the sum of the probabilities, where the sum is over all possible outcomes of the random variable, must be 1.

Often, probabilities come from prior experience. We may have looked at many items in the past and found that about 98 percent of the items are good and 2 percent are defective. We treat probabilities as relative frequencies and assume that the experiment can be repeated under more or less identical conditions. Sometimes, experiments cannot be repeated and probabilities are thought of as measuring one's prior belief about the occurrence of an event. For example, my prior belief of rain for tomorrow may be 0.60 (or 60 percent), and my prior belief for the event that I will learn piano within the next year may be 0.20. Probabilities measuring prior personal belief and probabilities arising from relative frequencies are fundamentally different; however, in most practical situations, both probabilities are being handled the same way.

EXAMPLE 2

Consider tossing a (fair) coin three times. Let X be the number of "heads" (H). Here the possible outcomes are $x = 0, 1, 2$, or 3. How should we assign the probabilities

$f(x) = P(X = x)$? Let us consider the following assignment:

x	0	1	2	3
$f(x) = P(X = x)$	1/8	3/8	3/8	1/8

Why is this a reasonable assignment? There are eight possible distinct outcomes: *TTT* (leading to $x = 0$); three distinct possibilities *TTH, THT,* and *HTT* (leading to $x = 1$); three distinct possibilities *THH, HTH,* and *HHT* (leading to $x = 2$); and *HHH* (leading to $x = 3$). If the coin is fair (meaning that it is not biased in any one direction), then each of the eight outcomes is equally likely and the probability of each possible sequence is 1/8. Since the outcome $x = 1$ can happen in three different ways, the probability $P(X = 1) = 3/8$. The other probabilities are obtained the same way. ■

EXAMPLE 3

X is the number of large contracts that are awarded to our company in a particular year. At the start of the new year we are uncertain about the number of contracts that we will receive. However, from previous years we know something about the distribution of X. We also have reason to believe that the business climate has not changed much since the last year and that the distribution obtained from prior years is still relevant for the current one. The distribution is given below:

x	0	1	2	3
$P(X = x)$	0.2	0.5	0.2	0.1

Note that these probabilities are nonnegative and that they sum to 1. ■

We use this last example to show how we can use the assigned probabilities to calculate probabilities of related events. For example, the probability of obtaining at most one contract (that is, either exactly one contract, or no contract) is given by

$$P(X \leq 1) = P(X = 0 \text{ or } X = 1) = P(X = 0) + P(X = 1) = 0.2 + 0.5 = 0.7.$$

We identify the basic outcomes that make up the related event: You can get at most one contract by either getting exactly zero contracts or exactly one contract. Here the basic outcomes are ($x = 0$; no contract) and ($x = 1$; exactly one contract). We call them *basic outcomes* as they cannot occur at the same time; we cannot be awarded exactly zero contracts and exactly one contract at the same time. The probability of the related event is then the sum of the probabilities of the basic outcomes that make up that event.

The probability of obtaining at least one contract (that is, one or more) is given by

$$P(X \geq 1) = P(X = 1 \text{ or } X = 2 \text{ or } X = 3) = P(X = 1) + P(X = 2) + P(X = 3)$$
$$= 0.5 + 0.2 + 0.1 = 0.8.$$

8.2.2 The Mean of a Distribution

We can describe a probability distribution by certain key characteristics. The most important ones are the *mean* and the *standard deviation of the distribution.* The mean measures the central location of the distribution, while the standard deviation measures the variability or dispersion.

Consider X, the number of contracts in Example 3. How many contracts can we expect for the next year? The mean of that distribution, denoted by the Greek letter μ, is given by

$$\mu = (0)(0.2) + (1)(0.5) + (2)(0.2) + (3)(0.1) = 1.2.$$

We weigh the possible outcomes by their probabilities. The mean of the distribution is the "balance point" of the distribution. If you mark the outcomes of the random variable on a ruler and place pennies on those marks in proportion to the probabilities, then the mean of the distribution is the fulcrum point at which the ruler is kept in perfect balance.

The mean of the distribution is also called the *expectation of the random variable*. The result $\mu = 1.2$ implies that we expect to be awarded 1.2 contracts per year. Of course, the number of awarded contracts can only be an integer; however, in the long run (that is, over many years) the number of contracts will average out to 1.2.

In general, the expression for the *mean of a discrete distribution* with outcomes $x_1, x_2, \ldots$ and associated probabilities $f(x_1) = P(X = x_1), f(x_2) = P(X = x_2), \ldots$ is given by

$$\mu = \Sigma_x x f(x) = x_1 f(x_1) + x_2 f(x_2) + \cdots.$$

It is a weighted average of the possible outcomes, where the weights are given by the probabilities of the outcomes.

In Example 2, where X is the number of heads among three coin tosses, the mean is

$$\mu = (0)(1/8) + (1)(3/8) + (2)(3/8) + (3)(1/8) = 1.5.$$

On average, we expect 1.5 heads among three coin tosses. Again, 1.5 heads is not a feasible number if you carry out this experiment once. However, over repeated applications of this experiment (that is, tossing three coins repeatedly and writing down the number of heads) the average number of heads is 1.5.

8.2.3 The Standard Deviation of a Distribution

In Chapter 7 we defined the standard deviation of a set of n observations as the square root of an average of the squared distances of the observations from their average. The standard deviation measures the "average distance" of the observations from their average.

The standard deviation of a discrete random variable (or a discrete distribution) is defined similarly. The *standard deviation of a discrete distribution*, denoted by the Greek letter σ, is given by

$$\begin{aligned}\sigma &= \sqrt{(x_1-\mu)^2 f(x_1) + (x_2-\mu)^2 f(x_2) + \cdots}\\ &= \sqrt{\Sigma_x (x-\mu)^2 f(x)}.\end{aligned}$$

Squared distances between the possible outcomes and their mean μ are weighted by their probabilities, and the weighted sum is taken over all possible outcomes. The square root is taken so that the standard deviation retains the same unit of the observations. The square of the standard deviation, σ^2, is called the *variance of the distribution*.

We can think of the standard deviation of a discrete random variable as an approximate "weighted" average distance of the possible x-values from their mean μ, where the weights are given by the probabilities. If the outcome is deterministic (that is, if there is no variation involved and one outcome occurs with probability 1), then the standard deviation σ is zero.

The standard deviation for the number of contracts in Example 3 on page 189 is

$$\begin{aligned}\sigma &= \sqrt{(0-1.2)^2(0.2) + (1-1.2)^2(0.5) + (2-1.2)^2(0.2) + (3-1.2)^2(0.1)}\\ &= \sqrt{(1.44)(0.2) + (.04)(0.5) + (.64)(0.2) + (3.24)(0.1)}\\ &= \sqrt{0.76} = 0.87 \text{ (contract).}\end{aligned}$$

8.2.4 Mean and Standard Deviation of a Linear Function of a Random Variable

Assume that a random variable X has mean μ and standard deviation σ. What happens to the characteristics of the distribution if we multiply the random variable by a constant b and if we consider the new random variable $Y = bX$? What is the mean of the random variable Y, and what is its standard deviation?

The new random variable Y can take on outcomes $bx_1, bx_2, \ldots,$ with probabilities $f(x_1), f(x_2), \ldots.$ Hence, the mean of the distribution of Y is given by

$$\mu_Y = (bx_1)f(x_1) + (bx_2)f(x_2) + \cdots = b[(x_1)f(x_1) + (x_2)f(x_2) + \cdots] = b\mu_X,$$

and the standard deviation of Y is

$$\begin{aligned}\sigma_Y &= \sqrt{(bx_1 - b\mu_X)^2 f(x_1) + (bx_2 - b\mu_X)^2 f(x_2) + \cdots}\\ &= \sqrt{b^2[(x_1-\mu_X)^2 f(x_1) + (x_2-\mu_X)^2 f(x_2) + \cdots]} = |b|\sigma_X.\end{aligned}$$

Similarly, we can show that the random variable $Y = a + bX$ has mean $\mu_Y = a + b\mu_X$ and standard deviation $\sigma_Y = |b|\sigma_X$. The addition of a constant to a random variable shifts the distribution by a constant amount. It changes the mean, but has no effect on the variability. The constant *a* does not affect the standard deviation.

EXAMPLE

Consider the random variable X with mean $\mu_X = 2$ and standard deviation $\sigma_X = 4$. Then the new random variable $Y = 3 + 5X$ has mean $\mu_Y = 3 + (5)(2) = 13$ and standard deviation $\sigma_Y = (5)(4) = 20$. ■

8.2.5 Data Summary Statistics as Estimates of the Corresponding Distribution Characteristics

It is important that you understand the difference between the average and the standard deviation of a *data set*, and the mean and the standard deviation of a *distribution*. Mean and standard deviation of a distribution characterize the distribution of possible outcomes, and no data is involved. We call these characteristics *parameters* of the distribution, and we use Greek symbols to denote them. We also say that the probability distribution describes the *population* of all possible outcomes, and hence we refer to μ and σ as the *population parameters*.

Note that the probability distribution provides a model that governs the generation of observations. For example, the probabilities in Example 2 on page 188 on the distribution of the number of heads among three coin tosses tell us how likely it is to obtain one of the four possible outcomes (0, 1, 2, or 3). It is easy to generate realizations, or observations, from this probability model. Just imagine tossing the three coins 20 times and recording the 20 realizations. You may get a "2" first (two heads among the first three coin tosses), a "3" next (three heads the next time), and so on, until perhaps a "0" for the twentieth toss of the three coins. We say that these 20 observations $x_1 = 2, x_2 = 3, \ldots, x_{20} = 0$ represent a *sample* from this distribution, and we refer to the average and the standard deviation of these 20 observations as the *sample average* (or *sample mean*) $\bar{x}$ and the *sample standard deviation* s. Note that we use ordinary letters to denote the sample characteristics, as compared to the Greek letters that we use for distribution or population characteristics.

The sample average $\bar{x}$ is an estimate of μ, the mean of the distribution; the sample standard deviation s is an estimate of σ, the standard deviation of the distribution. We say that the sample statistics $\bar{x}$ and s are *estimates* of the parameters of the distribution, μ and σ. Sampling errors will be involved with sample estimates of distribution characteristics. The estimates that we get from one particular sample and the population characteristics will usually differ, especially for small sample sizes; the sample average from 20 realizations in the coin toss example will not always be 1.5. Of course, for a very large sample the relative sample frequencies of the outcomes will approach the probabilities of the random variable, and the estimates $\bar{x}$ and s will converge to the distribution parameters μ and σ.

8.3 THE BINOMIAL DISTRIBUTION

In this and the next subsection we describe two special discrete distributions: the *binomial* distribution and the *Poisson* distribution. These two distributions arise in sampling inspection and in control charts for attribute data. We need to study these distributions if we want to understand the principles behind sample inspection plans and behind the construction of control limits in p- and c-charts. Let us start our discussion with the following two examples.

EXAMPLE 1

Consider a certain production process that produces at the 5 percent defect level. If we take a single item from the production line, then there is a 5 percent chance that the selected item is defective. That is, $P(\text{defective item}) = 0.05$ and $P(\text{good item}) = 0.95$. Now take $n = 20$ items from the production line. What is the probability that you get exactly two defectives? What is the chance that you get two or more defectives? What is the chance that you get no more than one defective? How many defectives do you expect? ■

EXAMPLE 2

Assume that the acceptable quality level for your production is 3 percent defectives. You are looking at a large lot of manufactured items and you have to decide whether the lot should be shipped. You base your decision on a *sampling inspection plan*. According to this plan you take a sample of size $n = 10$; if all items are good, then you accept the lot and ship it to your customer. If one or more of the sampled items is defective, then you reject the lot. What is the chance that you reject the lot even though the defect rate of your production does not exceed the acceptable level of 3 percent; that is, what is the probability of falsely rejecting a good lot? Furthermore, what is the chance that you accept and ship the lot if your production has slipped to a 5 percent defective level; that is, what is the probability of falsely accepting a bad lot? ■

8.3.1 Binomial Probabilities

Consider the following situation:

1. You conduct an experiment (also called a *trial*) that can result in only one of two outcomes. We shall call the outcomes "success" (S) and "failure" (F). The probability of a success is given by $P(S) = \theta$, while the probability of a failure is given by $P(F) = 1 - \theta$.
2. You are conducting n such trials. You carry them out *independently*, which means that there is no carryover from one trial to the next; having just observed a success in the last trial does not alter the probability of success in the subsequent ones.

3. Consider the random variable X, the *number of successes among these n trials.*

The possible values for X are $x = 0, 1, 2, \ldots, n$; you can have no success at all, but you can't have more than n successes in the n trials. One can show that the probabilities that are associated with these $n + 1$ outcomes are given by

$$f(x) = P(X = x) = \frac{n!}{x!(n-x)!}\, \theta^x (1-\theta)^{n-x} \quad \text{for } x = 0, 1, 2, \ldots, n$$

where for an integer x, $x!$ ("x factorial") is defined as $x! = (x)(x-1)\cdots(1)$. For example, $3! = (3)(2)(1) = 6$ and $5! = (5)(4)(3)(2)(1) = 120$. By definition, $0! = 1$.

We refer to this probability assignment as the *binomial distribution*. The sample size n and the probability of success in a single trial, θ, are needed for the calculation of these probabilities. We call n and θ the parameters of the distribution.

Explanation: The following discussion should help you understand where binomial probabilities come from. If we carry out n trials and we want x successes, then we must have $n - x$ failures. What is the probability of getting x successes in a row? The probability of success in a single trial is θ; hence the probability of getting x successes in a row is $\theta \cdot \theta \cdots \theta = \theta^x$. Here we use the independence from one trial to the next, and the fact that for independent events the probabilities can be multiplied. We will explain this multiplication rule for probabilities in more detail in Section 8.10. As an example, consider $\theta = 0.05$, where θ is the probability of a defect. If we take one item from the assembly line, what is the probability that it is defective? The answer is 0.05. If we take two items, what is the probability that the first and the second one are defective? The probability is $(0.05)(0.05) = 0.0025$. What is the chance that the first three are defective? It is $(0.05)(0.05)(0.05)$, and so on.

Similarly, the probability of failure in a single trial is $(1 - \theta)$, and the probability of $n - x$ failures in a row is $(1-\theta)^{n-x}$. Because of independence, the probability of having x successes followed by $n - x$ failures is the product of the two probabilities: $\theta^x (1-\theta)^{n-x}$. This explains the second factor in the binomial probabilities. The first factor, the ratio involving factorials, arises because there are many ways of getting x successes and $n - x$ failures. You can get the successes first (followed by the failures); you can get the failures first (followed by the successes); you can start with $x - 1$ successes, follow this by $n - x$ failures, and end with another success; and so on. It turns out that the number of different ways one can arrange the x successes and the $n - x$ failures is exactly equal to this first factor. For illustration, consider flipping three fair coins, and consider X, the number of heads. You can get two heads ($x = 2$) three different ways: *HHT, HTH,* and *THH.* Since each of these three ways has probability (0.5)(0.5)(0.5), it follows that $P(X = 2) = (3)(0.5)^3 = 3/8$. You can check that you get this result from the above formula with $n = 3, \theta = 0.5$, and $x = 2$.

The *mean* of the binomial distribution is given by

$$\mu = n\theta.$$

This result is not surprising. If you conduct n trials and if the chance of success in a single trial is θ, then you can expect $n\theta$ successes among the n trials. Formally, you can show this result by multiplying each possible outcome with its binomial probability and by adding the resulting products over all possible outcomes. You will find, after some algebra, that $\mu = n\theta$.

The *standard deviation* of the binomial distribution is given by

$$\sigma = \sqrt{n\theta(1-\theta)}.$$

This result is obtained be substituting the binomial probabilities into the general equation for the standard deviation (see Section 8.2). While this is not very difficult, the algebra is somewhat tedious. For us it will suffice to remember the result.

EXAMPLE

A large lot of items includes 10 percent defectives. Thus, the chance of getting a defective item is $\theta = 0.10$; the chance of selecting a good item is $1 - \theta = 0.9$.

We are sampling ten items ($n = 10$). What is the chance of getting exactly two defectives? It is

$$P(X = 2) = \frac{10!}{2!\,8!}(0.1)^2(0.9)^8 = \frac{(9)(10)}{(1)(2)}(0.1)^2(0.9)^8 = 0.1937.$$

Furthermore, the chance of getting exactly one defective item among the ten sampled items is

$$P(X = 1) = \frac{10!}{1!\,9!}(0.1)^1(0.9)^9 = (10)(0.1)^1(0.9)^9 = 0.3874.$$

Similarly, we can calculate all other probabilities of this distribution. The resulting probabilities are given in Table 8.1 (page 196). A graph of the distribution is given in Figure 8.1. On the horizontal axis of this line graph we plot the possible outcomes; the probabilities of the outcomes are graphed on the vertical axis.

The probabilities of these basic events can be used to calculate the probability of related events. For example, the probability that we get at most one defective is

$$\begin{aligned} P(X \le 1) &= P(X = 0 \text{ or } X = 1) = P(X = 0) + P(X = 1) \\ &= 0.3487 + 0.3874 = 0.7361. \end{aligned}$$

The probability that we get at least one defective is

$$\begin{aligned} P(X \ge 1) &= P(X = 1) + P(X = 2) + P(X = 3) + \cdots + P(X = 10) \\ &= 0.3874 + 0.1937 + 0.0574 + 0.0112 + 0.0015 + 0.0001 + \cdots \\ &= 0.6513. \end{aligned}$$

TABLE 8.1 Binomial Probabilities $P(X = x)$ for $n = 10$ and $\theta = 0.1$

Outcomes x	$P(X = x)$
0	0.3487
1	0.3874
2	0.1937
3	0.0574
4	0.0112
5	0.0015
6	0.0001
7	0.0000
8	0.0000
9	0.0000
10	0.0000

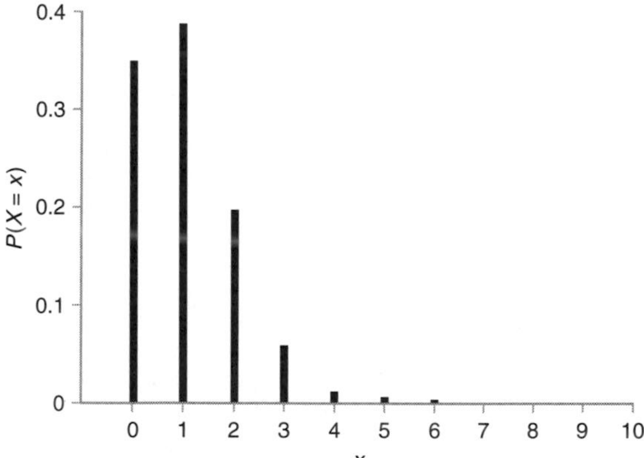

FIGURE 8.1 Binomial distribution for $n = 10$ and $\theta = 0.1$.

There is an alternative, and quicker, way to calculate this probability. Probabilities, summed over all possible outcomes, add to 1. The probability of an event and the probability of the complement of the event add to 1. Hence:

$$P(X \geq 1) = 1 - P(X < 1) = 1 - P(X = 0) = 1 - 0.3487 = 0.6513.$$

The mean of the binomial distribution with $n = 10$ and $\theta = 0.1$ is given by $\mu = (10)(0.1) = 1.0$. If we carry out 10 trials, and the success probability in a single trial is 0.1, then we expect one defective among a sample of 10 items. The standard deviation is

$$\sigma = \sqrt{(10)(0.1)(0.9)} = \sqrt{0.90} = 0.9487.$$

■

8.3.2 Tables of Binomial Probabilities

The probabilities of getting exactly x successes, $P(X = x; n, \theta)$, and the cumulative probabilities of getting x or fewer successes, $P(X \leq x; n, \theta)$, for all feasible values of x and for various parameter combinations of n and θ, are given in most introductory statistics textbooks. Furthermore, most statistical computer packages and spreadsheet programs include convenient functions that calculate binomial probabilities, usually individual probabilities as well as cumulative probabilities. Table 8.2 (page 198) gives the cumulative probabilities $P(X \leq x; n, \theta)$ for $n = 5$, 10 and 20 and θ from 0.05 to 0.50, in steps of 0.05. You can obtain the probabilities for θ larger than 0.50 by redefining success and failure; the binomial probability of obtaining x successes with success probability θ is the same as the probability of obtaining $n - x$ successes with success probability $1 - \theta$.

EXAMPLE

The chance that a good baseball batter connects with the ball is about $\theta = 0.3$. In a series of six games, our player has 20 at-bats. The chance that he has fewer than seven hits is

$$P(X < 7) = P(X \leq 6) = 0.608.$$

The chance that he has at least six hits (that is, six or more hits) is

$$P(X \geq 6) = 1 - P(X \leq 5) = 1 - 0.4164 = 0.5836.$$

We may be interested in the chance that he gets between five and eight hits:

$$P(5 \leq X \leq 8) = P(X \leq 8) - P(X \leq 4) = 0.8867 - 0.2375 = 0.6492.$$

One must be very careful about including and excluding the boundary values in probability calculations. For discrete distributions it makes a difference whether an endpoint is included.

How many hits do you expect? We expect $(20)(0.3) = 6.0$ hits among his 20 at-bats. The standard deviation is $\sigma = \sqrt{20(0.3)(0.7)} = \sqrt{4.20} = 2.05$ hits. ■

EXAMPLE

Consider the binomial distribution with $n = 20$ and $\theta = 0.5$: In this case

$$\mu = (20)(0.5) = 10$$

$$\sigma = \sqrt{(20)(0.5)(0.5)} = 2.24.$$

TABLE 8.2 Cumulative Binomial Probabilities $P(X \leq x; n, \theta)$ for $n = 5$, 10, and 20, and θ from 0.05 to 0.50

		θ									
n	x	0.05	0.10	0.15	0.20	0.25	0.30	0.35	0.40	0.45	0.50
5	0	0.7738	0.5905	0.4437	0.3277	0.2373	0.1681	0.1160	0.0778	0.0503	0.0312
	1	0.9774	0.9185	0.8352	0.7373	0.6328	0.5282	0.4284	0.3370	0.2562	0.1875
	2	0.9988	0.9914	0.9734	0.9421	0.8965	0.8369	0.7648	0.6826	0.5931	0.5000
	3	1.0000	0.9995	0.9978	0.9933	0.9844	0.9692	0.9460	0.9130	0.8688	0.8125
	4	1.0000	1.0000	0.9999	0.9997	0.9990	0.9976	0.9947	0.9898	0.9815	0.9688
	5	1.0000	1.0000	1.0000	1.0000	1.0000	1.0000	1.0000	1.0000	1.0000	1.0000
10	0	0.5987	0.3487	0.1969	0.1074	0.0563	0.0282	0.0135	0.0060	0.0025	0.0010
	1	0.9139	0.7361	0.5443	0.3758	0.2440	0.1493	0.0860	0.0464	0.0233	0.0107
	2	0.9885	0.9298	0.8202	0.6778	0.5256	0.3828	0.2616	0.1673	0.0996	0.0547
	3	0.9990	0.9872	0.9500	0.8791	0.7759	0.6496	0.5138	0.3823	0.2660	0.1719
	4	0.9999	0.9984	0.9901	0.9672	0.9219	0.8497	0.7515	0.6331	0.5044	0.3770
	5	1.0000	0.9999	0.9986	0.9936	0.9803	0.9527	0.9051	0.8338	0.7384	0.6230
	6	1.0000	1.0000	0.9999	0.9991	0.9965	0.9894	0.9740	0.9452	0.8980	0.8281
	7	1.0000	1.0000	1.0000	0.9999	0.9996	0.9984	0.9952	0.9877	0.9726	0.9453
	8	1.0000	1.0000	1.0000	1.0000	1.0000	0.9999	0.9995	0.9983	0.9955	0.9893
	9	1.0000	1.0000	1.0000	1.0000	1.0000	1.0000	1.0000	0.9999	0.9997	0.9990
	10	1.0000	1.0000	1.0000	1.0000	1.0000	1.0000	1.0000	1.0000	1.0000	1.0000
20	0	0.3585	0.1216	0.0388	0.0115	0.0032	0.0008	0.0002	0.0000	0.0000	0.0000
	1	0.7358	0.3917	0.1756	0.0692	0.0243	0.0076	0.0021	0.0005	0.0001	0.0000
	2	0.9245	0.6769	0.4049	0.2061	0.0913	0.0355	0.0121	0.0036	0.0009	0.0002
	3	0.9841	0.8670	0.6477	0.4114	0.2252	0.1071	0.0444	0.0160	0.0049	0.0013
	4	0.9974	0.9568	0.8298	0.6296	0.4148	0.2375	0.1182	0.0510	0.0189	0.0059
	5	0.9997	0.9887	0.9327	0.8042	0.6172	0.4164	0.2454	0.1256	0.0553	0.0207
	6	1.0000	0.9976	0.9781	0.9133	0.7858	0.6080	0.4166	0.2500	0.1299	0.0577
	7	1.0000	0.9996	0.9941	0.9679	0.8982	0.7723	0.6010	0.4159	0.2520	0.1316
	8	1.0000	0.9999	0.9987	0.9900	0.9591	0.8867	0.7624	0.5956	0.4143	0.2517
	9	1.0000	1.0000	0.9998	0.9974	0.9861	0.9520	0.8782	0.7553	0.5914	0.4119
	10	1.0000	1.0000	1.0000	0.9994	0.9961	0.9829	0.9468	0.8725	0.7507	0.5881
	11	1.0000	1.0000	1.0000	0.9999	0.9991	0.9949	0.9804	0.9435	0.8692	0.7483
	12	1.0000	1.0000	1.0000	1.0000	0.9998	0.9987	0.9940	0.9790	0.9420	0.8684
	13	1.0000	1.0000	1.0000	1.0000	1.0000	0.9997	0.9985	0.9935	0.9786	0.9423
	14	1.0000	1.0000	1.0000	1.0000	1.0000	1.0000	0.9997	0.9984	0.9936	0.9793
	15	1.0000	1.0000	1.0000	1.0000	1.0000	1.0000	1.0000	0.9997	0.9985	0.9941
	16	1.0000	1.0000	1.0000	1.0000	1.0000	1.0000	1.0000	1.0000	0.9997	0.9987
	17	1.0000	1.0000	1.0000	1.0000	1.0000	1.0000	1.0000	1.0000	1.0000	0.9998
	18	1.0000	1.0000	1.0000	1.0000	1.0000	1.0000	1.0000	1.0000	1.0000	1.0000

Subtract two standard deviations from the mean ($\mu - 2\sigma = 5.52$) and add two standard deviations to the mean ($\mu + 2\sigma = 14.48$). What is the chance that X will lie between these two values?

$$P(\mu - 2\sigma \leq X \leq \mu + 2\sigma) = P(5.52 \leq X \leq 14.48) = P(6 \leq X \leq 14)$$
$$= P(X \leq 14) - P(X \leq 5) = 0.9793 - 0.0207 = 0.9586.$$

This is a very useful result. We have seen this type of rule before (in Chapter 7) when we discussed data. The above result says that roughly 95 percent of the probability distribution of this particular binomial distribution lies within two standard deviations of the mean. This 95 percent rule holds for many distributions. For binomial distributions, this rule works best if the distribution is symmetric (θ around 0.50) and if n is reasonably large. ■

8.4 THE POISSON DISTRIBUTION

EXAMPLE 1

Calls at the University switchboard come in at a rate of four calls per minute. What is the probability that we get exactly six calls within the next minute? What is the probability that we get more than six calls? ■

EXAMPLE 2

The machine that fills toothpaste tubes jams on average three times during a shift. Today's shift experienced nine jams. Is this finding consistent with our prior experience? What is the probability that a shift experiences nine or more jams? ■

8.4.1 Poisson Probabilities

Consider the following situation. Let X stand for the *number of successes within a certain interval.* This could be the number of calls per minute arriving at the switchboard, the number of machine jams per shift, the number of fatal accidents per quarter on Iowa rural Interstates, the yearly number of plane crashes in the United States, and so on. It turns out that the Poisson distribution provides a good model for their distribution; more discussion of this will be given shortly.

The possible outcomes for X are: $x = 0, 1, 2, \ldots$, that is, every possible nonnegative integer. The Poisson probabilities are given by

$$P(X = x) = \frac{\lambda^x}{x!}e^{-\lambda} \quad \text{for } x = 0, 1, 2, \ldots$$

where λ is the parameter of the Poisson distribution, $e = 2.718$ (approximately) is Euler's number, and "x factorial" is $x! = (x)(x-1)\cdots(1)$. That is,

$$P(X=0) = e^{-\lambda}$$
$$P(X=1) = (\lambda)e^{-\lambda}$$
$$P(X=2) = (0.5)(\lambda)^2 e^{-\lambda}$$
$$\ldots$$

It can be shown, by substituting the Poisson probabilities into the general expression for the mean of a discrete distribution, that the mean of the Poisson distribution is given by

$$\mu = \lambda.$$

This result helps us interpret the parameter λ, as we now see that the parameter of the Poisson distribution stands for the mean of the distribution.

Similarly, we can show that the standard deviation of the Poisson distribution is

$$\sigma = \sqrt{\lambda}.$$

EXAMPLE 1 *(continued)*

Calls at the University switchboard arrive at an average rate of four calls a minute. That is, the mean number of calls in a one-minute interval is $\lambda = 4$.

The probability that we get exactly six calls within the next minute can be calculated from the Poisson distribution

$$P(X=6) = \frac{(4)^6}{6!}e^{-4} = 0.104.$$

The probability that we get more than six calls during the next minute is

$$P(X>6) = 1 - P(X \le 6) = 1 - [P(X=0) + \cdots + P(X=6)]$$
$$= 1 - 0.889 = 0.111.$$

You can calculate these probabilities with a calculator, or you can look them up in tables. Or, you can calculate them using statistical computer software. Most statistical computer packages and spreadsheet programs have functions that calculate individual and cumulative Poisson probabilities. In Table 8.3 (pages 202, 203) we have given a table of cumulative Poisson probabilities $P(X \le x; \lambda)$ for λ between 0.1 and 6. You can check that for $\lambda = 4, P(X \le 6) = 0.889$.

Similarly, the probability that between three and six calls (inclusive) arrive at the switchboard is

$$P(3 \le X \le 6) = P(X \le 6) - P(X \le 2) = 0.889 - 0.238 = 0.651.$$

■

EXAMPLE 2 *(continued)*

Assuming that the number of jams per shift has a Poisson distribution with parameter (mean) $\lambda = 3$, the probability of getting nine or more jams is

$$P(X \geq 9) = 1 - P(X \leq 8) = 1 - 0.996 = 0.004.$$

This probability is very small. Getting nine or more jams within a single shift is a very unlikely event, and such an event would make it very doubtful that the current process has stayed stable. Something unusual must have happened. ■

8.4.2 Justification of the Poisson Distribution

The Poisson distribution is also called the distribution of *rare events*. One can show that the binomial distribution with large n (that is, many trials) and small θ (that is, rare events) is well approximated by the Poisson distribution with parameter (mean) $\lambda = n\theta$. Exercise 8.12 will convince you that the approximation is quite good. Consider the quarterly number of fatal accidents on Iowa rural Interstates. There are many drivers (and many miles driven), and each driver has a very small probability of being involved in a fatal accident; hence it is not surprising that the Poisson distribution provides a good approximation for the number of fatal accidents.

There is yet another way to justify the Poisson distribution. Divide the time interval (for example, the shift in our example regarding the number of jams) into many small nonoverlapping subintervals and make the following, and very reasonable, assumptions: Assume that the chance of getting exactly one success (that is, one jam) within a small subinterval of time is proportional to the length of the interval, and suppose that the chance of getting two or more successes within that small interval is essentially zero. Moreover, assume that successes occur independently; the fact that you just observed a success in one interval does not influence the likelihood of getting a success in the next one. This setup implies that you are adding up the number of successes over many such intervals (that is, n large), where the probability of a success in each one of these intervals is very small (as the width of the interval is small). Under these conditions the number of successes within the given time interval follows a Poisson distribution.

8.5 USE OF THE BINOMIAL AND THE POISSON DISTRIBUTIONS

The binomial and Poisson distributions provide the theory behind the control limits in the p- and c-control charts. We will say more about those when we discuss control charts in Chapter 12.

These distributions also arise in sampling inspection, as the following example illustrates. A sample inspection plan may ask you to take a sample of 200 items

TABLE 8.3 Cumulative Poisson Probabilities $P(X \leq x; \lambda)$, for Feasible x and Various Values of λ between 0.1 and 6.0

	λ									
x	0.1	0.2	0.3	0.4	0.5	0.6	0.7	0.8	0.9	1.0
0	0.905	0.819	0.741	0.670	0.607	0.549	0.497	0.449	0.407	0.368
1	0.995	0.982	0.963	0.938	0.910	0.878	0.844	0.809	0.772	0.736
2	1.000	0.999	0.996	0.992	0.986	0.977	0.966	0.953	0.937	0.920
3	1.000	1.000	1.000	0.999	0.998	0.997	0.994	0.991	0.987	0.981
4	1.000	1.000	1.000	1.000	1.000	1.000	0.999	0.999	0.998	0.996
5	1.000	1.000	1.000	1.000	1.000	1.000	1.000	1.000	1.000	0.999
6	1.000	1.000	1.000	1.000	1.000	1.000	1.000	1.000	1.000	1.000
x	1.1	1.2	1.3	1.4	1.5	1.6	1.7	1.8	1.9	2.0
0	0.333	0.301	0.273	0.247	0.223	0.202	0.183	0.165	0.150	0.135
1	0.699	0.663	0.627	0.592	0.558	0.525	0.493	0.463	0.434	0.406
2	0.900	0.879	0.857	0.833	0.809	0.783	0.757	0.731	0.704	0.677
3	0.974	0.966	0.957	0.946	0.934	0.921	0.907	0.891	0.875	0.857
4	0.995	0.992	0.989	0.986	0.981	0.976	0.970	0.964	0.956	0.947
5	0.999	0.998	0.998	0.997	0.996	0.994	0.992	0.990	0.987	0.983
6	1.000	1.000	1.000	0.999	0.999	0.999	0.998	0.997	0.997	0.995
7	1.000	1.000	1.000	1.000	1.000	1.000	1.000	0.999	0.999	0.999
8	1.000	1.000	1.000	1.000	1.000	1.000	1.000	1.000	1.000	1.000
x	2.2	2.4	2.6	2.8	3.0	3.2	3.4	3.6	3.8	4.0
0	0.111	0.091	0.074	0.061	0.050	0.041	0.033	0.027	0.022	0.018
1	0.355	0.308	0.267	0.231	0.199	0.171	0.147	0.126	0.107	0.092
2	0.623	0.570	0.518	0.469	0.423	0.380	0.340	0.303	0.269	0.238
3	0.819	0.779	0.736	0.692	0.647	0.603	0.558	0.515	0.473	0.433
4	0.928	0.904	0.877	0.848	0.815	0.781	0.744	0.706	0.668	0.629
5	0.975	0.964	0.951	0.935	0.916	0.895	0.871	0.844	0.816	0.785
6	0.993	0.988	0.983	0.976	0.966	0.955	0.942	0.927	0.909	0.889
7	0.998	0.997	0.995	0.992	0.988	0.983	0.977	0.969	0.960	0.949
8	1.000	0.999	0.999	0.998	0.996	0.994	0.992	0.988	0.984	0.979
9	1.000	1.000	1.000	0.999	0.999	0.998	0.997	0.996	0.994	0.992
10	1.000	1.000	1.000	1.000	1.000	1.000	0.999	0.999	0.998	0.997
11	1.000	1.000	1.000	1.000	1.000	1.000	1.000	1.000	0.999	0.999
12	1.000	1.000	1.000	1.000	1.000	1.000	1.000	1.000	1.000	1.000

(continues)

TABLE 8.3 (*continued*)

	λ									
x	4.2	4.4	4.6	4.8	5.0	5.2	5.4	5.6	5.8	6.0
0	0.015	0.012	0.010	0.008	0.007	0.006	0.005	0.004	0.003	0.002
1	0.078	0.066	0.056	0.048	0.040	0.034	0.029	0.024	0.021	0.017
2	0.210	0.185	0.163	0.143	0.125	0.109	0.095	0.082	0.072	0.062
3	0.395	0.359	0.326	0.294	0.265	0.238	0.213	0.191	0.170	0.151
4	0.590	0.551	0.513	0.476	0.440	0.406	0.373	0.342	0.313	0.285
5	0.753	0.720	0.686	0.651	0.616	0.581	0.546	0.512	0.478	0.446
6	0.867	0.844	0.818	0.791	0.762	0.732	0.702	0.670	0.638	0.606
7	0.936	0.921	0.905	0.887	0.867	0.845	0.822	0.797	0.771	0.744
8	0.972	0.964	0.955	0.944	0.932	0.918	0.903	0.886	0.867	0.847
9	0.989	9.985	0.980	0.975	0.968	0.960	0.951	0.941	0.929	0.916
10	0.996	0.994	0.992	0.990	0.986	0.982	0.977	0.972	0.965	0.957
11	0.999	0.998	0.997	0.996	0.995	0.993	0.990	0.988	0.984	0.980
12	1.000	0.999	0.999	0.999	0.998	0.997	0.996	0.995	0.993	0.991
13	1.000	1.000	1.000	1.000	0.999	0.999	0.999	0.998	0.997	0.996
14	1.000	1.000	1.000	1.000	1.000	1.000	0.999	0.999	0.999	0.999
15	1.000	1.000	1.000	1.000	1.000	1.000	1.000	1.000	1.000	0.999
16	1.000	1.000	1.000	1.000	1.000	1.000	1.000	1.000	1.000	1.000

from a large lot of items (say 10,000 elements, or more), and direct you to accept the lot if your sample contains six or fewer defectives. The number 6 is called the *acceptable number of defectives* of the sample inspection plan; we denote it by $Ac = 6$. The lot is also referred to as the population from which the items are selected.

What is the probability of accepting the lot if the allowable fraction of defectives in the lot is 2.5 percent ($\theta = 0.025$)? We need to study the distribution of the number of defectives among the 200 items that are selected from the lot. We can think of this as carrying out $n = 200$ trials with a single trial success probability $\theta = 0.025$, and keeping track of the number of successes (defects). This fits the binomial framework, with one minor difference: The binomial assumptions specify independence among trials. In the sampling inspection this isn't exactly true, as a selected item is not returned to the lot, and hence is not eligible for the next draws. However, for reasonably large lots (the lot of 10,000 items in our illustration is certainly very large) this will make no difference and we can safely use the binomial probabilities.

In sampling inspection situations the assumed probability of a defect in the lot is usually quite small (such as 0.025 in our example) and the sample sizes are reasonably large ($n = 200$ in our case). Hence we can use the Poisson distribution as an approximation for the distribution of the number of defectives X. The parameter of the Poisson distribution is $\lambda = (200)(0.025) = 5$. Thus the probability of accepting the lot (that is, the probability of getting six or fewer defectives) is

$$P(X \leq 6; \lambda = n\theta = (200)(0.025) = 5) = 0.762.$$

That is, in 76 percent of the cases our sample inspection plan accepts a lot with an acceptable fraction of defectives of $\theta = 0.025$. But, this result implies that in 24 percent of the cases we reject a satisfactory lot. This latter probability is called the *producer's risk*. If you are the producer, you will think that this risk of 24 percent is certainly too high.

Similarly, we can obtain the probabilities of acceptance for lots that have higher (undesired) levels of defectives. The probability of acceptance as a function of the fraction of defectives is called the *operating characteristic curve* of the sampling plan. For our sampling plan the operating characteristic curve is given by $OC(\theta) = P(X \leq 6; \theta)$. Here we evaluate this function for several values of θ:

$$OC(\theta = 0.01) = P(X \leq 6; \lambda = n\theta = 2) = 0.995$$
$$OC(\theta = 0.025) = P(X \leq 6; \lambda = n\theta = 5) = 0.762$$
$$OC(\theta = 0.05) = P(X \leq 6; \lambda = n\theta = 10) = 0.130.$$

The last probability, for example, indicates that there is a 13 percent chance that a bad lot with 5 percent defectives will slip by our inspection. This probability, also called the *consumer's risk*, may be unacceptably high for the consumer who is satisfied with $\theta = 0.025$ but unhappy with $\theta = 0.05$.

How can we get a better sampling plan that doesn't reject very often if the production is acceptable, and that rejects most of the time if the production is poor? Note that the operating characteristic curve changes with different sample sizes n and acceptable numbers Ac. Thus we can select n and Ac such that we get a desired operating characteristic curve. We will say more on this topic in Chapter 11 when we discuss sample inspection.

8.6 CONTINUOUS RANDOM VARIABLES AND CONTINUOUS DISTRIBUTIONS

Data on dimensions such as the length and the width of a product, the fill weight of tubes, or the temperature of a process is continuous in nature. Continuous variables can take on any value in an interval. In this section we discuss distributions for continuous random variables. The *normal distribution* is described in detail.

We show how to calculate the proportion of (normally) distributed items that fall within specified limits, and the proportion of items that exceed certain values. For example, attaining the correct fill weight is a concern of all filling operations: Assume that the required fill weight for a tube of toothpaste is 2.7 ounces, but that the actual fill weight varies; suppose that the standard deviation of repeated fill weights is 0.05 ounce. In order to be on the safe side, the operator overfills on average and sets the mean fill weight of the filling process at 2.8 ounces.

Two questions are relevant: (1) What is the proportion of tubes that are still underfilled? That is, what is the probability that the fill weight is less than the required 2.7 ounces? (2) What is that extra material, which we give away by setting the process mean at 2.8, costing the company and how can we reduce the amount of that material? The cost not only involves the extra material given to each customer, but also reflects the fact that customers do not need to buy the product quite as often.

In order to introduce the concept of a probability distribution of a continuous random variable, let us consider the following illustration. Assume that we have obtained a very large set of measurements on fill weight, say measurements on 1,000 tubes. In Chapter 7 we learned how to construct histograms. We divided the range of fill weight into nonoverlapping intervals (with so many measurements it is certainly possible to consider many narrow intervals), determined the relative frequencies, and displayed the relative frequencies in the form of a bar chart (that is, a histogram). One can go one step further and normalize the histogram such that the area under the histogram is 1. This is easily done: One divides the relative frequency of each interval by the width of that interval, and displays this ratio on the y-axis of the bar chart. This ratio is called the density, and the resulting histogram is called a *density histogram*. In a density histogram the area of the bar over an interval, that is the product of (relative frequency/width) times (width), represents the relative frequency, and we know that the sum of the relative frequencies, and hence the sum of the areas of these bars, is 1. As the size of the data set becomes larger and the width of each interval is taken smaller, the density histogram becomes smoother and smoother in appearance, and eventually we are looking at a smooth curve. Because of the normalization, the area under the smooth curve is 1. We call this curve a *probability density function* and we denote it by $f(x)$. Figure 8.2 gives a picture of such a curve.

The area under this curve between the vertical lines at $x = a$ and $x = b$ is the proportion of the distribution that falls between $x = a$ and $x = b$. It expresses the

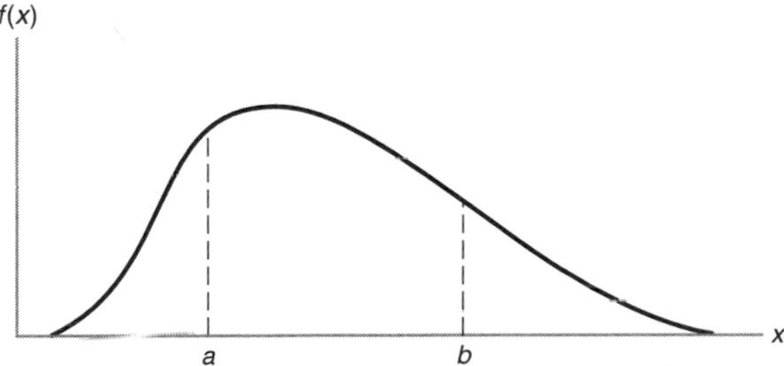

FIGURE 8.2 A probability density of a continuous random variable. The area under the curve is 1.

probability, $P(a \leq X \leq b)$, that a randomly selected item from this distribution will fall within the interval from a to b. Why don't you guess at the probability depicted in the above figure? It is somewhere around 0.60 (or 60 percent).

Areas under the probability density function represent probabilities. It is just as easy to obtain the percentiles of a distribution from the graph of the density function. If $P(X \leq a) = p$, where p is a number between 0 and 1, then we say that a is the *(100p)th percentile* of the distribution. Guessing from Figure 8.2, the value a is roughly the 20th percentile of the distribution.

8.7 THE UNIFORM DISTRIBUTION

Let us consider measurements that can only vary between c and d (where $c < d$) and let us assume that each value in that interval is equally likely to occur. This describes the *uniform distribution* on the interval from c to d. Its probability density function is given by

$$\begin{aligned} f(x) &= 1/(d-c) \quad \text{for } x \text{ between } c \text{ and } d, \\ &= 0 \quad \text{otherwise.} \end{aligned}$$

It is easy to check that the area under the curve is 1. A graph of this probability function is given in Figure 8.3.

The mean of this distribution is $\mu = (c + d)/2$. This is a very intuitive result; the mean is the point in the middle of the interval into which the random variable X can fall. Furthermore, one can show that the standard deviation of this distribution is given by $\sigma = (d - c)/\sqrt{12}$.

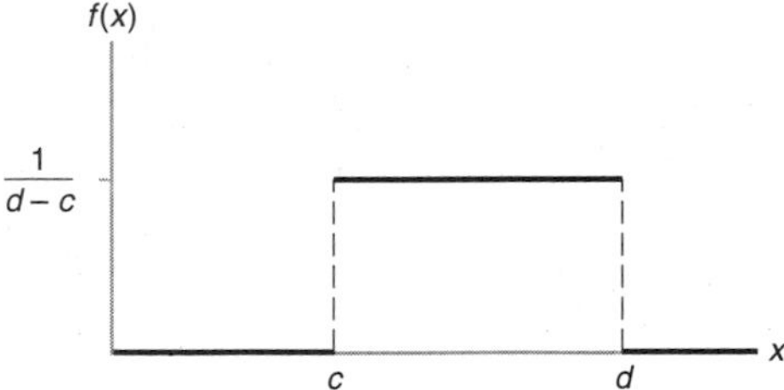

FIGURE 8.3 Probability density function of the uniform distribution on the interval from c to d.

EXAMPLE

Consider the uniform distribution between $c = 0$ and $d = 1$:

$$\begin{aligned} f(x) &= 1 \quad \text{for } 0 \leq x \leq 1 \\ &= 0 \quad \text{for } x \text{ outside the interval from 0 to 1.} \end{aligned}$$

The mean of this distribution is $\mu = 0.5$, and the standard deviation is $\sigma = 1/\sqrt{12}$. Probabilities can be calculated as the areas of relevant rectangles. For example,

$$P(0.2 < X < 0.4) = (1)(0.4 - 0.2) = 0.20,$$
$$P(X < 0.7) = (1)(0.7) = 0.70,$$
$$P(X > 0.1) = (1)(0.9) = 0.90.$$

Furthermore,

$$P(X = 0.1) = 0.$$

With continuous random variables there is no width to an interval of a single point; hence the last probability is zero. This result implies that for continuous random variables it does not matter whether we include or exclude the boundary value. For discrete random variables the situation is different. There it matters, and one has to be very careful about endpoints; the probability that a discrete random variable X exceeds six may well be different from the probability that X is six or larger.

You may think that the result, $P(X = x) = 0$ for the outcome x of a continuous random variable X, is very surprising. However, note that any continuously varying number x will always be rounded. For example, with rounding to three decimal points the number 0.234 stands for all values between 0.2335 and 0.2345. Hence the number 0.234 is represented by an interval of width 0.001, and the probability of X falling within that interval is certainly nonzero. ■

8.8 THE NORMAL DISTRIBUTION

The normal distribution with its characteristic bell-shaped probability density function is the most important distribution in statistics. It turns out that the distributions of many measurements are well-approximated by a normal distribution. We saw this in Chapter 7, where several histograms had such a characteristic bell-shaped appearance. An explanation of this useful fact is given in Chapter 10, when we discuss the Central Limit Effect.

The normal distribution is characterized by two values: its mean μ and its standard deviation σ. These are called the parameters of the distribution.

The probability density function is shown in Figure 8.4 (page 208). The distribution is *symmetric* around the mean, which is also its median; values below the mean are as likely as values above the mean. The density is *unimodal* with a single peak at the mean, and it has a very characteristic bell-shaped form. We could write down an algebraic equation for this function; however this information is not really needed for our subsequent discussion.

The standard deviation σ controls the spread of the distribution. Most of the distribution lies in the interval from $\mu - 2\sigma$ to $\mu + 2\sigma$; in fact 95 percent of the distribution is within two standard deviations of the mean. About 2/3 of the

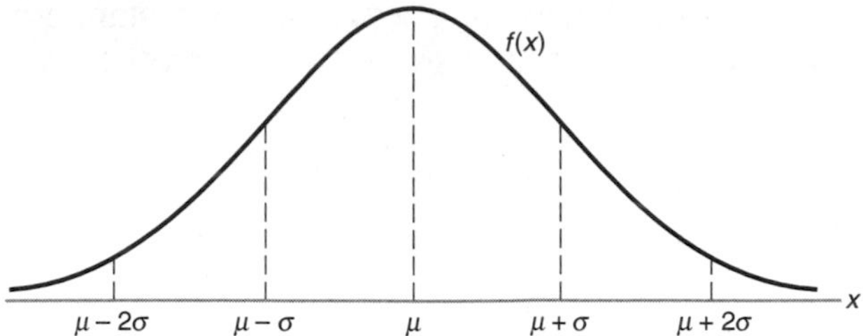

FIGURE 8.4 Probability density function of the normal distribution.

distribution lies between $\mu - \sigma$ and $\mu + \sigma$, and 99.7 percent of the distribution is between $\mu - 3\sigma$ and $\mu + 3\sigma$.

8.8.1 The Standard Normal Distribution with Mean 0 and Standard Deviation 1

The *standard normal distribution* is a normal distribution with mean 0 and standard deviation 1. We use uppercase Z to denote a standard normal random variable. A graph of its probability density function is given in Figure 8.5. The distribution is centered at zero. Most of the probability is over the area from -3 to $+3$.

How do we calculate probabilities for this distribution? For example, what is $P(Z < 0)$? The answer comes easily when we look at the graph in Figure 8.5. We need to obtain the area under the curve that lies to the left of the vertical line at 0 (remember, for continuous random variables it does not matter whether 0 is included or not). Since the distribution is symmetric and since the area under a probability density function is always 1, this area is 0.5. Thus, $P(Z < 0) = 0.5$.

What about $P(Z < 0.7)$? It should be larger than 0.5, but by how much? To answer this, one needs to calculate the area under the curve up to the point 0.7. We haven't given you the mathematical expression for the density function of a standard normal random variable, and even if we had, it would be difficult to carry out the calculation; the calculation would involve numerical integration. Fortunately, the calculation is not necessary as areas under this curve have been tabulated. Table 8.4 (pages 210–211) gives the cumulative probabilities, $P(Z < z)$, of the

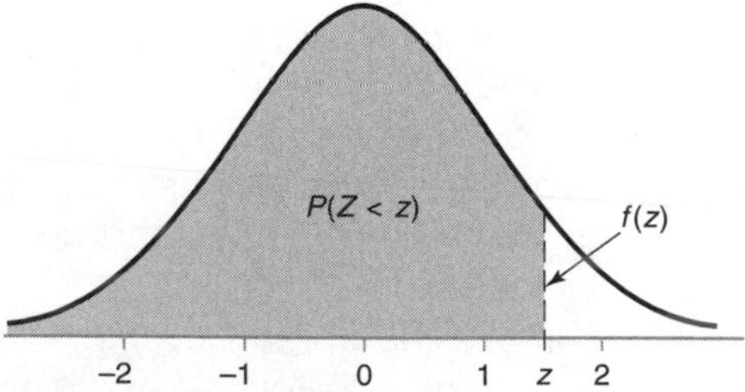

FIGURE 8.5 Probability density function of the standard normal distribution.

standard normal distribution. Statistical computer software and most spreadsheet programs include routines for calculating these probabilities.

The following examples illustrate the use of this table (note that it does not matter whether endpoints of the intervals are included):

$$P(Z < -0.6) = 0.2743,$$
$$P(Z > -0.6) = 1 - P(Z < -0.6) = 1 - 0.2743 = 0.7257.$$

The probability $P(Z > -0.6)$ is not a cumulative probability, and we cannot use the entries in Table 8.4 directly. Here we have used the fact that the probability of an event and the probability of the complement of the event add to 1. Also,

$$P(Z > 0.7) = 1 - P(Z < 0.7) = 1 - 0.7580 = 0.2420,$$
$$P(0.4 < Z < 1.2) = P(Z < 1.2) - P(Z < 0.4) = 0.8849 - 0.6554 = 0.2295.$$

We get this last probability by first determining $P(Z < 1.2)$, which represents the area to the left of 1.2, and then subtracting $P(Z < 0.4)$, which is the area to the left of 0.4; the difference represents the area under the curve from 0.4 to 1.2. The result implies that the chance of selecting an item with measurement somewhere between 0.4 and 1.2 is 22.95 percent. Furthermore,

$$\begin{aligned} P(-0.42 < Z < 1.23) &= P(Z < 1.23) - P(Z < -0.42) \\ &= 0.8907 - 0.3372 = 0.5535. \end{aligned}$$

Whenever you are in doubt on how to look up the relevant areas, we recommend that you draw a picture first.

The percentiles of the standard normal distribution can also be looked up in Table 8.4. For example, the 50th percentile is 0.00, the 95th percentile is 1.645, the 5th percentile is −1.645, the 97.5th percentile is 1.96, the 99th percentile is 2.326, and so on. You find these numbers by fixing the desired probability in the body of the table, and then locating the cutoff value in the margins of the table that lead to the desired probability.

8.8.2 Probability Calculations for the General Normal Distribution

Let us now calculate probabilities about a random variable X that follows a general normal distribution with mean μ and standard deviation σ. For example, let us calculate the probability $P(a < X < b)$. We reduce this to a problem involving a standard normal distribution by standardizing the limits in the inequality. That is,

$$\begin{aligned} P(a < X < b) &= P\left(\frac{a-\mu}{\sigma} < \frac{X-\mu}{\sigma} < \frac{b-\mu}{\sigma}\right) \\ &= P\left(\frac{a-\mu}{\sigma} < Z < \frac{b-\mu}{\sigma}\right) \end{aligned}$$

TABLE 8.4 Tables of the Probabilities $P(Z < z)$ for the Standard Normal Distribution

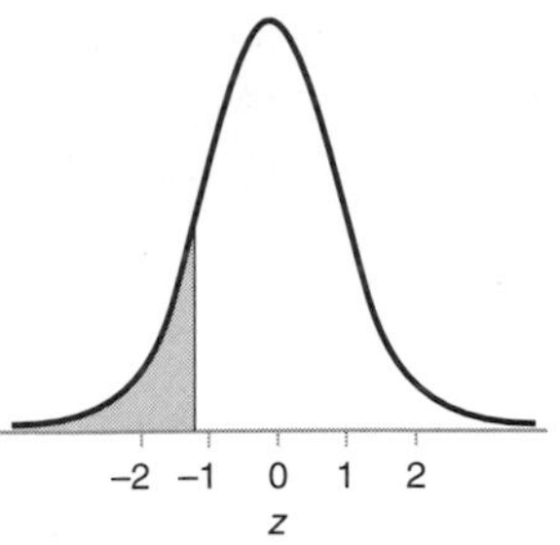

Normal Distribution Table (Each entry is the total area under the standard normal curve to the left of z, which is specified to two decimal places by joining the row value to the column value.)

z	0.00	0.01	0.02	0.03	0.04	0.05	0.06	0.07	0.08	0.09
−3.9	0.0000	0.0000	0.0000	0.0000	0.0000	0.0000	0.0000	0.0000	0.0000	0.0000
−3.8	0.0001	0.0001	0.0001	0.0001	0.0001	0.0001	0.0001	0.0001	0.0001	0.0001
−3.7	0.0001	0.0001	0.0001	0.0001	0.0001	0.0001	0.0001	0.0001	0.0001	0.0001
−3.6	0.0002	0.0002	0.0001	0.0001	0.0001	0.0001	0.0001	0.0001	0.0001	0.0001
−3.5	0.0002	0.0002	0.0002	0.0002	0.0002	0.0002	0.0002	0.0002	0.0002	0.0002
−3.4	0.0003	0.0003	0.0003	0.0003	0.0003	0.0003	0.0003	0.0003	0.0003	0.0002
−3.3	0.0005	0.0005	0.0005	0.0004	0.0004	0.0004	0.0004	0.0004	0.0004	0.0003
−3.2	0.0007	0.0007	0.0006	0.0006	0.0006	0.0006	0.0006	0.0005	0.0005	0.0005
−3.1	0.0010	0.0009	0.0009	0.0009	0.0008	0.0008	0.0008	0.0008	0.0007	0.0007
−3.0	0.0013	0.0013	0.0013	0.0012	0.0012	0.0011	0.0011	0.0011	0.0010	0.0010
−2.9	0.0019	0.0018	0.0018	0.0017	0.0016	0.0016	0.0015	0.0015	0.0014	0.0014
−2.8	0.0026	0.0025	0.0024	0.0023	0.0023	0.0022	0.0021	0.0021	0.0020	0.0019
−2.7	0.0035	0.0034	0.0033	0.0032	0.0031	0.0030	0.0029	0.0028	0.0027	0.0026
−2.6	0.0047	0.0045	0.0044	0.0043	0.0041	0.0040	0.0039	0.0038	0.0037	0.0036
−2.5	0.0062	0.0060	0.0059	0.0057	0.0055	0.0054	0.0052	0.0051	0.0049	0.0048
−2.4	0.0082	0.0080	0.0078	0.0075	0.0073	0.0071	0.0069	0.0068	0.0066	0.0064
−2.3	0.0107	0.0104	0.0102	0.0099	0.0096	0.0094	0.0091	0.0089	0.0087	0.0084
−2.2	0.0139	0.0136	0.0132	0.0129	0.0125	0.0122	0.0119	0.0116	0.0113	0.0110
−2.1	0.0179	0.0174	0.0170	0.0166	0.0162	0.0158	0.0154	0.0150	0.0146	0.0143
−2.0	0.0228	0.0222	0.0217	0.0212	0.0207	0.0202	0.0197	0.0192	0.0188	0.0183
−1.9	0.0287	0.0281	0.0274	0.0268	0.0262	0.0256	0.0250	0.0244	0.0239	0.0233
−1.8	0.0359	0.0351	0.0344	0.0336	0.0329	0.0322	0.0314	0.0307	0.0301	0.0294
−1.7	0.0446	0.0436	0.0427	0.0418	0.0409	0.0401	0.0392	0.0384	0.0375	0.0367
−1.6	0.0548	0.0537	0.0526	0.0516	0.0505	0.0495	0.0485	0.0475	0.0465	0.0455
−1.5	0.0668	0.0655	0.0643	0.0630	0.0618	0.0606	0.0594	0.0582	0.0571	0.0559
−1.4	0.0808	0.0793	0.0778	0.0764	0.0749	0.0735	0.0721	0.0708	0.0694	0.0681
−1.3	0.0968	0.0951	0.0934	0.0918	0.0901	0.0885	0.0869	0.0853	0.0838	0.0823
−1.2	0.1151	0.1131	0.1112	0.1093	0.1075	0.1056	0.1038	0.1020	0.1003	0.0985
−1.1	0.1357	0.1335	0.1314	0.1292	0.1271	0.1251	0.1230	0.1210	0.1190	0.1170
−1.0	0.1587	0.1562	0.1539	0.1515	0.1492	0.1469	0.1446	0.1423	0.1401	0.1379
−0.9	0.1841	0.1814	0.1788	0.1762	0.1736	0.1711	0.1685	0.1660	0.1635	0.1611
−0.8	0.2119	0.2090	0.2061	0.2033	0.2005	0.1977	0.1949	0.1921	0.1894	0.1867
−0.7	0.2420	0.2389	0.2358	0.2327	0.2296	0.2266	0.2236	0.2206	0.2177	0.2148
−0.6	0.2743	0.2709	0.2676	0.2643	0.2611	0.2578	0.2546	0.2514	0.2483	0.2451
−0.5	0.3085	0.3050	0.3015	0.2981	0.2946	0.2912	0.2877	0.2843	0.2810	0.2776
−0.4	0.3446	0.3409	0.3372	0.3336	0.3300	0.3264	0.3228	0.3192	0.3156	0.3121
−0.3	0.3821	0.3783	0.3745	0.3707	0.3669	0.3632	0.3594	0.3557	0.3520	0.3483
−0.2	0.4207	0.4168	0.4129	0.4090	0.4052	0.4013	0.3974	0.3936	0.3897	0.3859
−0.1	0.4602	0.4562	0.4522	0.4483	0.4443	0.4404	0.4364	0.4325	0.4286	0.4247
−0.0	0.5000	0.4960	0.4920	0.4880	0.4840	0.4801	0.4761	0.4721	0.4681	0.4641

(continues)

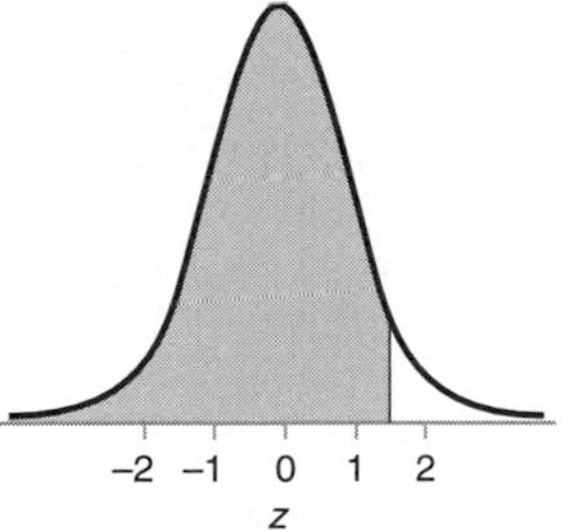

Normal Distribution Table (Each entry is the total area under the standard normal curve to the left of z, which is specified to two decimal places by joining the row value to the column value.)

z	0.00	0.01	0.02	0.03	0.04	0.05	0.06	0.07	0.08	0.09
0.0	0.5000	0.5040	0.5080	0.5120	0.5160	0.5199	0.5239	0.5279	0.5319	0.5359
0.1	0.5398	0.5438	0.5478	0.5517	0.5557	0.5596	0.5636	0.5675	0.5714	0.5753
0.2	0.5793	0.5832	0.5871	0.5910	0.5948	0.5987	0.6026	0.6064	0.6103	0.6141
0.3	0.6179	0.6217	0.6255	0.6293	0.6331	0.6368	0.6406	0.6443	0.6480	0.6517
0.4	0.6554	0.6591	0.6628	0.6664	0.6700	0.6736	0.6772	0.6808	0.6844	0.6879
0.5	0.6915	0.6950	0.6985	0.7019	0.7054	0.7088	0.7123	0.7157	0.7190	0.7224
0.6	0.7257	0.7291	0.7324	0.7357	0.7389	0.7422	0.7454	0.7486	0.7517	0.7549
0.7	0.7580	0.7611	0.7642	0.7673	0.7704	0.7734	0.7764	0.7794	0.7823	0.7852
0.8	0.7881	0.7910	0.7939	0.7967	0.7995	0.8023	0.8051	0.8078	0.8106	0.8133
0.9	0.8159	0.8186	0.8212	0.8238	0.8264	0.8289	0.8315	0.8340	0.8365	0.8389
1.0	0.8413	0.8438	0.8461	0.8485	0.8508	0.8531	0.8554	0.8577	0.8599	0.8621
1.1	0.8643	0.8665	0.8686	0.8708	0.8729	0.8749	0.8770	0.8790	0.8810	0.8830
1.2	0.8849	0.8869	0.8888	0.8907	0.8925	0.8944	0.8962	0.8980	0.8997	0.9015
1.3	0.9032	0.9049	0.9066	0.9082	0.9099	0.9115	0.9131	0.9147	0.9162	0.9177
1.4	0.9192	0.9207	0.9222	0.9236	0.9251	0.9265	0.9279	0.9292	0.9306	0.9319
1.5	0.9332	0.9345	0.9357	0.9370	0.9382	0.9394	0.9406	0.9418	0.9429	0.9441
1.6	0.9452	0.9463	0.9474	0.9484	0.9495	0.9505	0.9515	0.9525	0.9535	0.9545
1.7	0.9554	0.9564	0.9573	0.9582	0.9591	0.9599	0.9608	0.9616	0.9625	0.9633
1.8	0.9641	0.9649	0.9656	0.9664	0.9671	0.9678	0.9686	0.9693	0.9699	0.9706
1.9	0.9713	0.9719	0.9726	0.9732	0.9738	0.9744	0.9750	0.9756	0.9761	0.9767
2.0	0.9772	0.9778	0.9783	0.9788	0.9793	0.9798	0.9803	0.9808	0.9812	0.9817
2.1	0.9821	0.9826	0.9830	0.9834	0.9838	0.9842	0.9846	0.9850	0.9854	0.9857
2.2	0.9861	0.9864	0.9868	0.9871	0.9875	0.9878	0.9881	0.9884	0.9887	0.9890
2.3	0.9893	0.9896	0.9898	0.9901	0.9904	0.9906	0.9909	0.9911	0.9913	0.9916
2.4	0.9918	0.9920	0.9922	0.9925	0.9927	0.9929	0.9931	0.9932	0.9934	0.9936
2.5	0.9938	0.9940	0.9941	0.9943	0.9945	0.9946	0.9948	0.9949	0.9951	0.9952
2.6	0.9953	0.9955	0.9956	0.9957	0.9959	0.9960	0.9961	0.9962	0.9963	0.9964
2.7	0.9965	0.9966	0.9967	0.9968	0.9969	0.9970	0.9971	0.9972	0.9973	0.9974
2.8	0.9974	0.9975	0.9976	0.9977	0.9977	0.9978	0.9979	0.9979	0.9980	0.9981
2.9	0.9981	0.9982	0.9982	0.9983	0.9984	0.9984	0.9985	0.9985	0.9986	0.9986
3.0	0.9987	0.9987	0.9987	0.9988	0.9988	0.9989	0.9989	0.9989	0.9990	0.9990
3.1	0.9990	0.9991	0.9991	0.9991	0.9992	0.9992	0.9992	0.9992	0.9993	0.9993
3.2	0.9993	0.9993	0.9994	0.9994	0.9994	0.9994	0.9994	0.9995	0.9995	0.9995
3.3	0.9995	0.9995	0.9995	0.9996	0.9996	0.9996	0.9996	0.9996	0.9996	0.9997
3.4	0.9997	0.9997	0.9997	0.9997	0.9997	0.9997	0.9997	0.9997	0.9997	0.9998
3.5	0.9998	0.9998	0.9998	0.9998	0.9998	0.9998	0.9998	0.9998	0.9998	0.9998
3.6	0.9998	0.9998	0.9999	0.9999	0.9999	0.9999	0.9999	0.9999	0.9999	0.9999
3.7	0.9999	0.9999	0.9999	0.9999	0.9999	0.9999	0.9999	0.9999	0.9999	0.9999
3.8	0.9999	0.9999	0.9999	0.9999	0.9999	0.9999	0.9999	0.9999	0.9999	0.9999
3.9	1.0000	1.0000	1.0000	1.0000	1.0000	1.0000	1.0000	1.0000	1.0000	1.0000

where $Z = (X - \mu)/\sigma$ follows a standard normal distribution; we can use the tables of the standard normal distribution to obtain the probability. Note that the subtraction of the mean has led to a random variable, $X - \mu$, that varies around mean 0, with standard deviation σ. The division by σ results in a random variable $Z = (X - \mu)/\sigma$ with mean 0 and standard deviation 1. Furthermore, one can show that the distribution of Z is normal.

EXAMPLE 1

Assume that X follows a normal distribution with mean $\mu = 75$ and standard deviation $\sigma = 5$. Then, the probability

$$\begin{aligned} P(70 < X < 82) &= P\left(\frac{70 - 75}{5} < \frac{X - 75}{5} < \frac{82 - 75}{5}\right) = P(-1.00 < Z < 1.40) \\ &= P(Z < 1.40) - P(Z < -1.00) = 0.9192 - 0.1587 = 0.7605. \end{aligned}$$

■

EXAMPLE 2

Let X be the weight of a dentifrice fill in a 2.7-ounce tube. Typically our filling process will add, on average, more fill than is required. Assume that the fillweight X follows a normal distribution with mean $\mu = 2.8$ and standard deviation $\sigma = 0.05$. What fraction of the tubes are underfilled?

$$P(X < 2.7) = P\left(\frac{X - 2.8}{0.05} < \frac{2.7 - 2.8}{0.05}\right) = P(Z < -2.00) = 0.0228.$$

That is, a little more than 2 percent of the tubes are underfilled. If this percentage is too large, how can we reduce it? One strategy is to set the mean fill weight of our filling process to a higher level. For example, we could set it at 2.9 ounces. Then the proportion of underfilled tubes becomes considerably smaller; that is,

$$P(X < 2.7) = P(Z < -4.00) = 0.00003.$$

Of course, this strategy is expensive, as we need more filling material.

Another strategy is to reduce the variability of our filling process, while keeping the mean fill weight the same. For example, a reduction of the standard deviation to $\sigma = 0.025$ has the following effect:

$$P(X < 2.7) = P\left(\frac{X - 2.8}{0.025} < \frac{2.7 - 2.8}{0.025}\right) = P(Z < -4.00) = 0.00003.$$

The strategy of reducing the variation σ may be cheaper than that of increasing the mean fill weight μ, as we can save on fill material. ■

EXAMPLE 3

Percentiles of the normal distribution with mean μ and standard deviation σ can be determined from the percentiles of the standard normal distribution, after shifting the origin by the mean μ and expanding the scale by the standard deviation σ. The 50th percentile is μ, the 95th percentile is $\mu + (1.645)\sigma$, the 5th percentile is $\mu - (1.645)\sigma$, the 97.5th percentile is $\mu + (1.96)\sigma$, the 99th percentile is $\mu + (2.326)\sigma$, and so on. If in doubt, convince yourself through the following calculations: $P(X < \mu + (1.96)\sigma) = P(Z < [\mu + (1.96)\sigma - \mu]/\sigma = 1.96) = 0.975$. ■

8.8.3 An Important Property of the Normal Distribution

Previously we claimed that roughly 2/3 of the distribution falls within one standard deviation of the mean, and roughly 95 percent falls within two standard deviations of the mean. We can now show these claims.

Assume that X follows a normal distribution with mean μ and standard deviation σ. Then

$$
\begin{aligned}
P(\mu - \sigma < X < \mu + \sigma) &= P\left(-1 < \frac{X - \mu}{\sigma} < 1\right) = P(-1 < Z < 1) \\
&= P(Z < 1) - P(Z < -1) = 0.8413 - 0.1587 = 0.6826;
\end{aligned}
$$

about 2/3 of the observations are within one standard deviation of the mean. Similarly,

$$
\begin{aligned}
P(\mu - 2\sigma < X < \mu + 2\sigma) &= P\left(-2 < \frac{X - \mu}{\sigma} < 2\right) \\
&= P(-2 < Z < 2) = 0.9544,
\end{aligned}
$$

implying that about 95 percent of the observations are within two standard deviations of the mean. Furthermore,

$$
P(\mu - 3\sigma < X < \mu + 3\sigma) = 0.9973,
$$

implying that almost all (in fact, 99.73 percent) of the observations are within three standard deviations of the mean.

8.9 OTHER CONTINUOUS DISTRIBUTIONS

There are many other useful continuous distributions. The *exponential distribution*, for example, is frequently used to describe the distribution of failure times. It arises in reliability studies. Other frequently used distributions are the *chi-square distribution*, the *t-distribution*, and the *F-distribution*. We do not emphasize these distributions in this book. If you want to learn more about these other distributions, you should consult introductory texts in statistics such as Hogg and Ledolter, *Applied Statistics for Engineers and Physical Scientists*.

8.10 BIVARIATE PROBABILITY DISTRIBUTIONS

So far we have considered just a single random variable X and we have studied its distribution. What if we have two random variables? How can we describe their joint distribution? For example, consider tossing a coin and rolling a die at the same time. The random variable X represents the toss of the coin, with outcomes 0 and 1 depending on whether we get heads or tails. The random variable Y represents the roll of the die, with discrete outcomes 1 through 6 depending on the number of spots on the upside, each with probability 1/6. Or, consider Y, the future change in the stock value of your company, and X, the future change in the value of the overall market.

In order to simplify the discussion we explain the concept of a joint probability distribution in the discrete case. We describe the *joint distribution* of two discrete random variables X and Y by listing all possible outcomes and by assigning to these outcomes probabilities that add to 1. Consider, for example, a random variable X with three possible outcomes, say x_1, x_2, and x_3; and a random variable Y with outcomes y_1 and y_2. Here we have six possible outcomes. We display these outcomes and their assigned probabilities in the following two-way table:

		X		
	x_1	x_2	x_3	$P(Y = y_i)$
Y y_1	0.1	0.2	0.3	0.6
Y y_2	0.1	0.1	0.2	0.4
$P(X = x_i)$	0.2	0.3	0.5	1.0

For example, the joint probability $P(X = x_2 \text{ and } Y = y_2) = 0.1$. You may change the joint probabilities in the table, but note that the probabilities must add to 1.

By adding probabilities across each row, we obtain the probability distribution of the random variable $Y, P(Y = y_1)$ and $P(Y = y_2)$. This is called a *marginal distribution* as their probabilities are given in the margin of the above table. For example, $P(Y = y_1) = 0.6$, as we can obtain the event $Y = y_1$ by getting either ($X = x_1$ and $Y = y_1$), or ($X = x_2$ and $Y = y_1$), or ($X = x_3$ and $Y = y_1$). The probabilities of these three events, 0.1, 0.2, 0.3, are added to give $P(Y = y_1) = 0.6$. Similarly, by adding the probabilities down each column we obtain the (marginal) distribution of X.

There is one more set of distributions that is of interest. These are the *conditional distributions*. If you know that Y has just been observed and if you know that its outcome was y_1, what is the probability that $X = x_1, X = x_2$, or $X = x_3$? We denote these conditional probabilities by $P(X = x \mid Y = y_1)$. Note that the conditional probabilities have to add to 1 if we sum them over x_1, x_2, and x_3. Hence we need to normalize the probabilities in the first row of the above table, 0.1, 0.2,

0.3, by dividing through by their sum, which is 0.6. Similarly, by standardizing the joint probabilities in the second row by its row sum 0.4, we obtain the conditional distribution of X, given $Y = y_2$. That is, the two conditional distributions are

	x_1	x_2	x_3
$P(X = x \mid Y = y_1)$	1/6	2/6	3/6
$P(X = x \mid Y = y_2)$	1/4	1/4	2/4

We notice that the conditional probability distribution of X changes with different conditioning values for Y. We say that the random variables X and Y are *statistically dependent*. You could also obtain the conditional distribution $P(Y = y \mid X = x_i)$ by dividing the probabilities in each column by their column sum; for example, $P(Y = y_1 \mid X = x_2) = 0.2/0.3 = 2/3$ and $P(Y = y_2 \mid X = x_2) = 0.1/0.3 = 1/3$, and so on.

Consider another table of joint probabilities:

		X			
		x_1	x_2	x_3	$P(Y = y_i)$
Y	y_1	0.12	0.18	0.30	0.6
	y_2	0.08	0.12	0.20	0.4
$P(X = x_i)$		0.20	0.30	0.50	1.0

This is also a valid joint probability distribution, and you will notice that it results in the same marginal probability distributions as the previous table on page 214. What about the conditional distributions? Standardizing the rows of probabilities, you obtain

	x_1	x_2	x_3
$P(X = x \mid Y = y_1)$	12/60	18/60	30/60
$P(X = x \mid Y = y_2)$	8/40	12/40	20/40

The two conditional distributions are the same. We say that the random variables X and Y are *statistically independent*. You can see that independence for X and Y implies that $P(X = x_i \text{ and } Y = y_j) = P(X = x_i) \times P(Y = y_j)$, the product of the two marginal probabilities. For example, $P(X = x_1 \text{ and } Y = y_1) = P(X = x_1) \times P(Y = y_1) = (0.2)(0.6) = 0.12$. We have used this result for independent random variables earlier in our discussion of binomial probabilities. There the probability of success in a single trial was θ, and the trials were assumed independent. Hence the probability of getting x successes in a row was the product of the x individual success probabilities, that is, $(\theta)(\theta)\cdots(\theta) = \theta^x$.

8.10.1 The Standard Deviation of a Sum or Difference of Independent Random Variables

Often one is interested in the sum or the difference of two independent random variables X and Y. Assume that X has a distribution with mean μ_X and standard deviation σ_X, and Y has a distribution with mean μ_Y and standard deviation σ_Y. Furthermore, we assume that X and Y are independent. Then one can show that the standard deviation of the new random variables $X + Y$ and $X - Y$ is given by

$$\sigma_{X+Y} = \sigma_{X-Y} = \sqrt{(\sigma_X)^2 + (\sigma_Y)^2}.$$

This is a very important result. It indicates how to combine the variability. The standard deviation is not the sum of the standard deviations, but the square root of the sum of the squared standard deviations (that is, the variances). It is important to realize that this result holds only for independent random variables. The result would be wrong if the random variables were dependent. Also, note that the standard deviation of a sum and the standard deviation of a difference of two independent random variables are identical. This is obvious once you write $X - Y = X + (-Y)$ and realize that $(-Y)$ and Y have the same standard deviation; the multiplication by (-1) changes only the mean.

Note that a similar result holds for the sum of more than two independent random variables. The standard deviation of a sum of several, mutually independent random variables is the square root of the sum of the squared standard deviations.

Let us illustrate this result with two independent random variables X and Y, where X has the discrete distribution

X	0	1	2
$P(X = x)$	0.2	0.3	0.5

and Y has the discrete distribution

Y	0	1	2
$P(Y = y)$	0.4	0.4	0.2

The parameters of these distributions are:

$$\begin{aligned}
\mu_X &= (0)(0.2) + (1)(0.3) + (2)(0.5) = 1.3 \\
\sigma_X &= \sqrt{(-1.3)^2(0.2) + (-0.3)^2(0.3) + (0.7)^2(0.5)} = \sqrt{0.61} = 0.781 \\
\mu_Y &= (0)(0.4) + (1)(0.4) + (2)(0.2) = 0.8 \\
\sigma_Y &= \sqrt{(-0.8)^2(0.4) + (0.2)^2(0.4) + (1.2)^2(0.2)} = \sqrt{0.56} = 0.748.
\end{aligned}$$

Because of the independence between the random variables, the joint probabilities are given by the products of the respective marginal probabilities:

		X			
		0	1	2	$P(Y = y_i)$
	0	0.08	0.12	0.20	0.40
Y	1	0.08	0.12	0.20	0.40
	2	0.04	0.06	0.10	0.20
$P(X = x_i)$		0.20	0.30	0.50	1.00

Hence the distribution of $W = X + Y$ is given by

w	0	1	2	3	4
$P(X + Y = w)$	0.08	0.20	0.36	0.26	0.10

For example, the event $X + Y = 3$ can be obtained in two different ways: ($X = 1$ and $Y = 2$) and ($X = 2$ and $Y = 1$). Adding the probabilities of these two events, 0.06 and 0.20, leads to $P(X + Y = 3) = 0.26$; you can check the other entries.

The mean of $X + Y$ is given by

$$\mu_{X+Y} = (0)(0.08) + (1)(0.20) + (2)(0.36) + (3)(0.26) + (4)(0.10) = 2.1$$

which is the same as the sum of the two means, $\mu_X + \mu_Y = 1.3 + 0.8$.

The standard deviation of $X + Y$ is

$$\begin{aligned}\sigma_X &= \sqrt{(-2.1)^2(0.08) + (-1.1)^2(0.20) + (-0.1)^2(0.36) + (0.9)^2(0.26) + (1.9)^2(0.10)} \\ &= \sqrt{1.17} = 1.082\end{aligned}$$

which is the same as $\sqrt{(\sigma_X)^2 + (\sigma_Y)^2} = \sqrt{0.61 + 0.56} = \sqrt{1.17}$. This shows that the stated result works for this example. It will work for any other joint distribution (discrete or continuous), as long as the two random variables are statistically independent.

8.11 CHECKING MODEL ADEQUACY: WHICH DISTRIBUTION FITS THE DATA?

Observations can be viewed as realizations from a probability distribution; we sometimes refer to the probability distribution as our model. How can we check whether a set of observations has originated from a certain distribution? For example, how can we check whether quarterly numbers of fatal accidents on Iowa rural Interstates follow a Poisson distribution? How can we check whether certain measurement data has come from a normal distribution?

The relationship between the mean and the standard deviation of a Poisson distribution helps us check whether count data, such as the number of fatal accidents, follows a Poisson distribution. We learned earlier that the standard deviation of a Poisson distribution is the square root of its mean; see Section 8.4. For a given set of observations we can check this relation from the sample average $\bar{x}$ and the sample standard deviation s. If s is approximately equal to the square root of the average $\bar{x}$, then the Poisson distribution is a candidate for an acceptable model. Of course, instead of just relying on the two summary statistics, we can check this further by comparing the relative frequencies of the various outcomes with the expected frequencies that are implied by the Poisson distribution. The Poisson frequencies are obtained by multiplying the respective Poisson probabilities (which you obtain by using the sample average $\bar{x}$ as the Poisson parameter λ) by the number of observations. Statistical tests for deciding whether the agreement between the observed frequencies and the expected frequencies is close enough are available, and you may want to consult statistics texts on how to do this.

A simple way to check whether observations are described by a normal distribution is to draw the histogram and check whether the shape of the histogram resembles that of a normal distribution. It is usually not that difficult to check whether the distribution is unimodal, symmetric, and bell-shaped. However, determining whether observed frequencies in the tail area of the distribution are exactly as implied by the normal distribution is difficult, especially if the sample size is small. Here is where normal probability plots can help.

The *normal probability plot* provides a simple, but very useful graphical procedure for checking whether observations are from a normal distribution. A normal probability plot involves the following steps.

You first rank the n observations, $x_1, x_2, \ldots, x_n$, from the smallest observation to the largest. The smallest observation gets rank 1, and is denoted by $x_{(1)}$. Note that x_1 and $x_{(1)}$ are not the same; x_1 is the first listed observation, while $x_{(1)}$ is the smallest observation. The largest observation gets assigned rank n, and is denoted by $x_{(n)}$.

The observation with rank i, denoted by $x_{(i)}$, is the $100(i/(n+1))$th percentile; we also call this the percentile of order $i/(n+1)$. This follows from our earlier definition of percentiles in Chapter 7. There we defined the $(100p)$th percentile as the observation with rank $i = (n+1)p$; solving for p in terms of the rank i, leads to $p = i/(n+1)$. If some of the observations are identical, then we assign to each one the average rank.

If the observations follow a normal distribution with mean μ and standard deviation σ, then the observation with rank i, $x_{(i)}$, should be close to the normal percentile of order $i/(n+1)$, $\mu + z_{i/(n+1)}\sigma$; here $z_{i/(n+1)}$ is the $100(i/(n+1))$th percentile of the standard normal distribution; $z_{i/(n+1)}$ is also called the *(standardized) normal score* of the observation $x_{(i)}$. The normal probability plot is a scatter plot of the implied percentiles from the normal distribution, $z_{i/(n+1)}$, against the observed percentiles, $x_{(i)}$. Under normality, the observations should fall along a straight line;

the slope of the line is given by $(1/\sigma)$. This is easy to see, as $x_{(i)} = \mu + z_{i/(n+1)}\sigma$ implies $z_{i/(n+1)} = -(\mu/\sigma) + (1/\sigma)x_{(i)}$. If the scatter plot of the standardized normal scores, $z_{i/(n+1)}$, against the observed percentiles, $x_{(i)}$, exhibits a straight line pattern, then we accept normality as the generating model for our observations. On the other hand, if there are departures from linearity we would question the normal model.

For illustration, consider the failure times of the $n = 50$ light bulbs in Exercise 7.2 of Chapter 7. Failure times are usually not normally distributed; most failure time distributions are skewed to the right and have a long right tail. A simple histogram of these 50 observations indicates that this is true also in this particular example; the distribution is skewed to the right. We can anticipate that the normal probability plot will indicate departures from normality. Let us illustrate the construction of a normal probability plot. The smallest observation among the 50 observations is 77 hours; hence $x_{(1)} = 77$. It represents the observed percentile of order $1/51 = 0.0196$. The percentile of order $1/51 = 0.0196$ that is implied by the standard normal distribution is given by $z_{0.0196} = -2.06$. Hence the first point in the normal probability plot is given by $(x = 77, y = -2.06)$. The second smallest observation $x_{(2)} = 113$ is the percentile of order $2/51 = 0.0392$. The implied normal percentile (that is, the normal score) is $z_{0.0392} = -1.76$; hence the second point on the normal probability plot is $(x = 113; y = -1.76)$. The observation with rank 10, $x_{(10)} = 446$, is the observed percentile of order $10/51 = 0.1961$; the implied normal percentile is $z_{0.1961} = -0.86$; and so on. The largest observation $x_{(50)} = 4{,}015$ is the observed percentile of order $50/51 = 0.9804$; the implied normal percentile is $z_{0.9804} = 2.06$. Selected observed percentiles and their implied normal scores are given in Table 8.5 (page 220; note that not all of the observations are shown). The normal probability plot, the scatter plot of the implied normal percentiles against the observed percentiles, is given in Figure 8.6. We notice that the graph looks far from linear. The normal distribution does not provide a plausible model for this particular data set.

A normal probability plot for the 95 observations on width (as well as gauge) in Chapter 7 confirms that the points in this scatter plot follow a straight line relationship. The normal probability model is appropriate in this case.

Statistical computer software and most spreadsheet programs include functions for obtaining normal probability plots. Hence there is really no need to construct such plots from scratch as we have illustrated above. Note that the definition of a percentile may vary slightly from one package to the next. Here we have defined the observation with rank i, $x_{(i)}$, as the percentile of order $i/(n+1)$. Not all packages use the same definition. Some of them define $x_{(i)}$ as the percentile of order $(i - 0.5)/n$; others, such as Minitab, define it as the percentile of order $[i - (3/8)]/[n + (1/4)]$. Thus the implied percentile (that is, the normal score of the observation $x_{(i)}$) may differ slightly depending on which software is used. If n is reasonably large, all three definitions give very similar results. All three definitions can be justified on different theoretical grounds, so none of them is wrong.

TABLE 8.5 Rank-Ordered Observations and Their Implied Standardized Normal Scores $z_{i/(n+1)}$: Failure Times of Light Bulbs

Ordered data $x_{(i)}$	Rank i	$i/(n+1)$	Implied normal score $z_{i/(n+1)}$
77	1	0.0196	−2.06
113	2	0.0392	−1.76
120	3	0.0588	−1.56
240	4	0.0784	−1.42
241	5	0.0980	−1.29
.			
.			
446	10	0.1961	−0.86
.			
.			
602	20	0.3922	−0.27
.			
.			
774	30	0.5882	0.22
.			
.			
2243	49	0.9608	1.76
4015	50	0.9804	2.06

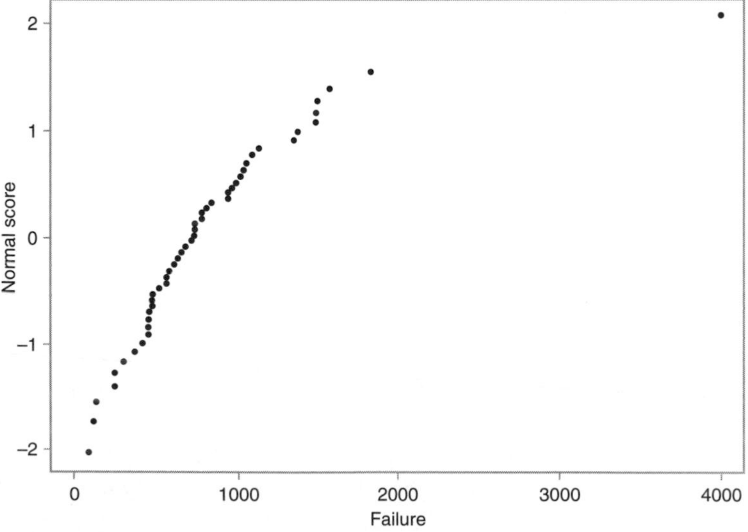

FIGURE 8.6 Normal probability plot: Failure times of light bulbs.

8.12 EXERCISES

8.1 Compute the mean and the standard deviation of the following discrete distribution:

x	1	2	3
$f(x)$	0.1	0.6	0.3

8.2 Compute the mean and the standard deviation of the following distribution:

x	0	1	2	3
$f(x)$	0.4	0.3	0.2	0.1

8.3 Consider X, the number of heads in four coin tosses. Justify the distribution given below. Calculate the mean and the standard deviation of this distribution:

x	0	1	2	3	4
$f(x)$	1/16	4/16	6/16	4/16	1/16

8.4 Consider the following probability distribution for X, the selling price of a $100 investment:

x	0	50	130
$f(x)$	0.2	0.3	0.5

(a) Calculate the mean of this discrete probability distribution. On average, is your investment successful?

(b) Calculate the standard deviation of this distribution.

8.5 The coin tossing experiment of Exercise 8.3 was performed $n = 25$ times resulting in the following numbers of heads:

$$3, 3, 2, 0, 1, 4, 3, 2, 2, 1, 3, 1, 2, 0, 3, 1, 1, 1, 2, 1, 2, 2, 0, 2, 3$$

Compute the average and the standard deviation of these 25 observations. Compare the sample estimates to the values that you would expect from theory (that is, the mean and standard deviation of the distribution of X, the number of heads among four coin tosses).

8.6 Let X have a binomial distribution with $n = 3$ trials and success probability $\theta = 0.25$. Calculate $P(X = 2)$ and $P(X \leq 2)$.

8.7 The probability of producing a high-quality print is $\theta = 0.15$. Let X be the number of high-quality prints among $n = 20$ prints (trials).

(a) What distribution would you expect for X? What are its mean and standard deviation?

(b) Find $P(X \leq 5)$ and $P(X = 2, 3, 4, 5, \text{ or } 6)$.

8.8 Your stock broker has a 65 percent success probability in picking stocks that will appreciate in value. You are investing in 20 securities that she has suggested.

(a) Obtain the probability that, among these 20 stocks, more than 13 stocks will appreciate.

(b) Obtain the probability that between 10 (inclusive) and 14 (inclusive) stocks will appreciate.

(c) How many stocks, among these 20 stocks, do you expect to appreciate?

8.9 Let X have a Poisson distribution with parameter $\lambda = 1.8$.

(a) Compute $P(X = 2)$.

(b) Using tables of the cumulative Poisson probabilities, find $P(X = 2) = P(X \leq 2) - P(X \leq 1)$.

8.10 The manufacture of a certain medical screen requires the drilling of 1000 small holes. The probability of producing a hole that is out of tolerance (that is, a defect) is 0.001, or 0.1 percent.

(a) What is the probability of producing a screen with no defects?

(b) What is the probability of producing a screen with fewer than two defects?

8.11 The number of defective bottles, X, among an hour's production follows a Poisson distribution with parameter $\lambda = 4$.

(a) What are the mean and the standard deviation of X, the number of defective bottles among an hour's production?

(b) Determine $P(X = 3)$, $P(X = 2 \text{ or } 3 \text{ or } 4 \text{ or } 5)$, and $P(X > 3)$.

8.12 Use computer software to carry out this exercise. Consider a binomial distribution with parameter $n = 100$ and $\theta = 0.01$. This describes a situation where n, the number of trials, is large and θ, the success probability in a single trial, is small. We know that the mean of this distribution is $\mu = (n)(\theta) = 1$.

(a) Using the computer, calculate the binomial probabilities $P(X = x)$, for $x = 0, 1, \ldots, 10$. Note that the probabilities, $P(X = x)$, for all $x > 10$ are essentially zero.

(b) Calculate, via computer, the approximating Poisson probabilities $P(X = x)$, for $x = 0, 1, \ldots, 10$.

(c) Interpret the results. For rare events (θ small and n large) the Poisson distribution provides a good approximation of the binomial probabilities.

(d) When would a normal distribution provide a good approximation to the binomial probabilities? Would it work in this case? (For a detailed discussion of this issue, see Chapter 10.)

8.13 On average, there are five fatal accidents on Iowa rural Interstates each quarter. Calculate the probability that there will be more than 15 accidents next quarter. What is the probability of fewer than five accidents? What is the probability that there will be between five and seven accidents (inclusive)?

8.14 A lot, consisting of a large number of items, is accepted if out of $n = 100$ sampled items we find $Ac = 3$ or fewer defectives. Compute the probabilities of accepting the lot if the proportion of defectives is **(a)** $\theta = 0.01$; **(b)** $\theta = 0.02$; **(c)** $\theta = 0.03$; **(d)** $\theta = 0.04$; **(e)** $\theta = 0.05$. The probabilities of accepting the lot, as a function of the proportion of defectives θ, is called the operating characteristic curve, $OC(\theta)$.

Plot this curve. Interpret the findings. Would this be a good sample inspection plan if your customer is satisfied with 1 percent defectives? How good is the plan at detecting unacceptable lots with 5 percent defectives?

Assume that the distribution of the number of defectives follows a Poisson distribution. This is reasonable, since n is large and θ is small (see Exercise 8.12).

8.15 The variable X follows a standard normal distribution; that is, a normal distribution with mean 0 and standard deviation 1. Determine:

(a) $P(X < 1.4)$
(b) $P(0.2 < X < 2.4)$
(c) $P(-0.3 < X < -0.1)$
(d) the 25th, the 75th, and the 80th percentile

8.16 The variable X follows a normal distribution with mean $\mu = 25$ and standard deviation $\sigma = 2$. Find

(a) $P(X < 26)$
(b) $P(23.5 < X < 25.3)$
(c) $P(X < 24.1)$
(d) the 25th and the 75th percentile, and the interquartile range

8.17 What percentage of tubes filled with TVC from a certain nozzle are above 84 grams if we can assume that the fill weight has a normal distribution with $\mu = 83.71$ grams and $\sigma = 0.15$ gram?

8.18 Assume that the sulfation end temperatures follow a normal distribution with mean $\mu = 108.4$ degrees and standard deviation $\sigma = 1.1$ degrees.

(a) What percentage of the items are above 110.5 degrees?
(b) What percentage of the items are between 107 and 109 degrees?
(c) Determine the 95th percentile of this distribution.

8.19 Measurements associated with the cap torque are normally distributed with $\mu = 36$ psi (pounds per square inch) and $\sigma = 6.5$ psi. The required specification limits for torque are a target of 30 and lower and upper specification limits of 20 and 40, respectively.

(a) What percentage of caps are outside the specification limits (that is, either below 20 or above 40)?
(b) What is this percentage if we succeed in centering the process at mean 30?
(c) What is this percentage if we succeed in centering the process at mean 30 and, furthermore, reduce the standard deviation to 4 psi?

8.20 The mean fill weight of a certain bottle-filling operation is μ. The standard deviation among fill weights is $\sigma = 0.02$ ounce. Determine the mean fill weight μ such that the fraction of underfilled bottles (that is, those weighing less than 22 ounces) is 0.01.

8.21 The fill weight follows a normal distribution with mean 2.8 and standard deviation 0.05. What is the proportion of tubes with fill weights between

(a) 2.7 and 2.9?
(b) 2.65 and 2.95?

8.22 The width dimensions on steel flats vary according to a normal distribution with mean 5.1 cm and standard deviation 0.1 cm.

(a) Obtain the 95th percentile of the distribution.
(b) The lower and upper specification limits for these steel flats are 4.8 and 5.2 cm. Calculate the probability that you exceed these specification limits.
(c) Will you reduce the probability of exceeding the specification limits if you adjust the process so that the width distribution is centered at 5.0 cm?

8.23 Assume that X follows a uniform distribution between 0 and 1.

(a) Obtain the cumulative probabilities $P(X \leq x)$, for any given x. Plot the cumulative probabilities as a function of x, for x between -3 and $+3$.

(b) Obtain the 25th and the 75th percentile of this distribution, and calculate the interquartile range.

8.24 Consider the 95 observations on width and gauge in Chapter 7. Construct normal probability plots and check whether the normal distribution provides a reasonable model.

8.25 Consider the data on compressive strength in Exercise 7.1. Construct a normal probability plot, using the locally available computer software. If none is available, construct a normal probability plot by hand, using the first 10 observations.

8.26 Consider two independent random variables X and Y with means 10.0 and 20.0, and standard deviations 3 and 5, respectively. Obtain

(a) the means and standard deviations of $X + Y$ and $X - Y$.

(b) the means and standard deviations of $X + 4Y$ and $X - 4Y$.

Hint: Use the fact that the standard deviation of $4Y$ is given by $4\sigma_Y$; see Section 8.2 of this chapter.

8.27 The maximum daily temperature for July follows a distribution with mean $\mu = 80$ degrees Fahrenheit and standard deviation $\sigma = 10$ degrees Fahrenheit. Obtain the mean and standard deviation of temperature expressed in Celsius. Note C = (5/9)(F − 32).

8.28 Write a brief report that summarizes the importance of the binomial, Poisson, and normal distributions in quality-related applications.

8.13 REFERENCES

Deming, W. E. *Out of the Crisis*, Cambridge, MA: MIT Center for Advanced Engineering Study, 1986.

Hogg, R. V., and J. Ledolter. *Applied Statistics for Engineers and Physical Scientists,* 2nd edition, New York: Macmillan, 1992.

CHAPTER 9

SAMPLE SURVEYS

9.1 SURVEYS

Industry and business need information, and much of the needed information comes from surveys. We carry out surveys on customers in order to obtain information on their level of satisfaction with particular products or services. We survey consumers on their buying intentions. We survey people to learn about their attitudes and opinions. We carry out surveys of company executives to assess their views on the current and the anticipated business climate. We conduct surveys on products through acceptance sampling plans, for deciding whether products should be shipped to customers.

Survey results, for example, may tell us that 68 percent of our customers are satisfied with our products, that the median income of our customers is $75,000, that the average length of life of a certain type of light bulb is 800 hours, that certain products contain no more than one percent defectives, and that the proportion of callers who are given incorrect advice on the Internal Revenue Service hotline is 38 percent.

In this book we use the term "survey" in a very general way. We think of a *survey* as a *process of systematically obtaining data on a universe of elements*. The *universe*, also called the *population*, is the collection of all *elements* about which we wish to obtain information. The universe may comprise 8,235 customers who purchased a certain foreign luxury car that our company imported to the United States in 1994. The universe may consist of the 1.5 million light bulbs that our company produced during the last month. The universe may consist of all telephone calls that were received on the IRS hotline during the first quarter of 1995.

The terms *process* and *systematic* are important elements in the above definition. A survey is a process in itself, and it is subject to its own inputs and errors.

The word "systematic" communicates the fact that one has to think about how to best obtain the information. A survey does not mean handing out haphazardly written questionnaires at convenient street corners! Much effort goes into the design and the execution of a survey. One must be clear about the type of information that one wishes to ascertain, the elements of the relevant universe, how one samples the elements if one does not wish to get the information on all elements, the instruments that are used to gather the information, the personnel that actually gathers the data, and the correct method of data analysis.

9.1.1 Census and Sample Surveys

If we get the information from every element of the universe, then we call the survey a *census*. The U.S. population census, which is carried out every ten years, is one example of a very large census. Its strengths lie in the great detail that the census results convey. However, in many cases a census is not feasible, because universes are often large and the cost of taking a census is usually prohibitive.

Most surveys are *sample surveys*. Instead of acquiring information on each and every element of the *population*, we select a (usually small) *sample* (part) of the population, obtain the information on the sampled elements, and use the sample information to make inferences on the complete population. Since sampling is involved, we refer to such surveys as *sample surveys*. We also refer to the activity of selecting the elements for the survey as *sampling*. Quite often we use the terms "samples" and "surveys" interchangeably, as we usually think about sample surveys.

One would think that a complete census should be preferable to a sample survey, as in a census information is obtained on all elements of the population, and not just on a subset of elements. What are some of the reasons for preferring a sample survey over a census or, in the language of inspection, for preferring a sample inspection over a 100 percent inspection? One major drawback of a census is its cost. However, there may be other drawbacks to a census as well, such as its lack of timeliness; it often takes a long time (several months, in the case of the population census) before results are available. Furthermore, the "quality" of a census may be inferior to that of a sample survey; in a census one must assess information on many elements (for example, millions of households in the population census) and it is not always possible to allocate much time and effort to each individual case. The quality of the interviewing, the coding of the information, and the supervision of the work can be superior in sample surveys, of course, provided that one takes advantage of the smaller job size.

9.1.2 Selection of Sample Units

The appropriate *selection* of the sample units is one important issue in sample surveys. One needs to select the sample such that one can make valid statements about the population. Assume, for example, that instead of contacting all 8,235 buyers of our luxury car our survey was sent to a sample of 100 buyers. Suppose that 68 of these 100 selected buyers, or 68 percent, were very satisfied with the car they bought. We then use this sample proportion to conjecture that also 68 percent of the population of the 8,235 customers are satisfied. This inference, however, is only appropriate if the 100 selected customers are representative of the whole population. They have to be selected in a certain way.

The concept of *equal complete coverage* is fundamental in sampling. The equal complete coverage result is the result that would be obtained from an examination of all units available for sampling, using the very same procedures that are used in the sample survey. Assume that we contact all 8,235 buyers and that we ask each one of them about their satisfaction, employing the same procedures of eliciting the information that are used under sampling. It may be that 5,920 of them, or 72 percent of the population, express satisfaction. Then we say that the equal complete coverage proportion is 72 percent. Our sample estimate, of 68 percent, is somewhat different. This difference arises because of our particular selection of the 100 sample elements. If we had sampled another set of 100 buyers, the resulting sample proportion would, in all likelihood, be somewhat different. Statistical theory can tell us about the margin of this "sampling error," provided that the elements are selected according to certain rules of probability. This issue is discussed in the next chapter on statistical inference.

Among sample surveys we distinguish *nonprobability sample surveys* and *probability sample surveys*. In probability sample surveys we use probability methods to control the selection of the elements that we sample; we will say much more about these in the remainder of the chapter. In nonprobability sample surveys we don't control the selection; we accept the elements as they are presented to us, not knowing the underlying mechanism that led to their selection.

Sampling procedures that rely on questionnaires left on restaurant tables or in hotel rooms are examples of nonprobability surveys. It is impossible to draw valid inferences to the overall customer population from this data, since it is unclear how the decision to fill out the questionnaire relates to the characteristic of the population that we want to ascertain. This is not to imply that information from nonprobability surveys is useless. They can lead to much useful information; in particular, they may bring important problems to our attention.

Sending a questionnaire to all customers (for example, the 8,235 buyers mentioned above), but compiling only the responses of customers who bothered to reply (say 1,000 of them), represents another example of a nonprobability survey. We, as the designer of this study, have no role in the selection of the elements for which we get information. The proportion of happy customers among those that returned the questionnaire may not be a good indication of the overall happiness of our customers. Some of the nonrespondents may have been so unhappy that they didn't want to communicate with our company at all. On the other hand, some of the nonrespondents may have been quite satisfied, but may have assumed that satisfaction is normal if one buys a luxury car. We just don't know why they did not respond. Roberts and Sergesketter express this well when they write: "Beware of haphazard customer sampling and low response rates. The resulting information may be misleading; for example, it may give undue influence to customers at the extremes of satisfaction, those most pleased and those most disgruntled." (See Roberts and Sergesketter, 1993, p. 100.)

Other examples of nonprobability samples are surveys taken by television news programs that depend on viewers to call in, often after paying a certain access charge. We don't know what prompts people to call in and whether their decision to call is related to how they feel on the issues they are responding to.

These examples illustrate the great difficulties that one faces when attempting to generalize the sample information from a nonprobability sample survey to the population from which the sample was taken. It is for this reason that our book does not cover these surveys in any detail. Our focus is on probability sample surveys.

9.1.3 Things to Watch When Constructing and Executing Surveys

Selection of the sample elements is certainly very important. However, many other important issues and problems arise when one designs a survey. Many of these issues arise well before one ever has to address the sampling issue; many times the actual probability selection of the sample elements is one of the easiest tasks in carrying out a sample survey.

If you want to know more about the theory and practice of sample surveys, you should study the classic books by W. Edwards Deming, *Sample Design in Business Research* and *Some Theory of Sampling*, as well as the book by M.H. Hansen, W.N. Hurwitz, and W.G. Madow, *Sample Survey Methods and Theory; Vol I: Methods and Applications; Vol II: Theory.* These texts give a comprehensive discussion of all the important issues that arise in sample surveys. The examples in these books are most instructive as they come from writers who draw on extensive practical experience.

Aim of the survey. One needs to be certain about the objectives of the survey. Survey questions need to be clear, unambiguous, and well-defined. Questionnaires need to be field-tested. Everyone who has written survey questions, or examination questions that cover a certain body of material, knows how easy it is to overlook the obvious. It always helps to conduct a pilot study and subject the questionnaire to a small field test. Usually it becomes obvious very quickly if some of the questions are ambiguous.

Construction of the relevant sample frame. One needs to construct the sample frame from which to draw the sample. A *(sample) frame* is made up of the relevant sample units. A sampling unit may be a household, a customer of a product, a firm, a farm, a dwelling, an individual industrial product, a lot of products for shipment, an entry in an accounting ledger, and so on. The sampling units need to be distinguishable and it helps to number them. Constructing the relevant sample frame is usually the most difficult and time-consuming part of a survey.

However, without a frame there can be no genuine probability sample survey, as otherwise there is no way of knowing and controlling the probability of selection. In fact, a frame is also needed for a census, as without such a list we wouldn't know whom to contact.

A frame is satisfactory if a complete 100 percent evaluation of its elements provides the relevant and desired characteristics of the population. Note that there could be gaps between the population of interest and the sample frame. The sample frame may miss parts of the population of interest and it may include parts that are not in the population. For example, a list of companies selected from tax records will miss companies that operate illegally without paying taxes. Or, a list of individuals by their home address will miss the homeless.

It is usually very difficult to establish the frame for a universe of elements that possess rare characteristics. Just imagine constructing a frame of people who have been deaf since birth. Or, think about establishing a frame for the population of drug users, or for people infected with HIV. In addition, in studies about future behavior (which Deming calls *analytic studies*; see Section 10.7) the frame is never complete, because the characteristics that one wishes to assess are in reference to future consumers, future products, and future processes.

Let us discuss several examples that illustrate the steps that are involved in the construction of a sample frame. Take our previous example about the level of satisfaction with regard to a recent car purchase. In this example our population consists of 8,235 buyers of a certain luxury car. Car companies keep good records of their buyers, and it is usually possible to get a list of the buyers, as well as their addresses and telephone numbers. The construction of the sample frame is straightforward and not too difficult. Our frame is basically a list of customers, numbered from 1 through 8,235. However, even in a simple case like this, difficulties are bound to arise. A large portion of the cars may be leased, and the dealership (or the company itself) may be listed as the "buyer." Special investigative effort will be necessary to locate the people who have leased the cars. Also, someone may have bought or leased the car, but may not drive it. You have to be specific whether the survey should be addressed to the buyer or to the driver.

For a survey of business establishments in a certain area we may have access to a very good list of "large" establishments. Here the sampling unit is the large firm, and it is rather easy to write down the sample frame. It contains a list of large establishments, numbered from 1 through N. However, no such list may exist for "small" establishments.

Deming, on page 90 of his book *Sample Design in Business Research*, discusses a survey which he used to study the employees' assessment of how management treats their suggestions. The question "Do you believe that management studies the suggestions offered by employees?" was given to a sample of 100 employees, drawn from the universe of 9,600 employees. This particular company had twelve different factories, and the number of employees in the various factories ranged from 100 to 2,000. Here the sampling unit is the employee and the sample frame is given by a list of all employees, numbered 1 through 9,600. This list could come from last month's payroll. However, note that the frame obtained from last month's payroll will not include recent hires, but will include former employees who no longer work for the company. This is another example where the sample frame and the population of interest are not exactly the same.

Deming, on page 102 of the book mentioned above, uses a survey to find out whether motels affiliated with the American Automobile Association (AAA) are in favor of instituting some system by which they could make reservations for motorists in advance of their arrival. Here the sample unit is an AAA affiliated motel, and the sample frame consists of all AAA affiliations. At the national AAA headquarters information on all affiliations was kept in several file drawers—172 of them, each filled with 64 index cards. Here the sample frame consists of the collection of index cards, numbered from the first through the last. Note that this survey was taken in the 1950s; today the information would be stored in computer files.

This example is also interesting for its detailed instructions for follow-up contacts. The original contact was with a questionnaire and an accompanying letter. A second notice, if necessary, was sent at the end of ten days. A third notice was sent at the end of 17 days. After 24 days a missing questionnaire was declared a nonresponse. In case of a nonresponse, field workers with automobiles were dispatched to contact the nonrespondents and the information was obtained through an interview. Note that a system is needed to track respondents. Without a tracking system, it would not be possible to conduct such a detailed follow-up of nonrespondents.

Deming, on page 165 of the above book, describes the problems that arise in a survey of a small urban area. He considers an area of 24 city blocks, with groups of three dwelling units as the sampling units. One objective of this particular survey was to obtain the number of children under age ten, the rent or the rental value of the apartment, and whether the dwelling was owned or rented. Block statistics for U.S. city blocks are available from the most recent census; census maps show street blocks and the locations of dwellings. This information can be used to construct the sample frame.

Method for obtaining the information. One needs to decide how to obtain the required information. Should we obtain the information through questionnaires that are sent through the mail, or should we rely on interviews? Of course, mail would be cheaper, but personal interviews may lead to more accurate and reliable information, especially if the questions are complicated. Furthermore, one needs to establish procedures for handling nonrespondents; for example, the frequency, the timing, and the method of follow-up contacts. One should think about strategies for increasing the response rate; for example, a monetary incentive may prompt individuals to return a mail survey.

Determining the sample size and selecting the sample. In the following sections we are going to discuss the commonly used probability sampling schemes, and we will show how the probability selection is carried out in practice. The required sample size depends on the margin of sampling error that one is willing to accept. If one wants to determine a certain characteristic of the population with absolute certainty, then one has to look at every single element. However, if one allows a certain margin of error for the sample estimate, then samples of small or moderate size may be sufficient. Of course, the larger the certainty one requires, the larger the sample size that one must take.

Executing the survey and analyzing the results. The quality of surveys depends, to a large extent, on the individuals who conduct the survey. A survey is usually not carried out by a single person; it is a process that can involve many individuals. It may involve statisticians who design the survey and develop the procedures; field workers who carry out the interviews; clerks who enter the information electronically; and data analysts who summarize and interpret the resulting information. It is important that all participants follow their instructions. However, before instructions can be followed, they must be given. It is also essential that everyone gets the right amount of training. For example, field workers must be taught to present the questions in a uniform way; this is essential for avoiding interviewer bias. Also, they must have clear instructions on how to locate their subjects and what to do if subjects cannot be found. It is usually not appropriate to substitute the answers of a neighbor for those of the missing subject. Uniformity is further enhanced by giving the interviewers preprinted worksheets for recording the relevant data.

One should also monitor the work of people as such monitoring may indicate the need for additional and different training. Deming, in Chapter 13 of *Sampling Design in Business Research*, talks about several simple graphical tools that can be used to monitor the uniformity of different field workers. For example, a simple scatter plot of the number of refusals against the number of nonrefusals, for each of several interviewers, will show whether certain interviewers are different from the rest. If this is the case, one should review the training procedures.

Once the raw data are collected, the data are usually entered into an electronic database. Various error-checking procedures should be used to catch errors in entering the information. For example, the data could be keyed in twice, preferably by different operators. A comparison of the two entries will flag possible inconsistencies.

After carefully checking the data entries, the information must be summarized using the appropriate statistical analyses, and the findings of the survey must be communicated to the customer who has commissioned and paid for the survey. Mistakes must be avoided.

9.2 PROBABILITY SAMPLE SURVEYS

We assume that a sample frame is in place and that the sample size (that is, the number of elements to be selected from the frame) has been determined. At issue is how the selection should be done.

9.2.1 Simple Random Sampling and Random Numbers

Simple random sampling is the most basic probability sampling process and many other, more complicated sampling procedures are based on it. In *simple random sampling* (often referred to as *random sampling*), the sampling is carried out in a manner such that each possible sample of size n has the same chance of being selected. For the implementation of simple random sampling it is essential that we have a sample frame that lists all elements of the population.

Assume that we wish to draw a simple random sample of size n from the N elements of the sample frame, which we have labeled 1 through N. In principle, the selection can be achieved by placing N slips of papers, with labels 1 through N, into a bowl, mixing the contents, and drawing one slip after the other, until we have selected n of them. For example, for a sample of size $n = 3$ from $N = 200$ elements, we may select elements numbered 28, 82, and 154. This sampling mechanism is known as *sampling without replacement*, as one doesn't put back the selected element into the bowl before the next element is drawn. This is different from *sampling with replacement* where the selected element is replaced before the subsequent one is selected. There it could happen that the same element is selected twice. In sampling practice one does not replace the selected item, as one doesn't want to select the same sample unit more than once. Usually it doesn't make sense to collect data on the same item more than once; of course, you may want to get replicate information if you want to assess the magnitude of the measurement error.

This sampling procedure is entirely equivalent to the one where we write out a slip of paper for each possible combination of $n = 3$ elements, taken from the $N = 200$ elements in the population. That is, we write out a slip for $(1, 2, 3)$, one for $(1, 2, 4), \ldots$, one for $(1, 2, 200), \ldots$, one for $(198, 199, 200)$. There are many possible combinations, and thus many slips. In fact, you can check that in this particular situation there are 1,313,400 such slips. For simple random sampling one could draw one slip from among these 1,313,400 slips; for example, we may get $(28, 82, 154)$. Note that this procedure follows the definition of random sampling that was given earlier, which says that in a random sample each possible subset of n elements has the same chance of being selected. We wrote out all of the possible subsets, and we picked one of them at random. However, this procedure is very tedious, and it certainly would not be used in practice. The procedure of sampling without replacement, as we have described it earlier, is much easier to carry out, and it, too, guarantees that each subset has the same chance of being selected.

While the procedure of drawing slips from a bowl is easy to understand, it would be quite cumbersome in practice. Instead, one uses tables of *random numbers*.

A table of 2,000 random digits between 0 and 9 is given in Table 9.1. Where do these digits come from? Here we give a simple but instructive procedure for generating such numbers. We put ten slips of paper with numbers 0 through 9

TABLE 9.1 Two Thousand Random Digits

98086	24826	45240	28404	44999	08896	39094	73407	35441	31880
33185	16232	41941	50949	89435	48581	88695	41994	37548	73043
80951	00406	96382	70774	20151	23387	25016	25298	94624	61171
79752	49140	71961	28296	69861	02591	74852	20539	00387	59579
18633	32537	98145	06571	31010	24674	05455	61427	77938	91936
74029	43902	77557	32270	97790	17119	52527	58021	80814	51748
54178	45611	80993	37143	05335	12969	56127	19255	36040	90324
11664	49883	52079	84827	59381	71539	09973	33440	88461	23356
48324	77928	31249	64710	02295	36870	32307	57546	15020	09994
69074	94138	87637	91976	35584	04401	10518	21615	01848	76938
09188	20097	32825	39527	04220	86304	83389	87374	64278	58044
90045	85497	51981	50654	94938	81997	91870	76150	68476	64659
73189	50207	47677	26269	62290	64464	27124	67018	41361	82760
75768	76490	20971	87749	90429	12272	95375	05871	93823	43178
54016	44056	66281	31003	00682	27398	20714	53295	07706	17813
08358	69910	78542	42785	13661	58873	04618	97553	31223	08420
28306	03264	81333	10591	40510	07893	32604	60475	94119	01840
53840	86233	81594	13628	51215	90290	28466	68795	77762	20791
91757	53741	61613	62269	50263	90212	55781	76514	83483	47055
89415	92694	00397	58391	12607	17646	48949	72306	94541	37408
77513	03820	86864	29901	68414	82774	51908	13980	72893	55507
19502	37174	69979	20288	55210	29773	74287	75251	65344	67415
21818	59313	93278	81757	05686	73156	07082	85046	31853	38452
51474	66499	68107	23621	94049	91345	42836	09191	08007	45449
99559	68331	62535	24170	69777	12830	74819	78142	43860	72834
33713	48007	93584	72869	51926	64721	58303	29822	93174	93972
85274	86893	11303	22970	28834	34137	73515	90400	71148	43643
84133	89640	44035	52166	73852	70091	61222	60561	62327	18423
56732	16234	17395	96131	10123	91622	85496	57560	81604	18880
65138	56806	87648	85261	34313	65861	45875	21069	85644	47277
38001	02176	81719	11711	71602	92937	74219	64049	65584	49698
37402	96397	01304	77586	56271	10086	47324	62605	40030	37438
97125	40348	87083	31417	21815	39250	75237	62047	15501	29578
21826	41134	47143	34072	64638	85902	49139	06441	03856	54552
73135	42742	95719	09035	85794	74296	08789	88156	64691	19202
07638	77929	03061	18072	96207	44156	23821	99538	04713	66994
60528	83441	07954	19814	59175	20695	05533	52139	61212	06455
83596	35655	06958	92983	05128	09719	77433	53783	92301	50498
10850	62746	99599	10507	13499	06319	53075	71839	06410	19362
39820	98952	43622	63147	64421	80814	43800	09351	31024	73167

SOURCE: Reprinted with permission from pages 1–2 of *A Million Random Digits with 100,000 Normal Deviates*, by The Rand Corporation. New York: The Free Press, 1955. Used by permission.

in a bowl, mix the slips thoroughly, and draw a slip of paper with a number on it. This is the first selected number. Then we return the slip to the bowl, mix the slips thoroughly, and draw another slip; this leads to the second number; and so on. Such drawing with replacement assures the complete randomness of the digits.

Although this particular mechanism for generating random numbers is instructive, it is not one that is used in practice. Computer software packages generate pseudorandom numbers with the characteristics of random numbers. Starting from a certain seed number, these computer packages determine the subsequent numbers through certain arithmetic operations. Despite their deterministic origin, these numbers behave as if they were truly randomly generated. Virtually all statistical software packages include routines for generating such pseudorandom numbers, and you can use them to generate your own table of random numbers.

How could you convince yourself that the numbers in Table 9.1 are truly random? First of all, the relative frequencies of these ten numbers should be roughly equal. This is easy to check; you will find that the relative frequencies are all around 0.1. Furthermore, there should be no carryover from one number to the next. Certain "runs" of numbers should not be more frequent than others. For example, the combination 75 should not come up more often than other pairs. You could confirm the absence of such runs by calculating relative frequencies for all 100 possible pairs of two numbers; their relative frequencies should be about 0.01. Similarly you could check whether adjacent triples, quadruples, and so on are equally likely.

How do we use tables of random numbers for simple random sampling? Assume, for example, that we want to randomly draw ten customers from a list of 860 customers. We all agree that it would be quite cumbersome to make up 860 slips of paper with numbers 1 through 860, put them in a bowl, and then draw ten of these slips at random and without replacement. It is much easier to use the random number table. First we select a random entry into that table, as we don't want to always start with the same number. Assume that we have selected the entry in the twenty-first row and the sixth column. Reading across the row, we see the digits 0 3 8 2 0 8 . . . . Since there are 860 elements in the sample frame, we need to work with nonoverlapping triples; the first triple is 038. Element 38 becomes the first element in our sample. Reading across rows, we find the next triple, 208. Thus element 208 becomes part of the sample. So do elements 686 and 429. The next triple is 901; however this number is ignored as we select from only 860 elements. You can check that the remaining six elements in our sample are 684, 148, 277, 451, 139, and 807. In this particular example each three-digit number occurred only once. If a number comes up more than once, the number is ignored the second time around.

We get our elements by reading across the rows of the table. Alternatively we could have read down the columns of the table, selecting 038, 371, 593, and so on. This would have led to another random sample. As long as we take *nonoverlapping* triples, it doesn't matter in which particular direction (row, column, across, up, or down) we take these numbers.

How would we select from a population with 2,056 elements? Here we would use nonoverlapping quadruples of numbers. Again, we would jump over numbers that are not part of our sampling frame, and we would ignore numbers that already have been selected.

Another important use of random numbers is in randomizing the run order of a sequence of experiments. We will say more on this in the chapter on the design of experiments (Chapter 14). How can we arrange eight experiments, experiments 1 through 8, in random order? Here we can use consecutive single digits. For example, we may start in row 3, column 16. Reading across the row we get: 70774 20151 23387 25016 25298 94624.... From this information we construct a sequence of digits 1 through 8 in the order they appear, ignoring repeats and ignoring digits 0 and 9. This results in the following random order for the eight experiments: 7, 4, 2, 1, 5, 3, 8, 6.

Benefits and Difficulties of Simple Random Sampling: Applying random sampling dispels the notion that a particular sample is particularly good or particularly bad. Random sampling provides a fair cross-section of the universe as each possible sample has the same chance of being selected. The random selection of the sample elements avoids *bias*. It may well be that the average for a particular sample is smaller than the true population characteristic that we want to estimate. But, this underestimation wouldn't necessarily happen with all other samples that one could draw from the population. In fact, if you look at the averages of all possible random samples from the population, then you find that these sample averages vary around the true population characteristic; no bias (that is, systematic over- or underestimation) is involved. You will see this in the next chapter when we study the sampling distribution of averages that are obtained from repeated random samples.

Our discussion emphasizes that for simple random sampling, as well as other probability sampling procedures, one must follow a strict protocol. In other words, one cannot just select items that are easily reached (such as oranges from the top layer of a crate, or ceramic components from the front row of a baking oven), or items from a particular portion of a shipping lot. The sample must be truly representative of the population.

Taking random samples is not always easy. For example, how would the plant manager of a steel mill take a random sample consisting of a ton of recycled metal scraps? It is not possible to follow a strategy of listing all the elements in the universe. In a case like this the manager would probably sample from the conveyer belt that transports the material into the melting furnace. He would carry out the selection as randomly as he could. For example, he may sample materials at random time periods. Or, consider the problem of selecting a random sample of 100 items from a warehouse that contains 10,000 packaged items. It may be quite difficult to draw a genuine random sample, especially if items are already packed in shipping lots; you don't want to open every package. However, it may be possible to select a few shipping lots at random and then select at random a few items from each chosen lot.

Taking random samples is often inconvenient for the one who collects the data. For example, it certainly takes more time to interview randomly selected households in a certain district than to interview households that are selected on the basis of convenience. Completing an interview schedule that is based on a predetermined random sample usually involves extra time to look up addresses as well as additional travel time. It would be much easier (for the interviewer) to select a starting place (probably in an area that is most accessible to the interviewer) and select neighboring households until a given quota is reached. However, this strategy wouldn't necessarily give a true picture of the population; it may very well be that, with regard to the variable that is being assessed, this "convenience" sample is quite different from the other elements in the population.

A similar problem arises if you ask an operator to carry out a sequence of experiments that involve changing certain experimental factors. There is always the temptation to select a sequential arrangement that involves as few factor changes as possible, that is, has few "changeovers." For example, in a two-factor experiment where factors are taken at high (+) and low (−) levels, an operator may be tempted to carry out the following sequence: $(-,-)$, $(-,+)$, $(+,+)$, $(+,-)$.

This means that the first experiment puts both factors at their low levels; the second experiment puts the first factor at its low level and the second factor at its high level; and so on. This particular sequential arrangement involves only three changeovers. On the other hand, a randomized arrangement may specify the following order: $(-,-)$, $(+,+)$, $(-,+)$, $(+,-)$. This sequence involves five changeovers. If you leave it up to the operator, you may end up with an arrangement that is more convenient, but one that is not randomized. It is important to make sure that the randomization protocol is followed.

9.2.2 Systematic Sampling

In *systematic sampling* one selects the items systematically from the sample frame, but starts this selection from a randomly chosen seed. Assume that we want to select 50 items from a list of 1,000 elements, labeled 1 through 1,000. This amounts to selecting one-twentieth of the population, or 5 percent. We select a number between 1 and 20 at random. This becomes our first element in the sample, and it serves as a seed for determining all subsequent ones; subsequent elements are obtained by adding 20 to that number. Assume that the initial random number is 12. Our systematic random sample selects items $12, 32, 52, 72, \ldots, 992$.

In the questionnaire for assessing management's view of employee suggestions, Deming (*Sample Design in Business Research*, p. 90) employed systematic (random) sampling to select 100 employees from the universe of 9,600. Each employee was assigned a number between 1 and 9,600. Deming selected systematic random samples of size 10, repeating this sampling procedure ten times.

In order to get the first sample of size 10, he selected at random a number between 1 and 960; this number was 502. His first sample consisted of sample units $502, 502 + 960 = 1462, 502 + (2)(960) = 2422, \ldots, 502 + (9)(960) = 9142$. For the second sample, he selected another random number between 1 and 960; this time the number was 147. The sample elements for this second sample were $147, 1107, \ldots, 8787$; and so on. Since this sampling strategy involves taking repeated samples, Deming refers to it as a *replicated sampling design*. It turns out that the results from these repeated samples can tell us about the variability of the estimates.

The fractions of "yes" responses (a "yes" means that management takes employees' suggestions seriously) in these ten samples were: 0.4, 0.5, 0.4, 0.6, 0.6, 0.4, 0.5, 0.5, 0.7, 0.6. The overall proportion of "yes" answers, $52/100 = 0.52$, indicated that 52 percent of the respondents believed that management takes employees' suggestions seriously.

Systematic sampling is in many instances easier than simple random sampling, especially if the items are already arranged on a readily available list. This is the advantage of the procedure. On the other hand, in systematic sampling most combinations of n elements cannot be drawn as samples. Systematic sampling restricts the choices, and it does not give each combination of n elements the same chance of being selected. However, if the arrangement of the items on the list is in random order, then systematic sampling and simple random sampling are the same.

9.2.3 Stratified Sampling

In many situations one has some prior knowledge that the population consists of two or more strata that are different with respect to the information that one wants to assess. Take, for example, the simple case where you want to estimate the mean salary, or the total payroll, of a department (population) of $N = 4$ employees. Here N is very small, but remember this example is just for illustration. Assume that you know that two of the employees are managers and two of them are line workers. That is, you know—prior to sampling—that you are dealing with two different groups (or strata). Within each stratum the salaries are similar, but between the strata you can expect big differences. For illustration, assume that monthly salaries (in thousands of dollars) are $a = 6$ and $b = 7$ (for managers), and $c = 2$ and $d = 3$ (for line workers). The mean salary in the population is 4.5, and the total payroll is 18.

Suppose that the sample size is $n = 2$. First, assume that we use simple random sampling. Table 9.2 (page 238) shows all possible and equally likely samples; there are six of them. It also shows their sample averages. Some of them are quite close to the population mean; but two of them (when both of the sampled elements are from the same group—either managers or line workers) are quite different from the population mean. The mean of the squared distances from the

TABLE 9.2 Illustration of Simple and Stratified Random Sampling

Simple random sampling	Stratified sampling
Sample average	Sample average
(ab) 6.5	
(ac) 4.0	(ac) 4.0
(ad) 4.5	(ad) 4.5
(bc) 4.5	(bc) 4.5
(bd) 5.0	(bd) 5.0
(cd) 2.5	

possible sample averages to the population mean, 4.5, is a measure of how close our estimate is, on average, to the unknown population characteristic. We call this the *mean square error* (MSE). For simple random sampling,

$$\text{MSE} = [(6.5 - 4.5)^2 + (4.0 - 4.5)^2 + (4.5 - 4.5)^2 + (4.5 - 4.5)^2 + (5.0 - 4.5)^2 + (2.5 - 4.5)^2]/6 = 1.417.$$

In stratified random sampling we split the population into the two strata—managers and line workers—and we take a random sample from each. Since the sample size is $n = 2$, we take one manager and one line worker at random. Table 9.2 shows the four equally likely pairs and their sample averages. It is obvious from this table that, on average, the estimate from stratified sampling will be closer to the population mean, as we will never select two employees from the same group. One can calculate the mean square error for stratified random sampling. We find that

$$\text{MSE} = [(4.0 - 4.5)^2 + (4.5 - 4.5)^2 + (4.5 - 4.5)^2 + (5.0 - 4.5)^2]/4 = 0.125$$

is much smaller than the mean square error for simple random sampling. It is pretty obvious that stratified sampling is preferable.

In general, it pays to stratify if one can identify strata where the elements within each stratum are homogeneous, but where differences from one stratum to the other are large. In stratification we separate the elements of the population, as listed on the sample frame, into two or more groups. Then, random samples are selected from each stratum.

As another illustration, assume that we are involved in filling tubes of toothpaste. Our filling machine accommodates ten nozzles which fill ten tubes at the same time. As part of a larger study we are taking a sample of 50 tubes over a 20-minute production span. Our interest is to learn about the mean fill weight during this particular 20-minute time span. We could collect the total production from this 20-minute time span in a huge container, sample from that container at random, and determine the average weight. This sample average would then be taken as an estimate of the fill weight of the process. Alternatively, we could collect the output from each of the ten nozzles in separate containers, sample five tubes from each container, and use the average fill weight of these 50 tubes as our estimate. We know from prior experience that fill weights of tubes that originate from the same nozzle tend to be more alike than those that come from different nozzles. Each nozzle represents a fairly homogeneous stratum. If each stratum is homogeneous and if differences between the strata are large, then the stratified sampling procedure will lead to a smaller error in our estimate.

As another example, assume that a firm employs $N_1 = 500$ managers, $N_2 = 1{,}500$ engineers, and $N_3 = 7{,}000$ line workers. Suppose that you want to estimate the total annual payroll for the company. You take a stratified random sample, selecting 5 managers, 15 engineers and 70 line workers. Assume that the sample averages (in thousands of dollars) for the three groups are 60, 45, and 20, respectively. Then an estimate of the total annual payroll is

$$\text{Estimated Total Payroll} = (500)(60) + (1{,}500)(45) + (7{,}000)(20) = 237{,}500$$

and an estimate of the mean salary in the company is given by $237{,}500/9{,}000 = 26.389$. Note that in this example the sample sizes in the strata are chosen proportional to the size of the strata. There are three times as many engineers as managers in the population; hence we also sample three times as many engineers as managers (5 versus 15); there are 14 times as many line workers as managers in the company; hence we sample 14 times as many line workers as managers (5 versus 70). It can be shown that such a proportional allocation works well if the variability of the variable of interest is about the same in each stratum. If there are differences in variability, then it is preferable to increase the sample sizes of strata with larger variability.

Market segmentation is another example of stratification. There we divide our potential customers according to characteristics such as age, income, and occupation. Instead of taking simple random samples from the complete population, we take random samples from the various strata. Again, the resulting estimates will be more precise. In addition, stratification allows us to study possible differences among the strata.

9.2.4 Cluster Sampling

Clusters are groupings of elements of the population that represent all aspects of the population in equal proportions. Each cluster is representative of the whole. Cluster sampling selects several of these clusters at random; all elements in the selected clusters become part of the sample. Consider, for example, a sample to be selected from the population of third graders in the State of Iowa. We could view each school in Iowa as a cluster of the basic sampling units (the third-grade students). In cluster sampling we choose a random sample of clusters (schools), and then select all units (third-graders) in the sampled clusters.

Cluster sampling works best if the clusters are representative of the population and if there are few or no differences between clusters. The results from cluster surveys are usually less precise than those of simple random sampling.

In practice, the grouping is often carried out according to the physical closeness of the elements. For example, a large geographic region may be divided into smaller subregions, and the clustering of the elements is done according to their geographic proximity. The appeal of cluster sampling lies in cost savings, as it will be easier to reach elements that are in close geographic proximity.

9.2.5 Two-Stage Sampling

Here the sampling consists of two stages. During the first stage of a two-stage sampling strategy we select primary sample units from the population. During the second stage, we take secondary samples from the sampled primary units. For example, packages in a warehouse may already be organized in larger groups or lots. We may select several of these lots at random (primary stage), and then select several items from each of the selected lots (secondary stage).

9.3 ERRORS INVOLVED IN SAMPLE SURVEYS

Assume that we want to estimate a certain proportion, for example, the proportion of customers who are satisfied with our product. We collect a sample of 100 customers and find that the proportion of satisfied customers is 68 percent. We take this as an estimate of the proportion of satisfied customers in the population. Usually there will be an error associated with this inference, as our estimate will, in all likelihood, miss the true proportion. Let us describe the components of this error.

One part of this error is the *pure sampling error*. The sampling error is there because of our selection mechanism. In our particular random sample we found 68 satisfied customers. However, another sample with another set of 100 customers may find 75 satisfied customers; another may find 63, and so on. Because of the nature of randomness, the sample results from one sample to the next will vary around the true population characteristic. Sampling distributions of sample averages and proportions, taken from random samples, will be discussed in the next chapter. There we will study the standard deviation of the sampling distribution and we will provide interval estimates of the population characteristics that furnish a margin of error for our estimate.

However, there are also *nonsampling errors* involved, and these errors may have a large impact on the accuracy of the estimates. Nonsampling errors arise because of coverage problems, problems with the survey instruments, personnel problems, and poor error control.

A coverage problem means that our survey doesn't reach all elements of the population. Assume that we select residents of a certain area on the basis of their telephone numbers. Some people may not have a telephone and our survey will miss them. Or, consider the homeless population with no address. They are missed by virtually every survey that is based on addresses or telephone numbers. Or, consider the nonrespondents in a survey who don't respond even after repeated attempts to reach them. These coverage problems may "bias" our estimate in one direction or the other.

Problems with the survey instruments also affect the error. Unclear wording of survey questions is a frequent problem. Assume that a question asks about "income," but leaves it open whether it refers to individual or family income. Or, in a question about the number of siblings, the question is unclear on how to count step-brothers and step-sisters. Or, a question on grade-point average may leave the grading scale unclear; some people may list the grade-point average on a five-point scale, while others report it on a four-point scale. Such misunderstandings introduce errors.

Personnel problems are another major source of nonsampling error. If more than one person carries out interviews or gathers data, you may get differences from one person to the next. This is especially true if there is little and inconsistent training. Lack of uniformity introduces variability and affects the error.

Nonsampling errors can play a major role, but they are usually difficult to measure. They can be much larger than the pure sampling error which, on the other hand, is easy to measure. However, it would be very misleading to ignore the nonsampling errors, just because they are difficult to measure. You should keep in mind that the margin of error that is based on the pure sampling error provides just a lower bound for the combined sampling and nonsampling error.

9.4 EXERCISES

9.1 Give examples of simple random sampling, stratified sampling, cluster sampling, and systematic sampling. Write down a sampling protocol for each of your examples.

9.2 (Individual or group project) The N students in this class make up the population of interest. Ask them about their body weight. You are interested in the population mean of weight and in the total body weight for the class.

(a) Write down the sample frame.

(b) Use the random number table to draw a random sample of size $n = 6$ from the population. Calculate the sample average $\bar{x}$ and use it as an estimate of the population mean. Use the product $(N)(\bar{x})$ as an estimate of the total class weight. How large are the sample errors?

(c) Divide the population into males and females; there are N_1 males and N_2 females in your class. Draw a stratified random sample of 3 male and 3 female students, and use the sample averages for the two groups, $\bar{x}_m$ and $\bar{x}_f$, to calculate estimates of the population characteristics. Use $(N_1\bar{x}_m + N_2\bar{x}_f)$ to estimate the total class weight, and

$(N_1\bar{x}_m + N_2\bar{x}_f)/(N_1 + N_2)$ to estimate the population mean. How large are the sampling errors?

(d) Discuss which of the two sampling procedures (random sampling or stratified random sampling) can be expected to give the more accurate estimates, and discuss why.

9.3 (Individual or group project)

(a) Construct a very short survey questionnaire of your own choosing.

(b) Administer this survey to randomly selected residences in the community you live in. Discuss how to construct the sample frame of residences. The residence section of your local telephone book is a good place to start. Discuss its shortcomings.

(c) Take a random sample of 50 residences by selecting $n = 50$ phone numbers at random. Describe your selection procedure in detail.

(d) After selecting the sample units, make the calls, obtain the relevant information, and summarize the information. Describe how you handled situations when no one was at home or when a child answered the phone, and discuss who at the residence was asked to answer the questions.

9.4 (Individual or group project) Select a large-section course at your University; for example, you may want to select an introductory statistics, accounting, or economics course. Develop and administer a questionnaire that addresses the "quality" of the course as it was taught last semester. Develop the sample frame; the instructor or the University registrar can give you a list of students who were registered in this course. Draw a random sample of size 30, using the table of random numbers in Table 9.1. Collect the information. Use the techniques that you learned in Chapter 7 to summarize the information.

9.5 (Individual or group project)

(a) Write a short questionnaire that can be used to assess the faculty's interest in teaching. For example, you may want to ask professors how many hours (per week) they teach this semester, how many hours they prepare for each hour of class instruction, how they perceive the rewards for good teaching, the professor's department, as well as other relevant background information such as the gender of the professor, rank, age, and so on.

(b) Construct the sample frame of all professors at your University; usually payroll or the University President's office will furnish this information. You may want to stratify the population according to faculty rank (instructor, assistant, associate, full professor), or gender.

(c) Use the random number table and draw a random sample of 60 professors, possibly stratified. Give a detailed description of your procedure.

(d) Mail the questionnaire via campus mail. Carefully draft an accompanying letter to maximize the response rate. Devise a system that allows you to keep track of nonresponding professors, but which protects the confidentiality of the respondents. Discuss follow-up procedures for nonrespondents.

(e) Analyze the results and write a short report.

(f) Discuss the benefits and drawbacks of the mail survey as compared with a telephone survey. If you feel that a telephone survey will be just as good or better, use a telephone survey.

9.6 As part of an investigation we carry out 16 experimental runs, runs 1 through 16, in which four factors are studied at low and high levels. For example, the run (−, − , + , −) sets factors 1, 2, and 4 at their low levels, and factor 3 at its high level. Use the table of random numbers to write down a random arrangement of these 16 experiments. Give reasons why one should use the randomized arrangement.

9.7 Consider the experiment of rolling two dice. Record the number of spots on the upside of the dice as an ordered pair: (x = spots on first die; y = spots on second die).

(a) Simulate $n = 10$ outcomes from this experiment. Use two adjacent columns in the table of random digits. For example, start in row 8 of Table 9.1 and use columns 9 and 10.

(b) Simulate $n = 10$ outcomes from this experiment, but use a single column of random digits. For example, start in row 8 of column 9. Simulate digits between 1 and 6, and then group the digits into nonoverlapping pairs.

(c) Convince yourself that either procedure provides random realizations from this experiment. Which of the two procedures is more "economical," in terms of minimizing the number of draws that don't lead to feasible outcomes?

9.8 A population of 1,000 students is stratified into 500 males and 500 females. Under stratified random sampling we select 10 male students and 10 female students at random from their respective strata.

(a) Convince yourself that each student has the same chance of being selected into the stratified sample (in fact, the chance is 10/500, or 2 percent).

(b) Explain why the result in (a) is not sufficient to make the stratified random sample a simple random sample from the population of 1,000 students. Note that in a simple random sample each subset (of size 20 in this case) has to have the same chance of being selected. Is this the case here?

9.9 You are using the table of random numbers to select $n = 2$ numbers from among the numbers between 00 and 99. You find a random entry in the table; for example row 6 and column 1. You read across the row and select *overlapping* pairs of random digits. The digits in row 6 of the table, "7 4 0 2 9 . . . ," become the numbers 74 and 40.

(a) Convince yourself that this procedure gives *each number* between 00 and 99 the same chance of being selected.

(b) Does this procedure lead to random samples? That is, does *each pair of numbers* between 00 and 99 have the same chance of being selected? Why or why not?

9.10 People are called up to service according to the results of a lottery that operates on the person's birthday. The lottery proceeds by first selecting at random a month, and then selecting at random a day from within that month. Discuss whether this sampling procedure can be used to generate random samples.

9.11 In the previous chapter we discussed discrete distributions, including the binomial and the Poisson distributions. The table of random digits can be used to simulate observations from these distributions.

Generate 50 realizations from a Binomial distribution with parameters $n = 3$ and $\theta = 0.4$.

(a) Convince yourself that the binomial probabilities for the four outcomes 0, 1, 2, and 3 are given by: $P(X = 0) = 0.216$, $P(X = 1) = 0.432$, $P(X = 2) = 0.288$, and $P(X = 3) = 0.064$.

(b) From the table of random digits select nonoverlapping triples, starting in a certain row and column. For numbers between 000 and 215, the realization is $x = 0$; for numbers between 216 and 647, the realization is $x = 1$; for numbers between 648 and 935, the realization is $x = 2$; and for numbers between 936 and 999, the realization is $x = 3$. This will generate the four possible outcomes with the correct probabilities.

For example, in Table 9.1 with columns 2, 3 and 4, and reading down from row 11 onwards, we get the following realizations: 2 (arising from 918), 0 (arising from 004), 1 (arising from 318), and so on.

(c) There is another, and equivalent, approach to generating these numbers. Use three nonoverlapping columns to represent the outcomes of the $n = 3$ trials. Code the trial as a success if the random digit is between 0 and 3 (as $\theta = 0.4$); code it as a failure if the digit is between 4 and 9. Then count up the successes across the three trials. For example, with columns 2, 3, and 4 and reading down from row 11 the realizations are: 1 (as 918 represents "FSF"), 2 (as 004 represents "SSF"), 2 (as 318 represents "SSF"), and so on.

9.12 Consider two independent random variables, X and Y. Assume that the random variable X has mean μ_X and standard deviation σ_X; the random variable Y has mean μ_Y and standard deviation σ_Y. We showed in Section 8.10 that the standard deviation of the sum $X + Y$, and also of the difference $X - Y$, is given by $\sigma_{X+Y} = \sigma_{X-Y} = \sqrt{(\sigma_X)^2 + (\sigma_Y)^2}$.

Use simulations to convince yourself of this fact. For example, roll a fair die for a total of 200 times. Enter the first 100 realizations into column 1, and the next 100 realizations into column 2. The first column represents realizations of X; the second column represents realizations of Y. Observe that these two columns are independent, as there is no carryover from one roll to the next. Calculate the standard deviations of the numbers in each column. Next, form two additional columns. The third column includes the sum and the fourth column includes the difference of the first two columns. Calculate the standard deviations of the numbers in these two columns.

Check that for the coin toss distribution the mean is 3.5 and the standard deviation is 1.71. Then, in theory, the standard deviation of $X + Y$ and of $X - Y$ is given by $\sqrt{(1.71)^2 + (1.71)^2} = 2.42$. Check whether the above claim holds for your simulated data. Note that you cannot expect exact agreement as you are dealing with sample statistics.

Instead of rolling your die by hand you may want to use computer software to generate random variables from this as well as various other distributions. You will notice that the result about the standard deviation of sums and differences does not depend on the particular distribution that you select.

9.13 The book *Mail and Telephone Surveys: The Total Design Method* by Don A. Dillman discusses the step-by-step details of how to conduct successful mail and telephone surveys. The book *Survey Questions: Handcrafting the Standardized Questionnaire* by Jean M. Converse and Stanley Presser gives much useful advice on how to write survey questions. Read and comment on these books.

9.14 Read the paper, "Listening to the Voice of the Employee," by Ronald D. Snee. *Quality Progress*, January 1995, pp. 91–95. Discuss the value of surveys and summarize Snee's ideas on how to plan and conduct surveys.

9.5 REFERENCES

Converse, J. M., and S. Presser. *Survey Questions: Handcrafting the Standardized Questionnaire*. Newbury Park, CA: Sage Publications, 1986.

Deming, W. E. *Some Theory of Sampling*. New York: Dover, 1950.

Deming, W. E. *Sample Design in Business Research*. New York: Wiley, 1960.

Dillman, D. A. *Mail and Telephone Surveys: The Total Design Method*. New York: Wiley, 1978.

Hansen, M. H., W. N. Hurwitz, and W. G. Madow. *Sample Survey Methods and Theory; Vol. I: Methods and Applications; Vol. II: Theory*. New York: Wiley, 1953.

Roberts, H., and B. Sergesketter. *Quality Is Personal: A Foundation for Total Quality Management*. New York: The Free Press, 1993.

Snee, R. D. "Listening to the Voice of the Employee," *Quality Progress*, January 1995, 91–95.

CHAPTER 10

STATISTICAL INFERENCE UNDER SIMPLE RANDOM SAMPLING

10.1 INTRODUCTION

We use sample statistics, calculated from a set of observations, to estimate characteristics of the population. We use the sample average as an estimate of the population mean, the sample standard deviation as an estimate of the population standard deviation, and the sample proportion as an estimate of the population proportion. The population characteristics are the equal complete coverage values that one would obtain by a complete evaluation of all elements in the population. We usually assume that the size of the population is large. The terms "population" and "process" are used interchangeably in this book. In many industrial settings the population is generated by a process, for example, a fill process that puts the required amount of fill into tubes of toothpaste; a chemical batch process that generates certain yields; or a manufacturing process that produces steel flats of certain desired dimensions and strength. Process outcomes are variable and we use distributions to describe the population of possible outcomes from such processes. These distributions are characterized by their process mean μ and their process standard deviation σ.

In order to make inferences from a sample to the population, one must have a sample that provides a "fair picture" of the population. While we only select one particular sample, we realize that there are many, many other samples that could have been selected. This chapter shows how to assess the margin of error that we make when using sample results to estimate population characteristics. The following discussion assumes that the observations have come from simple random sampling. Under random sampling each possible sample has the same chance of being selected. How this is carried out in practice is the subject of the previous chapter.

Let us start with several illustrations of the concepts that are being covered in this chapter.

Illustration 1 Assume that we take a random sample of 25 tubes of toothpaste from today's production and find that for this particular sample the average fill weight is 6.7 ounces and the sample standard deviation is 0.5 ounce. What can we say about today's process mean? Because of the sample information our best guess of the process mean is 6.7 ounces. However, this is just an estimate, as we have selected only 25 tubes. With a different set of 25 tubes the sample average would have been different. How can we construct an interval estimate that contains the process mean with high probability? We will call such intervals *confidence intervals*.

We may be interested in the following related question. In the past the mean fill weight of this particular process has been 6.5 ounces. How can we use the sample information (that is, sample average 6.7 ounces and sample standard deviation 0.5 ounce from a random sample of 25 tubes) to test whether the process level has shifted? We will refer to this as the *testing of a hypothesis*.

Illustration 2 As another example, assume that the mean level of a particular airborne pollutant is 10.0 parts per million (ppm). A change is made in how the pollutant is measured, as the air is now heated before measurements are taken. We suspect that the change in the measurement procedure may have led to a reduction in the level. In order to test our suspicion, we took 100 measurements under the new procedure. These measurements led to a sample average of 9.32 ppm and a sample standard deviation 0.8 ppm. Is this enough evidence to say that the process mean has decreased? The sample average is an estimate of the population mean, and it is lower than 10 ppm. However, keep in mind that the sample average is only an estimate of the process level. Is this estimate really small enough to toss out the status quo?

Illustration 3 We are interested in estimating the fraction of defectives of a certain process. We take a random sample of 200 items from today's production and find that 3.5 percent are defective. The sample fraction, 0.035, is our best estimate or guess of the unknown fraction of defectives among today's products. However, we could have taken many other random samples, and with each sample the sample proportion would have been somewhat different. What is the reliability of our estimate? How can we get an interval estimate (that is, a confidence interval) for the unknown population proportion of defectives?

Furthermore, in the past the average fraction of defectives of this process has been 3 percent. Our random sample of 200 items has shown that 3.5 percent are defective. How likely is it to get such a large sample proportion of defectives if the population proportion is still at 3 percent? Does the sample result of 3.5 percent defectives among a random sample of size 200 indicate that the fraction of defectives in the population (process) has gone up?

Illustration 4 The mean yield of a certain production process is 6.2 tons for an eight-hour shift. Modifications on the process are made, with the intent to increase the mean yield. The yields for the next 30 shifts after the modifications have been implemented average 6.305 tons, with a standard deviation of $s = 0.5$ ton. Is this enough evidence to conclude that the process mean has increased?

Illustration 5 X-bar control charts, which are discussed in Chapter 12, are time sequence plots of successive subgroup averages. Small random samples from the process, also called subgroups, are taken at periodic intervals, and the averages of these subgroups are plotted. Control limits are an integral part of these charts. These control limits help us assess whether a particular sample average is unusual, when compared with the past in-control history of the process.

In all of the above problems (the calculation of interval estimates or confidence intervals; the testing of hypotheses; and the determination of control limits in x-bar control charts) one needs to know something about the variability of sample statistics from one random sample to the next. In particular, we need to understand the variability of the sample average

$$\bar{X} = (X_1 + \cdots + X_n)/n,$$

calculated from a random sample of observations that is taken from an underlying population or process with mean value μ and standard deviation σ. The *Central Limit Effect*, discussed in the next section, gives us the answer to this question.

10.2 THE CENTRAL LIMIT EFFECT FOR AVERAGES

Consider a process that generates certain measurements. Let us call the variable of interest X, and let us assume that the variability among the measurements can be described by a distribution with mean μ and standard deviation σ. The distribution need not be normal, nor does it have to be symmetric. The distribution describes the population from which we sample. The population could also consist of a finite collection of elements, and then the population mean and standard deviation are the equal complete coverage values; for a finite population we require that the population size is large.

Take a random sample of size n from this process and calculate the sample average

$$\overline{X} = (X_1 + X_2 + \cdots + X_n)/n.$$

Prior to sampling, the sample average itself is a random variable. This is because random draws from the population can lead to many different samples, and samples that include different elements imply different sample averages. We say that the sample average $\overline{X}$ has a *sampling distribution*. For a population with a finite number of elements (N of them) one can, in theory, write out all possible random samples of size n, and one can calculate the sample averages of these equally likely samples (they are equally likely because of random sampling). One can display the distribution of the possible sample averages through a histogram, and one can calculate the average and the standard deviation of all possible sample averages. Of course, if the population size N is large then there would be millions or billions of possible samples.

Very general and extremely useful results can be established about the sampling distribution of sample averages. For random samples one can show that:

1. The mean of the sampling distribution of $\overline{X}$ is given by μ. This says that sample averages from repeated random samples vary around the process mean. This makes perfect sense: If individual observations vary around μ, then we can expect that sample averages vary around μ also. Let us denote the mean of the sampling distribution of $\overline{X}$ by Mean($\overline{X}$). Then this result says that

$$\text{Mean}(\overline{X}) = \mu.$$

2. The standard deviation of the sampling distribution of $\overline{X}$ is given by

$$\text{StdDev}(\overline{X}) = \frac{\sigma}{\sqrt{n}}.$$

The standard deviation of the sampling distribution of $\overline{X}$ is also called the *standard error* of the sample average. It tells us about the variability of averages from repeated random samples. Averaging reduces the variability. The variability of an average is smaller than the variability of individual observations; we see that the standard deviation of an average decreases with the square root of the sample size n. This makes sense, as $\overline{X}$ averages out high and low values.

3. For reasonably large sample sizes, the distribution of $\overline{X}$ is *approximately normal*, whether or not the individual measurements come from a normal distribution. The approximation becomes better with increasing sample size. A sample size of $n = 30$ is usually large enough; however, in many cases the Central Limit Effect already works for much smaller sample sizes.

This last result explains why so many measurements are, in fact, normally distributed. Measurements are affected by a multitude of factors; some of the factors decrease the measurements, while others increase them. The influences of these factors average out to create normally distributed variables.

Putting results 1 through 3 together, we can state the *Central Limit Effect for Averages* as follows:

> *For reasonably large random samples from a population with mean μ and standard deviation σ, the sampling distribution of the sample average $\bar{X}$ follows (approximately) a normal distribution with mean μ and standard deviation $\sigma/\sqrt{n}$.*

A formal proof of the Central Limit Effect is beyond the scope of this book. However, you can convince yourself that this result is true by carrying out the following simulation experiment. Roll a single die and record X, the number of dots on the upside of the die. The variable X can take on outcomes $x = 1, 2, \ldots, 6$, with equal probabilities 1/6. This discrete distribution describes the population. It is a simple exercise to calculate the mean and the standard deviation of the distribution of X. The mean is $\mu = 3.5$ and the standard deviation is $\sigma = 1.71$; see Exercise 10.1.

Rolling the die is the same as drawing an element from this distribution. Now roll the die five times and record the average number of dots; that is, calculate the average $\bar{X} = (X_1 + X_2 + \cdots + X_5)/5$. In order to learn more about the distribution of sample averages, repeat the experiment (the experiment of rolling a die five times) and calculate the sample average for each of these replications. In Table 10.1 we illustrate this for three experiments.

We repeated the experiment 5,000 times, which resulted in 5,000 subgroup averages that were calculated from 5 observations each. (We didn't actually do this by hand, but used a computer program; see Chapter 9, and in particular the exercises at the end of this chapter for an explanation how this is done.) It is quite easy to do this within spreadsheet software; just generate 5 columns of 5,000 random draws each and then average across the five columns. The histogram of the 5,000 simulations is given in Figure 10.1 (page 252). It represents the sampling distribution of $\bar{X}$. It shows a bell-shaped distribution centered right at $\mu = 3.5$. In fact, the average of the 5,000 averages of size 5 is 3.4977, which is very close to $\mu = 3.5$. The standard deviation calculated from the 5,000 averages of size 5 is 0.7677; this is very close to what we expected as $\text{StdDev}(\bar{X}) = (1.71/\sqrt{5}) = 0.7647$.

These results illustrate that the Central Limit Effect is working. Averages (from samples of size 5) vary around the process mean; the standard deviation of averages decreases with the square root of the number of observations; and the shape of the distribution is already approximately normal, despite the facts that the distribution of individual observations is uniform (which is far from normal) and that

TABLE 10.1 Three Replications of the Experiment of Rolling a Die Five Times

	Outcomes						
	1	2	3	4	5	6	
Roll 1		2					
2				4			$\bar{x} = 4.0$ in our first sample of size $n = 5$
3			3				
4					5		
5						6	

	Outcomes						
	1	2	3	4	5	6	
Roll 6	1						
7				4			$\bar{x} = 3.2$ in our second sample of size $n = 5$
8			3				
9						6	
10		2					

	Outcomes						
	1	2	3	4	5	6	
Roll 11		2					
12						6	$\bar{x} = 3.4$ in our third sample of size $n = 5$
13					5		
14			3				
15	1						

the sample size ($n = 5$) is small. If we had averaged more than five observations, the normal approximation would have been even better (in Exercise 10.2 we ask you to carry out these simulation experiments with a larger sample size).

In Figure 10.2 (page 252) we display the population distribution from which we sample; the distribution gives equal probabilities to discrete outcomes 1 through 6. We also display the approximate normal sampling distribution of averages from random samples of size five; this distribution is centered at the population mean 3.5 and its standard deviation is $1.71/\sqrt{5} = 0.76$. For comparison, we also display the sampling distribution of averages from random samples of size 25. The variability is considerably smaller; the standard deviation for averages from random samples of size 25 is $1.71/\sqrt{25} = 0.34$.

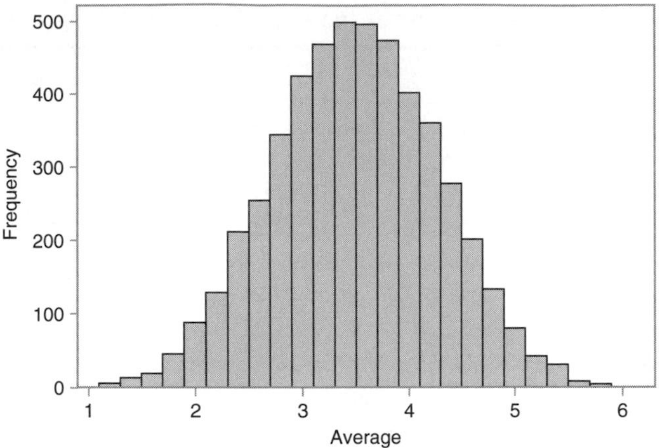

FIGURE 10.1 Histogram of 5,000 averages of size 5, where individual observations are the outcomes of the roll of a die.

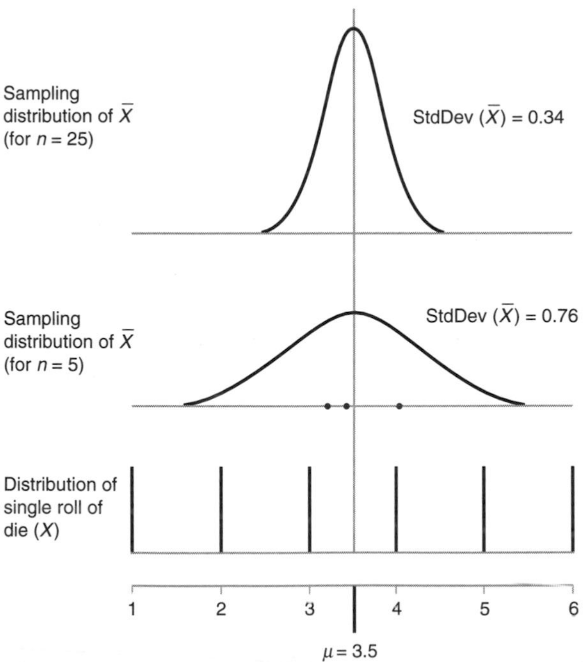

FIGURE 10.2 The population distribution for the roll of a die, and the approximating sampling distributions of averages from random samples of size 5 and 25.

EXAMPLE 1

Let X be a measurement that follows a distribution with mean $\mu = 10$ and standard deviation $\sigma = 2$. Note that no assumptions about the shape of the distribution are made. We are planning to take a random sample of size $n = 49$ and calculate the sample average. What can we say about the distribution of sample averages from samples of size 49?

The sample size $n = 49$ is reasonably large. The Central Limit Effect tells us that the sampling distribution of averages $\overline{X}$, calculated from random samples of size 49 from such a population, is approximately normal with mean $\mu = 10$ and standard deviation $\sigma/\sqrt{n} = 2/7 = 0.286$.

What, then, is the probability that a sample average of 49 observations will fall within the interval between 9.5 and 10.5? Using the normal table, we find that this probability is approximately

$$P(9.5 \le \overline{X} \le 10.5) \approx P\left(\frac{9.5 - 10}{0.286} \le Z \le \frac{10.5 - 10}{0.286}\right)$$
$$= P(-1.75 \le Z \le 1.75) = 0.9198.$$

■

10.3 CONFIDENCE INTERVALS FOR THE PROCESS MEAN AND TESTS OF HYPOTHESES

The Central Limit Effect is very useful as it tells us about the variability that can be expected among sample averages; it shows us how far the sample average can be from the process mean that we are trying to estimate. Assume that we have obtained a sample of size n from a process with mean μ and standard deviation σ. From this particular sample we calculate the sample average $\bar{x}$ and the sample standard deviation s. Note that these are numbers such as $\bar{x} = 20.7$ and $s = 2$; hence our lowercase notation. We use the sample average $\bar{x}$ as our estimate of the unknown process mean μ. However, we are aware of the sampling error; our estimate is based on the result of just a single sample and we know that under random sampling the average of one such sample can differ from the process mean. Instead of quoting just a single number as a point estimate it would be preferable to take account of the sampling variability and quote interval estimates. Such intervals, called *confidence intervals*, are introduced in this section.

The sampling error is the difference between the estimate and the process mean. The sampling error $\overline{X} - \mu$ has a sampling distribution. The Central Limit Effect says that this distribution is approximately normal with mean zero and standard deviation StdDev($\overline{X}$) $= \sigma/\sqrt{n}$. Therefore, the standardized sampling error, $(\overline{X} - \mu)/\text{StdDev}(\overline{X})$, is approximately standard normal. For normal distributions we know that

$$P\left(-2 \leq \frac{\overline{X} - \mu}{\text{StdDev}(\overline{X})} \leq 2\right) \approx 0.95.$$

We now rearrange the terms in the above inequality. We multiply each term by $\text{StdDev}(\overline{X})$, we subtract $\overline{X}$ from each term, and we multiply the components by (-1), which reverses the inequality. Then we find that

$$P(\overline{X} - 2\ \text{StdDev}(\overline{X}) \leq \mu \leq \overline{X} + 2\ \text{StdDev}(\overline{X})) \approx 0.95,$$

or, after substituting $\text{StdDev}(\overline{X}) = \sigma/\sqrt{n}$,

$$P(\overline{X} - 2\sigma/\sqrt{n} \leq \mu \leq \overline{X} + 2\sigma/\sqrt{n}) \approx 0.95.$$

This result says that the random interval

$$[\overline{X} - 2\ \text{StdDev}(\overline{X}), \overline{X} + 2\ \text{StdDev}(\overline{X})] \quad \text{or} \quad [\overline{X} - 2\sigma/\sqrt{n}, \overline{X} + 2\sigma/\sqrt{n}]$$

covers the unknown mean μ in approximately 95 percent of the samples. In other words, among repeated random samples, intervals constructed in this particular way cover the mean μ about 95 percent of the time.

We observe the outcomes of just a single sample, with sample average $\bar{x}$. Using the sample results we calculate the interval $[\bar{x} - 2\sigma/\sqrt{n}, \bar{x} + 2\sigma/\sqrt{n}]$. We call this a 95 percent *confidence interval for the process mean* μ. The interval, calculated from a single sample, will either miss or cover the unknown mean μ. However, the sampling distribution for sample averages tells us that in repeated samples from that process about 95 percent of intervals constructed in that way will cover the process mean μ. Thus we are "95 percent confident" that our single interval will cover the process mean.

There is still one problem with this interval. We probably can't calculate it, as we won't know the population standard deviation σ. The best we can do is replace σ in that interval with the sample standard deviation s, and use

$$[\bar{x} - 2s/\sqrt{n}, \bar{x} + 2s/\sqrt{n}]$$

as an *approximate 95 percent confidence interval.* It is an approximate 95 percent confidence interval for two reasons: First, we rely on the Central Limit Effect, which says that the sampling distribution can be approximated by the normal distribution. Second, we replace the unknown standard deviation σ with its sample estimate s, the sample standard deviation. We estimate the standard deviation of the sample average by $s/\sqrt{n}$.

If the sample size is very small (less than 20 or so) then the sample standard deviation s is not a very reliable estimate of the population standard deviation σ. By replacing a fixed population parameter with an uncertain, possibly unreliable estimate we introduce additional variability into our interval. In order to be on the safe side one should stretch the confidence interval and make it a bit wider. Instead of using the constants ± 2 in the 95 percent confidence interval, one could use slightly larger cutoffs such as ± 2.1 or ± 2.2, depending on the size of the random sample. Under certain additional assumptions (namely that the population distribution is normal) one can obtain these revised cutoffs from a t-distribution. The *t-distribution* is very similar to the standard normal (it is symmetric around zero and roughly bell-shaped), except that it has slightly heavier tails than the normal. In fact, there is a whole family of t-distributions, indexed by a parameter called *degrees of freedom*, with differing heaviness of the tails. The 97.5th percentile of a t-distribution is slightly larger than 1.96; for example, for a sample of size 10 the cutoff from a t-distribution is 2.26; for a sample of size 20 it is 2.09; for a sample of size 30 it is 2.04.

In most practical applications these small differences will matter very little. For our purposes, it will be sufficient to use cutoffs ± 2. It is then easy to remember how to get a 95 percent confidence interval for the mean μ. We take the point estimate, which is the sample average $\bar{x}$, and add and subtract two times the estimated standard deviation of this estimate, which is $s/\sqrt{n}$.

How would we construct a 99.73 percent confidence interval? We know from tables for the standard normal distribution that 99.73 percent of the probability lies between -3 and $+3$. Thus an approximate 99.73 percent confidence interval for the process mean μ is given by $[\bar{x} - 3s/\sqrt{n}, \bar{x} + 3s/\sqrt{n}]$. This result makes sense: If we want a higher level of confidence for our interval, then we have to make the interval wider.

How would we get a 90 percent confidence interval? This means that we have to find cutoffs such that 90 percent of the distribution of the standardized sampling error is within these values. For this, we need the 5th and the 95th percentiles of the standard normal distribution; they are -1.645 and $+1.645$. Thus the approximate 90 percent confidence interval for μ is given by $[\bar{x} - (1.645)s/\sqrt{n}, \bar{x} + (1.645)s/\sqrt{n}]$.

EXAMPLE 2

A random sample of 25 tubes of toothpaste from today's production led to an average fill weight of 6.7 ounces; the sample standard deviation among these 25 observations is $s = 0.10$ ounce. Based on these sample results, our estimate for the mean weight of today's filling process is 6.7 ounces. An approximate 95 percent confidence interval for today's process mean μ is

$$[6.7 - (2)(0.10/\sqrt{25}), 6.7 + (2)(0.10/\sqrt{25})],$$

or [6.66, 6.74]. We are very confident (in fact, 95 percent confident) that this interval will cover the unknown mean μ. ■

EXAMPLE 3

In the past the mean yield of a certain process during an 8-hour shift has been 6.2 tons. Modifications on the process have been made recently, and we are not sure whether these modifications have changed the process mean. After the modifications have been implemented, we measure the yield during the next 30 shifts. We find that the sample average from these 30 numbers is 6.305 tons, and the standard deviation is 0.5 ton. Is this enough evidence to say that there has been a change in the mean yield of the process?

Let us calculate an approximate 95 percent confidence interval for the mean yield μ. It is given by

$$[6.305 - (2)(0.5/\sqrt{30}), 6.305 + (2)(0.5/\sqrt{30})]$$

or [6.12, 6.49]. We are pretty confident that this interval will cover the true unknown process mean. Notice that the old status quo value, 6.2 tons, is included in this interval. Thus, we cannot conclude that the process mean has changed from its previous value 6.2. ■

In the above example we "test" a certain hypothesis about the population mean; namely that the process mean has stayed at 6.2 tons. Statisticians call this hypothesis the *null hypothesis*, and write it as $\mu = 6.2$. We test whether the sample data is consistent with this hypothesis. Now it is true that the sample average is different (it is 6.305 tons); but this is sample information and thus subject to sampling error. Is this sample information from just 30 shifts enough evidence to say that the process level μ has changed? In the previous example we answered this by obtaining a 95 percent confidence interval and checking whether this interval includes 6.2 tons. In our case the interval did cover 6.2. Thus we could not rule out that the mean has stayed at 6.2. In other words, we concluded that the mean has not shifted.

Before the law, you are innocent until proven guilty. In statistics, the null hypothesis is retained until the evidence suggests otherwise. The burden of proof is carried by those who want to prove that the null hypothesis is incorrect.

We mentioned before that the length of a confidence interval changes with the confidence level. If we want to be extremely confident (such as 99 percent, or 99.99 percent), the corresponding confidence interval gets wider. Thus, we are more likely to retain the null hypothesis.

By making a decision on the basis of sample information we are bound to make errors. For example, our sample data may reject the null hypothesis ($\mu = 6.2$), when, in fact, the process mean is 6.2. We call this a *type I error*. We know that a 95 percent confidence interval will fail to cover the true mean 5 percent of the time. Thus, by using the 95 percent confidence interval in our testing approach, we keep the probability of a type I error at 5 percent. A decision based on a 99 percent confidence interval keeps the chance of making such an error at 1 percent.

Keeping the probability of making a type I error (that is, rejecting the null hypothesis when, in fact, it is true) small, is a good idea. However, keeping it too small can also be bad, because with the resulting very wide confidence interval our decision will be conservative. With a very wide confidence interval we would rarely reject the hypothesized value, even if the null hypothesis were wrong. Such a conservative strategy would constitute a serious error as we would fail to recognize that the level has changed. We would be likely to make the mistake of accepting the null hypothesis (and conclude that the mean is 6.2 tons) even though the process level has shifted. We call the error of accepting the null hypothesis when, in fact, the null hypothesis is wrong, a *type II error*.

10.4 TEST STATISTICS AND PROBABILITY VALUES

Calculating a confidence interval for the population (or process) mean and checking whether it includes a certain hypothesized value is an excellent approach to testing a hypothesis, especially if the alternative to the null hypothesis is two-sided. We talk about a *two-sided alternative* if we test whether the population mean is *different* from a hypothesized value. We talk about a *one-sided alternative* if we test whether the population mean has *increased* or *decreased*. For example, we may be interested in testing whether the mean of a modified process is larger than 6.2 tons.

There is another, and equivalent way of testing statistical hypotheses. This approach argues through *test statistics* and *probability values*.

Let us test whether the mean concentration of a certain pollutant for the current year has *increased* above the previous year's level of 20.0 parts per million. The mean value for the previous year is well established; it has been determined through numerous measurements. Here we want to decide between the null hypothesis $\mu = 20.0$ and the alternative hypothesis $\mu > 20.0$. Sample information for the current year was obtained. Fifty observations were taken, leading to a sample average of 20.7 ppm and a sample standard deviation of $s = 2$ ppm. Is this enough evidence to reject the null hypothesis in favor of the alternative hypothesis?

The test statistic for this problem is pretty straightforward to obtain. We calculate the difference between the sample average and the hypothesized value, and we standardize this difference by the standard error of the average. That is, we calculate the (standardized) *test statistic*

$$TS = \frac{\bar{x} - 20}{s/\sqrt{n}} = \frac{20.7 - 20.0}{2/\sqrt{50}} = 2.47.$$

This result tells us that our sample average is 2.47 standard errors larger than the hypothesized value. Large values of the test statistic support the alternative hypothesis. However, is this value large enough to doubt the null hypothesis $\mu = 20.0$? We can argue as follows: If the null hypothesis were true (that is, the mean is really 20.0), then the sampling distribution of this test statistic is approximately standard normal; this is a consequence of the Central Limit Effect. We can calculate the probability that a standard normal variable is as large as or larger than 2.47. This probability is $P(Z > 2.47) = 0.0068$. It is called the *probability value* or the *p-value*. In this example it is very small. This says that it is quite unlikely to get such a large test statistic if the process mean had indeed stayed at 20.0. In other words, we don't believe in our null hypothesis. We reject it, and conclude that the mean has increased.

Typically we compare the p-value with a value of 0.05. If the p-value is smaller than 0.05, then it is unlikely that our sample result has originated from the null hypothesis. In this case we reject the null hypothesis. We say that the difference between the sample information and the null hypothesis is *statistically significant*. On the other hand, if the probability value is larger than 0.05, then our test statistic is not extreme and it is quite likely that it has come from the distribution that is specified by the null hypothesis. Hence there is not enough evidence to reject the null hypothesis, and we decide to retain it. A choice of 0.05 for the comparison allows for a type I error of 5 percent. This value is also called the *significance level of the test*. It is akin to working with 95 percent confidence intervals.

For this analysis to be applicable, the data must represent a random sample. For example, in the context of the present example a sample of just the January observations wouldn't necessarily constitute a random sample. If there were seasonality in the population levels and if the mean for January were different from the means of other months, then the sample results would be biased. A sample of January measurements would tell us about the mean level for January, but not about the overall mean level for the whole year. If there were no seasonality, and thus no systematic differences in the measurements from one month to the next, then a sample of January measurements alone may be representative. But the absence of seasonality is a rather strong assumption which is better checked by taking data for different months. Another possible violation of random sampling is to take all measurements close together in time—say 50 measurements within an hour period on the very same day, say January 10. This sampling scheme will tell us about the process mean for that particular hour on January 10. While this is quite a lot of information to pin down the mean for this particular short time interval, the information may not be representative of the whole month of January, or the whole year. The variability among measurements that are taken close together in time reflects the short-time variability; however, the long-term variability in the measurements may be much larger.

EXAMPLE 4

Let us revisit an example that we mentioned in the introduction. Assume that the mean level of the currently used measurement procedure when applied to certified test samples of an airborne pollutant is 10.0 ppm. A change is made in how we measure the pollutant; the air is now heated before the measurements are taken. We are interested in whether this change in the procedures has decreased the level of the measurement. We take 100 measurements under the new procedures and we find that the sample average is 9.32 ppm; the standard deviation of the 100 observations is $s = 0.8$ ppm. Can we conclude that the mean concentration has *decreased?*

Here the null hypothesis is $\mu = 10.0$ and the alternative is that the mean has decreased; that is $\mu < 10.0$. We calculate the test statistic

$$TS = \frac{9.32 - 10.0}{0.8/\sqrt{100}} = -8.5.$$

Large negative values of the test statistic support the alternative hypothesis, which claims that the new procedure leads to a smaller mean. The probability value is the probability of getting such a small statistic, or one that is even smaller, by chance. Since $P(Z < -8.5)$ is essentially zero, it is extremely unlikely that one gets such a small value by chance alone. Thus there is very strong evidence that the mean has decreased from 10.0 ppm. ■

EXAMPLE 5

As a last illustrative example let us reanalyze Example 3. There we investigated whether the mean output *changed* from its previous standard of 6.2 tons. The null hypothesis is $\mu = 6.2$ tons; the alternative hypothesis is *two-sided*, as our problem does not specify a particular direction for the alternative.

The sample average from the next 30 shifts is 6.305 tons; the standard deviation is 0.5 ton. Is this enough evidence that there has been a change in the mean output?

We calculate the test statistic

$$TS = \frac{6.305 - 6.2}{0.5/\sqrt{30}} = 1.15.$$

What is its probability value? Recall that the probability value is the probability of observing such a large (or larger) statistic by chance if the null hypothesis is true. Since this is a two-sided test we question the null hypothesis for large positive as well as small negative values of the test statistic. Thus the probability value is $P(Z > 1.15) + P(Z < -1.15) = (2)P(Z > 1.15) = (2)(0.1251) = 0.2502$. The probability value is considerably larger than 0.05. There is not enough evidence to reject the null hypothesis that $\mu = 6.2$. ■

10.5 NORMAL APPROXIMATION OF THE BINOMIAL DISTRIBUTION AND CONFIDENCE INTERVALS FOR A POPULATION PROPORTION

The Central Limit Effect can also be used to approximate the sampling distribution of the *sample total*

$$Y = (X_1 + X_2 + \cdots + X_n) = n\bar{X}.$$

The total is just a fixed multiple of the sample average, and we already know that $\bar{X}$ has an approximate normal distribution with mean μ and standard deviation $\sigma/\sqrt{n}$. Hence it follows that the sample total Y has an approximate normal distribution, with mean $n\mu$ and standard deviation $(n)(\sigma/\sqrt{n}) = (\sqrt{n})\sigma$. Here we have used the results of Section 8.2 in Chapter 8. There we showed that the mean and the standard deviation of a multiple of a random variable, $Y = bX$, are obtained by multiplying the mean and the standard deviation of X by this multiple; that is $\mu_Y = b\mu_X$ and $\sigma_Y = |b|\sigma_X$.

The Central Limit Effect for the total can be used to approximate the binomial distribution by the normal distribution. A binomial variable Y, the number of successes in n trials, is nothing more than a sum of zeros and ones; that is $Y = X_1 + X_2 + \cdots + X_n$, where X_i is either 0 or 1. Thus, provided n is large, the distribution of Y can be approximated by the normal distribution. In the previous chapter we learned that the mean of a binomial distribution with parameters n and θ is $n\theta$, and that its standard deviation is $\sqrt{n\theta(1-\theta)}$. Using the Central Limit Effect, we can approximate the binomial distribution by the normal distribution with the same mean, $n\theta$, and the same standard deviation, $\sqrt{n\theta(1-\theta)}$. This approximation works well if n is reasonably large and if θ is not too close to either zero or 1. It wouldn't work if θ is close to zero; in that case the binomial distribution is much better approximated by a Poisson distribution with parameter $n\theta$; see our discussion in Section 8.4.

EXAMPLE 6

Assume that 40 percent ($\theta = 0.4$) of all companies utilize control charts in their everyday work. Assume that we randomly sample $n = 100$ companies. What is the distribution of Y, the number of control chart users among a random sample of size 100?

Y will vary depending upon which companies we select for our sample. The above result implies that Y follows a binomial distribution with $n = 100$ and $\theta = 0.40$. Its mean is $100(0.40) = 40$ and its standard deviation is $\sqrt{(100)(0.40)(0.60)} = 4.9$.

What if you had to calculate the probability that in a random sample of 100 companies the number of control chart users is between 35 and 45? It could be done; you could use tables or a computer to carry out the calculation. You would calculate $P(Y = 35), P(Y = 36), \ldots, P(Y = 45)$, and add up these numbers. If you do this you get $P(35 \leq Y \leq 45) = 0.7386$. Alternatively, you could use the normal approximation with mean 40 and standard deviation 4.9. However, since we approximate a discrete (the binomial) by a continuous distribution (the normal), we have to include a continuity correction. The probability that $Y = 35$ is approximated by the probability that the normal approximating variable Y_{app} is between 34.5 and 35.5. Thus the probability

$$P(35 \leq Y \leq 45) \approx P(34.5 \leq Y_{\text{app}} \leq 45.5)$$
$$= P\left(\frac{34.5-40}{4.9} \leq Z \leq \frac{45.5-40}{4.9}\right) = P(-1.12 \leq Z \leq 1.12) = 0.7372.$$

Note that the approximation by the normal distribution is quite accurate. ■

Similarly, we can approximate the distribution of the sample proportion, Y/n, where Y is the number of successes in n trials. Dividing the mean and standard deviation of the distribution of Y by n, we find that the approximating distribution for the sample proportion Y/n is normal with mean θ and standard deviation $\sqrt{\theta(1-\theta)/n}$.

We can use this result to obtain confidence intervals for a proportion. Let y be the observed number of occurrences (successes) in the selected sample of size n. Then the sample proportion $p = y/n$ is our best estimate of the population proportion θ. An approximate 95 percent confidence interval for the population proportion θ is given by

$$\left[p - (2)\sqrt{\frac{(p)(1-p)}{n}},\, p + (2)\sqrt{\frac{(p)(1-p)}{n}}\right].$$

When constructing this interval estimate, we follow the standard approach for calculating confidence intervals. We start with the sample estimate (the sample proportion p) and add and subtract two times the standard deviation of the sample proportion. Note that the standard deviation of the sample proportion, $\sqrt{\theta(1-\theta)/n}$, involves the unknown population proportion θ. However, we can replace the unknown θ in this expression with its estimate $p = y/n$, and use the estimated standard deviation $\sqrt{(p)(1-p)/n}$. This is exactly what we did in the above equation.

EXAMPLE 7

A random poll of 400 companies found that 300 of the 400 engage in downsizing their companies; that is $p = 300/400 = 0.75$. Our best estimate for the population proportion of all companies engaged in downsizing is 75 percent. A 95 percent confidence interval for the population proportion is given by

$$[0.75 - (2)(\sqrt{(0.75)(0.25)/400}), 0.75 + (2)(\sqrt{(0.75)(0.25)/400})]$$

or [0.707, 0.793]. We are 95 percent confident that the interval from 70.7 to 79.3 percent will cover the unknown population proportion. This information is certainly strong enough to reject the claim that no more than 50 percent are downsizing. ■

10.6 DETERMINING THE SAMPLE SIZE IN SIMPLE RANDOM SAMPLING

We want to estimate the population (process) mean from the results of a random sample. We would like to obtain a reliable estimate; our goal is to have our estimate within a certain specified distance from the population mean. Because of the random nature of sample averages we cannot achieve this goal with certainty. However, we can require that the probability of this event is very large. How large must the sample size be so that we are 95 percent confident that the sampling error, in absolute value, is not larger than a given value d? In other words, we want

$$P(|\bar{X} - \mu| \leq d) = 0.95.$$

We learned earlier that the standardized estimation error, $(\bar{X} - \mu)/\text{StdDev}(\bar{X})$, follows an approximate standard normal distribution. The requirement

$$0.95 = P\left(\frac{|\bar{X} - \mu|}{\text{StdDev}(\bar{X})} \leq \frac{d}{\text{StdDev}(\bar{X})}\right)$$

implies

$$\frac{d}{\text{StdDev}(\bar{X})} = \frac{d}{\sigma/\sqrt{n}} = 2.$$

Solving this equation for n, we obtain the required sample size,

$$n = (2/d)^2\sigma^2.$$

What about if we wanted to be 99.7 percent confident that our estimate is within d units of the population mean? Then we need to replace the 2 by a 3, and the required sample size is $n = (3/d)^2\sigma^2$.

The required sample size depends on the variability of the individual measurements. In many cases a good planning value for σ is available; we may have access to prior data that can tell us about the standard deviation σ.

EXAMPLE 8

A new procedure for measuring the breaking strength of a steel flat is being considered. From experiments with other related measurement procedures we know that the standard deviation of individual measurements is about 3 lb/sqft. We want to be 95 percent confident that our estimate is within 0.5 lb/sqft of the unknown process mean. How many measurements do we need? Here $\sigma = 3$, and $n = (2/0.5)^2(3)^2 = 144$. We have to take 144 measurements. ■

The same approach can be used to obtain the sample size for estimating a population proportion. Assume that we want to be 95 percent confident that the sample proportion, Y/n, is within d units of the population proportion. That is

$$0.95 = P(|Y/n - \theta| \leq d).$$

In large samples the sample proportion has an approximate normal distribution with mean θ and standard deviation $\text{StdDev}(p) = \sqrt{\theta(1-\theta)/n}$. The requirement

$$0.95 = P\left(\frac{|Y/n - \theta|}{\text{StdDev}(p)} \leq \frac{d}{\sqrt{\theta(1-\theta)/n}}\right)$$

implies that

$$2 = \frac{d}{\sqrt{\theta(1-\theta)/n}}.$$

Solving this equation for n we obtain the required sample size,

$$n = (2/d)^2\theta(1-\theta).$$

We need a planning value for the population proportion, just as we needed a planning value for the standard deviation σ in the earlier case. One can show that $\theta(1-\theta)$ reaches its largest value when $\theta = 1/2$; any other value for θ leads to a smaller product. Just try $\theta = 1/3$; then $\theta(1-\theta) = 2/9$, which is smaller than $(1/2)(1/2) = 1/4$. This implies that

$$n \leq (1/d)^2.$$

A sample size of $(1/d)^2$ will be sufficient for any θ.

EXAMPLE 9

How many people do we have to poll such that the sample proportion is within four percentage points of the population proportion? Here $d = 0.04$, and $n = (1/0.04)^2 = 625$. Of course, if we knew that θ is somewhere in the neighborhood of 0.3, then we could achieve this precision with a smaller sample size, as $n = (2/0.04)^2(0.3)(0.7) = 525$. It is amazing how close we can get to θ, with a rather moderate sample size. This is the reason why winners in elections are predicted from a surprisingly small number of election returns. Of course, this only works if we take random samples. If those early returns come from a particular region of the country that is not representative of the whole population, then this inference could be seriously wrong. ■

10.7 DISCUSSION

10.7.1 Statistical Significance versus Practical Significance

How likely is it that a particular sample result (that is, a certain sample average $\bar{x}$) has come from a population with mean μ? This is what a test statistic and its associated probability value can tell us. For example, the probability value 0.0068 in the earlier example in Section 10.4 expressed the fact that it was extremely unlikely that a sample average of 20.7 ppm has come from a distribution with a mean 20.0 ppm.

We should not make the mistake of confusing statistical significance with practical significance. The practical significance of an increase in the mean pollution from 20.0 ppm to 20.7 ppm depends on the costs and savings that are associated with this change. While a 0.7 ppm increase in mean pollution may imply considerable savings for industry, the benefits to industry have to be balanced with the costs that are paid by society. An increase of 0.7 ppm may be extremely relevant, or it may be relatively unimportant. The costs need to be known before we can assess the practical significance.

10.7.2 Enumerative versus Analytic Studies

The results in this chapter are directly applicable in studies where our objective is to make inferences about parameters of a well-defined population. W. Edwards Deming (*Out of the Crisis*, 1986) calls such studies *enumerative studies*, as in such studies it is possible to enumerate the elements of the population; the list of elements in the population was called the sample frame. From this list one can draw a random sample, and one can use the resulting information for point and interval estimates of population parameters, such as a population mean or a population proportion.

Enumerative studies are quite common. For example, the 1,000 steel billets that are stored in our inventory may represent the population of interest, and the goal of our study may be to estimate the mean depletion of carbon of the 1,000 billets in storage, or the proportion of unacceptable pieces in the inventory. It is common that each billet gets assigned an identification number, in which case it is easy to sample, say 25 of them, at random. From the sample average of these 25 billets we can obtain a 95 percent confidence interval for the population mean. While there is no guarantee that this one interval will include the population mean, the confidence level that is associated with this interval is high.

Many other examples of enumerative studies can be given. A large company may be interested in the mean educational background of its employees. The population consisting of all employees is easily enumerated by using the Social Security numbers that can be obtained from payroll. A random sample can be taken from this sample frame, and inferences on population characteristics, such as the mean number of years beyond high school or the proportion of college graduates among all employees, can be based on the results of a rather small random sample. Other examples of enumerative studies include customer surveys that assess characteristics of the customer population, such as their mean income, their average family size, and the proportion of repeat buyers. For big-ticket items such as cars or durable goods, the sales department will have a list of past buyers that can be enumerated and from which a random sample can be selected.

Deming distinguishes enumerative studies from *analytic studies*. He argues that in many industrial settings the population of interest cannot be enumerated. Furthermore, he contends that many quality-related applications of statistics do not involve confidence intervals of characteristics of populations that can be enumerated; instead they deal with predictions, such as predictions of future improvements or assessments whether a certain relationship will carry over to other times and different places.

Consider the following two illustrative examples. The first is about a continuous production process that involves the rapid filling of tubes with toothpaste. A sample of 25 tubes is taken at a certain point of time and their average fill weight is evaluated. Note that in this particular situation it would be difficult to enumerate the elements of the population, and without a sample frame it would be difficult to draw a genuine random sample. Furthermore, and more importantly, we are dealing with a process that includes a time-component and the parameter of the population (that is, the process mean μ) may actually shift with time. Instead of a confidence interval for the process mean at a particular point in time, we may be more interested in predicting the fill weight at future points in time.

The second example of an analytic study deals with the information that arises from an experiment that is conducted in one particular lab. Experiments in this one lab show rather convincingly that certain polymers mixed for 60 minutes work better in a subsequent manufacturing process than the same polymers mixed for 30 minutes. Such a finding is normally backed by sophisticated statistical inference; for example, the statistical analysis may confirm that the observed difference in the sample means would be very unlikely to occur if the population means were equal. This is useful information, but one must realize that this inference applies only to polymers that are mixed in one particular lab. One could argue that for purposes of planning, it would be unwise to put too much emphasis on this particular inference. Instead, one should be looking for evidence that this result is repeatable, or predictable, and that it applies to other places and other times. For example, does it still hold in a production situation when polymers are mixed on-site, is the result affected by temperature or other factors, and so on? Different data and different analyses are needed to answer this question.

10.8 PREDICTION INTERVALS FOR FUTURE OBSERVATIONS

One could argue that standard statistical inference is inappropriate in analytic studies as it provides no immediate basis for prediction. However, this would be a rather extreme position as it is possible to obtain predictions and prediction intervals if certain additional assumptions are made. We need to make assumptions about the evolution of the process throughout time, as without these assumptions there is no way to extrapolate. The simplest assumption is to assume *stability over time*. Of course, one should never believe assumptions blindly, and one should always check them whenever possible. Constructing time-sequence plots and plotting observations over time is a good first step to learn about violations of stability. The chapter on control charts (Chapter 12) has much to say on whether a process is stable over time.

How does one predict a future observation X_{n+1} if the observations do, in fact, come from a stable system? Let us assume that the observation at time t can be modeled by (1) a fixed level μ that is constant over time and (2) a noise (or error) component with mean zero and standard deviation σ that, furthermore, is unrelated to errors at all other times. Let us also assume that the distribution of the noise is normal.

The natural predictor of the next observation $X_{n+1} = \mu + \text{noise}_{n+1}$ is the mean μ. This is because we assumed that noise terms at different times are unrelated, implying that the noise component of a future observation cannot be predicted from the past observations. A 95 *percent prediction interval* for the next observation X_{n+1} is given by $(\mu - 2\sigma, \mu + 2\sigma)$; there is a 95 percent chance that the future observation will fall in this interval. Prediction intervals with different coverage can be obtained by replacing the factor 2 in the above expression with the corresponding percentiles of the standard normal distribution; for example, for a 90 percent prediction interval one replaces the 2 with 1.645.

The prediction and the prediction intervals depend on μ and σ, and in the above discussion we have assumed that they are known. In practice, they have to be estimated from a sample of previous observations. We then replace μ and σ by the sample average $\bar{x}$ and the sample standard deviation s. Then the prediction of the future X_{n+1} is given by $\bar{x}$, and an approximate 95 percent prediction interval is given by

$$(\bar{x} - 2s, \bar{x} + 2s).$$

This approach works well if the sample size is reasonably large. However, for small samples one should make the prediction interval wider, in order to take account of the estimation error that we make when replacing the population parameters by their sample estimates. Exercise 10.15 shows that the estimation error for μ increases the width of the prediction interval by a factor of $\sqrt{1 + (1/n)}$. With this modification, the approximate 95 percent prediction interval for a future observation is

$$\left(\bar{x} - 2s\sqrt{1 + (1/n)}, \bar{x} + 2s\sqrt{1 + (1/n)}\right).$$

For reasonably large samples the extra factor in the prediction interval becomes negligible. Even for $n = 50$, the difference between $2s$ and $2s\sqrt{1.02}$ is inconsequential. Note, however, that the above equation incorporates only the error in estimating the level μ, but not the error in estimating σ. Approaches that incorporate estimation errors for μ as well as σ have been studied; we refer you to the literature on tolerance intervals. The book by Hahn and Meeker, *Statistical Intervals: A Guide for Practitioners*, is an excellent reference.

A confidence interval for a population parameter such as the mean μ and a prediction interval for a future observation are different, and they *must not be confused*. A confidence interval for μ assesses the reliability of the estimate $\bar{x}$ in estimating the population characteristic μ. For large sample sizes n the confidence interval shrinks to zero; with larger and larger sample sizes we obtain more and more information on the parameter, and eventually our uncertainty about that parameter shrinks to zero. A prediction interval for the next observation X_{n+1} assesses the uncertainty of a future individual observation. For a stable system and for large sample sizes the 95 percent prediction interval $(\bar{x} - 2s, \bar{x} + 2s)$ approaches $(\mu - 2\sigma, \mu + 2\sigma)$. Note that it will never shrink to zero, as there is variability in individual observations even if one knows the population parameters exactly.

Our prediction and prediction interval have assumed stability of the process. That is, the process parameters μ and σ do not change over time. Many times stability is violated and often the process mean changes over time. The sample average, which gives every observation the same importance in calculating the prediction, is not appropriate for processes with changing levels. A predictor that gives more weight to more recent observations and less weight to observations in the past may be preferable. Various exponential smoothing and time series forecast methods for data with or without trend and seasonality are discussed in the forecasting literature. For a detailed discussion of forecast methods we refer you to the books by Abraham and Ledolter (*Statistical Methods for Forecasting*) and Newbold and Bos (*Introductory Business Forecasting*).

10.9 EXERCISES

10.1 Roll a die and record X, the number of spots on the upside. Assume that the die is fair; that is, the distribution of X is given by outcomes $1, 2, \ldots, 6$, with equal probabilities 1/6. Check that the mean of this distribution is given by $\mu = 3.5$ and the standard deviation by $\sigma = 1.71$. (Use the results in Section 8.2.)

10.2 Your experiment consists of rolling the die three times. Record the number of spots X_1, X_2, and X_3, and calculate the average $\bar{X}$. Repeat this experiment 50 times. This will give you 50 averages. Construct a histogram and calculate the mean and the standard deviation of these 50 averages. Comment on the results and check whether the conclusions of the Central Limit Effect are confirmed by the results of this example. The Central Limit Effect implies that averages vary around $\mu = 3.5$; the standard deviation of averages of size 3 is $(1.71)/\sqrt{3}$. Realize that the sample size is only $n = 3$, and that we started with a distribution which is far from normal.

(a) Repeat the experiment using ten rolls of your die. That is, calculate the average from 10 rolls of your die.

(b) If you have access to computer software, you may want to generate variables from the discrete uniform distribution that takes on integers between 1 through 6 with equal probability. This would save you rolling the die.

10.3 Let $\bar{X}$ be the average of a random sample of size $n = 17$ from a distribution with mean 42 and standard deviation 8. Approximate

(a) $P(\bar{X} < 43.2)$

(b) $P(40.2 < \bar{X} < 42.8)$

10.4 The burst strength of a certain sampling container has mean 33 and standard deviation 4. Let $\bar{X}$ be the average of a random sample of size $n = 25$ such tubes. Determine $P(\bar{X} \leq 32.5)$.

10.5 Let $\bar{X}$ be the sample average of a random sample of size n from a normal distribution with an unknown mean μ and standard deviation $\sigma = 3$. How large should the sample size n be so that $P(\mu - .5 < \bar{X} < \mu + .5) = 0.95$?

Note that the above expression states that you want to be 95 percent confident that your estimate (the sample average) is within 0.5 unit of the unknown μ.

10.6 It takes on average 93 minutes to repair breakdowns of a certain type of copying machine (this is the status quo). The company claims that breakdowns of its new and improved copying machine take less time to fix. In order to test this claim, 68 breakdowns of the new model were observed, resulting in an average repair time of 88 minutes and a standard deviation of 26 minutes. Discuss the company's claim. Obtain a 95 percent confidence interval for the mean repair time. Calculate the test statistic and the corresponding probability value. What is your conclusion at the 0.05 significance level?

10.7 A commuter was recently told that it takes on average 22 minutes to commute from Branford, Connecticut, to the parking lot of the Yale University School of Organization and Management ($\mu = 22$ is the hypothesized value). Anxious to learn whether this is correct, our commuter takes measurements on 20 consecutive week days. She finds that the average commuting time is 27 minutes with a standard deviation of 3 minutes. Discuss the validity of the claim. Obtain a 95 percent confidence interval; test the hypothesis at the 0.05 significance level. What other factors would you investigate if you wanted to predict the commuting time?

10.8 The mean yield of a certain product during an 8-hour shift is 6.2 tons. The standard deviation of yields from shift to shift is 0.7 ton. You have made some modifications on your process, with the intent of increasing the mean yield. You take measurements on $n = 25$ shifts (under the modified process) and you find that the sample mean is $\bar{x} = 6.3$ tons.

Calculate the probability of observing a sample average $\bar{x} = 6.3$ tons (or even larger) when, in fact, the true process mean has stayed the same (at $\mu = 6.2$ tons).

10.9 A random sample of one hundred tubes of toothpaste are taken from today's production line and their fill weights are determined. The sample average is 6.7 ounces and the standard deviation is 0.5 ounce. Calculate an approximate 95 percent confidence interval for the mean fill weight of the process. Interpret the interval, clearly stating all assumptions.

10.10 Let Y be binomial with parameters $n = 100$ and $\theta = 0.1$.

(a) Approximate $P(Y \leq 3)$, using the Poisson distribution.

(b) Approximate $P(Y \leq 3)$, using the normal approximation (apply the continuity correction).

(c) Which approximation would you prefer in this case?

10.11 In a *New York Times*/CBS poll, 56 percent of 2,000 randomly selected voters in New York City said that they would vote for the incumbent in a certain two-candidate race. Calculate a 95 percent confidence interval for the population proportion. Discuss its implication. Carefully discuss what is meant by the population, how you would carry out the random sampling, and what other factors could lead to differences between the responses to the surveys and the actual votes on the day of the election.

10.12 Assume that the population proportion, θ, of people voting for one of two candidates is around $1/2 = 0.5$ (as it is in most presidential elections). We want to determine the sample size n so that we can be 95 percent confident that our sample proportion is within 3 percentage points of the population proportion. How large does the sample size have to be if we want to be 99.7 percent confident?

10.13 Let θ be the fraction of all industrial engineers who do not understand basic statistical concepts. Unfortunately, this number has been quite high, at about 73 percent. A new program to improve the situation was started and it was expected that under this program the fraction θ would change (hopefully decrease). To test whether it does, $n = 300$ engineers were tested and 180 among them had difficulties with statistics. Calculate a 90 percent confidence interval for the proportion θ. Do you feel that the new program has changed the understanding? Has it been cost effective? Discuss.

10.14 A sample of $n = 50$ bread loaves is taken from the sizable production that left our bakery this morning. We find that the average weight of the 50 loaves is 1.05 pounds; the standard deviation is $s = 0.06$ pound.

(a) Obtain a 95 percent confidence interval for the mean weight of this morning's production.

(b) One of the employees claims that the current process produces loaves which are heavier than one pound, on average. Is there enough information in our sample to reject the null hypothesis that $\mu = 1.00$ lb in favor of the alternative that $\mu > 1.00$ lb?

(c) Assume that the distribution of weights is normal; furthermore assume that the sample average and standard deviation are good estimates of the corresponding population characteristics μ and σ. Calculate the proportion of loaves that are underweight (that is, weigh less than 1.0 pound).

(d) Predict the weight of a single loaf from this morning's production. Obtain an approximate 95 percent prediction interval.

10.15 Assume that the observation at time t can be expressed by a fixed level μ that does not depend on time and a noise (or error) component with mean zero and standard deviation σ. Suppose that the noise at a certain point in time is unrelated to errors at all other times and assume that the distribution of the noise is normal. You are given the past history $(X_1, X_2, \ldots, X_n)$ of the process, and you have to predict the next observation X_{n+1}. You are using the sample mean $\overline{X}$ as your prediction.

(a) Show that the prediction error is $X_{n+1} - \overline{X} = \text{noise}_{n+1} + (\mu - \overline{X})$. It consists of two components: The first represents the variability of an individual observation around the mean level; the second represents the estimation error that we make when we replace the unknown mean μ by the sample average. Obtain the standard deviations of these two components.

(b) Obtain the standard deviation of the forecast error. You can use the result in Section 8.10, which showed that the standard deviation of the sum of two independent random variables is given by the square root of the sum of the squared standard deviations.

(c) Use the standard deviation in part (b) to show that a 95 percent prediction interval for X_{n+1} is given by

$$\left[\overline{X} - 2\sigma\sqrt{1 + (1/n)}, \overline{X} + 2\sigma\sqrt{1 + (1/n)}\right].$$

10.16 A random sample of 50 teaching assistants at the University of Iowa in the fall of 1996 indicated that 30 of them were planning to join the union for teaching assistants. Calculate a 95 percent confidence interval for the proportion of University of Iowa teaching assistants who are in favor of joining a union.

10.17 The American Association of University Professors claims that the mean income of tenured professors at public universities is \$62,000. Our hypothesis is that the mean salary is actually lower than \$62,000. In order to test whether or not the mean salary is lower than \$62,000, we take a random sample of $n = 36$ professors. Their salaries led to a sample average of \$59,000 and a sample standard deviation $s = \$8,000$.

(a) Calculate the test statistic and obtain its probability value.

(b) Assuming a significance level of 5 percent, what is your conclusion?

10.18 The side effects of a new drug are thoroughly investigated before the drug is allowed into the market. Data is collected to test the following two hypotheses:

Null hypothesis: New drug is unsafe
Alternative hypothesis: New drug is safe

(a) Describe the type I error.

(b) Describe the type II error.

(c) On which side lies the burden of proof? Which error do you control by setting the significance level at 0.01?

10.19 We asked undergraduate students at the University of Iowa about the number of hours they study per week. A random sample of 64 students gave us a sample mean of 7.6 hours, and a standard deviation of 4 hours. Calculate a 90 percent confidence interval for the population mean (that is, the average number of hours studied for all undergraduate UI students). What do we assume about the sampling procedure, and how would you carry it out in practice?

10.20 Prior studies showed that the standard deviation among individual measurements on a certain air pollutant is 0.6 ppm. You are planning on using the information from a random sample (that is, the sample average) to estimate the unknown process (population) mean μ. How large do you have to select the sample size if you want to be 95 percent certain that your sample average is within plus or minus 0.2 ppm of the unknown process mean?

10.21 The profits from equal investments in individual stocks over the same time period follow a distribution with mean 5 and standard deviation 30.

(a) If you pick one stock at random, what is the probability that you make money?

(b) If you buy a portfolio of 16 stocks, what is the probability that you are making money? Why is this larger than the probability in (a)?

(c) Assume that the mean of the distribution of profits from individual stocks has changed to 0. Repeat the calculation in (a) and (b). Are there still reasons to prefer the portfolio? If so, what are they?

10.22 Thirty light bulbs were selected randomly from among a very large production batch, and they were put on test to determine the time until they burn out. The average failure time for these thirty bulbs was 1,080 hours; the sample standard deviation was 210 hours.

The light bulbs are advertised as having a mean life length of 1,200 hours. Test this hypothesis against the alternative that the mean life length of this batch is actually smaller than 1,200 hours.

10.23 Discuss, in your own words, the difference between enumerative and analytic studies. For additional reference, you may want to read the paper, "On Probability as a Basis for Action," by W. Edwards Deming (*American Statistician*, Vol. 29, 1975, pp. 146–152), or his book *Out of the Crisis*.

10.24 Read and discuss the paper, "Surveys: Thank You for Your Support—I Think," by Bert Gunter (*Quality Progress*, December 1990, pp. 111–112). Discuss, in your own words, the difference between sampling variability and survey bias. Confidence intervals for a population proportion are easily calculated. But what assumptions must be met before one can use such intervals as uncertainty measures for sample estimates?

10.10 REFERENCES

Abraham, B., and J. Ledolter. *Statistical Methods for Forecasting*. New York: Wiley, 1983.

Deming, W. E. *Out of the Crisis*. Cambridge, MA: MIT Center for Advanced Engineering Study, 1986.

Deming, W. E. "On Probability as a Basis for Action," *American Statistician*, Vol. 29, 1975, 146–152.

Gunter, B. "Surveys: Thank You for Your Support—I Think," *Quality Progress*, December 1990, 111–112.

Hahn, G. J., and W. Meeker. *Statistical Intervals: A Guide for Practitioners*. New York, Wiley, 1991.

Newbold, P., and T. Bos. *Introductory Business Forecasting*, 2nd edition, Cincinnati: South-Western Publishing, 1994.

CHAPTER 11

ACCEPTANCE SAMPLING PLANS

11.1 INTRODUCTION

The control of incoming as well as outgoing products is often performed through a final acceptance inspection. The purpose of such an inspection is to decide whether a group of items, also referred to as an inspection *lot*, satisfies the requirements that were put upon them. A lot usually consists of product units of a single type and grade, manufactured under essentially the same conditions.

One hundred percent final inspection is one possible inspection approach; there each and every item is inspected, and nonconforming (defective) items are removed from the lot before its shipment. One hundred percent inspection, however, is often impractical, particularly if the testing is destructive. It is also unwarranted and usually much too expensive if relatively inexpensive products are involved that are made in large quantities and at large speeds, such as screws, nuts, or widgets. One hundred percent inspection is also impractical if goods of long lengths are involved, such as rolls of textiles or coils of wire, which are difficult to unroll for inspections. Furthermore, the accuracy of a 100 percent inspection if carried out by human inspectors is often compromised by the boredom and fatigue associated with repetitive inspections of large groups of items. Some studies have shown that often only 80 percent of nonconforming units are detected during a 100 percent final inspection.

Acceptance sampling is another, and often preferable strategy. This approach involves taking a random sample from each lot and using a decision rule to determine whether a lot should be accepted or rejected. Corrective action is taken whenever lots are rejected; generally this takes the form of a 100 percent screening of the rejected lot, and the subsequent removal of all defective items.

Acceptance sampling plans help us decide whether a lot should be shipped to the customer. Before we go any further, we should clarify the meaning of a lot. The lot is the population from which we sample. Usually a lot is a collection of items that is ready to be shipped by the producer, or a collection of items that is being received by the customer. Individual products are often grouped into larger units; for example, into boxcars or truck loads. We refer to these larger units as lots. A lot may be a shipment of 2,000 pounds of fish; a container of 10,000 toothbrushes; a truck loaded with 500 crates of apples; a shipment of 1,000 office chairs; or a shipment of 5,000 shock absorbers for light-duty trucks. We usually assume that N, the number of items in the lot, is large.

In this chapter we discuss commonly used sample inspection plans for attribute data. Attribute data is obtained by classifying items as either defective or acceptable. We review (1) single sample inspection plans, (2) double sample inspection plans, and (3) sequential sample inspection plans. In addition we describe the MIL-STD-105E acceptance sampling plans for attribute data, which are commonly used sample inspection plans. Let us start with three examples.

EXAMPLE 1: *A Single Sample Inspection Plan*

We take a sample of size $n = 50$. If none or one of the items is defective, we accept the lot. If two or more items are defective, we reject the lot. Here the acceptance number is 1; this number is usually denoted by $Ac = 1$. The acceptance number is the maximum allowable number of defective units that still leads to an acceptance of the lot.

Assume that we find one defective in the sample of size 50. Hence we accept the lot. ■

EXAMPLE 2: *A Double Sample Inspection Plan*

We take a sample of size $n = 50$. If no item is defective, we accept the lot. If two or more items are defective, we reject the lot. If one item is defective, we take another sample of size 25. If all elements in that second sample are good, we accept the lot. Otherwise (that is, if one or more of the items in the second sample are defective), we reject the lot.

Assume that we find one defective item among the first 50 sampled elements. In the second sample we find one defective item among the 25. We reject the lot. ■

EXAMPLE 3: *A Sequential Sample Inspection Plan*

We sample from the lot by successively taking one item after the other. We keep track of the cumulative number of defectives. After each item we compare the number of defective items to numbers that come from two linear equations: an acceptance line and a rejection line. The acceptance line, for a certain application,

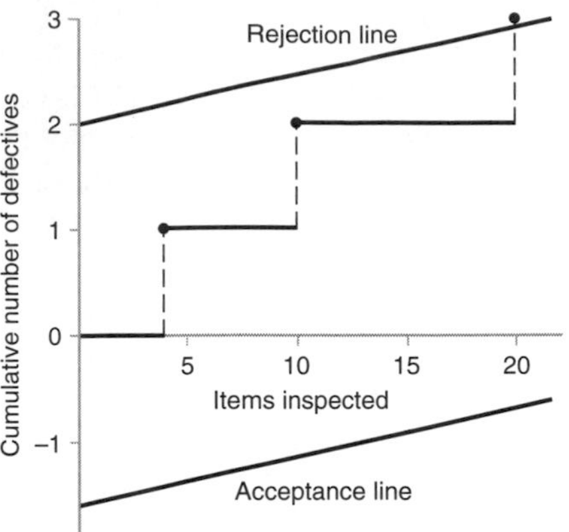

FIGURE 11.1 Cumulative numbers of defectives, and acceptance and rejection lines for the sequential sample inspection plan.

may be given by $-1.553 + (0.0463)(n)$, where $n = 1, 2, \ldots$ denotes the count of the sampled items. The rejection line may be given by $1.994 + (0.0463)(n)$. In Section 11.4 we will explain how one gets these two equations. According to this particular sample inspection plan, we reject the lot at item number n if the number of defectives among the first n items exceeds the rejection line for the first time. We accept the lot if the number of defectives falls below the acceptance line. We continue to sample as long as the number of defectives stays between the two lines; see Figure 11.1.

Assume that our third defective item arrives with the twentieth sampled item ($n = 20$). Suppose that defective items were also found at item number 4 and 10. At $n = 4$, the rejection line has the value 2.18; at $n = 10$, it is 2.46; at $n = 20$, it is 2.92. Since the number of defectives at sample 20 is 3 and since this exceeds 2.92, we reject the lot. We have reached a decision, and there is no need to take further items. Note that the number of defectives never dipped below the acceptance line, because for n smaller than 33 the acceptance line is negative. Thus the inspection had to continue until the lot was eventually rejected at the twentieth sampled item. ■

These three examples illustrate the main features of sample inspection plans. The next question that needs to be addressed is how we determine the parameters of these plans. In particular, how do we decide the sample size n, the maximum allowable number of defective items Ac, and the acceptance and rejection lines in the sequential inspection plan?

The *operating characteristic curve* is the key tool that helps us decide the parameters of sample inspection plans. Operating characteristic curves were introduced in Section 8.5 when we discussed applications of the binomial and Poisson distributions. A more detailed discussion is given in this chapter.

11.2 SINGLE SAMPLE INSPECTION PLANS

Denote the lot size by N (it is usually a large number) and the sample size of the acceptance sampling plan by n. The *operating characteristic curve* of the plan depicts the probability of accepting a lot, viewed as a function of the fraction of defectives θ. We denote it by $OC(\theta)$; that is,

$$OC(\theta) = P(\text{accepting the lot; } \theta).$$

The operating characteristic curve describes the properties of the sampling plan. We often summarize the characteristics of a sampling plan by evaluating its operating characteristic curve at two values of θ. One value, θ_1, denotes the largest fraction of defectives that, for purpose of sampling inspection, is still acceptable to the customer. We refer to this value as the upper limit of the acceptable fraction of defectives, or simply the *acceptable quality level (AQL).*

The other value, θ_2, represents the smallest fraction of defectives that defines unacceptable or poor quality. We refer to this value as the lower limit of the rejectable fraction of defectives, or simply as the *lot tolerance percent defective (LTPD).* This value is also known as the limiting quality (LQ).

A sampling plan should accept a lot with high probability if its fraction of defectives is θ_1. In other words, the probability of rejecting an acceptable lot should be small. The probability of rejecting an acceptable lot (with fraction of defectives θ_1) is called the *producer's risk*, as the producer loses out if an acceptable lot is rejected. We also call this the α *(alpha) risk*. On the other hand, the probability of accepting an unacceptable lot (with fraction of defectives θ_2) should be small. This probability is referred to as the *consumer's risk*, as the consumer is being shipped a rejectable lot. We call this the β *(beta) risk*.

When designing an acceptance sampling plan one fixes producer's and consumer's risks at certain small values and finds the sample size n and the acceptance number Ac such that $OC(\theta = \theta_1) = (1 - \alpha)$ and $OC(\theta = \theta_2) = \beta$. For example, $AQL = \theta_1 = 0.02$ may be based on the consumer's desire to accept lots 95 percent of the time when the proportion of nonconforming items is no worse than 2 percent. The $LTPD = \theta_2 = 0.08$ may reflect the consumer's desire to accept lots with 8 percent defectives or more no more than 10 percent of the time. Here the alpha risk is $\alpha = 0.05$ at the acceptable quality level $AQL = 0.02$, and the beta risk is $\beta = 0.10$ at $LTPD = 0.08$.

11.2.1 Evaluating the Operating Characteristic Curve of a Single Sample Inspection Plan

Let us first fix the parameters of the acceptance sampling plan (that is, the sample size n and the acceptance number Ac) and let us discuss the properties of that plan. In particular, let us find its operating characteristic curve, its consumer risk α at a certain AQL, and its producer risk β at a certain $LTPD$.

Assume that the lot size N is large, that we sample $n = 100$ items, and that the acceptance number is $Ac = 4$. That is, we accept the lot if we have four or fewer defectives in a sample of size $n = 100$. Let X be the number of defectives in a sample of size n. Then the operating characteristic curve is given by

$$OC(\theta) = P(X \leq 4; \theta) = P(X = 0; \theta) + P(X = 1; \theta) + P(X = 2; \theta) \\ + P(X = 3; \theta) + P(X = 4; \theta).$$

The number of defectives, X, in a sample of size n has a binomial distribution with parameter $n = 100$ and θ. We assume that the lot size N is large, which implies that the result of one draw is approximately independent from that of any other; since N is large, the result of one draw does not change appreciably the probability of getting a defective the next time around. For a fixed θ, the probability of acceptance can be calculated from the binomial probabilities in Chapter 8, preferably through the use of computer software. Alternatively, since n is large and the fractions θ of interest are small (usually in the range between 0.01 and 0.10), we can use the Poisson approximation with parameter $\lambda = (n)(\theta) = (100)\theta$.

For example, for $\theta = 0.02$ and using the Poisson distribution with parameter $\lambda = (100)(0.02) = 2$, we obtain from the Poisson probabilities in Table 8.3:

$$OC(\theta = 0.02) = P(X \leq 4; \lambda = 2) = 0.9473.$$

The same calculations are carried out for different values of θ. The resulting operating characteristic function is given in Table 11.1. The function is graphed in Figure 11.2. To show that there is not much difference between the Poisson and the binomial probabilities we have shown both values in Table 11.1.

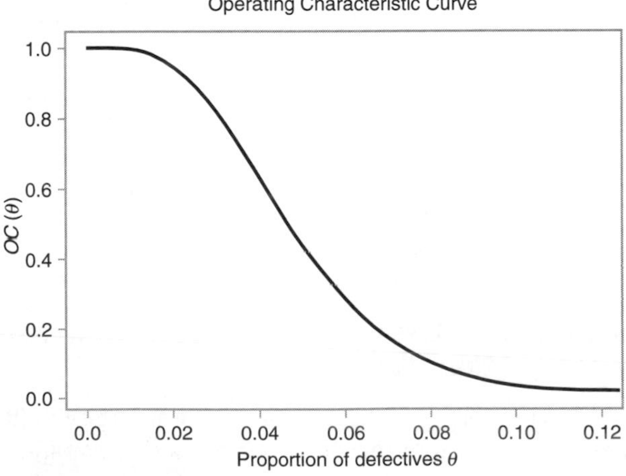

FIGURE 11.2 Operating characteristic curve of the single sample inspection plan with $n = 100$ and $Ac = 4$.

TABLE 11.1 Operating Characteristic Curve $OC(\theta) = P(X \leq 4; n = 100, \theta)$ of the Single Sample Inspection Plan: Binomial Distribution and Poisson Distribution

	$OC(\theta)$	
θ	Binomial	Poisson
0.005	0.9998	0.9998
0.010	0.9966	0.9963
0.015	0.9823	0.9814
0.020	0.9492	0.9473
0.025	0.8937	0.8912
0.030	0.8179	0.8153
0.035	0.7272	0.7254
0.040	0.6289	0.6288
0.045	0.5299	0.5321
0.050	0.4360	0.4405
0.055	0.3509	0.3575
0.060	0.2768	0.2851
0.065	0.2143	0.2237
0.070	0.1632	0.1730
0.075	0.1223	0.1321
0.080	0.0903	0.0996
0.085	0.0658	0.0744
0.090	0.0474	0.0550
0.095	0.0337	0.0403
0.100	0.0237	0.0293
0.105	0.0165	0.0211
0.110	0.0114	0.0151
0.115	0.0078	0.0107
0.120	0.0053	0.0076

Assume that our specifications for the acceptance sampling plan require an alpha risk $\alpha = 0.05$ at $AQL = 0.02$, and a beta risk $\beta = 0.10$ at the $LTPD = 0.08$. The operating characteristic curve in Table 11.1 shows that our plan with $n = 100$ and $Ac = 4$ does just that; its alpha risk is $\alpha = 1 - 0.9492 = 0.0508$, and its β risk is $\beta = 0.0903$. This is a good plan!

11.2.2 Impact of the Parameters of a Single Inspection Plan on the Operating Characteristic Curve

The operating characteristic curve, and thus the alpha and beta risks at specified *AQL* and *LTPD*, change with different sample sizes and acceptance numbers.

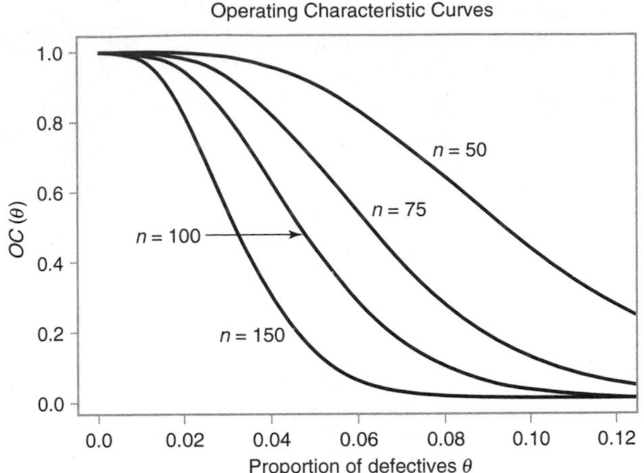

FIGURE 11.3 Operating characteristic curves of the single sample inspection plans with $Ac = 4$ and $n = 50, 75, 100,$ and 150.

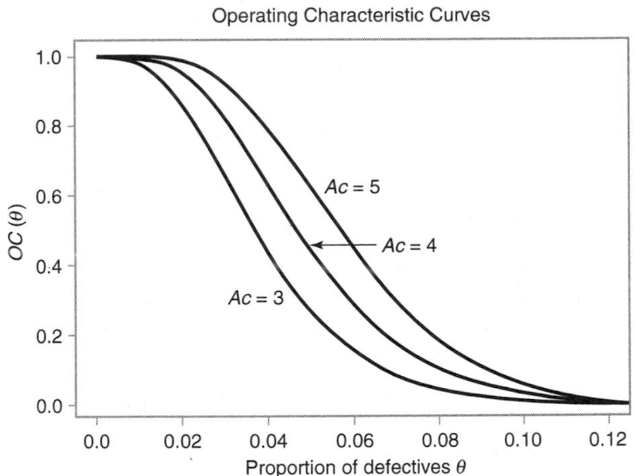

FIGURE 11.4 Operating characteristic curves of the single sample inspection plans with $n = 100$ and $Ac = 3, 4,$ and 5.

This is illustrated in Figures 11.3 and 11.4. Figure 11.3 compares the operating characteristic curves for plans with $Ac = 4$ and sample sizes $n = 50, 75, 100, 150$. Figure 11.4 compares sampling plans with $n = 100$ and varying acceptance numbers $Ac = 3, 4, 5$.

Keeping the acceptance number fixed and decreasing the sample size shifts the whole operating characteristic curve to the right. With small sample sizes, for example $n = 50$, we accept lots far too often. The beta risk of accepting rejectable lots with a $LTPD = 0.08$ is 0.63, or 63 percent.

Keeping the sample size fixed and increasing the acceptance number has a similar effect. We are accepting lots, good as well as bad ones, too often. For $n = 100$ and $Ac = 5$ the beta risk at $LTPD = 0.08$ is about 18 percent; this value is larger than desired. While it is true that the alpha risk for this particular plan is even smaller than 0.05 (which is good, as then we almost never reject a good lot), the plan does not have the required power of signaling problems if the percent defective is large.

When designing an acceptance sampling plan, one has to select values for n and Ac such that the risk specifications are satisfied. There are several ways to do this:

1. One approach is by trial and error. One fixes n and Ac, obtains the operating characteristic curve, and experiments with various n and Ac until one gets a satisfactory plan. This is not difficult, especially with today's computer software. However, it is time consuming.
2. Another approach is to consult tables in books on acceptance sampling. For example, Table 11.2 (page 280) shows the required sample sizes and acceptance numbers for plans with $\alpha = 0.05$ and $\beta = 0.10$. You can check that the plan for $AQL = 0.02$ and $LTPD = 0.08$ requires $n = 100$ and $Ac = 4$. This is the plan we studied in this section. This table, also known as the Japanese standard JIS Z 9002 for single sample inspection by attributes, is taken from page 124 of the book by Kaoru Ishikawa, *Guide to Quality Control*. Similar tables are included in the book by Larry E. Shirland, *Statistical Quality Control with Microcomputer Applications*. This second book also includes computer software, which makes it very easy to calculate the complete operating characteristic curves for any specified plan.

11.2.3 Average Outgoing Quality of a Rectifying Sample Inspection Plan

Corrective action is required whenever lots are rejected. This generally takes the form of a 100 percent inspection of the rejected lots, with subsequent removal of all defective items. We call such a strategy of replacing defective items with good ones a *rectifying sample inspection plan*. It is called rectifying, as it corrects the quality of the outgoing lots after lots have gone through the sample inspection procedure.

Suppose that incoming lots include a fraction of defectives θ; we can think of this as the *incoming lot quality*. Some of the lots will be accepted by our sampling inspection plan; the probability of this happening is $OC(\theta)$. Yet other lots will be rejected, and this will occur with probability $1 - OC(\theta)$. Since each and every item of a rejected lot is inspected and rectified, outgoing lots that were initially rejected will include zero percent defectives. This implies that the *outgoing quality* is either θ with probability $OC(\theta)$, or zero with probability $1 - OC(\theta)$. Hence the *average outgoing quality* that originates from this sample inspection

TABLE 11.2 Table of Single Sample Inspection Plans by Attributes

θ_1 (%) \ θ_2 (%)	0.71 ~ 0.90	0.91 ~ 1.12	1.13 ~ 1.40	1.41 ~ 1.80	1.81 ~ 2.24	2.25 ~ 2.80	2.81 ~ 3.55	3.56 ~ 4.50	4.51 ~ 5.60	5.61 ~ 7.10	7.11 ~ 9.00	9.01 ~ 11.2	11.3 ~ 14.0	14.1 ~ 18.0	18.1 ~ 22.4	22.5 ~ 28.0	28.1 ~ 35.5	θ_2 (%) / θ_1 (%)
0.090 ~ 0.112	*	400 1	↓	←	↓	→	60 0	50 0	←	↓	↓	←	↓	↓	↓	↓	↓	0.090 ~ 0.112
0.113 ~ 0.140	*	↓	300 1	↓	←	↓	→	↓	40 0	←	↓	↓	←	↓	↓	↓	↓	0.113 ~ 0.140
0.141 ~ 0.180	*	500 2	↓	250 1	↓	←	↓	→	↑	30 0	←	↓	↓	←	↓	↓	↓	0.141 ~ 0.180
0.181 ~ 0.224	*	*	400 2	↓	200 1	↓	←	↓	→	↑	25 0	←	↓	↓	←	↓	↓	0.181 ~ 0.224
0.225 ~ 0.280	*	*	500 3	300 2	↓	150 1	↓	←	↓	→	↑	20 0	←	↓	↓	←	↓	0.225 ~ 0.280
0.281 ~ 0.355	*	*	*	400 3	250 2	↓	120 1	↓	←	↓	→	↑	15 0	←	↓	↓	←	0.281 ~ 0.355
0.356 ~ 0.450	*	*	*	500 4	300 3	200 2	↓	100 1	↓	←	↓	→	↑	15 0	←	↓	↓	0.356 ~ 0.450
0.451 ~ 0.560	*	*	*	*	400 4	250 3	150 2	↓	80 1	↓	←	↓	→	↑	10 0	←	↓	0.451 ~ 0.560
0.561 ~ 0.710	*	*	*	*	500 6	300 4	200 3	120 2	↓	60 1	↓	←	↓	→	↑	7 0	←	0.561 ~ 0.710
0.711 ~ 0.900	*	*	*	*	*	400 6	250 4	150 3	100 2	↓	50 1	↓	←	↓	→	↑	5 0	0.711 ~ 0.900
0.901 ~ 1.12		*	*	*	*	*	300 6	200 4	120 3	80 2	↓	40 1	↓	←	↓	↑	↑	0.901 ~ 1.12
1.13 ~ 1.40			*	*	*	*	500 10	250 6	150 4	100 3	60 2	↓	30 1	↓	←	↓	↑	1.13 ~ 1.40
1.41 ~ 1.80				*	*	*	*	400 10	200 6	120 4	80 3	50 2	↓	25 1	↓	←	↓	1.41 ~ 1.80
1.81 ~ 2.24					*	*	*	*	300 10	150 6	100 4	60 3	40 2	↓	20 1	↓	←	1.81 ~ 2.24
2.25 ~ 2.80						*	*	*	*	250 10	120 6	70 4	50 3	30 2	↓	15 1	↓	2.25 ~ 2.80
2.81 ~ 3.55							*	*	*	*	200 10	100 6	60 4	40 3	25 2	↓	10 1	2.81 ~ 3.55
3.56 ~ 4.50								*	*	*	*	150 10	80 6	50 4	30 3	20 2	↓	3.56 ~ 4.50
4.51 ~ 5.60									*	*	*	*	120 10	60 6	40 4	25 3	15 2	4.51 ~ 5.60
5.61 ~ 7.10										*	*	*	*	100 10	50 6	30 4	20 3	5.61 ~ 7.10
7.11 ~ 9.00											*	*	*	*	70 10	40 6	25 4	7.11 ~ 9.00
9.01 ~ 11.2												*	*	*	*	60 10	30 6	9.01 ~ 11.2
θ_1 (%) / θ_2 (%)	0.71 ~ 0.90	0.91 ~ 1.12	1.13 ~ 1.40	1.41 ~ 1.80	1.81 ~ 2.24	2.25 ~ 2.80	2.81 ~ 3.55	3.56 ~ 4.50	4.51 ~ 5.60	5.61 ~ 7.10	7.11 ~ 9.00	9.01 ~ 11.2	11.3 ~ 14.0	14.1 ~ 18.0	18.1 ~ 22.4	22.5 ~ 28.0	28.1 ~ 35.5	θ_1 (%) \ θ_2 (%)

Small type = n, bold type = Ac

Use the first column of n, Ac in the direction of the arrow. There are no sampling methods for the blank columns.

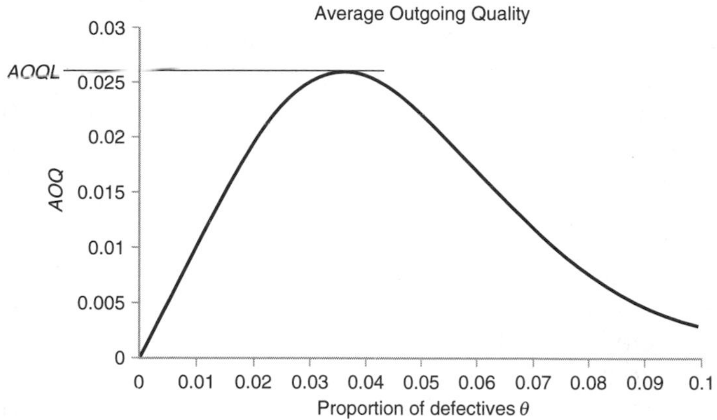

FIGURE 11.5 Average outgoing quality curve of the rectifying single sample inspection plan with $n = 100$ and $Ac = 4$.

scheme is

$$AOQ(\theta) = [\theta][OC(\theta)] + [0][1 - OC(\theta)] = [\theta][OC(\theta)].$$

We have already determined the operating characteristic curve, $OC(\theta)$, of the sampling inspection plan; hence it is easy to calculate $AOQ(\theta)$ and graph the average outgoing quality as a function of θ. We have done this for the single sample inspection plan with $n = 100$ and $Ac = 4$. Figure 11.5 shows the average outgoing quality curve for this particular plan.

For lots with good incoming quality (that is, small θ), the average outgoing quality will be good also. If the incoming quality is poor, then many lots will be rejected by our sample inspection plan. However, the outgoing quality will also be very good, as the rejected lots are 100 percent rectified. In between these two extremes the *AOQ* curve rises, reaches a maximum, and then descends. The maximum of the average outgoing quality curve (that is, the largest y-ordinate on that graph) is called the *average outgoing quality limit (AOQL)*. It expresses the worst possible average outgoing quality that will originate from our rectifying sampling plan. For our plan the maximum value of the *AOQ* curve is about 2.55 percent. No matter how bad the quality of the incoming lots, the percent defectives of the outgoing lots will be at most 2.55 percent, on average.

11.3 DOUBLE SAMPLE INSPECTION PLANS

In a double sampling inspection plan we first select a sample of size n_1. We accept the lot if the number of defective items is less than or equal to Ac_1. We reject the lot if the number of defectives is greater than or equal to Re_1. If the number of defectives in the first sample is larger than Ac_1, but less than Re_1, then we take another sample of size n_2. We accept the lot if the combined number of defectives from the first and second sample is less than or equal to Ac_2. On the other hand, we reject the lot if the number of defectives in the two samples is greater than Ac_2.

A double sampling plan is characterized by the two sample sizes n_1 and n_2; the acceptance number Ac_1 and the rejection number Re_1 at the first stage; and the acceptance number Ac_2 for the combined number of defectives from the first and second sample.

Let us consider the following example with $n_1 = 50$, $Ac_1 = 1$ and $Re_1 = 5$, and $n_2 = 50$ and $Ac_2 = 4$. Here we take an initial sample of size 50 and accept the lot if there is at most one defective. We reject the lot if there are five or more defectives in the first sample. We take a second sample if there are 2, 3, or 4 defectives in the first sample. We reject the lot at the second stage if the combined number of defectives from the first and second sample exceeds four.

Let us write out all possible ways that the lot can be accepted. Let X be the number of defectives in the first sample and Y be the number of defectives in the second sample. Then we accept the lot

1. At stage 1: if ($X = 0$), or ($X = 1$)
2. At stage 2: if ($X = 2$ and $Y = 0$), ($X = 2$ and $Y = 1$), or ($X = 2$ and $Y = 2$)
   if ($X = 3$ and $Y = 0$), or ($X = 3$ and $Y = 1$)
   if ($X = 4$ and $Y = 0$)

One can calculate the acceptance probability by computing and adding the probabilities of all possible ways of accepting the lot. Because of random sampling, the results of the first and second draw are independent. Hence the probability of an event such as ($X = 3$ and $Y = 1$) is obtained by multiplying the probability of ($X = 3$) and the probability of ($Y = 1$). That is, $P(X = 3 \text{ and } Y = 1) = [P(X = 3)] \times [P(Y = 1)]$; see Section 8.10 in Chapter 8.

The operating characteristic curve for this double sampling plan is shown in Table 11.3. It is fairly similar to the one of the single inspection plan with $n = 100$ and $Ac = 4$. This is not very surprising as both plans use the same combined sample size and the same combined acceptance number. For the double sample inspection plan the alpha risk at $AQL = 0.02$ is $\alpha = 0.0443$, and the beta risk at $LTPD = 0.08$ is $\beta = 0.1347$. The double sampling plan has a slightly larger beta risk than the single sample inspection plan, which means that more unacceptable lots slip through inspection. On the other hand, the double sampling plan requires, on average, the inspection of fewer items, as a decision may already be reached after the first 50 items have been inspected. Note that many other possible double sample inspection plans could have been constructed. Even for the same sample sizes n_1 and n_2, one could have varied Ac_1, Re_1 and Ac_2 in many different ways.

One appeal of double sample inspection plans is that they give a second chance of acceptance. Furthermore, if the result of the first sample is either very

TABLE 11.3 Operating Characteristic Curve $OC(\theta)$ of the Double Sample Inspection Plan: Binomial Distribution and Poisson Distribution

	$OC(\theta)$	
θ	Binomial	Poisson
0.005	0.9999	0.9999
0.010	0.9971	0.9970
0.015	0.9851	0.9845
0.020	0.9569	0.9557
0.025	0.9091	0.9075
0.030	0.8427	0.8414
0.035	0.7620	0.7618
0.040	0.6729	0.6746
0.045	0.5814	0.5855
0.050	0.4925	0.4992
0.055	0.4099	0.4190
0.060	0.3359	0.3469
0.065	0.2716	0.2840
0.070	0.2171	0.2303
0.075	0.1717	0.1852
0.080	0.1347	0.1479
0.085	0.1049	0.1176
0.090	0.0813	0.0930
0.095	0.0626	0.0734
0.100	0.0481	0.0578
0.105	0.0368	0.0454
0.110	0.0282	0.0357
0.115	0.0215	0.0280
0.120	0.0164	0.0220

good or very poor, then there is no reason to take a second sample. This saves cost, as one reaches a decision with a smaller sample size.

11.4 SEQUENTIAL SAMPLE INSPECTION PLANS

An extension of double sample inspection that provides the possibility of taking several samples was developed by Abraham Wald (*Sequential Analysis*, 1947). In this section we discuss the item-by-item sequential sampling plan where we inspect one item after another, as compared to groups in group-by-group sequential sampling plans. If at item number n the number of defective items is equal to or less than a certain "acceptance number," then the lot is accepted. If the number of defective items at this stage is equal to or greater than a certain "rejection number," then the lot is rejected. If the number of defectives is larger than the acceptance number but smaller than the rejection number, then we continue to sample and we inspect another item. Wald shows that for given α risk at $AQL = \theta_1$ and β risk at $LTPD = \theta_2$, the acceptance and rejection lines are given by

$$Ac(n) = -a_1 + (b)(n)$$
$$Re(n) = a_2 + (b)(n)$$

where

$$a_1 = \ln[(1-\alpha)/\beta]/K$$
$$a_2 = \ln[(1-\beta)/\alpha]/K$$
$$b = \ln[(1-\theta_1)/(1-\theta_2)]/K$$
$$K = \ln\{[\theta_2(1-\theta_1)]/[\theta_1(1-\theta_2)]\}$$

and where ln is the natural logarithm. Wald shows that the sequential plan reaches, on average, a decision within fewer samples than the fixed-size sample plans.

It is easy to calculate these lines. For our particular example with $\theta_1 = 0.02$, $\theta_2 = 0.08$, $\alpha = 0.05$, and $\beta = 0.10$, we find that $K = 1.45$, $a_1 = 1.553$, $a_2 = 1.994$, and $b = 0.0436$. Thus, the acceptance and rejection lines in this example are given by

$$Ac(n) = -1.553 + (0.0436)(n)$$
$$Re(n) = 1.994 + (0.0436)(n)$$

These are the very lines that are shown in Figure 11.1.

11.5 COMMONLY USED ACCEPTANCE SAMPLING PLANS: MILITARY STANDARD 105E PLANS

A widely used sample inspection system for attribute data is provided by the U.S. Military Standard 105E plans. Originally developed as MIL-STD-105A in 1950, this inspection system has gone through several revisions. The current MIL-STD-105E sample inspection system (of April 1989) is a revision of MIL-STD-105D that was adopted in 1963. It has been accepted by national and international quality associations, including the American National Standards Institute (ANSI), the American Society for Quality Control (ASQC), and the International Standards Organization (ISO). It has become an ANSI/ASQC standard (ANSI/ASQC Z1.4-1981), as well as

TABLE 11.4 MIL-STD-105E: Sample Size Code Letters

	Special inspection levels				Normal inspection levels		
Lot size	S-1	S-2	S-3	S-4	I	II	III
2–8	A	A	A	A	A	A	B
9–15	A	A	A	A	A	B	C
16–25	A	A	B	B	B	C	D
26–50	A	B	B	C	C	D	E
51–90	B	B	C	C	C	E	F
91–150	B	B	C	D	D	F	G
151–280	B	C	D	E	E	G	H
281–500	B	C	D	E	F	H	J
501–1,200	C	C	E	F	G	J	K
1,201–3,200	C	D	E	G	H	K	L
3,201–10,000	C	D	F	G	J	L	M
10,001–35,000	C	D	F	H	K	M	N
35,001–150,000	D	E	G	J	L	N	P
150,001–500,000	D	E	G	J	M	P	Q
Over 500,000	D	E	H	K	N	Q	R

an international standard (ISO 2859). Note that in 1997 ASQC changed its name to the American Society for Quality (ASQ).

Detailed steps describe the planning and execution of the MIL-STD-105E acceptance sampling plans. One distinguishes among three *levels of inspection*. Inspection level I refers to cases when the inspection costs are relatively high; inspection level II refers to ordinary cases, and inspection level III refers to cases when the inspection costs are relatively low. The lower the level of inspection, the smaller the required sample size. In addition to these three normal inspection levels, there are four special inspection levels that refer to destructive testing involving different levels of cost.

The level of inspection and the size of the lot determines the sample size code letters in Table 11.4. These code letters are used to determine the sample sizes and the acceptance numbers. Information on n and Ac is obtained from Table 11.5a for normal inspection, Table 11.5b for tightened inspection, and Table 11.5c for reduced inspection. Usually the inspection starts with a sampling plan that is taken from the normal inspection table. A set of switching rules tells the user when to switch from one inspection regime to the other. When normal inspection is in effect, tightened inspection is instituted when two out of five consecutive lots are rejected. When tightened inspection is in effect, normal inspection is instituted after five consecutive lots are found acceptable. If the inspection records show that the producer consistently submits products of better quality than the *AQL*,

TABLE 11.5a MIL-STD-105E (Normal Inspection): Table of Sample Sizes and Acceptance Numbers

Sample size code letter	Sample size (n)	AQLs (normal inspection)																									
		0.010	0.015	0.025	0.040	0.065	0.10	0.15	0.25	0.40	0.65	1.0	1.5	2.5	4.0	6.5	10	15	25	40	65	100	150	250	400	650	1000
		Ac Re	Ac Re	Ac Re	Ac Re	Ac Re	Ac Re	Ac Re	Ac Re	Ac Re	Ac Re	Ac Re	Ac Re	Ac Re	Ac Re	Ac Re	Ac Re	Ac Re	Ac Re	Ac Re	Ac Re	Ac Re	Ac Re	Ac Re	Ac Re	Ac Re	Ac Re
A	2	↓	↓	↓	↓	↓	↓	↓	↓	↓	↓	↓	↓	↓	↓	0 1	↓	↓	1 2	2 3	3 4	5 6	7 8	10 11	14 15	21 22	30 31
B	3	↓	↓	↓	↓	↓	↓	↓	↓	↓	↓	↓	↓	↓	0 1	↑	↓	1 2	2 3	3 4	5 6	7 8	10 11	14 15	21 22	30 31	44 45
C	5	↓	↓	↓	↓	↓	↓	↓	↓	↓	↓	↓	↓	0 1	↑	↓	1 2	2 3	3 4	5 6	7 8	10 11	14 15	21 22	30 31	44 45	↑
D	8	↓	↓	↓	↓	↓	↓	↓	↓	↓	↓	↓	0 1	↑	↓	1 2	2 3	3 4	5 6	7 8	10 11	14 15	21 22	30 31	44 45	↑	↑
E	13	↓	↓	↓	↓	↓	↓	↓	↓	↓	↓	0 1	↑	↓	1 2	2 3	3 4	5 6	7 8	10 11	14 15	21 22	30 31	44 45	↑	↑	↑
F	20	↓	↓	↓	↓	↓	↓	↓	↓	↓	0 1	↑	↓	1 2	2 3	3 4	5 6	7 8	10 11	14 15	21 22	↑	↑	↑	↑	↑	↑
G	32	↓	↓	↓	↓	↓	↓	↓	↓	0 1	↑	↓	1 2	2 3	3 4	5 6	7 8	10 11	14 15	21 22	↑	↑	↑	↑	↑	↑	↑
H	50	↓	↓	↓	↓	↓	↓	↓	0 1	↑	↓	1 2	2 3	3 4	5 6	7 8	10 11	14 15	21 22	↑	↑	↑	↑	↑	↑	↑	↑
J	80	↓	↓	↓	↓	↓	↓	0 1	↑	↓	1 2	2 3	3 4	5 6	7 8	10 11	14 15	21 22	↑	↑	↑	↑	↑	↑	↑	↑	↑
K	125	↓	↓	↓	↓	↓	0 1	↑	↓	1 2	2 3	3 4	5 6	7 8	10 11	14 15	21 22	↑	↑	↑	↑	↑	↑	↑	↑	↑	↑
L	200	↓	↓	↓	↓	0 1	↑	↓	1 2	2 3	3 4	5 6	7 8	10 11	14 15	21 22	↑	↑	↑	↑	↑	↑	↑	↑	↑	↑	↑
M	315	↓	↓	↓	0 1	↑	↓	1 2	2 3	3 4	5 6	7 8	10 11	14 15	21 22	↑	↑	↑	↑	↑	↑	↑	↑	↑	↑	↑	↑
N	500	↓	↓	0 1	↑	↓	1 2	2 3	3 4	5 6	7 8	10 11	14 15	21 22	↑	↑	↑	↑	↑	↑	↑	↑	↑	↑	↑	↑	↑
P	800	↓	0 1	↑	↓	1 2	2 3	3 4	5 6	7 8	10 11	14 15	21 22	↑	↑	↑	↑	↑	↑	↑	↑	↑	↑	↑	↑	↑	↑
Q	1250	0 1	↑	↓	1 2	2 3	3 4	5 6	7 8	10 11	14 15	21 22	↑	↑	↑	↑	↑	↑	↑	↑	↑	↑	↑	↑	↑	↑	↑
R	2000	↑	↑	1 2	2 3	3 4	5 6	7 8	10 11	14 15	21 22	↑	↑	↑	↑	↑	↑	↑	↑	↑	↑	↑	↑	↑	↑	↑	↑

↓ = Use first sampling plan below arrow. When sample size equals or exceeds lot size, do total (100 percent) inspection.
↑ = Use first sampling plan above arrow.
Ac = Acceptance number
Re = Rejection number
AQL: Values of 10 or less may be interpreted as percent defectives or defects per hundred units. Values above 10.0 must be interpreted as defects per hundred units.

TABLE 11.5b MIL-STD-105E (Tightened Inspection): Table of Sample Sizes and Acceptance Numbers

Sample size code letter	Sample size (n)	AQLs (tightened inspection) 0.010	0.015	0.025	0.040	0.065	0.10	0.15	0.25	0.40	0.65	1.0	1.5	2.5	4.0	6.5	10	15	25	40	65	100	150	250	400	650	1000
		Ac Re	Ac Re	Ac Re	Ac Re	Ac Re	Ac Re	Ac Re	Ac Re	Ac Re	Ac Re	Ac Re	Ac Re	Ac Re	Ac Re	Ac Re	Ac Re	Ac Re	Ac Re	Ac Re	Ac Re	Ac Re	Ac Re	Ac Re	Ac Re	Ac Re	Ac Re
A	2	↓	↓	↓	↓	↓	↓	↓	↓	↓	↓	↓	↓	↓	↓	↓	↓	↓	↓	1 2	2 3	3 4	5 6	8 9	12 13	18 19	27 28
B	3	↓	↓	↓	↓	↓	↓	↓	↓	↓	↓	↓	↓	↓	↓	0 1	↓	↓	1 2	2 3	3 4	5 6	8 9	12 13	18 19	27 28	41 42
C	5	↓	↓	↓	↓	↓	↓	↓	↓	↓	↓	↓	↓	↓	0 1	↓	↓	1 2	2 3	3 4	5 6	8 9	12 13	18 19	27 28	41 42	↑
D	8	↓	↓	↓	↓	↓	↓	↓	↓	↓	↓	↓	↓	0 1	↓	↓	1 2	2 3	3 4	5 6	8 9	12 13	18 19	27 28	41 42	↑	↑
E	13	↓	↓	↓	↓	↓	↓	↓	↓	↓	↓	↓	0 1	↓	↓	1 2	2 3	3 4	5 6	8 9	12 13	18 19	27 28	41 42	↑	↑	↑
F	20	↓	↓	↓	↓	↓	↓	↓	↓	↓	↓	0 1	↓	↓	1 2	2 3	3 4	5 6	8 9	12 13	18 19	↑	↑	↑	↑	↑	↑
G	32	↓	↓	↓	↓	↓	↓	↓	↓	↓	0 1	↓	↓	1 2	2 3	3 4	5 6	8 9	12 13	18 19	↑	↑	↑	↑	↑	↑	↑
H	50	↓	↓	↓	↓	↓	↓	↓	↓	0 1	↓	↓	1 2	2 3	3 4	5 6	8 9	12 13	18 19	↑	↑	↑	↑	↑	↑	↑	↑
J	80	↓	↓	↓	↓	↓	↓	↓	0 1	↓	↓	1 2	2 3	3 4	5 6	8 9	12 13	18 19	↑	↑	↑	↑	↑	↑	↑	↑	↑
K	125	↓	↓	↓	↓	↓	↓	0 1	↓	↓	1 2	2 3	3 4	5 6	8 9	12 13	18 19	↑	↑	↑	↑	↑	↑	↑	↑	↑	↑
L	200	↓	↓	↓	↓	↓	0 1	↓	↓	1 2	2 3	3 4	5 6	8 9	12 13	18 19	↑	↑	↑	↑	↑	↑	↑	↑	↑	↑	↑
M	315	↓	↓	↓	↓	0 1	↓	↓	1 2	2 3	3 4	5 6	8 9	12 13	18 19	↑	↑	↑	↑	↑	↑	↑	↑	↑	↑	↑	↑
N	500	↓	↓	↓	0 1	↓	↓	1 2	2 3	3 4	5 6	8 9	12 13	18 19	↑	↑	↑	↑	↑	↑	↑	↑	↑	↑	↑	↑	↑
P	800	↓	↓	0 1	↓	↓	1 2	2 3	3 4	5 6	8 9	12 13	18 19	↑	↑	↑	↑	↑	↑	↑	↑	↑	↑	↑	↑	↑	↑
Q	1250	↓	0 1	↓	↓	1 2	2 3	3 4	5 6	8 9	12 13	18 19	↑	↑	↑	↑	↑	↑	↑	↑	↑	↑	↑	↑	↑	↑	↑
R	2000	0 1	↑	↓	1 2	2 3	3 4	5 6	8 9	12 13	18 19	↑	↑	↑	↑	↑	↑	↑	↑	↑	↑	↑	↑	↑	↑	↑	↑
S	3150		↑	1 2								↑	↑	↑	↑	↑	↑	↑	↑	↑	↑	↑	↑	↑	↑	↑	↑

↓ = Use first sampling plan below arrow. When sample size equals or exceeds lot size, do 100 percent inspection.
↑ = Use first sampling plan above arrow.
Ac = Acceptance number
Re = Rejection number
AQL: Values of 10 or less may be interpreted as percent defectives or defects per hundred units. Values above 10.0 must be interpreted as defects per hundred units.

TABLE 11.5c MIL-STD-105E (Reduced Inspection): Table of Sample Sizes and Acceptance Numbers

Sample size code letter	Sample size (*n*)	AQLs (reduced inspection)[†]																									
		0.010	0.015	0.025	0.040	0.065	0.10	0.15	0.25	0.40	0.65	1.0	1.5	2.5	4.0	6.5	10	15	25	40	65	100	150	250	400	650	1000
		Ac Re	Ac Re	Ac Re	Ac Re	Ac Re	Ac Re	Ac Re	Ac Re	Ac Re	Ac Re	Ac Re	Ac Re	Ac Re	Ac Re	Ac Re	Ac Re	Ac Re	Ac Re	Ac Re	Ac Re	Ac Re	Ac Re	Ac Re	Ac Re	Ac Re	Ac Re
A	2	↓	↓	↓	↓	↓	↓	↓	↓	↓	↓	↓	↓	↓	↓	0 1	↓	↓	1 2	2 3	3 4	5 6	7 8	10 11	14 15	21 22	30 31
B	2	↓	↓	↓	↓	↓	↓	↓	↓	↓	↓	↓	↓	↓	0 1	↑	↓	0 2	1 3	2 4	3 5	5 6	7 8	10 11	14 15	21 22	30 31
C	2	↓	↓	↓	↓	↓	↓	↓	↓	↓	↓	↓	↓	0 1	↑	↓	0 2	1 3	1 4	2 5	3 6	5 8	7 10	10 13	14 17	21 24	↑
D	3	↓	↓	↓	↓	↓	↓	↓	↓	↓	↓	↓	0 1	↑	↓	0 2	1 3	1 4	2 5	3 6	5 8	7 10	10 13	14 17	21 24	↑	↑
E	5	↓	↓	↓	↓	↓	↓	↓	↓	↓	↓	0 1	↑	↓	0 2	1 3	1 4	2 5	3 6	5 8	7 10	10 13	14 17	21 24	↑	↑	↑
F	8	↓	↓	↓	↓	↓	↓	↓	↓	↓	0 1	↑	↓	0 2	1 3	1 4	2 5	3 6	5 8	7 10	10 13	↑	↑	↑	↑	↑	↑
G	13	↓	↓	↓	↓	↓	↓	↓	↓	0 1	↑	↓	0 2	1 3	1 4	2 5	3 6	5 8	7 10	10 13	↑	↑	↑	↑	↑	↑	↑
H	20	↓	↓	↓	↓	↓	↓	↓	0 1	↑	↓	0 2	1 3	1 4	2 5	3 6	5 8	7 10	10 13	↑	↑	↑	↑	↑	↑	↑	↑
J	32	↓	↓	↓	↓	↓	↓	0 1	↑	↓	0 2	1 3	1 4	2 5	3 6	5 8	7 10	10 13	↑	↑	↑	↑	↑	↑	↑	↑	↑
K	50	↓	↓	↓	↓	↓	0 1	↑	↓	0 2	1 3	1 4	2 5	3 6	5 8	7 10	10 13	↑	↑	↑	↑	↑	↑	↑	↑	↑	↑
L	80	↓	↓	↓	↓	0 1	↑	↓	0 2	1 3	1 4	2 5	3 6	5 8	7 10	10 13	↑	↑	↑	↑	↑	↑	↑	↑	↑	↑	↑
M	125	↓	↓	↓	0 1	↑	↓	0 2	1 3	1 4	2 5	3 6	5 8	7 10	10 13	↑	↑	↑	↑	↑	↑	↑	↑	↑	↑	↑	↑
N	200	↓	↓	0 1	↑	↓	0 2	1 3	1 4	2 5	3 6	5 8	7 10	10 13	↑	↑	↑	↑	↑	↑	↑	↑	↑	↑	↑	↑	↑
P	315	↓	0 1	↑	↓	0 2	1 3	1 4	2 5	3 6	5 8	7 10	10 13	↑	↑	↑	↑	↑	↑	↑	↑	↑	↑	↑	↑	↑	↑
Q	500	0 1	↑	↓	0 2	1 3	1 4	2 5	3 6	5 8	7 10	10 13	↑	↑	↑	↑	↑	↑	↑	↑	↑	↑	↑	↑	↑	↑	↑
R	800	↑	↑	0 2	1 3	1 4	2 5	3 6	5 8	7 10	10 13	↑	↑	↑	↑	↑	↑	↑	↑	↑	↑	↑	↑	↑	↑	↑	↑

↓ = Use first sampling plan below arrow. When sample size equals or exceeds lot size, do 100 percent inspection.
↑ = Use first sampling plan above arrow.
Ac = Acceptance number
Re = Rejection number
[†]If the figure exceeds the acceptance number but is below rejection number, this lot is passed, but switch to normal inspection for the next lot.
AQL: Values of 10 or less may be interpreted as percent defectives or defects per hundred units. Values above 10.0 must be interpreted as defects per hundred units.

then it is permissible to switch to reduced inspection. The rules require that none of the preceding ten lots on normal inspection have been rejected and that the total number of defectives in the samples from the preceding ten lots is less than a certain acceptable number. Tables for such acceptable numbers are given in the MIL-STD-105E documentation, but they are not shown here. When reduced inspection is in effect, normal inspection is instituted if there is a single rejection.

EXAMPLE

Assume that the lot size is $N = 2000$ and that our acceptable quality level is $AQL = 0.01$. Furthermore, suppose that we operate under inspection level II where inspection costs are ordinary. Table 11.4 shows that the appropriate sample code letter is "K". Under the normal inspection regime (see Table 11.5a) we take samples of size $n = 125$ and accept the lot whenever we have 3 or fewer nonconforming items in the sample, that is, $Ac = 3$. For tightened inspection the acceptance number is reduced to two, $Ac = 2$. For reduced inspection, the plan calls for a sample of size 50. If there is no more than one defective ($Ac = 1$) among the $n = 50$ items, we accept the lot. If there are four or more defectives, we reject the lot and go back to the normal inspection regime. If we find 2 or 3 defectives, then we accept this lot, but switch to normal inspection for the subsequent inspections.

The use of MIL-STD-105E sample inspection plans is often dictated by the federal government. A requirement to use a particular set of plans eliminates the need to construct such plans from first principles; this is an advantage. However, while it makes life easier, it also presents a danger as the Military Standard plans may not lead to the desired alpha and beta risks. One can look at the operating characteristic curves that are implied by these plans, and such curves are provided in the MIL-STD-105E documentation. Simple probability calculations for our example show that for normal inspection ($n = 125$ and $Ac = 3$) the alpha risk at $AQL = 0.01$ is 0.0374; for tightened inspection ($n = 125$ and $Ac = 2$) it is 0.1307, and for reduced inspection ($n = 50$ and $Ac = 4$) it is 0.0006. The beta risk at $LTPD = 0.05$ is 0.1238 for normal inspection, 0.0477 for tightened inspection, and 0.2396 for reduced inspection. You can get these risks from the binomial probabilities. Note that under reduced inspection the consumer risk is quite large. The alpha and beta risks for plans that switch among the various inspection levels according to the prescribed rules are combinations of the risks for the fixed inspection regimes. However these calculations are beyond an introduction to this topic. Interested readers can consult the book by Anders Hald, *Statistical Theory of Sampling Inspection Plans by Attributes*.

Here we have illustrated the Military Standard procedure for a single sample inspection plan for attribute data. Similar tables are available for double and multiple sampling plans, as well as for sampling plans that involve variables data instead of attribute data. ■

11.6 FURTHER COMMENTS

While important historically, acceptance sampling has lost some of its significance in today's climate of continuous quality improvement. This is because one cannot inspect quality into a product; the quality of an item has already been determined by the time the item reaches the inspection stage. The focus of inspection is on the product, with little concern for the process of creating the product. While inspection keeps bad products from being shipped, it does little to keep bad products from being manufactured.

Sample inspection is oriented in the past; detecting flaws and nonconforming items that already have been produced comes too late. Furthermore, much time has usually elapsed since the onset of the quality problem and the time of the final inspection; most likely many more unacceptable items will have been produced before inspection becomes aware of the problem. Moreover, it is usually not possible to reconstruct the exact circumstances that existed at the time the flawed item was produced. As a consequence, little information is available that allows us to fix the problem and make sure that things get done right the next time around.

The modern way to achieve quality involves the continual stabilization and improvement of processes. Statistical process control monitors the stability of processes through timely inspections. Processes are monitored with the aid of control charts; the presence of unusual observations triggers investigations aimed at detecting the root causes of unusual events. Control charts give us timely information on our processes, and corrective action can be taken immediately. The monitoring of processes is an important component of any quality improvement effort, and an extensive discussion of control charts is given in the next chapter. Of course, just being stable over time is not sufficient. One must also check whether the process is capable of producing according to the specified requirements.

There is yet another reason why sampling inspection is often not very useful. In many high-quality applications the proportion of defectives is very low, and no amount of inspection can provide the required information. If the defect rates are small (say, one defective among 100,000 items), then sampling plans will not be very effective. In order to detect even a 100-fold increase in the rate of defectives, one will need extremely large sample sizes (see Exercise 11.7 for further discussion).

These are some of the reasons why the traditional inspection approaches of certifying quality are being replaced by monitoring approaches that examine the stability of the underlying processes. If processes are in control and within their required specifications, then there is little reason to check the final products through inspection. Inspection of the final goods will become superfluous if suppliers actively monitor their processes.

Nevertheless, inspection plays a role in many industries where customers still inspect incoming materials or, alternatively, require producers to certify the quality through inspection. Many receiving departments determine the acceptability of products through inspection. Since 100 percent inspection is usually too expensive or often impossible, acceptance sampling plans are used in practice.

11.6.1 Another Criticism of Acceptance Sampling Plans

Statistical acceptance sampling plans can also be criticized on grounds that these decision rules make no reference to the costs that are involved. There are two types of costs: the cost of inspection, k_1, and the cost of failing to detect that a certain part is defective, k_2. In most assembly-type operations the item under question becomes part of a much larger component. The failure of an item can imply a large loss for the assembly, usually much larger than the value of the item. For example, integrated circuits become components of a television set. It may cost 30 cents to inspect an integrated circuit ($k_1 = 30$). However, the next opportunity of detecting the failure of a circuit may be at the subassembly level, and at that stage a considerable amount of value will have been added. The value of the subassembly may be 100 times the inspection cost; that is, \$30 (or $k_2 = 3000$). Or, for another illustration, consider the production of certain hard disks. One component of the construction of those disks involves an aluminum substrate that is received in lots of 1,000 pieces. It costs seven cents to visually inspect the substrate ($k_1 = 7$). On the other hand, the value added to the disk is \$11 (that is, $k_2 = 1100$). In other words, we are losing eleven dollars if we fail to detect the defect in the substrate.

These costs should be reflected in one's decision whether to carry out zero inspection, 100 percent inspection, or something in between (that is, sample inspection). Standard acceptance sampling plans make no reference to these costs. Deming, in Chapter 15 of his book *Out of the Crisis* (p. 431), is very critical of acceptance sampling plans. He writes:

> *Unfortunately, standard acceptance plans occupy a prominent place in textbooks on statistical methods of quality control .... It is time that we realize what the problem really is, and solve that problem as well as we can, instead of inventing a substitute problem that can be solved exactly, but is irrelevant. It is time to talk about total cost and the problems of practice.*

Let us illustrate what he means by this. Let us assume the cost of inspection is k_1, and the cost of failing to detect that a certain part is defective is k_2. Deming shows that the average total cost is minimized by an "*all or none rule*": No inspection should be carried out if the best lot to come in has fraction defective less than k_1/k_2. On the other hand, 100 percent inspection is indicated if the best lot to come in has fraction defective greater than k_1/k_2.

This result is fairly easy to show. Draw at random a part from the lot with fraction defective θ. Should we subject this item to inspection, or should we place it into production without any inspection? If we inspect, then the average cost per item is k_1. If we don't inspect the part, then the average cost per item is $(\theta)(k_2)$. These two average costs are equal if $\theta = k_1/k_2$. For $\theta < k_1/k_2$, a "no inspection" strategy will give the lesser total cost, while for $\theta > k_1/k_2$ the 100 percent inspection approach will achieve minimal cost. The ratio k_1/k_2 is called the "break-even quality."

For illustration, assume that past experience with the incoming circuit boards that go into television sets indicates a defect rate of about 1.5 defects per 10,000 boards; that is $\theta = 0.00015$. The costs $k_1 = 30$ and $k_2 = 3000$ imply that $k_1/k_2 = 0.01$. Since $\theta = 0.00015 < k_1/k_2 = 0.01$, no inspection should be done at all. In our second illustration involving the aluminum substrate, $k_1 = 7$, $k_2 = 1100$, and $k_1/k_2 = 0.0064$. Past experience with the quality of the incoming substrates has shown that 2.5 percent of the incoming pieces were defective. Since $\theta = 0.025$ is larger than $k_1/k_2 = 0.0064$, we are better off with 100 percent inspection.

Deming also shows that in cases where the incoming quality is predominantly on one side of the break-even quality, the adoption of any plan of inspection other than the all-or-none rule runs the risk of increasing the total cost. Suppose that we inspect a fraction f of incoming items from a lot with fraction defective θ. Then the average cost per item for the inspection of the incoming material and to repair and retest an assembly that failed because of a faulty component is

$$\text{Average Cost} = (f)(k_1) + (1 - f)\theta k_2.$$

How should one set the sampling fraction, f, such that the average cost is minimized? If $\theta < k_1/k_2$, then the average cost, $\theta k_2 + (f)(k_1 - \theta k_2)$, is smallest if $f = 0$. We should not inspect at all; any other sampling fraction will increase the average cost. On the other hand, if $\theta > k_1/k_2$, then the average cost, $k_1 + (1 - f)(\theta k_2 - k_1)$, is minimized for $f = 1$. We should apply 100 percent inspection; inspection short of 100 percent will increase the average cost above the minimum.

Let us illustrate this with the example involving the aluminum substrates in the construction of hard disks. Past experience with the quality of the incoming substrates has shown that 2.5 percent of the incoming pieces were defective. An acceptance sampling plan that selects 65 of the 1,000 substrates at random was employed. According to this plan a lot was rejected whenever five or more items failed. Very few lots were ever rejected. With this sampling plan the average proportion of defective items that were put into the production process was $[(0.025)(1000) - (0.025)(65)]/1000 = 0.023$; this is because the sampling procedure screens out (0.025)(65) defective items on average. Alternatively, you can check that for $\theta = 0.025$ the outgoing quality for a rectifying inspection plan is 0.0244. What about the costs of the various plans? The average cost per incoming piece for 100 percent inspection is 7 cents (since $k_1 = 7$). The average cost if no inspection takes place is $(0.025)(1{,}100) = 27.5$ cents (as $\theta = 0.025$ and $k_2 = 1{,}100$). The average cost per piece for the sampling inspection plan is $(0.065)(7) + (0.023)(1{,}100) = 25.75$ cents. These numbers show that there is a very large difference in costs between the sampling approach and the 100 percent inspection strategy. Inspection short of 100 percent increases the average cost by a considerable amount. The sampling plan should be avoided.

11.7 EXERCISES

11.1 A single sample inspection plan uses sample size $n = 15$ and acceptance number $Ac = 1$. Calculate the operating characteristic curve and determine the alpha risk at $AQL = 0.03$ and the beta risk at $LTPD = 0.10$. Discuss whether this is a good plan.

11.2 A single sampling plan uses sample size $n = 100$ and acceptance number $Ac = 3$.

(a) Obtain the operating characteristic curve, the alpha risk at $AQL = 0.02$, and the beta risk at $LTPD = 0.08$.

(b) Calculate and graph the average outgoing quality curve, $AOQ(\theta)$, and find its maximum (that is, the average outgoing quality limit, $AOQL$). Interpret your findings.

11.3 **(a)** Design a single sample inspection plan for $AQL = 0.03$ and $LTPD = 0.07$. Control the risks at $\alpha = 0.05$ and $\beta = 0.10$, respectively.

(b) Calculate and graph the average outgoing quality curve, $AOQ(\theta)$, and find its maximum (that is, the average outgoing quality limit, $AOQL$). Interpret your findings.

(c) Discuss a sequential sampling procedure that controls the very same risks. Comment on the advantages of a sequential approach.

(d) Discuss how you would use the tables for the MIL-STD-105E plans. Assume that the lot size is 2000, that inspection costs are ordinary, and that you are at the beginning of your sampling procedure. What is your sampling plan?

11.4 A destructive test is used to determine whether a product meets the required specifications. The current inspection scheme is to take $n = 4$ items from a large lot. If all four items meet the specifications, then we accept the lot. If two or more fail, then we reject the lot. If exactly one item fails, then we take another sample of size 2. If both of the items pass the test, we accept the lot; otherwise we reject it.

(a) Write out all possible ways that we can accept the lot.

(b) Obtain and sketch the operating characteristic curve for this double sample inspection plan. What is the chance that we accept a lot that contains 5 percent defectives?

11.5 Consider the single sample inspection plan that takes a sample of size $n = 10$ and rejects the lot if one or more items are defective. Obtain the operating characteristic curve $OC(\theta)$, the average outgoing quality curve $AOQ(\theta)$, and the average outgoing quality limit $AOQL$. Note that with a binomial distribution for the number of defectives X, the operating characteristic curve is given by $OC(\theta) = P(X = 0) = (1 - \theta)^{10}$. It is possible to find an explicit expression for the $AOQL$. Interpret the results.

11.6 Assume that defects are very rare; say one per 100,000 items. Discuss whether sample inspection plans would be useful in such a situation. How would you design a sampling plan for such a small AQL?

(a) Start with a single sample inspection plan with sample size n and $Ac = 0$; a larger value for Ac would make it even more unlikely to reject an acceptable lot with $AQL = 0.00001$. How large do you have to select the sample size to achieve a producer risk of 0.05 at

$AQL = 0.00001$? Use the binomial distribution (or its Poisson approximation as the sample size will be large and the θ is very small) to obtain the operating characteristic curve $OC(\theta) = (1 - \theta)^n$. Solve the equation, $0.05 = 1 - (1 - AQL)^n$, in terms of n.

(b) How large do you have to set the sample size n in order to achieve a consumer risk of 0.08 at $LTPD = 0.0010$ (which is 100 times as large as the AQL)? Solve $0.08 = (1 - LTPD)^n$ for the sample size n. Interpret your results.

11.7 Verify the calculations in Table 11.1.

11.8 Assume that it is desirable to have a producer risk of $\alpha = 0.05$ at $AQL = 0.01$ and a consumer risk of $\beta = 0.10$ at $LTPD = 0.07$. Determine the acceptance and rejection lines in the sequential sample inspection plan.

11.9 Discuss the statement, "You cannot inspect quality into a product," and investigate its implications for the usefulness of acceptance sampling procedures.

11.10 The book by E.G. Schilling, *Acceptance Sampling in Quality Control*, is an excellent reference. Read and comment on this book. Furthermore, look at various issues of *Quality Progress* to learn more on the issues that surround sample inspection.

11.11 Transactions at a bank move from one section to another. The cost to review one transaction while it is being carried out is 25 cents, while the average cost to correct a mistake that is made at the transaction stage at a point further down the line is \$500. Past experience shows that you can expect no fewer than one error among 1,000 entered transactions. What inspection strategy would you recommend?

11.12 The inspection of an automobile transmission costs about \$0.60 per unit. If a defective transmission becomes part of an assembly, the cost to disassemble and repair the unit is \$240. The fraction of defective transmissions is about 0.3 percent (that is, $\theta = 0.003$). Which inspection strategy would you recommend?

11.8 REFERENCES

Deming, W. E. *Out of the Crisis*, Cambridge, MA: MIT Center for Advanced Engineering Study, 1986.

Hald, A. *Statistical Theory of Sampling Inspection Plans by Attributes*. New York: Academic Press, 1991.

Ishikawa, Kaoru. *Guide to Quality Control*, 2nd edition. Tokyo: Asian Productivity Organization, 1982 (available through UNIPUB, New York).

Schilling, E. G. *Acceptance Sampling in Quality Control*. New York: Marcel Dekker, 1982.

Shirland, Larry E. *Statistical Quality Control with Microcomputer Applications*. New York: Wiley, 1993.

Wald, A. *Sequential Analysis*. New York: Wiley, 1947.

PROJECTS FOR SECTION 2

PROJECT 3

The table below provides data on the assembly defects of a car air-conditioning evaporator. The data is taken from Victor E. Kane, *Defect Prevention: Use of Simple Statistical Tools* (Marcel Dekker, 1989, p. 366). Defect information is given for two successive weeks. The number of defects are summarized by the hour they occurred within an eight-hour shift.

	Week 1								Week 2								
Defective item	**1**	**2**	**3**	**4**	**5**	**6**	**7**	**8**	**1**	**2**	**3**	**4**	**5**	**6**	**7**	**8**	**Total**
Sealer		1															1
Defective housing	4	1	10	4	3	4	3			2	2	1	5	1	3		43
Foreign material									1				1	1			3
Welding																	
Missing screws	13	7	11	3	16	8	15	12	24	25	20	15	35	30	25	15	274
Missing doors																	
Cams loose/missing		1	1						1								3
Missing spring																	
Cam screws loose	2								6	4							12
Missing gasket	1		1		1	2	4	3	5	6	3	4	6	4		1	41
Missing door arm									3								3
Missing studs	1		1		3	3	4	1	1								14
Door shaft arm	1		1														2
Missing recirc duct	1					2	1	2			1				2		9
Scrap	4	1	9	1	2							1		1			19
Unconn motor wires	9	5	3		1												18
Missing motor clips									5	15	7	3	7	7	10	5	59
Incomplete parts										1	3		1	3	5		13
Total	36	16	37	8	26	19	27	18	46	53	36	24	55	47	45	21	514
Units repaired				105								161					266
Units produced				1395								1440					2835

Analyze the information, using the statistical tools that you learned in Section 2. Think hard about the best ways of presenting the material. In particular:

Questions

1. Use the summary information (total number of defects, summed over weeks and hours) and construct a Pareto chart. Interpret the information. Is it true that the three most prevalent causes constitute approximately 80 percent of all defects?
2. Compare the defect frequencies for Week 1 and Week 2. Discuss changes, if any, among the frequencies of certain defects from one week to the next.
3. Compare the frequencies of defects across hours within the shift. Are there differences from one hour to the next? Discuss.
4. Write a brief report that summarizes and explains your findings.

PROJECT 4

Victor E. Kane, *Defect Prevention: Use of Simple Statistical Tools*, p. 393, lists the number of weekly "burr rejects" on two machines, machine 3 and machine 4. Burr rejects occur when the manufactured edge of a piece of material shows small indentations, called burrs. The following information is given for twelve consecutive weeks.

Week	Machine	Units produced	Number of rejects
1	3	263	11
	4	244	20
2	3	285	5
	4	336	14
3	3	201	10
	4	221	11
4	3	435	21
	4	257	6
5	3	133	2
	4	275	8
6	3	375	3
	4	422	13
7	3	321	10
	4	281	20

(*continues*)

(continued)

Week	Machine	Units produced	Number of rejects
8	3	307	4
	4	317	15
9	3	294	3
	4	299	15
10	3	348	13
	4	358	11
11	3	331	0
	4	312	6
12	3	296	1
	4	328	7

Questions

1. Analyze the information using the statistical tools that you learned in Section 2 of this book. In particular, use bar charts and time series displays to compare the defect information (1) across machines; (2) across weeks; (3) across weeks, separately for machines 3 and 4.
2. Write a short report summarizing your conclusions. Support your conclusions with the appropriate tables and figures.

PROJECT 5

This project is taken from Victor E. Kane, *Defect Prevention: Use of Simple Statistical Tools*, p. 513. A grinding operation is used to manufacture a small aluminum valve that becomes part of an automobile transmission. After grinding, the valves are tumbled in a deburring medium to remove any remaining burrs. After that, the valves are anodized. Anodization is a continuous chemical process that places a thin coating of aluminum oxide on the valve; the purpose of the coating is to increase the valve's wear characteristics.

The deburring process removes material, while the anodization process adds material. The net change in material was designed to be zero. In this particular application the targeting problem was made more difficult as it was necessary to balance two part characteristics. Two diameters, at different locations on the valve, were of interest; here we call them the large and the small diameter. Measurements before deburring and after anodizing were made at these two locations on 50 parts collected randomly over a representative period of time. The data given below is in coded units. The original measurements can be calculated from the coded values according to:

$$\text{Actual (in mm)} = 12.99 + (0.0001)(\text{coded value}) \quad \text{for the large diameter}$$
$$\text{Actual (in mm)} = 10.36 + (0.0001)(\text{coded value}) \quad \text{for the small diameter}$$

For example, the measurements on the first valve are: $12.99 + (0.0001)(-5) = 12.9895$ (before deburring) and $12.99 + (0.0001)(5) = 12.9905$ (after anodizing) for the large diameter, and $10.36 + (0.0001)(35) = 10.3635$ (before deburring) and $10.36 + (0.0001)(50) = 10.3650$ (after anodizing) for the small diameter.

	Large		Small			Large		Small	
Part	**Before deburr**	**After anod**	**Before deburr**	**After anod**	**Part**	**Before deburr**	**After anod**	**Before deburr**	**After anod**
1	−5	5	35	50	26	25	25	25	35
2	15	10	35	65	27	20	20	30	25
3	15	20	50	45	28	25	25	30	25
4	15	20	40	75	29	35	40	45	55
5	0	20	30	70	30	25	25	25	75
6	0	5	30	45	31	10	15	40	75
7	20	20	15	25	32	20	20	40	70
8	15	25	30	40	33	65	60	30	55
9	10	5	45	75	34	10	20	30	45
10	30	25	40	90	35	35	30	15	45
11	65	50	15	75	36	65	70	45	70
12	20	15	20	90	37	15	30	30	50
13	40	25	30	85	38	20	15	35	60
14	40	30	25	80	39	60	40	35	45
15	50	35	30	80	40	55	50	20	65
16	40	40	55	50	41	15	25	35	75
17	25	25	45	60	42	10	30	20	65
18	35	50	25	65	43	50	70	25	55
19	25	40	40	50	44	40	60	30	65
20	35	55	35	55	45	−5	10	30	45
21	20	40	40	55	46	95	110	35	75
22	20	40	30	45	47	25	40	30	55
23	45	55	20	50	48	10	30	25	60
24	25	35	15	45	49	40	55	40	70
25	20	35	45	75	50	50	60	15	75

Coded measurements.

Analyze the information using the techniques that you learned in Section 2 of this book. In particular:

Questions

1. Summarize the diameter measurements before deburring and after anodizing, separately for small and large diameters. Calculate averages and standard deviations. Is it true that the large-diameter variability is the same before deburring and after anodizing? Does the same hold for the small-diameter variability? Support your conclusions with the relevant summary statistics and graphical displays of the data.
2. For each location, two measurements are taken from the same valve: a measurement before deburring and a measurement after anodizing. Remember that the net material change was planned to be zero. Decide whether the mean difference in material is indeed zero. (Since two measurements are taken on the same part, you should obtain the difference in these measurements for each part, calculate the average and the standard deviation from those differences, and test whether the observed distance of the sample average of the differences from the hypothesized value zero is statistically significant. Do this for both small and large diameters.)

   What do you conclude? Is it true that deburring and anodizing adds material? Does your answer depend on whether you look at small or large diameters?
3. Construct a scatter diagram where you plot the diameter measurement after anodizing against the diameter measurement before deburring. Do this for small and large diameters separately. Calculate the correlation coefficients that go with these two graphs.

   What can you learn from these displays? Are the conclusions that you reached in questions 1 and 2 the same as your findings in question 3? Explain.

PROJECT 6

The data for this project is taken from Levine, David, Ramsey, Patricia, P., and Berenson, Mark L., *Business Statistics for Quality and Productivity*, p. 756.

The Antilope Pass Mining Company operates a large heap leach gold mine in the western United States. The company utilizes a giant computer-controlled stacker that was designed to load each day 35,000 tons of crushed ore onto the leaching pad. A chemical solution is then sprinkled over the heap, and the gold is recovered from the solution after it seeps through the gold-bearing ore. The following information was collected:

Day	Ore stacked (in tons)	Downtime (in minutes)					
		Total	By category				
			ME	EL	TR	OP	NF
1	9,612	1,093	1,093	0	0	0	0
2	15,417	877	13	740	0	102	22
3	30,259	321	0	0	0	0	321
4	36,345	30	0	0	30	0	0
5	21,553	671	480	0	76	115	0
6	35,658	154	0	0	0	51	103
7	37,047	93	0	0	0	31	62
8	28,222	237	0	0	0	46	191
9	28,698	412	184	0	0	175	53
10	29,049	226	0	0	0	216	10
11	9,105	931	0	0	0	0	931
12	4,448	1,051	480	0	0	15	556
13	12,660	647	0	27	0	124	496
14	17,157	487	0	0	0	0	487
15	31,563	149	0	0	0	55	94
16	30,801	261	0	0	0	68	193
17	18,710	892	255	386	0	113	138
18	36,568	66	28	0	0	26	12
19	12,889	804	480	0	0	171	153
20	25,637	305	0	0	0	182	123
21	21,390	504	0	24	0	424	56
22	32,006	291	0	0	0	7	284
23	33,449	238	0	0	0	30	208
24	23,392	456	0	0	0	355	101
25	25,842	388	0	0	0	25	363
26	20,192	572	525	0	0	0	47
27	14,907	784	0	0	0	588	196
28	19,587	681	20	0	0	511	150
29	20,237	536	0	0	0	388	148
30	11,222	727	152	195	0	314	66
31	10,053	1,022	922	0	0	100	0
32	9,158	822	95	230	0	250	247
33	18,298	606	480	0	0	0	126
34	20,003	444	60	0	0	277	107
35	31,762	59	0	10	0	9	40

ME = Mechanical
EL = Electrical
TR = Tonnage restriction
OP = Operator
NF = No feed

Questions

1. Column 2 of the table lists the daily amount of stacked ore over a five-week period. What do you see when you look at the past history of the daily amounts of stacked ore? Is the stacking process in statistical control, or do you see patterns or trends in the data? (You can use a time-sequence plot of the individual observations to assess stability.)

   Since the data is from consecutive days, you can check for (weekly) seasonality. Are there differences due to the day of the week? Justify your conclusion with summary statistics and appropriate graphs.

   Based on this data, do you believe that the stacker can achieve its goal of 35,000 tons per day?
2. Column 3 of the table displays the daily amount of downtime of the stacker. Explore how the throughput (that is, the amount of stacked ore) is related to the amount of downtime. Graph throughput against downtime. Interpret the graph. Calculate and interpret the correlation coefficient. What do you conclude? What steps would you recommend for improving the daily throughput?
3. Your analysis in question 2 implies that the amount of ore processed by the stacker would probably increase if downtime could be reduced. An Ishikawa cause-and-effect diagram to assess the possible causes of downtime was developed. It showed that the causes of downtime could be organized into five broad categories:

   Mechanical failures
   Electrical failures
   Tonnage restrictions (because of plant shutdowns due to environmental restrictions such as dust control)
   Operator failures
   No available feed (because of problems upstream in the process that prevent the ore from reaching the stacker)

   The downtimes that can be attributed to these causes are also given in the above table. Summarize and compare the amount of downtime attributable to the different causes. Display the information in the most appropriate graphs.
4. Write a brief report that summarizes your findings and that outlines an action plan for improvement.

PROJECT 7

Collect and analyze data on traffic along a busy road of your choice. You may want to collect data on vehicle frequencies, the car/truck mix, the number of passengers riding in a vehicle, and other factors that you find useful.

Questions

1. Establish the appropriate operational definitions; for example, define what you mean by a car and a truck. Develop a sampling strategy that allows you to learn about possible "time-of-the-day" and "day-of-the-week" effects.
2. Carry out your sampling strategy, collect the information, and analyze the data using the statistical tools that you learned in Section II of this book. Summarize your findings.
3. Enumerate and discuss possible reasons for traffic congestion, using an Ishikawa cause-and-effect diagram. Discuss strategies for easing traffic bottlenecks.

PROJECT 8

Investigate the annual compensation that is paid to Chief Executive Officers of large U.S. companies. Study whether the compensation paid is a reflection of performance.

Questions

1. Develop operational definitions of the variables. What do you mean by "compensation"? What do you mean by "performance"?
2. Collect the information for one of the recent years. You may want to check for this information in libraries (issues of business magazines and publications) or on relevant Web sites. Depending on the available data, you may have to change your operational definition. How did you select the CEOs and their companies?
3. Analyze the data graphically and through summary statistics. What can you say about CEO compensation? What does the distribution of compensation look like? Why are the mean and median compensations different?
4. What can you say about the relationship between compensation and performance? Discuss.
5. Develop a cause-and-effect diagram that helps explain differences in compensation. What does your data say about performance as a cause?
6. Would it help to stratify CEOs according to gender? according to type of company? according to the size of the company? Discuss.

References for Projects for Section 2

Kane, V. E. *Defect Prevention: Use of Simple Statistical Tools.* New York, NY: Marcel Dekker, 1989.

Levine, D., P. P. Ramsey, and M. L. Berenson. *Business Statistics for Quality and Productivity.* Englewood Cliffs, N.J.: Prentice Hall, 1995.

SECTION 3

PROCESS STABILIZATION: MAKING PROCESSES PREDICTABLE

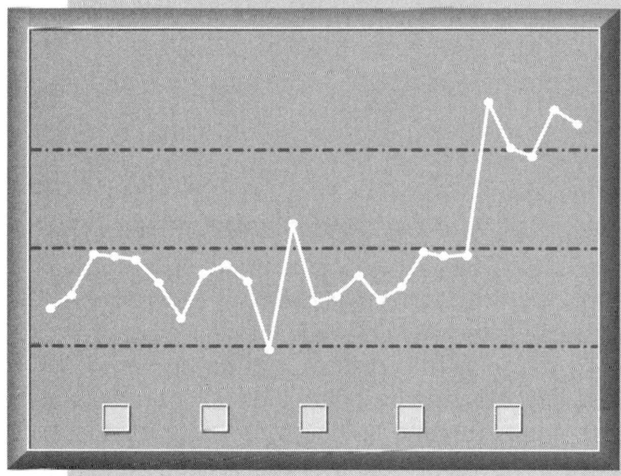

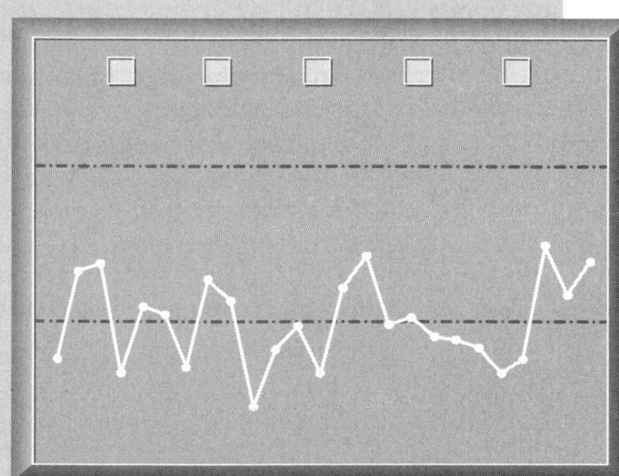

CHAPTER 12

STATISTICAL PROCESS CONTROL: CONTROL CHARTS

12.1 INTRODUCTION

Variation is a natural part of all processes. *Statistical Process Control* (SPC in short, also known under the alternative term, Statistical Quality Control or SQC) is the application of statistics to the control of process variability. Control of process variability encompasses the control of the motion in the process mean, as well as of changes in process variability. Statistical process control techniques help us detect unusual behavior in the process and determine whether process outcomes are affected by special events. They help us decide whether a process is stable over time. Achieving stability is an important first step in any quality improvement program.

12.1.1 Control Charts

Control charts are the basic tools of statistical process control. A control chart is a time-sequence plot of important product (or process) characteristics that are obtained from the process at periodic intervals. Such a time-sequence graph is

- A graphical method for determining whether a process is *stable* (or, as it is also called, *in statistical control*).

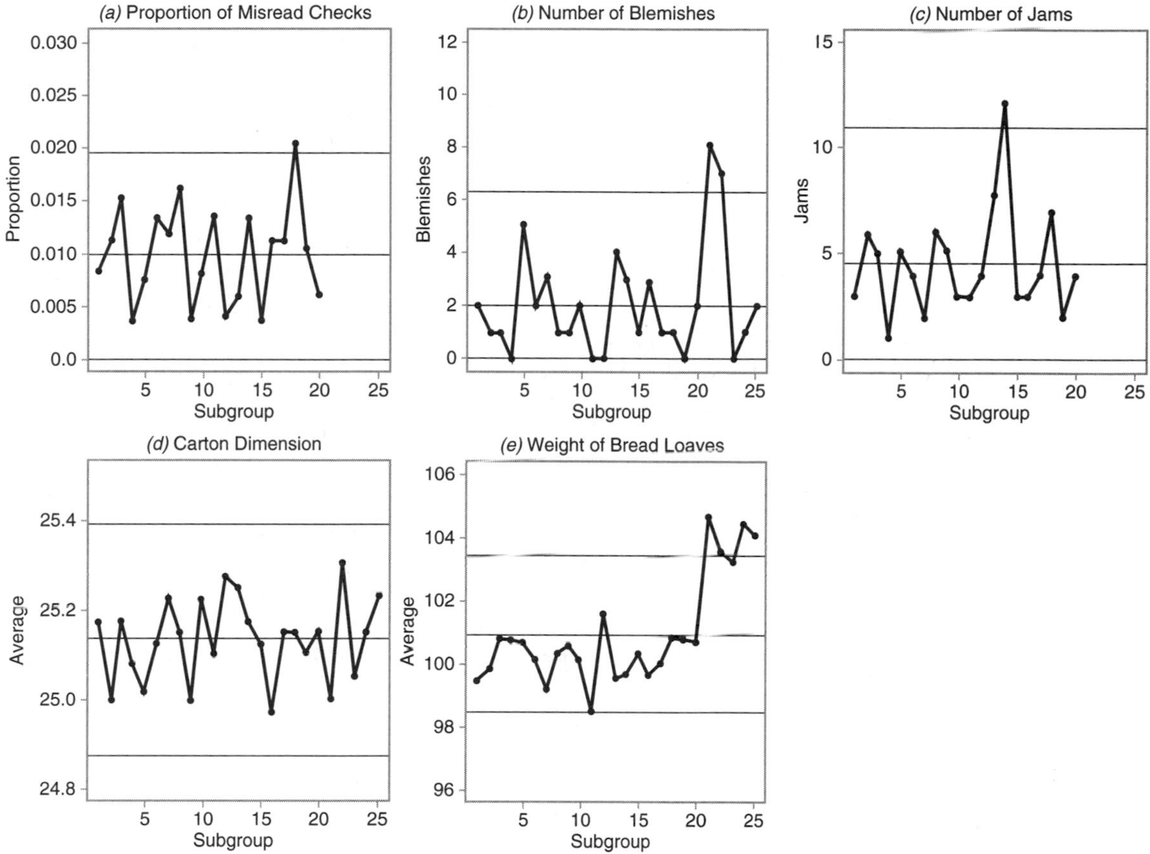

FIGURE 12.1 Examples of control charts and control limits.

- A tool for distinguishing usual (or *common*) variability from unusual (*special*, or *assignable*) causes.
- An alarm system signaling the need for an analysis of the causes of problems.
- An aid to understanding and improving processes. The identification and elimination of sources of unusual events help us stabilize and improve the process. Control charts help our process reach the best level that can be achieved without altering its basic underlying structure.

Examples of control charts are given in Figures 12.1a through e. Figure 12.1a is a time-sequence plot of daily proportions of misread items from an automatic check reading machine. Figure 12.1b shows the number of blemishes on a ten-inch-wide section of a thin aluminum strip; a continuous aluminum strip is sampled at half-hour intervals and the number of blemishes is recorded. Figure 12.1c shows the number of machine jams over a period of 20 consecutive shifts.

Figure 12.1d shows average dimensions of packing cartons; averages are calculated from subgroups of four cartons that are taken from the production line every hour. Figure 12.1e shows average weights of loaves of bread; five bread loaves are taken at 10-minute intervals and the resulting sample averages are displayed in Figure 12.1e. Many other examples from manufacturing as well as the service sector can be given. We can track daily numbers of purchase orders, number of trouble calls, dimensions of manufactured goods, absentee times, and so on.

The lines that are superimposed on these time-sequence plots are known as the *control limits*. The meaning and the calculation of control limits are explained in this chapter. These limits are action limits. Points outside the control limits are an indication that something unusual has happened to the process. They prompt us to investigate the process and initiate actions.

Several of the charts in Figure 12.1 exhibit features that suggest the presence of unusual events. For example, on the first graph (which displays proportions of misread checks) the observation at time period 18 exceeds the upper control limit. What happened at that particular time? There are two unusual observations in Figure 12.1b: the observations at times 21 and 22. There is one unusual observation in Figure 12.1c: the number of blemishes (12 of them) in period 14 is unusually high. The chart in Figure 12.1e shows a shift in the mean level. After period 20 the weight of bread loaves has gone up. What could have accounted for such a shift?

Control charts talk to us. A major advantage of a control chart is that, even without the control limits, it brings unusual events to the attention of the observer. Unusual points lead to the response: "What the heck happened here?"

12.1.2 A Brief History of Statistical Quality Control

For several decades, statistical quality control was the main technique for improving product quality in the manufacturing area. In the 1920s, Walter A. Shewhart of the Bell Telephone Laboratories originated the concept of statistical quality control (Shewhart, 1931). In subsequent years, it spread through the manufacturing segment of the U.S. economy, slowly at first, but rapidly during World War II when sudden heavy demand was placed on industry.

After the war, Japan turned to quality as a fundamental strategy for recovering from the devastation wrought by the war and for regaining world markets. American experts, such as W. Edwards Deming and Joseph M. Juran, were invited to help; and they introduced statistical quality control to the Japanese. For at least a decade, statistical process control was their chief tool in promoting quality. Gradually the growth of other concepts and techniques, such as the importance of management in achieving quality, eclipsed the importance of statistical quality control in Japan. But it remains a fundamental tool for quality, one that the Japanese thoroughly mastered and regularly apply.

12.1.3 Basic Concepts of Control Charts

As its name suggests, statistical quality control is a branch of applied statistics, dealing with statistical tools that can be used to monitor and control the quality of products. Careful monitoring of products and reacting to unusual events by finding and eliminating their root causes leads to quality improvements in the processes that generate the products.

A control chart is a graphical tool that can be used to understand a process and help assure the quality of products produced by that process. There are several reasons why these charts have been used successfully for more than half a century.

A fundamental reason for the success of control charts is that they raise important issues and force their resolution. To apply control chart techniques, it is necessary to decide specifically what is to be controlled, the standards to be used, the measurements to be taken, how they are to be taken, and what will be done with them. The use of control charts forces communication and establishes responsibility on these important issues.

A second reason for the success of control charts is that they focus *attention on the process* rather than the product. There are two fundamental causes of poor products, and it is important to distinguish between them. A poor product can result from operator error; that is, it can result from improper operation of a satisfactory production process. More often, however, a poor product is not due to poor workmanship, but to a poor production process—a process that is just not capable of meeting requirements and standards on a consistent basis. The distinction between poor workmanship and a poor process is highlighted by the use of control charts. W. Edwards Deming, in his book *Out of the Crisis* (p. 314), says this very eloquently when he writes:

> *A fault in the interpretation of observations, seen everywhere, is to suppose that every event (defect, mistake, accident) is attributable to someone (usually the nearest at hand), or is related to some special event. The fact is that most troubles with service and production lie in the system. Sometimes the fault is indeed local, attributable to someone on the job or not on the job when he should be. We shall speak of faults of the system as common causes of trouble, and faults from fleeting events as special causes.*

In Deming's view, 94 percent of all troubles belong to the system (and are responsibility of management), while only 6 percent are special.

A third reason for the success of control charts is that they constitute a set of techniques that can be taught to people and that people can apply in a specified manner. As much as one might devalue a "cookbook" approach to quality, experience shows that people want a prescribed procedure to assist them in achieving quality. In much the same way, the technique of using control charts serves as a guide for people who otherwise might not be able to take effective actions toward quality improvement.

12.1.4 Statistical Control: Common Causes and Special Causes

Being in statistical control means that the variability in our process measure is determined by a stable, predictable chance system. There is always going to be variability in the system. In a stable system the process that generates this variability is constant over time. We say that the process is *in statistical control.* On the other hand, if the laws that govern the variability change over time, then we say that the process is *not in* (or is *out of*) *statistical control.*

W. Edwards Deming ("Some Principles of the Shewhart Methods of Quality Control," pp. 173–177) expresses this very clearly:

> *There is no such thing as constancy in real life. There is, however, such a thing as a constant-cause system. The results produced by a constant-cause system vary, and, in fact, may vary over a wide band or a narrow band. They vary, but they exhibit an important feature called stability. . . . It is the distribution of results that is constant or stable. . . . When a manufacturing process behaves like a constant cause system. . . it is said to be in statistical control. The control chart will tell you whether your process is in statistical control.*

As an illustration, take the number of calls that are received by the technical support system of a mail-order computer store. There is variability among the daily numbers of incoming calls. We may get, on average, 1,000 calls a day and the standard deviation may be 100 calls a day. If the process is in statistical control (that is, stable), it is very easy to predict the number of calls for any other day. We are pretty certain that the number of calls will be somewhere between 700 and 1,300 calls. This is because counts, as long as they are reasonably large, follow an approximate normal distribution. We know that the interval that we get by adding and subtracting three standard deviations from the mean covers more than 99 percent of the distribution of the number of incoming calls. What would you conclude if you saw a day with 1,600 calls? Such an event would definitely be very unusual, and we would very much doubt that only the constant-cause system was operating.

In a constant-cause system the variability in our measurements is considered to be the effect of many individually small, unobserved influences. Deming calls these the *common causes.* Examples of common causes are slight variations among different machines, poor instruction and poor supervision, variation among skill levels of workers, poor design of products and services, variability among raw materials, variations in environmental conditions in the plant such as fluctuating temperature or relative humidity, uncomfortable working conditions and poor lighting, and failure to provide workers with information that shows them where they can improve their performance. Common causes represent the myriad of ever-present factors that contribute to small shifts in the process.

Deming distinguishes common causes from *special causes*. Special causes or, as Shewhart calls them, *assignable causes* arise because of special circumstances and they affect the process only some of the time. Examples of special causes are a temporary change to a new supplier, a temporary worker who did not get properly trained, a sudden shift in the power supply, a sudden breakdown of an air conditioning unit, a sudden contamination of the incoming water supply, breakage of a tool, and so on. Special effects usually introduce large and sudden changes into the process.

A process is said to be in statistical control if only common causes operate on the process and no special causes influence the variability of the process result. Common causes are the ones that make up the variability in a constant cause system. Special (or assignable) causes are those that are different from the usual system. We need to remove these special causes from the system.

Several comments should be made on what statistical control and control charts are, and what they are not:

A process in statistical control is not necessarily a good process which satisfies the required specifications. Our process may be in statistical control, but the constant-cause variation may be so large that the process fails to meet the requirements that are demanded by the customer. Control charts provide information about how the process *is* running, not about how it *should* run.

Control charts help us detect unusual variation; they do not detect the *reason*. Special causes need to be detected and flagged, and control charts allow us to do this. However, we need to do more: Once we have identified unusual results, we need to find an explanation for them. Causes for the unusual events must be found through an investigation of the process. If the unusual measurements are undesirable, then one must make sure that the causes are prevented in the future. Of course, if they represent unusually good results, then one must make sure that the causes stay present.

12.1.5 React to Special Causes, but Avoid Tampering with a Stable System

It is very important to react to special causes and attempt to remove them so that they do not occur again. Reacting to common causes of variation that cannot be controlled, however, is unwise as unnecessary *tampering* with a process that is in control will increase the variation.

This assertion can be explained with Deming's *funnel experiment* (Deming, *Out of the Crisis*, p. 327), which we describe here in the following, slightly altered, form. The experiment involves dropping a light ball through a holder (a funnel) onto a target on the floor. Assume that the release position is fixed optimally, directly over the desired target. Of course, the actual "hit" is not always exactly on target. The ball may come to rest at point $z = (x, y)$, where x and y are the coordinates of the hit as measured from the target. For example, (1, −3) indicates that the hit is one unit to the right of the target and three units below the target. Suppose that the experiment is repeated, say 100 times. The variability of the process can be displayed graphically by marking the impact positions in relation to the target; the variability in the process can be summarized numerically by averaging the Euclidian distances, $\sqrt{(x_k)^2 + (y_k)^2}$, of the impact positions $z_k = (x_k, y_k), k = 1, \ldots, 100$. The observed variability reflects the common cause variability of the process. The outcome of the process (that is, the impact position of the dropped ball) is affected by many random factors such as the stability of the air, drafts in the room, and so on. Variability is present, but the system is in statistical control. The only way to reduce the variability is to make changes to the system. For example, one can make sure that the doors are closed at all times and that there are no drafts in the room. Perhaps the use of a different, heavier material for the ball would get us closer to the target, and so on.

Someone unfamiliar with the concept of common cause variation may think that they can do better by adjusting the release position on the basis of the location of the previous impact. One such strategy (strategy 1) revises the release position as follows: If the kth ball hits at $z_k = (x_k, y_k)$ as measured from the target, then the release position for the next drop is moved by $-z_k = (-x_k, -y_k)$ from its *last release position*. This particular adjustment remembers the previous release position (as Deming says, it has "memory"), and the adjustment is in the opposite direction of the last error as measured from the target. Carry out a sequence of such adjustments and plot the results on graph paper; you will find that this strategy increases the distances from the target. We are tampering with a stable system by reacting to and chasing after the random components in the system. We are much better off leaving things alone!

Another conceivable tampering strategy (strategy 2), and one that is even worse than the previous one, is to adjust the new release position by moving it by $-z_k = (-x_k, -y_k)$ from the *initial release position* that was determined at the outset of the experiment. In our case the initial release position has coordinates (0, 0), and hence the holder for the $(k + 1)$st experiment is moved to the position $-z_k = (-x_k, -y_k)$. This is different from the first strategy, where the adjustment is made in relation to the previous release position; under the second strategy the adjustment does not remember the previous position of the funnel; it has no memory. One can show that the hits under this strategy oscillate back and forth around the target, and as time goes on this strategy will lead us further and further away from the target. As W. Edwards Deming says, the process is "off to the Milky-Way." Figure 12.2 illustrates these two tampering procedures. Figure 12.3 (page 312) shows the outcomes that result from a strategy that leaves the process alone and those that arise from each of the two tampering strategies. Exercise 12.3

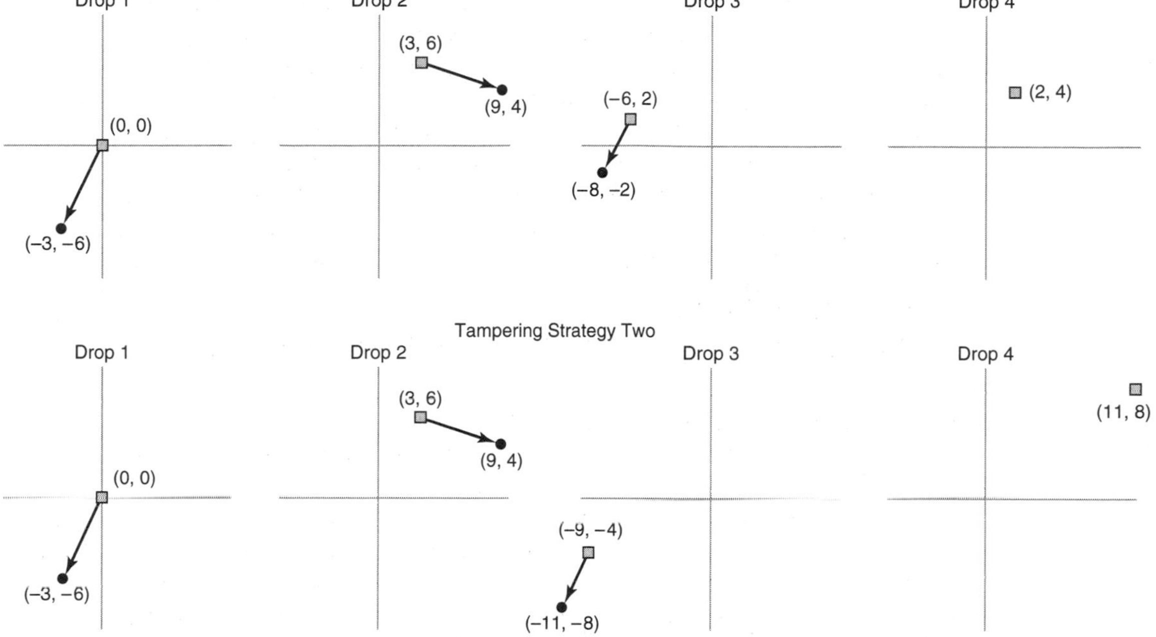

FIGURE 12.2 Two tampering strategies in the funnel experiment using the same random errors in both plans.
□ Release position
• Hit

asks you to confirm these results by simulation. Exercise 12.4 is a one-dimensional modification of this exercise which can be carried out without the funnel equipment; all that is needed is a pair of dice.

Tampering is clearly bad if the system is stable. However, this discussion does not imply that one should never make adjustments to a process. Of course, one should make the necessary adjustments if there are clearly identified causes that affect the system. The tool wear example in Section 7.2 of Chapter 7 is a good example. There we knew that the drift in the process was due to tool wear. In this case it made perfect sense to adjust the position of the tool; a simple feedback algorithm was effective in reducing the variability.

This discussion shows that there are two kinds of mistakes: Ascribing a variation or a mistake to a special cause, when in fact the cause belongs to the system, leads to overadjustment and tampering. However, there is also the mistake of ascribing a variation or a mistake to the system, when in fact the cause is special. A consequence of this mistake is that we fail to detect the presence of an assignable cause.

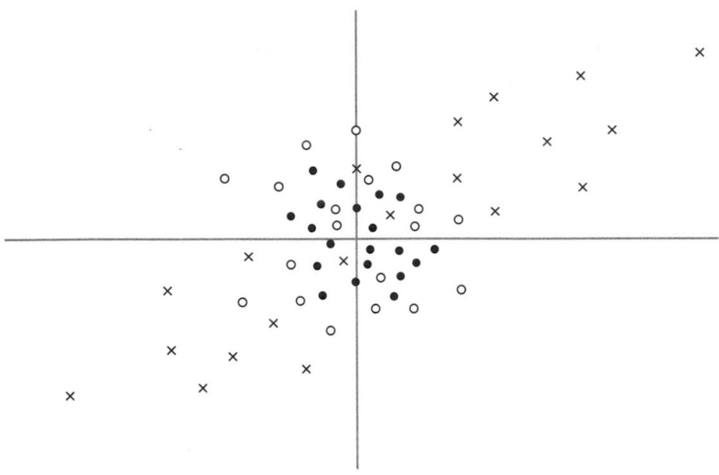

FIGURE 12.3 Results of the funnel experiment.
• No tampering
○ Strategy 1
× Strategy 2.

12.1.6 Process Monitoring versus Sample Inspection

The old way of assuring quality through sample inspection prior to shipping is oriented toward the past. Detecting flaws or nonconforming items that have been produced already comes *too late*. Significant time may have passed since the process has gone out of control and much scrap may have been produced since the onset of the problem. Finding the problem at the sample inspection stage prior to shipment comes too late.

Furthermore, sample inspection is *not enough*. At the sampling inspection stage it may not be possible to reconstruct the exact circumstances that existed at the time the problem started. As a consequence, not much can be done to fix the problem, and the results of the sample inspection do not help us make the appropriate changes. In summary, sample inspection is *too little, too late*.

The modern way to think about quality involves process control where the process is controlled through timely inspection. The process is monitored through control charts and processes are adjusted as needed. If observations are judged not consistent with the usual common-cause variability, then we look for causes of the additional variability, and we attempt to prevent those causes from occurring again.

Control charts are a first important step; they bring our processes to stability. Stable processes are predictable. Once we establish a stable and thus predictable process, then we can address the next question whether the process is also acceptable. The process may or may not be acceptable. If the process is unacceptable, adjustments may be needed to (1) bring the process on-target and (2) reduce the variation such that the process satisfies the specifications of our customers.

Statistical control of a process is not an end in itself. Once statistical control is established, serious work to improve the quality and the economy of production can begin. The important problems of improvement commence once one has established statistical control. For process improvement we need to identify the common causes of variation and remove them from the system. For example, we may have to stabilize the fluctuations in the incoming raw materials, or the fluctuations in certain environmental conditions in the plant if our process is very much affected by such variation. Or, we may want to try to make the process *more robust*, in the sense that it is insensitive to such variation. Discussion on robust processes and products is given in Chapter 16.

12.2 CONTROL CHARTS FOR CONTINUOUS MEASUREMENT DATA

Control charts are designed for different situations. Some charts are used to monitor the proportion of defective items; they are called *p-charts*. Some charts are used to keep track of the number of defects or flaws on a product, such as the number of defects on a car, the number of blemishes on a section of aluminum foil, or the number of flaws on a piece of woven fabric; such charts are referred to as *c-charts*. The p- and c-charts are used for attribute data, which is data that describes the presence or absence of a certain characteristic. These charts will be discussed in Section 12.4.

12.2.1 *X*-Bar Charts, *S*-Charts, and *R*-Charts

Control charts are used to monitor fill weight or fill volume, such as the weight of ice cream or the volume of shampoo. Measurements on dimensions such as length, volume, or weight are taken on a continuous scale, as compared with attribute measurements, which are categorical in nature. The *x-bar chart* (also called the *mean chart*), the *s-chart* (also called the *standard deviation chart*), and the *R-chart* (also called the *range chart*) are used to monitor continuous measurement or variables data. An important question is whether the filling process is stable over time—in particular, whether the *levels* of the fill weights are stable over time and whether the *variability* in the filling process is stable over time. The first question is addressed by the mean chart, whereas standard deviation and range charts are used to monitor the variability. In order to construct x-bar, s-, and R-charts, we take small samples from the process in question at periodic points of time. The subgroup (or sample) size, n, is usually small, typically of the order of four or five observations. For example, we may take a sample of four items at 10:00 a.m., four items at 10:30, and so on; here the subgroup size is $n = 4$. The average, the standard deviation, and the range of each subgroup are computed. Successive

TABLE 12.1 Dimensions of Packing Cartons (in Centimeters, from Front to Back)

Time	Measurements				Average	Std. dev	Range
6:30 am	25.1	25.5	25.0	25.1	25.175	0.222	0.50
7:30	24.8	25.2	25.1	24.9	25.000	0.183	0.40
8:30	25.1	25.2	25.2	25.2	25.175	0.050	0.10
9:30	25.1	25.4	24.8	25.0	25.075	0.250	0.60
10:30	25.2	24.7	24.9	25.3	25.025	0.275	0.60
11:30	25.2	25.2	25.0	25.1	25.125	0.096	0.20
12:30 pm	25.2	25.2	25.2	25.3	25.225	0.050	0.10
1:30	25.2	25.1	25.3	25.0	25.150	0.129	0.30
2:30	24.9	25.1	25.2	24.8	25.000	0.183	0.40
3:30	25.1	25.1	25.3	25.4	25.225	0.150	0.30
4:30	25.4	25.0	25.1	24.9	25.100	0.216	0.50
5:30	25.3	25.2	25.1	25.5	25.275	0.171	0.40
6:30	25.2	25.1	25.5	25.2	25.250	0.173	0.40
7:30	25.0	24.9	25.6	25.2	25.175	0.310	0.70
8:30	25.1	25.2	25.1	25.1	25.125	0.050	0.10
9:30	25.0	25.0	24.9	25.0	24.975	0.050	0.10
10:30	25.3	25.1	25.3	24.9	25.150	0.191	0.40
11:30	25.2	25.1	25.2	25.1	25.150	0.058	0.10
12:30 am	25.1	25.1	25.4	24.8	25.100	0.245	0.60
1:30	25.4	25.0	25.2	25.0	25.150	0.191	0.40
2:30	24.8	25.2	25.0	25.0	25.000	0.163	0.40
3:30	25.3	25.4	25.2	25.3	25.300	0.082	0.20
4:30	25.1	24.8	25.2	25.1	25.050	0.173	0.40
5:30	25.0	25.4	25.1	25.1	25.150	0.173	0.40
6:30	25.1	25.3	25.3	25.2	25.225	0.096	0.20
Average					25.134	0.1572	0.352

Twenty-five subgroups of size $n = 4$, taken every hour.

sample averages are plotted against time; we call such a time-sequence plot an *x-bar chart.* A time-sequence plot of successive standard deviations is referred to as an *s-chart*; and a time-sequence plot of successive ranges is called an *R-chart.*

As an example, consider the process of manufacturing paper containers for a certain household detergent. We are interested in the container dimensions (centimeters, from front to back). Each hour four cartons are selected and their dimensions are measured. Table 12.1 lists the measurements for 25 consecutive subgroups of size $n = 4$, together with their averages, standard deviations, and ranges.

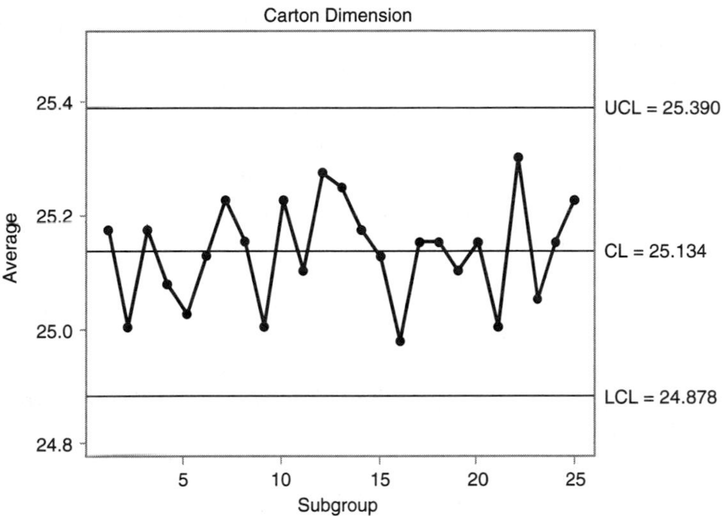

FIGURE 12.4a X-bar chart: Carton dimensions.

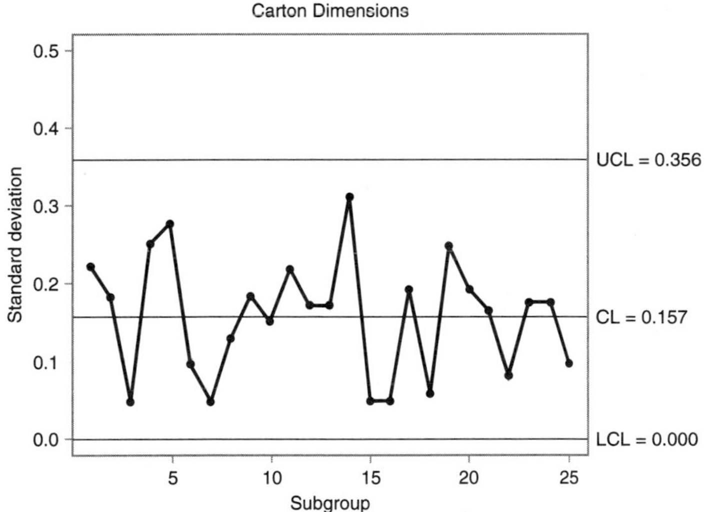

FIGURE 12.4b S-chart: Carton dimensions.

Time-sequence plots of subgroup averages and subgroup standard deviations are shown in Figures 12.4a and b. Standard deviations and ranges measure the variability. The *standard deviation chart*, and also the *range chart*, indicate whether the variability in the process is stable over time. We certainly would want to know of any changes in the variability (or the precision) of the filling operation. Unusually large or small variability in some of the subgroups would indicate that something may have changed. While causes of unusually large variability must be removed, we would like to maintain the conditions that give rise to unusually small variability. The *mean chart*, on the other hand, indicates whether the process is able to achieve stability with respect to its level. We certainly would want to know whether the changes in the mean level from one subgroup to the next are usual, or whether there have been shifts in the mean levels. A stable process should be stable with regard to both its variability and its level. Thus, it is important to look at both aspects of the process. It is important to understand that the mean and the standard deviation charts measure different aspects of the process. Stability of an x-bar chart means that the central tendency of the process is not changing; however, there could be frequent, wild variations in individual observations that are masked by the averaging process. Such variations would show up in an s-chart. Conversely, a process could have very consistent variation so that the s-chart remains stable. But the levels may shift over time, the process levels may fluctuate up and down, and there may be trends.

So far we have not discussed the lines on these charts. There are three lines: The middle one is called the *center line*; the other two are known as the *lower and upper control limits*. Their meaning and their calculation are discussed next.

We start our discussion with the x-bar chart, which is a time-sequence plot of sample averages. Using statistical guidelines, an upper control limit and a lower control limit are drawn on the chart. The control limits of the x-bar chart are calculated so that for a stable process 99.73 percent of the observed sample averages—that is to say, practically all of them—fall between these limits. A sample average that falls outside these limits represents a rare event for such a stable process. Thus there is strong evidence that a special event must have occurred and caused this sample average to differ that much from its typically expected level.

For a process to be in statistical control, all of the observed averages should fall between the lower and upper control limits. If this is the case, then we say that our process is stable. Then we are dealing with a constant cause system, and there is no evidence of assignable causes of variation. What this means is that the process that is generating the observations is behaving in a consistent manner, and the observed variation in the measurements is due to the inherent randomness of the process, and not to some outside unusual influence.

On the other hand, if some of the observed averages fall outside the control limits, then we conclude that the process is not under statistical control. This means that there was a change in the process. That is, a special (or assignable) cause of the aberrant behavior may have occurred. In this event, the task is to look for and find the cause of this behavior. To assist in this effort, it is standard practice in statistical quality control to match the unusual observations with the production conditions that were present at that time.

How do we construct the control limits? The x-bar chart graphs sample averages of size n. We know something about the distribution of sample averages if the observations are drawn from a stable process with mean μ and standard deviation σ. The Central Limit Effect (discussed in Chapter 10) says that the distribution of averages from samples of size n taken from such a stable process is approximately normal, with mean μ and standard deviation $\sigma/\sqrt{n}$. Hence, there is a 99.73 percent chance that a sample average from a stable process falls within the interval from $\mu - 3\sigma/\sqrt{n}$ to $\mu + 3\sigma/\sqrt{n}$. It is quite rare that a sample average falls outside that interval; the probability of falling beyond the control limits is 0.0027 (0.27 percent), or one out of 370 cases.

If we don't know the mean and the standard deviation of the in-control process, we use past data to estimate μ and σ. Let us assume that we have taken several subgroups, say k of them, from a process that can be considered in control. It is usually recommended that one calculates the control limits from at least 20 or 25 subgroups. Table 12.1 lists the measurements of $k = 25$ subgroups, each of size $n = 4$, as well as the subgroup averages and subgroup standard deviations. The sample information from the k subgroups is used to calculate the limits. We use the *grand average*,

$$\bar{\bar{x}} = (\bar{x}_1 + \bar{x}_2 + \cdots + \bar{x}_k)/k$$

in place of μ, and the *average standard deviation*

$$\bar{s} = (s_1 + s_2 + \cdots + s_k)/k$$

in place of σ. The grand average $\bar{\bar{x}}$ determines the center line of the x-bar chart. The control limits can be calculated as $\bar{\bar{x}} - (3/\sqrt{n})\bar{s}$ and $\bar{\bar{x}} + (3/\sqrt{n})\bar{s}$. Even simpler, we can calculate the lower and upper control limits according to

$$\text{LCL} = \bar{\bar{x}} - A_3\bar{s}$$
$$\text{UCL} = \bar{\bar{x}} + A_3\bar{s}$$

where the constant A_3 is given in Table 12A in the Appendix to this chapter. Here we have followed the standard notation that is commonly used in the control chart literature. The constant A_3 depends on the subgroup size. For subgroup size $n = 4, A_3 = 1.628$. You can check that the number A_3 is close to $3/\sqrt{n}$, but they are not exactly equal. Why? There are theoretical reasons why they are slightly different and why the constant A_3 in the table is preferable to $3/\sqrt{n}$. The small difference arises because for small sample sizes the mean of the sampling distribution of s is not the same as σ; it is slightly smaller. One says that the sample standard deviation is a "biased" estimate of σ. The constant A_3 is chosen so that it corrects for this small bias. For large n, there is little difference. Take $n = 20$; then $A_3 = 0.680$ and $3/\sqrt{20} = 0.671$ are very close.

Table 12.1 shows a total of $kn = (25)(4) = 100$ measurements. We find that

$$\bar{\bar{x}} = (25.175 + 25.000 + \cdots + 25.225)/25 = 25.134$$
$$\bar{s} = (0.222 + 0.183 + \cdots + 0.096)/25 = 0.1572.$$

Hence,

$$\begin{aligned} \text{CL} &= 25.134 \\ \text{LCL} &= 25.134 - (1.628)(0.1572) = 24.878 \\ \text{UCL} &= 25.134 + (1.628)(0.1572) = 25.390. \end{aligned}$$

The x-bar chart in Figure 12.4a shows that none of the sample averages falls outside the control limits. Thus there is little concern that special effects are impacting the process. What we observe is the common cause variation of the process.

Similarly, we can draw a center line and lower and upper control limits on the s-chart. The center line is given by the average of the k subgroup standard deviations; that is $\text{CL} = \bar{s}$. Again, lower and upper control limits are selected such that for a stable process 99.7 percent of the standard deviations fall within these limits. A standard deviation beyond the upper control limit is an indication that the variability in our process has increased. A value below the lower control limit points to a decrease in the variability.

For setting these limits we need to know the sampling distribution of standard deviations from repeated samples that are drawn from a stable process. The control limits have been worked out in the literature and virtually every book on statistical process control lists the relevant constants. These constants are also incorporated into SPC computer software. It can be shown that the control limits for the s-chart are given by:

$$\text{LCL} = B_3\bar{s} \quad \text{and} \quad \text{UCL} = B_4\bar{s},$$

where the constants B_3 and B_4 can be looked up in Table 12A in the Appendix to this chapter. These constants depend on the subgroup size n. In our example with $n = 4, B_3 = 0$ and $B_4 = 2.266$. Therefore,

$$\begin{aligned} \text{CL} &= 0.1572 \\ \text{LCL} &= (0)(0.1572) = 0 \\ \text{UCL} &= (2.266)(0.1572) = 0.356. \end{aligned}$$

The s-chart in Figure 12.4b shows that also the variability is stable. None of the subgroup standard deviations exceed either limit.

An alternative to the standard deviation chart is the *range chart* (R-*chart*), where we plot the ranges of successive subgroups. The control limits for the range chart are selected such that for a stable process 99.7 percent of the sample ranges fall within these limits. A process is considered out of control if a sample range falls outside the control limits.

The center line for the R-chart is given by the average of the subgroup ranges; that is, $\text{CL} = \bar{R}$. The lower and upper control limits are determined from

$$\text{LCL} = D_3\bar{R} \quad \text{and} \quad \text{UCL} = D_4\bar{R}$$

where D_3 and D_4 are given in Table 12A in the Appendix to this chapter. In order to derive these constants one needs the sampling distribution of the sample range, and this has been studied by statisticians. For $n = 4$, the constants are $D_3 = 0$ and $D_4 = 2.282$. With $\bar{R} = 0.352$ from Table 12.1, we find that

$$\begin{aligned} \text{CL} &= 0.352 \\ \text{LCL} &= (0)(0.352) = 0 \\ \text{UCL} &= (2.282)(0.352) = 0.803. \end{aligned}$$

The R-chart in Figure 12.4c confirms the findings from the s-chart. All sample ranges are within the control limits, and there is no indication of any unusual events.

Both the R-chart and the s-chart monitor the variability of the process. In practice, only one chart is needed. Historically, people preferred the R-chart to the s-chart, as they felt that it was easier to calculate a range than a standard deviation. Arguments in favor of R-charts are pertinent if calculations are carried out by hand and by workers on the factory floor. However, with today's computer software it is just as easy to calculate the standard deviations. There are also theoretical advantages to the s-chart. The sample range is quite sensitive to individual outliers and, in general, the standard deviation is a much better measure of variability. For this reason we prefer the s-chart over the R-chart.

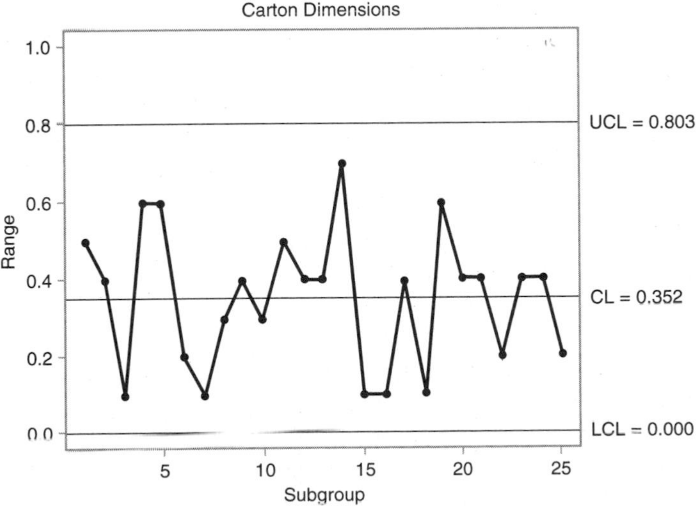

FIGURE 12.4c *R*-chart: Carton dimensions.

For subgroups of size six or less, the constants D_3 in Table 12A and hence the lower limits in the R-chart are always equal to zero. This says that an R-chart constructed from small subgroups cannot tell us whether the variability has decreased. While it is important to detect increases in variability, it is also significant to detect decreases, as such decreases are an indication of improvements in our process. A similar criticism can be leveled against the s-chart; however, the constants B_3 in Table 12A show that an s-chart constructed with subgroups of size six would already be capable of recognizing decreases. This is another indication that the s-chart is more effective than the R-chart and a further reason why we prefer it.

An additional comment: We have used the average standard deviation, $\bar{s}$, to calculate the control limits in the x-bar chart. Since the standard deviation and the range are both measures of variability, it is possible to use the average range, $\bar{R}$, in the calculation of the control limits. The control limits of the x-bar chart can also be calculated from

$$\text{LCL} = \bar{\bar{x}} - A_2\bar{R}$$

$$\text{UCL} = \bar{\bar{x}} + A_2\bar{R}.$$

Sampling theory shows that the sampling distribution of the range, calculated from n observations that are taken from a normal distribution with mean μ and standard deviation σ, is centered at $d_2\sigma$. The constant d_2, which changes with the sample size n, is listed in Table 12A. Consequently, $\bar{R}$ is an estimate of $d_2\sigma$, and $(3/\sqrt{n})\sigma$ is estimated by $(3/\sqrt{n})(\bar{R}/d_2) = A_2\bar{R}$. The constant $A_2 = 3/(d_2\sqrt{n})$, for various sample sizes n, is listed in Table 12A. In most situations the control limits that use the average range are quite similar to the ones that use the average standard deviation.

12.2.2 Another Illustration of *X*-Bar, *S*-, and *R*-Charts

Table 12.2 lists the weight of bread loaves that leave a large bakery. Every ten minutes, five loaves are selected from the cooling trays and their weights are determined. The unit of weight here is decagram; 1 kilogram equals 100 decagrams. The last three columns contain the averages, standard deviations, and ranges for subgroups of five measurements each. The x-bar, s-, and R-charts are given in Figures 12.5a,b,c (pages 322–323). The constants in Table 12A (for $n = 5$) are used to calculate the control limits.

The center line and the control limits of the x-bar chart are given by CL = 100.92, LCL = 100.92 − (1.427)(1.74) = 98.44, and UCL = 100.92 + (1.427)(1.74) = 103.41. Here we have used the average standard deviation $\bar{s} = 1.74$, and the constant $A_3 = 1.427$ for subgroup size $n = 5$.

The center line and the control limits for the s-chart are given by CL = 1.74, LCL = (0)(1.74) = 0, and UCL = (2.089)(1.74) = 3.63, using the constants $B_3 = 0$ and $B_4 = 2.089$ (for $n = 5$) from Table 12A.

TABLE 12.2 Weight of Bread Loaves in Decagrams (1 kilogram = 100 decagrams)

Group	Measurements					Average	Std. dev.	Range
1	99.2	100.7	100.9	98.2	98.3	99.46	1.29	2.70
2	101.9	98.0	100.0	102.3	96.8	99.80	2.39	5.50
3	97.8	99.4	103.0	103.7	100.2	100.82	2.48	5.90
4	100.9	100.1	101.1	99.4	102.3	100.76	1.09	2.90
5	98.1	102.3	99.9	100.1	102.9	100.66	1.95	4.80
6	100.2	100.4	101.8	97.0	101.1	100.10	1.84	4.80
7	99.8	99.4	97.3	99.1	100.4	99.20	1.17	3.10
8	97.5	100.6	102.7	102.3	98.5	100.32	2.29	5.20
9	101.0	97.6	100.8	100.1	103.2	100.54	2.01	5.60
10	100.1	101.2	99.6	100.2	99.5	100.12	0.68	1.70
11	98.4	96.3	100.2	98.8	98.3	98.40	1.40	3.90
12	102.9	102.9	101.5	98.8	101.8	101.58	1.68	4.10
13	97.9	100.7	99.3	100.3	99.8	99.60	1.09	2.80
14	98.5	97.0	99.4	102.3	101.5	99.74	2.17	5.30
15	101.1	104.1	100.1	97.4	98.6	100.26	2.57	6.70
16	102.4	100.0	99.2	98.2	98.4	99.64	1.70	4.20
17	101.8	99.2	100.7	101.0	97.3	100.00	1.78	4.50
18	99.3	100.6	103.3	101.1	99.9	100.84	1.54	4.00
19	98.2	101.3	101.3	102.1	100.8	100.74	1.49	3.90
20	99.6	102.9	99.4	100.8	100.9	100.72	1.40	3.50
21	105.7	105.6	104.5	104.0	103.2	104.60	1.07	2.50
22	103.9	102.2	103.1	105.4	102.8	103.48	1.24	3.20
23	104.1	105.9	105.1	99.5	101.5	103.22	2.66	6.40
24	100.8	104.9	105.8	104.8	105.7	104.40	2.06	5.00
25	101.8	102.1	103.0	107.4	105.9	104.04	2.48	5.60
Average						100.92	1.74	4.31

Twenty-five subgroups of size 5.

The center line and the control limits for the R-chart are CL = 4.31, LCL = 0, and UCL = (2.115)(4.31) = 9.12, using the constants $D_3 = 0$ and $D_4 = 2.115$ from Table 12A.

We should always start the investigation by checking whether the variability of the process is stable over time. This is because the control limits in the x-bar chart make use of the average variability, and without stability of the variability the control limits of the x-bar charts make little sense. The s-chart and the R-chart confirm that the variability in the process is stable; neither the standard deviations nor the ranges exceed their respective control limits.

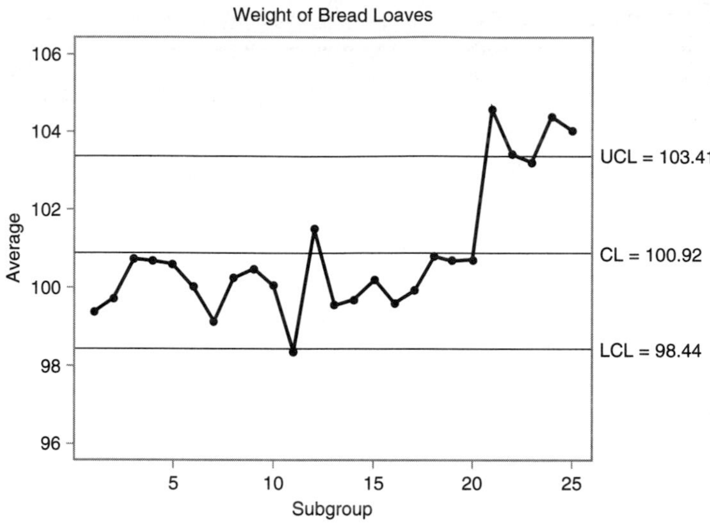

FIGURE 12.5a *X*-bar chart: Weight of bread loaves.

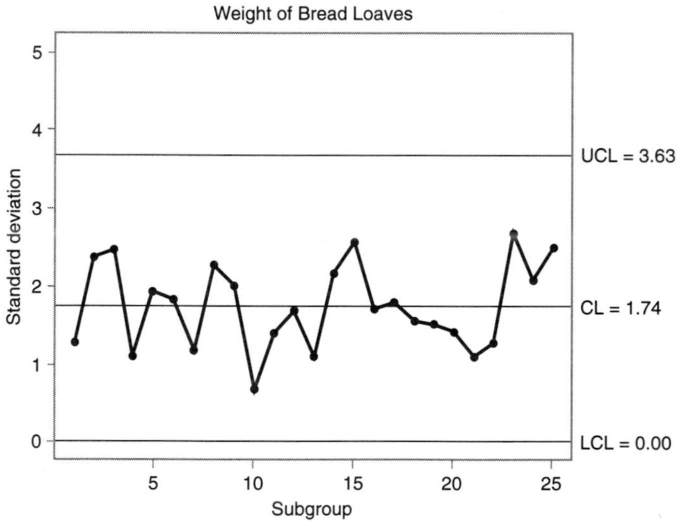

FIGURE 12.5b *S*-chart: Weight of bread loaves.

However, the *x*-bar chart shows that stability with respect to the levels is lacking. It is quite obvious that the levels of the last five subgroups have increased. The fact that these subgroup averages exceed the upper control limit (the one for subgroup 23 is only slightly below the upper control limit) is a clear indication that the process has gone out of statistical control. There has been a shift in the level after subgroup 20. A subsequent investigation into possible causes for this shift

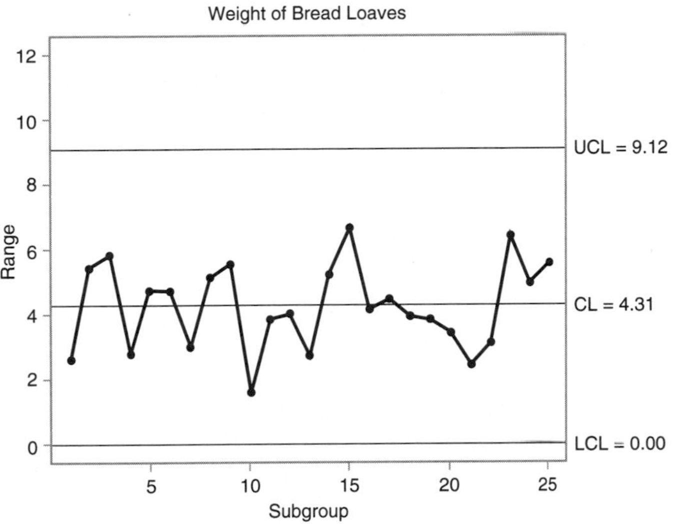

FIGURE 12.5c *R*-chart: Weight of bread loaves.

in the levels revealed that an improperly calibrated scale was at fault. The scale was recalibrated and the problem disappeared.

12.3 THE DESIGN OF CONTROL CHARTS

12.3.1 The Average Run Lengths of Control Charts

The performance of control charts is usually characterized by their run length distribution. The *run length* (RL) of a control chart procedure is defined as the number of samples that have to be plotted until the plotted process characteristic exceeds the control limits for the first time. Because of the random nature of the observations, the run length follows a probability distribution. The run length can take on any positive integer $1, 2, \ldots,$ and the corresponding probabilities are easily calculated. Let us denote the probability that a plotted process characteristic (that is, the control chart signal) will fall outside the control limits by w. That is,

$$w = P(\text{control chart signal falls outside the control limits}).$$

Then the probabilities in the run length distribution are

$$\begin{aligned}
P(\text{RL} = 1) &= w, \text{ as RL} = 1 \text{ is realized if the very first signal is outside the control limits;} \\
P(\text{RL} = 2) &= P(\text{1st signal inside and 2nd signal outside}) = (1 - w)w; \\
P(\text{RL} = 3) &= P(\text{1st signal inside; 2nd signal inside; 3rd signal outside}) \\
&= (1 - w)(1 - w)w = (1 - w)^2 w;
\end{aligned}$$

and, in general,

$$P(\text{RL} = k) = (1 - w)^{k-1} w \quad \text{for } k = 1, 2, \ldots .$$

The mean of this distribution is called the *average run length* (ARL). It is given by

$$\begin{aligned}\text{ARL} &= (1)P(\text{RL} = 1) + (2)P(\text{RL} = 2) + (3)P(\text{RL} = 3) + (4)P(\text{RL} = 4) + \cdots \\ &= w + 2w(1 - w) + 3w(1 - w)^2 + 4w(1 - w)^3 + \cdots \\ &= w[1 + 2(1 - w) + 3(1 - w)^2 + 4(1 - w)^3 + \cdots] \\ &= w/[1 - (1 - w)]^2 = 1/w .\end{aligned}$$

Here we have used the result in Exercise 12.16 that shows us how to obtain the sum of such a convergent series. The average run length tells us how many subgroups are needed, on average, before the signal exceeds the control limits.

Let us evaluate the average run length for the x-bar chart. First, assume that the process is in control at a certain mean value μ_0. The standard deviation for individual measurements is given by σ, and hence the control limits for subgroup averages from random samples of size n are set at $\text{LCL} = \mu_0 - (3/\sqrt{n})\sigma$ and $\text{UCL} = \mu_0 + (3/\sqrt{n})\sigma$. We already know that for a process that is in control,

$$w = 1 - P(\text{LCL} \leq \overline{X} \leq \text{UCL}) = 0.0027;$$

this follows from the normal distribution. Hence the average run length of an in-control process is $\text{ARL} = 1/0.0027 = 370$. This says that sample averages from a stable process can be plotted for quite some time before these averages will give us an incorrect signal—in fact, for 370 subgroups, on average.

But what happens if the process goes out of control? How long does it take until the control chart recognizes this fact? Assume that the process goes out of control by having its mean *shift* to a new value. Assume that the mean shifts by δ standard deviations; that is, from the in-control value μ_0 to a new value $\mu_0 + (\delta)\sigma$. The constant δ expresses the magnitude of the shift; if $\delta = 0.5$, the mean shifts by half a standard deviation. Let us calculate the probability that averages from the changed process exceed the control limits. That is,

$$\begin{aligned}w &= 1 - P(\text{LCL} = \mu_0 - (3/\sqrt{n})\sigma \leq \overline{X} \leq \mu_0 + (3/\sqrt{n})\sigma = \text{UCL}) \\ &= 1 - P\left(\frac{\mu_0 - (3/\sqrt{n})\sigma - (\mu_0 + \delta\sigma)}{\sigma/\sqrt{n}} \leq Z \leq \frac{\mu_0 + (3/\sqrt{n})\sigma - (\mu_0 + \delta\sigma)}{\sigma/\sqrt{n}}\right) \\ &= 1 - P(-3 - \delta\sqrt{n} \leq Z \leq 3 - \delta\sqrt{n}) = 1 - P(Z \leq 3 - \delta\sqrt{n}) + P(Z \leq -3 - \delta\sqrt{n}).\end{aligned}$$

Under the shifted process, the subgroup average follows a normal distribution with mean $\mu_0 + \delta\sigma$ and standard deviation $\sigma/\sqrt{n}$. Because Z has a standard normal distribution, the above probabilities can be looked up from the table of normal probabilities.

TABLE 12.3 Probability of an Out-of-Control Signal (w) and Average Run Length (ARL) for Level Shifts of δ Standard Deviations

	$n = 1$		$n = 5$		$n = 10$	
δ	w	ARL	w	ARL	w	ARL
0.00	0.0027	370.4	0.0027	370.4	0.0027	370.4
0.10	0.0028	352.9	0.0034	295.7	0.0041	244.1
0.20	0.0032	308.4	0.0056	177.7	0.0091	110.0
0.30	0.0040	253.1	0.0100	99.5	0.0202	49.6
0.40	0.0050	200.1	0.0177	56.6	0.0414	24.2
0.50	0.0064	155.2	0.0299	33.4	0.0780	12.8
0.60	0.0084	119.7	0.0486	20.6	0.1351	7.4
0.70	0.0108	92.3	0.0757	13.2	0.2158	4.6
0.80	0.0140	71.6	0.1129	8.9	0.3191	3.1
0.90	0.0179	55.8	0.1617	6.2	0.4388	2.3
1.00	0.0228	43.9	0.2225	4.5	0.5645	1.8
1.25	0.0401	25.0	0.4188	2.4	0.8297	1.2
1.50	0.0668	15.0	0.6384	1.6	0.9594	1.0
1.75	0.1057	9.5	0.8194	1.2	0.9944	1.0
2.00	0.1587	6.3	0.9295	1.1	0.9996	1.0

X-bar charts with subgroup sizes of $n = 1$, $n = 5$, and $n = 10$.

For a given plan with specified sample size n we can calculate these probabilities for various shifts δ, and from these probabilities we can obtain the average run lengths of the control chart. Table 12.3 lists the probabilities and average run lengths for plans with subgroup sizes $n = 1$ (individual observations), $n = 5$, and $n = 10$.

As expected, large shifts are easier to detect and the average run lengths decrease with increasing magnitudes δ of the shift. Furthermore, a large subgroup size increases our chance of detecting a level shift of a certain magnitude. It is quicker to detect the same-size level shift with a sample of $n = 5$ observations than with a single observation ($n = 1$). The average run lengths in this table show this very clearly. A level shift of one half of the standard deviation ($\delta = 0.5$) is detected, on average, after 155 observations (if the subgroup size is $n = 1$), after 33.4 subgroups of $n = 5$ observations, and after 12.8 subgroups of $n = 10$ observations. Note that the average run length is expressed in terms of the number of subgroups that are needed to detect a certain level shift. Since each subgroup requires n measurements, it would be more equitable to make the comparisons across the sample sizes in terms of the *expected number of individual units*, $I = n\text{ARL}$, that need to be plotted before the first out-of-control signal is encountered.

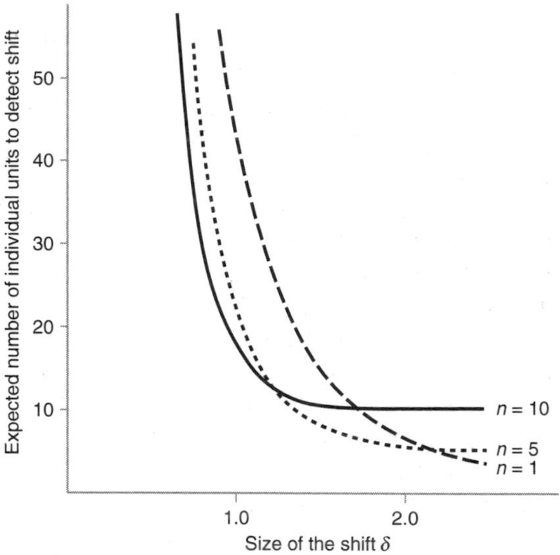

FIGURE 12.6 Plot of the expected number of individual units ($I = n\text{ARL}$) to detect a shift of δ standard deviations; subgroup sizes of $n = 1, n = 5$, and $n = 10$.

A graph of $I = n\text{ARL}$ against the size δ of the level shift, for each of the three sample sizes, is shown in Figure 12.6. This figure and the numbers in Table 12.3 provide a supportive argument for the use of small subgroup sizes. In order to detect a fairly large level shift of say 1.25 standard deviations, a chart with subgroup size $n = 5$ will, on average, require fewer individual observations than a chart with $n = 10$. Hence there are some savings when using the chart with $n = 5$. On the other hand, for a small shift (of $\delta = 0.5$ standard deviation) the chart with $n = 5$ requires, on average, (5)(33.4) = 167 individual measurements, while the chart with subgroup size 10 needs only (10)(12.8) = 128.

12.3.2 Selection of the Sampling Interval and Formation of Rational Subgroups

How often should you sample your process, how many items should you sample each time, and how should you carry out the sampling? These are three very important questions. Ideally, the sampling scheme that would provide the most information for detecting special causes and shifts in the process parameters would consist of taking large samples and doing that quite often. However, because of the costs involved this may not be feasible, and one has to decide among large samples at infrequent intervals or small samples at more frequent intervals. The current industry practice is to take relatively small samples (typically 4 or 5 units) at rather frequent intervals. The information in Figure 12.6 shows that small samples work well if we can tolerate small changes in the process parameters. Of course, if it is important to detect small changes in the process parameters, then a larger sample size will be needed.

Decisions on the sample size and the frequency of sampling depend on the costs that are involved. There is the cost of obtaining the measurements; it may be relatively cheap and easy to measure each item, or it may be very expensive, as is often the case in destructive testing. There are also the costs that are incurred for failing to stop a process that has changed. If this cost is high, then one should sample more frequently; otherwise, many poor items could slip by, and the associated wasted production could amount to a sizable loss. One should certainly sample more often if critical expensive items are involved.

The frequency of sampling also depends on one's experience with the process. If one has little reason to fear sudden changes in the process, then there is not much harm in extending the time between samples. While one can get by with infrequent samples if the process is quite stable, one should monitor volatile processes more frequently.

The literature discusses theoretical models that balance the various economic costs. Under certain idealized conditions one can find optimal sampling times and optimal sample sizes.

We also have to decide on *how* to carry out the sampling. How should we plan our samples? It is recommended that the samples are taken in such a way that, to the best of our knowledge, the units in any one sample form a *rational subgroup*. By that we mean a subgroup that represents a homogeneous set of conditions and is as free as possible from assignable causes. A rational subgroup should consist of similar units; it should include units that are made under nearly identical conditions as far as materials, equipment, manufacturing methods, and process conditions are concerned. Rational subgroups should be selected so that there is little chance that items within a subgroup are affected by special effects. The variability among the units of a rational subgroup can then be attributed to the constant-cause factors; it represents the smallest variability that is inherent in the system. Rational subgroups selected to minimize the within-subgroup variability provide the maximum opportunity for differences between subgroups that are caused by special effects to be made apparent by the control charts.

In general we know that manufacturing conditions tend to change from time to time as a result of factors of which we may not be aware. For this very reason, we usually create the subgroups according to the time order. This is a reasonable strategy because it allows us to detect assignable causes that occur over time. However, there is more than one way of collecting the information. Let us assume that we plan to obtain data in 30-minute time intervals. One approach is to take observations at every thirty minutes and group *consecutive* units of production into the sample; that is, units that have been produced closely together in time. It is quite easy to carry this out in practice, and this sampling strategy provides a good snapshot of the process at certain points in time. It is a good approach for detecting shifts in the process parameters. This sampling strategy results in minimum variability within the elements of a subgroup and in maximum variability between subgroups if assignable causes are present. This is because with items that are produced close in time either all or none are affected by the assignable cause; in either case, the within-subgroup variability is a measure of just the common-cause variability.

The other approach to forming subgroups is to take *random samples* from among all the products that have been produced within the last 30 minutes. If one's objective is to determine whether all the products that have been produced since the previous sample was drawn are acceptable, then this is a good approach. However, if the process goes in and out of control at periodic intervals, then the samples that are obtained with the random sampling approach may represent a mixture of the overall process condition. In this case one may miss the fact that the process switches between being in and out of control.

The following example shows that it is not always easy to make the correct decision regarding the appropriate rational subgroup. In Exercise 12.15 we discuss an injection molding process where control charts are used to monitor part weight over time. The data collection consisted of taking and weighing five *consecutive* parts per shift. Standard x-bar and R-charts were produced, and these charts revealed many out-of-control signals. However, subsequent investigations of conditions during out-of-control signals uncovered nothing unusual, and no special effects could be found. Furthermore, subsequent runs with the same unchanged process turned out parts that were consistently acceptable. Operators lost confidence in the control charts, and pretty soon control charts were ignored altogether.

A review of the control charts was carried out to investigate whether modifications of these charts could lessen the number of investigations and hence give the control charting method a higher degree of acceptance. Recall that the upper and lower control limits of an x-bar chart are supposed to represent the limits of variation of averages. These limits are to be determined from the normal process variation that takes place during the shift, as well as from shift to shift; the limits are supposed to reflect the common cause variability. However, in this particular application the time period for collecting the five observations was very short. The variation among observations that are collected within such a short time interval is very small, and certainly much smaller than the normal variability that is present throughout a shift or from one shift to the next. There is uncontrolled common-cause variation due to changes in the raw material (the plastic for the injection). However, this variability takes place over a much larger time frame and thus this variability is not apparent in consecutive items. Within a very short time interval the input material is essentially constant, while over the duration of a shift or from shift to shift the raw material varies. The adopted sampling procedure of selecting five consecutive parts picks up only the short-term variability, and this short-term variability will underestimate the true common-cause variability. Hence the control limits that are based on the average range are much too narrow, and they will lead to many signals for which no special effects can be found.

This example shows the importance of selecting appropriate rational subgroups. In this particular example, it would have been much better to use the second sampling approach where we would sample these five items from among all items that have been produced during the shift.

A further comment: The choice of the correct rational subgroup is also relevant if the process involves several machines, several operators, or several shifts. It is usually preferable to select a single operator or a single machine as the appropriate rational subgroup, and use control charts to display the information for each machine and each operator, separately. If you sample from the overall output, and hence fail to stratify according to operator or machine, then the sample information could be a mixture of possibly different processes and it may not be sensitive enough to show instability.

12.4 CONTROL CHARTS FOR ATTRIBUTE DATA

X-bar, s-, and R-charts are used to monitor continuous measurement (or variables) data. The charts that are discussed in this section are used to monitor attributes of a process. Attribute measurements are satisfactory when one deals with a very large number of relatively simple products, where it is often sufficient to simply classify each product as satisfactory or defective.

In most situations it is fairly obvious whether to consider attribute or variables control charts. For example, if we observe the presence or absence of a condition (such as whether or not an item works as it should), or if we monitor a finished product for surface scratches or a fabric for its color, then we are naturally led to attribute data and attribute charts. Attribute data is also useful as it allows us to monitor several quality characteristics at the same time by classifying a unit as unacceptable whenever one of the monitored characteristics fails its specifications. However, if we measure the dimensions of a product (such as the width, length, or weight of an item) then we have a choice of what to do: We can control the product on the dimensions, or we can control the product on its attribute of whether the dimensions exceed the specification limits. In general, variables data provides more useful information about process performance. With variables data we can construct one chart to monitor the levels, and another chart to monitor the variability. These charts give us a better chance to detect the potential causes of out-of-control signals. Furthermore, these charts can give us an indication of forthcoming trouble, usually well before the process starts producing defectives. In other words, the x-bar and R-charts are leading indicators of future trouble, while the attribute charts only react to changes in the rate of defective products. Furthermore, the sample sizes that are used with variables charts are usually much smaller (most of the time we sample about $n = 5$ products) than those needed for attribute charts. Hence there are also economic advantages to using the variables charts.

12.4.1 Control Charts for Proportions of Defectives: *P*-Charts and *NP*-Charts

The *p-chart* graphs the proportions, $p_1, p_2, \ldots,$ of defective items from successive subgroups. The following example illustrates the construction and use of p-charts. The example is taken from the banking industry, which uses automated procedures to handle checks. Mechanization of the check processing operation is achieved through *Magnetic Ink Character Recognition* (MICR). Checks contain magnetic ink characters and virtually all banks use these characters to process their checks in both their demand deposit and transit operations.

Although MICR characters printed on checks can be read by automatic equipment, a small percentage of the characters are defective and cannot be read. When this occurs, the reading equipment "rejects" the document, placing it in a special pocket for subsequent correction. Handling these rejected checks is quite costly.

William J. Latzko, in his book *Quality and Productivity for Bankers and Financial Managers*, analyzes daily data on the proportion of checks that were "rejected" by the reader. Table 12.4 shows the number of processed checks on a given day (subgroup size n), as well as the number of checks that were rejected (defects d). Note that the numbers of processed checks vary somewhat from day to day. However, the subgroup sizes are fairly close to their average number, $\bar{n} = 1000$.

The p-chart for this example is given in Figure 12.7. The center line for the p-chart is taken as the average proportion of defectives $\bar{p}$. Among the 20,000

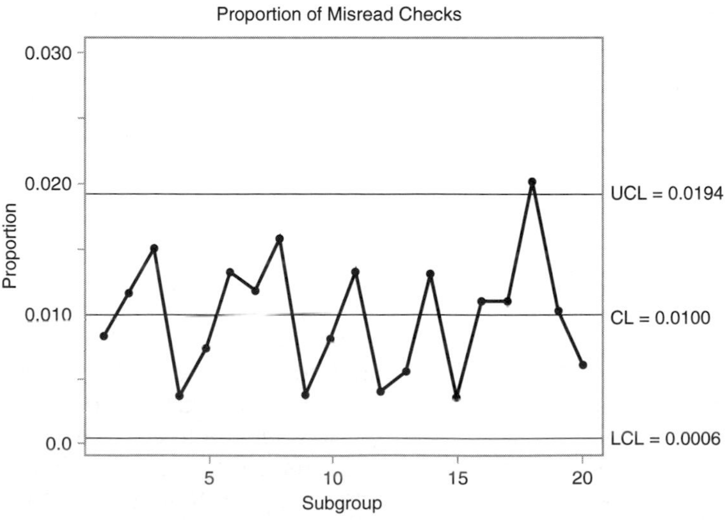

FIGURE 12.7 *P*-chart: Proportion of misread checks.

TABLE 12.4 Magnetic Ink Character Recognition

Day	n	d	Proportion (in percent)
Monday	930	8	0.86
Tuesday	1080	12	1.11
Wednesday	1050	16	1.52
Thursday	1020	4	0.39
Friday	1050	8	0.76
Monday	1040	14	1.35
Tuesday	920	11	1.20
Wednesday	1000	16	1.60
Thursday	990	4	0.40
Friday	950	8	0.84
Monday	970	13	1.34
Tuesday	950	4	0.42
Wednesday	1030	6	0.58
Thursday	980	13	1.33
Friday	1050	4	0.38
Monday	1070	12	1.12
Tuesday	980	11	1.12
Wednesday	940	19	2.02
Thursday	1050	11	1.05
Friday	950	6	0.63
Total	20000	200	
Average	1000		1.00

Number of checks read (n), number of checks misread (d), and proportion of checks misread (in percent).

checks, we counted 200 defectives. Hence

$$\text{CL} = \bar{p} = 200/20{,}000 = 0.01.$$

The control limits on the p-chart are chosen so that for a stable process 99.73 percent of the observed sample proportions—that is to say, practically all of them—fall between these limits. A proportion that falls outside these limits represents a rare event for a stable process and is an indication of a special event.

The Central Limit Effect for sample proportions (discussed in Section 10.5 in Chapter 10) helps us set the control limits. The proportions of defectives vary from subgroup to subgroup. For a stable process with defect rate $\bar{p}$, the proportion of defectives in a sample of size n_i varies around $\bar{p}$ with standard deviation $\sqrt{\bar{p}(1-\bar{p})/n_i}$. Thus the lower and upper control limits for a proportion based on a random sample of n_i observations are given by

$$\text{LCL} = \bar{p} - (3)\sqrt{\frac{\bar{p}(1-\bar{p})}{n_i}}$$

$$\text{UCL} = \bar{p} + (3)\sqrt{\frac{\bar{p}(1-\bar{p})}{n_i}}.$$

In this particular example, the sample sizes vary from one subgroup to the next, and hence the control limits for the various subgroups are not exactly the same. However, for small differences in the sample sizes, such as is the case here, not much is lost by using the average sample size in the construction of a single set of control limits; this makes the picture easier to interpret. Of course, it is more accurate to use the exact sample size for each sample; fortunately, most computer software packages allow for unequal sample sizes.

The following rule of thumb seems to work well in practice. According to this rule we use the average sample size $\bar{n}$ provided that the smallest and the largest individual sample sizes are not more than 20 to 25 percent from the average sample size. Alternatively, one could use the largest individual sample size; this would result in tighter control limits and draw attention to borderline cases. These borderline cases could then be investigated further by calculating the exact limits that use the correct sample size.

The sample sizes in our example in Table 12.4 range from 920 to 1080. Since the smallest and the largest sample size are only about 10 percent from the average sample size, we use $\bar{n} = 1000$ in the subsequent calculations. Consequently,

$$\text{LCL} = 0.01 - 3\sqrt{\frac{(0.01)(0.99)}{1000}} = 0.0006$$

$$\text{UCL} = 0.01 + 3\sqrt{\frac{(0.01)(0.99)}{1000}} = 0.0194.$$

If the calculation of the LCL had led to a negative number, then we would have set the lower control limit equal to zero, as proportions cannot be negative. The control limits are given in Figure 12.7. We notice that the proportion on Wednesday of the last week ($p = 0.0202$, or 2.02 percent) exceeds the upper control limit. One should probe into the causes for this unusually large proportion and try to prevent them from occurring again.

The *np-chart* is a slight modification of the p-chart. Instead of plotting the fraction of defectives p_i, we plot the *number of defectives* np_i. Some users prefer this chart as the number of defectives can be plotted directly, without having to carry out a division to obtain the fraction of defectives. For the number of defectives to be comparable across the different subgroups we must assume that the sizes of the subgroups are all the same. Then the plotted signal in the np-chart is a simple multiple of the signal in the p-chart. We obtain the center line and the control limits of the np-chart by multiplying the corresponding values in the p-chart by the sample size n. The control limits in the np-chart are given by

$$\begin{aligned} \text{CL} &= n\bar{p} \\ \text{LCL} &= n\bar{p} - (3)\sqrt{n\bar{p}(1-\bar{p})} \\ \text{UCL} &= n\bar{p} + (3)\sqrt{n\bar{p}(1-\bar{p})}. \end{aligned}$$

12.4.2 Control Charts for the Number of Defects: *C*-Charts and *U*-Charts

In applications where we inspect large products such as a car or a piece of computer software, one usually measures quality in terms of the number of defects; in the literature on statistical process control defects are also referred to as *nonconformities*. To monitor the quality, we sample products and record the number of defects on each product. Similarly, we may record the number of jams on a certain machine over several consecutive shifts, or we may sample a piece of woven material of a certain specified size and count the number of flaws. Table 12.5 (page 334) lists the number of jams on a filling machine over 20 consecutive shifts.

On a c-chart we plot successive numbers of defects (flaws, nonconformities) $c_1, c_2, \ldots$. Assume that we have obtained k such measurements and that we have calculated the average, $\bar{c}$. Then the center line and the control limits of the c-chart are

$$\begin{aligned} \text{CL} &= \bar{c} \\ \text{LCL} &= \bar{c} - 3\sqrt{\bar{c}} \\ \text{UCL} &= \bar{c} + 3\sqrt{\bar{c}}. \end{aligned}$$

The control limits can be justified as follows. The distribution of the number of defects on an item, or the number of blemishes observed over a certain area of fabric can be approximated by a Poisson distribution; see the discussion in Section 8.4 in Chapter 8. There we also learned that the standard deviation of the Poisson distribution is the same as the square root of its mean. With $\bar{c}$ as the estimate of the mean and $\sqrt{\bar{c}}$ as the estimate of the standard deviation, we find that the three-sigma control limits are given by $\bar{c} - 3\sqrt{\bar{c}}$ and $\bar{c} + 3\sqrt{\bar{c}}$.

For the data in Table 12.5, the average number of jams is $\bar{c} = 4.5$. Therefore $\text{CL} = 4.5$, $\text{LCL} = 4.5 - (3)\sqrt{4.5} = -1.86$, and $\text{UCL} = 4.5 + (3)\sqrt{4.5} = 10.86$. The lower control limit is set equal zero ($\text{LCL} = 0$), as the number of jams cannot be negative.

We question the stability of the process if the number of jams is 11 or more. The c-chart in Figure 12.8 (page 335) flags one unusual observation, namely the one for the second shift on September 7. Twelve jams are quite unusual for this process. Something must have happened during this particular period.

TABLE 12.5 Number of Machine Jams When Filling Bottles of Shampoo

Date	Number of jams	Shift
3	3	1
3	6	2
3	5	3
4	1	1
4	5	2
4	4	3
5	2	1
5	6	2
5	5	3
6	3	1
6	3	2
6	4	3
7	8	1
7	12	2
7	3	3
8	3	1
8	4	2
8	7	3
9	2	1
9	4	2

Twenty consecutive shifts. Data taken in September 1992.

The *u-chart* is a modification of the c-chart. In the c-chart the sample size is 1 as we determine the number of nonconformities on exactly one inspection unit—that is, the number of defects on one car, the number of blemishes on a ten-by-ten-foot section of aluminum, and so on. The single inspection unit is often chosen to simplify the data collection. However, there is really no good reason why the sample size has to be exactly one unit all the time. On the contrary, we may want to inspect more than one unit at each inspection point (for example, $n = 3$ cars), as this would increase the area of opportunity for the occurrence of a nonconformity. Moreover, the inspection unit n need not be an integer, and it does not have to be the same for all inspection points; for example, at the next inspection the number of blemishes may come from a 10-by-20-foot aluminum section.

In the u-chart we plot the *number of nonconformities per unit.* We plot $u_i = c_i/n_i$, where n_i represents the number of inspection units at time i. The plotted

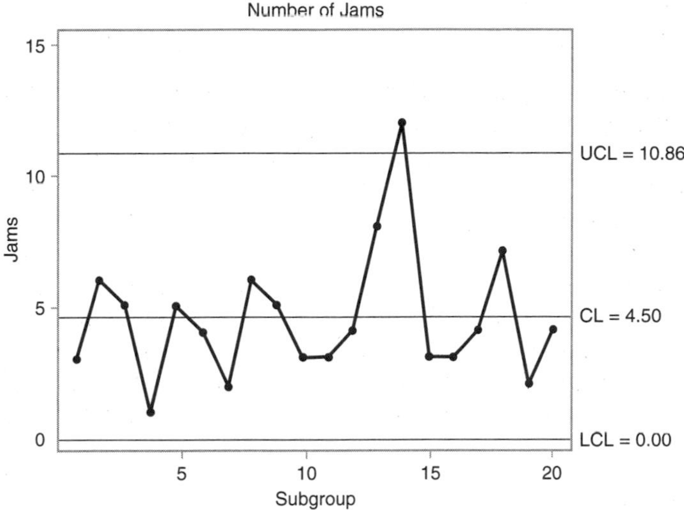

FIGURE 12.8 *C*-chart: Number of machine jams.

signal in the u-chart is a simple fraction of the signal in the c-chart. We obtain the center line and the control limits of the u-chart by dividing the corresponding values in the c-chart by the sample size n_i. Hence the control limits in the u-chart are given by

$$\begin{aligned} \text{CL} &= \bar{u} \\ \text{LCL} &= \bar{u} - 3\sqrt{\bar{u}/n_i} \\ \text{UCL} &= \bar{u} + 3\sqrt{\bar{u}/n_i} \end{aligned}$$

where $\bar{u}$ represents the average number of nonconformities per unit of inspection. The results of prior inspections can be used to obtain this value. For example, if k inspections lead to c_i nonconformities on n_i inspection units, for $i = 1, 2, \ldots, k$, then the average number of nonconformities per unit inspection is estimated as $\bar{u} = (c_1 + \cdots + c_k)/(n_1 + \cdots + n_k)$.

12.5 FURTHER DISCUSSION

12.5.1 Other Out-of-Control Conditions

Up to now, the only way that a process is declared out of control is when a subgroup statistic falls outside the control limits. However, there are other patterns that one would not expect if the observations were coming from a stable process. For example, even if subgroup statistics were within the control limits, one would not expect to find all of them crowded near one of the two control limits. Nor would

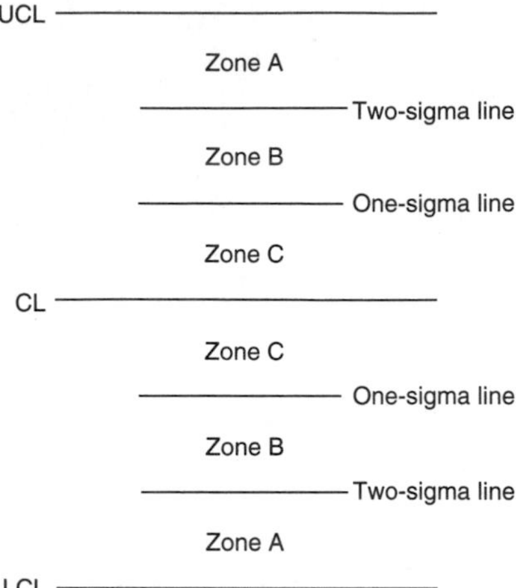

FIGURE 12.9 Division of the area between the control limits into six equal zones.

one expect to find them alternating up and down. These and other "nonrandom" patterns would give cause to reject the notion that the process is stable.

Various rules for interpreting control charts have been proposed. A simple set of rules is illustrated below; see the Western Electric Company *Statistical Quality Control Handbook* (1956), and the paper by Andrew C. Palm in the *Journal of Quality Technology*, Vol. 22, 1990, pages 289–298. Divide the area between each control limit and the center line into three equal-sized zones (zones A, B, and C) by drawing in additional one-sigma and two-sigma lines. This leads to the six areas that are given in Figure 12.9.

A process is considered out of statistical control if any of the following conditions holds:

Condition 1: A single statistic lies outside the control limits (that is, beyond zone A). This is the usual rule.

Condition 2: At least two of three successive statistics fall on the same side of the center line, and are outside the two-sigma limits (that is, in zone A or beyond).

Condition 3: At least four out of five successive statistics fall on the same side of the center line, and are outside the one-sigma limits (that is, in zone B or beyond).

Condition 4: At least eight successive statistics fall on the same side of the center line.

One can list several other unnatural patterns that suggest that the process is not completely stable. For the following discussion it makes no difference whether the statistic falls in the zone above or below the center line; thus, "points in Zone C" means points in Zone C above or below the center line.

Condition 5: At least 15 consecutive observations fall inside Zone C. We call this "hugging the center line."

Condition 6: At least eight consecutive observations fall outside Zone C. This suggests a "mixture" situation, where we sample from more than one process.

Condition 7: A long record where sample statistics alternate between high and low. We call this a "sawtooth" pattern.

Condition 8: Cycles or trends indicated by an increasing or decreasing sequence of consecutive statistics.

The more of these rules that are used simultaneously, the more sensitive the chart is to shifts in the level. For example, if the level shifts by one standard deviation, then the simultaneous use of the first four rules stops the process after 9 observations, on average. With rule 1 alone, one can show that the process is stopped after 44 observations, on average; see the results in Table 12.3. However, the more rules used, the higher the probability that the process is stopped unnecessarily. If rule 1 alone is followed, then the probability of finding lack of control when in fact the process is in control is 0.0027 and the average run length is ARL $= 1/0.0027 = 370$. Using rules 1 through 4 together, this probability increases to about 0.01, and the average run length is reduced to ARL $= 1/0.01 = 100$.

12.5.2 Process Stability and Process Capability

It is important to observe that the definition of statistical control does not make mention of the product requirements. This means that a process can be in statistical control, and yet the products that it produces may not meet the requirements. Think of it this way: A process is in control if it produces consistent products; whether these products meet requirements or not depends on the use to which they will be put. For one application where the requirements are lenient, the products might be quite appropriate; for another with stricter requirements, they might not be. A stable process need not be a capable one! This point was made previously. However, it is such an important point that there is no harm in saying it again.

It is also possible for a process to be out of statistical control and yet have its products meet the specified requirements. This is most likely to happen when there is a wide tolerance for the products. When the products meet requirements, there is a temptation not to worry whether the process is in control. However, this may be a mistake. The fact that the process is not under control means that some outside factor is causing variation; you really don't know what it is. Since you don't know, what guarantee do you have that the unexplained variation will stay in a range where the products are still satisfactory? If a process is not under control, then you can't be sure what it will produce next (more on that in the next chapter when we discuss pre-control). Control charts and their control limits are unrelated to the process target and the process specification limits that are specified by the consumer. Because of that, specifications should not be shown on a control chart.

12.5.3 Process Surveillance

The data in Table 12.2 raises the following important issue. The x-bar chart in Figure 12.5a shows that the weight of bread loaves increased after the 20th subgroup. An assignable cause for this shift was actually found, and the process was improved by adjusting a scale that was used to weigh one of the ingredients.

When we first calculated the control limits for the x-bar chart we also used the observations (subgroups 21 through 25) that were not in statistical control. These out-of-control observations certainly affected the control limits as they increased the grand average and consequently the upper control limit. As a result, the upper control limit is too large, and large subgroup averages that would be recognized as special events if the limits for the stable system were used may not be recognized as special events.

It is recommended that one recalculate the control limits without the observations from the out-of-control samples, if one finds a subgroup statistic that is outside the control limits *and* if one can determine its cause and prevent it from occurring again. In our example we found and eliminated the cause for the out-of-control behavior; hence we are justified in excluding the last five subgroups from the calculation of the control limits. Without the last five subgroups in Table 12.2, the grand average and the average standard deviation are 100.17 and 1.70, respectively. The revised center line and the revised control limits on the x-bar chart are $\text{CL} = 100.17$, $\text{LCL} = 100.17 - (1.427)(1.70) = 97.74$ and $\text{UCL} = 100.17 + (1.427)(1.70) = 102.60$. Note that these control limits are tighter. Hence they make it easier to spot unusual observations. With these revised control limits it becomes even more obvious that the level of the last five subgroups has shifted.

In this particular situation it makes sense to recalculate the limits. However, we should emphasize that one would *not* recalculate the limits if one cannot find and eliminate the reason for the special event. If we can't eliminate a cause, then that cause will be part of the process also in the future.

The question of recalculating the limits also arises if one applies process control procedures to *new processes* that are not yet in statistical control. Control limits for such processes are typically wide and, because of that, it is not easy to recognize special effects. However, a strategy of systematically removing special effects from the system and recalculating the control limits each time a special cause gets identified and prevented from occurring in the future, reduces the variability of our processes. This strategy leads to tighter and tighter control limits, and one ends up with better processes.

For well-established processes that are already in control the control chart procedures can be used as surveillance instruments. Once the control limits are established for a stable system, they can be used for quite some time. Nevertheless, it is always a good idea to recalculate these limits periodically.

12.6 MORE ON CONTROL CHARTS FOR CONTINUOUS MEASUREMENT DATA

The purpose of this chapter is to acquaint you with control charts and to introduce you to the importance of the concept and its potential usefulness. By now you know how to apply these tools to many different settings. There is a very large literature on control charts, and other charts, beyond those that have been discussed here, are used in practice.

The variables charts discussed in this chapter are based on subgroup information. The x-bar chart, for example, tracks subgroup means and its control limits are calculated from standard deviations (or ranges) within the subgroups. However, there are many situations where only a single observation is taken at each sampling period and where individual observations are plotted over time. The resulting control charts are known as *individual observations charts* or *x-charts*.

Cumulative sum (CUSUM) charts, exponentially weighted moving average (EWMA) charts, and multivariate control charts are other useful charting techniques that are in common use. Instead of plotting sample averages and basing one's decision on just the last recorded average, one can plot a cumulative sum or a weighted average of previous sample statistics. This is the idea behind CUSUM and EWMA charts. *Multivariate control charts* are used to monitor several response variables simultaneously.

In this chapter we give an introduction to several of these charts. If you want to learn more about them, then you should consult texts on *statistical quality control.* Good references are the books by D.C. Montgomery *(Introduction to Statistical Quality Control)*, E.L. Grant and R.S. Leavenworth *(Statistical Quality Control)*, and T.P. Ryan *(Statistical Methods for Quality Improvement)*. Journals, foremost *Technometrics* and the *Journal of Quality and Technology*, include many technical articles on statistical process control. Descriptions of successful applications can be found in *Quality Progress*.

12.6.1 Control Charts for Individual Measurements

An individual observations chart is appropriate in cases where the production rate is very slow, and where it would take too long to accumulate more than one unit before analysis. It is also suitable in cases where automatic measurement and analysis equipment makes it feasible to actually analyze every observation. Furthermore, individual observations charts are indicated in situations where the subgroups consist of consecutive measurements, but where the variation among the consecutive measurements would underestimate the common-cause variability. Exercise 12.15 is a good example of this. There the variability from consecutive part weights in an injection molding process is much smaller than the common-cause variability across the production shift, or from shift to shift. A similar situation arises in many coating operations where thickness differs very little across each roll, and where a sample taken from the same roll could seriously underestimate the uncontrolled common-cause variability.

Note that the control limits in an x-bar chart do not use the standard deviation that is obtained by averaging the deviations of the kn observations from their overall grand average. Instead, we calculate and average subgroup standard deviations that are obtained from observations that are close in time; each subgroup standard deviation measures the variability around the local subgroup level. With sample information at each time period we are able to separate the variability from the level changes. However, in the absence of subgroup information it is difficult to calculate an independent estimate of the process variability. From a single observation it is not possible to obtain both an estimate for the level and an estimate for the variability. One possible approach for calculating the control limits in an individual observation chart is to use the sample standard deviation, s, of the k individual measurements around their time average, $\bar{x}$; this results in control limits $\bar{x} - 3s$ and $\bar{x} + 3s$. However, when doing this one makes the rather strong assumption that the mean level of the series has not shifted; and this is exactly what we want to detect. There is a danger with this particular approach of setting the control limits because for a process with time-varying levels the calculated standard deviation will be large also. Hence there is a good chance that the resulting control limits are too wide to catch the instability in the levels.

The literature discusses another approach for monitoring the stability of individual observations. It is common to calculate moving ranges by considering differences of adjacent observations. The *moving range* is defined as $\text{MR}_i = |x_i - x_{i-1}|$; it is the absolute value of the difference between two adjacent observations. From the k individual observations we can calculate the $k - 1$ moving ranges, $\text{MR}_2 = |x_2 - x_1|$, $\text{MR}_3 = |x_3 - x_2|, \ldots, \text{MR}_k = |x_k - x_{k-1}|$. A *moving-range chart* is a time sequence plot of the moving ranges $\text{MR}_2, \text{MR}_3, \ldots, \text{MR}_k$. This chart monitors the stability of the variability across time. It plots ranges that are obtained from (overlapping) samples of size $n = 2$, and we can use the constants $D_3 = 0$ and $D_4 = 3.267$ for the range chart in Table 12A to set the control limits. The center line of the moving-range chart is given by $\overline{\text{MR}} = (\text{MR}_2 + \cdots + \text{MR}_k)/(k - 1)$, and the control limits are $\text{LCL} = (0)\,\overline{\text{MR}}$ and $\text{UCL} = (3.267)\,\overline{\text{MR}}$.

The moving-range chart monitors the variability of the observations across time. However, you should be aware that with just a single observation at each time period it is not possible to get an estimate of the variation without making an additional assumption. In our interpretation of the moving-range chart we implicitly assume that the levels of the two adjacent observations have not changed. Consequently, the difference between the two observations is taken as a measure of the process variability and not of any level change. In order to appreciate this assumption more fully, assume that the level of the process shifts halfway through the series from one value to another. Then one moving range, namely the one where this shift has taken place, will be unusually large. The moving-range chart indicates that at this point in time something unusual has happened to the "variability." But keep in mind that in this particular illustration the one very large moving range is really due to a level shift; a single unusual point on a moving-range chart is often an indication that the level has shifted. Another difficulty with the visual interpretation of a moving range chart is the fact that the moving ranges come from overlapping samples and hence they are not independent; each measurement enters into the calculation of two moving ranges.

One should interpret the moving-range chart in conjunction with the *individual observations chart* (also called the *x-chart*). An x-chart is a time-sequence plot of the individual observations; it is used to monitor the stability of the levels of the series. The center line in the x-chart is the time average of the observations $\bar{x} = (x_1 + x_2 + \cdots + x_k)/k$. The average of the moving ranges, $\overline{\text{MR}} = (\text{MR}_2 + \cdots + \text{MR}_k)/(k-1)$, is used in the calculation of the control limits. We learned earlier that the sampling distribution of a range, calculated from n observations that are taken from a normal distribution with mean μ and standard deviation σ, is centered at $d_2\sigma$. The constant d_2, which depends on the sample size n, is given in Table 12A; for $n = 2$, this constant is $d_2 = 1.128$. The average moving range $\overline{\text{MR}}$ is an estimate of 1.128σ and hence $\overline{\text{MR}}/1.128$ is an estimate of the process standard deviation σ. The control limits for the individual observation charts are then given by

$$\text{LCL} = \bar{x} - (3)(\overline{\text{MR}}/1.128)$$
$$\text{UCL} = \bar{x} + (3)(\overline{\text{MR}}/1.128).$$

Note that normality is assumed here. One ought to check this assumption by displaying the histogram or the normal probability plot of the observations.

EXAMPLE

The concentration of an active ingredient in a liquid detergent, expressed in grams/gallon, was measured on consecutive batches. As each batch takes several hours to produce and since the production rate is very slow, it was not possible to take sample sizes greater than one. The data is listed in Table 12.6 (page 342). We use the information on the first 20 batches to construct a moving-range chart and an individual observation chart.

The moving ranges are given in the last column of this table. The average moving range from the first 20 batches is given by $\overline{\text{MR}} = 1.947$. This becomes the center line on the moving-range chart; the control limits are given by LCL $= (0)(1.947) = 0$ and UCL $= (3.267)(1.947) = 6.36$. The average of the 20 observations, $\bar{x} = 50.035$, becomes the center line in the individual observations chart; the control limits in the x-chart are given by LCL $= 50.035 - (3)(1.947/1.128) = 44.86$ and UCL $= 50.035 + (3)(1.947/1.128) = 55.21$. The moving-range chart and the individual observations chart are shown in Figure 12.10 (page 343). Both charts indicate that the observations from the first 20 batches are stable over time.

TABLE 12.6 Concentration of an Active Ingredient in a Liquid Detergent (Grams/Gallon)

	Concentration x_i	Moving range $\lvert x_i - x_{i-1} \rvert$
Sample 1	49.3	*
Sample 2	51.1	1.8
Sample 3	47.7	3.4
Sample 4	46.9	0.8
Sample 5	48.5	1.6
Sample 6	48.4	0.1
Sample 7	50.1	1.7
Sample 8	48.2	1.9
Sample 9	48.2	0.0
Sample 10	52.2	4.0
Sample 11	53.7	1.5
Sample 12	49.9	3.8
Sample 13	51.3	1.4
Sample 14	51.0	0.3
Sample 15	52.0	1.0
Sample 16	48.7	3.3
Sample 17	50.6	1.9
Sample 18	48.2	2.4
Sample 19	53.0	4.8
Sample 20	51.7	1.3
Average	50.035	1.947
New data		
Sample 21	44.9	6.8
Sample 22	49.3	4.4
Sample 23	46.7	2.6
Sample 24	46.8	0.1
Sample 25	49.6	2.8
Sample 26	47.8	1.8
Sample 27	42.1	5.7
Sample 28	46.7	4.6
Sample 29	46.4	0.3
Sample 30	47.2	0.8

Thirty consecutive batches.

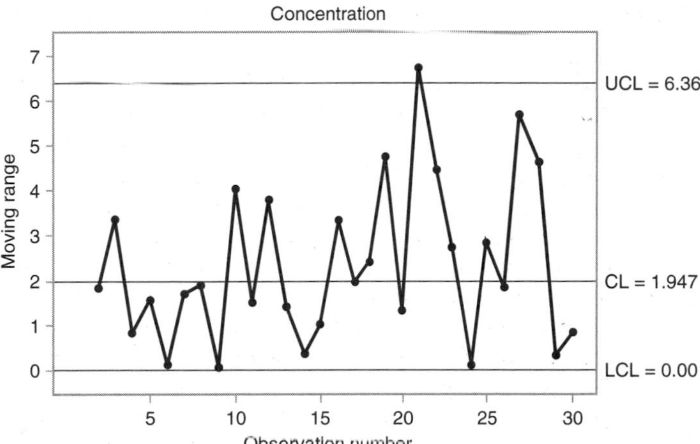

FIGURE 12.10a Moving-range chart for the concentration measurements in Table 12.6. Control limits are obtained from the first twenty batches.

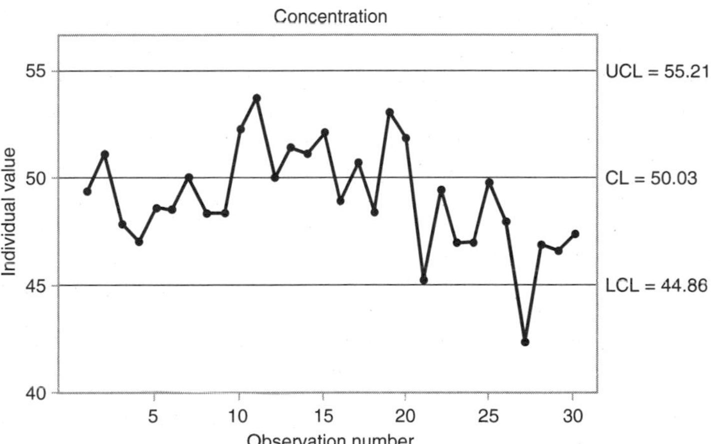

FIGURE 12.10b Individual observations chart for the concentration measurements in Table 12.6. Control limits are obtained from the first twenty batches.

The observations and the moving ranges for batches 21 through 30 are added on the charts. We recognize that there must have been a level shift after the first 20 observations. The moving-range chart shows one unusually large range, $MR_{21} = |x_{21} - x_{20}| = 6.8$, a pattern that is consistent with a level shift after the first 20 batches. Note that very few observations on the x-chart fall below the lower control limit. However, the figure shows that the concentration of every single batch among the last 10 batches is below the center line. ■

12.6.2 Exponentially Weighted Moving Average Charts

Instead of plotting individual observations on an x-chart (or sample averages on an x-bar chart in case of subgroups) and basing one's decision on just the last recorded observation, one can also plot a cumulative sum (CUSUM) or a weighted average of previous values. The CUSUM cumulates the deviations of the observations from the center line, while the weighted average gives more weight to the more recent observations and less to those in the past. We talk about an exponentially weighted moving average (EWMA) if the weights that are given to the observations decrease geometrically with the age of the observations.

CUSUM and EWMA charts are designed to detect small level shifts in the process. An x-bar chart is quite good in detecting large changes in the level; however, it takes quite a long time to detect small changes in the process level; we refer you to the average run lengths in Table 12.3. The CUSUM chart and the EWMA chart detect small shifts much quicker. The performance of CUSUM and EWMA charts is similar to that of charts that incorporate the "added run rules" discussed in Section 12.5. For example, these added run rules declare a process out of control if eight successive subgroup averages are on the same side of the center line. If eight observations are on the same side of the center line, then also a plot of the cumulative deviations from the center line in the CUSUM chart would indicate a very prominent trend.

Let us discuss the *EWMA chart* in more detail. Let us assume that we are dealing with individual measurements x_i that become available sequentially; if we deal with subgroup information then we simply replace x_i by $\bar{x}_i$, the subgroup average of the n measurements. The *exponentially weighted moving average* (EWMA) is given by

$$\text{EWMA}_i = \lambda x_i + (1-\lambda)\text{EWMA}_{i-1}.$$

We start the recursion with $\text{EWMA}_0 = \mu_0$, where μ_0 is the in-control level of the process. We can use past data on the process to estimate this value; for example, we can use the time average in the individual observations chart or the grand average in the x-bar chart. The recursive nature makes the calculation of the EWMA signals particularly easy. However, in order to gain more understanding into the technique, one can express the EWMA as a weighted linear combination of current and past observations. That is,

$$\begin{aligned}
\text{EWMA}_1 &= \lambda x_1 + (1-\lambda)\text{EWMA}_0 \\
\text{EWMA}_2 &= \lambda x_2 + (1-\lambda)\text{EWMA}_1 = \lambda x_2 + (1-\lambda)[\lambda x_1 + (1-\lambda)\text{EWMA}_0] \\
&= \lambda x_2 + \lambda(1-\lambda)x_1 + (1-\lambda)^2\text{EWMA}_0,
\end{aligned}$$

and in general, through repeated substitution,

$$\begin{aligned}
\text{EWMA}_i &= \lambda x_i + (1-\lambda)\text{EWMA}_{i-1} = \cdots \\
&= \lambda x_i + \lambda(1-\lambda)x_{i-1} + \lambda(1-\lambda)^2 x_{i-2} + \cdots + \lambda(1-\lambda)^{i-1}x_1 + (1-\lambda)^i\text{EWMA}_0.
\end{aligned}$$

The constant λ in this recursion is between 0 and 1; $0 < \lambda \leq 1$. It is called the *smoothing constant*. You can see why EWMA_i is called an exponentially weighted moving average. Since $1 - \lambda$ is less than one, the weights that are given to past observations decrease geometrically (or exponentially) with the age of the observation. If λ is 1, then only the most recent observation is incorporated into the EWMA signal; that is, $\text{EWMA}_i = x_i$. On the other hand, if λ is small, then the weights decrease only very slowly and the EWMA signal is essentially an average of all previous observations; in this case the EWMA is very similar to the CUSUM.

In an EWMA chart we plot the consecutive EWMA_i's. The center line on the EWMA chart is the in-control level of the process μ_0. The standard deviation of EWMA_i is needed for the calculation of the control limits. The standard deviation of EWMA_i is given by

$$\begin{aligned}\text{StdDev}(\text{EWMA}_i) &= \{[\lambda\sigma]^2 + [\lambda(1-\lambda)\sigma]^2 + [\lambda(1-\lambda)^2\sigma]^2 + \cdots + [\lambda(1-\lambda)^{i-1}\sigma]^2\}^{1/2} \\ &= \sigma\lambda\{1 + (1-\lambda)^2 + (1-\lambda)^4 + \cdots + (1-\lambda)^{2(i-1)}\}^{1/2}.\end{aligned}$$

Here we have used the result in Section 8.10 on the standard deviation of a sum of independent components. Exercise 12.16 shows how to simplify the above sum. This leads to

$$\text{StdDev}(\text{EWMA}_i) = \sigma\sqrt{\frac{\lambda}{2-\lambda}}\sqrt{1-(1-\lambda)^{2i}}.$$

Hence the lower and upper control limits for EWMA_i in the EWMA chart are given by

$$\begin{aligned}\text{LCL} &= \mu_0 - 3\sigma\sqrt{\frac{\lambda}{2-\lambda}}\sqrt{1-(1-\lambda)^{2i}} \\ \text{UCL} &= \mu_0 + 3\sigma\sqrt{\frac{\lambda}{2-\lambda}}\sqrt{1-(1-\lambda)^{2i}}.\end{aligned}$$

If i becomes large, then the last term $\sqrt{1-(1-\lambda)^{2i}}$ approaches 1, and the control limits are simply given by $\text{LCL} = \mu_0 - 3\sigma[\lambda/(2-\lambda)]^{1/2}$ and $\text{UCL} = \mu_0 + 3\sigma[\lambda/(2-\lambda)]^{1/2}$.

Past data must usually be employed to estimate the in-control level of the process μ_0 and the standard deviation of the plotted signal. In case of individual observations (sample size $n = 1$), we estimate μ_0 by the time average $\bar{x}$, and σ by the sample standard deviation s or by $\overline{\text{MR}}/1.128$. If the EWMA signal involves subgroup averages, then we estimate μ_0 by the grand average and the standard deviation of subgroup averages by $(A_3\bar{s})/3$ or by $(A_2\bar{R})/3$; the constants A_2 and A_3 depend on the subgroup size n. This follows from the fact that the factors $(A_3\bar{s})$ and $(A_2\bar{R})$ in the x-bar chart estimate three times the standard deviation of subgroup averages.

One can show that a smoothing constant in the range between 0.1 and 0.2 works well in practice, facilitating the detection of rather small level shifts within a short period of time. For further discussion and refinements in the selection of the smoothing constant and the control limits, we refer the reader to the papers by Hunter (1986), Crowder (1989), and Lucas and Saccucci (1990).

EXAMPLE

The data in Table 12.6 that lists individual concentrations on consecutive batches of detergent is used to illustrate the EWMA chart with smoothing constant $\lambda = 0.2$. The center line and the control limits of the EWMA chart are determined from the first 20 batches with average $\bar{x} = 50.035$ and standard deviation $s = 1.923$; note that the alternative estimate of σ, $\overline{\text{MR}}/d_2 = 1.947/1.128 = 1.73$, is quite similar. Table 12.7 shows the calculated EWMA control signals:

$$\text{EWMA}_1 = (0.2)(49.3) + (0.8)(50.035) = 49.888$$
$$\text{EWMA}_2 = (0.2)(51.1) + (0.8)(49.888) = 50.130,$$

and so on. It also shows the lower and upper control limits for the EWMA chart. The EWMA chart with its control limits is plotted in Figure 12.11. At batch number 27 the EWMA signal dips below the lower control limit. At that point we conclude that the process has shifted to a lower level. This confirms our findings from the individual observations chart in Figure 12.10. ■

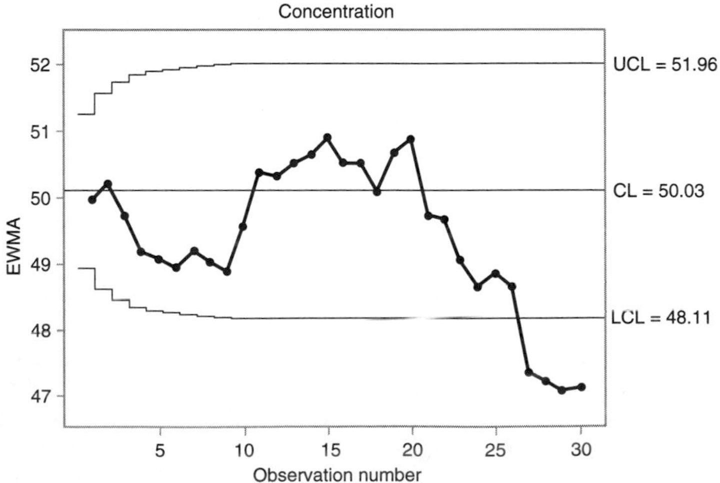

FIGURE 12.11 EWMA chart for the concentration measurements in Table 12.6. Center line and control limits are calculated from the first twenty batches.

TABLE 12.7 EWMA Signals and Control Limits for the Concentration Data in Table 12.6

			Control limits		
Sample	x_i	$EWMA_i$	Lower	Upper	
1	49.3	49.888	48.88	51.19	
2	51.1	50.130	48.56	51.51	
3	47.7	49.644	48.38	51.69	
4	46.9	49.095	48.28	51.79	
5	48.5	48.976	48.22	51.85	
6	48.4	48.861	48.18	51.89	
7	50.1	49.109	48.15	51.92	
8	48.2	48.927	48.14	51.93	
9	48.2	48.782	48.13	51.94	
10	52.2	49.465	48.12	51.95	
11	53.7	50.312	48.12	51.95	
12	49.9	50.230	48.12	51.95	
13	51.3	50.444	48.11	51.96	
14	51.0	50.555	48.11	51.96	
15	52.0	50.844	48.11	51.96	
16	48.7	50.415	48.11	51.96	
17	50.6	50.452	48.11	51.96	
18	48.2	50.002	48.11	51.96	
19	53.0	50.601	48.11	51.96	
20	51.7	50.821	48.11	51.96	
21	44.9	49.637	48.11	51.96	
22	49.3	49.570	48.11	51.96	
23	46.7	48.996	48.11	51.96	
24	46.8	48.557	48.11	51.96	
25	49.6	48.765	48.11	51.96	
26	47.8	48.572	48.11	51.96	
27	42.1	47.278	48.11	51.96	**** out of control
28	46.7	47.162	48.11	51.96	
29	46.4	47.010	48.11	51.96	
30	47.2	47.048	48.11	51.96	

Smoothing constant $\lambda = 0.2$, starting value $EWMA_0 = 50.035$, and standard deviation $s = 1.923$.

12.7 APPLICATIONS OF STATISTICAL PROCESS CONTROL IN THE SERVICE AND INFORMATION SYSTEMS AREAS

We end this chapter by discussing applications of statistical quality control in service operations and information systems (IS) areas. Statistical process control is widely practiced in manufacturing, and its use has grown in the service sector of the economy as well. However, little use has been made of it so far by the information systems community.

12.7.1 Statistical Process Control in the Service Sector: IBM Kingston

The following discussion is based on an article by W.J. McCabe, "Improving Quality and Cutting Costs in a Service Organization," in the June 1985 issue of *Quality Progress* (pp. 85–89). This discussion shows the initial difficulties, but also the benefits of introducing statistical process control ideas into the service sector.

Each department at IBM Kingston (purchasing, security, administration, maintenance, personnel) was asked to identify objectives for their operations and develop a set of measurements. As part of this program the company decided to apply control charts to their operations.

Challenges were that people had little knowledge of or skills with control charts. Furthermore, most texts on control charts covered production, but had little to say about the service industry. People had to take concepts from the statistical literature and make them practical. They had to develop examples.

People found that the most significant gains came from the *process of developing the control chart*, not the chart itself. In the process of developing control charts they had to answer questions such as "What aspect of the process is really important to its success?" The very act of examining the process for possible control-chart applications produced a multitude of improvements.

Most groups had little difficulty in finding several key indicators, but they quickly found that there was little data. What data was available was highly aggregated (for example, only quarterly summary information was available) and was of little use. Hence they had to start collecting data. Four areas are highlighted in the article:

1. **Suggestion Program:** The response time to suggestions was identified as a critical variable, as employees must have confidence that the company will respond to their suggestions in a timely fashion. The response time to suggestions was tracked by functional areas. Differences were found, indicating that some groups were slower than others in responding to requests. Workshops on how to respond in a timely fashion were held. These efforts

were found to lower response times. Response times were monitored with control charts. Out-of-control situations were investigated and their causes were identified; vacation coverage and failure to attend workshops were the main reasons.

2. **Pre-employment Medical Exams:** The company felt that pre-employment medical exams took too long and that they put a heavy burden on the medical staff. The first step in this investigation was to figure out how to measure the length of time of a medical examination. Interestingly enough, examination times had never been analyzed. The times of 100 exams were obtained and they were divided into subgroups of size 5. From this information x-bar and R-charts were constructed. The average time was 74 minutes, and the range varied greatly. Analysis of this information pointed out a need for new equipment and for additional staff training. With new equipment and additional staff training the times were reduced to around 40 minutes.
3. **Purchase Orders:** The company realized that considerable time and money were being lost by nonconforming documents issued by the purchase department. Data on weekly purchase orders and orders that were in error was kept for 20 weeks. A p-chart was constructed and it was found that the average error rate was about 5.9 percent. Buyers were asked to look at this assembled information and over the next 6 weeks the average dropped to 3.7 percent (presumably just by buyers' individual efforts). The control limits were revised according to this new lower proportion. Use of the p-chart indicated a serious out-of-control condition in week 35. It was subsequently found that many buyers were on vacation that week, and that replacement staff had made more mistakes, mainly because of heavy work load and lack of experience. Preventive measures were put in place to avoid these problems for the next peak vacation period.
4. **Rearrangements:** Rearrangements have to do with transfer of people and changes in space and facilities. Customers were asked to report the number of moving problems they experienced. It was found that the average number of problems was 4.3 per move. A c-chart was established with an upper control limit of 11 errors per move. Whenever this limit was exceeded, the mover was given a warning. If the mover exceeded that limit a second time, that mover was removed from the list of approved bidders. One contractor was put on notice. In more than 20 subsequent moves, problems with all contractors virtually disappeared.

Other applications included janitorial inspection, telephone trouble reports, misaddressed mail, and accident rates. This work convinced the company that control chart methodology is widely applicable to nonproduct (that is, service) quality. In fact, they found that control charts provide a common language to discuss service quality.

12.7.2 Statistical Process Control in the Information Systems Area

Very little use of statistical process control has been made so far by the information systems community. The reason for this is unclear, but it seems to have more to do with it being an unfamiliar concept than with the lack of suitable areas for application. Several suggestions outlining potentially useful applications are discussed in this section.

Control Charts and the IS Application Development Process: One way that statistical quality control can be used in the IS area is to monitor the application development process. For that process, the resulting product is a module of code. One attribute that one wants to control is the number of errors. Errors could be measured by the number of "bugs" per module, and those could be plotted on a *c*-chart. For this to be appropriate, modules should be approximately of the same size; otherwise, a *u*-chart should be used. From the chart a determination could be made as to whether the process is under control. If not, an investigation into the possible causes could be started.

If you apply this technique in your organization, don't be surprised to discover that your development process is under statistical control but that the products you produce are not of satisfactory quality. It is likely that you will find that your process is under statistical control, because most shops have a fairly standard way of developing products which is probably the same today as it was last month or last year. However, you are very likely to find that your products are not satisfactory—that on average there are too many defects in the code you are producing. One important reason for this can be that your requirements have become more stringent in recent years because of a greater concern about data quality. Your process might well have been satisfactory when it was installed several years ago, but it might be unable to deliver the products that your present requirements demand.

Control Charts and IS Operations: Statistical quality control can also be applied in the operations area of IS. Applications in this area are generally easier to identify because IS operation is analogous to manufacturing, in fact highly automated manufacturing. Measurements that could be analyzed through statistical quality control procedures are:

- Time to failure of a system
- Response time of a system
- Time to repair a system that failed
- Tape mounting time
- Tape reading errors

- Production volume
- Production quality

This list suffices to show that there are many problems in operations that can be investigated through statistical quality control.

Control charts can also be applied to general problems: tracking the quality level of an area, measuring the effectiveness of different procedures and standards, tracking the performance of vendors, and other problems that often are thought of as management issues. As a general rule, if a process can be measured, then statistical quality control should be considered as a tool for investigating and tracking the measurements.

12.7.3 Guidelines for Setting Up Statistical Process Control Systems

Implementing statistical quality control is not a trivial task. The paper by T. Pyzdek, "A Ten-Step Plan for Statistical Process Control Studies," in *Quality Progress*, July 1985, pages 18–21, discusses useful guidelines on how to set up a statistical process control system. We summarize the basic ideas, and ask you to read the paper as one of the exercises.

1. Select a candidate for study. Pick an important problem that is accessible to solution. Picking a "winner" motivates people to stay with the program.
2. Define the scope of the study and the processes that are to be examined. Avoid solving the wrong problem.
3. Procure management backing and resources. Decide who is monitoring what.
4. Determine the adequacy of the measurement system.
5. Provide a control system. Identify sources of variation and establish a system that keeps track of changes.
6. Select a method for analysis. Normally this is a control chart, but other techniques may be used.
7. Gather and analyze data. Train the people who gather and analyze data.
8. Track down and remove special causes. In other words, fix the problem.
9. Estimate process capability. For this to be meaningful, you need to have a stable process.
10. Establish a quality control plan for the process. This may include surveillance of important process variables, periodic inspection of control dimensions, sorting inspection if the process does not provide the desired level of quality, and pursuit of process improvement programs.

12.8 EXERCISES

12.1 Consider the number of blemishes on a 10-inch wide section of aluminum strip. Measurements on the aluminum strip are taken every 30 minutes (read across):

2 1 1 0 5 2 3 1 1 2 0 0 4 3 1 3 1 1 0 2 8 7 0 1 2

Construct the appropriate control chart and calculate the control limits. Is this process stable? (The control chart is shown in Figure 12.1b.)

12.2 The data given below contains the sample size, the number of defectives, and the date at which the subgroup was taken:

Sample size	**Number of defectives**	**Date**
120	7	April 20
100	7	22
120	2	23
144	5	24
98	3	25
120	2	29
120	7	30
120	1	May 1
144	3	2
100	5	3
144	6	6
120	4	7
80	7	8
120	2	9
100	3	10
100	5	13
120	3	14
120	7	15
120	6	16
108	1	17
120	4	20
120	4	21
100	3	22
80	0	23
120	6	24

Construct the appropriate control chart and calculate its control limits. Are we observing a stable process?

12.3 (Group project) Consider the funnel experiment discussed in Section 12.1.

(a) Carry out the experiment with a fixed release position, repeating it 100 times. Plot the results, measure the distances to the target, and summarize the results.

(b) Use each of the two adjustment (tampering) procedures discussed in the text. Use 100 replications in each case and show, graphically as well as numerically, that tampering makes things worse.

12.4 If you don't have access to the equipment to carry out the funnel experiment, you may want to replace Exercise 12.3 with the following exercise. This exercise is based on the paper by T.C. Krehbiel, "Tampering with a Stable Process," in *Teaching Statistics*, Vol. 16, No. 3, 1994, pp. 75–79. Its advantage is the ease of execution, as it requires no equipment except a pair of dice. The experiment illustrates that tampering with a stable system will not decrease the common cause variability and, in fact, will make things even worse.

The objective of this experiment is to minimize the process variation around the target 7. The stable process is described by rolling two dice and calculating the total, T, of the spots on the upsides of the two dice. You can convince yourself that the possible outcomes from this experiment are the integers between 2 and 12, with probabilities $P(T = 2) = P(T = 12) = 1/36; P(T = 3) = P(T = 11) = 2/36; P(T = 4) = P(T = 10) = 3/36; P(T = 5) = P(T = 9) = 4/36; P(T = 6) = P(T = 8) = 5/36$; and $P(T = 7) = 6/36$. The mean of this distribution is 7 and the standard deviation is 2.415 (see Section 8.2).

Three strategies are pursued: *Strategy 1* takes no adjustment action, and leaves the process alone. That is, the process value at time k, P_k, is the same as the dice total at time $k, P_k = T_k$. *Strategy 2* compensates on the basis of the *last dice total.* That is, you adjust the process value to $P_k = T_k + (7 - T_{k-1})$. If you have rolled a 4 at time $k - 1$ (that is, on the prior roll you were three units below your target), then you adjust the new process value by adding 3 units to the next roll total. This adjustment is a univariate counterpart of the first tampering strategy in Deming's funnel experiment in Section 12.1. *Strategy 3* compensates on the basis of the *last process value*, that is, $P_k = T_k + (7 - P_{k-1})$. If your previous (adjusted) process value was 9 (that is 2 units above your target), then you adjust the new process value by subtracting 2 from the total in the current dice roll. This adjustment is a univariate counterpart of the second tampering strategy in Deming's funnel experiment.

Roll the two dice for a total of 100 times and calculate the process outcomes under each of the three strategies. Discuss the results. Plot the process values in form of a time-sequence plot. Calculate the average and the standard deviation of the process values under each of the three strategies.

Attempt to explain the results theoretically. In the first strategy, $P_k = T_k$. It is straightforward to obtain the mean and the standard deviation of the distribution of P_k. In the second strategy, $P_k = T_k + (7 - T_{k-1})$. You know that the rolls, and hence T_{k-1} and T_k, are independent; calculate the mean and the standard deviation of P_k. You can use the result in Section 8.10 on the standard deviation of a difference of two independent random variables. For the third strategy you can show, through repeated substitution into the adjustment formula, that $P_k = T_k - T_{k-1} + T_{k-2} - T_{k-3} \cdots + T_1$, if k is an odd number. Calculate the standard deviation of P_k. Can you understand now what Deming meant when he said that "the process is off to the Milky Way"?

12.5 Discuss other examples of tampering. For another, somewhat different view on the funnel experiment, read and discuss the paper "A Different View of the Funnel Experiment," by John F. MacGregor in the *Journal of Quality Technology*, 1990, pp. 255–259.

12.6 Read the paper "Don't Touch That Funnel!" by Thomas J. Boardman and Eileen C. Boardman, in *Quality Progress*, December 1990, pp. 65–69. Relate the results of their experiments to our discussion of tampering in Section 12.1.

12.7 The table below shows the results of hardness determinations on 25 samples of four titanium buttons, the samples being drawn at regular intervals from a chemical process. (This data set is taken from G.B. Wetherill, *Sampling Inspection and Quality Control*, p. 46.) Construct x-bar, s-, and R-charts. Discuss the results; in particular, describe the actions that you would take after seeing these plots.

Sample	Hardness			
1	125.8	128.4	129.0	121.0
2	125.2	127.0	130.4	124.6
3	121.8	126.8	127.0	129.8
4	131.0	130.0	127.2	127.0
5	128.6	122.8	125.4	126.4
6	122.0	123.8	131.2	121.8
7	122.8	129.8	126.2	128.8
8	120.2	130.0	125.6	144.0
9	124.8	123.8	130.2	128.8
10	127.0	126.4	122.2	129.0
11	131.8	127.6	123.8	123.2
12	129.8	125.6	128.2	127.6
13	127.6	125.6	128.2	126.8
14	124.2	122.8	124.8	124.6
15	125.4	129.4	123.6	127.2
16	130.8	122.8	125.4	126.2
17	127.4	131.0	123.0	122.8
18	124.8	122.6	122.8	123.6
19	123.8	130.0	128.4	130.0
20	128.8	141.2	138.8	136.2
21	126.4	123.8	128.8	129.6
22	130.8	127.4	126.0	125.2
23	129.6	128.4	123.2	125.8
24	124.4	127.0	130.0	122.8
25	129.2	126.2	128.0	123.2

12.8 The data given below represents the number of dry cell batteries on test and the number of defective units for 14 consecutive samples (Wadsworth, Stephens, and Godfrey, 1986). Construct and interpret the appropriate control chart.

Sample	Number on test	Number of defectives
1	312	4
2	356	6
3	412	6
4	260	7
5	465	12

(*continues*)

(continued)

Sample	Number on test	Number of defectives
6	362	4
7	508	11
8	241	5
9	216	9
10	292	4
11	396	6
12	452	8
13	480	7
14	405	5

12.9 In May 1979, Manitoba introduced a very stringent drinking and driving legislation. The question is whether this bill has significantly reduced the proportion of alcohol-related traffic fatalities or whether any change in the proportions is simply attributable to random variation. Use a *p*-chart to investigate this claim. (The data is taken from F.A. Spiring, "A Bill's Effect on Alcohol-Related Traffic Fatalities," *Quality Progress*, February 1994, pp. 35–38.)

Year	No. of motor vehicle fatalities	No. of alcohol-related fatalities
1973	249	123
1974	220	98
1975	226	121
1976	226	122
1977	185	90
1978	208	84
1979	179	115
1980	184	82
1981	224	120
1982	160	72
1983	155	62
1984	143	56
1985	144	64
1986	184	99
1987	186	80
1988	156	74
1989	173	74
1990	38	16 (partial data)

12.10 Carbon fibers of a certain type used in fibrous composite materials are being manufactured. A sample of five fibers, each 50 mm in length, is periodically selected from the process and the breaking strength (in GPa, or giga-Pascals) is measured for each fiber. (Data is taken from W.J. Padgett and J.D. Spurrier, "Shewhart-Type Charts for Percentiles of Strength Distributions," *Journal of Quality Technology*, 1990, pp. 283–288.) Construct the appropriate control charts and discuss the stability of this process.

Sample	Breaking strength (in GPa) of carbon fibers				
1	3.70	2.74	2.73	2.50	3.60
2	3.11	3.27	2.87	1.47	3.11
3	4.42	2.41	3.19	3.22	1.69
4	3.28	3.09	1.87	3.15	4.90
5	3.75	2.43	2.95	2.97	3.39
6	2.96	2.53	2.67	2.93	3.22
7	3.39	2.81	4.20	3.33	2.55
8	3.31	3.31	2.85	2.56	3.56
9	3.15	2.35	2.55	2.59	2.38
10	2.81	2.77	2.17	2.83	1.92
11	1.41	3.68	2.97	1.36	0.98
12	2.76	4.91	3.68	1.84	1.59
13	3.19	1.57	0.81	5.56	1.73
14	1.59	2.00	1.22	1.12	1.71
15	2.17	1.17	5.08	2.48	1.18
16	3.51	2.17	1.69	1.25	4.38
17	1.84	0.39	3.68	2.48	0.85
18	1.61	2.79	4.70	2.03	1.80
19	1.57	1.08	2.03	1.61	2.12
20	1.89	2.88	2.82	2.05	3.65

12.11 Take measurements on personal characteristics, such as your blood pressure or your pulse in the morning, the time it takes you to drive or walk to work, the number of students failing to attend class, the number of pieces of mail that you receive, and so on. Take data for a number of consecutive periods (20 or so). Construct the appropriate control charts and discuss the results.

12.12 Consider your attention span in class and think about ways of measuring this factor. Most likely you will notice variability in your attention span. Is your attention span stable from class to class? List common causes for this variability and write down possible special causes. Repeat this exercise for your teacher's level of preparedness.

12.13 The following papers discuss various aspects of control charts. Read and comment on these papers:

R.G. Maki and M.R. Milota, "Statistical Quality Control Applied to Lumber Drying," *Quality Progress*, December 1993, pp. 75–79.

C. Woznlak, "Proactive vs. Reactive SPC," *Quality Progress*, February 1994, pp. 49–50.

A.J. Barnett and R.W. Andrews, "Are You Getting the Most Out of Your Control Charts?" *Quality Progress*, November 1994, pp. 75–80.

T. Pyzdek, "A Ten-Step Plan for Statistical Process Control Studies," *Quality Progress*, July 1985, pp. 18–21.

L.B. Hare, R.W. Hoerl, J.D. Hromi, and R.D. Snee, "The Role of Statistical Thinking in Management," *Quality Progress*, February 1995, pp. 53–60.

J. Stalter, "Process in Control for Conformance," *Quality Progress*, April 1984, pp. 18–21.

J.W. Leppelmeier, "A Common-Sense Approach to SPC," *Quality Progress*, October 1987, pp. 62–64.

12.14 Our plant produces small circuit boards that go into electronic consumer products. Our company has managed to stabilize the production process around 2 percent defectives. The process is monitored on a continuous basis and control charts are used for surveillance. Each shift 200 circuit boards are taken from the production line and are visually inspected. The last few samples led to the following number of defectives (among samples of size 200):

Sample 1: 3 defectives
Sample 2: 1 defective
Sample 3: 6 defectives
Sample 4: 3 defectives
Sample 5: 7 defectives
Sample 6: 8 defectives
. . . .

Has the process gone out of control? If so, when?

12.15 Read Jim Whitney, "Developing Control Limits to Accommodate a Fixed Sampling Plan," pp. 3–5.

Control charts are applied to an injection molding process to monitor part weight with the objective to keep part weight consistent over time. The data collection consists of taking five *consecutive* parts per shift and obtaining the weight of each part. The results of 25 consecutive shifts (averages and ranges of samples of five parts each) are given below.

Sample	Average	Range
1	1964	3
2	1949	18
3	1960	18
4	2061	30
5	2045	5
6	2035	1
7	2042	17
8	2070	29
9	1986	21
10	2006	30
11	2137	6
12	2002	30
13	2000	10
14	2065	7
15	2109	20
16	2106	16
17	2102	2
18	2010	9

(*continues*)

(continued)

Sample	Average	Range
19	2080	8
20	2079	19
21	2069	27
22	2016	11
23	1990	4
24	2027	9
25	2090	15

(a) Construct the x-bar chart and the R-chart. You will notice that there are several out-of-control signals where averages fall outside the upper and the lower control limits.

Comment: Whitney reports that subsequent investigations of conditions during out-of-control signals uncovered nothing unusual. No special effects could be found. Furthermore, subsequent runs with the same unchanged process turned out parts that were consistently acceptable. Operators of the process continued to construct time sequence plots of sample averages, mainly to assess whether part weight had been running high or low. Pretty soon the control charts and especially the control limits were ignored.

A review of the control charts was carried out to investigate whether a certain modification of these chart could lessen the number of investigations and hence give the control charting method a higher degree of acceptance. Recall that the lower and upper control limits of an x-bar chart are supposed to represent the limits of variation of the observed averages. These limits are determined from the normal process variation that takes place during the shift as well as from shift to shift; the limits reflect the common-cause variability. However, in this particular application the time period for collecting the five observations was very short. The variation in the observations that are collected within such a short time interval is very small, and much smaller than the normal variability that happens during a shift or from one shift to the next. For example, there is uncontrolled common-cause variation due to changes in the raw material (that is, the plastic for the injection), but this variability takes place over a much larger time frame. Within each short time interval it is very likely that the input material is essentially constant, whereas over the duration of a shift or from shift to shift the common-cause variability will be much larger. The adopted sampling procedure of selecting five consecutive parts picks up only the short-term variability, and it will underestimate the true common-cause variability. Hence the control limits that are based on the average range are much too narrow, and will lead to many signals for which no special effects can be found. This is a good example, as it shows how important it is to select rational subgroups in the right way (see Section 12.3 for further discussion). In this particular example, nothing could be done about the sampling strategy. In order to alleviate the problem of too many incorrect signals, Whitney recommended to treat the sample averages as individual observations and to construct an individual observations chart where the control limits are calculated from the moving ranges.

(b) Use the sample averages and construct an individual observations chart. Calculate the moving ranges and use the average moving range to construct the control limits. Interpret your results.

Why is there a difference in the findings in (a) and (b)? Discuss and relate your answer to the discussion of rational subgroups in Section 12.3.

Comment: The sampling scheme of taking five consecutive parts and measuring their weight could not be changed. The R chart from the five consecutive measurements monitors the stability of the short-term variation in the process. It was felt that this information was still useful as a trend of increasing ranges points to machine problems and the need for maintenance. The averages of successive shifts were plotted, but the averages were treated as individual observations and the control limits on that chart were calculated with the average of the moving ranges. This was necessary as the within-subgroup variability was much smaller than the common-cause variability of the process.

12.16 Take x between -1 and $+1$ (that is, $-1 < x < 1$). Show that:

(a) $1 + 2x + 3x^2 + 4x^3 + \cdots = 1/(1-x)^2$.

Hint: Calculate the product $(1 + 2x + 3x^2 + 4x^3 + \cdots)(1 - 2x + x^2)$ and show that it is 1.

(b) $1 + x + x^2 + x^3 + \cdots + x^{i-1} = (1 - x^i)/(1 - x)$.

Hint: Calculate the product $(1 + x + x^2 + x^3 + \cdots + x^{i-1})(1 - x)$ and show that it is $(1 - x^i)$.

12.17 The computer operations department of a large company whose job is the processing of information from government surveys keeps track of the daily number of jobs that were executed on the company's mainframe computer system, as well as the number of jobs that ended abnormally. The data for January 1996 is listed below. Analyze the stability of the failure rates.

Date	Jobs executed	Abnormal endings
1/1/96	1191	11
1/2/96	206	1
1/3/96	613	8
1/4/96	590	5
1/5/96	604	2
1/8/96	1017	32
1/9/96	606	3
1/10/96	594	1
1/11/96	599	3
1/12/96	579	2
1/15/96	1008	17
1/16/96	607	12
1/17/96	637	1
1/18/96	503	4
1/19/96	652	7
1/22/96	1035	23
1/23/96	593	2
1/24/96	564	4
1/25/96	539	2
1/26/96	558	4
1/29/96	976	10
1/30/96	578	4
1/31/96	558	2

12.18 Shampoo is produced in large batches by mixing together various ingredients. The pH value of these batches is of great importance. Measurements on the last 15 batches resulted in the following pH values.

Batch 1	6.04
Batch 2	6.01
Batch 3	5.81
Batch 4	5.95
Batch 5	6.12
Batch 6	6.04
Batch 7	6.13
Batch 8	6.17
Batch 9	6.28
Batch 10	6.11
Batch 11	6.16
Batch 12	5.87
Batch 13	6.15
Batch 14	5.86
Batch 15	6.06

(a) Calculate the moving ranges, and construct the moving-range and the individual observations charts.

(b) Construct an EWMA chart, using smoothing constant $\lambda = 0.2$. Use the sample average from the 15 batches to initialize the EWMA (that is, $\text{EWMA}_0 = \bar{x}$).

(c) Concentrations of the next five batches are: 6.12, 5.82, 5.81, 5.75, 5.88. Plot these new measurements on the charts that you had constructed in (a) and (b).

12.19 The data given below represents the amount of force needed to pull apart certain wood-laminates that are produced in large quantities in a furniture production facility. Ten samples of size $n = 4$, taken at 30-minute intervals, are given below:

Sample 1	43.94	44.12	45.70	44.13
Sample 2	44.02	45.95	44.12	44.01
Sample 3	42.56	43.61	44.38	45.59
Sample 4	45.05	43.73	45.56	45.40
Sample 5	45.83	44.56	44.52	44.17
Sample 6	44.85	45.51	45.30	44.23
Sample 7	44.36	45.81	44.36	43.86
Sample 8	46.52	46.50	45.69	44.40
Sample 9	44.47	45.00	44.33	44.15
Sample 10	45.91	44.36	44.37	44.88

Construct the x-bar and the R-charts, and discuss your findings.

12.20 The following data represents response times (in seconds) of an on-line system. Samples of size $n = 5$ were taken at 10-minute intervals. Discuss whether the process is in statistical control.

Sample	Observations					Mean	Range
1	1.41	1.42	1.44	1.47	1.50	1.448	0.09
2	1.45	1.50	1.50	1.52	1.53	1.500	0.08
3	1.40	1.46	1.46	1.54	1.55	1.482	0.15
4	1.44	1.45	1.47	1.48	1.50	1.468	0.06
5	1.42	1.43	1.49	1.49	1.52	1.470	0.10
6	1.43	1.43	1.44	1.50	1.51	1.462	0.08
7	1.44	1.45	1.49	1.49	1.54	1.482	0.10
8	1.44	1.44	1.45	1.50	1.52	1.470	0.08
9	1.47	1.47	1.48	1.49	1.54	1.490	0.07
10	1.39	1.44	1.47	1.49	1.52	1.462	0.13
11	1.42	1.44	1.44	1.49	1.54	1.466	0.12
12	1.44	1.47	1.49	1.49	1.53	1.484	0.09
13	1.46	1.48	1.49	1.49	1.49	1.482	0.03
14	1.44	1.44	1.47	1.51	1.52	1.476	0.08
15	1.42	1.49	1.50	1.51	1.51	1.486	0.09
16	1.39	1.47	1.48	1.51	1.52	1.474	0.13
17	1.44	1.44	1.48	1.49	1.50	1.470	0.06
18	1.44	1.49	1.49	1.50	1.51	1.486	0.07
19	1.42	1.47	1.49	1.49	1.50	1.474	0.08
20	1.43	1.44	1.46	1.47	1.49	1.458	0.06
21	1.45	1.47	1.49	1.50	1.51	1.484	0.06
22	1.46	1.46	1.47	1.50	1.53	1.484	0.07
23	1.44	1.46	1.47	1.49	1.52	1.476	0.08
24	1.41	1.48	1.49	1.50	1.54	1.484	0.13
25	1.44	1.45	1.48	1.48	1.52	1.474	0.08
26	1.45	1.47	1.50	1.51	1.52	1.490	0.07
27	1.44	1.45	1.47	1.52	1.52	1.480	0.08

12.21 The April 1997 issue of the *Journal of Quality Technology* includes a panel discussion on statistically-based process monitoring and control. In this article, several expert researchers and practitioners give an up-to-date overview of the field of control charts and other related statistical process monitoring techniques. Read their contributions on pages 121–162, and discuss the following questions:

(a) What are some of the new frontiers of control chart applications?

(b) Compare process monitoring to detect special effects with the feedback adjustments of engineering process control.

(c) Discuss autocorrelations in time-series observations. Do the autocorrelations have an impact on the properties of the ordinary control charts?

(d) What do they mean by multivariate SPC? Discuss whether this is a worthwhile technique. Can you think of applications where multivariate control charts would be useful?

(e) What do they mean by the economic modeling for statistical process control? How do costs enter the picture?

12.22 Read the paper, "Control Charts Based on Attribute Data: Bibliography and Review," by W.H. Woodall in the *Journal of Quality Technology*, 1997, pp. 172–183. Relate the discussion in the paper to the material that you learned in Chapter 12. The bibliography in Woodall's paper shows you the many different ways that one can extend the basic *p*- and *c*-charts.

12.23 Eugene L. Grant, in his book *Statistical Quality Control* (1952, p. 23), analyzes the dimensions of molded plastic rheostat knobs which have to fit into a certain assembly. The targets for the dimension were set by the engineering department as 0.140 ± 0.003 inch. A special gauge was developed to permit quick measurement of the actual value of this dimension. Five knobs from each hour's production were selected at random and measured. The averages and ranges (expressed in units of 0.001 inch) for the first 20 hours are given below:

Hour	Average	Range
1	137.8	9
2	143.0	8
3	141.2	15
4	139.8	6
5	140.0	10
6	139.2	8
7	141.2	10
8	140.0	8
9	142.0	7
10	139.2	13
11	139.6	12
12	141.4	9
13	141.2	3
14	140.6	8
15	141.6	9
16	140.4	13
17	140.0	6
18	141.8	8
19	140.4	8
20	138.8	6

(a) Analyze the stability of the process through *x*-bar and *R*-charts. In addition, construct an exponentially weighted moving average chart (with $\lambda = 0.3$). Interpret your results.

(b) Do you believe that this process satisfies the engineering requirements? How capable is the process? Discuss.

(c) Discuss the difference between process stability and process capability.

12.24 Read the paper, "Planning a Control Chart," by Kevin M. Nolan, in *Quality Progress*, December 1990, pp. 51–55. Discuss the author's views of the development and maintenance of control charts.

12.25 Read and discuss the paper "Are Acceptance Sampling and SPC Complementary or Incompatible?" by V.E. Sower et al., in *Quality Progress*, September 1993, pp. 85–89.

12.9 REFERENCES

Barnett, A. J., and R. W. Andrews. "Are You Getting the Most Out of Your Control Charts?" *Quality Progress*, Vol. 27, November 1994, 75–80.

Boardman, T. J., and E. C. Boardman. "Don't Touch That Funnel!" *Quality Progress*, Vol. 23, December 1990, 65–69.

Crowder, S. V. "Design of Exponentially Weighted Moving Average Schemes," *Journal of Quality Technology*, Vol. 21, 1989, 155–162.

Deming, W. E. "Some Principles of the Shewhart Methods of Quality Control," *Mechanical Engineering*, Vol. 66, 1944, 173–177.

Deming, W. E. *Out of the Crisis*. Cambridge, MA: MIT Center for Advanced Engineering Study, 1986.

Grant, E. L. *Statistical Quality Control*, 2nd edition, New York: McGraw-Hill, 1952.

Grant, E. L., and R. S. Leavenworth. "*Statistical Quality Control*," 6th edition. New York: McGraw-Hill, 1988.

Hare, L. B., R. W. Hoerl, J. D. Hromi, and R. D. Snee. "The Role of Statistical Thinking in Management," *Quality Progress*, Vol. 28, February 1995, 53–60.

Hunter, J. S. "The Exponentially Weighted Moving Average," *Journal of Quality Technology*, Vol. 18, 1986, 203–210.

Krehbiel, T. C. "Tampering with a Stable Process," *Teaching Statistics*, Vol. 16, No. 3, 1994, 75–79.

Latzko, W. J. *Quality and Productivity for Bankers and Financial Managers*. New York: Marcel Dekker, 1986.

Leppelmeier, J. W. "A Common-Sense Approach to SPC," *Quality Progress*, Vol. 20, October 1987, 62–64.

Lucas, J. M., and M. S. Saccucci. "Exponentially Weighted Moving Average Control Schemes: Properties and Enhancements," *Technometrics*, Vol. 32, 1990, 1–12.

MacGregor, J. F. "A Different View of the Funnel Experiment," *Journal of Quality Technology*, Vol. 22, 1990, 255–259.

Maki, R. G., and M. R. Milota. "Statistical Quality Control to Lumber Drying," *Quality Progress*, Vol. 26, December 1993, 75–79.

McCabe, W. "Improving Quality and Cutting Costs in a Service Organization," *Quality Progress*, Vol. 18, June 1985, 85–89.

Montgomery, D. C. *Introduction to Statistical Quality Control*, 3rd edition. New York, Wiley, 1996.

Nolan, K. M. "Planning a Control Chart," *Quality Progress*, Vol. 23, December 1990, 51–55.

Padgett, W. J., and J. D. Spurrier. "Shewhart-Type Charts for Percentiles of Strength Distributions," *Journal of Quality Technology*, Vol. 22, 1990, 283–288.

Palm, A. C. "Tables of Run Length Percentiles for Determining the Sensitivity of Shewhart Control Charts for Averages with Supplementary Runs Rules," *Journal of Quality Technology*, Vol. 22, 1990, 289–298.

Pyzdek, T. "A Ten-Step Plan for Statistical Process Control Studies," *Quality Progress*, Vol. 18, July 1985, 18–21.

Ryan, T. P. *Statistical Methods for Quality Improvement*. New York: Wiley, 1989.

Shewhart, W. A. *Economic Control of Quality of Manufactured Product.* New York: Van Nostrand, 1931.

Sower, V. E., et al. "Are Acceptance Sampling and SPC Complementary or Incompatible?" *Quality Progress*, Vol. 26, September 1993, 85–89.

Spiring, F. A. "A Bill's Effect on Alcohol-Related Traffic Fatalities," *Quality Progress*, Vol. 27, February 1994, 35–38.

Stalter, J. "Process in Control for Conformance," *Quality Progress*, Vol. 17, April 1984, 18–21.

Wadsworth, H. M., K. S. Stephens, and A. B. Godfrey. *Modern Methods for Quality Control and Improvement.* New York: Wiley, 1986.

Western Electric Company: *Statistical Quality Control Handbook*, Indianapolis, 1956.

Wetherill, G. B. *Sampling Inspection and Quality Control*, 2nd edition. London: Chapman and Hall, 1977, p. 46.

Whitney, Jim. "Developing Control Limits to Accommodate a Fixed Sampling Plan," Institute for Improvement in Quality and Productivity (IIQP), University of Waterloo, *Fall Newsletter*, 1996, pp. 3–5.

Woodall, W. H. "Control Charts Based on Attribute Data: Bibliography and Review," *Journal of Quality Technology*, Vol. 29, 1997, 172–183.

Wozniak, C. "Proactive vs. Reactive SPC," *Quality Progress*, Vol. 27, February 1994, 49–50.

APPENDIX TO CHAPTER 12: SUMMARY OF CONTROL CHARTS: CENTER LINES AND LOWER AND UPPER CONTROL LIMITS

Consider k subgroups of n (continuous) measurements each. Typically, we consider 20 or 25 subgroups ($k = 20$ or 25) of 4 or 5 measurements ($n = 4$ or 5). For each subgroup i we calculate the average $\bar{x}_i$, the standard deviation s_i, and the range R_i. The averages of these quantities, averaged over the k subgroups, are denoted by $\bar{\bar{x}}$, $\bar{s}$, and $\bar{R}$.

Mean Chart

For the x-bar chart we plot successive subgroup averages $\bar{x}_1, \bar{x}_2, \ldots$. The center line and the lower and upper control limits are determined by

$$\text{CL} - \bar{\bar{x}}$$
$$\text{LCL} = \bar{\bar{x}} - A_3\bar{s}$$
$$\text{UCL} = \bar{\bar{x}} + A_3\bar{s}$$

where A_3 is a function of the subgroup size n, and is given in Table 12A (page 366).

An alternative version of the x-bar chart uses the average range to determine the control limits. In this version the control limits are calculated from

$$\text{LCL} = \bar{\bar{x}} - A_2\bar{R}$$
$$\text{UCL} = \bar{\bar{x}} + A_2\bar{R}.$$

The constants A_2 for various subgroup sizes are given in Table 12A.

Standard Deviation Chart

For the s-chart we plot successive subgroup standard deviations $s_1, s_2, \ldots$. The center line and the lower and upper control limits are given by

$$\text{CL} = \bar{s} \qquad \text{LCL} = B_3\bar{s} \qquad \text{UCL} = B_4\bar{s}$$

where B_3 and B_4 depend on the subgroup size n. They are given in Table 12A.

Range Chart

In an R-chart we plot successive subgroup ranges $R_1, R_2, \ldots$. The center line and the control limits of this chart are given by

$$\text{CL} = \bar{R} \qquad \text{LCL} = D_3\bar{R} \qquad \text{UCL} = D_4\bar{R}$$

where D_3 and D_4 depend on the subgroup size. They are also given in Table 12A.

P-Chart

In a p-chart we plot successive subgroup proportions of defectives $p_1 =$ (number of defectives in subgroup 1)/(number of items sampled in subgroup 1), $p_2 =$ (number of defectives in subgroup 2)/(number of items sampled in subgroup 2), and so on. Assume that we have k subgroups; typically k is of the order 20 or 25. In the ith subgroup we inspect n_i elements. With attribute data we need to take larger samples than the samples we take for continuous measurement data. The sample sizes n_i should be reasonably large—usually 50 or more elements. Also note that the sample sizes need not be the same. If sample sizes are different, but reasonably close, then we can use the average sample size, $\bar{n}$, in the calculations of the control limits.

From the k subgroups we calculate the overall proportion of defectives, $\bar{p}$, by dividing the total number of defectives by the total number of items sampled. Then the center line for the p-chart is given by $\text{CL} = \bar{p}$ and the control limits for the ith subgroup proportion are

$$\text{LCL} = \bar{p} - (3)\sqrt{\frac{\bar{p}(1-\bar{p})}{n_i}}$$
$$\text{UCL} = \bar{p} + (3)\sqrt{\frac{\bar{p}(1-\bar{p})}{n_i}}.$$

C-Chart

This chart is used when we monitor the number of defects or flaws on sampled items. We plot successive numbers of flaws $c_1, c_2, \ldots$. Assume that we have obtained k such measurements and we have calculated the average, $\bar{c}$. The center line and the control limits of the c-chart are

$$\text{CL} = \bar{c} \qquad \text{LCL} = \bar{c} - 3\sqrt{\bar{c}} \qquad \text{UCL} = \bar{c} + 3\sqrt{\bar{c}}.$$

TABLE 12A Constants for Selected Control Charts

Subgroup	Mean chart		*S*-chart		Range chart		
	Using $\bar{s}$	Using $\bar{R}$					
n	A_3	A_2	B_3	B_4	D_3	D_4	d_2
2	2.659	1.880	0	3.267	0	3.267	1.128
3	1.954	1.023	0	2.568	0	2.575	1.693
4	1.628	0.729	0	2.266	0	2.282	2.059
5	1.427	0.577	0	2.089	0	2.115	2.326
6	1.287	0.483	0.030	1.970	0	2.004	2.534
7	1.182	0.419	0.118	1.882	0.076	1.924	2.704
8	1.099	0.373	0.185	1.815	0.136	1.864	2.847
9	1.032	0.337	0.239	1.761	0.184	1.816	2.970
10	0.975	0.308	0.284	1.716	0.223	1.777	3.078
11	0.927	0.285	0.321	1.679	0.256	1.744	3.173
12	0.886	0.266	0.354	1.646	0.283	1.717	3.258
13	0.850	0.249	0.382	1.618	0.307	1.693	3.336
14	0.817	0.235	0.406	1.594	0.328	1.672	3.407
15	0.789	0.223	0.428	1.572	0.347	1.653	3.472
16	0.763	0.212	0.448	1.552	0.363	1.637	3.532
17	0.739	0.203	0.466	1.534	0.378	1.622	3.588
18	0.718	0.194	0.482	1.518	0.391	1.608	3.640
19	0.698	0.187	0.497	1.503	0.403	1.597	3.689
20	0.680	0.180	0.510	1.490	0.414	1.586	3.735

The constant d_2 is such that, for normally distributed observations, Mean$(R) = d_2\sigma$.

CHAPTER 13

PROCESS CAPABILITY AND PRE-CONTROL

13.1 INTRODUCTION

One must check whether processes are capable of producing products that satisfy the required specifications. In this chapter we introduce several measures of *process capability*, and we discuss various issues that arise in their operation. We also discuss the pre-control chart, which is a tool to monitor process capability over time, and we examine the circumstances under which this chart provides useful information.

Typically the customer requires that certain product specifications are being met. Specifications are usually given in terms of a *target value* (T_g), a *lower specification limit* (LSL) and an *upper specification limit* (USL). They are called the "specs" or the "tolerances" of the product. The specifications are determined by translating customer requirements into suitable product requirements; engineering considerations and the intended use of the product play important roles in setting the specifications. Once these specifications are set, one must monitor the production process to make sure that the products meet the specifications. If the products do, then we say that we are dealing with a process that is *capable* of producing according to the given specifications.

In the next section we introduce several process capability indexes; we examine their importance as well as their shortcomings and discuss their implementation. These capability measures are expressed in terms of the specifications (that is, the target value and the lower and upper specification limits) and the process characteristics (that is, the process mean μ and the process standard deviation σ). Capability indexes are estimated by taking samples from the process under study and by replacing the process characteristics with their sample estimates.

Probably the simplest way to check conformance is to construct a dot diagram of the measurements, or if the data set is large, a histogram. The target value and the lower and upper specification limits can be added to this graph, and the proportion of values that are outside these limits are easily calculated. Of course, no (or very few) values should be outside these limits.

We illustrate this approach with the data on width and gauge of steel flats discussed in Chapter 7. The target for width is 4 inches, with specification limits LSL = 3.97 and USL = 4.03. The target for gauge is 0.25 inch, with lower and upper specification limits LSL = 0.235 and USL = 0.265, respectively. The dot diagrams for width and gauge are shown in Figure 13.1. These are actually bar charts as the frequency on the vertical axis is displayed as a bar instead of a stack of unconnected dots. We notice that 2 of the 95 width measurements (that is, 2.1 percent) are outside the specification limits. One of the 95 gauge measurements (or 1 percent) is outside the specification limits. These figures also show that for both dimensions the center of the process distribution is somewhat smaller than the required target. Our production is slightly off target.

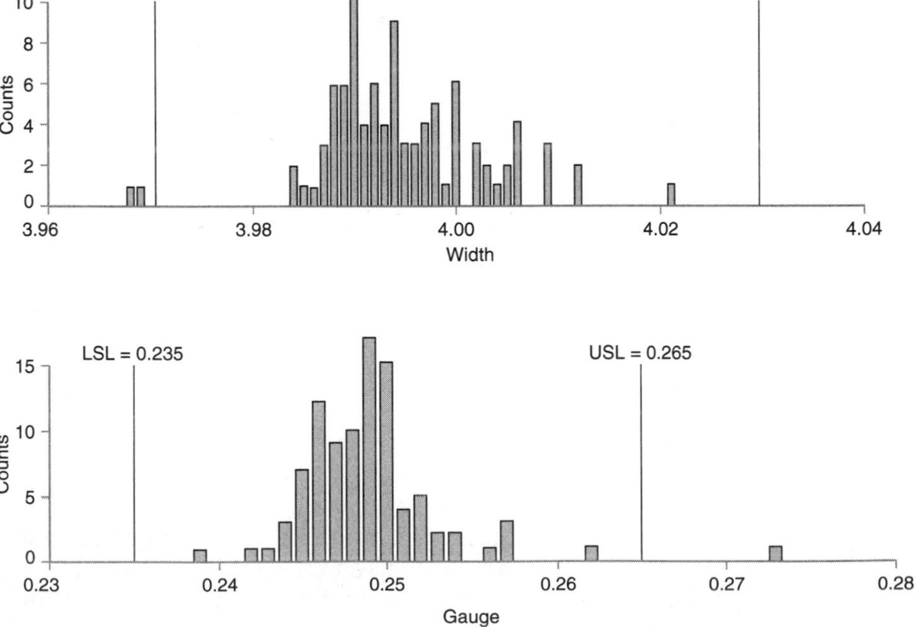

FIGURE 13.1 Dot plots (bar charts) of width and gauge measurements.

13.2 PROCESS CAPABILITY INDEXES

Dot diagrams or histograms are instructive in displaying the capability graphically, and we recommend their use. However, it is common practice to calculate various capability indexes, and many companies require their suppliers to use these measures to document the capability of their processes. Capability indexes quantify the capability or, in other words, the conformance of a process to the required specifications.

13.2.1 The C_p Capability Index

A commonly used measure of capability is the C_p *capability index.* It is given by

$$C_p = \frac{\text{USL} - \text{LSL}}{6\sigma} = \frac{\text{Allowable Spread}}{\text{Actual Spread}}.$$

LSL and USL are the lower and upper specification limits, and σ is the process standard deviation. Note that for the time being we assume that the process characteristics are known. Of course, we will have to estimate them from historic process information.

Why is this a reasonable index? For many distributions the interval $(\mu - 3\sigma, \mu + 3\sigma)$ covers virtually all of the distribution—in fact, 99.73 percent if the distribution is normal. Hence an interval of length 6σ measures the extent of the process variability; in other words, 6σ is a measure of the *actual process spread.* USL − LSL is the *allowable process spread*, and the C_p relates the allowable spread to the actual process spread. For capable processes we expect that the actual process spread is smaller than the allowable spread, and that C_p is larger than one. A large value of C_p indicates that the process variability is small when compared to the width of the specification interval. The larger this index, the better. For normal distributions that are centered at the target, $C_p = 1$ corresponds to 0.27 percent defectives, or 2700 defective parts per million. This is easy to see, as in this case the specification limits are three standard deviations from the target value; we learned earlier that for a normal distribution the probability beyond the three sigma limits is 0.0027. Many companies require that the C_p is at least 1.33 (which implies no more than 63 defective parts per million, as calculations with the normal distribution show), or 1.5 (or 7 defective parts per million). Some companies (for example, Motorola) require that this index is at least 2.0 (implying no more than 0.1 defective part per million).

We estimate this capability index by replacing the process standard deviation σ by its estimate s that we obtain from past data on the process. There are various ways of estimating σ, and we will say more about this issue in the next section.

The estimated C_p is given by

$$\hat{C}_p = \frac{\text{USL} - \text{LSL}}{6s}.$$

We use the caret on top of C_p to denote that it is a sample estimate. For illustration we use the width and gauge measurements on the 95 steel flats. The summary statistics on these observations were given in Table 7.8. For *width* we found a sample average of 3.9947 and a standard deviation of $s = 0.0080$. Thus

$$\hat{C}_p \text{ (width)} = \frac{4.03 - 3.97}{6(0.008)} = 1.25.$$

For *gauge* the sample mean is 0.24894 and the standard deviation is 0.00421. Thus

$$\hat{C}_p \text{ (gauge)} = \frac{0.265 - 0.235}{6(0.00421)} = 1.19.$$

These values are somewhat smaller than what we would like to see. We would have preferred values at least as large as 1.33.

Problems with the C_p Capability Index: The argument that we used to explain and justify the C_p capability index assumes that the process is *on target*, which means that the process level μ and the target value are the same. The C_p index provides a good assessment of capability when the process is on target, as is illustrated by case 1 in Figure 13.2. However, it can be very misleading when the process is off target, as illustrated by case 2 where the defective products

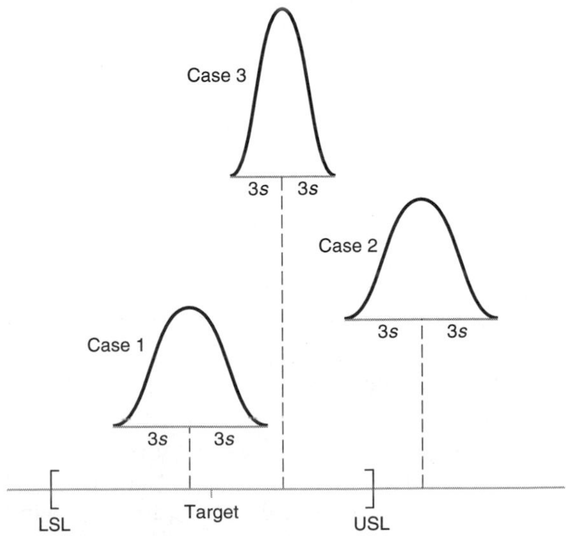

FIGURE 13.2 Illustrating problems with C_p.

far outnumber the acceptable ones. There the process is causing a considerable fraction of defectives. However, the actual process spread, 6σ, is small when compared to the allowable spread. The C_p value is deceptively large, despite the fact that the process is not capable of meeting the specifications. Because C_p makes no reference to the target value, we recommend against its use.

13.2.2 The C_{pk} Capability Index

Processes with small variability but poor proximity to the target have sparked the development of several indexes similar to the C_p. These indexes take into account process variability, as well as the process mean and its deviation from the target value. One of them is the C_{pk} *capability index*, given by

$$C_{pk} = \text{minimum}\left\{\frac{\text{USL} - \mu}{3\sigma}; \frac{\mu - \text{LSL}}{3\sigma}\right\}.$$

C_{pk} relates the distances between each specification limit and the process mean to three standard deviations. For capable processes we expect that the difference between the upper specification limit and the process mean is at least three standard deviations. We expect the same for the difference between the process mean and the lower specification limit. Therefore, we expect the smaller of these two differences to be larger than 3σ, hopefully much larger. A C_{pk} index that is smaller than the usual cutoff of 1.00 or 1.33 is taken as an indication that the process fails to satisfy the required specifications.

The C_{pk} is a much better measure of capability than the C_p. Convince yourself that the C_{pk} index for case 2 in Figure 13.2 is unacceptable; in fact, it is negative as the process mean is larger than the upper specification limit.

In practice we need to replace the process characteristics by their estimates. We estimate the C_{pk} capability index as

$$\hat{C}_{pk} = \text{minimum}\left\{\frac{\text{USL} - \bar{x}}{3s}; \frac{\bar{x} - \text{LSL}}{3s}\right\},$$

where $\bar{x}$ and s are the estimates of μ and σ. For illustration we use the width and gauge measurements on the same 95 steel flats.

For *width* we find that

$$\begin{aligned}\hat{C}_{pk}\,(\text{width}) &= \text{minimum}\left\{\frac{4.03 - 3.9947}{3(0.008)}, \frac{3.9947 - 3.97}{3(0.008)}\right\}\\ &= \text{minimum}\{1.47, 1.03\} = 1.03.\end{aligned}$$

For *gauge* we find that

$$\begin{aligned}\hat{C}_{pk}\,(\text{gauge}) &= \text{minimum}\left\{\frac{0.265 - 0.24894}{3(0.00421)}, \frac{0.24894 - 0.235}{3(0.00421)}\right\}\\ &= \text{minimum}\{1.27, 1.10\} = 1.10.\end{aligned}$$

These capability indexes are also somewhat smaller than what one would have hoped for.

13.2.3 The C_{pm} Capability Index

The C_{pm} capability index is defined as

$$C_{pm} = \frac{\text{USL} - \text{LSL}}{6\sigma^*}.$$

It is similar to C_p, except that σ^* measures the variability of process measurements around the *target* T_g, and not around the process mean μ. The distance of a measurement X from the target T_g can be written as $(X - \text{T}_g) = (X - \mu) + (\mu - \text{T}_g)$. We can think of it as the sum of the distance of the observation from the process mean and the distance of the process mean from the target; the second component is referred to as the bias. It can be shown that

$$\sigma^* = \sqrt{\sigma^2 + (\mu - \text{T}_g)^2}.$$

Hence

$$C_{pm} = \frac{\text{USL} - \text{LSL}}{6\sqrt{\sigma^2 + (\mu - \text{T}_g)^2}} = \frac{\text{USL} - \text{LSL}}{6\sigma\sqrt{1 + \frac{(\mu - \text{T}_g)^2}{\sigma^2}}} = \frac{C_p}{\sqrt{1 + \frac{(\mu - \text{T}_g)^2}{\sigma^2}}}.$$

For processes on target with $\mu = \text{T}_g$, C_{pm} reduces to C_p. If the process mean is different from the target, then the denominator in C_{pm} increases and the capability index decreases.

With n sample observations, we estimate C_{pm} in the above equation by replacing σ^* by its sample estimate $s^* = \sqrt{\Sigma(x_i - \text{T}_g)^2/(n-1)}$; s^* is like the sample standard deviation, except that the target has replaced the sample average that is used in s. Alternatively, we can estimate C_{pm} from

$$\hat{C}_{pm} = \frac{\text{USL} - \text{LSL}}{6\sqrt{s^2 + (\bar{x} - \text{T}_g)^2}}.$$

For illustration we use the width and gauge measurements on the 95 steel flats. For *width* the mean is 3.9947 and the standard deviation is 0.008. Hence

$$\hat{C}_{pm}\ (\text{width}) = \frac{4.03 - 3.97}{(6)\sqrt{(.008)^2 + (3.9947 - 4.00)^2}} = 1.04.$$

For *gauge* we find that

$$\hat{C}_{pm}\ (\text{gauge}) = \frac{0.265 - 0.235}{(6)\sqrt{(.00421)^2 + (0.24894 - 0.25)^2}} = 1.15.$$

13.2.4 Capability Ratio and Target-Z

Several other indexes are in use. Some companies (Procter & Gamble, for example) use the reciprocal of C_p,

$$CR = \frac{1}{C_p} = \frac{\text{Actual Spread}}{\text{Allowable Spread}}.$$

This measure is known as the *capability ratio*. If multiplied by 100, it represents the proportion of the allowable spread that is taken up by the actual process spread. Small values for CR are good; Procter & Gamble requires that the capability ratio of most of their processes is less than 0.75. Note that this is equivalent to requiring that C_p is greater than 1.33.

The capability ratio has the same drawbacks as the C_p. It must be supplemented by a measure that assesses whether the process mean is close to the target.

$$\text{Target-}Z = \frac{T_g - \mu}{\sigma}$$

is such a measure. It is the standardized difference between the target value T_g and the process mean μ. Procter & Gamble, for example, requires that Target-Z lies between -0.5 and 0.5. This says that the process mean must be within one-half of a standard deviation of the target. The Target-Z is estimated from sample data by replacing μ and σ with the sample mean and sample standard deviation.

In summary, capable processes at Procter & Gamble satisfy *both* CR < 0.75 and $-0.5 <$ Target-$Z < 0.5$.

Case 3 in Figure 13.2 illustrates a process that leads to acceptable C_p and C_{pk} indexes, but fails the requirements on Target-Z. One could argue that the process depicted in case 3 is a good one, as the process variability is well within the acceptable range. Nevertheless, it is also true that the process is clearly off target; a level adjustment would make things even better.

For our width and gauge measurements, we find that the estimates are

$$\widehat{CR}\text{ (width)} = 0.80$$
$$\widehat{\text{Target-}Z}\text{ (width)} = (4.0 - 3.9947)/(0.008) = 0.66$$

and

$$\widehat{CR}\text{ (gauge)} = 0.84$$
$$\widehat{\text{Target-}Z}\text{ (gauge)} = (0.25 - 0.24894)/(0.00421) = 0.25.$$

Neither width nor gauge would satisfy Procter & Gamble's capability standards.

13.2.5 Motorola's Six Sigma Concept

Motorola, in announcing the achievement of Total Customer Satisfaction as the corporation's fundamental objective, introduced the concept of *six sigma* as a statistical way of measuring quality. Motorola views its failure rates in terms of parts per million (ppm). Motorola's six sigma goal is a 3.4 ppm defect level!

How does the six sigma requirement translate into a defect level of 3.4 ppm? Obviously, Motorola requires very capable processes. In fact, they require that processes are on target and that the specification limits are at least six sigmas away from the target; hence the name "six sigma." Such a requirement on the process translates into a capability index C_p of 2.0; this is better than the usually adopted standard.

Motorola, however, also realizes that the process is not always exactly on target. In practice, mean levels shift dynamically over time. Motorola allows drifts away from the target of at most 1.5 sigma. Under the six sigma goal and assuming that the observations are from a normal distribution with (shifted) mean $T_g + (1.5)\sigma$ and standard deviation σ, one can calculate the probability that an individual observation falls outside the interval $(T_g - 6\sigma, T_g + 6\sigma)$. The probability is given by

$$
\begin{aligned}
&P \text{ (observation outside specification limits)} \\
&= 1 - P(T_g - 6\sigma \le X \le T_g + 6\sigma) \\
&= 1 - P\left(\frac{T_g - 6\sigma - (T_g + 1.5\sigma)}{\sigma} \le Z \le \frac{T_g + 6\sigma - (T_g + 1.5\sigma)}{\sigma}\right) \\
&= 1 - P(-7.5 \le Z \le 4.5) \approx 1 - P(Z \le 4.5) = 0.0000034,
\end{aligned}
$$

or 3.4 parts per million. (You have to use more elaborate normal probability tables than the one we have given in Chapter 8, which only goes to $P(Z < 4.0)$. You may want to use a spreadsheet program to calculate this probability.) Note that in this situation the process mean is 4.5 standard deviations below the upper specification limit, and hence $C_{pk} = 1.5$.

13.2.6 Process Capability Indexes for One-Sided Tolerances

Consider the situation where the tolerances on a product are *one sided.* For example, the product requirements may specify that the concentration of a certain ingredient must be at least 50 mg/liter (here LSL = 50); or that the weight of an item can be at most 80 grams (here USL = 80); or that the proportion of items with minor color variations can be at most 2 percent (USL = 0.02). In a situation where one-sided tolerance is prescribed, one calculates one-sided C_{pk} capability indexes:

$$
C_{pk} \text{ (upper)} = \frac{\text{USL} - \mu}{3\sigma}
$$

$$
C_{pk} \text{ (lower)} = \frac{\mu - \text{LSL}}{3\sigma}.
$$

For illustration, assume that the process characteristics are given by $\mu = 53$ mg/liter and $\sigma = 0.5$ mg/liter. Then the capability index for the process, relative to a one-sided lower tolerance LSL = 50 mg/liter, is C_{pk} (lower) = (53 − 50)/3(0.5) = 2.0; this indicates a very capable process.

13.3 DISCUSSION OF PROCESS CAPABILITY INDEXES

Capability indexes, such as the C_{pk} or C_{pm} indexes, summarize the process information in a succinct manner. They establish a common language that is dimensionless (that is, it does not depend on the particular units of the observations) and that assesses the potential and the actual performance of production processes. Engineering and manufacturing can communicate through these measures and they can identify processes with high (or low) capability. Capability measures are also useful tools for monitoring the capability over time; they indicate improvements as well as deteriorations in the process.

However, keep in mind that a capability index is just a single summary statistic and can never bring out all features of a distribution. As with any other single summary statistic, there are potential problems. One needs to be aware of these problems when interpreting this statistic.

13.3.1 Specification Limits

Capability indexes depend on the specifications, which usually are determined by the customers and engineers. It is important that careful thought goes into the selection of the specifications. It is wrong to select them too wide, as this may allow inferior products. Usually products are part of a complicated assembly that involves many components. If there is too much variability in one component (because specification limits or tolerances are set too wide), the parts may not fit together as they should. Take, for example, car doors and car frames. If there is too much variability in the door and/or the frame, the door will not close correctly. We refer to this as tolerance stackup. However, the specifications should not be taken as too narrow either. Unnecessary expenses are incurred with narrow specification limits if tight tolerances are not needed.

13.3.2 Assumption of Normality

Capability indexes are designed for normal distributions; we assumed a normal distribution when we related the C_p index to the proportion of unacceptable parts. It is questionable whether capability indexes are meaningful for distributions that are very different from the normal distribution. In order to illustrate this point, assume that the process variability is described by a *uniform* distribution over −1 and +1. The mean of this distribution is given by 0, and the standard deviation is 0.577; refer to Section 8.7. Suppose that the specification limits are given by $-a$ and $+a$; consider $a = 1.5$, for example. The probability that our process exceeds the specification limits is zero, as for the uniform distribution there is no probability beyond −1 and +1. However, $C_{pm} = C_{pk} = C_p = (3)/[(6)(0.577)] = 0.87$, which is rather poor. In this situation the capability index raises unnecessary concerns. Keep in mind that a capability index is just a single summary statistic and can never bring out all features of a distribution. It is always useful to supplement these indexes by a histogram of the measurements.

The uniform distribution is a flat distribution; we also call it "short-tailed," "light-tailed," or "platykurtic"; its density looks like a platypus. Next, consider a symmetric distribution that has very heavy tails (that is, the distribution allows for considerable probability that an observation falls far beyond its mean. For illustration, start with a bell-shaped normal density, but draw it so that the tails are heavier than the normal). For such distributions, the capability index may look quite "good," whereas the probability of exceeding the specifications is large (certainly larger than those implied by the normal distribution). The references in Exercise 13.8 at the end of this chapter discuss this point in more detail.

13.3.3 The Difference Between Process Stability and Process Capability

Let us repeat several comments that we made in Chapter 12 on process control:

Specification limits and control limits are *not* the same. The former reflect the requirements of the customer, while the latter provide bounds on the common-cause variability of the process. These two sets of limits must not be confused!

A process should be in control first, before one assesses its capability. A capable process that is not in control is not very reassuring. It is capable of surprising you! The fact that the process is not under control means that some outside factors are causing the process to be unstable. Since you don't know what these factors are, there is no guarantee that the unexplained variation will stay in a range where the products are still satisfactory. If the process is not in control, you don't know how well you will produce in the future.

13.3.4 Estimation of Capability Indexes

Capability indexes depend on the process parameters, in particular the mean μ and the standard deviation σ. These parameters must be estimated from past data. If a sample taken from past data is representative of the population, then the information from this particular sample will give us a good picture of what the production is like. Using the sample statistics we can obtain an estimate of the C_{pk} of the items from which the sample was drawn. However, in general a single, onetime sample is not sufficient to assess the capability of the *process*. Many companies report the capability daily to their customers. It is important to know that the process is stable over time. If one has no idea whether the process is in statistical control, then a single sample can be quite misleading.

For a stable process that is monitored through control charts there is a direct way to obtain these estimates. Recall that the control limits on an x-bar chart are calculated from LCL $= \bar{\bar{x}} - A_3\bar{s}$ and UCL $= \bar{\bar{x}} + A_3\bar{s}$, where A_3 is a constant which we looked up in Table 12A. The grand average $\bar{\bar{x}}$ is the natural estimate of μ and the product $A_3\bar{s}$ is an estimate of $3(\sigma/\sqrt{n})$, where n is the subgroup size and σ is the standard deviation of the process. Hence it follows that $(\sqrt{n})(A_3)(\bar{s})/3$ is an estimate of σ. This estimate can be used in the calculation of the capability indexes.

Let us illustrate this calculation with the example from Section 12.2. There we found that the carton dimensions in Table 12.1 came from a stable process. We calculated $\bar{\bar{x}} = 25.134$ and $A_3\bar{s} = (1.628)(0.1572) = 0.256$. Thus, $(\sqrt{4})(1.628)(0.1572)/3 = 0.512/3 = 0.171$ is an estimate of σ. Assume that the target is specified at 25, with specification limits of 24 and 26. Then the C_{pk} process capability index is given by

$$\hat{C}_{pk} = \min\left\{\frac{26 - 25.134}{(3)(0.171)}, \frac{25.134 - 24}{(3)(0.171)}\right\} = 1.69;$$

it is quite satisfactory.

Alternatively, one can work with the control limits that use the average range, LCL $= \bar{\bar{x}} - A_2\bar{R}$ and UCL $= \bar{\bar{x}} + A_2\bar{R}$. In this case, $A_2\bar{R}$ is an estimate of $3\sigma/\sqrt{n}$, and $(\sqrt{n})A_2\bar{R}/3$ is used to estimate σ.

Note that the control chart approach of estimating the process parameters pools the standard deviations (or ranges) that are calculated from the n observations in each subgroup across the k subgroups. Another possibility is to combine all $(k)(n)$ observations and calculate the sample mean and the sample standard deviation s. The sample mean and the grand average $\bar{\bar{x}}$ in the x-bar chart are the same, but there may be a large difference between the pooled standard deviation $\bar{s}$ from the control chart and the standard deviation s. Which one should we use for the calculation of the capability indexes? If the process is in control, then there is no or little difference between the two estimates, and it doesn't really matter which estimate we use. However, if the process is not in statistical control, then the estimate $\bar{s}$, which we get by averaging subgroup standard deviations, is usually much smaller than the standard deviation s that is calculated from all $(k)(n)$ observations. This is because $\bar{s}$ measures only the common cause variability, whereas s involves the common-cause variability as well as the variability from special causes which are present because the process is out of control. It would be misleading to use the small $\bar{s}$ in this case, as it would imply large capability indexes which could not be sustained in the long run.

13.3.5 Confidence Intervals for Capability Indexes

When calculating capability coefficients we replace the process parameters (μ and σ) with sample estimates. Hence the calculated capability index is just an estimate of the unknown process capability index, and it is important to evaluate its margin of error, especially if the sample size n, from which these statistics are calculated, is not very large. Assuming that the process is stable and assuming that the measurements are normally distributed, it is possible to obtain approximate confidence intervals for the various capability indexes. A useful, and also rather simple, approximate 95 percent confidence interval for C_{pk} is given by

$$\hat{C}_{pk}\left[1 \pm 2\sqrt{\frac{1}{9n(\hat{C}_{pk})^2} + \frac{1}{2(n-1)}}\right],$$

where n is the number of observations that are used to estimate the capability index. For example, in the steel flat illustration we had 95 observations to estimate the process characteristics. Be careful not to confuse the number of available observations in the above equation with the subgroup size n (4 or 5) in the variables control charts.

The paper by R.H. Kushler, and P. Hurley, "Confidence Bounds for Capability Indices," in the *Journal of Quality Technology*, pp. 188–195, gives an in-depth review of this and several other approaches of approximating confidence intervals for C_{pk} and C_{pm}.

13.4 PRE-CONTROL CHARTS

Dorian Shainin, a well-known quality consultant, has developed several tools for product control and quality improvement. The *pre-control chart*, which is a chart for monitoring the capability of processes over time, is one of his innovations. Pre-control charts are described in Shainin (1984). Further discussion is given in Juran and Gryna (1988; Section 24), Bhote (1988), Shainin and Shainin (1989), Mackertich (1990, with subsequent discussion by Shainin), and Ledolter and Swersey (1997).

13.4.1 Description of Pre-Control

1. In the case of two-sided tolerance, pre-control divides the specification interval into four equal areas. *Pre-control lines (PC lines)* are drawn at the midpoints between the target and the lower (and upper) specification limit. The area between the two pre-control lines is called the green zone. The area between the pre-control lines and the specification limits is called the yellow zone; the area outside the specification limits is referred to as the red zone. See Figure 13.3 for a graphical display. In one-sided tolerance a single

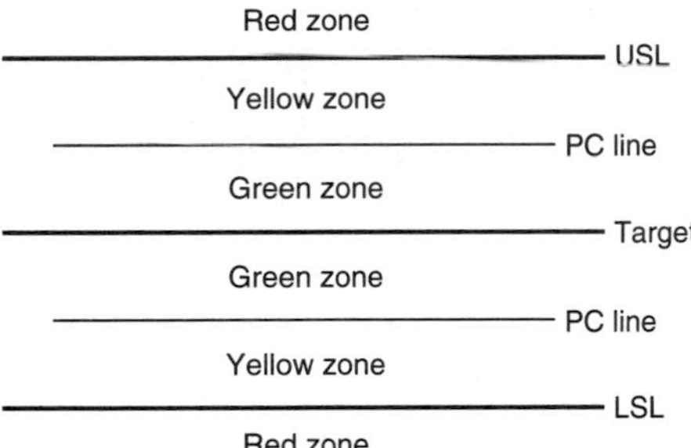

FIGURE 13.3 Green, yellow, and red zones in pre-control.

pre-control line is usually placed at the midpoint between the target and the maximum (or minimum) specification limit.

2. Initial process capability (also called *setup approval*) is established by taking five consecutive units from the process. Production is implemented full-force if all five measurements fall within the green zone. If one gets a single yellow among the five measurements, additional units are inspected and the count of greens is started over. If two consecutive yellows or one red are encountered, then adjustments are made to the process and the qualification procedure is restarted.
3. Following the setup approval, two consecutive units are sampled from the process at periodic intervals: (a) If both units fall in the green zone, production is continued. (b) Production also continues if one unit is in the green zone and the other is in one of the yellow zones. (c) If both units fall in the same yellow zone, the process is stopped and adjustments are made. Deviations from the target are commonly used to adjust the process through feedback control. After the adjustment one needs to confirm its success by checking that the next five items fall into the green zone. (d) If the consecutive yellows are on opposite sides of the target, then it is likely that the variability has increased. The process is stopped; causes for the extra variability need to be identified and their occurrence must be prevented in the future. This usually involves more than just a simple feedback adjustment as the cause of the extra variation must be found. (e) If one unit falls in the red zone, production is stopped immediately and the process is investigated.

   After stopping the process (as in 3c, d, and e) one must find the cause of the problem and take action. Afterward rule 2 (setup approval) must be applied; five consecutive units must be in the green zone before production can resume.
4. The frequency of sampling is set so that the average number of sample pairs between stoppages (that is, between reds or two pairs of yellows) is 6. For example, if a stoppage occurs at 9 a.m., and the process is corrected and restarted soon thereafter, and this is followed by another stoppage at

12 noon, then the frequency of sampling should be 3/6 = 0.5 hour. That is, samples of size 2 should be taken in half-hour increments. If one wants higher protection against continuing a process that should be stopped, then the frequency of sampling can be increased so that the average number of sample pairs between stoppages is a higher number, such as 10, 12, or 24.

13.4.2 Example

Bhote (1988, p. 228) describes an example of a pre-control chart used in controlling the thickness of chrome and gold deposits on glass in a sputtering machine. Samples of two units each are taken and the thickness of chrome and gold deposits is recorded. The data is given in Table 13.1 (page 381). For chrome the target thickness is 9 units, and the specification limits are 6 and 12, respectively. Hence the PC lines on the pre-control chart in Figure 13.4a (page 382) are 7.5 and 10.5. For gold the target thickness is 32, and the specification limits are 23 and 41. Hence the PC lines of the pre-control chart in Figure 13.4b are 27.5 and 36.5.

Pre-control does not signal any problems with the capability of the thickness of gold deposits. However, problems are signaled for chrome deposits. On April 4 we observe two consecutive yellows on the same side of the target. The first sample on April 5 leads to two consecutive yellows on opposite sides; in the second sample one of the observations is in the red zone. This indicates that the capability of the process has become unacceptable. Something must have happened to the process at that time. One must investigate the process and find the reasons for its behavior. We can only speculate with regard to the reasons, as Bhote's discussion does not reveal whether and how the process was adjusted.

13.4.3 An Evaluation of Pre-Control

Motorola, a recipient of the Malcolm Baldrige Quality Award, reportedly makes widespread use of pre-control. Although we know of no surveys that document the extent to which pre-control is used, it is claimed that this approach is fairly common in industry, although control charts remain the dominant tool. Pre-control has several attractive features, but also has some drawbacks. A detailed evaluation of pre-control is given in Ledolter and Swersey (1997); the following discussion summarizes the findings that are reported in this paper.

The objectives of pre-control and control charts differ. Pre-control is an algorithm for controlling a process on its *tolerances* (without explicit consideration of stability), while control charts monitor the *stability* of the process over time (without specifically looking at its capability).

Pre-control was developed originally with machining operations in mind. There an operator is faced with the problem of first setting up the machine, and then deciding whether the setup has been properly done and whether the machine is ready for full production. In many machining operations, each piece takes

TABLE 13.1 Thickness of Chrome (Cr) and Gold (Au) Deposits for 28 Subgroups of Size Two

	Sample 1		Sample 2		
	Cr	Au	Cr	Au	
March 20	11.2	35.0	8.6	30.5	
March 21	9.1	32.5	9.6	31.5	
March 21	9.6	33.0	7.6	33.0	
March 21	9.6	34.0	9.6	32.0	
March 22	8.6	36.5	9.6	31.0	
March 22	8.1	34.5	9.6	33.5	
March 22	6.6	32.0	10.2	34.0	
March 23	7.1	31.0	10.2	32.0	
March 27	9.6	34.0	10.2	31.5	
March 28	10.2	33.0	10.2	32.0	
March 29	10.2	33.0	9.6	34.0	
April 2	10.2	33.5	11.2	33.0	
April 3	9.6	32.0	10.2	30.0	
April 4	10.2	33.0	9.6	33.5	
April 4	10.7	33.5	11.2	35.0	2 yellows on same side (Cr)
April 4	7.6	30.5	8.6	25.4	
April 5	10.5	34.0	6.5	34.5	2 yellows on opposite sides (Cr)
April 5	12.2	30.5	10.2	32.0	one red (Cr)
April 6	7.6	33.5	9.6	35.0	
April 6	10.2	32.0	6.6	33.0	
April 9	10.2	35.0	10.2	34.0	
April 9	10.2	34.5	10.2	33.0	
April 9	10.2	32.5	9.1	33.0	
April 9	10.2	34.0	9.1	32.0	
April 10	9.6	34.0	9.1	32.0	
April 10	10.2	32.0	8.6	30.5	
April 11	9.1	32.5	11.2	34.5	
April 11	7.6	33.0	9.6	33.0	

Specification limits for chrome are 6 and 12; specification limits for gold are 25 and 41.

a considerable amount of time to produce and lot sizes are relatively small. Furthermore, it is usually difficult, if not impossible, to maintain statistical control: Tools wear, machine components and fixtures heat up and cool down, and so forth. The operator has the capability to make continuous adjustments with the aim of producing parts that (1) meet specifications, and (2) exhibit as little variability as possible. The developers and proponents of pre-control would argue that in such

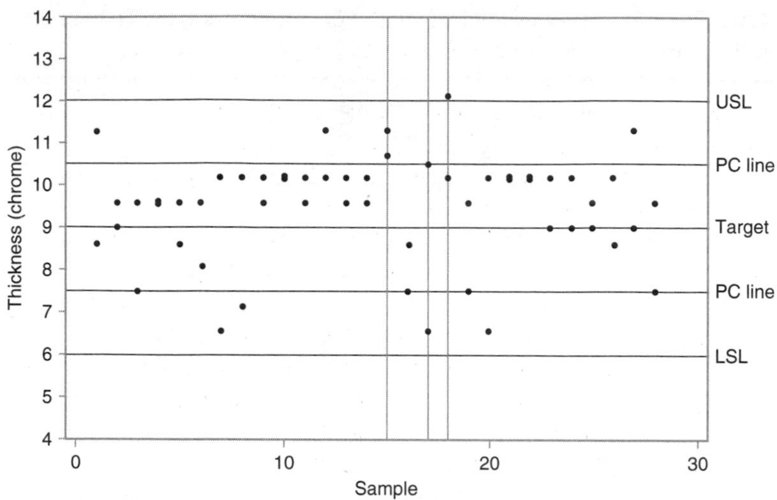

FIGURE 13.4a Pre-control chart: Thickness of chrome.

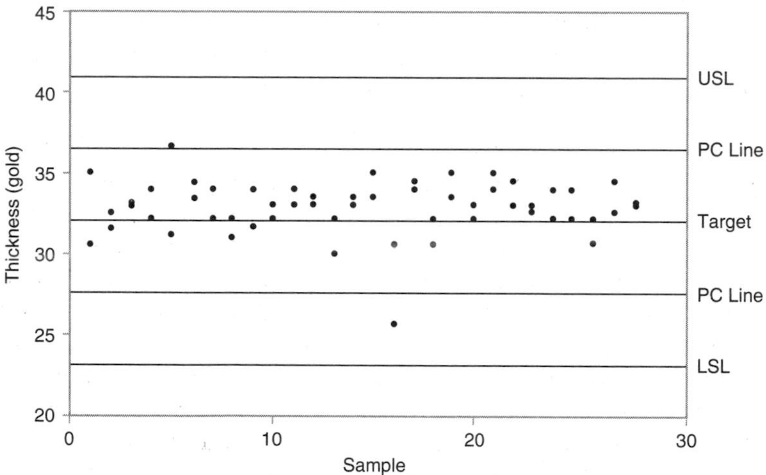

FIGURE 13.4b Pre-control chart: Thickness of gold.

an environment it should be accepted that statistical control is usually not possible, and that the focus should be directly on meeting specifications. Furthermore, in many machining situations it is just not feasible to produce data for 20 or 25 subgroups, which is the common standard for constructing control charts.

Of course, making continuous adjustments requires that the user actually knows *how* to adjust the process. Pre-control is typically well-suited for machining operations where one can devise simple feedback algorithms that bring the process back to its target. For example, the bore size of a metal cutting operation may drift with tool wear, implying that the bore of the part becomes over- (or under-) sized. In either case it becomes necessary to offset the tool in the opposite direction of the observed change with such a magnitude that the dimensions of the parts are restored to acceptable limits. Operators with considerable experience usually know how to make such feedback adjustments. Also, there are several statistical approaches that allow one to find the optimal feedback strategy.

Control charts, on the other hand, are devised as a means for identifying and eliminating assignable causes of variation. A process which is in control is operating at "its best." Capability, or whether "best is good enough," is another question. If a process is not sufficiently capable, then it must be improved by reducing the inherent variability (that is, the common-cause variability).

Pre-control is not concerned with whether the process is in control, but only whether it is meeting specifications. If the process is very capable, pre-control will not intervene. But, what if process capability is poor, but the process is in control? Here pre-control will stop the process more often than the control charts. But no assignable causes will be found. If adjustments are made, such adjustments will, most likely, represent "tampering," that is, adjusting a process when no change is needed or adjusting incorrectly. The process variability will increase as a consequence of tampering. Proponents of pre-control imply that once it is determined that a process is not capable, it is a relatively easy matter to improve it. But this is not always the case.

In statistical process control one usually insists that specification limits are *not* drawn on control charts. One reason is that x-bar control charts display the behavior of averages, while the specification limits are for individual observations. The variability of averages is automatically smaller than the variability of individual observations, and placing specification limits for individual observations on a control chart for successive averages would be misleading. Just because of averaging, subgroup averages would usually be well within the specification limits.

However, what if individual observations are plotted? Is there some good reason to add specification limits? We believe that this practice has a certain value, as such displays can draw attention to emerging process capability problems. If many processes are followed, such a practice helps us decide which of the processes need to be worked on first. While we believe that specification limits on such individual observations charts have value, we are also aware of a possible danger. A finding that the observations are well within the specification limits may inhibit continual process improvement and variability reduction of the process, which is the ultimate goal of process control.

Despite differences, pre-control and control charts have important common features. Both force the operator to take measurements on the process at periodic intervals and display them on a chart. Quite often it is not the limits (or the zones) on these charts that are important, but the fact that the information is plotted for everyone to see. Such charts tell us about sudden shifts, slow trends, cycles, and the presence of overcompensation. Graphs are important!

13.4.4 Summary

In general, pre-control is not an adequate substitute for control charts. Control charts are highly useful for identifying and removing assignable (special) causes of variation, and for distinguishing between special and common causes. This is particularly important in the early stages of process control and improvement when a given process may have low capability. In contrast, pre-control is poorly suited for processes with low capability where it is likely to lead to unnecessary tampering and consequently an increase in process variability. The pre-control rules will signal very quickly, but if the process is in control searches for assignable causes will be fruitless, and process adjustments are likely to increase the variability and make matters worse. Although pre-control may shut down processes of low capability, because it cannot distinguish between special and common causes it will provide no or little guidance for process improvement.

Pre-control was originally developed for use with machining operations, and it is in this context that it has most value. In situations such as machining, where product characteristics are easily monitored and feedback adjustments are readily available, pre-control is useful for monitoring process capability over time. The procedure will not flag unstable processes (that is, processes out of statistical control), as long as they remain capable. The approach has the virtue of drawing management attention only to priority problems.

As companies introduce statistical process control, it is not unusual for control charts to proliferate. In situations for which processes are highly capable, pre-control offers a useful alternative.

13.5 EXERCISES

13.1 Consider the carton dimensions in Table 12.1. Assume that the target for our process is 25 and that the lower and upper specification limits are given by 24 and 26, respectively.

(a) Use the 100 measurements in Table 12.1. Calculate the sample mean and the sample standard deviation from these 100 observations and use them as estimates of μ and σ. Estimate the capability coefficients C_p, C_{pk}, C_{pm}, CR, and Target-Z. Interpret your findings.

(b) Use the control chart method to estimate the process variability σ, and repeat part (a).

(c) Comment on any differences between (a) and (b). Discuss the advantages and disadvantages of these two approaches.

13.2 Use the first 20 subgroups of the data in Table 12.2 (weight of bread loaves). Repeat Exercise 13.1 with these $(20)(5) = 100$ measurements. Assume that the target is 100 decagrams, and the lower and upper specification limits are 95 and 105, respectively.

13.3 The target value for the pH content of a certain shampoo is 6.15. The lower specification limit is LSL $= 5.85$ and the upper specification limit is UCL $= 6.45$. A sample of 298 bottles was taken and the pH value for each bottle was determined. It was found that the minimum value was 5.66, the maximum 6.91, the sample average 6.212, and the sample standard deviation 0.123. In addition, it was found that the distribution of pH was well approximated by a normal distribution.

(a) Calculate and interpret C_p and C_{pk}. Are you satisfied with the capability of your process? What could you do to increase the capability? Is there a problem with not being on target, or is there a problem with excessive variability?

(b) Assuming that the distribution is normal, obtain an estimate of the probability of getting an observation (i) above the upper specification limit, (ii) below the lower specification limit, (iii) outside the specification limits.

13.4 A sample ($n = 150$) from another production run of shampoo resulted in a minimum pH value of 5.89, a maximum of 7.12, an average of 6.44, and a standard deviation of 0.15. Repeat Exercise 13.3.

13.5 Use the measurements in Table 12.1. Assume that the target for our process is 25 and that the lower and upper specification limits are 24 and 26, respectively. For purposes of this exercise take only the first two observations in each subsample. Construct a pre-control chart using such samples of size two. Interpret your findings. Explain the differences between your pre-control chart and the x-bar chart in Chapter 12.

13.6 The plant manager has set up a pre-control chart for the fill weight of certain tubes. The specifications on the fill weight are a target of 2.75 ounces, with specification limits 2.70 and 2.80. Every 30 minutes he takes a sample of size 2 and enters the measurements on a pre-control chart. Since this chart fails to give any warning signals, he proclaims that the process is perfectly in control. Discuss this assertion.

13.7 Read and comment on the paper by P.R. Tadikamalla, "The Confusion Over Six-Sigma Quality," in *Quality Progress*, Vol. 27, November 1994, pp. 83–85. The paper includes a table that relates the proportion of defectives to the C_p capability index and the difference of the process mean from the target. Check some of the entries in this table. In particular, calculate the proportion of defectives with:

(a) $C_p = 2$ and a process mean that is 1.5 standard deviations off-target

(b) $C_p = 1.5$ and a process mean that is 0.5 standard deviation off-target

(c) $C_p = 1.5$ and a process mean that is 1.0 standard deviation off-target

Hint: $C_p = 2$ implies that the specification limits are six standard deviations from the target. Calculate $1 - P[\mathrm{T}_g - 6\sigma < X < \mathrm{T}_g + 6\sigma]$, where X follows a normal distribution with mean $\mathrm{T}_g + (1.5)\sigma$ and standard deviation σ. For part (b), calculate $1 - P[\mathrm{T}_g - (4.5)\sigma < X < \mathrm{T}_g + (4.5)\sigma]$, where X follows a normal distribution with mean $\mathrm{T}_g + (0.5)\sigma$ and standard deviation σ.

13.8 Discuss why capability indexes may not be meaningful with nonnormal distributions. For example, assume that the process variability can be described by a uniform distribution over -1 and $+1$. One can show that the mean of this distribution is given by 0, and the standard deviation is given by 0.577; refer to Section 8.7. Assume that the specification limits are given by $-a$ and $+a$. Consider several values of a (for example, vary a from $a = 0.5$, which means that the specification limits are considerably narrower than the extent of the process variability; $a = 1, a = 1.5, a = 2$, etc.). Calculate, for each a, (i) the C_p capability index and (ii) the probability that the specification limits are exceeded. Interpret your findings. You will find that for moderate-sized $a > 1$ the capability index is rather low, despite the fact that there is no chance that the specifications are exceeded. Thus, the C_p looks not very good, despite the fact that the probability of exceeding the specifications is zero.

Next, consider a symmetric distribution that has very heavy tails. For such distributions, the opposite result is true. That is, the capability index may look "good," whereas the probability of exceeding the specifications is larger than that implied by the normal distribution.

Read the papers by B.H. Gunter, "The Use and Abuse of C_{pk}: Parts 1–4," in *Quality Progress*, January 1989, pp. 72–73; March 1989, pp. 108–109; May 1989, pp. 79–80; July 1989, pp. 86–87; and "The Use and Abuse of C_{pk} Revisited," January 1991, pp. 90–94.

13.9 The October 1992 issue of the *Journal of Quality Technology* is devoted to the topic of process capability analysis. Read and discuss the basic ideas in the introductory article on "Recent Developments in Process Analysis," by R.N. Rodriguez (pp. 176–187), and the four papers that follow his article.

One important issue with capability indexes has to do with the sampling variability of capability coefficients. The papers by V.E. Kane, "Process Capability Indices," *Journal of Quality Technology*, 1986, pp. 41–52; R.H. Kushler and P. Hurley, "Confidence Bounds for Capability Indices," *Journal of Quality Technology*, 1992, pp. 188–195; and L.A. Franklin and G.S. Wasserman, "Bootstrap Lower Confidence Limits for Capability Indices," *Journal of Quality Technology*, 1992, pp. 196–210, are particularly relevant.

13.10 Read and discuss the following papers:

P. McCoy, "Using Performance Indexes to Monitor Production Processes," *Quality Progress*, February 1991.

L.J. Chan, S.W. Cheng, and F.A. Spiring, "A New Measure of Process Capability: C_{pm}," *Journal of Quality Technology*, 1986, pp. 41–52.

F.A. Spiring, "The C_{pm} Index," *Quality Progress*, February 1991.

13.11 Show the following relationship between C_{pk} and C_p:

$$C_{pk} = (1 - k)C_p,$$

where

$$k = 2|\mathrm{T}_g - \mu|/(\mathrm{USL} - \mathrm{LSL}),$$

$\mathrm{T}_g = \frac{\mathrm{USL}+\mathrm{LSL}}{2}$ is the specified target, and LSL and USL are the specification limits.

13.12 The target value for one of the ingredients of a certain liquid detergent is 50 grams/gallon. The specification limits are 46 and 54 grams/gallon. Individual observations and moving-range charts on the last 20 batches show that the process is in statistical control. The average concentration of these 20 batches is 49.8 grams/gallon, and the average of the moving ranges is 0.8 gram/gallon. Calculate and interpret the appropriate capability indexes.

Hint: Use the fact that $\overline{\mathrm{MR}}/d_2 = \overline{\mathrm{MR}}/1.128$ is an estimate of the process standard deviation σ.

13.13 The requirements on the dimensions of steel flats specify a target of 100 mm (millimeters), with lower and upper specification limits of 97 mm and 103 mm, respectively. The stability of the process is well-established and is being monitored with x-bar and R-charts that use rational subgroups of size $n = 5$. It turns out that the process mean is 0.2 mm below the target; the lower and upper control limits on the x-bar chart are given by 98.8 and 100.8. Calculate and interpret the C_p, the C_{pk}, and the C_{pm} capability indexes.

Hint: Use the fact that $(A_2\bar{R})$ in the control limits of the x-bar chart is an estimate of $3(\sigma/\sqrt{n})$. Use this to solve for σ.

13.14 (Continuation of Exercise 12.20 in Chapter 12) The requirements for this particular on-line system call for a response time of 1.5 seconds or better. Does the process meet this requirement?

13.6 REFERENCES

Bhote, Keki R. *Strategic Supply Management*. New York: American Management Association, 1988.

Chan, L. J., S. W. Cheng, and F. A. Spiring. "A New Measure of Process Capability: C_{pm}," *Journal of Quality Technology*, Vol. 18, 1986, 41–52.

Franklin, L. A., and G. S. Wasserman. "Bootstrap Lower Confidence Limits for Capability Indices," *Journal of Quality Technology*, Vol. 24, 1992, 196–210.

Gunter, B. H. "The Use and Abuse of C_{pk}: Parts 1–4," *Quality Progress*, January 1989, 72–73; March 1989, 108–109; May 1989, 79–80; July 1989, 86–87; "The Use and Abuse of C_{pk} Revisited," January 1991, 90–94.

Juran, J. M., and F. M. Gryna. *Quality Control Handbook* (4th edition). New York: McGraw Hill, 1988 (Section 24 on pre-control).

Kane, V. E. "Process Capability Indices," *Journal of Quality Technology*, Vol. 18, 1986, 41–52.

Kushler, R. H., and P. Hurley. "Confidence Bounds for Capability Indices," *Journal of Quality Technology*, Vol. 24, 1992, 188–195.

Ledolter, J., and A. Swersey. "An Evaluation of Pre-Control," *Journal of Quality Technology*, Vol. 29, 1997, 163–171.

Mackertich, N. A. "Precontrol versus Control Charting: A Critical Comparison" (with discussion by Dorian Shainin), *Quality Engineering*, Vol. 2, 1990, 253–268.

McCoy, P. "Using Performance Indexes to Monitor Production Processes," *Quality Progress*, February 1991, Vol. 24.

Rodriguez, R. N. "Recent Developments in Process Analysis," *Journal of Quality Technology*, Vol. 24, October 1992, 176–187.

Shainin, D. "Better Than Good Old Xbar and R Charts Asked by Vendees," *ASQC Quality Congress Transactions*, Chicago, 1984, pp. 302–307.

Shainin, D., and P. Shainin. "Pre-Control versus Xbar & R Charting: Continuous or Immediate Quality Improvement?" *Quality Engineering*, Vol. 1, 1989, 419–429.

Spiring, F. A. "The C_{pm} Index," *Quality Progress*, February 1991, Vol. 24.

Tadikamalla, P. R. "The Confusion Over Six-Sigma Quality," *Quality Progress*, Vol. 27, November 1994, 83–85.

PROJECTS FOR SECTION 3

PROJECT 9

The following data were taken from Levine, David, Ramsey, Patricia, P., and Berenson, Mark L., *Business Statistics for Quality and Productivity.* Englewood Cliffs, NJ: Prentice Hall, 1995, p. 749.

Companies involved in the processing of milk products must be concerned about the freshness and safety of their products. Bacteria growth can shorten the shelf life and, in extreme cases, can result in serious health hazards. A common test of quality in the dairy industry is a standard plate bacteria count. A small amount of milk is plated on a specified culture medium and bacteria growth is monitored over a given period of time. In this particular case study the quality of the milk was measured by the number of colonies of bacteria present per millimeter of processed whole milk after holding the sample for two days under refrigeration at 45 degrees Fahrenheit. The results for samples from 36 consecutive days are given below. The measurements were obtained by taking a single one-gallon container of milk from all those packaged that day, and by plating a small amount of milk from the selected container.

Bacteria plate counts for milk samples from 36 consecutive days: Colonies/ml of whole milk (read across)

290	260	270	230	300	310	300	280	230	300
260	300	270	230	290	310	260	270	240	310
270	260	270	310	280	260	300	290	270	270
250	240	280	260	250	280				

Questions

1. Is the process in a state of statistical control? Why or why not?

   Hint: You can use the c-chart to assess statistical control. The measurement, colonies/ml, is like the numbers of failures per unit, and in such a situation the use of a c-chart is recommended.

2. What can you say about the distribution of your measurements?
3. What questions should you ask about the adopted sampling procedure? Would it be better to sample more than one container per day? What

information would you need to make a decision on how many containers to sample? Discuss.

4. The plant manager thought that the daily plate counts were unacceptably high. She believed that an increased emphasis on sanitation could reduce those levels and started a rigorous training program for all employees. After completion of the training, she collected another set of 36 daily measurements. The new data is given below:

Bacteria plate counts for milk samples from 36 consecutive days after new training methods were instituted: Colonies/ml of whole milk (read across):

245	210	215	175	255	265	240	225	185	255
205	260	220	190	230	260	210	200	300	265
215	210	220	255	235	240	200	235	210	195
220	190	240	230	210	200				

Check whether the new process is in statistical control.

5. How successful was the new training program in reducing the plate counts? Compare the plate counts under the old and the new process. Make your comparison in terms of graphs. Make your comparisons by carrying out a statistical test; assess whether or not the observed difference in the average plate counts (before and after) is statistically significant.

6. Write a brief report that summarizes your findings.

PROJECT 10

The following data were taken from Wheeler, Donald J., *Advanced Topics in Statistical Process Control: The Power of Shewhart Charts*, Knoxville, TN: SPC Press, 1995, p. 144.

An injection molding process is used to make a particular socket; four pieces are made at the same time. One mold, with four cavities for the four pieces, one press, and one operator are involved. The recorded data consists of the effective thickness of the socket, measured in hundredths of a millimeter. A special gauge had to be designed to measure the thickness. Four times a day the supervisor went to the press and gathered up the parts that were produced by five consecutive cycles of the press. Since each cycle produces four parts (one from each cavity), a total of 20 parts is measured every two hours. The supervisor kept track of the cycle and the cavity from which each part came.

Below we have listed the results (thickness in excess of 12.75 millimeters, recorded in hundredths of a millimeter) for five consecutive days. Twenty time periods are involved, and at each of these periods 20 measurements (four cavities and five cycles) are recorded. This leads to a total of 400 measurements:

Time 1:	A	B	C	D	E
	Cycle of press				
Cavity I	15	16	17	16	18
Cavity II	10	13	11	10	10
Cavity III	7	8	10	7	10
Cavity IV	8	9	10	10	10

Time 2:	A	B	C	D	E
	Cycle of press				
Cavity I	13	18	15	15	15
Cavity II	9	10	11	8	9
Cavity III	7	11	10	10	9
Cavity IV	10	13	13	10	9

Time 3:	A	B	C	D	E
	Cycle of press				
Cavity I	14	14	18	14	14
Cavity II	9	10	10	12	9
Cavity III	8	10	9	10	8
Cavity IV	8	9	10	8	9

Time 4:	A	B	C	D	E
	Cycle of press				
Cavity I	14	15	15	15	14
Cavity II	10	10	11	11	10
Cavity III	7	9	12	10	10
Cavity IV	11	12	11	10	13

Time 5:	A	B	C	D	E
	Cycle of press				
Cavity I	12	13	13	12	13
Cavity II	8	7	8	7	7
Cavity III	5	6	8	5	4
Cavity IV	4	4	5	3	4

Time 6:	A	B	C	D	E
	Cycle of press				
Cavity I	14	15	17	14	13
Cavity II	7	11	12	8	6
Cavity III	6	4	7	6	5
Cavity IV	4	7	6	5	4

Time 7:	A	B	C	D	E
	Cycle of press				
Cavity I	12	12	13	13	11
Cavity II	6	6	6	6	7
Cavity III	4	5	4	4	6
Cavity IV	4	4	5	4	5

Time 8:	A	B	C	D	E
	Cycle of press				
Cavity I	13	15	16	14	13
Cavity II	9	8	7	7	8
Cavity III	10	8	6	7	5
Cavity IV	6	6	8	6	5

Time 9:	A	B	C	D	E
	Cycle of press				
Cavity I	15	16	17	14	13
Cavity II	11	13	11	13	8
Cavity III	9	9	6	8	10
Cavity IV	9	10	11	9	5

Time 10:	A	B	C	D	E
	Cycle of press				
Cavity I	13	13	14	13	13
Cavity II	7	8	7	6	7
Cavity III	4	5	6	5	5
Cavity IV	5	5	6	6	5

	Cycle of press				
Time 11:	**A**	**B**	**C**	**D**	**E**
Cavity I	13	16	13	16	18
Cavity II	10	8	10	10	11
Cavity III	8	7	8	7	11
Cavity IV	11	10	9	10	10

	Cycle of press				
Time 12:	**A**	**B**	**C**	**D**	**E**
Cavity I	16	18	18	16	13
Cavity II	13	8	8	10	7
Cavity III	13	10	10	6	7
Cavity IV	9	6	8	7	7

	Cycle of press				
Time 13:	**A**	**B**	**C**	**D**	**E**
Cavity I	13	18	18	14	13
Cavity II	11	10	9	10	10
Cavity III	14	9	10	9	7
Cavity IV	9	12	11	11	6

	Cycle of press				
Time 14:	**A**	**B**	**C**	**D**	**E**
Cavity I	13	13	14	14	14
Cavity II	7	8	9	8	8
Cavity III	6	6	7	6	6
Cavity IV	6	7	6	6	6

	Cycle of press				
Time 15:	**A**	**B**	**C**	**D**	**E**
Cavity I	13	15	18	15	14
Cavity II	7	12	10	10	7
Cavity III	7	8	12	12	6
Cavity IV	11	12	12	12	6

	Cycle of press				
Time 16:	**A**	**B**	**C**	**D**	**E**
Cavity I	15	14	15	14	12
Cavity II	6	7	8	6	10
Cavity III	7	10	8	6	6
Cavity IV	6	8	7	9	7

	Cycle of press				
Time 17:	**A**	**B**	**C**	**D**	**E**
Cavity I	14	16	14	13	14
Cavity II	9	10	13	7	6
Cavity III	6	5	5	7	5
Cavity IV	7	7	4	7	5

	Cycle of press				
Time 18:	**A**	**B**	**C**	**D**	**E**
Cavity I	12	15	15	15	14
Cavity II	9	7	8	10	9
Cavity III	5	7	6	6	10
Cavity IV	6	8	7	12	12

	Cycle of press				
Time 19:	**A**	**B**	**C**	**D**	**E**
Cavity I	17	15	18	18	17
Cavity II	10	10	12	12	6
Cavity III	5	9	7	8	7
Cavity IV	7	7	5	12	8

	Cycle of press				
Time 20:	**A**	**B**	**C**	**D**	**E**
Cavity I	18	16	17	14	13
Cavity II	8	10	11	10	7
Cavity III	7	7	7	10	5
Cavity IV	10	7	9	8	8

Check whether the injection molding process is stable over time. A quick look at the data in the above table shows that the magnitude of the measurements depends very much on the cavity from which the part originates; measurements on units from the first cavity are consistently higher. For this reason it can be expected that stratification (that is, separate control charts, one for each of the four cavities) will increase the likelihood of detecting changes over time.

Questions

1. Construct x-bar and R-charts, separately for each of the four cavities. Use the five press cycles as the rational subgroups; this generates samples of size $n = 5$ for each of the 20 sampled hours. The cycle-to-cycle differences make up the within-sample variability, while the hour-to-hour differences become the between-sample variability. This particular rational subgroup selection maximizes the opportunity to detect hour-to-hour differences.

Put the four x-bar charts on a single graph. Use the same scale on all four charts as this will reveal the fact that the magnitudes of the measurements vary with cavity. Check that measurements for items pulled from cavity I are consistently higher than all others.

Discuss whether the levels of the process are stable over time (hour). (You will notice instability in the levels over time.)

Discuss whether the variability of the process is stable over time. (You will notice that the process is in statistical control as far as its variability is concerned.)

You will notice that the magnitudes of the measurements vary with cavity. What about the variability? Do you see differences in variability among the four cavities?

2. There are other ways of forming rational subgroups. For example, you could use an arrangement where the columns in the above table represent the subgroups. This leads to $(20)(5) = 100$ samples of size $n = 4$. Under this arrangement, the variability within the subgroups comes from the cavity-to-cavity differences; the between-subgroup variability originates from the hour-to-hour and the cycle-to-cycle differences.

Construct the x-bar chart and the R-chart, using this particular arrangement for the rational subgroups. (There are considerable size differences among the four cavities from the same mold. The within-subgroup variability is huge, and hence the control limits on the x-bar chart are quite wide; all subgroup averages fall well within the control limits.)

For this choice of rational subgroups the control charts try to answer the following questions:

Are the cavity-to-cavity differences (that is, the within-subgroup variability) consistent over time? (They clearly are! You can see this from the R-chart.)

Are there detectable differences from one hour to the next, and are there detectable differences from one cycle to the next? The plotted averages on the x-bar chart fall within the limits, and from this analysis alone one would conclude that the process is stable with respect to different cycles and hours. However, note that this particular analysis is much less sensitive than the one you have done in Question 1; the reason is that it puts the large, and *explainable* cavity-to-cavity differences into the natural variability of the process.

3. Still another way to look at this data is to use the rows in the above table as the rational subgroups. The rows represent the five consecutive cycles, and hence the within-subgroup variation arises because of cycle-to-cycle differences. In this case we end up with $(20)(4) = 80$ samples of size 5, representing the results from cavity I, cavity II, cavity III, cavity IV at the first hour, cavity I, cavity II, ..., at the second hour, and so on.

Construct the x-bar and R-charts that correspond to this particular subgroup choice. Note that for a fixed hour there really is no natural time order among the cavity subsamples, as the observations on the four cavities are taken at the same time. Nevertheless, it is instructive to treat them as a time series as it allows us to recognize differences among the cavities.

Here the within-subgroup variability consists of the cycle-to-cycle differences, while the between-subgroup variability is made up by the cavity-to-cavity and hour-to-hour differences. These charts address the following questions:

Are there detectable differences from one cavity to the next? (Yes, there are clear differences. The within-subgroup variability is very small as for a given cavity and fixed hour the measurements from consecutive cycles are very similar. Hence the control limts on the x-bar chart are very tight. Since measurements on the four cavities are quite different, the averages for different cavities will exceed these limits. Also, note the very pronounced "seasonal" pattern; the averages representing the four cavities repeat themselves in groups of four. The message from this chart is that the measurements for the four different cavities are clearly different.)

The limits on the x-bar chart are tight, and most of the subgroup averages are outside the control limits. Hence this chart is not very useful for assessing the stability of the process with respect to time (hour). This choice for the natural subgroups is not very useful if you want to assess whether the process is stable over time (hour).

The R-chart assesses whether the within-variability (that is, the cycle-to-cycle differences) is stable with respect to cavity and time. What is your conclusion?

4. Discuss which of the three subgroup arrangements in Questions 1–3 is the more sensitive. Which one would you use if your objective is to assess stability with respect to time (hour)?

5. Write a short report discussing the importance of the correct selection of rational subgroups.

PROJECT 11

Pork producers keep detailed records on their operations. HOGLOT, the Iowa-based company that we examine in this case study, is concerned about their breeding operation. In large-scale breeding operations, the female pigs (sows) of the breeding herd are artificially inseminated at carefully monitored times. For our particular breeder about 200 inseminations, called "services," are carried out each week. Weekly records on the breeding herd are kept, including the number of pigs weaned per mated female per year, the number of pigs born alive per litter, the preweaning mortality, the number of litters per mated female per year, and the farrowing rate. Weekly data for the period from July 1995 through June 1996 is listed below:

Week	Var1	Var2	Var3	Var4	Var5	Var6	Var7
7/1/95	20.0	9.8	10.2	2.64	62.5	3	26
7/8/95	20.9	9.1	8.2	2.51	70.0	0	121
7/15/95	20.5	9.4	9.4	2.41	68.0	0	80
7/22/95	19.3	8.8	9.0	2.33	69.8	0	88
7/29/95	17.2	8.3	12.5	2.26	66.5	0	84
8/5/95	14.7	9.3	14.6	2.18	67.5	0	114
8/12/95	17.4	9.4	15.1	2.12	72.2	0	119
8/19/95	17.8	10.1	14.6	2.10	77.0	0	71
8/26/95	18.6	9.6	9.2	2.05	79.4	0	105
9/2/95	18.8	9.4	9.3	2.06	81.0	9	49
9/9/95	17.5	9.4	7.7	2.02	73.0	10	21
9/16/95	17.8	8.7	12.0	2.06	78.1	72	5
9/23/95	19.2	9.1	1.4	2.06	78.2	45	5
9/30/95	17.9	9.0	4.8	2.13	81.0	41	0
10/7/95	17.9	9.4	6.2	2.16	79.8	48	9
10/14/95	16.7	8.9	13.9	2.13	84.7	75	2
10/21/95	18.0	9.3	10.3	2.15	72.7	118	0
10/28/95	18.6	9.6	6.3	2.20	63.5	196	0
11/4/95	19.1	10.0	5.1	2.20	69.9	201	0
11/11/95	18.7	9.5	9.1	2.17	58.6	241	0
11/18/95	19.4	8.7	9.7	2.20	58.0	203	0
11/25/95	19.6	9.3	9.7	2.21	48.4	226	0
12/2/95	19.1	9.6	3.2	2.34	47.0	234	0
12/9/95	19.6	8.6	11.6	2.40	55.5	336	0
12/16/95	19.8	9.3	12.9	2.49	49.4	261	0
12/23/95	20.8	9.1	9.0	2.48	62.2	280	0
12/30/95	20.7	9.3	10.8	2.47	73.6	301	0
1/6/96	20.1	9.5	7.3	2.47	80.2	309	0
1/13/96	21.6	9.3	11.0	2.52	74.8	270	0

(*continues*)

(continued)

Week	Var1	Var2	Var3	Var4	Var5	Var6	Var7
1/20/96	22.8	9.9	3.3	2.49	73.5	346	0
1/27/96	20.3	9.1	9.6	2.47	66.3	466	0
2/3/96	20.7	9.0	11.3	2.40	70.4	323	0
2/10/96	20.5	9.3	10.4	2.37	74.8	255	0
2/17/96	20.6	9.1	3.3	2.36	69.8	215	0
2/24/96	20.8	9.5	5.2	2.36	69.4	247	0
3/2/96	20.1	9.0	10.8	2.40	61.0	330	0
3/9/96	20.2	9.4	10.0	2.40	74.5	171	0
3/16/96	19.5	9.4	9.8	2.40	75.8	209	0
3/23/96	20.8	9.7	6.1	2.37	77.1	199	0
3/30/96	20.1	9.9	8.3	2.36	78.1	160	0
4/6/96	21.3	9.6	8.3	2.39	82.1	130	4
4/13/96	21.4	9.5	12.6	2.41	80.4	107	0
4/20/96	21.8	9.3	8.4	2.42	82.2	96	0
4/27/96	19.6	9.0	11.3	2.45	77.7	125	0
5/4/96	20.3	9.7	12.1	2.46	73.1	61	1
5/11/96	19.1	9.2	9.8	2.47	77.6	74	17
5/18/96	20.7	8.7	14.4	2.44	75.1	15	26
5/25/96	20.8	9.5	4.0	2.44	67.7	64	0
6/1/96	19.6	9.1	11.9	2.44	77.2	29	1
6/8/96	20.8	9.4	2.8	2.46	77.9	2	43
6/15/96	21.8	9.5	7.9	2.45	76.9	0	61
6/22/96	20.8	9.2	8.9	2.46	73.1	0	71

Var1: Number of pigs weaned per mated female per year
Var2: Number of pigs born alive per litter
Var3: Preweaning mortality (in percent)
Var4: Number of litters per mated female per year
Var5: Farrowing rate
Var6: Number of heating degree days
Var7: Number of cooling degree days

Questions

1. The manager of HOGLOT wants to describe and summarize the variability in his operation. In particular, he wants to know whether his processes are in statistical control.

   Use the appropriate control charts to check whether the processes are in statistical control. Use individual observations and moving range charts. Would an exponentially weighted moving average chart lead to different conclusions? Use dot diagrams or histograms to display the variability. Calculate the relevant summary statistics.

2. The manager in charge of the breeding operation believes that some of the herd characteristics are affected by the weather. His breeding barns are not air-conditioned in the summer and they are poorly heated during the winter. Hence he suspects that process characteristics such as the preweaning mortality may change with adverse weather conditions. The above table also includes information on weekly heating and cooling degree days for Des Moines, Iowa. Explore whether there are any relationships among the breeding herd characteristics and the weather variables.
3. You may find no (or at most, very weak) relationships. But, assume for the moment that there are strong relationships. Also suppose that you are not able or willing to control your operation for adverse meteorological variables as you decided that adding more efficient heaters and an airconditioning system is too expensive.

   How would the variability in the weather variables affect the control charts that you completed in Question 1? Can you think of ways of adjusting your control charts for the uncontrolled weather characteristics? For example, assume that an observation is outside the control limits. What is the logical next question that you would ask?

   You may want to delay your answer to this question until you have had a chance to study regression analysis in Chapter 17.

References for Projects to Section 3

Levine, D., P. P. Ramsey, and M. L. Berenson. *Business Statistics for Quality and Productivity*, Englewood Cliffs, NJ: Prentice Hall, 1995, p. 749.

Wheeler, Donald J. *Advanced Topics in Statistical Process Control: The Power of Shewhart Charts*, Knoxville: SPC Press, 1995, p. 144.

SECTION 4

IMPROVEMENT THROUGH DESIGNED EXPERIMENTS

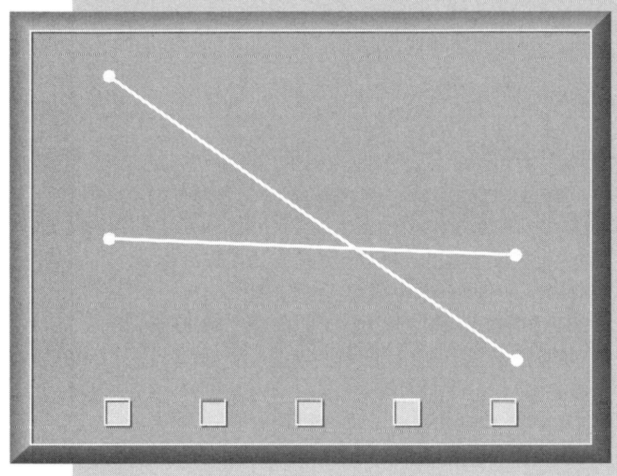

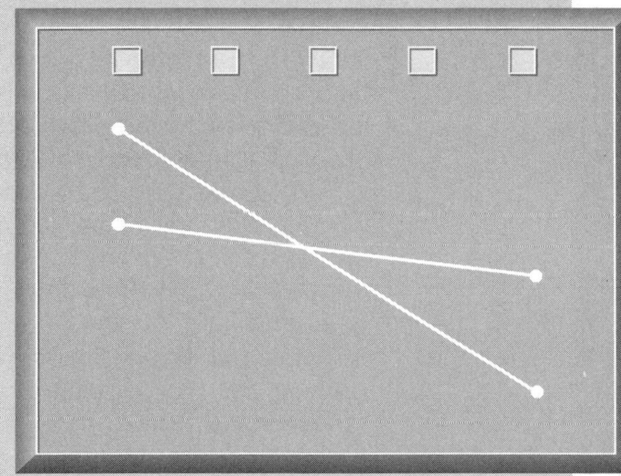

CHAPTER 14

PRINCIPLES OF EFFECTIVE EXPERIMENTAL DESIGN

14.1 INTRODUCTION

Advancement of knowledge is an iterative process. So is the improvement of quality. Several possible explanations and causes usually come to mind when one is faced with a certain quality problem. In the first few chapters of this book we outlined a general problem-solving strategy, and we studied several procedures that help us identify possible causes and explanations. Flow diagrams, cause-and-effect diagrams, and group-based techniques that tap the creativity of employees are important components of this strategy.

The next step in a problem-solving strategy is to collect data and to check which one, if any, of several competing hypotheses is supported by data. Now data usually doesn't just "happen." One must go out and collect it. How should this be done? It is important to understand how data can be collected in the best possible way.

In the previous chapters we discussed the analysis of data that comes from surveys, data that originates from acceptance sampling plans, and data that arises from process control and process capability studies. Control charts are important as they assist us in bringing processes under statistical control. They help us identify special effects and, by preventing these special effects from occurring in the future, processes become stable. There are important advantages to stability. The performance of a stable process is predictable, and a process that is in statistical control performs at its best possible level. This is not to say that this best possible level is always good enough. It may be that the stable process is not quite on target, and its common-cause variability may be too large. If the process at its very best is not good enough, then one needs to change (that is, improve) the process! This is where experimentation and the design of experiments come in. Designed experiments help us find ways of reducing the common-cause variability.

Stability is an important prerequisite for designed experiments to work. Without stability, the observed effects of planned changes could be very misleading as one wouldn't know for sure whether the observed effects are due to the planned changes or due to some other special effect that happened to occur at the same time.

In *comparative experiments* we change the settings of process factors and study how these changes influence our variable of interest. In terms of the information that can be gained from such experiments, there are good ways of changing factors around and there are bad ones. We must learn how to carry out these experiments in a way that maximizes the information that we get from the data. This and the next two chapters on the *statistical design of experiments* introduce you to this area. The present chapter discusses the general principles that are behind effective experimental designs. Chapter 15 explains how to carry out factorial and fractional factorial experiments and shows how to analyze the resulting information. Chapter 16 introduces you to Taguchi design ideas, which are useful for product and process improvement. At the end of Chapter 16 we provide an extensive list of references that you can use for further study.

We want answers to questions such as:

- Which material is better for a certain purpose: material A or material B?
- Several methods of performing an operation are suggested. Which one of the methods will give us the most satisfactory results?
- How can we improve the yield of a chemical process? Does the yield vary with the temperature of the process? Does it vary with the pressure? What happens if we change both the temperature and the pressure? How should we set the input factors such that the process yield is maximized?
- A long list of factors is suggested as conceivably having an effect on our variable of interest. Which factors are the most important ones? For example, which factors affect the hardness of the steel flats that are produced in our factory?
- How should we choose the input factors such that our production process is right on target and that the process variability around the target is as small as possible?

Before we can answer these questions, we must collect data. We have to collect the data according to a well-thought-out plan; we call this an *experimental plan*. There are good and bad experimental plans. Bad experimental plans will increase our cost of obtaining relevant data and, in the worst case, the obtained data may be totally irrelevant for answering the posed question.

R.A. Fisher, an eminent 20th-century British statistician, shaped the discipline of statistical design of experiments. He said (in *Statistical Methods for Research Workers*, 1925):

> *The results of a well-planned experiment are obvious from simple statistical (graphical) analyses.... However, the most sophisticated of all statistical methods cannot salvage a poorly designed experiment.... A complete overhaul of an experimental design often increases the precision of the results 10- to 12-fold for the same cost in time and labor.*

Much of the discussion in this and the next chapter was greatly influenced by the thoughts and writings of George Box, who has made pivotal contributions to the philosophy and the practice of the statistical design of experiments. The book by Box, Hunter, and Hunter, *Statistics for Experimenters* (1978), gives a wonderful introduction to the design of experiments and the analysis of the resulting information.

14.2 ACTIVE AND PASSIVE WAYS OF COLLECTING DATA

We can collect data through an *active* or a *passive* mode. A passive way of collecting information is to merely observe the process without actively intervening. The control charts in Chapter 12 are a good example of passive data collection. There, small samples of the production are taken at periodic time intervals, usually once an hour, or once during a shift, or once every ten minutes. For example, in an x-bar chart one plots successive subgroup averages in the form of a time-sequence plot. If a sample average exceeds the control limits or if there is a pattern in the graph, then one searches for explanations of this unusual event. Once the causes are found, one tries to prevent them from occurring in the future.

An active way to collect data is to intervene in the process by changing deliberately some of the factors that influence the process. For example, we may change the temperature and the pressure of a certain chemical reaction and observe the response of the process. Or, we may switch to a different supplier and observe whether the rate of defectives changes. Or, we may try five new ways of doing a certain operation, check whether the results change, and decide which of the five methods is the best.

Listening to (that is, monitoring) the process is very important and can lead to much useful information. However, we can learn even more by actively changing the factors and by observing how the process reacts to changes. Relying exclusively on data obtained through passive listening is often inefficient, as it may take a long time until changes in important process factors occur on their own. Hence it is quite useful to "kick the process," and make it respond to changes that are deliberately introduced.

14.3 THREE EXAMPLES OF GOOD (AND POOR) EXPERIMENTAL DESIGNS

14.3.1 Example 1: Comparing the Durability of Two Different Synthetic Shoe Soles*

A First Experimental Plan We are interested in comparing the wear characteristics of two different materials commonly used for shoe soles: material A made of rubber, and material B made from a mixture of certain plastic components. We are using the students in this class to carry out an experiment. We divide the group of students (assume, for the moment, that there are 20 students in this course) into two equally sized groups. The division into the two groups is carried out *at random*. Each student gets assigned a number between 1 and 20. Twenty slips of papers, with numbers 1 through 20, are placed in a bowl and drawn, one after the other. The first ten selected students (numbers) are given pairs of shoes with material A; the remaining students get pairs of shoes made with material B.

Randomization is an important feature of this design. Randomization is vital as it avoids possible biases in the comparisons. Every student has the same chance of being assigned one of the materials. This is much better than assigning, for example, students in the front rows to material A, or all female students to B, or letting the students themselves select the material they want to try. These latter assignments could lead to biases. For example, students in the front rows may use their shoes less than those in the back rows, and hence the wear on their shoes may be smaller, irrespective of whether they use A or B. Or, female students may take better care of their equipment and, as a consequence, their wear may be smaller; and so on. Such biases can be avoided by randomizing, and giving each student the same chance of being assigned to one of the materials. We call the resulting design a *completely randomized design*.

After four weeks we measure the wear on their shoes. The results (that is, the average wear from the right and the left shoe) for the 20 students are displayed in the form of two dot plots, one for material A and one for material B. For easy comparisons we have put these two graphs in Figure 14.1 (page 402) on the same scale.

From this picture it is virtually impossible to determine whether one material shows less wear than the other. Sophisticated statistical analyses wouldn't help either. The averages of the two groups are slightly different, but the difference in the averages is small compared to the sizable variability that exists in both groups.

Why is there so much variability? The explanation is simple. It is because within each group the activity levels of the subjects vary greatly. Some students are more active than others. This activity level is responsible for much of the variability in the results.

A Second (and Better) Experimental Plan Under the better experimental plan, every student tries *both* materials. With two materials and two feet on each person,

*This example is patterned after an example in Section 4.2 of Box, Hunter, and Hunter, *Statistics for Experimenters*, New York: Wiley, 1978.

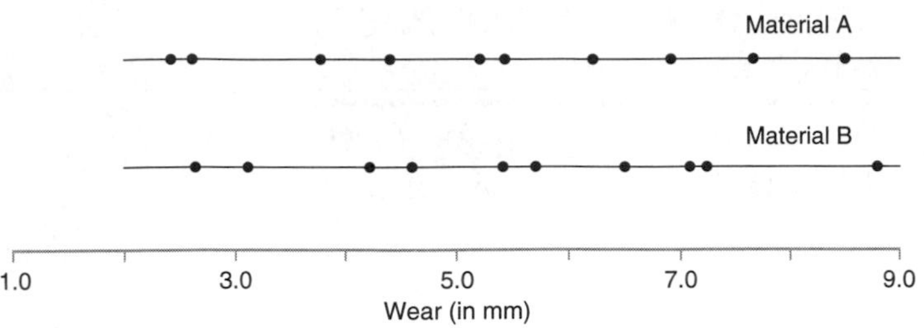

FIGURE 14.1 Dot diagrams for wear: Material A and material B. Completely randomized design.

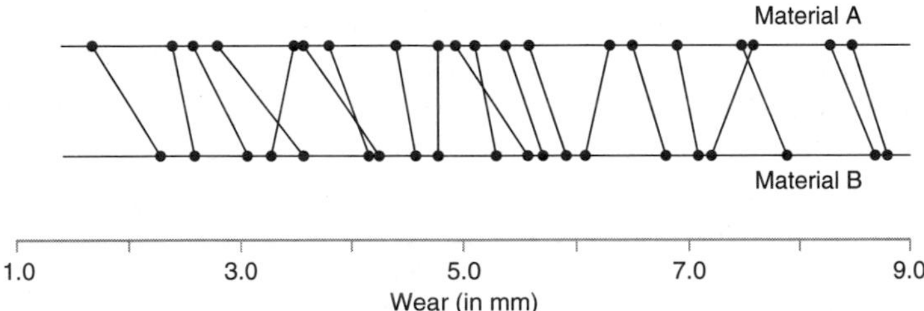

FIGURE 14.2 Dot diagrams for wear: Material A and material B. Randomized block design.

this is easily done. We put material A on one foot and material B on the other. Each participant in this study is viewed as a unit (or, as it is called in statistical terminology, a *block*) and gets assigned both materials. In order to avoid a possible right/left bias in the assignment, we randomize the assignment. We flip a coin: If the coin comes up "heads," we put material A on the right foot; otherwise material A gets put on the left foot. [Note that under this particular randomization it is possible that more A's are assigned to either the right or left foot. If one wanted to assign the same number of A's and B's to the right and left foot, then one would select 10 subjects from the 20 at random, and assign treatment A to the right (or left) foot of those selected.]

Using the 20 subjects and assigning both A and B to each subject, we end up with 20 pairs of measurements (the data is listed in Table 15.1 of the following chapter). These measurements are shown on the dot diagrams in Figure 14.2. One is for material A and the other is for material B; both are displayed on the same scale. We have connected the points that come from the same subject. While we see tremendous variability from one subject to the other, it is now the *difference* between wear under A and wear under B on each subject that is of importance. Because of our experimental design we can get these differences for all our subjects. While it is true that our measurements include a very large "activity" component, taking the difference between the two measurements on a subject will in effect "cancel" out this component. This is because one leg gets pretty much the same exercise as the other.

In Figure 14.2 we have connected the points that come from the same subject. We see from this comparison that among the 20 pairs, in 17 cases the wear for material A is less than the wear for material B; 17 of the 20 connecting lines have negative slopes. From this data it is obvious that wear for material A is less than that for B. We conclude that A is the better material. This is what R.A. Fisher had in mind when he said that the results of a well-planned experiment are obvious from simple statistical graphical analyses.

A comparison of these dot diagrams, without any information on which of the two dots come from the same subject, does not give us much information on which material is better. If you just compare the two dot diagrams, then there is no chance whatsoever to be able to conclude that one material is better than the other; even the most sophisticated statistical methods cannot salvage a poorly designed experiment. Knowing that the experiment was carried out in pairs helps tremendously, as we now can compare the two treatments within each block. A simple overhaul of the experimental design has, for the same cost in time and labor, increased the information content of our data.

We learned two important principles: the principle of *blocking* and the principle of *randomization*. If there is an important factor that separates our subjects (in our example it was the activity level of our subjects), then we want to utilize this factor and think about running the experiment in blocks, or pairs. In our case, the subject became the block, and we assigned both treatments (materials A and B) to each block. Randomization of the treatments is also important, as within each block we want to avoid a possible right/left allocation bias. Thus we flip a coin to randomize the assignment. We call such a design a *randomized block design*.

14.3.2 Example 2: Yield of a Chemical Process under Various Operating Conditions

We suspect that the yield of a chemical process depends on the following three factors: the temperature of the reaction, the pressure of the reaction, and the type of catalyst that is used. The operator knows that temperature should be somewhere between 500 degrees (the lower level, usually denoted by "−") and 600 degrees (the upper level, denoted by "+"); pressure should be between 60 (−) and 80 (+) kg/cm^2; and we have the choice of two catalysts: catalyst A (−) and catalyst B (+).

A good experimental design asks for experiments at all eight possible factor-level combinations. That is, we should obtain the yield for the following eight process settings:

temperature 500 degrees, pressure of 60 kg/cm^2, catalyst A
temperature 500 degrees, pressure of 60 kg/cm^2, catalyst B
temperature 500 degrees, pressure of 80 kg/cm^2, catalyst A
temperature 500 degrees, pressure of 80 kg/cm^2, catalyst B
temperature 600 degrees, pressure of 60 kg/cm^2, catalyst A

temperature 600 degrees, pressure of 60 kg/cm^2, catalyst B
temperature 600 degrees, pressure of 80 kg/cm^2, catalyst A
temperature 600 degrees, pressure of 80 kg/cm^2, catalyst B.

Graphically, these eight experiments can be displayed as the corner points of a cube; see Figure 14.3.

How should we carry out these eight experiments? In which time-order? There may be time trends, carryover effects and cycles, but we may know very little about them. For example, we may have an increasing time-trend unrelated to temperature; now if we conducted all four experiments under temperature of 500 degrees first, then we would conclude incorrectly that lowering temperature decreases the yield. Of course if the trend was decreasing, the opposite conclusion would be reached. We really don't know whether a trend is there, and if it were there, we wouldn't know whether it is increasing or decreasing. Hence we randomize the order of the experiments as this helps us avoid biases in the comparisons. We can do this by labeling the eight experiments with numbers 1 through 8, putting eight slips of paper with numbers 1 through 8 in a bowl, and drawing slips at random. The experiments are then carried out in the order in which these slips are drawn. If 3 is the first number, then our first experiment is the one with temperature at 500 degrees, pressure of 80 kg/cm^2, and catalyst A. Of course, you can also use random numbers to decide on the random order; see our discussion in Chapter 9.

Should we just carry out a single experiment (often referred to as a "run") at each of these eight factor-level combinations, or should we think about *replications*? We could replicate the experiment once and consider a design with 16 runs. That is, we could conduct two experiments at each of the eight factor-level combinations. Replication helps reduce the uncertainty. We are going to increase our certainty about the true response if we can work with average yields that come from more than one run.

How should we carry out these 16 experiments? Again, it is preferable to randomize the order among these 16 experiments, and we can do this by drawing

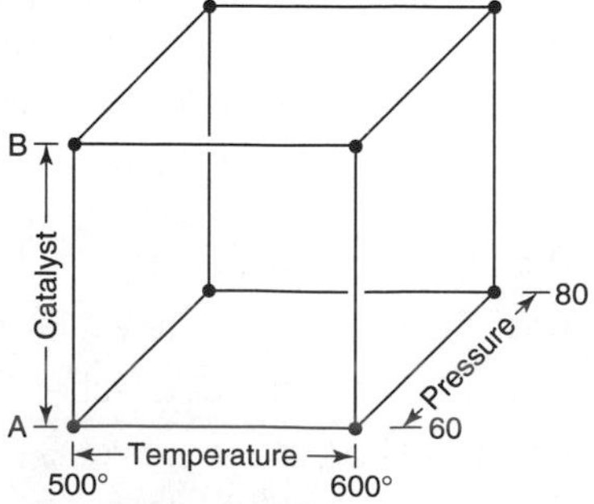

FIGURE 14.3 Graphical representation of the eight factor-level combinations.

16 slips of paper, or by using nonoverlapping pairs of digits in a random number table. But what should we do if we can only run at most eight experiments on a given day? In such a case we could run a full set of eight runs (like the ones listed above) on the first day, and a second set of eight on the second day. The order of the experiments within each day should be randomized, and it most likely would not be the same on both days.

14.3.3 Example 3: Production of Gypsum Plaster

This example, described by J. Pignatiello in the notes for a short course on Statistical Methods for Quality and Productivity Improvement held at the University of Iowa, is based on the University of Arizona Master's thesis by Alberto Garza. The process of manufacturing gypsum plaster is relatively simple. The process is illustrated in the flowchart in Figure 14.4. Gypsum rock is crushed in the primary crusher, and then ground in a grinder. Citric acid is added to the ground material and the mixture is heated; this is referred to as the calcination process. Then the material is cooled and packaged in paper bags.

Gypsum plaster is used in adobe-type construction. Contractors are concerned about the variability in the hardening time (also called the setting time), which is the time it takes for gypsum plaster to harden. In the past contractors have complained frequently about excessive variation in the hardening time from one bag of gypsum plaster to another.

The manufacturer of gypsum plaster started an investigation into the possible causes for this undesirable variability. Pignatiello gives a cause-and-effect

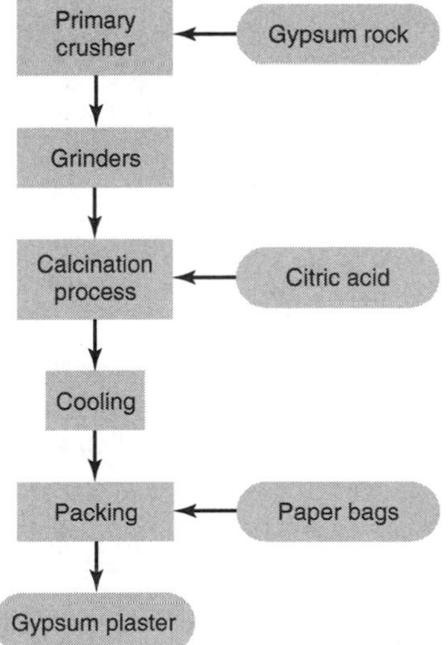

FIGURE 14.4 Flow chart: Manufacture of gypsum plaster. Boxes show operations; ovals show materials.

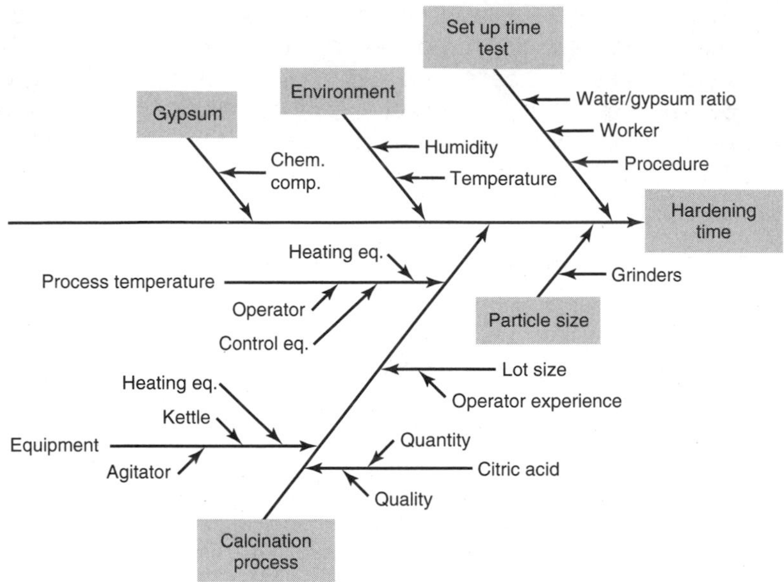

FIGURE 14.5 Cause-and-effect diagram: Manufacture of gypsum plaster.

diagram that lists several suspected causes for this variability, and this diagram is shown in Figure 14.5. The calcination process was mentioned as one possible major cause. Three factors were thought to have a major impact: the batch or lot size (either small or large); the temperature (either low or high), and the concentration of the citric acid that is added (either low or high).

With two levels on each of these three factors, one is led to eight different factor-level combinations. One combination considers a small batch size, low temperature, and low concentration of citric acid; another considers a small batch size, low temperature, and high concentration, and so on. The eight factor-level combinations were replicated six times, and the hardening times of the resulting $(8)(6) = 48$ runs were recorded. The results from the six replications were used to calculate the mean and the standard deviation of the hardening times for each of the eight different factor-level combinations.

Much was learned from the results of this rather simple experiment. The results showed small variability among hardening times for low concentration of citric acid and small batch sizes. Hence, variability in the hardening time could be reduced by using less citric acid and smaller batch sizes. It was also found that temperature had little influence on the variability. Since process temperature was not found to be an important factor, lower process temperatures could be used in the manufacturing process, thus lowering energy costs. Smaller batch sizes and lower temperatures also reduced the production time per batch and thus increased the throughput (productivity). Yet another benefit from switching to smaller batch sizes was a reduction in agitator equipment breakdowns.

14.4 IMPORTANT FACTS ABOUT EXPERIMENTS

14.4.1 Important Reasons for Experimentation

Prior to carrying out any experiment, we should be clear about the objectives of the experiment. The purpose of the experiment may include one or more of these objectives:

- Comparing two or more methods (as in Example 1)
- Optimizing the yield of a process (as in Example 2)
- Minimizing the variability of a response variable (as in Example 3)
- Adjusting factors so that a response variable is closer to its target

14.4.2 Generalizing the Results of an Experiment

We must be aware of the *range of validity* of an experiment, and the dangers that are associated with extrapolating the findings from one experiment to other circumstances. One must be aware of the risks that are associated with extrapolations. Assume, for example, that one experimental plan calls for changes in temperature over a range from 500 to 600 degrees. The results from this experiment show how the process yield reacts to such changes in temperature. However, these results do not tell us how the process would react to a temperature of 1000 degrees, as no data is available for this range of temperature.

We need to be clear about the factors that are used in an experiment. If we study the strength of concrete blocks, all of which come from one large lot, we may not be able to say much about blocks that come from a different lot. If the experiments for the gypsum plaster example are performed in Mexico, we have to consider whether the results would apply equally to construction in the northeast United States.

Usually experiments are carried out under tightly controlled conditions. For example, when we vary factors such as temperature, pressure and type of catalyst, we do our best to keep all other conditions the same. We try to keep the relative humidity and the temperature in the plant at constant levels, and we try to use the same carefully trained operators throughout the experiment. Most *off-line experiments* (that is, experiments that are not part of the normal production process) are carried out under tightly controlled conditions. We have to think how these experiments perform on the factory floor (that is, *on-line*) where many other factors and conditions are not so tightly controlled. How robust are the results from an experiment with respect to changes in environmental conditions, variability among raw materials, and variability among the workers?

14.4.3 Response Variables

Response variables are the factors that we study. Often we are interested in only a single response variable. For example, we may be interested in the weight gain in an experiment comparing different feeds, the hardening time of gypsum plaster, the yield of a chemical process, or the tear strength of aluminum foil. Sometimes we are interested in more than one response variable. We may be interested in the yield of a process, but at the same time wanting to achieve a certain level of quality or a certain level of cost. For example, we may want to maximize the yield of a certain process, but at the same time produce materials that are of acceptable quality (as far as smoothness of its surface and clarity of the product are concerned) and at a cost that does not exceed a certain threshold.

Response variables can be *quantitative* (such as amount, volume, dimensions) or *qualitative* (such as taste: excellent, good, poor, terrible; or quality: acceptable, defective).

14.4.4 Factors Influencing the Response

Group discussions, cause-and-effect diagrams, and flowcharts help us learn about factors that may have an influence on a response. Usually, such discussions lead to a long list of possible factors that are thought to have an influence on the response.

It is useful to distinguish among *primary* and *secondary* factors. *Primary factors* are variables of main interest. In experiments we change their levels deliberately and we observe their effects on the response. Examples are temperature, pressure, concentration, types of production methods, different raw materials, and so on.

Secondary factors, on the other hand, are not of main interest; our interest is in the primary factors. However, we don't want these secondary factors to influence our comparison unduly. In some respects, secondary factors are nuisances. We like to exclude their effects so that we can focus on the effects of the primary factors.

The following example will clarify this distinction. Assume that we are a major producer of ball point pens. Our objective is to keep the defect rate as small as possible.

We are investigating the effect of the ink on the defect rates. We have two different suppliers for our ink: supplier A (ink A) and supplier B (ink B). In order to find out whether there is a difference in the defect rates for these two inks, we produce 20 lots of pens with ink A and 20 lots of pens with ink B. Here a lot is a large production unit of 10,000 pens. We can produce only ten lots per day. Thus it takes us four days to carry out the comparison. We use ink A for our production on Thursday and Friday. Our defect rate on these days is 1.5 percent. We use ink B for our production on Saturday and Sunday; the defect rate is 5.8 percent.

On first sight, it looks like the defect rate for material B is quite a bit higher than the one for ink A. However, we also know that on weekdays and weekends different workers use the machines. On weekdays it is our well-trained regular work crew, while on weekends it is our temporary staff. It is not clear how much of the difference in defect rates, $5.8 - 1.5 = 4.3$, is due to the different inks, and how much is due to the different workforce. Our experiment cannot tell us, as we completely *confounded* the effects of material (ink A or B) and the effects of the workforce (weekday or weekend crew).

Our conclusions about the primary factor may very well be affected by the levels of the secondary factor. If this is true, then this was a bad experiment. Can we do better? Yes, we can! It is much better to treat each production day as a block, and on each day carry out 5 experiments with ink A and 5 experiments with ink B. This allows us to compare inks A and B directly.

Also, within a work day, there are many different factors that may have an effect on the defect rates. One doesn't want these factors to influence our comparison. For example, conditions in the plant may change during the day; workers may become tired, there may be startup problems in the morning, and so on. We already know about the benefits of randomization. In order to be safe and not to bias our comparisons, it is preferable to randomize the order of the experiments within each day. For example, we prepare ten slips of paper: five with the letter A, and five with the letter B. We put these slips in a bowl and draw them at random. (Of course, we could also use random numbers from a random number table). The selected sequence determines the order of the experiments. We may get the following arrangement:

Thursday:	B	A	B	A	B	B	A	A	A	B
Friday:	B	B	A	B	B	A	A	B	A	A
Saturday:	A	A	A	B	B	B	A	B	B	A
Sunday:	B	A	A	B	B	A	A	B	A	B

This means that on Thursday we start with ink B, then switch to ink A, then ink B again, and so on.

14.5 STATISTICAL PRINCIPLES FOR CONSTRUCTING GOOD EXPERIMENTAL DESIGNS

Here we summarize what we have learned so far and we also provide an additional illustrative example.

14.5.1 Blocking the Experiment

If you have reasons to believe that certain secondary factors have an influence on the response, then you should conduct the experiment in blocks. A block is a region (or a group) of experimental units which provides fairly uniform conditions for the comparison of the primary factors. For example, "day" in our previous example provides fairly uniform conditions for comparing the different settings of the primary factors (which in this case, is the type of ink). Most likely there are large differences between days; this is because of differences in the workforce, different weather conditions, and so on. However, within the same day the conditions can be expected to be fairly uniform.

14.5.2 Randomization

There are many background factors that will affect our response variable. For example, the defect rates in our ink example are affected by a variety of small events that happen throughout the day. The conditions within a day may change according to a pattern that we can't even anticipate. In order to be fair to the various levels of our primary factors (in this case, the type of ink) and to avoid a possible bias in the comparisons, we arrange the experiments within each day at random. Randomization, in some sense, compensates for the many factors that cannot be controlled.

A good rule of thumb for any experimental design is: *Block whatever you can block, and randomize whatever you can't block.*

14.5.3 A Further Example

The following example illustrates the importance of a good blocking arrangement. Here we study the wear of automobile tires and investigate the differences among four different brands of tires: A, B, C, and D. Experiments are carried out on four automobiles. They are the same model cars, but we are somewhat concerned that slight differences among the cars could lead to different results. Also, there are four wheel positions on each car: right front, left front, right back, and left back. We are also concerned that the different positions may have an impact on the comparisons. Clearly, the car and the wheel position are secondary factors. Our primary factor is the type of tire. We want to block the experiment such that the car and the type of wheel position have little influence on the brand comparisons.

The following two experimental designs are not very good:

	Car			
Position	**1**	**2**	**3**	**4**
R/F	A	B	C	D
L/F	A	B	C	D
R/B	A	B	C	D
L/B	A	B	C	D

	Car			
Position	**1**	**2**	**3**	**4**
R/F	A	A	A	A
L/F	B	B	B	B
R/B	C	C	C	C
L/B	D	D	D	D

The first arrangement is bad as there could be differences among cars. Confounding the type of tire with the car could be dangerous. Also the second arrangement is not very good because it confounds the type of tire with the wheel position.

The following arrangement is much better as it blocks the experiment with respect to both the car and the wheel position. It is called a *Latin square* arrangement:

	Car			
Position	**1**	**2**	**3**	**4**
R/F	A	B	C	D
L/F	B	C	D	A
R/B	C	D	A	B
L/B	D	A	B	C

Every tire is used on every car and in every position. This is the defining property of a Latin square experiment.

14.5.4 Sequential Nature of Experimentation

It would be nice to have unlimited time and unlimited resources to find answers to posed questions, but this is never the case. As students, we have a limited amount of time to complete our assignments. In the work place, time and budget constraints affect and limit our investigations. Thus it is important to think very carefully about how best to use one's resources. It would be unwise to spend all of one's budget at the beginning of an investigation and to plan too comprehensive an experiment at the outset. It is much better to perform a sequence of smaller-sized experiments, and to run the experiments in successive order. This is because of the paradox that the best time to design an experiment is after it is finished; the worst time to design an experiment is at the outset of an investigation when one knows least. After an experiment we usually know much about the factors that are important, we know the ranges of the factors that should be studied, and we know the metrics in which the factors should be expressed. In the beginning, before running the experiment, we are very uncertain about all such issues.

At the end of a project, on looking back on one's initial experiments, one is often struck by the poor choices and assumptions that were made in the beginning. At the end of our investigation, our knowledge usually doesn't look at all like what we started with. One shouldn't be too embarrassed by this fact, because this reflects the natural learning process. We learn by doing. If we knew it all from the very outset, then there would be little reason to experiment.

We must make sure that we allow for learning to take place. For that reason, we prefer a sequence of smaller-sized experiments to one giant, all-encompassing experiment. Box, Hunter, and Hunter (1978) talk about *the 25 percent rule*. They suggest that not more than one quarter of the experimental effort (or budget) should be invested in a first design.

There are definite advantages to adopting a *sequential approach to experimentation*, and to carrying out a sequence of moderately-sized designs. After each stage of our experimentation more information about the question at hand becomes available. Some of the variables that were considered initially may drop out. Other variables may enter our investigation. The range of the variables may change; for example, we may start out by changing temperature in the 400 to 500 degree range, but after a few experiments it may become clear that a temperature around 700 degrees is preferable. The objective of our experiments may shift; for example, we may start out looking at a certain issue, but in the process of experimentation we may make a discovery that cannot be ignored and that changes the scope of our experiment. At the end of each experiment we gain knowledge. This knowledge helps us to design the next stage. The gaining of knowledge is a sequential process. One huge comprehensive experiment at the outset with no possibility of follow-up would not allow for learning to take place. Also, if surveys are involved, it is always a good idea to run a pilot study to examine the appropriateness and clarity of the survey questions.

14.6 PROBLEMS WITH EXPERIMENTS THAT CHANGE ONLY ONE FACTOR AT A TIME

Response variables are usually affected by more than one factor, and most often these factors interact in their effects on the response. A frequent and, as we show in this section, wrong approach to learning about these effects is to experiment by changing only one factor at a time, and leaving all other factors fixed. Authors refer to this approach as the *change-one-factor-at-a-time approach* to experimentation. George Box, through his work on response surface methodology, was among the first to point out the perils of this approach.

The following example is adapted from Hogg and Ledolter (1992). It illustrates that the change-one-factor-at-a-time approach to experimentation is seriously flawed. Assume that we are interested in optimizing the yield of a chemical process. Two factors are thought to have an influence on yield: temperature and pressure. The graph in Figure 14.6 connects the levels of temperature and pressure that lead to the same yield. For example, a yield of 60 is achieved by all points that lie on the curve (in this case, an ellipse) labeled 60. We call such a graph a *contour plot.* A contour plot connects points of equal response. In practice, because of variability, we wouldn't expect identical yields from experiments for which temperature and pressure lie on that particular contour line; instead, the results would vary around a mean value of 60. The graph in Figure 14.6 shows that the yield is largest if temperature is set at 270 degrees and pressure at 85 psi.

Assume that we don't know where the optimum occurs and that it is the aim of the investigation to uncover this information through a sequence of experiments. How would we proceed under the change-one-factor-at-a-time approach? We would fix the temperature, say at 220 degrees. Then we would change pressure and conduct experiments at different levels of pressure, say at 80, 90, 100, 110, and 120 psi. We would look for the pressure that maximizes yield. Figure 14.7a (page 414) shows how the yield varies with changing pressure if temperature

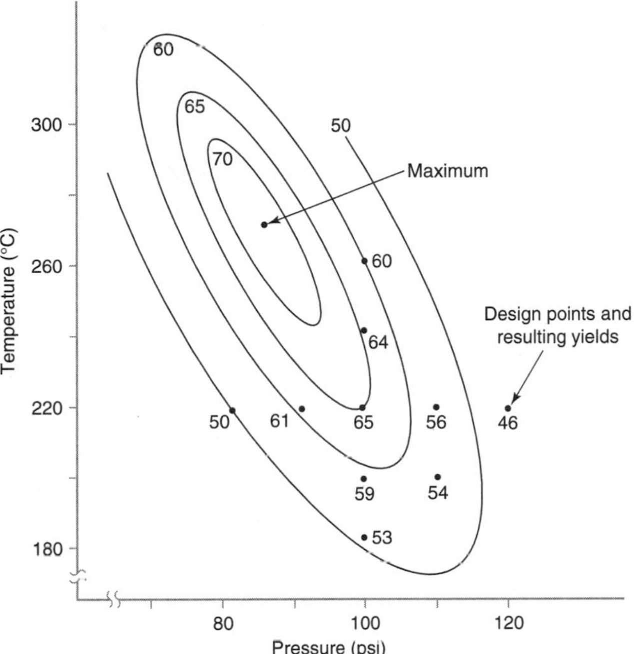

FIGURE 14.6 Contour plot of yield as a function of temperature and pressure.

is fixed at 220 degrees. We get this graph by interpolating the contour lines in Figure 14.6. We find that the yield is maximized if the pressure is set at 100 psi.

Next, we fix pressure at 100 psi (which is the optimal value for a temperature of 220 degrees) and we vary temperature. We conduct experiments with temperature 180, 200, 220, 240, and 260 degrees and obtain the yields for these experimental conditions. Figure 14.7b illustrates how the yield responds to changes in temperature, at fixed pressure of 100 psi. We have obtained this graph by interpolating the contour lines in Figure 14.6. From that graph we find that the best value of temperature is not far from a temperature of 220 degrees, possibly a little bit higher.

A conclusion that the overall process maximum is achieved at a pressure of 100 psi and a temperature of about 220 degrees (or somewhat higher) is obviously incorrect since, according to Figure 14.6, the optimum occurs for temperature of 270 degrees and pressure of 85 psi. Of course, one could keep on iterating the change-one-factor-at-a-time procedure. But without finer intervals for temperature and pressure one would not move away from the region that the first stage had identified as "optimal"; you can see this from Figure 14.6. With finer intervals there would be some movement to the overall optimum, but it certainly would be a very slow one.

The change-one-factor-at-a-time approach didn't work here. We can do much better by conducting a sequence of experiments in which the factors temperature

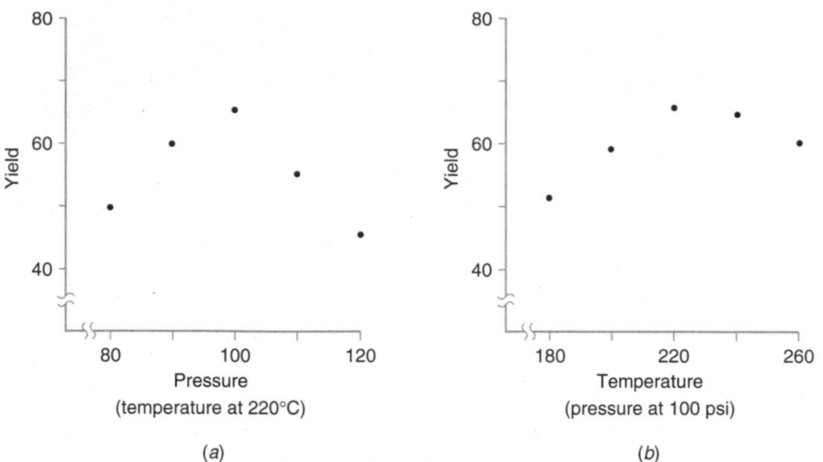

FIGURE 14.7 (*a*) Yield as a function of pressure, with temperature fixed at 220 degrees. (*b*) Yield as a function of temperature, with pressure fixed at 100 psi.

and pressure are changed *together*. It would be much better to run experiments at the four factor-level combinations of a two-level factorial experiment. Factorial designs are described in detail in the next chapter. Our initial design could consist of the following four runs:

(Temperature = 200 degrees, Pressure = 100 psi)
(Temperature = 220 degrees, Pressure = 100 psi)
(Temperature = 200 degrees, Pressure = 110 psi)
(Temperature = 220 degrees, Pressure = 110 psi)

The yields from these four runs (indicated by the numbers on the contour plot in Figure 14.6) tell us that we should move into a new region, by increasing the temperature and decreasing the pressure. The results from this factorial experiment tell us about the *path of steepest ascent* (that is, the path on which the yields go up fastest). Additional experiments could be performed on this path, and usually with very few runs we would locate the maximum.

Why didn't the change-one-factor-at-a-time approach work in this example? It failed because there was *interaction* among the two factors. An interaction between temperature and pressure means that the effect on yield of a temperature change varies with the level of pressure. You can see this interaction from the contour plot in Figure 14.6. At a pressure of 110 psi, the effect of a 20-degree temperature change from 200 to 220 degrees is $56 - 54 = 2$ units. The effect is $65 - 59 = 6$ units, if pressure is at 100 psi.

For the change-one-factor-at-a-time approach to work, one must assume that the effects of changes in one factor do not depend on the values of the other factors. However, since interactions are more the rule than the exception, we strongly recommend against using this approach.

14.7 EXERCISES

(Can be group projects) Discuss and plan an experiment of your choice. Identify the response variable and the factors that influence the response. Identify primary and secondary factors. Discuss how best to measure the variables. Write down the experimental plan. Is there a reason to block the experiment? How does randomization enter into your experimental design?

Carry out the experiment and record the data. Analyze the results through a few well-chosen graphs. Write a report in which you state your design, data collection, and conclusions. You may have to wait until the next chapter to carry out a complete analysis of the data. Comment on any shortcomings in your experiments and discuss how a follow-up experiment could help you remove some of the ambiguities you are left with at the end of your initial experiment.

Here are several suggestions:

14.1 Helicopter experiment: Use a sheet of paper and make a paper helicopter. Change the width and the length of the rotors and experiment with different weights (in the form of paper clips and pennies). Drop the helicopter (a high lobby of a building works well) and record the time it takes the helicopter to reach the ground. Assume that you are interested in maximizing the flying time. Study how the length, width, and weight affect the time. Feel free to add any other design changes that you believe are useful.

14.2 Think of simple experiments with rubber rings, rulers, paper clips, and tape. For example, use rubber rings and rulers to shoot at a target. You are interested in accuracy. How do the distance from the target, and the length, width, and color of the rubber rings affect the accuracy? Does it matter who carries out the experiment?

14.3 Use tape to attach empty film containers to the wall. Put pennies into these containers and determine when the containers fall from the wall. Vary the texture of the wall and the method of attaching the containers. Does it make a difference? If so, how?

14.4 Expansion of pinto beans (see Project 13 at the end of Section 4): Use five tablespoons of soaking fluid to soak each bean for two hours. Consider two soaking fluids (water and beer). Design an experiment that allows you to learn about the effects of the soaking fluid. Discuss how you would set up the experiment. Discuss how you would allocate the beans, taken from a bag of pinto beans, to the two different soaking fluids. Discuss how you would measure the "expansion" of a pinto bean. Carry out your experimental plan and obtain the results. Analyze the results graphically. Discuss whether you can generalize the results from this experiment. For example, do your results still apply if the beans were soaked in refrigerated fluids?

14.5 (Continuation of Exercise 14.4) Consider two additional factors: the soaking temperature (refrigerator or room temperature), and the soaking time (two hours or six hours). Design an experiment that can show you the effects of soaking fluid, soaking temperature, and soaking time. Carry out the experiment and describe the results. (You will learn in the next chapter how to analyze the resulting data.)

14.6 Consult past issues of *Quality Progress* and locate and discuss articles on the design of experiments. For example, read the article by Bert Gunter, "Statistically Designed Experiments: Quality Improvement, the Strategy of Experimentation, and the Road to Hell," *Quality Progress*, December 1989.

14.8 REFERENCES

Note that many more references on the design of experiments are given at the end of Chapter 16.

Box, G. E. P., W. G. Hunter, and J. S. Hunter. *Statistics for Experimenters.* New York: Wiley, 1978.

Fisher, R. A. *Statistical Methods for Research Workers.* Edinburgh: Oliver & Boyd, 1925.

Gunter, B. "Statistically Designed Experiments: Quality Improvement, the Strategy of Experimentation, and the Road to Hell," *Quality Progress*, Vol. 22, December 1989, 63–64.

Hogg, R. V., and J. Ledolter. *Applied Statistics for Engineers and Physical Scientists.* New York: Macmillan, 1992.

CHAPTER 15

ANALYSIS OF DATA FROM EFFECTIVE EXPERIMENTAL DESIGNS AND AN INTRODUCTION TO FACTORIAL EXPERIMENTS

The previous chapter introduced you to several important principles in the design of experiments. We learned about completely randomized designs, randomized block designs, and factorial designs where we vary more than one factor at a time. In this chapter we illustrate how to analyze the resulting information, and we show how to draw inferences from these experiments to the underlying population or process.

15.1 COMPARISON OF AVERAGES FROM TWO UNRELATED EXPERIMENTS

The experiment that we describe in this section involves the comparison of the breaking strengths of two different types of leads used in mechanical pencils.*

*This particular example is adapted from lecture notes by Russell V. Lenth for a University of Iowa short course on Statistical Methods for Quality and Productivity Improvement. In order to appreciate the practical challenges of experimentation, we recommend that you replicate this, or a similar experiment.

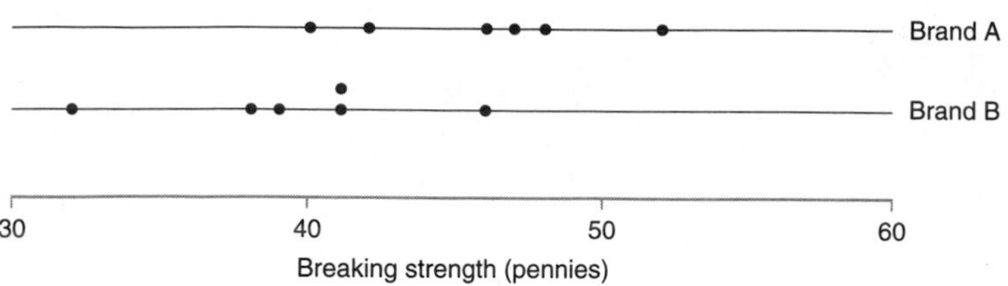

FIGURE 15.1 Dot diagrams for breaking strength of lead pencils: Brand A and brand B.

One type is manufactured by Company A, the other by Company B. All leads have diameter of 0.5 mm. Several packages of each brand were purchased and the leads were subjected to a simple strength test. Pairs of leads from the same manufacturer were placed across the gap between two books to form a bridge. Pennies were added onto the middle of this bridge until one of the leads broke. The number of pennies at which one of the leads broke was taken as a measure of strength.

An experiment with twelve pairs of leads was carried out; six pairs came from brand A, and six pairs came from brand B. The student who conducted the experiment carried out the twelve tests in random order. Furthermore, he did not know which brand he was testing. The results of these twelve trials are as follows:

BRAND A: 46, 42, 47, 48, 52, 40
BRAND B: 32, 46, 41, 39, 38, 41

Dot diagrams of the observations, shown on the same scale, are given in Figure 15.1.

Summary statistics (averages and standard deviations) for both groups are given below:

Group 1: (Brand A): $n_1 = 6, \quad \bar{x}_1 = 45.8, \quad s_1 = 4.31$
Group 2: (Brand B): $n_2 = 6, \quad \bar{x}_2 = 39.5, \quad s_2 = 4.59$

A comparison of the two group averages leads to an average brand difference:

$$\text{Brand A} - \text{Brand B} = 45.8 - 39.5 = 6.3.$$

15.1.1 Statistical and Practical Significance of a Difference of Two Averages

What does an average brand difference of 6.3 pennies, determined from two unrelated samples of size 6, signify?

Let us decide whether this observed average difference of 6.3 pennies is *statistically significant*. Could it be that this observed difference of 6.3 pennies is merely due to the random sampling mechanism? In other words, could it be that this difference would disappear if we had selected other samples of leads and repeated the experiment? Is this difference of 6.3 pennies just an artifact of our sampling and testing procedure, or is the difference "real"? Is this a real difference, in the sense that the difference would persist in experiments with other leads from these two brands?

Note that the concept of statistical significance as described above is very different from the concept of *practical relevance*. We may conclude that the difference of 6.3 pennies is statistically significant (meaning that this difference is not just a sampling artifact that would go away if we carry out the experiment again), but at the same time conclude that a difference of 6.3 pennies is irrelevant from a practical point of view. When the leads are used in mechanical pencils, people may not notice a difference in the breaking strength of 6.3 pennies. Or, if they did, such a difference may not be worth the extra cost. The cost of producing the stronger lead A may exceed the premium customers are willing to pay. The answer to the question of practical significance depends on the particular situation at hand. It can only be answered if one knows the associated costs and benefits.

The answer to the question of statistical significance depends on the variation of the measurements from their respective sample averages. Consider the two illustrations in Figure 15.2. In both illustrations the difference between the two sample averages is 6.3. But the illustrations differ by the magnitude of the variability within each of the two groups. There is little doubt in the first illustration: Brand A is stronger than Brand B. The deviations of the observations from their respective group averages are all very small, compared to the large difference in the group averages. The two groups don't even overlap. All six measurements for brand B are smaller than the measurements for brand A. In the second illustration, on the other hand, it is difficult to tell whether Brand A is better than Brand B. The large

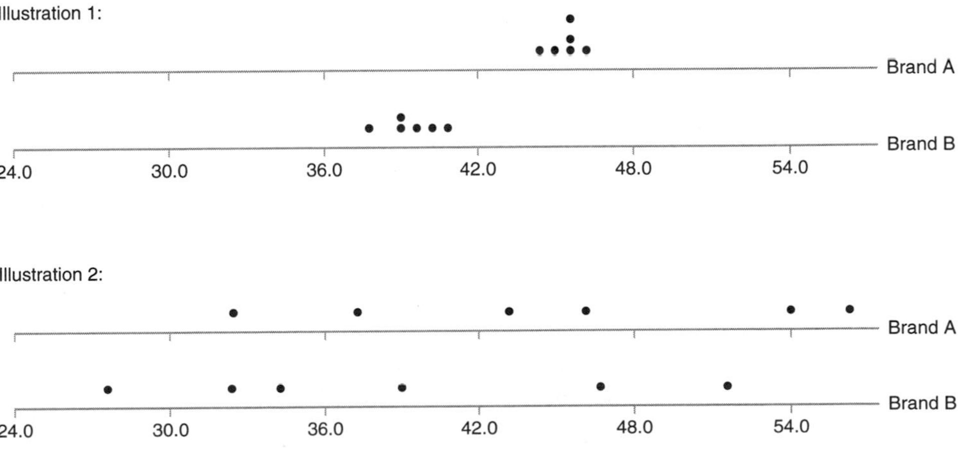

FIGURE 15.2 Two dot diagrams of six observations each: Illustration 1 and Illustration 2.

variability of the observations from their respective group averages makes it very difficult to form any firm conclusion. While some measurements for Brand B are smaller than some for A, there are also some measurements for Brand A that are smaller than some for B.

How can we assess statistical significance? For that we need to know the distribution of the difference of two sample averages that would result from repeated applications of the experimental procedure. We can think of this as random sampling from two unrelated populations and study the variability of the difference of two sample averages in repeated samples from these two populations. However, the analogy to random sampling from two unrelated distributions is not always perfect, as experiments are usually carried out over time and the conditions that are present in today's experiment may differ from those tomorrow. This is exactly the reason why randomization in experimentation is so important, as this randomization allows us to view the data as the result of two unrelated random samples.

In Chapter 10 we studied the sampling distribution of the sample average $\bar{X}$, obtained from n items that are sampled at random from a population with mean μ and standard deviation σ. We learned that for reasonably large sample sizes, the sampling distribution of $\bar{X}$ is approximately normal with mean μ and standard deviation $\sigma/\sqrt{n}$.

Here we have two populations and two unrelated random samples. Let us assume that the first sample of size n_1 is taken from a population with mean μ_1 and standard deviation σ_1. Then sample averages $\bar{X}_1$, calculated from random samples of size n_1 taken from that population, vary around the population mean μ_1; the standard deviation, or standard error of such averages is given by $\sigma_1/\sqrt{n_1}$. Similarly, sample averages $\bar{X}_2$, calculated from random samples of size n_2 taken from population 2 with mean μ_2 and standard deviation σ_2, vary around μ_2; the standard deviation, or standard error of such averages is $\sigma_2/\sqrt{n_2}$.

Here we consider the difference of two such averages that come from unrelated distributions. In Section 8.10 in Chapter 8 we learned how to calculate the standard deviation of a difference of two independent random variables. Applying this result to the present situation, we find that the sampling distribution of differences between two sample means, $\bar{X}_1 - \bar{X}_2$, is centered at mean $\mu_1 - \mu_2$ and its standard deviation, or standard error is given by

$$\begin{aligned}\text{StdDev}(\bar{X}_1 - \bar{X}_2) &= \sqrt{[\text{StdDev}(\bar{X}_1)]^2 + [\text{StdDev}(\bar{X}_2)]^2} \\ &= \sqrt{\frac{(\sigma_1)^2}{n_1} + \frac{(\sigma_2)^2}{n_2}}.\end{aligned}$$

For this result to hold we need to assume that the experiments are carried out independently and under similar conditions. That is, the results must come from two unrelated experiments where there is no carryover from one experiment to the next, and also no carryover from the experiments in one group to the other. In other words, we assume that the observations come from a *completely randomized design*.

Of course, we usually don't know the population standard deviations, and we need to replace σ_1 and σ_2 by the sample standard deviations s_1 and s_2. The estimated standard deviation, or the estimated standard error of the difference $\bar{X}_1 - \bar{X}_2$, is given by

$$\text{StdDev}(\bar{X}_1 - \bar{X}_2) = \sqrt{\frac{(s_1)^2}{n_1} + \frac{(s_2)^2}{n_2}}.$$

It is used in the calculation of confidence intervals for the difference in the population means, $\mu_1 - \mu_2$. An approximate 95 percent confidence interval for $\mu_1 - \mu_2$ is obtained by adding and subtracting two standard errors from the observed difference $\bar{x}_1 - \bar{x}_2$; it is given by the interval

$$\bar{x}_1 - \bar{x}_2 \pm (2)\sqrt{\frac{(s_1)^2}{n_1} + \frac{(s_2)^2}{n_2}}.$$

This is approximate, as we use the normal approximation to the sampling distribution. For small sample sizes and with sample standard deviations replacing the population standard deviations, the coverage may be somewhat different from 95 percent. Nevertheless such intervals work well with reasonably-sized samples, even in a case like the one considered here ($n_1 = n_2 = 6$).

For our data set, the estimated standard deviation of the difference $\bar{X}_1 - \bar{X}_2$ is given by

$$\text{StdDev}(\bar{X}_1 - \bar{X}_2) = \sqrt{\frac{(4.31)^2}{6} + \frac{(4.59)^2}{6}} = 2.57,$$

and an approximate 95 percent confidence interval for the difference of the two population means is given by the interval 6.3 ± 5.1, or (1.2, 11.4). We are 95 percent confident that the interval from 1.2 to 11.4 pennies covers the difference of the true breaking strengths. Note that this interval does not cover the value 0. Recall that $\mu_1 - \mu_2 = 0$ implies that there is no difference among the two process or population means. Thus we are fairly confident that Brand A is stronger than Brand B. We say that the distance of the observed difference 6.3 from zero is *statistically significant*. If the value 0 were included in the confidence interval, then we could not say that there is a statistically significant difference among the two averages. In such a case the difference between 6.3 pennies and zero could be explained by sampling variability.

Formally, we could have tested the null hypothesis that $\mu_1 - \mu_2 = 0$ against the two-sided alternative hypothesis that $\mu_1 - \mu_2 \neq 0$. The standardized test statistic for this two-sided test is given by $(6.3 - 0)/2.57 = 2.45$. The probability of obtaining such a large test statistic or one that is even more extreme, if in fact $\mu_1 - \mu_2 = 0$, is given by $(2)P(Z > 2.45) = 0.0143$; this is the probability value of the test statistic. Since the probability value is smaller than the usually adopted 0.05 significance level, we have evidence against the null hypothesis. The data indicates that the mean strengths of these two brands are different.

15.2 COMPARISON OF TWO AVERAGES FROM A BLOCKED EXPERIMENT

In Section 14.3 of the previous chapter we described an experiment in which we compared the wear characteristics of two different types of synthetic soles. In this experiment we gave each of the 20 participants material A, as well as material B. We flipped a coin to decide whether A was put on the right or the left foot.

Each subject in this experiment is a block. The two observations which come from the same subject (block) are *related*; they are certainly *not* independent. They both depend on the activity level of the person. If a subject runs a lot, then that person's wear on A, as well as his wear on B, will be large. For this reason we cannot use the approach of the previous section, as it assumes that observations from different groups are independent.

In this section we analyze the data from this blocked experiment. The data on A and B, as well as the differences B – A, are given in Table 15.1.

Dot diagrams of the observations on A and B were shown in Figure 14.2. Since the experiment is blocked and since each pair of observations comes from the same subject, it is natural to consider their differences. The twenty differences, $d_1, d_2, \ldots, d_{20}$, are listed in Table 15.1; a dot diagram of the differences is shown in Figure 15.3. The dot diagram shows that 17 of 20 differences (B – A) are positive. The average of these twenty differences is $\bar{d} = 0.27$, and the standard deviation is $s_d = 0.2975$. Note that we have used the subscript d to remind us that this is the standard deviation of the differences.

The sample average $\bar{d} = 0.27$ is our best estimate of the mean difference in the population, μ_d. We want to obtain a confidence interval for μ_d, and for this we need the standard deviation of averages, $\bar{D}$, that are calculated from repeated random samples of size n. We know that the standard deviation of such averages is estimated by

$$\text{StdDev}(\bar{D}) = s_d/\sqrt{n} = 0.2975/\sqrt{20} = 0.0665.$$

Section 10.3 in Chapter 10 showed us how to obtain confidence intervals. An approximate 95 percent confidence interval for the unknown mean difference μ_d in the population is given by $0.27 \pm (2)(0.0665)$, or $(0.14, 0.40)$. Note that this interval does not include the value 0. Therefore, we can conclude that the difference between these two materials is statistically significant. The difference of 0.27 from zero cannot be shrugged off as a sampling artifact. We have considerable evidence that the wear of material B is greater than the wear on A. We decide that A is better than B.

TABLE 15.1 Shoe Wear Example: Soles A and B

	A	*B*	*B* − *A*
Subject 1	8.3	8.7	0.4
Subject 2	6.3	6.1	−0.2
·	7.5	7.9	0.4
·	2.6	3.1	0.5
	8.5	8.8	0.3
	7.6	7.2	−0.4
	5.4	5.7	0.3
	4.4	4.6	0.2
	3.6	4.3	0.7
	3.8	4.2	0.4
	2.4	2.6	0.2
	5.6	5.9	0.3
	3.5	3.3	−0.2
	6.5	6.8	0.3
	2.8	3.6	0.8
	4.8	4.8	0.0
	6.9	7.1	0.2
·	1.7	2.3	0.6
·	5.1	5.3	0.2
Subject 20	5.2	5.6	0.4

Twenty subjects in a paired experiment.

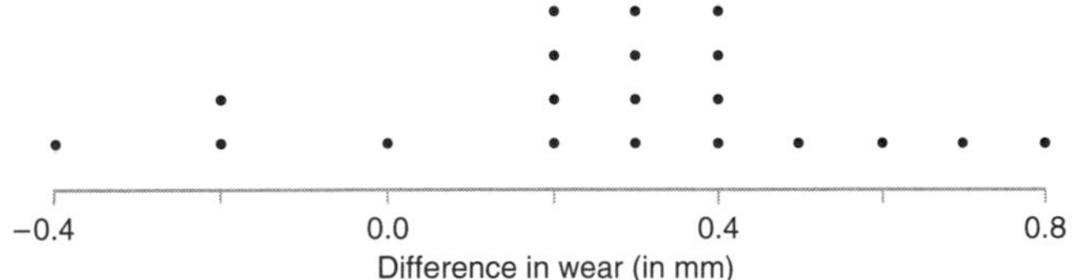

FIGURE 15.3 Dot diagram of difference in wear ($B - A$).

15.3 INTRODUCTION TO TWO-LEVEL FACTORIAL EXPERIMENTS

15.3.1 A Factorial Experiment in Two Factors

So far we have studied the effects of a *single* factor (brand of pencil lead in the first example, and shoe sole material in the second), and we have compared two groups (levels, or settings) of this one factor. In many applications we are interested in more than one factor and we investigate the influence of several factors on a response variable.

Assume that temperature and reaction time are expected to have an effect on the yield of a certain chemical process. Suppose we carry out a sequence of experiments in which we observe the yield of the process under different temperature conditions and different levels of reaction time. Operators familiar with the process can certainly tell us about the feasible ranges for temperature and reaction time. In the following example we selected two levels for temperature T: a low level of 110 degrees (−) and a high level of 130 degrees (+). We also selected two levels for reaction time R: a low level of 50 minutes (−) and a high level of 70 minutes (+). We use "−" and "+" codes to abbreviate the low and high values.

We carried out a simple *factorial experiment*. In a factorial experiment one investigates all possible factor-level combinations. Since each of the two factors is studied at two levels, there is a total of four factor-level combinations. These combinations (in the original factor levels, as well as in the coded units "+" and "−" for high and low levels) are listed in Table 15.2. We carried out eight runs as we replicated the experiment once, and we randomized the order of the eight runs. The yields of the two runs at each of the four factor-level combinations, as well as their average, are listed in Table 15.2.

It is quite easy to write down the factor levels for these four runs. We create a table; in the first column (for the first factor) we enter the sequence: "− + − +". The column starts with a "−" sign, and the signs alternate each time. The second

TABLE 15.2 Replicated 2^2 Factorial Experiment

		Yield (in percent)		
Temperature	Time	Average	Run1	Run2
110 Degr	50 Min	55.0	(55.5	54.5)
130 Degr	50 Min	60.6	(60.2	61.0)
110 Degr	70 Min	64.2	(64.5	63.9)
130 Degr	70 Min	68.2	(67.7	68.7)

T	R	Yield (in percent)		
Temperature	Time	Average	Run1	Run2
−	−	55.0	(55.5	54.5)
+	−	60.6	(60.2	61.0)
−	+	64.2	(64.5	63.9)
+	+	68.2	(67.7	68.7)

Average yields are listed first. Yields of replicates are shown in parentheses.

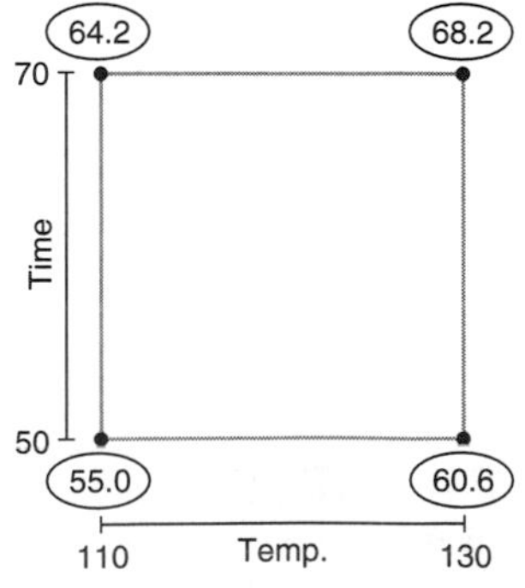

column (for the second factor) is written as "$- - + +$". It starts with 2 minus signs, "$- -$", and signs alternate in groups of two. The rows of this table give us the levels of the four runs. The first run is the one where both factors are at their low levels; the second run is the one where the first factor is at its high level and the second factor is at its low level; and so on. This particular arrangement of the four runs is referred to as the *standard order*. This arrangement is useful as it gives us a simple rule for writing down all possible factor-level combinations. However, we wouldn't necessarily conduct the four runs always in this particular order. In practice, we have to randomize the order.

Geometrically, the four factor-level combinations represent the corners of the square in Table 15.2.

15.3.2 A Factorial Experiment in Three Factors

Assume that three factors, temperature T, concentration C, and type of catalyst K, are thought to have an effect on the yield of a chemical process. We study the process at two different levels of temperature (160 and 180 degrees), and two different levels of concentration (20 and 40 percent), and we investigate two different catalysts (catalyst A and B). A two-level factorial design studies all possible factor-level combinations of these three factors; it leads to a total of $2^3 = 8$ runs. The factor levels of the eight different runs (in coded units) are listed in Table 15.3.

The factor levels of these eight runs, arranged in standard order, are easy to remember. Generate a table where the first column (first factor) is given by "$- + - + - + - +$". It starts with a minus sign, and the signs alternate until the eighth entry is reached. The second column (second factor) is "$- - + + - - + +$". It starts with two minus signs, and the signs alternate in blocks of two. The third

TABLE 15.3 A 2^3 Factorial Experiment

Temp. T	Conc. C	Catalyst K	Result
−	−	−	60
+	−	−	72
−	+	−	54
+	+	−	68
−	−	+	52
+	−	+	83
−	+	+	45
+	+	+	80

Levels for temperature are 160 (−) and 180 (+) degrees; levels for concentration are 20 (−) and 40 (+) percent; 2 catalysts ($A = -$ and $B = +$).

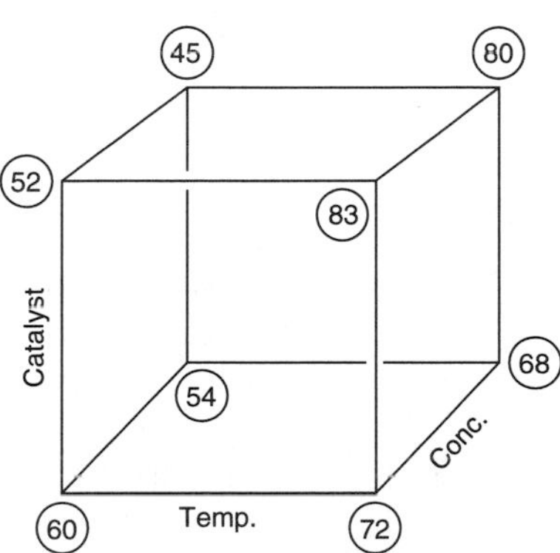

column (third factor) is "$- - - - + + + +$". It starts with four minus signs, and the signs alternate in blocks of four. Each row of this table gives us the factor levels of one of these eight runs. Geometrically, the eight runs represent the corners of a cube.

15.3.3 A Factorial Experiment in k Factors

Our experiment may involve k factors, where each factor is studied at two different levels. A two-level factorial design requires a total of 2^k runs. It is easy to write down the factor levels for these 2^k runs in standard order:

Generate a table where the first column (for the first factor) is given by 2^k alternating signs, "$- + - + - + - + - \cdots - +$". The signs of the second column (for the second factor) alternate in groups of two, "$- - + + - - + + - \cdots + +$". The signs of the third column (for the third factor) alternate in groups of four, "$- - - - + + + + - \cdots + +$", and so on. Column (factor) k consists of 2^{k-1} minus signs, followed by 2^{k-1} plus signs, "$- - - - \cdots + + + +$". Each row in this table represents one of the 2^k different runs; the runs are arranged in standard order.

With this procedure it is easy to remember all runs. Of course, one would not carry out the runs in this particular (standard) order. To guard against possible time trends, one should always randomize the order of the runs.

15.4 ANALYSIS OF DATA FROM TWO-LEVEL FACTORIAL DESIGNS

15.4.1 Analysis of a 2^2 Factorial Experiment

Here we analyze the results of the 2^2 factorial experiment given in Table 15.2. There we study the effects of temperature and reaction time on the yield of a chemical process. Eight experiments were carried out in random order, resulting in two observations for each of the four factor-level combinations. The average yields at the four factor-level combinations of the 2^2 factorial experiment are used to estimate the effects of the two factors on the response; the replications are used later when we assess the statistical significance of these estimates.

The average yields, depicted at the four corners of the square in Table 15.2, are used to estimate the effects of temperature and reaction time. Figure 15.4 expresses the same information graphically. There we plot yields for the two levels of temperature, separately for each level of reaction time; observations that come from the same reaction time are connected.

The entries in Table 15.2 and their display in Figure 15.4 show us how to estimate the effect of temperature. The *effect of a 20-degree change in temperature* from 110 degrees ($-$) to 130 degrees ($+$) is estimated by the difference of the yield averages at temperature 130 and 110. The yields at temperature 130 degrees are 60.6 and 68.2; those at temperature 110 degrees are 55.0 and 64.2. Thus, the

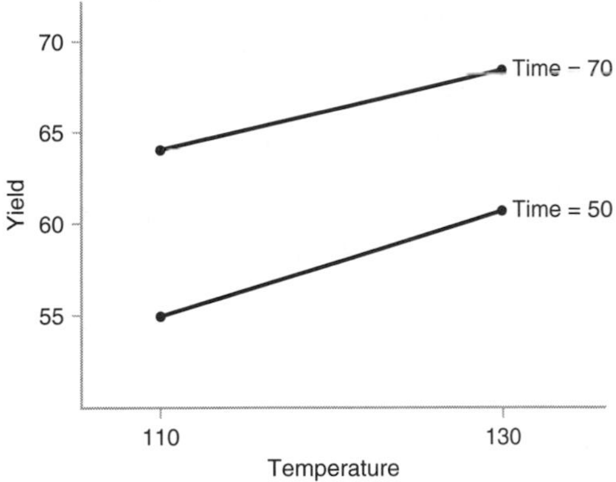

FIGURE 15.4 Graphical display of the results of the 2^2 factorial experiment.

estimated effect T of temperature is

$$T = \frac{60.6 + 68.2}{2} - \frac{55.0 + 64.2}{2} = 64.4 - 59.6 = 4.8$$
$$= (-55.0 + 60.6 - 64.2 + 68.2)/2 = 4.8.$$

Here we have calculated the temperature effect by referring back to the displays in Table 15.2 and Figure 15.4. However, there is also an easy algorithmic rule for calculating the temperature effect: Responses (in this case, the yields) are multiplied by the signs (the coded units) in column 1 (temperature) of Table 15.2; the resulting products are added up and divided by 2. The number 2 represents the number of minus signs (or, equivalently, + signs) in that column. This is exactly what was done in the second line of the above equation.

The estimated effect $T = 4.8$ implies that a 20-degree temperature change from 110 to 130 degrees increases the yield by 4.8 units (in this case, percent).

Similarly, the *effect R of a reaction time change* from 50 minutes (−) to 70 minutes (+) is estimated as the difference of the yield averages at 70 (+) and 50 (−) minutes:

$$R = \frac{64.2 + 68.2}{2} - \frac{55.0 + 60.6}{2} = 66.2 - 57.8 = 8.4$$
$$= (-55.0 - 60.6 + 64.2 + 68.2)/2 = 8.4.$$

Again, the calculation is easy to remember. Multiply the responses in Table 15.2 by the signs in column 2 (reaction time), add up the numbers, and divide by 2. Again, 2 is the number of minus signs in that column. The result, $R = 8.4$, implies that an increase in the reaction time from 50 to 70 minutes increases the yield by 8.4 units (percent).

The effects T and R are called *main effects*. They express how a change in the levels of one factor affects the response. In the calculation of the main effect of one factor we average over all levels of the other factor(s). That is, to obtain the main effect of temperature we average over the two levels of reaction time.

In many cases it happens that the effect of a change in one factor depends on the level of the other factor(s); in our particular case the temperature effect may change dependent on the level of reaction time. It could be that the impact of a temperature change at a reaction time of 50 minutes is very different from the impact of a temperature change at a reaction time of 70 minutes.

We can check whether this is the case. Presence or absence of an interaction between the factors temperature and reaction time can be seen from Figure 15.4. In this graph the two yield lines, for low and high levels of R, are almost parallel. This means that the temperature effects at the two levels of R are pretty much the same.

The *interaction* between the factors temperature and reaction time, $T \times R$, is quantified as one half of the difference of the main effect of temperature at reaction time of 70 minutes (+) and the main effect of temperature at reaction time of 50 minutes (−). The temperature effect at reaction time of 70 minutes is given by $68.2 - 64.2 = 4.0$; the temperature effect at reaction time of 50 minutes is $60.6 - 55.0 = 5.6$. Hence,

$$T \times R = [(68.2 - 64.2) - (60.6 - 55.0)]/2 = -0.8.$$

If this coefficient is 0 or small in absolute value, then we say that there is no interaction between the two factors. The presence of an interaction influences our interpretation of main effects. If there is little or no interaction among the two factors, then it makes good sense to interpret the main effects as in this case it is appropriate to average the results over the levels of the second factor. However, if there is considerable interaction among the factors, implying that the effect of temperature depends very much on the level of the reaction time, then it makes little sense to interpret the main effects. A main effect of one factor is obtained by averaging over the levels of the other factor(s). Hence it may be that at reaction time 50 minutes the yield increases by 5 units with a change in temperature, and that at reaction time of 70 minutes it decreases by 5 units. Talking about a main effect of temperature, which in this case is zero, does not make sense. Temperature does have an impact in this case, but its impact depends on the level of the other factor.

The presence of an interaction is easily seen in a plot like the one in Figure 15.4. We call such a plot an *interaction plot*. There we plot and connect yields for the same reaction time. If these two lines are parallel (or almost parallel), then there is no (or little) interaction. If they are not parallel, then interaction is present.

It is not always necessary to calculate the interaction from first principles, as we have done here. There is another easy way to carry out the calculation. You form a new column (the column TR) which you get by multiplying the coded units (the + and − signs) in columns T and R in Table 15.2 that lists the four factor-level combinations. This leads to the column: "+ − − +". This column of signs gets multiplied with the column of the responses, the products are added up, and the sum is divided by 2. That is,

$$T \times R = (+55.0 - 60.6 - 64.2 + 68.2)/2 = -0.8.$$

15.4.2 Analysis of a 2^3 Factorial Experiment

As an example, we analyze the 2^3 factorial experiment discussed in Section 15.3.2. The first three columns in Table 15.4 contain the coded levels of the three factors: temperature T, concentration C, and catalyst K. The next four columns (TC, TK, CK, TCK) contain all possible products of these columns. For example, the column TC is the result of multiplying the minus and plus signs in columns T and C. The column TCK is the product of the three columns T, C, and K; you should check the calculations in Table 15.4. These columns will become useful when we estimate interaction effects. The last column contains the results.

TABLE 15.4 The 2^3 Factorial Experiment; Design and Calculation Columns

T	C	K	TC	TK	CK	TCK	Result
−	−	−	+	+	+	−	60
+	−	−	−	−	+	+	72
−	+	−	−	+	−	+	54
+	+	−	+	−	−	−	68
−	−	+	+	−	−	+	52
+	−	+	−	+	−	−	83
−	+	+	−	−	+	−	45
+	+	+	+	+	+	+	80

Estimation of Main Effects The effect of a temperature change from 160 (−) to 180 (+) degrees is estimated by the difference of the response averages at temperature 180 (+) and 160 (−) degrees. Table 15.4 and also the cube in Table 15.3 show that the results for runs with temperature at 180 degrees are 72, 68, 83, 80. The observations for runs at a temperature of 160 degrees are 60, 54, 52, 45. Thus,

$$T = \frac{72 + 68 + 83 + 80}{4} - \frac{60 + 54 + 52 + 45}{4} = 75.75 - 52.75$$
$$= (-60 + 72 - 54 + 68 - 52 + 83 - 45 + 80)/4 = 23.0.$$

The calculation is easy to remember: The entries in the results column are multiplied by the signs in the first column (temperature, T), added up, and the sum is divided by 4. The number 4 represents the number of minus (or plus) signs in the first column. The result implies that a 20-degree temperature increase, from 160 to 180 degrees, increases the yield by 23 units.

The effect of a change in the concentration from 20 (−) to 40 (+) percent is estimated by the difference of the response averages at concentration 40 (+) and 20 (−) percent:

$$C = \frac{54+68+45+80}{4} - \frac{60+72+52+83}{4} = 61.75 - 66.75$$
$$= (-60-72+54+68-52-83+45+80)/4 = -5.0.$$

The entries in the results column of Table 15.4 are multiplied with the signs in the second column, added up, and their sum is divided by 4. An increase in the concentration from 20 to 40 percent reduces the yield by 5 units.

The effect of changing the catalyst from A (−) to B (+) is estimated by the difference in the average results for catalyst B (+) and catalyst A (−):

$$K = \frac{52+83+45+80}{4} - \frac{60+72+54+68}{4} = 65.0 - 63.5$$
$$= (-60-72-54-68+52+83+45+80)/4 = 1.5.$$

The responses are multiplied with the signs in the third column, added, and divided by 4. A change from catalyst A to catalyst B increases the yield by 1.5 units.

Estimation of Two-Factor Interaction Effects Next, we estimate the interaction effect between temperature and catalyst. In this case we ignore, and average over, the information on concentration.

At catalyst B, the responses at high temperature are 80 and 83. The responses at low temperature and catalyst B are 52 and 45. Therefore, at catalyst B (+) the effect of a temperature change from 160 to 180 degrees is estimated by

$$T(\text{Catalyst } B) = (80+83)/2 - (52+45)/2$$
$$= 81.5 - 48.5 = 33.$$

At catalyst A (−), the responses for runs at the high temperature are 72 and 68; the responses for runs at the low temperature and catalyst A are 60 and 54. Therefore, at catalyst A the effect of a temperature change from 160 to 180 degrees is given by

$$T(\text{Catalyst } A) = (72+68)/2 - (60+54)/2$$
$$= 70 - 57 = 13.$$

The interaction effect between temperature and catalyst, $T \times K$, is one half of the difference between these two temperature effects. That is,

$$T \times K = (33 - 13)/2 = 10.$$

The calculation is easy to remember. The results in the last column are multiplied with the signs in the TK column (which we get by multiplying the coded units in columns T and K), the products are added up, and the sum is divided by 4. That is,

$$T \times K = (+60 - 72 + 54 - 68 - 52 + 83 - 45 + 80)/4 = 10$$

The other two interaction effects (temperature and concentration $T \times C$, and concentration and catalyst $C \times K$) are estimated similarly, multiplying the results by the signs in the corresponding product column in Table 15.4, and dividing the resulting sum by 4. That is,

$$T \times C = (+60 - 72 - 54 + 68 + 52 - 83 - 45 + 80)/4 = 1.5$$
$$C \times K = (+60 + 72 - 54 - 68 - 52 - 83 + 45 + 80)/4 = 0.0.$$

What is one to make of the two-factor interactions? If a two-factor interaction is close to zero, then the main effect of one factor does not depend on the levels of the second factor.

Estimation of a Three-Factor Interaction Effect The interaction effect between temperature and catalyst may depend on the level of the third factor, concentration. The interaction effect $T \times K$ at concentration of 40 percent (+) is given by

$$T \times K \text{ (for } C = +) = [(80 - 45) - (68 - 54)]/2 = 10.5.$$

The first component, $80 - 45$, is the temperature effect at $K = +$ and $C = +$. The second component, $68 - 54$, is the temperature effect at $K = -$ and $C = +$. One half of their difference is the interaction between T and K for $C = +$.

Similarly, the interaction effect $T \times K$ at concentration of 20 percent (−) is given by

$$T \times K \text{ (for } C = -) = [(83 - 52) - (72 - 60)]/2 = 9.5.$$

The three-factor interaction, $T \times C \times K$, is one half of the difference between these two-way interactions. For our data the three-factor interaction is

$$T \times K \times C = (10.5 - 9.5)/2 = 0.5.$$

If a three factor interaction is zero or reasonably small, then the interaction of two factors does not depend on the levels of the third factor. If the three-way interaction is appreciably different from zero, then the two-way interactions depend on the level of the third factor.

In the calculation of a three-factor interaction we have conditioned two-factor interactions on the level of a third factor. Our choice of "concentration" as this third factor is arbitrary and does not affect the value of the three-factor interaction. Alternatively, we could have conditioned on "temperature," or on "catalyst"; the results would have been all the same.

It is useful, but not necessary to remember the calculation of a three-factor interaction from first principles. The calculation can be remembered from the following rule: The observations in the results column are multiplied with the signs in the *TCK* column, added up, and their sum is divided by 4. That is,

$$T \times C \times K = (-60 + 72 + 54 - 68 + 52 - 83 - 45 + 80)/4 = 0.5.$$

Summary of the Results The results (estimated main effects and interaction effects) of this example are summarized in Table 15.5. We have also added the average of the eight observations, 64.25, and have indicated the effects that are statistically significant. In the next section we explain how to determine the statistical significance of the effects.

Concentration ($C = -5.0$) has an influence on the response. The impact of concentration does not depend on the other factors, as its interaction effects with the other factors are all small. Raising the concentration by 20 units (from 20 percent to 40 percent) reduces the yield by 5 units.

Temperature and the type of catalyst interact in their effects on the yield. Because of this interaction ($T \times K = 10.0$), we must interpret their effects jointly. The interaction diagram in Figure 15.5 shows how these two factors influence the response. The effect of catalyst switches with changing temperature; yield is largest at temperature 180 degrees and catalyst *B*.

TABLE 15.5 Estimated Effects in the 2^3 Factorial Experiment

Effects	Estimates	
Average	64.25	
T	23.0	***
C	−5.0	***
K	1.5	
$T \times C$	1.5	
$T \times K$	10.0	***
$C \times K$	0.0	
$T \times C \times K$	0.5	

Significant effects are indicated by ***.

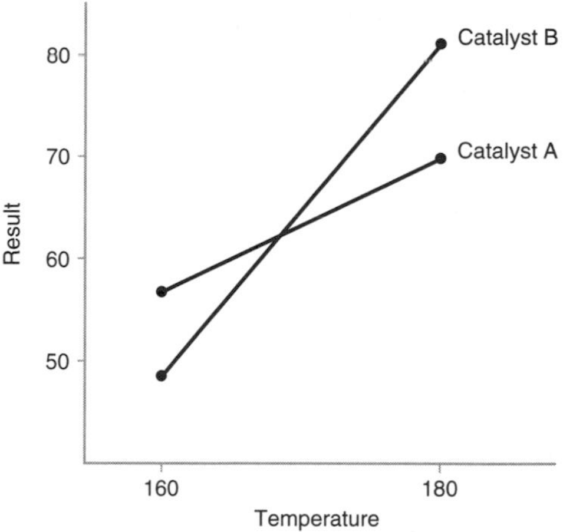

FIGURE 15.5 Interaction plot for temperature and catalyst. (Results are averaged over concentration.)

15.5 DETERMINATION OF THE STATISTICAL SIGNIFICANCE OF ESTIMATED EFFECTS

We have shown how to estimate main and interaction effects from the outcomes of two-level factorial experiments. The outcomes of the experiments are affected by factors other than those that are controlled in the experiment; hence the experimental outcomes are subject to variation. As a consequence the estimated effects are subject to sampling variability. Before we can assess the statistical significance of the estimates of the effects we need to understand their sampling variability.

15.5.1 The Unreplicated Situation

Let us first consider the case when there are no replications of the factorial experiment. As a very simple way to check whether the estimated effects amount to more than just random variation or noise, we recommend plotting all estimated main and interaction effects on a dot diagram. If none of the factors have an influence on the response, then the estimated main and interaction effects should scatter around zero. The estimated effects involve sums and differences of the responses, and because of the Central Limit Effect, their distribution should look normal. If some of the estimated effects are too large to fit a normal distribution around zero, then we say that these larger estimated effects are statistically significant. R.V. Lenth, in his paper "Quick and Easy Analysis of Unreplicated Factorials" (1989, pp. 469–473), discusses a quick method for deciding which of the estimated effects are unusually large.

Normal probability plots are often used to make this determination. There one graphs the estimated effects on normal probability paper. We conclude that none of the effects are statistically significant if all estimated effects plot on a straight line through the origin. Effects that don't fall on a straight line through the origin are taken as statistically significant. Normal probability plots are explained in Section 8.11 in Chapter 8. For additional discussion of normal probability plots in the context of factorial experiments we refer you to Box, Hunter, and Hunter (1978).

Sometimes it is rather difficult to recognize whether an estimated effect is sufficiently different from zero. This is especially true if our experiments involve only two or three factors, as there are only three estimated effects in the 2^2 and seven estimated effects in the 2^3 factorial.

15.5.2 The Replicated Situation

Let us consider the case when the 2^k factorial experiment is replicated, say n times. This means that we have n replicates at each of the 2^k factor-level combinations, and a total of $n2^k$ observations. From each set of n replicates at a given factor-level combination we can estimate a standard deviation. We can pool these 2^k standard deviations, $s_1, s_2, \ldots, s_{2^k}$, to obtain an even better estimate of the standard deviation of individual observations. We could take a straight average of the 2^k standard deviations. However, it turns out that it is preferable to use the pooled estimate

$$s_{\text{pooled}} = \sqrt{\frac{1}{2^k} \sum_{i=1}^{2^k} (s_i)^2},$$

which we get by averaging the variances (that is, the squared standard deviations) and then taking the square root. This pooled standard deviation measures the variability, or the noise in individual observations. We can use it to obtain standard deviations, or standard errors of the estimated effects. One can show that the standard deviation, or the standard error of each estimated effect, is given by

$$\text{StdDev(effect)} = s_{\text{pooled}} \sqrt{\frac{1}{n2^{k-2}}}.$$

Approximate 95 percent confidence intervals of the effects can be obtained by adding and subtracting from the estimated effects two standard errors, resulting in the interval [effect − (2)StdDev(effect); effect + (2)StdDev(effect)].

15.5.3 An Example

Consider the results of the replicated 2^2 factorial experiment in Table 15.2. Two experiments were carried out at each of the four factor-level combinations. We can use these two observations to calculate a standard deviation.

The standard deviations at the four factor-level combinations are given by

$$(\text{TEMP} = -; \text{TIME} = -): \quad s_1 = \sqrt{\frac{1}{2-1}[(55.5-55.0)^2 + (54.5-55.0)^2]} = \sqrt{0.50}$$

$$(\text{TEMP} = +; \text{TIME} = -): \quad s_2 = \sqrt{\frac{1}{2-1}[(60.2-60.6)^2 + (61.0-60.6)^2]} = \sqrt{0.32}$$

$$(\text{TEMP} = -; \text{TIME} = +): \quad s_3 = \sqrt{\frac{1}{2-1}[(64.5-64.2)^2 + (63.9-64.2)^2]} = \sqrt{0.18}$$

$$(\text{TEMP} = +; \text{TIME} = +): \quad s_4 = \sqrt{\frac{1}{2-1}[(67.7-68.2)^2 + (68.7-68.2)^2]} = \sqrt{0.50}.$$

This yields the pooled estimate

$$s_{\text{pooled}} = \sqrt{(0.50 + 0.32 + 0.18 + 0.50)/4} = \sqrt{0.375} = 0.61,$$

and the standard error of each estimated effect

$$\text{StdDev(effect)} = (0.61)\sqrt{\frac{1}{(2)2^{2-2}}} = 0.44.$$

Approximate 95 percent confidence intervals for the effects are obtained by adding and subtracting (2)(0.44) = 0.88 from the estimates. The $T \times R$ interaction effect (which was −0.8) is not statistically significant. This is because the interval -0.8 ± 0.88, or (−1.68, 0.08), includes 0. Thus there is no (or at the most, very minor) interaction between temperature and reaction time. The absence of any appreciable interaction is also evident from the interaction plot in Figure 15.4; the two lines in that graph are almost parallel.

The two main effects (4.8 for temperature, and 8.4 for reaction time) are both larger than two standard errors. Thus there is considerable evidence that these effects are larger than zero. These factors influence the yield of the process.

15.6 ANOTHER ILLUSTRATIVE EXAMPLE: ANALYSIS OF A 2^4 FACTORIAL EXPERIMENT

Lynne Hare, in the paper "In the Soup: A Case Study to Identify Contributors to Filling Variability" (1988, pp. 36–43), addresses a problem that originated in the filling of dry soup mix packages at Lipton Soup. Customers of dry soup expect consistent products; hence it is important that mix packages are uniform. Lipton had experienced considerable fill variation for their "intermix," which is one component of their dry soup mix. The intermix is a mixture of flavorful ingredients, vegetable oil, salt, and so on, mixed together in a mixer that is capable of holding

TABLE 15.6 Fill-Weight Experiment

					Calculation columns										
STD	P	T	W	D	PT	PW	PD	TW	TD	WD	PTW	PTD	PWD	TWD	$PTWD$
1.18	−	−	−	−	+	+	+	+	+	+	−	−	−	−	+
1.70	+	−	−	−	−	−	−	+	+	+	+	+	+	−	−
1.13	−	+	−	−	−	+	+	−	−	+	+	+	−	+	−
1.28	+	+	−	−	+	−	−	−	−	+	−	−	+	+	+
1.85	−	−	+	−	+	−	+	−	+	−	+	−	+	+	−
2.10	+	−	+	−	−	+	−	−	+	−	−	+	−	+	+
1.09	−	+	+	−	−	−	+	+	−	−	−	+	+	−	+
1.36	+	+	+	−	+	+	−	+	−	−	+	−	−	−	−
0.97	−	−	−	+	+	+	−	+	−	−	−	+	+	+	−
0.98	+	−	−	+	−	−	+	+	−	−	+	−	−	+	+
1.47	−	+	−	+	−	+	−	−	+	−	+	−	+	−	+
1.25	+	+	−	+	+	−	+	−	+	−	−	+	−	−	−
0.76	−	−	+	+	+	−	−	−	−	+	+	+	−	−	+
0.62	+	−	+	+	−	+	+	−	−	+	−	−	+	−	−
0.78	−	+	+	+	−	−	−	+	+	+	−	−	−	+	−
1.10	+	+	+	+	+	+	+	+	+	+	+	+	+	+	+

Standard deviation (STD) is the response variable; P is number of ports (1 or 3 ports); T is temperature (ambient or cool); W is batch weight (1500 or 2000 pounds); D is delay (1 or 7 days).

over 2,000 pounds. Too much intermix in a packet gives too strong a flavor, while too little makes the soup too weak.

Researchers responsible for the product identified several intermix processing factors which, according to their opinion, were expected to have an influence on fill control. These factors were: the number of ports through which vegetable oil is added (factor P); the temperature of the jacket surrounding the mixer (factor T); the batch weight (factor W); and the delay (in days) between mixing and packing (factor D). The results of a 2^4 factorial design in these four factors are given in Table 15.6. For each of the 16 factor-level combinations a batch of material was prepared. From each batch five packages were taken every 15 minutes, and their fill weight was recorded. A standard deviation was calculated from about 25 to 30 sets of five measurements; the standard deviation from these 125 to 150 observations reflects both the within-sample variability as well as the variability from sample to sample. The variable of interest in this particular example is the variability within each batch. The standard deviations (STD) that correspond to the 16 different experimental conditions are listed in Table 15.6 in standard error; the actual order in which the experiments were carried out was randomized.

For this illustration we have simplified the discussion considerably. You should consult the original paper for many interesting and relevant details. For example, our abbreviated discussion ignores the mixing time, which was another factor that was varied in this experiment. We will say more about this factor in Section 15.7.

Estimation of Main and Interaction Effects The main effect of P, the number of ports, is estimated by multiplying the results (the standard deviations, STD) with the minus and plus signs in column P, adding the terms, and dividing by eight (as there are eight minus signs in column P). You can check that this gives

$$P = (-1.18 + 1.70 - 1.13 + 1.28 - \cdots - 0.78 + 1.10)/8 = 1.16/8 = 0.145.$$

The two-factor interaction between the number of ports (P) and temperature (T) is estimated by multiplying the results with the signs in the product column PT, adding the terms, and dividing by eight. That is,

$$P \times T = (+1.18 - 1.70 - 1.13 + 1.28 + \cdots - 0.78 + 1.10)/8 = -0.12/8 = -0.015.$$

Similarly, we estimate all other main and interaction effects. For example, we obtain the three-factor interaction between P, W, and D by multiplying the results with the signs in column PWD; for the four-factor interaction we multiply the results with the signs in $PTWD$. Considerable calculation is involved. However, the calculations are easily programmed and computer software is available for the computations. The computations can take advantage of a short-cut method, known as the Yates algorithm. You may want to consult one of the references such as Box, Hunter, and Hunter (1978) or Hogg and Ledolter (1992) for details.

Estimates of the main and interaction effects are given in Table 15.7 (page 438). A dot diagram of the estimates is given in Figure 15.6. The three largest effects warrant further investigation, as they are clearly different from the remaining ones scattered around zero. They are the main effect of delay ($D = -0.470$), which is by far the largest, and the two-factor interactions of delay with temperature ($T \times D = 0.405$) and with weight of the batch ($W \times D = -0.315$). The negative sign of the main effect of D implies that a seven-day delay reduces the variability, making the intermix within the batch more uniform. The interaction plots in Figure 15.7 (for delay and temperature, and delay and weight of batch) illustrate the nature of the interactions. If a seven-day delay is adopted, then these plots indicate that larger batches are preferable and that no cooling is necessary. The number of ports does not appear to affect the variability.

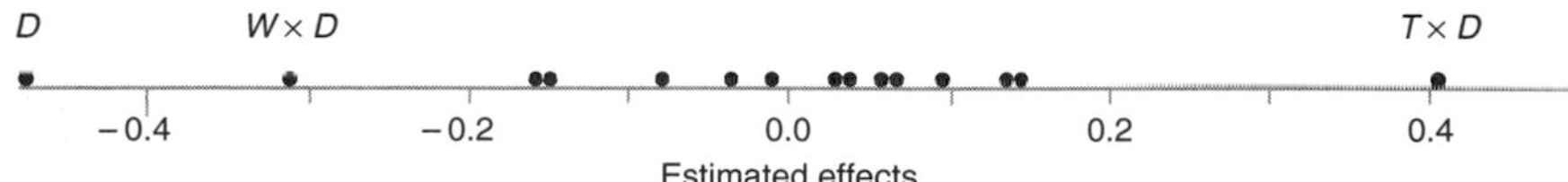

FIGURE 15.6 Dot diagram of the 15 estimated main and interaction effects in the fill-weight experiment.

TABLE 15.7 Estimated Main and Interaction Effects in the Fill-Weight Experiment

	Estimated effects	
Average	1.22625	
P (Port)	0.1450	
T (Temp.)	−0.0875	
W (Weight)	−0.0375	
D (Delay)	−0.4700	***
$P \times T$	−0.0150	
$P \times W$	0.0300	
$P \times D$	−0.1525	
$T \times W$	−0.1625	
$T \times D$	0.4050	***
$W \times D$	−0.3150	***
$P \times T \times W$	0.1350	
$P \times T \times D$	0.0725	
$P \times W \times D$	0.0675	
$T \times W \times D$	0.0950	
$P \times T \times W \times D$	0.0375	

Large effects are indicated by ***.

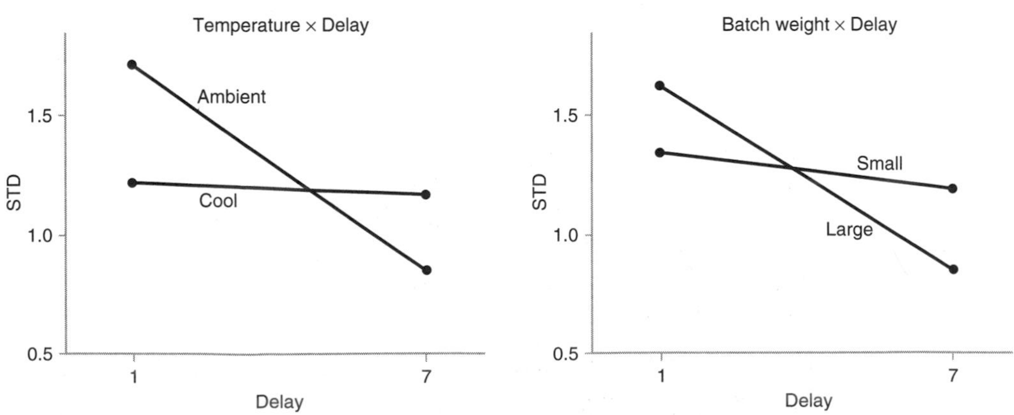

FIGURE 15.7 Interaction plots in the fill-weight experiment.

15.7 INTRODUCTION TO FRACTIONAL FACTORIAL EXPERIMENTS

Assume that we have identified several factors that are thought to have an influence on the response variable. We may have identified seven factors, or ten factors, or even more. It would be quite unwieldy and expensive to carry out a full factorial experiment. For 7 factors, a full factorial experiment involves $2^7 = 128$ runs; for 10 factors, the experiment consists of $2^{10} = 1024$ runs.

Fractional factorial experiments use certain well-chosen fractions of full factorial experiments. Instead of investigating all 2^k factor-level combinations, we study a certain subset (or fraction) of these runs. Obviously, such an approach is more economical. However, we pay a price by not being able to estimate all main and interaction effects.

Here we give only a very brief introduction to fractional factorial experiments. If you want to learn more about this topic, we recommend that you consult Box, Hunter, and Hunter (1978) and the references that are given in their book.

15.7.1 A Fractional Factorial Experiment for Seven Factors in Eight Runs

We call a fractional factorial experiment with seven factors in eight runs a 2^{7-4} fractional factorial experiment, since we consider only a 2^{-4} (or a sixteenth) fraction of the original factorial experiment of $2^7 = 128$ runs. The arrangement of the eight runs is given in Table 15.8. For example, in the first run factors 1, 2, 3, and 7 are at their low levels, while factors 4, 5, and 6 are at their high levels; in the second run factors 2 through 5 are at low levels, while factors 1, 6, and 7 are at

TABLE 15.8 The 2^{7-4} Fractional Factorial Design

Factors						
1	2	3	4 (= 12)	5 (= 13)	6 (= 23)	7 (= 123)
−	−	−	+	+	+	−
+	−	−	−	−	+	+
−	+	−	−	+	−	+
+	+	−	+	−	−	−
−	−	+	+	−	−	+
+	−	+	−	+	−	−
−	+	+	−	−	+	−
+	+	+	+	+	+	+

high levels; and so on. The arrangement in Table 15.8 is in standard order; when carrying out the experiment, one should randomize the order.

It is interesting to learn how such fractional factorials are constructed. We start by writing down a full factorial in eight runs; we can accommodate three factors, factors 1 through 3. The levels of the remaining four factors are determined from the calculation columns in the 2^3 factorial; these are the product columns 12, 13, 23, 123. It is obvious from this construction that the design in Table 15.8 will confound main effects with interactions (for example, the main effect of factor 4 is confounded with the interaction effect of factors 1 and 2; the main effect of factor 5 is confounded with the interaction of factors 1 and 3, and so on). Nevertheless, if one is willing to ignore the interactions, the fractional factorial in Table 15.8 will provide good estimates of the main effects of the seven factors.

15.7.2 A Fractional Factorial Experiment for Five Factors in Sixteen Runs

The analysis of fill weight of dry soup mix packages in Section 15.6 used the data from a 16-run design involving four factors. The four factors were the number of ports (P), the temperature (T), the batch weight (W), and the delay between mixing and packing (D). In fact there was a fifth factor, the mixing time (factor M), but we ignored it in our previous analysis.

The analysis involving all five factors is given next; the 16-run design in five factors is listed in Table 15.9. A full 2^5 factorial requires 32 runs. Hence the 16 runs in Table 15.9 represent a half-fraction of the 2^5 factorial, or a 2^{5-1} fractional factorial. The levels of the first four factors represent a full 2^4 factorial. The levels of the fifth factor M are the same as the product $PTWD$; you can see this by multiplying the first four design columns, and by comparing the design column for M with the $PTWD$ column in Table 15.6. We call $M = PTWD$ the *generator* of the 2^{5-1} fractional factorial. The design confounds M with $PTWD$; hence estimates of the main effect of M and of the four-factor interaction $P \times T \times W \times D$ are confounded. We can't really tell whether the estimate 0.0375 in Table 15.7 estimates the main effect of M, or the four-factor interaction $P \times T \times W \times D$, or any combination of the two. In practice, it is reasonable to ignore higher-order interactions. We usually believe that main effects and two-factor interactions are important, but we are willing to ignore interactions of order three or higher. Ignoring the four-factor interaction, we interpret 0.0375 as an estimate of the main effect of M.

What about the other estimates in Table 15.7? What do they estimate? Take P, for example. Since $M = PTWD$, we find that $TWDM = P$. (You can see this by multiplying both sides of the equation by TWD, and realizing that products such as TT, WW, etc., lead to columns of plus signs. You can also show the identity by multiplying the columns T, W, D, and M in Table 15.9 and convincing yourself that it is the same as P.) This identity says that the main effect of P is confounded with the four-factor interaction $T \times W \times D \times M$.

TABLE 15.9 Fill-Weight Experiment

STD	P	T	W	D	$M = PTWD$
1.18	−	−	−	−	+
1.70	+	−	−	−	−
1.13	−	+	−	−	−
1.28	+	+	−	−	+
1.85	−	−	+	−	−
2.10	+	−	+	−	+
1.09	−	+	+	−	+
1.36	+	+	+	−	−
0.97	−	−	−	+	−
0.98	+	−	−	+	+
1.47	−	+	−	+	+
1.25	+	+	−	+	−
0.76	−	−	+	+	+
0.62	+	−	+	+	−
0.78	−	+	+	+	−
1.10	+	+	+	+	+

Standard deviation (STD) is the response variable; P is number of ports (1 or 3 ports); T is temperature (ambient or cool); W is batch weight (1500 or 2000 pounds); D is delay (1 or 7 days); M is mixing time (60 or 80 seconds).

What about PT? Since $M = PTWD$, we find that $WDM = PT$. This says that the two-factor interaction between P and T is confounded with the three-factor interaction $W \times D \times M$. What about the three-factor interaction $P \times T \times W$? Again, since $M = PTWD$, we find that $PTW = DM$, confounding these two interactions. It is usually reasonable to ignore interactions of order three or higher; if we do this, then we can view the estimate 0.135 in Table 15.7 as estimating the two-factor interaction $D \times M$. The estimates in Table 15.7 are repeated in Table 15.10 (page 442). However, we have added the fifth factor M and the confounding patterns. The effects in bold are obtained after ignoring interactions of order three or higher.

Changes in mixing time (M) do not affect the variability. Table 15.10 shows that the main effect of M as well as all two-factor interactions involving M are small. It is the main effect of D and its interactions with T and W that are important. Our earlier conclusions in Section 15.6 are still valid. But the fractional factorial design has allowed us to study one additional factor in the same number of runs. Or, to say this differently, the fractional factorial design has allowed us to economize the number of runs of a full factorial, and study five factors in only 16 runs.

TABLE 15.10 Estimated Main and Interaction Effects in the 2^{5-1} Fractional Factorial Experiment with $M = PTWD$

Estimated effects		
Average	1.22625	
$P(T \times W \times D \times M)$	0.1450	
$T(P \times W \times D \times M)$	−0.0875	
$W(P \times T \times D \times M)$	−0.0375	
$D(P \times T \times W \times M)$	−0.4700	***
$P \times T(W \times D \times M)$	−0.0150	
$P \times W(T \times D \times M)$	0.0300	
$P \times D(T \times W \times M)$	−0.1525	
$T \times W(P \times D \times M)$	−0.1625	
$T \times D(P \times W \times M)$	0.4050	***
$W \times D(P \times T \times M)$	−0.3150	***
$P \times T \times W\ (D \times M)$	0.1350	
$P \times T \times D\ (W \times M)$	0.0725	
$P \times W \times D\ (T \times M)$	0.0675	
$T \times W \times D\ (P \times M)$	0.0950	
$P \times T \times W \times D\ (M)$	0.0375	

The estimates are the same as in Table 15.7. Effects in bold are estimated if interactions of order three or higher are ignored. Large estimated effects are indicated by ***.

15.8 EXERCISES

15.1 Many of the exercises in Chapter 14 involved two-level factorial designs. Analyze the data that you obtained. Estimate main and interaction effects. Explain your findings. Use graphical procedures, as well as numerical estimates.

15.2 B. H. Gunter, A. L. Tadder, and C. M. Hemak (1985, pp. 54–59) use factorial designs to improve the picture-tube phosphor screening process at RCA's picture-tube manufacturing facility. This process involves applying, exposing, and developing a photosensitive phosphor slurry to the inside of the picture tube faceplate. Surfactants are added to the slurry to help make it smoother. As part of their investigation they varied three surfactant additives according to a 2^3 factorial experiment and studied their effects on the manufacturing losses. The current settings of the three additives were varied slightly, and low (−) and high (+) levels were determined. The losses were measured by the screen-room process rejects.

The losses from the 2^3 factorial runs were as follows:

Surfactant additive			
A	**B**	**C**	**Loss**
−	−	−	1.28
+	−	−	1.93
−	+	−	0.94
+	+	−	1.31
−	−	+	0.36
+	−	+	1.11
−	+	+	1.16
+	+	+	1.58

Interpret the results, both graphically and numerically. How would you change the surfactant additives to reduce your losses?

15.3 R.V. Hogg and J. Ledolter (1992) include the following case study written by B.H. Gunter.

Three components of an emulsion are thought to affect the line width of a photolithographic process. Photolithography uses chemicals to etch patterns on a substrate by sensitizing the substrate through a photographic exposure process. Three components are studied. They are T, D, and F, comprising 5, 12, and 1.5 percent by volume of the total emulsion. A 2^3 factorial experiment was conducted and the line widths at the center and the corners of a rectangle were measured. The results are given below:

			Line width	
T	**D (in percent)**	**F**	**Center (in mils or 0.001 inch)**	**Corners**
3	8	0	6.62	4.11
7	8	0	7.00	4.74
3	16	0	9.68	7.17
7	16	0	9.38	7.35
3	8	3	7.24	5.06
7	8	3	7.56	5.58
3	16	3	10.02	7.65
7	16	3	9.84	7.92

Analyze the information and interpret the results. For further study, refer to the case study on pages 424–434 of the above book.

15.4 Two different fabrics are tested on a wear tester that can compare two materials in a single run. A wear tester is a mechanical device that rubs a material against an object. The weight losses (in milligrams) from seven runs are as follows:

	Run						
Fabric	**1**	**2**	**3**	**4**	**5**	**6**	**7**
A	36	26	31	38	28	37	22
B	39	27	35	42	31	39	21

Analyze the data and determine whether the mean wear of fabric *A* is different from that of *B*. If it is different, how does it differ? Comment on the required randomization.

15.5 The cap torque is a critical component in a bottle filling operation. Thirty-two bottles were sampled from our standard production line and it was found that the average cap torque was 38.1 units, with a standard deviation of 3.1. After making certain changes to this process, we selected 28 bottles and found that the average cap torque was 34.2 units, with a standard deviation of 2.8. Analyze the data and discuss whether the modified process has lowered the cap torque.

15.6 The same applied statistics course is taught to both undergraduate and graduate students. You believe that, on average, graduate students should score higher on a standardized test that assesses students' understanding of basic statistical concepts. In order to test your claim, you select random samples of both undergraduate and graduate students, and you give them the same test.

For the random sample of 30 undergraduates you find that the average is 70 points, and the standard deviation is 15 points. For the random sample of 15 graduate students the average is 74 points, and the standard deviation is 10 points.

Test whether or not the mean score for graduate students exceeds the mean score for undergraduates. Use a 0.05 significance level.

15.7 Two different brands of dandruff shampoo are compared with regard to their ability to get rid of dandruff. Twenty-five males were recruited for this study. They applied shampoo *A* to one side of their head and brand *B* to the other. The amount of remaining dandruff was measured on a 100 point scale. The averages for shampoo *A* and *B* were 36.4 and 41.5, respectively. The standard deviations for shampoo *A* and *B* were 15.2 and 18.5, respectively. The standard deviation of the 25 differences between *A* and *B* was 6.5 units.

Analyze the data. Comment on any practical difficulties that you see with this experiment.

15.8 A new procedure was developed to improve the yield (measured in ounces) of a chemical process. The data for the current and the new process are given below:

Current Process

3.3, 5.5, 7.6, 3.3, 5.4, 3.8, 7.1, 5.8, 3.9, 3.5, 4.1,
8.3, 2.3, 4.0, 3.6, 6.0, 4.1, 2.8, 4.2, 3.1, 4.7, 3.6,
4.9, 2.1, 5.2

New Process

4.8, 5.6, 4.9, 6.1, 3.9, 4.6, 4.8, 3.6, 5.3, 6.1, 6.9,
5.6, 7.0, 5.9, 5.4

(a) Compare the yields of the current and the new process. Are there differences in the means or in the variabilities? Discuss, using appropriate graphs and summary statistics. (Note that in this book we have not discussed how to *test* whether two variances are the same.)

(b) The new process is more expensive than the current process, so a careful evaluation is necessary. Discuss whether you would switch to the new process.

15.9 D.C. Montgomery (1996, p. 543) discusses the application of a 2^4 factorial experiment in developing a nitride etch process on a plasma etcher. The etching process uses C_2F_6 (perfluoroethane) as the reactant gas. Four factors can be varied: the gas flow, the power applied to the cathode, the pressure in the reaction chamber, and the gap between the anode and the cathode. The response variable is the etch rate for silicon nitride (in Angstroms per minute). Each factor was varied at a high- and a low-level setting. The objective is to find the factor-level settings that maximize the etch rate. The levels for gap (factor *A*) are 0.8 and 1.2 cm; the levels for pressure (factor *B*) are 450 and 550 mTorr; the levels for the C_2F_6 flow (factor *C*) are 125 and 200 sccm (standard cc/minute); the levels for power (factor *D*) are 275 and 325 watts. For further background on the etching process and details of the experiment, you can consult the original source for this exercise (Gerald Z. Yin and Don W. Jillie, *Solid State Technology*, 1987).

Run	*A* (Gap)	*B* (Pressure)	*C* (Flow)	*D* (Power)	Response (Etch rate)
1	−1	−1	−1	−1	550
2	1	−1	−1	−1	669
3	−1	1	−1	−1	604
4	1	1	−1	−1	650
5	−1	−1	1	−1	633
6	1	−1	1	−1	642
7	−1	1	1	−1	601
8	1	1	1	−1	635
9	−1	−1	−1	1	1037
10	1	−1	−1	1	749
11	−1	1	−1	1	1052
12	1	1	−1	1	868
13	−1	−1	1	1	1075
14	1	−1	1	1	860
15	−1	1	1	1	1063
16	1	1	1	1	729

Analyze the results of the 2^4 factorial experiment. Find the important main effects and interactions. How would you select the factor-level settings so that you achieve high etch rates?

15.10 Read and discuss the paper "In the Soup: A Case Study to Identify Contributors to Filling Variability," by Lynne Hare (1988, pp. 36–43). Estimate the main and interaction effects, checking the results in Sections 15.6 and 15.7.

15.9 REFERENCES

Box, G. E. P., W. G. Hunter, and J. S. Hunter. *Statistics for Experimenters*. New York: Wiley, 1978.

Gunter, B. H., A. L. Tadder, and C. M. Hemak. "Improving the Picture Tube Phosphor Screening Process with EVOP," *RCA Engineer*, Vol. 30(3), 1985, 54–59.

Hare, L. "In the Soup: A Case Study to Identify Contributors to Filling Variability," *Journal of Quality Technology*, Vol. 20, 1988, 36–43.

Hogg, R. V., and J. Ledolter. *Applied Statistics for Engineers and Physical Scientists*. New York: Macmillan, 1992.

Lenth, R. V. "Quick and Easy Analysis of Unreplicated Factorials," *Technometrics*, Vol. 31, 1989, 469–473.

Montgomery, D. C. *Introduction to Statistical Quality Control*, 3rd edition. New York: Wiley, 1996.

Yin, G. Z., and D. W. Jillie. "Orthogonal Design for Process Optimization and Its Application in Plasma Etching," *Solid State Technology*, May 1987, 127–132.

CHAPTER 16

TAGUCHI DESIGN METHODS FOR PRODUCT AND PROCESS IMPROVEMENT

16.1 INTRODUCTION

Genichi Taguchi is a Japanese engineer who has contributed greatly to the improvement of Japan's industrial products and processes. He has developed both a *philosophy* and an *experimental design methodology* directed to the improvement of processes and products. He is the author of a well-known and widely adopted Japanese text on experimental design which has been translated into English (Taguchi and Wu, 1980).

Many Japanese firms have achieved great success by applying his ideas. It has been reported that thousands of engineers have performed tens of thousands of experiments based on his teaching. Taguchi has received some of Japan's most prestigious awards for quality achievement, including the Deming Prize. Taguchi and his associates have given seminars in the United States since the early 1970s. Starting around 1980 several major United States companies, such as AT&T, Ford, and Xerox, began applying his ideas. The new quality technology based on Taguchi methods was first introduced in the U.S. automotive industry. In the beginning, this effort was fostered by an aggressive Ford drive to improve quality and reduce cost. Ford set up an institute in 1981 to teach Taguchi methods to its suppliers. The institute has since been incorporated as the independent "American Supplier Institute." Its courses are open to all industry.

Taguchi's philosophy of quality engineering has been readily accepted, but his design methodology and his recommended statistical techniques have been somewhat controversial. Writers have debated the efficacy of several of his statistical methods. Reactions to Taguchi methods have ranged from praise to disapproval. Proponents argue that Taguchi has changed U.S. quality thinking and engineering technology. Associates of Taguchi claim that Taguchi methods for improving industrial productivity and quality are one of the most important developments in decades. Others are more critical of Taguchi's contributions and point out that where Taguchi's use of experimental design comes into play, many ideas are neither new nor Taguchi's. They argue that Taguchi uses old and largely discredited techniques and they contend that standard experimental designs are more efficient. For an excellent discussion of these issues, you should refer to the papers by Berton Gunter (1987, pp. 44–52) and George Box and Soren Bisgaard (1987, pp. 54–61). The message in these papers is that one should listen to and respect Taguchi's philosophy, but that one should be skeptical of his statistical methodology.

16.2 TAGUCHI'S CONTRIBUTIONS

The following two concepts are fundamental to the Taguchi approach: (1) his concept of a *loss function*, and (2) his idea of making products and processes more *robust* to uncontrolled environmental conditions. There is general agreement that the development of these two concepts represents a very important contribution.

16.2.1 Quality Loss Function

Quality losses must be defined as deviations from the target. It is more than conformance or nonconformance to often rather arbitrary specifications. Furthermore, quality losses must be measured by systemwide losses, not just by the local costs at points of defect detection. The cost of failure of a five-cent component that is put into a \$100 assembly is not just the five cents it costs to produce a good one; it also includes the cost of fixing the assembled product worth \$100.

The following example, taken from the article by Berton Gunter (1987, p. 46), illustrates the first point:

> *A major Ford subassembly operation used domestic as well as Japanese suppliers. Both suppliers were required to produce to the same given specifications. The specifications were given in terms of a target value and lower and upper specification limits. Warranty complaints for products that contained domestically made parts far exceeded those made by the Japanese supplier. In particular, noisiness was a frequent complaint for U.S. products, while practically none were raised for Japanese products.*

Ford collected samples from domestic and Japanese subassemblies and took measurements on the individual components. Both suppliers met the specifications, and zero defects were found. But Japanese subassemblies had reduced the variability, and their products were closer to the target value than the domestic subassemblies. Also Japanese production reported less scrap, less rework, and lower inventory. In other words, their costs were lower.

Until recently, American engineers would have had a hard time justifying the cost of efforts to do better rather than simply staying within specifications. The notion was that there was no economic loss as long as a part was within the required tolerances (specifications).

Taguchi challenges this belief and provides an economic basis for doing better. All variation from ideal values causes a loss of quality and imposes cost. Anything short of ideal dimensions results in some economic loss, Taguchi argues, whether it is in greater warranty costs, consumer dissatisfaction, or a loss of reputation for the company. A high-quality product performs near the target value consistently throughout the product's life span and under all different operating conditions. Notice the three important components of this statement: 1. The product must be near the target value; 2. It must be near the target value throughout the life span of the product; 3. It should be close to the target under all operating conditions.

16.2.2 Robust Products and Designs

Quality means meeting requirements. For items that are supposed to achieve certain requirements, any variation from the target is undesirable. It follows that improvement in the quality of any process is largely an effort to reduce variation in the items produced by the process. This reduction can be achieved in many ways, for instance, by improved inspection or through tighter control of the manufacturing process. Taguchi uses yet another approach. The Taguchi method aims to reduce variation through *improved design*—improved design of the items being manufactured and improved design of the manufacturing process that produces these items. Frequently the idea is expressed by saying that "quality must be designed in."

The Taguchi method, in its broad sense, focuses on improving product quality through better design of products and better design of the processes that are used at the manufacturing stage. The basic idea behind the Taguchi method is to minimize the adverse effects of factors that are not directly controlled during the manufacturing process or during the product's actual use.

The Taguchi method, in its narrow interpretation, is a statistical method involving the design of experiments and the analysis of the variation in the outcome of these experiments. In this book we don't attempt to give a full discussion of the details of the statistical procedures that are involved in the method; rather we shall look only at the basic concepts and several illustrative examples. Details can be obtained from various references. For example, you may want to refer to the book by Taguchi and Wu (1980).

16.3 THE ENGINEERING DESIGN PROCESS

An understanding of the Taguchi method starts with an understanding of the engineering design process. The basic inputs to this process are a set of requirements for some physical item to be manufactured and constraints on the way in which it will be manufactured. The design process has two basic outputs, namely, a design for the physical item and a design for a manufacturing process to produce that physical item. Under the Taguchi method, a design process has three stages: *system design, parameter design*, and *tolerance design*. Although the Taguchi method is mostly concerned with the second of these stages, we shall review all three.

16.3.1 Stage 1: System Design

During the system design stage of the design process, the designer must specify materials, parts, manufacturing equipment, manufacturing steps, and other components that, when properly combined, will result in a manufacturing process that will consistently produce the required physical items. Faced with many choices and complex interactions among the various components of his design, it is impossible for the designer to achieve an optimal configuration. Rather the goal usually is to find a design that meets the requirements and is "good," perhaps even "elegant." "Tuning" the design is done later.

Every manufacturing operation is affected by a large number of influences or "factors" that determine the functional characteristics of the items being produced. Some factors relate to the manufacturing process and its inputs (process factors), and some to the product itself (product factors). Typical factors are the temperature, humidity, and lighting of the location in which manufacturing takes place; the dimensions, weight, or chemical composition of parts and components used by the process; variation in the output from the manufacturing equipment; the skill and experience of operators; the volume of production; and the physical characteristics of the item being produced. Faced with such a multitude of factors, the designer must decide which factors will be controlled during the manufacturing process and which will be ignored or left uncontrolled. Factors that are left uncontrolled are referred to as "noise factors," as they contribute to the variability (or noise) in the output.

Important characteristics of factors, both the controlled factors and the noise factors, can usually be quantified and described by "parameters" that range over some set of values. Factors and their parameters are closely associated so that control of a factor usually amounts to control of its parameters. Thus the terms "controlled factor" and "controlled parameter" often are used interchangeably.

During system design, an acceptable range of values is established for each controlled parameter. Also, each parameter is assigned a tentative value that will allow the system to "work," but might not give optimal performance.

16.3.2 Stage 2: Parameter Design

During the parameter design stage of the design process, these controlled parameters are "tuned," so as to reduce variation in the manufacturing process. This activity is where the Taguchi use of experimental design comes into play. For example, a controlled factor might be "temperature of the oven," and an acceptable range for the parameter describing temperature might be from 300 to 400 degrees Fahrenheit. A tentative value of 350 might be established for the temperature; during the parameter design stage this value might be adjusted to reduce variation in the process.

Noise can cause a manufacturing process to produce faulty items; in other words, noise can be a cause of failure. One general technique for improving quality is to search for causes of failure and eliminate them; using this technique, an appropriate response to troublesome noise would be to eliminate or at least control it. In other words, the cause-removal approach would call for moving the offending factor from the uncontrolled to the controlled category. At times this might be an appropriate action. But another tactic is also available: The parameters of the controlled factors are selected so as to minimize the impact of the noise. In other words, instead of removing the cause of defects, adjustments are made so as to minimize the impact of the cause. This tactic for improving quality is at the core of the Taguchi approach.

The rationale for the Taguchi approach to quality improvement is that not all factors of a process can be controlled; there are just too many factors for this to be practical. Moreover, control of some factors might be very expensive, and for some it may be virtually impossible. Part of the design process, therefore, is to make a judgment as to which factors should be controlled and which are the noise factors that one must learn to live with. Having made this judgment, parameter values for the controlled factors are then chosen so as to make the manufacturing process robust. A manufacturing process is robust if the variation in the noise factors has little impact on its output.

16.3.3 Stage 3: Tolerance Design

Careful design of parameters will reduce variation in the output of a manufacturing process, but in some cases this reduction will not be sufficient for the process to satisfy the required specifications. In such cases, it is necessary to go on to the third stage in the design process, tolerance design. This stage calls for tightening the tolerances on some controlled factors, which may be product factors as well as process factors, so as to reduce the variation in the output of the manufacturing process. For example, this stage might call for using better-grade components, more skilled operators, or higher-precision equipment.

Generally, tolerance design results in more costly decisions than those made during parameter design, hence it adds more to the cost of production. At times this added cost must be incurred to obtain the necessary reduction in variation. However, quite often designers simply skip the parameter design stage and solve their problem through tolerance design. This action amounts to "throwing money at the problem" to make it go away. It can be an effective, but very costly, solution. Consequently, it can lead to a production process that is no longer competitive.

16.4 A CLOSER LOOK AT PARAMETER DESIGN

Let us look more closely at parameter design, the second stage of the design process and the centerpiece of Taguchi's experimental design strategy. Parameter design involves a series of experiments to determine the effects of controlled factors and the most important noise factors. During such experiments, the noise factors are controlled even though they would not be controlled under ordinary operating conditions.

The activities involved in parameter design are these:

1. For each parameter of the controlled factors, a finite set of "levels" is selected. Usually there will be from two to four levels for each parameter. These levels cover the range of values that the parameter is likely to be assigned. For example, for the controlled factor "temperature of oven," the parameter might be assigned the values 300, 350, and 400, which might be described informally as "low," "medium," and "high" temperature, respectively. Taguchi refers to the experimental design for the controlled factors as the *inner array*.
2. From all noise factors, a finite set is selected as the most important noise factors. These are the noise factors judged to have the greatest impact; in other words, they are expected to cause the greatest variation in the manufacturing process. For each important noise factor, a finite set of "levels" is defined. Usually from two to four levels are selected for each noise factor; these levels are selected so as to cover the range of values that the noise factor is likely to assume. Taguchi refers to the experimental design for the noise factors as the *outer array*.
3. An experiment is designed. This design calls for operating the manufacturing process at various combinations of levels for the controlled factors and the noise factors, and then measuring the resulting output. It is not necessary to examine every combination, which is fortunate because the number of such combinations can be very large. Instead it is possible to take advantage of statistical theory and construct economical designs that allow us to identify

the effect of each factor within a reasonable number of experiments. Taguchi uses *orthogonal array designs* for his experiments. The family of orthogonal array designs, a very flexible class of designs, has been studied extensively in the statistical literature. The factorial and fractional factorial designs of Chapter 15 and the Latin square designs studied in Chapter 14 are all examples of orthogonal array designs.

4. The experiments called for by the experimental design are conducted. Experimental results are analyzed to determine the combination of levels that will minimize the effect of the noise factors.

The design process is finished if a combination of levels of the controlled factors can be found that results in a process that achieves production (1) close to the target and (2) at an acceptable level of variation. If the variation is still unacceptably high, then it is necessary to take further action. One possible action is to examine other ranges for the controlled factors. Another approach is to move one or more noise factors into the controlled category and then conduct further experiments to determine acceptable levels. Failing these efforts, it might be necessary to move to stage 3 of the design process and examine tolerances.

16.4.1 An Example

The following example illustrates these concepts. It also shows why it is important to distinguish between controlled factors that affect the level and controlled factors that affect the variability. It shows why a situation where different controlled factors affect the level and the variability can be used to one's advantage: Factors that affect the level only can be used to adjust the level; we call these factors the *level-adjustment factors*. Similarly, *variability-adjustment factors* can be used to reduce the variability.

The example that is discussed here is taken from the book by Peter John (1990). The output resistance of a certain electrical circuit is the variable of interest. The target output resistance is 73 ohms, and this target is to be achieved with as little variability as possible.

An experiment with three factors, A, B, and C, is conducted. A simple two-level factorial design (as described in Chapter 15) is used. Furthermore, four experiments are conducted at each of the eight factor-level combinations. The variability among these four experiments reflects the influence of the noise variables that one is unable or unwilling to control. The four replications come from an experiment that varies each of two noise factors between a low and a high setting. The results of the experiment are given in Table 16.1 (page 454). For each of the eight factor-level combinations we list the replications, y_1, y_2, y_3, y_4, the average $\bar{y}$, the sample variance s^2 (which is the square of the sample standard deviation), and the logarithm (base 10) of the sample variance.

We can analyze the data in several different ways. We can investigate the effects of the three factors on the *average* from the four replications. Such an

TABLE 16.1 Results of an Experiment with Three Controlled Factors

A	B	C	Observations				Average	Variance	$\log_{10}$(variance)
−	−	−	60.5	61.7	60.5	60.8	60.875	0.323	−0.491
+	−	−	47.0	46.3	46.7	47.2	46.800	0.153	−0.814
−	+	−	92.1	91.0	92.0	91.6	91.675	0.249	−0.604
+	+	−	71.0	71.7	71.1	70.0	70.950	0.497	−0.304
−	−	+	65.2	66.8	64.3	65.2	65.375	1.083	0.034
+	−	+	49.5	50.6	49.5	50.5	50.025	0.369	−0.433
−	+	+	91.2	90.5	91.5	88.7	90.475	1.576	0.198
+	+	+	76.0	76.0	78.3	76.4	76.675	1.209	0.082

analysis tells us about the effects that the controlled factors have on the level of the output resistance. Taking the average $\bar{y}$ as the response and using the tools of Chapter 15, we obtain the following estimates of main and interaction effects:

Average $= 69.1$

Main effects: $A = -16.0$; $B = 26.7$; $C = 3.1$

Interactions: $A \times B = -1.3$; $A \times C = 1.4$; $B \times C = -0.8$; $A \times B \times C = 2.1$

This analysis tells us that factors A and B influence the average output resistance, and that there is little interaction among these two factors. Factor C does not appear to have much influence on the average output.

We can also analyze the effects of these three controlled factors on the *variability*. Taking the variance s^2 as the response, we get the following main and interaction effects:

Average $= 0.68$

Main effects: $A = -0.25$; $B = 0.40$; $C = 0.75$

Interactions: $A \times B = 0.19$; $A \times C = -0.29$; $B \times C = 0.27$;
$A \times B \times C = -0.02$

Factor C has by far the largest effect on the variability. While factors A and B have an impact on the average, their effects on the variability are relatively minor. In summary, factors A and B can be used for level adjustments, while factor C can be used to reduce the variability.

The average variance for the low level of factor C is 0.31 (you get this by averaging 0.323, 0.153, 0.249, and 0.497); the average variance at the high level of C is 1.06. In order to reduce the variability, it is best to set factor C at its low level.

Since C has little effect on the level, we can safely average over the results from the two settings of C when investigating the effects of A and B on the level of output. Averages for low and high values of A and B are given by:

A (low) and B (low): 63.13	A (low) and B (high): 91.08
A (high) and B (low): 48.41	A (high) and B (high): 73.81

In order to get close to the desired target value of 73 ohms, we set both A and B at their high values. In summary, it is best to set A and B at their high levels, and C at its low level.

How would we proceed if our target value were 55.5 ohms? We can adjust the average level by varying the factors A and B. Since there is little interaction between A and B, we can obtain the desired level adjustments by simple linear interpolation. For example, we could set B at its low level and set A at value zero (which is the level halfway between its low and high values); this is because the average level at the low level of B is 55.77 (which is close to the required 55.5). Or, we could set A at its high value and set B at the value -0.5; we get this value by solving the interpolating equation $[(48.41 + 73.81)/2] + [(73.81 - 48.41)/2]x = 55.5$, which gives us $x = -0.44$. In fact, there are many other combinations of A and B that lead to an average output level of 55.5 ohms. Any point on the line going through ($A = 0$; $B = -1$) and ($A = +1$; $B = -0.5$) gives us the desired level adjustment.

A word of caution: You should not take this analysis alone as definite proof that one or the other of these combinations leads to the desired target. You should always conduct a confirmative experiment and check whether the implied results are, in fact, upheld by the data.

A further comment: Here we have analyzed the sample variances. It is sometimes recommended to analyze the logarithm of the variances, as this particular transformation makes the measure more normally distributed. You can check that, in this particular example, the conclusions are not affected when considering a logarithmic transformation of the variances.

16.4.2 Signal-to-Noise Ratios

In the above example we have analyzed the average and the variation, separately. Taguchi discusses various ways of combining these two pieces of information, through the use of a *signal-to-noise ratio*. The signal-to-noise ratio (usually tailor-made for the particular application at hand) is calculated for each factor level combination, and the levels of the controlled factors that maximize the signal-to-noise ratio are determined. Taguchi has proposed many different signal-to-noise ratios. The following ratios are commonly used.

The ratio

$$SN_{\text{small}} = -10 \log_{10} \left[\sum (y_i)^2 / n \right]$$

is recommended if one wishes to make the response y as small as possible. For each factor-level combination one calculates the signal-to-noise ratio from the n replications $(y_1, y_2, \ldots, y_n)$ of the noise array. One determines the levels of the controlled factors such that SN_{small} is maximized.

The maximization of the ratio

$$SN_{\text{large}} = -10 \log_{10}\left[\sum (1/y_i)^2/n\right]$$

is recommended if one wishes to make y as large as possible.

The maximization of the ratio

$$SN_{\text{target}} = 10 \log_{10}[(\bar{y}^2/s^2) - (1/n)]$$

or

$$SN_{\text{target}} = 10 \log_{10}[(\bar{y}^2/s^2)]$$

is recommended if the response y is to attain a specific target value; $\bar{y}$ and s are the average and the standard deviation of the replicates within a fixed factor-level combination.

Engineers like these signal-to-noise criteria as they transform two statistics (the average and the standard deviation) into a single one (the signal-to-noise ratio). However, these criteria are not always intuitive and they have been criticized on various grounds. For example, SN_{target} makes no mention of the specific target value. This fact makes it hard to justify the signal-to-noise ratio as a measure of deviation from a target. Closer inspection of the last two ratios show that they are related to the minimization of the coefficient of variation, $CV = s/\bar{y}$. While it is a good idea to minimize s, it is not obvious why a particular function of the coefficient of variation should be of interest. Many statisticians argue that because of these shortcomings one should not bother with signal-to-noise ratios. Instead, one should separately investigate measures that carry information on the level and measures that focus on the variability. We have done that in the previous example. Taguchi, on the other hand, would probably have adopted one of the signal-to-noise ratios SN_{target}.

16.5 BASIC ASSUMPTIONS BEHIND THE TAGUCHI METHODOLOGY

An examination of the Taguchi method reveals several basic assumptions, which are not always made explicit. Let us examine these assumptions.

First, there is an implicit assumption that a manufacturing process and manufactured items are inherently random. Few would question this. A chemical is rarely 95 percent pure, but might be consistently between 94 percent and 96 percent pure. The length of a rod might vary normally about a desired value. The output of a machine might "drift" slightly between settings. Variability is the norm in manufacturing; deterministic behavior is the exception.

A second assumption is that controllable factors and noise factors can be described by parameters, and that these behave in a "consistent" manner. More precisely, usually it is assumed tacitly that a factor can be described by a parameter with one of three characteristics: the larger the parameter value, the better; the smaller the parameter value, the better; the closer the parameter to some nominal value, the better (deviation in either direction being bad). The effect of this assumption is to limit the amount of experimentation needed to establish optimal parameter values. For example, suppose that a manufacturing process depends on a noise factor called "relative humidity," and this factor is to be considered at the two levels, low (25%) and high (75%). In considering only these two levels, there is an implicit assumption that behavior of the manufacturing process between the low and high humidity levels can be inferred from the behavior at the two extremes. That is to say, there is an implicit assumption that if, say, low is good and high is bad, then process response deteriorates monotonically as humidity increases from low to high. For many physical processes, an assumption such as this is reasonable.

A third assumption is that experiments can be conducted during the design stage to determine how a proposed manufacturing system would react to different parameter settings. In effect, this assumption, which is usually made implicitly, amounts to saying that an experimental version or prototype of the system can be constructed, and that this prototype can be used to learn how the proposed system would respond to different values of the controlled and noise parameters. The prototype might involve a laboratory model, a pilot plant, or simply an analysis of scientific knowledge about the factors involved. However achieved, there is an assumption that reasonable predictions about the behavior of a proposed manufacturing system can be made before the system is actually built. It frequently happens that the findings from off-line experiments differ from the results of on-line investigations. Confirmative experiments must be carried out to see whether the findings from off-line experiments carry over to the actual production process.

16.6 CRITIQUE OF THE TAGUCHI METHODOLOGY

People agree that Taguchi's philosophy of quality engineering has been very influential, and undoubtedly it has contributed to many quality improvements. His concept of a loss function, his idea of making products and processes robust to uncontrolled variability, his emphasis on the process upstream, and his use of experimentation to improve the quality of products and processes represent major contributions to quality engineering. The controversy about Taguchi is centered not on his philosophy, but on his experimental designs and his statistical approach for analyzing the resulting data. Taguchi's statistical design methods are not always the best. Many statisticians argue that Taguchi fails to take full advantage of standard and well-developed statistical techniques that are more efficient than the ones he proposes. A lack of communication between engineers and statisticians is, in part, to blame for this. Engineers learn from engineers and they may not be aware of the contributions statisticians have made to the area of design of experiments, just as statisticians are often not aware of the work that has been done by engineers. Box, Bisgaard, and Fung (1988, pp. 123–131) have expressed this very well:

> *Taguchi has emphasized the importance of statistically designed experiments to improve the quality of the engineering design of products and processes. He is to be congratulated for the major accomplishment of getting more people to run experiments. However, a separate issue is the choice of statistical methods for solving the important problems he raises. Here we often part company with Professor Taguchi. His methods are frequently statistically inefficient and cumbersome. Lack of statistical efficiency is not a minor technical detail. For example, an analysis which is 50 percent efficient is equivalent to throwing away half of the hard-won data, meaning in turn that important effects may be overlooked, and that the experimenter may have to run further costly experiments to make up for this loss. We recommend that the reader take Taguchi's engineering ideas very seriously, learn about them, and understand what he is trying to do; but in implementing the ideas we recommend the use of simpler and more modern data analytic methods.*

Techniques for experimental design go back to the early 1920s when R.A. Fisher, through his work at the Rothamsted agricultural research station in England, laid the foundations for all future work in this area. Design techniques were later extended to industry, but application has been patchy in the West, usually because of lack of management understanding and support. This is different from Japan, where engineers routinely conduct experiments on processes, both on-line and off-line. In Japan management is convinced of the value of experimentation, and well-planned experiments have contributed to the development of high-quality products and processes that will rarely go wrong. The greatest contribution of Taguchi and his followers may not be the introduction of a novel methodology, but their relentless emphasis on the value of experimentation and their success in packaging and marketing methods for the statistical design of experiments that are readily accessible to the nonexpert user.

16.7 ILLUSTRATIVE EXAMPLES

16.7.1 Example 1: Integrated Circuit Fabrication

Kackar and Shoemaker (1986, pp. 39–50) used the following designed experiment to improve certain aspects of an integrated-circuit fabrication process. They investigated eight factors in a 16-run two-level orthogonal array design. The measure of interest was the thickness of the epitaxial layer of the manufactured wafer. The studied factors were the susceptor rotation method (A); the code of the wafers (B); the deposition temperature (C); the deposition time (D); the arsenic gas flow rate (E); the HCl etch temperature (F); the HCl flow rate (G); and the nozzle position (H). The objective of the experiment was to learn how these factors affect the thickness of the epitaxial layer. For each experimental run the thickness of the epitaxial layer of 14 wafers was measured at five places, leading to 70 measurements in all. Averages and sample variances from the 70 measurements were calculated for each of the 16 factor-level combinations. The averages and the logarithms of the sample variances for the 16 experimental runs are given in Table 16.2.

The design in Table 16.2 represents a two-level fractional factorial design in eight factors and 16 runs; see the discussion in Chapter 15. Inspection of the arrangements of the levels in the above table shows that the columns for factors

TABLE 16.2 Results for Example 1: Integrated Circuit Fabrication

A	B	C	D	E	F	G	H	$\bar{y}$	$\log(s^2)$
−	−	−	+	−	−	−	−	14.821	−0.4425
−	−	−	+	+	+	+	+	14.888	−1.1989
−	−	+	−	−	−	+	+	14.037	−1.4307
−	−	+	−	+	+	−	−	13.880	−0.6505
−	+	−	−	−	+	−	+	14.165	−1.4230
−	+	−	−	+	−	+	−	13.860	−0.4969
−	+	+	+	−	+	+	−	14.757	−0.3267
−	+	+	+	+	−	−	+	14.921	−0.6270
+	−	−	−	−	+	+	−	13.972	−0.3467
+	−	−	−	+	−	−	+	14.032	−0.8563
+	−	+	+	−	+	−	+	14.843	−0.4369
+	−	+	+	+	−	+	−	14.415	−0.3131
+	+	−	+	−	−	+	+	14.878	−0.6154
+	+	−	+	+	+	−	−	14.932	−0.2292
+	+	+	−	−	−	−	−	13.907	−0.1190
+	+	+	−	+	+	+	+	13.914	−0.8625

E, C, B, and A are written in the standard order of a full 2^4 factorial in four factors. The levels of the remaining four factors are obtained by equating their levels to certain three-factor calculation columns. You can convince yourself that $D = -ABC$; $F = ABE$; $G = ACE$; and $H = CBE$. One can show that such a design allows the estimation of all main effects, free of any confounding with two-factor interactions.

We calculate the main effects of these eight factors, separately for the level (that is, using the sample average of the 70 measurements as the response) and the variability (using the logarithm of the sample variance as the response). The results are as follows:

Level

Average = 14.389

$A = -0.055$	$B = 0.056$	$C = -0.109$	$D = 0.836$
$E = -0.067$	$F = 0.060$	$G = -0.098$	$H = 0.142$

Variability

Average = −0.648

$A = 0.352$	$B = 0.122$	$C = 0.105$	$D = 0.249$
$E = -0.012$	$F = -0.072$	$G = -0.101$	$H = -0.566$

The results show that factor D has by far the largest impact on the level of the measurements. Factors A and H (and also to a lesser extent factor D) affect the variability. In order to achieve reductions in the variability, we should set factor A at its low level (since the main effect of A is positive) and factor H at its high level (since the main effect of H is negative).

Factor D (deposition time) can be used for level adjustment. Assume that we want to obtain a mean thickness of 14.5 μm. When D is at its low level, the average thickness is 13.97 μm. When D is at its high level, the average thickness is 14.81 μm. In order to achieve an average level of 14.5, we should set D at about 0 (linear interpolation tells us to set it at 0.26; in coded units). Confirmative experiments should be conducted to check whether this setting has the desired effect.

16.7.2 Example 2: Nylon Tubing

D.M. Byrne and S. Taguchi (1987, pp. 19–26) as well as F.B. Alt (1988, pp. 165–167) discuss the following experiment. The objective of the experiment is to maximize the pull-off force of nylon tubing inserted into an elastomeric connector. These connectors are used in automotive engine components. The four controllable factors in this experiment are the interference between the tubing and the connector (factor A); the wall thickness of the connector (factor B); the insertion depth of the tubing into the connector (factor C); and the percent adhesive (factor D). Three levels were chosen for each of the controllable factors. A nine-run orthogonal array design for four factors at three levels each was selected. The levels of these nine

TABLE 16.3 Results for Example 2: Nylon Tubing

A	*B*	*C*	*D*	Observations								SN-ratio	Average
1	1	1	1	19.1	20.0	19.6	19.6	19.9	16.9	9.5	15.6	24.025	17.525
1	2	2	2	21.9	24.2	19.8	19.7	19.6	19.4	16.2	15.0	25.522	19.475
1	3	3	3	20.4	23.3	18.2	22.6	15.6	19.1	16.7	16.3	25.335	19.025
2	1	2	3	24.7	23.2	18.9	21.0	18.6	18.9	17.4	18.3	25.904	20.125
2	2	3	1	25.3	27.5	21.4	25.6	25.1	19.4	18.6	19.7	26.908	22.825
2	3	1	2	24.7	22.5	19.6	14.7	19.8	20.0	16.3	16.2	25.326	19.225
3	1	3	2	21.6	24.3	18.6	16.8	23.6	18.4	19.1	16.4	25.711	19.850
3	2	1	3	24.4	23.2	19.6	17.8	16.8	15.1	15.6	14.2	24.832	18.338
3	3	2	1	28.6	22.6	22.7	23.1	17.3	19.3	19.9	16.1	26.152	21.200

runs are given in Table 16.3. The numbers 1, 2, and 3 stand for the low, medium, and high levels of each factor. This arrangement of runs represents the inner array of the experiment. The design in Table 16.3 is a generalization of the two-level factorial and fractional factorial designs that we discussed in Chapter 15. Such three-level designs are commonly used in Taguchi-type experiments.

Three noise factors were considered: the conditioning time (factor $N1$); the conditioning temperature (factor $N2$); and the conditioning relative humidity (factor $N3$). Each noise factor was studied at two levels (a low and a high one), representing the conditions that the product would experience in the engine. The noise factors were varied according to a 2^3 factorial experiment. This represented the outer array (the noise array) of the experiment. The eight realizations that were obtained by varying the noise factors are listed in Table 16.3.

The objective of this investigation was to find the settings of the controlled factors that maximize the pull-off force. Byrne and Taguchi use the signal-to-noise ratio

$$SN_{\text{large}} = -10 \log_{10} \left[\sum (1/y_i)^2 / n \right]$$

which is recommended if one wants to make the response as large as possible. Taguchi often recommends to pick the "winner," that is, the factor-level combination that leads to the optimal (maximal) signal-to-noise ratio. The signal-to-noise ratio is maximized in run 5: medium interference (level 2 of factor A); medium wall thickness (level 2 of factor B); deep insertion (level 3 of factor C); and low percent adhesive (level 1 of factor D). Of course, confirmative experiments should be conducted at this particular factor-level setting, or at settings that are close to them.

A word of caution: There is one data point in the above table that raises suspicion. The seventh observation in the first run, 9.5, is quite different from the rest. It must be scrutinized before it is included in the analysis. Questions should be asked about the particular conditions that were present at the time this experiment was carried out. It is impossible for us to address this question now, as we did not carry out the experiment ourselves. However, it appears that there could have been a recording error and that the first digit could have been dropped; the number may well have been 19.5. Using 19.5 as the observation, we recalculate the *SN* ratio and find that its value changes to 25.37. However, this change is not large enough to alter the conclusion from our "pick the winner" analysis.

In addition to several more formal analyses, Taguchi recommends an analysis where one calculates the average of the signal-to-noise ratios as well as of the average mean responses, for each level of each controlled factor. We have calculated the averages of the *SN* ratios and of the averages (given in the last two columns of Table 16.3) for the three levels of each controlled factor. We find that both the *SN* ratio and the average are maximized at level 2 of *A*, level 2 of *B*, level 3 of *C*, and level 1 of *D*. This confirms the earlier conclusion from the "pick the winner" strategy.

	***SN* ratio**				**Average**		
	Level 1	**Level 2**	**Level 3**		**Level 1**	**Level 2**	**Level 3**
A	24.96	26.05	25.57	*A*	18.68	20.73	19.80
B	25.21	25.75	25.60	*B*	19.17	20.21	19.81
C	24.73	25.86	25.98	*C*	18.36	20.27	20.57
D	25.70	25.52	25.36	*D*	20.52	19.51	19.17

16.7.3 Example 3: Leaf Springs for Trucks

Our third illustrative example is taken from a discussion contribution by J.J. Pignatiello and J.S. Ramberg (1985, pp. 198–206). The process that is described in their paper involves the heat treatment of leaf springs for trucks. The leaf spring assembly is transported on a conveyor through a high-temperature furnace. After being heated in the furnace, the part is transferred to a forming machine where the camber (that is, the curvature) of the spring is created by holding the spring in a high-pressure press for a very short time. Next, the spring is submersed in an oil quench and then removed from the processing area. An important characteristic of the leaf spring is its free height (that is, the height of the spring in an unloaded condition). The free height of a spring is created during the heat treatment process while the camber is being formed. The target value for this particular spring is 8 inches. Deviations above or below this nominal value are considered undesirable.

The experiment includes four controllable factors and one noise factor. The controllable factors are:

B: Furnace temperature (that is, the temperature at which the heat furnace is set). The low (−) setting is at 1840 degrees F; the high (+) is at 1880 degrees F.

C: Heating time (that is, the length of time a part is heated). The low (−) setting is at 25 seconds; the high (+) is at 23 seconds.

D: Transfer time (that is, the length of time to transfer a part from the heat furnace to the camber former). The low (−) setting is at 12 seconds; the high (+) is at 10 seconds. [Note that the low (−) setting for factor D (as well as factor C) corresponds to longer times. We have retained the same coding that was used in the original reference.]

E: Hold-down time (that is, the length of time that the camber former is closed on a hot part). The low (−) setting is at 2 seconds; the high (+) is at 3 seconds.

The engineers felt that the temperature of the oil quench (factor O) would be difficult to control during the actual production, and hence this factor was treated as a noise variable. In this particular experiment temperature was varied between a low value somewhere between 130 and 150 degrees F and a high value somewhere between 150 and 170 degrees F. Even under the controlled conditions of the experiment it was difficult to set the temperature at exactly the desired value.

Pignatiello and Ramberg maximize the signal-to-noise ratio $SN = 10 \times \log_{10}(\bar{y}^2/s^2)$, which is one of the signal-to-noise ratios that is recommended if one wants to attain a certain target. The design and the results of the experiments are given in Table 16.4. The inner array is a 2^{4-1} fractional factorial design, where the levels of factor E are selected according to $E = BCD$. You can check that this design does not confound the main effects with two-factor interactions. The outer (noise) array consists of six runs each. The observations, as well as the sample averages, variances, and signal-to-noise ratios are listed in Table 16.4.

Using the signal-to-noise ratio in the last column of the table, we calculate the individual effects of the four controllable factors. They are given by

$$B = -0.3325 \quad C = 9.2675 \quad D = -4.5675 \quad E = 2.9425$$

TABLE 16.4 Results for Example 3: Leaf Springs for Trucks

B	*C*	*D*	*E*	High *O*			Low *O*			Average	Variance	SN-ratio
−	−	−	−	7.78	7.78	7.81	7.50	7.25	7.12	7.54	0.09004	28.00
+	−	−	+	8.15	8.18	7.88	7.88	7.88	7.44	7.90	0.07074	29.46
−	+	−	+	7.50	7.56	7.50	7.50	7.56	7.50	7.52	0.00096	47.70
+	+	−	−	7.59	7.56	7.75	7.63	7.75	7.56	7.64	0.00792	38.67
−	−	+	+	7.94	8.00	7.88	7.32	7.44	7.44	7.67	0.09084	28.11
+	−	+	−	7.69	8.09	8.06	7.56	7.69	7.62	7.79	0.05291	30.59
−	+	+	−	7.56	7.62	7.44	7.18	7.18	7.25	7.37	0.03802	31.55
+	+	+	+	7.56	7.81	7.69	7.81	7.50	7.59	7.66	0.01728	35.31

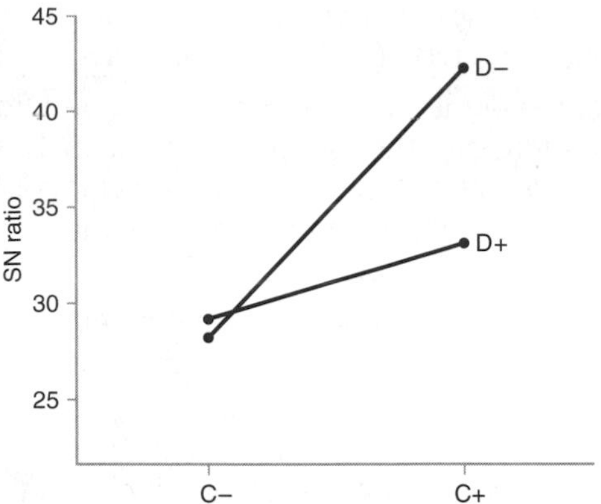

FIGURE 16.1 Interaction diagram for factors C and D: SN-ratio of Example 3.

It appears that factors B and E have little influence on the signal-to-noise ratio. The factors C and D influence the signal-to-noise ratio, as can be seen by their individual effects, as well as by the interaction diagram in Figure 16.1. The average of the signal-to-noise ratio at the low level of D is 28.73 (when C is at its low level), and 43.18 (when C is at its high level). At the high level of D, the average is 29.35 (when C is at its low level), and 33.43 (when C is at its high level). We see that there is an interaction between the factors C and D. In order to maximize the signal-to-noise ratio we should select C (the heating time) at its "+" level (that is, 23 seconds) and D (the transfer time) at its "−" level (that is, 12 seconds). Additional confirmative experiments at these factor levels should be conducted in order to check whether these findings hold up in further experiments.

The two factors that do not have an influence on the signal-to-noise ratio can be used to adjust the average free height to the required level. Analyzing the averages in Table 16.4, we find that the mean effects are: $B = 0.2200$; $C = -0.1775$; $D = -0.0275$; and $E = 0.1025$. These results indicate that one should change B and E in order to reach the desired free spring height of 8 inches. You can check that the average level for experiments at the high level of B and the high level of E is 7.78; hence one must increase B and E in order to reach the desired 8 inches.

16.8 EXERCISES

16.1 Peter W.M. John (1990) describes an experiment that involves five controllable factors, each studied at three levels. The inner array, describing the arrangement of the 18 experimental conditions, is given below. We have listed sample averages and sample variances that are calculated from an outer array of nine replications that are obtained by varying the noise factors.

A	*B*	*C*	*D*	*E*	Average	Variance
1	1	1	1	1	39.08	10.1767
1	2	2	2	2	41.82	7.8668
1	3	3	3	3	39.77	10.1985
2	1	2	3	2	42.15	9.1639
2	2	3	1	3	46.82	9.5696
2	3	1	2	1	43.05	12.1668
3	1	3	2	2	46.28	11.3950
3	2	1	3	3	46.80	9.3032
3	3	2	1	1	45.67	7.8275
1	1	3	3	1	39.30	7.8870
1	2	1	1	2	42.65	10.6673
1	3	2	2	3	41.37	8.6670
2	1	1	2	3	39.91	9.3533
2	2	2	3	1	45.21	10.8302
2	3	3	1	2	45.51	8.4237
3	1	2	1	3	43.47	8.8222
3	2	3	2	1	46.07	9.6859
3	3	1	3	2	46.67	11.3564

(a) Calculate the average of the levels and the average of the variances (or their logarithms) for the three levels of each controlled factor. Determine the factors that affect the average. Determine the factors that affect the variability. (Note: Follow the discussion of Example 2 in Section 16.7.)

(b) Assume that you want to maximize the average response. Determine the best values for each of the five factors.

(c) Calculate the signal-to-noise ratio $SN_{\text{target}} = 10 \log_{10}[(\bar{y}/s)^2 - (1/n)]$. Find the best levels of the five factors (that is, those that maximize this signal-to-noise ratio). Is your conclusion different from that reached in (b)?

16.2 E.W. Karlin (1987, pp. 54–57) discusses an experiment with five controllable factors in eight different arrangements. (You will recognize that a fractional factorial was used.) At each of the eight design conditions of the inner array, an experiment with five replications was carried out. The data is given below.

A	*B*	*C*	*D*	*E*	Observations				
−	−	−	+	+	4.5	9.0	0.5	5.0	3.5
+	−	−	−	−	9.5	8.0	3.5	7.0	4.5
−	+	−	−	+	0.5	4.0	1.5	6.0	7.0
+	+	−	+	−	11.5	9.5	6.6	17.5	9.5
−	−	+	+	−	7.0	8.5	19.5	15.5	16.0
+	−	+	−	+	2.5	5.0	1.0	7.0	4.5
−	+	+	−	−	9.0	13.5	0.5	5.5	7.0
+	+	+	+	+	10.5	4.5	4.0	1.5	2.5

(a) Analyze the data. Calculate the sample averages and the sample variances for each of the eight experimental conditions. Identify the factors that affect the level. Identify the factors that affect the variability. Assume that you want to minimize the response. How would you set the levels of the five controllable factors?

(b) Calculate the signal-to-noise ratio that is recommended if one wants to minimize the response. That is, calculate and maximize $SN_{\text{small}} = -10\log_{10}[\sum(y_i)^2/n]$. How would you set the levels of the five controllable factors? Is your conclusion different from the one you reached in (a)?

16.3 Reanalyze the information in Example 3 of Section 16.7. Instead of analyzing the signal-to-noise ratio (which is a function of the sample average and the sample variance), analyze the average and the logarithm of the variance separately. Check whether you reach the same conclusion.

16.4 Confirm the data analysis for Examples 1 and 2 in Section 16.7.

16.5 Read and discuss the following articles on the Taguchi methodology. The first six papers are in *Quality Progress*. The first four papers emphasize the benefits of Taguchi methods. The last three papers are more critical, comparing the efficacy of Taguchi's statistical design methods with that of standard experimental designs.

L. P. Sullivan, "Reducing Variability: A New Approach to Quality," Vol. 17, July 1984, pp. 15–21.

L. P. Sullivan, "The Power of Taguchi Methods," Vol. 20, June 1987, pp. 76–79.

R. N. Kackar, "Taguchi's Quality Philosophy: Analysis and Commentary," Vol. 19, December 1986, pp. 21–29.

T. B. Barker, "Quality Engineering by Design: Taguchi's Philosophy," Vol. 19, December 1986, pp. 32–42.

Berton Gunter, "A Perspective on the Taguchi Methods," Vol. 20, June 1987, pp. 44–52.

G. E. P. Box, and S. Bisgaard, "The Scientific Context of Quality Improvement," Vol. 20, June 1987, pp. 54–61.

G. E. P. Box, S. Bisgaard, and C. Fung, "An Explanation and Critique of Taguchi's Contributions to Quality Engineering," *Quality and Engineering Reliability International*, Vol. 4, 1988, pp. 123–131.

Additional discussion on the Taguchi philosophy and methodology is given in the Vol. 13, September 1987 issue of *Quality Assurance*.

16.6 Read and discuss the paper "Top Ten Triumphs and Tragedies of Genichi Taguchi," by Joseph J. Pignatiello and John R. Ramberg in *Quality Engineering*, Vol. 4, 1992, pp. 221–225.

16.9 REFERENCES

Alt, F. B. "Taguchi Method for Off-Line Quality Control," *Encyclopedia of Statistical Sciences*, Vol. 9, 1988, 165–167.

Barker, T. B. "Quality Engineering by Design: Taguchi's Philosophy," *Quality Progress*, Vol. 19, December 1986, 32–42.

Box, G. E. P., and S. Bisgaard. "The Scientific Context of Quality Improvement," *Quality Progress*, Vol. 20, June 1987, 54–61.

Box, G. E. P., S. Bisgaard, and C. Fung. "An Explanation and Critique of Taguchi's Contributions to Quality Engineering," *Quality and Engineering Reliability International*, Vol. 4, 1988, 123–131.

Byrne, Diane M., and Shin Taguchi. "The Taguchi Approach to Parameter Design," *Quality Progress*, Vol. 20, December 1987, 19–26.

Gunter, Berton. "A Perspective on the Taguchi Methods," *Quality Progress*, Vol. 20, June 1987, 44–52.

John, P. W. M. *Statistical Methods in Engineering and Quality Assurance*. New York: Wiley, 1990.

Kackar, R. N. "Taguchi's Quality Philosophy: Analysis and Commentary," *Quality Progress*, Vol. 19, December 1986, 21–29.

Kackar, R. N., and A. C. Shoemaker. "Robust Design: A Cost-Effective Method for Improving Manufacturing Processes," *AT&T Technical Journal*, Vol. 65, 1986, Issue 2, 39–50.

Karlin, E. W. "Software on Review," *Quality Progress*, Vol. 20, January 1987, 54–57.

Pignatiello, J. J., and J. S. Ramberg. "Discussion of a paper by R. N. Kackar," *Journal of Quality Technology*, Vol. 17, 1985, 198–206.

Pignatiello, J. J., and J. S. Ramberg. "Top Ten Triumphs and Tragedies of Genichi Taguchi," *Quality Engineering*, Vol. 4, 1992, 221–225.

Sullivan, L. P. "Reducing Variability: A New Approach to Quality," *Quality Progress*, Vol. 17, July 1984, 15–21.

Sullivan, L. P. "The Power of Taguchi Methods," *Quality Progress*, Vol. 20, June 1987, 76–79.

Taguchi, G., and Y. Wu. *Introduction to Off-Line Quality Control*. Nagoya, Japan: Central Japan Quality Control Association (available from the American Supplier Institute, Dearborn, MI), 1980.

APPENDIX TO SECTION 4

USEFUL BOOKS ON DESIGN OF EXPERIMENTS

For further study we recommend the following books on design of experiments:

References

Anderson, V. L., and R. A. McLean. *Design of Experiments: A Realistic Approach*. New York: Marcel Dekker, 1974.

Box, G. E. P., and N. R. Draper. *Empirical Model Building and Response Surfaces*. New York: John Wiley & Sons, 1986.

Box, G. E. P., W. G. Hunter, and J. S. Hunter. *Statistics for Experimenters*. New York: John Wiley & Sons, 1978.

Cochran, W. G., and D. R. Cox. *Experimental Designs*, 2nd ed. New York: John Wiley & Sons, 1957.

Cornell, J. A. *Experiments with Mixtures*. New York: John Wiley & Sons, 1981.

Daniel, C. *Applications of Statistics to Industrial Experimentation*. New York: Macmillan, 1976.

Davies, O. L. *Design and Analysis of Industrial Experiments*, 2nd ed. New York: Longman, 1978.

Davies, O. L., and P. L. Goldsmith. *Statistical Methods in Research and Production*, 4th ed. New York: Longman, 1984.

Diamond, W. J. *Practical Experimental Designs*. Belmont, CA: Wadsworth, 1981.

Hogg, R. V., and J. Ledolter. *Applied Statistics for Engineers and Physical Scientists*, 2nd ed. New York: Macmillan, 1992.

John, P. W. M. *Statistical Methods in Engineering and Quality Assurance*. New York: John Wiley & Sons, 1990.

Mason, R. L., R. F. Gunst, and J. L. Hess. *Statistical Design and Analysis*. New York: John Wiley & Sons, 1989.

Montgomery, D. C. *Design and Analysis of Experiments*, 3rd ed. New York: John Wiley & Sons, 1991.

Myers, R. H., and D. C. Montgomery. *Response Surface Methodology: Process and Product Optimization Using Designed Experiments*, New York: John Wiley & Sons, 1995.

Ostle, B., and L. C. Malone. *Statistics in Research*, 4th ed. Ames: Iowa State University Press, 1988.

Snee, R. D., L. B. Hare, and J. R. Trout. *Experiments in Industry.* Milwaukee, WI: Quality Press, 1985.

Taguchi, G., and Y. Wu. *Introduction to Off-Line Quality Control.* Nagoya, Japan: Central Japan Quality Control Association (available from the American Supplier Institute, Dearborn, MI), 1980.

PROJECTS FOR SECTION 4

PROJECT 12

The Web site "http://www.macomb.k12.mi.us/math/web1.htm" is concerned with linking mathematics/science with statistical design of experiments. It is designed to make science and math more exciting and relevant to issues that students can see and understand. The underlying pedagogical theme is the essential importance of *doing* real science. It exploits the simplicity and power of basic design of experiments strategies to allow students to systematically investigate practically any issue that they can experiment with.

The Web site contains a useful glossary of important concepts in design of experiments. Many illustrative examples and student projects are listed.

Another useful reference on simple experiments that can be assigned as projects is the article by W.G. Hunter (1977, pp. 12–17).

Use this information to come up with your own experiment. Conduct the experiment, analyze the resulting data, and write a brief report that summarizes your findings. Discuss what you have learned.

PROJECT 13

This is an extension of Exercise 14.4 in Chapter 14. See Hogg and Ledolter (1992, p. 342).

Investigate the effects of the following five factors on the expansion of pinto beans:

Soaking fluid: water (−) or beer (+)

Salinity: no salt (−) or salt (+)

Acidity: no vinegar (−) or vinegar (+)

Soaking temperature: refrigerator temperature (−) or room temperature (+)

Soaking time: 2 hours (−) or 6 hours (+)

Carry out the following experiment. Select a pinto bean, measure its size, put the bean into a soaking fluid, and—after a certain amount of elapsed time—measure its size again. Use five tablespoons of soaking fluid to soak each bean. Make sure that the liquid covers the bean. Use regular beer because light beer might act like water. For salt, add 1/4 teaspoon to the soaking fluid. For vinegar, add 1 teaspoon to the soaking fluid.

Questions

1. Discuss how you measure the "size of a pinto bean" and its "expansion." Give a detailed description of your measurement procedure, so that it can be carried out by other people; that is, give an operational definition.
2. Design, set up, and execute the experiment as a 2^5 factorial experiment. Conduct two replications, which may be run concurrently. Analyze the effects of the five factors. Write a short report that summarizes your findings. Support your findings with appropriate graphs and calculations. What have you learned? What was the most difficult part of your experiment (apart from wasting the beer)? If you had to do it over again, what would you change?

   Note: In carrying out this experiment, you need $(64)(2) = 128$ small paper containers for soaking the beans.
3. Instead of carrying out a full factorial with 64 runs and two replications, economize on the number of runs and conduct only a half-fraction (or a quarter-fraction) of the 2^5 factorial design. What would you give up in terms of your analysis? How would you carry out a quarter-fraction? What are its advantages and what is the price that you pay compared with the full 2^5 factorial experiment?

PROJECT 14

You will have to consult references to carry out the analysis of the fractional factorial experiments. The books by Box, Hunter, and Hunter (1978) and Hogg and Ledolter (1992), which were mentioned in the Appendix to Section 4, are good references.

S. Eibl, U. Kess, and F. Pukelsheim (1992, pp. 22–26) report a case study of how the response variable, paint coat thickness, depends on a set of six input factors. Their objective was to find factor settings that achieve a desired target value of 0.8 mm paint coat thickness. Read the paper for a detailed description of the process and the experiment.

Eibl et al. consider the following six input factors *A* through *F* (listed here in decreasing order of their assumed importance): belt speed, tube width, pump pressure, paint viscosity, tube height, and heating temperature. All factors could be varied continuously. Level 0 stands for the standard operating condition. All factors were scaled so that levels between -3 and $+3$ were technically feasible, without increasing cost.

Part I: The first experiment varied the factor levels between -1 and $+1$; it was expected that this experiment could detect the effect of these changes. The table given below lists the observed paint thickness (in mm) for a two-level fractional factorial experiment with four replications at each factor-level combination. The order of the 32 experiments was fully randomized (refer to the discussion in the paper).

A	*B*	*C*	*D*	*E*	*F*	Thickness of paint coat (mm)			
−1	−1	1	−1	1	1	1.62	1.49	1.48	1.59
1	−1	1	−1	−1	−1	1.09	1.12	0.83	0.88
−1	1	−1	−1	1	−1	1.83	1.65	1.71	1.76
1	1	−1	−1	−1	1	0.88	1.29	1.04	1.31
−1	−1	−1	1	−1	1	1.46	1.51	1.59	1.40
1	−1	−1	1	1	−1	0.74	0.98	0.79	0.83
−1	1	1	1	−1	−1	2.05	2.17	2.36	2.12
1	1	1	1	1	1	1.51	1.46	1.42	1.40

Questions

1. Convince yourself that this design is a 2^{6-3} fractional factorial design.
2. Calculate the averages from the replications, and analyze these averages. Find the important effects and interpret your findings.
3. Calculate the standard deviations from these replications, and analyze the variation. It is common practice to analyze $\log(s^2)$. Repeat the analysis in question 2, but now use $\log(s^2)$ as the response.

Hint: Notice that factors *A*, *B* and *D* form a full 2^3 factorial design. Write out the calculation columns and discuss how the levels of the remaining factors *C*, *E*, and *F* were selected. You will find that $C = BD$, $E = AD$, and $F = AB$. There is only one calculation column, namely *ABD*, that is not taken up as a design variable. In addition to the average, you can estimate seven effects from these eight runs. Since this design represents only 1/8 of a full 2^6 factorial, it is not possible to get unconfounded estimates of main and interaction effects. However, if you ignore two-factor interactions, you can get estimates of the main effects. You get them by applying the plus and minus signs in the corresponding factor level column to the observations, adding the results, and dividing by four. The effect that uses the *ABD* calculation column confounds several interactions of order two or higher.

Part II: A follow-up experiment focused on the first four factors (factors *A* through *D*). Note that this experiment is a 2^{4-1} fractional factorial, however, with slightly changed experimental settings. The levels of the factors were changed because of the findings in the initial experiment. When analyzing the data you can transform the factor levels into -1 and $+1$; the -1 in your new coding of factor *A* corresponds to -1.5 on the original scale; the $+1$ in the new coding corresponds to 0.5 in the old one. You can do the same for the other factors. Repeat the analysis in Part I with this new data set.

A	*B*	*C*	*D*	**Thickness**	
−1.5	−2	−2	−2	1.51	1.18
0.5	−2	−2	−2	0.64	0.78
−1.5	0	0	−2	1.74	1.98
0.5	0	0	−2	1.33	1.06
−1.5	−2	0	0	1.71	1.60
0.5	−2	0	0	1.15	1.29
−1.5	0	−2	0	1.71	1.61
0.5	0	−2	0	0.91	1.30

Can you think of another, and better, 2^{4-1} fractional factorial design?

Hint: After recoding, you will find that $C = -BD$. Write down the 2^3 factorial design in factors A, B, and D, and estimate the three main and four interaction effects. There will be confounding because of the fractional nature of the design. For example, since $A = -ABCD$ (you get this by multiplying both sides of the above equation, $C = -BD$, by AC), the main effect of factor A can be estimated clearly; it is only confounded with the negative of the four-factor interaction $ABCD$, which we are willing to ignore. Since $B = -CD$, we find that the main effect of B is confounded with the negative of the two-factor interaction between C and D. Hence in interpreting the estimate of B there is some uncertainty whether it is the main effect or the negative of the two-factor interaction. Check that $D = -BC$, $AB = -ACD$, $AD = -ABC$, $BD = -C$, and $ABD = -AC$. Hence the $B \times D$ interaction from the 2^3 factorial is also an estimate of the negative main effect of C; the three-factor interaction $A \times B \times D$ is also the negative of the two-factor interaction between A and C.

Part III: Another follow-up experiment was conducted with just the first three factors. The results from this 2^3 factorial experiment are given below. Again, you can transform the new factor levels into -1 and $+1$. Repeat the analysis.

A	*B*	*C*	**Thickness**	
1.0	−2	−2	0.57	0.58
1.5	−2	−2	0.51	0.66
1.0	−1	−2	0.62	0.74
1.5	−1	−2	0.69	0.49
1.0	−2	−1	0.75	0.58
1.5	−2	−1	0.53	0.64
1.0	−1	−1	0.79	1.04
1.5	−1	−1	0.78	0.79

Part IV: Summarize your findings from all experiments. Can you find the factor settings that achieve the desired target value of 0.8 mm paint coat thickness?

PROJECT 15

Think about the following experiments aimed at the improvement of *personal processes*.

Cardiovascular Fitness: Possible measurements include resting pulse, exercise pulse, and postexercise pulse. Describe how you measure these variables. Give a detailed description of your measurement procedure. Design an exercise program that is aimed at improving fitness. For example, design a stair-climbing exercise that is repeated several times during an exercise program. Set an exercise schedule and keep careful records of your data. Display your data over time. Write a report that summarizes your findings.

Improvement of Sports Skills: Can you improve your basketball free-throw shooting percentage by varying some of the key factors (such as shooting angle, use of backboard, relaxation before shot)? Design an experiment where you vary these factors. Discuss your findings.

References for Projects for Section 4

Box, G. E. P., W. G. Hunter, and J. S. Hunter. *Statistics for Experimenters.* New York: John Wiley & Sons, 1978.

Eibl, S., U. Kess, and F. Pukelsheim. "Achieving a Target Value for a Manufacturing Process: A Case Study," *Journal of Quality Technology*, Vol. 24, 1992, 22–26.

Hogg, R. V., and J. Ledolter. *Applied Statistics for Engineers and Physical Scientists.* New York: Macmillan, 1992, p. 342.

Hunter, W. G. "Some Ideas about Teaching Design of Experiments with 2^5 Examples of Experiments Conducted by Students," *American Statistician,* Vol. 31, 1977, 12–17.

SECTION 5

OTHER USEFUL STATISTICAL TECHNIQUES

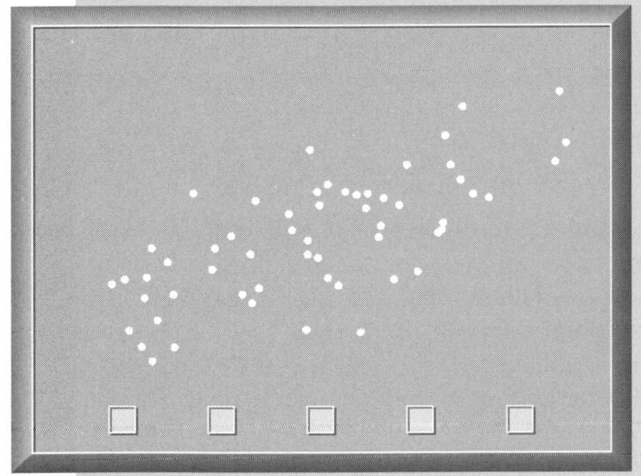

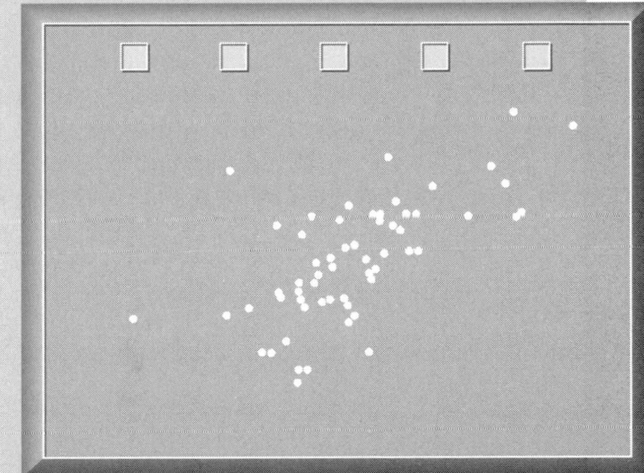

CHAPTER 17

REGRESSION ANALYSIS: A USEFUL TOOL FOR MODELING RELATIONSHIPS

17.1 INTRODUCTION

The values of one variable often depend on the levels of several others. For example, the fuel efficiency of an automobile depends on, among other factors, the weight of the car and the characteristics of its engine. The yield of a certain production process may depend on temperature, pressure, catalyst, and the rate of throughput. The number or the rate of defectives on an assembly line may depend on the speed of the production line. The number of defective seals on toothpaste tubes may depend on the temperature and the pressure of the sealing process. The volume of a tree is related to the diameter at breast height, the height of the tree, and the taper of the tree.

Many more examples can be given: The tensile strength may be related to hardness and density of the stock; tool life may depend on the hardness of the stock to be machined and the depth of the cut; the weight of the coating of an electrolytic tin plate may be affected by the current, acidity, rate of travel of the strip, and distance from the anode; employee efficiency may be related to the performance on employment tests, years of training, and educational background; diameter of a condenser coil may be affected by the thickness of the coil, number of turns and tension in the winding; moisture content of lumber depends on the speed of drying, the temperature, and the dimension of the pieces; the performance of a foundry may be affected by atmospheric conditions; the life of a light bulb may be related to the results of a quality test on the filament; the tile finish may depend on the temperature of firing; and so on.

The first step in exploring and modeling relationships is to display the observations in the form of scatter diagrams. In a scatter plot we plot the levels of one variable against the levels of an other. Scatter plots were reviewed in Chapter 7. There we also discussed the *correlation coefficient*, which provides a measure of the strength and the direction of the linear association among two variables.

Regression methods are used to model and estimate the functional relationship between a response variable (which we denote by Y) and one or more explanatory variables (say p of them, $X_1, X_2, \ldots, X_p$). Modeling the relationship is useful for many reasons:

- We learn which of the explanatory variables have an effect on the response. This tells us which explanatory variables need to be changed in order to affect the response. A finding that certain explanatory variables are not related to the response is also useful as this allows us to omit these variables from the list of possible causes. We can stop taking measurements on these variables, and this saves money.
- The functional relationship between the response and the explanatory variables allows us to estimate the response for given values of the explanatory variables. It makes it possible to infer the value of the response for settings of the explanatory variables that were not studied directly. Let us illustrate this with an example from the steel industry. (See *Real Life Statistics: Regression Analysis and Quality Control in Manufacturing*, Films for the Humanities and Sciences.) The removal of sulphur is an important step in the production of steel. The sulphur in a batch of iron ore is removed by adding magnesium to the molten mixture. However, magnesium is expensive, and one wants to add only as much magnesium as is really needed. Given the sulphur content of a batch of iron ore, what amount of magnesium should be added? A regression model with the needed amount of magnesium as the response variable and the sulphur content as the explanatory variable is extremely useful. The operator takes a sample from the batch of iron ore, determines its sulphur content, and adds the amount of needed magnesium that he obtains by plugging the measured sulphur content into the regression equation.
- Regression models can tell us how to change the explanatory variables so that the response variable reaches an optimum. We may want to make the response as small as possible, or as large as possible, or have it close to a specified target. For example, the regression model may relate the yield of a process to the settings of the input factors, say reaction time and temperature. The fitted regression model can tell us how to change the input factors so that the yield of the process is moved toward a more optimal region. Response surface methodology is the area of statistics that deals with

such issues. A brief introduction to response surface methods is given in Section 17.8.

- A regression analysis may show that a variable that is difficult and expensive to measure can be explained to a large extent by variables that are easy and cheap to obtain. This is important information, as we can substitute the cheaper measurements for the more expensive ones. Here is an example: Tensile strength of a certain final product may be very expensive to measure, because of the destructive nature of the measurement procedure. It may be much easier and also quite inexpensive to measure the hardness and the density of the product. If hardness and density are good indicators of the tensile strength, then one may get around measuring tensile strength altogether. The regression analysis can tell us whether the two explanatory variables, hardness and density, are good predictors of tensile strength. Similarly, one may be interested in the hardness of an item at a location which is difficult to reach; it may be much more convenient to measure hardness at another location. If the measurements on hardness taken at the two different locations are closely related, then we can use the one that is cheaper to obtain as a proxy for the other.
- Regression methods can be used for extrapolation and prediction. We may have past data on the actual production time (the response) and the number and type of products that were produced (the explanatory variables), and we may have fitted a regression model relating these variables. Our production schedule for the coming month may call for certain manufacturing targets. We can use the regression model to predict the production time that is needed to satisfy next month's production goals.

17.2 THE SIMPLE LINEAR REGRESSION MODEL

17.2.1 The Model

In the simplest modeling situation we relate the response Y to a single explanatory variable X, and we do so through a straight line model. Consider the data set in Table 17.1, which contains the fuel efficiency (in gallons per hundred miles, GPM) and the weight (in 1,000 pounds) of a sample of ten cars. The scatter plot of GPM on Weight is given in Figure 17.1. It shows an approximate linear relationship between GPM and the weight of the car.

We consider a linear model to represent the relationship between the response $Y = \text{GPM}$ and the explanatory variable $X = \text{Weight}$:

$$\text{GPM} = \beta_0 + \beta_1 \text{ Weight} + \text{Noise}.$$

The first component, $\beta_0 + \beta_1$ Weight, represents the regression line. It is also referred to as the *signal* of the model. The slope, β_1, tells us about the effect of

TABLE 17.1 Data on Weight (in 1,000 pounds) and Fuel Consumption (in gallons per 100 miles)

Weight	GPM	Car
3.4	5.5	AMC Concord
3.8	5.9	Chevy Caprice
4.1	6.5	Ford Country Squire Wagon
2.2	3.3	Chevette
2.6	3.6	Toyota Corona
2.9	4.6	Ford Mustang Ghia
2.0	2.9	Mazda GLC
2.7	3.6	AMC Sprint
1.9	3.1	VW Rabbit
3.4	4.9	Buick Century

SOURCE: Data was taken from *Consumer Reports* (1978–79 model years).

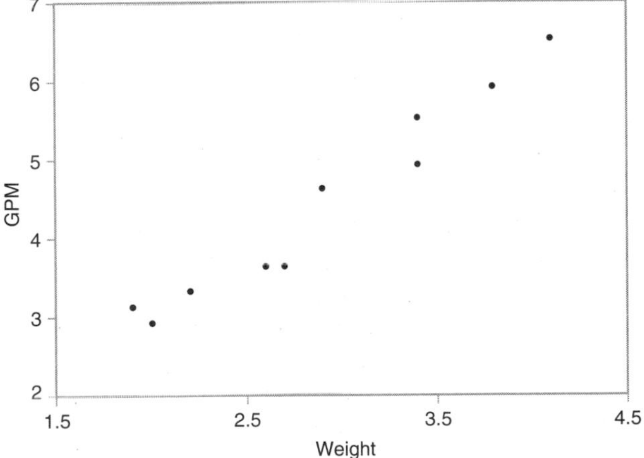

FIGURE 17.1 Scatter plot of GPM versus weight.

Weight on GPM. A one-unit change in Weight (say from 3,000 to 4,000 pounds) translates into a change in GPM of β_1 units. The linearity of the model implies that the impact on GPM of a unit change in Weight is the same for all values of Weight; that is, changing Weight from 2,000 to 3,000 pounds has the same effect as changing Weight from 3,000 to 4,000 pounds. The intercept of the regression line, β_0, has little meaning. It tells us about the GPM of a car with zero weight.

However, the regression line that we consider for this data set is probably only good for weights in the range between 1,900 and 4,000 pounds (see Figure 17.1). This model is certainly not appropriate for cars that weigh much less than 1,900 pounds.

There is a *noise*, or error component in the model as the relationship is not exact. The GPM of a car of certain weight will fluctuate around the regression line. This is because many other factors contribute to a car's fuel efficiency, not just the weight of the automobile. There is test variability; repeated tests on the very same car will, most likely, lead to different results. Even among cars that come from the same model line there will be variability from one car to the next; tests on seemingly identical cars will, most likely, lead to different results. Furthermore, cars that weigh the same will be different on other characteristics that have an impact on fuel efficiency.

17.2.2 Estimates of the Regression Coefficients

How do we get estimates of the regression coefficients β_0 and β_1? How do we determine a line that fits the data best? It is common to measure "best" through the *least squares criterion.* We select estimates of the regression coefficients such that the sum of the squared vertical distances from the observations to the regression line is minimized. Take the ith case (x_i, y_i), where x_i is the value of the explanatory variable and y_i is the measured response. The distance from the observation y_i to the value that is implied by the regression line, $\beta_0 + \beta_1 x_i$, is given by $[y_i - (\beta_0 + \beta_1 x_i)]$. The sum of the squared distances is given by

$$\text{Sum of Squares } (\beta_0, \beta_1) = \sum_{i=1}^{n} [y_i - (\beta_0 + \beta_1 x_i)]^2$$

We select values for β_0 and β_1 such that this sum of squares is as small as possible. The values that achieve this are called the *least squares estimates*, and we denote them by b_0 and b_1. Note that we use Greek symbols for the unknown parameters, and Roman letters for their estimates; this is consistent with our earlier use of Greek symbols for population parameters μ and σ, and Roman letters $\bar{x}$ and s for their estimates.

Explicit expressions can be given for the least squares estimates. For the simple linear regression model it turns out that

$$b_1 = \frac{\sum_{i=1}^{n}(x_i - \bar{x})(y_i - \bar{y})}{\sum_{i=1}^{n}(x_i - \bar{x})^2} = \frac{\sum_{i=1}^{n}(x_i - \bar{x})y_i}{\sum_{i=1}^{n}(x_i - \bar{x})^2} = \frac{s_y}{s_x} r$$

$$b_0 = \bar{y} - b_1 \bar{x}$$

where $\bar{y}$ and $\bar{x}$ are the sample averages and where s_y and s_x are the sample standard deviations of the response and the explanatory variable, respectively. The quantity r denotes the sample correlation coefficient between X and Y; it was discussed in Section 7.8 in Chapter 7. It is not very important to remember the exact calculation of these estimates; statistical computer packages and even some hand-held calculators give you these estimates with a few keystrokes. However, it is useful to remember where these estimates come from; they minimize the sum of the squared vertical distances from the observations to the regression line. Furthermore, there exists an easy mathematical expression that allows us to calculate these estimates.

The calculations for the mileage example show

i Car	x_i Weight	y_i GPM	$(x_i - \bar{x})(y_i - \bar{y})$	$(x_i - \bar{x})^2$
1	3.4	5.5	0.555	0.250
2	3.8	5.9	1.359	0.810
3	4.1	6.5	2.532	1.440
4	2.2	3.3	0.763	0.490
5	2.6	3.6	0.237	0.090
6	2.9	4.6	0.000	0.000
7	2.0	2.9	1.341	0.810
8	2.7	3.6	0.158	0.040
9	1.9	3.1	1.290	1.000
10	3.4	4.9	0.255	0.250
Average	2.9	4.39		
Sum			8.490	5.180

Here $\bar{x} = 2.9$, $\bar{y} = 4.39$, $\sum(x_i - \bar{x})(y_i - \bar{y}) = 8.490$, and $\sum(x_i - \bar{x})^2 = 5.180$. The least squares estimates are $b_1 = (8.490/5.180) = 1.639$ and $b_0 = 4.39 - (1.639)(2.9) = -0.363$.

17.2.3 Fitted Values and Residuals

From these least squares estimates we can calculate the *fitted regression line* $\hat{Y} = b_0 + b_1 X$. For our mileage example $\widehat{\text{GPM}} = -0.363 + 1.639$ Weight. The slope 1.639 implies that for each 1,000 pounds of weight, an additional 1.639 gallons of fuel is required to travel 100 miles. We mentioned earlier that the estimate of the intercept has little meaning as it does not make sense to extrapolate the least squares line to cars with Weight = 0.

If we evaluate this equation at the values of our explanatory variable X (which are $x_1, x_2, \ldots, x_n$), we obtain n *fitted values*

$$\hat{y}_i = b_0 + b_1 x_i \quad \text{for } i = 1, 2, \ldots, n.$$

We are using the caret on top of y to distinguish between observations and fitted values. The differences between the observations and the fitted values are called the *residuals*,

$$e_i = y_i - \hat{y}_i = y_i - (b_0 + b_1 x_i) \quad \text{for } i = 1, 2, \ldots, n.$$

The observations, fitted values, and residuals for the mileage example are given below:

Car	x_i Weight	y_i GPM	$\hat{y}_i$ Fitted value	$e_i = y_i - \hat{y}_i$ Residual
1	3.4	5.5	5.2095	0.2905
2	3.8	5.9	5.8651	0.0349
3	4.1	6.5	6.3568	0.1432
4	2.2	3.3	3.2427	0.0573
5	2.6	3.6	3.8983	−0.2983
6	2.9	4.6	4.3900	0.2100
7	2.0	2.9	2.9149	−0.0149
8	2.7	3.6	4.0622	−0.4622
9	1.9	3.1	2.7510	0.3490
10	3.4	4.9	5.2095	−0.3095

You can check that the residuals add to zero, subject to possible rounding error. This fact is not just a coincidence for this particular data set, but holds for all regression models that are fitted by least squares. Some of the residuals around the least squares line are negative and some of them are positive, but on average they are zero. Exercise 17.7 at the end of this chapter asks you to show this fact formally for the simple linear regression model.

17.2.4 Assessing the Fit: Sum of Squares Decomposition and the Coefficient of Determination

The observations on the response variable Y, which are $y_1, y_2, \ldots, y_n$, vary. A natural measure for the variability in the y's is given by the *total sum of squares*,

$$SSTO = \sum_{i=1}^{n} (y_i - \bar{y})^2.$$

The total sum of squares for Y = GPM, calculated from the ten cars, is $SSTO = [(5.5 - 4.39)^2 + \cdots + (4.9 - 4.39)^2] = 14.589$. One may also want to calculate the standard deviation of the y's, which is $s_y = \sqrt{14.589/(10-1)} =$ 1.273 gallons per 100 miles. There is quite a bit of variability among the fuel efficiencies of these 10 cars. This is because cars differ with respect to their size; some of them are large and heavy, while others are small.

When we fit the regression model, we explain the response variable $Y =$ GPM by $X =$ Weight, through the fitted linear equation $\hat{Y} = b_0 + b_1 X$.

Factoring in the weight of the car reduces our uncertainty about the fuel efficiency. We certainly are better equipped to predict a car's GPM once we know its weight. However, even after knowing a car's weight there is still uncertainty left about its fuel efficiency. The leftover variability (that is, the variability that is not explained by the regression model) is expressed by the *residual sum of squares* (also called the *error sum of squares*),

$$SSE = \sum_{i=1}^{n} e_i^2 = \sum_{i=1}^{n} (y_i - \hat{y}_i)^2.$$

It expresses the variability in the responses $y_1, y_2, \ldots, y_n$, after one has accounted for the effect of the explanatory variable X. If there is a perfect fit and if all observations lie on the fitted line, then $SSE = 0$. For our data set, $SSE = [(0.2905)^2 + \cdots + (-0.3095)^2] = 0.674$. The calculation of the error sum of squares is straightforward; we square the residuals in the above table, and add them up.

The third sum of squares that is of interest is the *regression sum of squares*,

$$SSR = \sum_{i=1}^{n} (\hat{y}_i - \bar{y})^2.$$

It measures the variability among the fitted values. If there is a perfect fit, then $\hat{y}_i = y_i$ and $SSR = SSTO$. This means that the variability among the fitted values is the same as the variability among the original observations. In other words, the model explains the variability in the observations perfectly. This is the reason why we refer to this sum of squares as the regression sum of squares, or the sum of squares that is explained by the regression model. For our data,

$$SSR = [(5.2095 - 4.39)^2 + (5.8651 - 4.39)^2 + \cdots + (5.2095 - 4.39)^2] = 13.915.$$

It can be shown that

$$SSTO = SSR + SSE.$$

The total sum of squares can be partitioned into a sum of squares that is due to regression (the part that is explained by the fitted line) and a sum of squares that is due to error (the part that is unexplained by the fitted line). This identity makes it easy to calculate SSR, as we can obtain it from $SSR = SSTO - SSE$. For our data set, $SSR = 14.589 - 0.674 = 13.915$.

The *coefficient of determination* R^2 measures the proportion of variation that is explained by the regression model. It is defined as

$$R^2 = \frac{SSR}{SSTO} = \frac{SSTO - SSE}{SSTO} = 1 - \frac{SSE}{SSTO}.$$

Quite often this coefficient is multiplied by 100. Then it expresses the proportional reduction in the sum of squares that is due to the regression model. In other words, it tells us how much of the variability in the response variable is picked up by the explanatory variable.

R^2 must be between 0 and 1. If the above equation is multiplied by 100 and the coefficient is expressed in percent, then $100R^2$ must be between 0 and 100 percent. $R^2 = 0$ says that our model (the simple linear regression model) explains none of the variability in Y. $R^2 = 1$ says that 100 percent (that is, all) of the variation in Y is explained by the simple linear regression model.

For the mileage data set we find that $SSTO = 14.589$, $SSE = 0.674$, and $SSR = 13.915$. Therefore $R^2 = 13.915/14.589 = 0.954$. This says that 95.4 percent of the variability in GPM is explained by the variable Weight. A very considerable proportion of the variability is explained by the regression on Weight.

Another, and very similar way of assessing the importance of the regression is as follows: Start with the standard deviation of the response Y,

$$s_y = \sqrt{SSTO/(n-1)}.$$

It measures the variability in the y's before we factor in the information from the corresponding x-values. In the mileage data set, we find that $s_y = 1.273$ gallons per 100 miles. The variability is large because the fuel efficiency of cars depends on their weight, and because the weights of the cars in our sample vary over a wide range (from 1,900 to 4,000 pounds).

How much variability is there in GPM if we adjust for the different weights of the cars? The unexplained variability is reflected in the residuals $e_1, \ldots, e_n$. The *standard deviation of the residuals* is

$$s_e = \sqrt{\sum(e_i - \bar{e})^2/(n-2)} = \sqrt{\sum e_i^2/(n-2)} = \sqrt{SSE/(n-2)}.$$

We mentioned earlier that the residuals from the least squares regression line always add to zero, and hence $\bar{e} = 0$ and $\sum(e_i - \bar{e})^2 = \sum e_i^2$. Note that we divide the error sum of squares by $n-2$, as compared to the usual $n-1$ in the definition of the sample standard deviation. The reason for $n-2$ in the expression for s_e is that we must estimate two regression parameters in order to get the residuals, as compared to estimating a single mean in the sample standard deviation.

The quantity s_e is an estimate of the variability in the y's, after having accounted for the effect of the explanatory variable X. In the mileage example, $s_e = 0.29$ gallon per 100 miles. This represents quite a big reduction from the standard deviation $s_y = 1.273$ gallons per 100 miles. In fact, it amounts to a 77.2 percent reduction.

17.2.5 Standard Errors of Estimates

Recall our discussion in Chapter 10, where we took random samples from a population of values with mean μ and standard deviation σ, and where we discussed the sampling variability of sample averages. We expressed the sampling variability of sample averages from repeated samples through the standard deviation, or standard error of the sample average. The standard error of a sample average is given by $\sigma/\sqrt{n}$, and we estimate it with $s/\sqrt{n}$ where s is the standard deviation of the sample.

The same concept applies to regression. Assume that we observe a response Y for a fixed value of the explanatory variable X—say the GPM of a car that weighs 3,000 pounds. If we look at another car that weighs 3,000 pounds and determine its GPM, we will encounter variability; its GPM is not going to be the same. This is because of test variability (even the same car will not give us the identical GPM in repeated trials), and because cars that weigh 3,000 pounds will differ with respect to other characteristics that may have an effect on their fuel efficiencies. Thus repeating the experiment will lead to different measurements, and hence different estimates b_0 and b_1.

Or, to say it somewhat differently: Imagine that you have a large population of N pairs (x_i, y_i), and that you take from this large population a random sample of n pairs from which you calculate the least squares estimates. Different samples of size n will lead to different values of the least squares estimates. Hence, there is sampling variability associated with the least squares estimates.

We can derive and estimate the standard deviations, or *standard errors of the least squares estimates*. However, the resulting expressions are more complicated than the standard error of a sample average, and we won't emphasize their calculation in this book. All we would like you to understand is that there is sampling variability associated with the least squares estimates, and that this variability can be expressed through the standard deviations, or standard errors of these estimates.

Any regression software package will give you the least squares estimates b_0 and b_1, as well as their standard errors StdDev(b_0) and StdDev(b_1). Standard errors are important for obtaining *confidence intervals* for the unknown regression coefficients. An approximate 95 percent confidence interval for β_1 is given by the interval

$$[b_1 - (2)\text{StdDev}(b_1), b_1 + (2)\text{StdDev}(b_1)].$$

For confidence intervals with confidence other than 95 percent, we replace the "2" in the above equation by the appropriate percentiles of the standard normal distribution. For example, in a 90 percent confidence interval we use 1.645, and for a 99 percent confidence interval we use 2.576.

Comment: The above approximation works well if the sample size n is reasonably large. For small sample sizes, where the Central Limit Effect hasn't had a chance to apply fully, the limits of the confidence interval should be taken a bit wider. In fact, it turns out that the percentiles shouldn't be taken from the normal distribution, but from a t-distribution with $n-2$ degrees of freedom. In Section 10.3 in Chapter 10 we mentioned the t-distribution, but only very briefly. The t-distribution is very similar to the standard normal; it is centered at zero and it is symmetric. However, the t-distribution has heavier tails than the normal distribution, and hence its percentiles are slightly larger than those of the normal. For example, the

97.5th percentile of a t-distribution with 8 degrees of freedom is 2.306, and hence a bit larger than the factor "2" which we have used above; note that we use 8 degrees of freedom, as $n = 10$ and $n - 2 = 8$. For moderately small sample sizes it matters very little whether we use the percentiles of the normal or the appropriate t-distribution. Hence we don't emphasize this distinction.

The standard errors are also useful for testing the hypothesis that the regression coefficient β_1 is zero. This is an important hypothesis, as with $\beta_1 = 0$ the explanatory variable X has no influence on the response. The appropriate (standardized) test statistic is given by

$$TS = \frac{b_1 - 0}{\text{StdDev}(b_1)} = \frac{b_1}{\text{StdDev}(b_1)}.$$

It is usually called the "t-ratio." Computer programs also calculate the probability value of this test statistic; that is, the probability that one would get such a statistic or one that is even larger if the true regression coefficient were indeed zero.

The t-ratios and their probability values are part of any standard regression output. They are useful for assessing the statistical significance of the estimated regression coefficients. A small probability value for the regression coefficient (smaller than the usually adopted significance level of 0.05) implies that β_1 is different from zero; in this case the regressor variable has a significant influence on the response. An alternative, and somewhat approximate rule of thumb is to compare the absolute value of the t-ratio with a cutoff of 2; if the t-ratio exceeds 2, in absolute value, then we conclude that the regression coefficient β_1 is different from zero.

The computer output for our example shows that the standard error of the least squares estimate $b_1 = 1.639$ is given by $\text{StdDev}(b_1) = 0.1275$. Hence an approximate 95 percent confidence interval for β_1 is given by $1.639 \pm (2)(0.1275)$, or (1.38, 1.89). This interval does not include zero. It provides strong evidence that the regression coefficient is positive; heavier cars need more fuel. The t-ratio for b_1 is $TS = b_1/\text{StdDev}(b_1) = 1.639/0.1275 = 12.85$; it is considerably larger than the critical cutoff 2.

17.2.6 Estimating the Mean Response for a Given Value of the Explanatory Variable

In many applications we are interested in estimating the *mean response* for a given value of the explanatory variable X. For example, we may be interested in estimating the average fuel efficiency for cars with a weight of 3,000 pounds. The estimate of the mean response for a given value of the explanatory variable, say $x_0 = 3.0$ (as X is measured in units of 1,000 pounds), is given by

$$\hat{y}_0 = b_0 + b_1 x_0$$

where b_0 and b_1 are the calculated least squares estimates. If we could be absolutely certain that the least squares estimates were identical to the parameters β_0 and β_1, then there would be no uncertainty about this estimate of the mean response. However, the values b_0 and b_1 in $\hat{y}_0 = b_0 + b_1 x_0$ are only estimates and they are subject to sampling variation. Taking the variability of the estimates into account, one can show that an approximate 95 percent confidence interval for the mean response at x_0 is given by

$$(b_0 + b_1 x_0) \pm (2) s_e \sqrt{\frac{1}{n} + \frac{(x_0 - \bar{x})^2}{\sum (x_i - \bar{x})^2}};$$

$s_e = \sqrt{SSE/(n-2)} = \sqrt{\sum e_i^2/(n-2)}$ is the standard deviation of the residuals. Intervals with different confidence coefficients can be obtained using the appropriate percentiles of the standard normal distribution.

For the mileage example we find that an approximate 95 percent confidence interval for the average GPM for cars with 3,000 pounds is

$$-0.363 + (1.639)(3) \pm (2)(0.29)\sqrt{\frac{1}{10} + \frac{(3 - 2.9)^2}{5.180}}$$

or 4.554 ± 0.185. The confidence interval for the mean fuel efficiency for cars weighing 3,000 pounds extends from 4.37 to 4.74 gallons per hundred miles.

17.2.7 Prediction Intervals

For large sample sizes, the width of the *confidence interval for the mean response* shrinks toward zero, as with large n we can estimate the regression coefficients very accurately. But what about a *prediction interval for an individual observation*? How would we predict the fuel efficiency of a single car with a weight of 3,000 pounds? First consider the situation where we can estimate the regression coefficients very precisely; in this case we know the mean response for $x_0 = 3.0$ exactly. However, due to the noise component in the model, the fuel efficiency of an individual car will scatter around this value. The variability around the regression line is estimated by the standard deviation of the residuals s_e. Hence an approximate 95 percent prediction interval for the response at x_0 is $(b_0 + b_1 x_0) \pm 2 s_e$. Of course, if the sample size is not very large, then we are better off also incorporating the standard error of the regression estimates. With that, an approximate 95 percent interval is given by

$$(b_0 + b_1 x_0) \pm (2) s_e \sqrt{1 + \frac{1}{n} + \frac{(x_0 - \bar{x})^2}{\sum (x_i - \bar{x})^2}}.$$

You notice that the prediction interval differs from the confidence interval by the addition of 1 to the term under the radical sign; the prediction interval is always wider. You can check that for $x_0 = 3.0$, the approximate 95 percent prediction interval is given by (3.94, 5.16).

17.3 EXAMPLES OF SIMPLE LINEAR REGRESSION MODELS

17.3.1 Example 1: Traction Coefficients of 25 Lubricating Oils

T. Koyotani, H. Yoshitake, T. Ito, and Y. Tamai (1986, pp. 102–106) study the variation in the traction coefficients of 25 lubricating oils. Traction measurements were obtained on a special two-disk machine. After applying oil to the cleaned faces of the two disks, the disks are pressed into contact by a spring. A certain load is applied and the rotating speed of one disk is increased from 45 centimeters per second (cm/sec) to 52 cm/sec, while the speed of the other disk is kept constant at 45 cm/sec. The variation in the traction coefficients with sliding speed is measured, and the maximum is recorded. The results for loads of 100 kg and 150 kg are given in Table 17.2.

It is hypothesized that the traction coefficient increases with the rigidity of the molecular structure of the lubricating fluid. Flow activation volume (*FAV*) is taken as a measure of rigidity. It measures the average size of the holes into which the flow segments are required to move. Since flexible molecules can separate into small flow segments with ease, flexible molecules have small values of *FAV*. Conversely, rigid molecules have large values of *FAV*.

Plots of the maximum traction coefficients against the flow activation volume of 25 lubricating oils, both for loads at 100 and at 150 kg, are shown in Figures 17.2a,b (page 490). These figures show that the traction coefficients increase with *FAV*. The relationship is roughly linear, even though there is some indication of curvature, especially for smaller loads of 100 kg. In this section we fit the simple linear regression model; in a subsequent section we extend the analysis to the quadratic model, $Y = \beta_0 + \beta_1 FAV + \beta_2 (FAV)^2 + \text{noise}$.

Here we use the maximum traction coefficients at 150 kg as our response variable Y, and fit the simple linear regression model $Y = \beta_0 + \beta_1 FAV + \text{noise}$. Virtually all statistical computer package and spreadsheet programs include regression routines; the output from such programs will include:

1. The estimated regression equation: $\widehat{\text{Tract}150} = 38.205 + 0.585\ FAV$.
2. The estimated regression coefficients, their standard errors (referred to as StdDev), their t-ratios, and the associated probability values:

Predictor	**Coef**	**StdDev**	***t*-ratio**	***p*-value**
Constant	$b_0 = 38.205$	3.586	10.66	0.000
FAV	$b_1 = 0.585$	0.055	10.72	0.000

3. The various sums of squares, usually expressed in the form of a table. Since this table displays variation (or variances), it is referred to as the *analysis of variance table*:

Source	Sum of squares	Degrees of freedom	Mean square
Regression	2,736.5	1	2,736.5
Error	547.5	23	23.8
Total	3,284.0	24	

TABLE 17.2 Maximum Traction Coefficients under Loads of 100 kg and 150 kg, respectively

Load at 100 kg	Load at 150 kg	FAV (in cm^3/mol)
66	74	51.8
65	68	50.7
65	70	51.0
59	60	40.1
54	56	40.4
58	58	39.5
63	63	39.5
57	57	39.7
83	77	76.1
74	75	61.5
91	93	67.8
92	93	92.2
90	88	80.5
88	87	87.8
88	89	88.7
91	93	91.5
87	88	94.4
69	75	57.2
67	68	53.0
69	72	53.9
66	66	57.6
76	75	58.7
76	74	73.5
76	78	61.2
85	83	71.9

Flow activation volume (*FAV*; in cm^3/mol) for the 25 lubricating fluids used in this experiment is given in the third column.
SOURCE: Koyotani, T., Yoshitake, H., Ito, T., and Tamai, Y., "Correlation Between Flow Properties and Traction of Lubricating Oils," in *Transactions of the American Society of Lubricating Engineers*, Vol. 2, 1986, pp. 102–106.

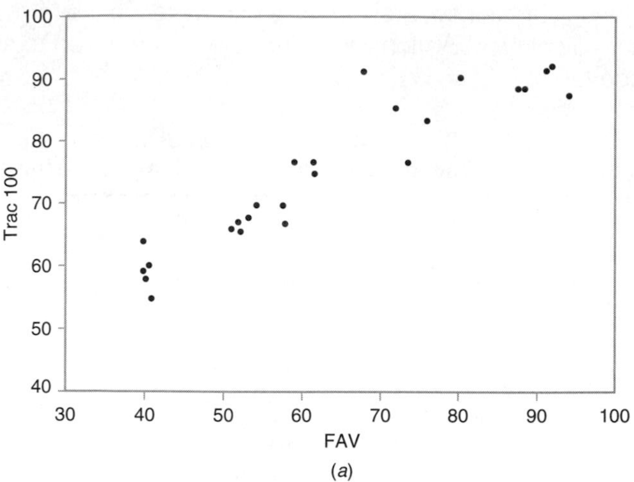

FIGURE 17.2(a) Scatter plot of traction coefficients against *FAV*, at 100 kg load.

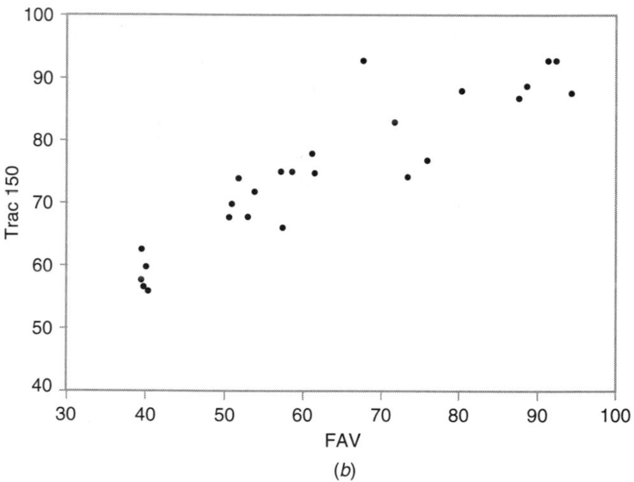

FIGURE 17.2(b) Scatter plot of traction coefficients against *FAV*, at 150 kg load.

This table shows that the total sum of squares is $SSTO = 3{,}284.0$. The standard deviation for the 25 traction measurements is $s_y = \sqrt{3{,}284.0/(25-1)} = 11.70$; the degrees of freedom in the row for "Total" are given by $n - 1 = 24$; it reminds us of the correct denominator for the standard deviation. The error sum of squares is $SSE = 547.5$; it is obtained by adding the squared residuals. Note that $(s_e)^2 = SSE/(n-2) = 547.5/23 = 23.8$; here we divide SSE by the degrees of freedom in the row for "Error," which is $n - 2 = 23$. This ratio is usually referred to as the mean square due to error, or the *mean square error*. Taking the square root of the mean square error results in the standard deviation of the residuals, $s_e = 4.88$; in this case s_e is considerably smaller than $s_y = 11.70$. The third row in the analysis of variance table displays the regression sum of squares $SSR = 3{,}284.0 - 547.5 = 2{,}736.5$. Its associated degree of freedom is 1, as there is only a single explanatory variable in the regression.

Regression programs also calculate the coefficient of determination R^2. From the analysis of variance table, we see that $R^2 = 2{,}736.5/3{,}284.0 = 0.833$, or 83.3 percent. This says that *FAV*, through its linear association with Y, explains 83.3 percent of the variation in the traction coefficients. The fitted model explains a considerable proportion of the variation. However, before we accept the model, we should check whether the model has any shortcomings. We mentioned earlier that there is some evidence of curvature when one looks at the scatter plots of traction against *FAV*. How can we check whether the fitted linear model is good enough?

A good model should produce residuals that contain no information that can be explained further. The usable components should all have been accounted for by the model. Thus, a plot of the residuals against the explanatory variable in the model, or any other explanatory variable that one may think of, should show no patterns (such as trends, curvature, etc.). Also, a plot of the residuals against the fitted values should contain no information.

Virtually all regression programs let you store the residuals and fitted values. It is then quite easy to plot the residuals against the values of the explanatory variable or against the fitted values. Figures 17.3a,b (page 492) show these scatter plots. It does appear that curvature is present in these graphs. Thus one should seriously think about enlarging the model by including a $(FAV)^2$ term; more on that in Section 17.5. The scatter plots in Figure 17.3 also reveal a rather large residual for the lubricating oil with *FAV* of 67.8.

Observe that in this particular example the two residual plots (residuals against fitted values, and residuals against the values of the explanatory variable) are almost identical. This is not true in general. Here it is the case because the response is closely related to the explanatory variable *FAV*, and hence fitted values and *FAV* contain very similar information.

17.3.2 Example 2: Tensile Strength as a Function of Hardness (or Density)

Measurements of tensile strength, hardness, and density on sixty specimens of a certain aluminum die casting are given in Table 17.3 (page 493). These data are taken from W.A. Shewhart (1931, p. 42). Obtaining a measurement on tensile strength was quite expensive, certainly more costly than getting measurements on hardness and density. The aim of Shewhart's investigation was to predict the tensile strength in terms of both the hardness and the density of the product. For that he needed a regression model that related the tensile strength of a product to its hardness and density.

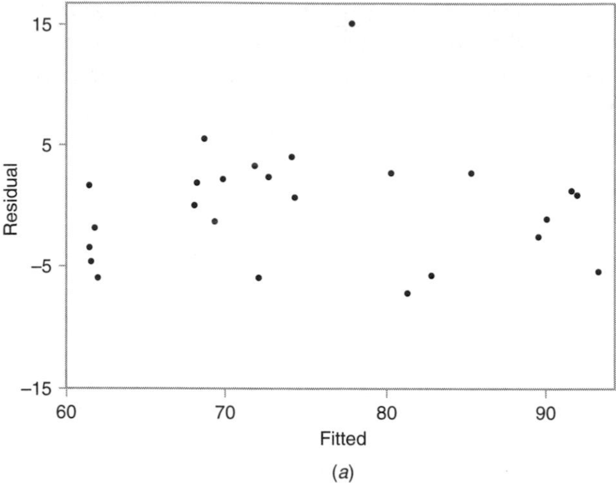

FIGURE 17.3(a) Scatter plot of residuals against fitted values. (Traction coefficients of 25 lubricating oils at a load of 150 kg.)

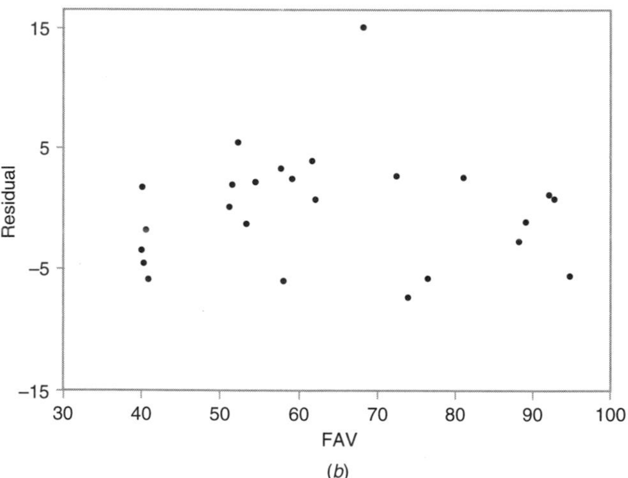

FIGURE 17.3(b) Scatter plot of residuals against *FAV*. (Traction coefficients of 25 lubricating oils at a load of 150 kg.)

Scatter plots of tensile strength against hardness, and of tensile strength against density are given in Figures 17.4a,b (page 494). Both plots reveal an approximate linear association. Here we estimate the following two simple regression models: Strength on Hardness, and Strength on Density. The model that includes both explanatory variables is described in the next section.

TABLE 17.3 Data on Tensile Strength of Sixty Aluminum Specimens

Y Tensile strength	X_1 Hardness	X_2 Density	Y Tensile strength	X_1 Hardness	X_2 Density
29.314	53.0	2.666	29.250	71.3	2.648
34.860	70.2	2.708	27.992	52.7	2.400
36.818	94.3	2.865	31.852	76.5	2.692
30.120	55.3	2.627	27.646	63.7	2.669
34.020	78.5	2.581	31.698	69.2	2.628
30.824	63.5	2.633	30.844	69.2	2.696
35.396	71.4	2.671	31.988	61.4	2.648
31.260	53.4	2.650	36.640	83.7	2.775
32.184	82.5	2.717	41.578	94.7	2.874
33.424	67.3	2.614	30.496	70.2	2.700
37.694	69.5	2.524	29.668	80.4	2.583
34.876	73.0	2.741	32.622	76.7	2.668
24.660	55.7	2.619	32.822	82.9	2.679
34.760	85.8	2.755	30.380	55.0	2.609
38.020	95.4	2.846	38.580	83.2	2.721
25.680	51.1	2.575	28.202	62.6	2.678
25.810	74.4	2.561	29.190	78.0	2.610
26.460	54.1	2.593	35.636	84.6	2.728
29.070	77.8	2.639	34.332	64.0	2.709
24.640	52.4	2.611	34.750	75.3	2.880
25.770	69.1	2.696	40.578	84.8	2.949
23.690	53.5	2.606	28.900	49.4	2.669
28.650	64.3	2.616	34.648	74.2	2.624
32.380	82.7	2.748	31.244	59.8	2.705
28.210	55.7	2.518	33.802	75.2	2.736
34.002	70.5	2.726	34.850	57.7	2.701
34.470	87.5	2.875	36.690	79.3	2.776
29.248	50.7	2.585	32.344	67.6	2.754
28.710	72.3	2.547	34.440	77.0	2.660
29.830	59.5	2.606	34.650	74.8	2.819

Column 1: tensile strength in 1,000 pounds per square inch; Column 2: hardness in Rockwell "E"; Column 3: density in grams per square centimeter.
SOURCE: Shewhart, W.A., *Economic Control of Quality of Manufactured Product*. New York: Van Nostrand, 1931, p. 42.

The results for the first model are:

(i) Regression equation: $\widehat{\text{Strength}} = 16.0 + 0.226$ Hardness.

(ii) Estimated regression coefficients, standard errors of the estimates, t-ratios, and probability values:

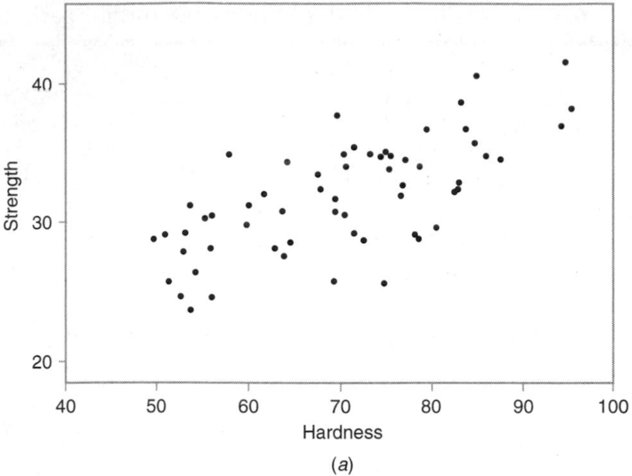

FIGURE 17.4(a) Scatter plot of tensile strength against hardness.

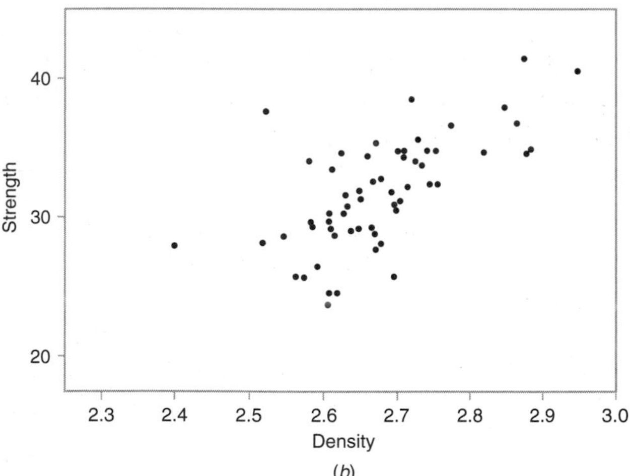

FIGURE 17.4(b) Scatter plot of tensile strength against density.

Predictor	**Coef**	**StdDev**	***t*-ratio**	***p***
Constant	$b_0 = 16.047$	2.212	7.25	0.000
Hardness	$b_1 = 0.226$	0.031	7.26	0.000

This information implies that Hardness is definitely needed as an explanatory variable in the regression model. An approximate 95 percent confidence interval for β_1 is given by the interval from $0.226-(2)(0.031)$ to $0.226+(2)(0.031)$, or 0.164 to 0.288; this interval is far from zero. Alternatively, the t-ratio, 7.26, is very large and positive, indicating that the regression coefficient β_1 is definitely positive.

(iii) The coefficient of determination $R^2 = 47.6\%$. Roughly half of the variation in tensile strength is explained by Hardness.

The results for the second model are:

(i) Regression equation: $\widehat{\text{Strength}} = -38.7 + 26.4$ Density.

(ii) Estimated regression coefficients, standard errors of the estimates, t-ratios, and probability values:

Predictor	**Coef**	**StdDev**	***t*-ratio**	***p***
Constant	$b_0 = -38.69$	10.62	−3.64	0.001
Density	$b_1 = 26.35$	3.96	6.65	0.000

The t-ratio of the coefficient for Density is quite a bit larger than 2, and the associated probability value is zero. The small probability value indicates that it is extremely unlikely that the sample estimate $b_1 = 26.35$ could have originated from $\beta_1 = 0$. Hardness is definitely needed as a predictor in the regression model.

(iii) The coefficient of determination $R^2 = 43.3\%$. This model is only slightly worse than the model that includes Hardness as the predictor variable.

17.4 THE GENERAL LINEAR REGRESSION MODEL

So far we have only considered the simple linear regression model which specifies a linear model of the form

$$Y = \beta_0 + \beta_1 X + \text{noise}.$$

Sometimes it is necessary to consider *quadratic components* (see Example 1 in Section 17.3). This leads to models of the form

$$Y = \beta_0 + \beta_1 X + \beta_2 (X)^2 + \text{noise}.$$

Furthermore, in many situations there is more than one explanatory variable. For example, in the tensile strength example (Example 2 in Section 17.3) we have available both Hardness and Density as possible explanatory variables. In the fuel efficiency example discussed in Section 17.2, we may want to consider weight of the car, number of cylinders, and horse power as possible explanatory variables; this would lead to a model of the form

$$\text{GPM} = \beta_0 + \beta_1\,\text{Weight} + \beta_2\text{Cyl} + \beta_3\text{HP} + \text{noise}.$$

In general, let us consider p explanatory variables and let us discuss the general linear regression model:

$$Y = \beta_0 + \beta_1 X_1 + \beta_2 X_2 + \cdots + \beta_p X_p + \text{ noise}.$$

Each regression coefficient, β_2 for example, measures the (partial) effect on the response Y of a unit change in the related explanatory variable (X_2 in this case), assuming that all other explanatory variables in the model are fixed at certain values. Note that the explanatory variables may include functions of explanatory variables, such as squares $(X_1)^2$ or cross products (X_1X_2). The square $(X_1)^2$ allows for curvature in the regression model. The cross product (X_1X_2) reflects an interaction effect. Take, for example, the model $Y = \beta_0 + \beta_1X_1 + \beta_2X_1X_2 + \text{noise}$. Since we can rewrite this model as $Y = \beta_0 + (\beta_1 + \beta_2X_2)X_1 + \text{noise}$, we see that the effect on Y of a change in X_1 depends on the level of X_2; similarly, the effect on Y of a change in X_2 depends on the level of X_1.

17.4.1 Inference in the General Linear Regression Model

Least squares estimates are calculated via statistical computer software; hand-calculations are far too tedious. The least squares estimates minimize the sum of the squared distances from the observations to the regression surface. Consider the ith case (for example, the ith car or the ith lubricating fluid) with observation y_i on the response Y, and $x_{1i}, x_{2i}, \ldots, x_{pi}$ as the levels of the p explanatory variables $X_1, X_2, \ldots, X_p$. Then the distance from the response to the regression function is $[y_i - (\beta_0 + \beta_1x_{1i} + \beta_2x_{2i} + \cdots + \beta_px_{pi})]$, and the method of least squares minimizes the sum of the n squared distances. Let us denote the least squares estimates by $b_0, b_1, \ldots, b_p$.

From the least squares estimates we can calculate the *n fitted values*

$$\hat{y}_i = b_0 + b_1x_{1i} + b_2x_{2i} + \cdots + b_px_{pi},$$

and the *n residuals*

$$e_i = y_i - \hat{y}_i = y_i - (b_0 + b_1x_{1i} + b_2x_{2i} + \cdots + b_px_{pi}).$$

We can calculate the *total sum of squares*,

$$SSTO = \sum_{i=1}^{n}(y_i - \bar{y})^2,$$

the *error sum of squares*,

$$SSE = \sum_{i=1}^{n} e_i^2 = \sum_{i=1}^{n}(y_i - \hat{y}_i)^2,$$

and the *regression sum of squares*,

$$SSR = \sum_{i=1}^{n}(\hat{y}_i - \bar{y})^2.$$

Just as in the simple linear regression situation, it is true in general that

$$SSTO = SSR + SSE.$$

This says that we can break up the total variation ($SSTO$) into a part that is explained by the regression model (SSR) and a part that is left unexplained (SSE). This decomposition is usually expressed in an analysis of variance table. The degrees of freedom for the regression sum of squares are now p, as there are p explanatory variables. The degrees of freedom for the error sum of squares are given by $[n - (p + 1)]$. The degrees of freedom for the error sum of squares are easy to remember; they are the difference between the number of observations n and the number of estimated regression coefficients $(b_0, b_1, \ldots, b_p)$.

The *standard deviation of the residuals* is given by

$$s_e = \sqrt{SSE/(n - p - 1)}.$$

The *coefficient of determination* R^2 is given by

$$R^2 = \frac{SSR}{SSTO} = \frac{SSTO - SSE}{SSTO} = 1 - \frac{SSE}{SSTO}.$$

It expresses the proportional reduction in the sum of squares that is due to the regression model. In other words, it tells us how much of the variability in the response variable is picked up by the p explanatory variables.

How do we know whether the explanatory variables $X_1, X_2, \ldots, X_p$, taken as a group, are useful in explaining the variability? For one, we can look at the coefficient of determination, R^2. If it is large, then we conclude that the regression model explains a good portion of the variability in the response Y.

Another, more formal way is to calculate what is called the *F-statistic*. It is given by

$$F = \frac{SSR/(\text{number of regressors in model})}{SSE/(\text{sample size} - \text{number of est reg coef})} = \frac{SSR/p}{SSE/(n - p - 1)},$$

and is part of the usual analysis of variance table output, available in virtually every statistics package. The F-statistic is functionally related to R^2. If R^2 is large, F is large also; if R^2 is small, F is small too. Next to the F-statistic, you will see its probability value—that is, the probability of obtaining such a large F-statistic or one that is even larger by chance, when not even a single explanatory variable has an effect on the Y. If this probability value is small (say smaller than the significance level 0.05), then there is evidence that the explanatory variables $X_1, X_2, \ldots, X_p$, taken as a group, have an influence on the response Y. In such a case, one must go further and sort out which of the p explanatory variables $X_1, X_2, \ldots, X_p$ are important. It could be that only a single explanatory variable is important; or that a certain pair is important; or that each one of the explanatory variables has an influence on the response Y.

We can learn about the effects of the individual regression coefficients by looking at the estimates, their standard errors, their t-ratios, and their probability values. The computer output will include information such as

b_0	StdDev(b_0)	t-ratio = b_0/StdDev(b_0)	p-value of b_0
b_1	StdDev(b_1)	t-ratio = b_1/StdDev(b_1)	p-value of b_1
b_2	StdDev(b_2)	t-ratio = b_2/StdDev(b_2)	p-value of b_2
...			
b_p	StdDev(b_p)	t-ratio = b_p/StdDev(b_p)	p-value of b_p

From this information it is easy to calculate confidence intervals and test hypotheses. For example, a 95 percent confidence interval for β_2 is given by

$$[b_2 - (2)\text{StdDev}(b_2), b_2 + (2)\text{StdDev}(b_2)].$$

If this interval includes zero, then we conclude that the regression coefficient in the population β_2 is zero. This says that after having adjusted the response for all other explanatory variables in the model, the explanatory variable X_2 does not affect the response Y. Always remember to interpret these coefficients as partial regression coefficients.

Alternatively, you can look at the t-ratio and the associated probability value. If the t-ratio exceeds 2 (in absolute value), or if the probability value is smaller than 0.05, then you can conclude that X_2 has an effect on the response Y. Again, this effect must be understood as partial in the sense that, prior to assessing the importance of X_2, we have made adjustments for the relationship between the response and the other explanatory variables in the model.

You should always look at the signs and the magnitudes of the estimated regression coefficients and assess whether they make sense. For example, if an estimated regression coefficient has the "wrong" sign (that is, a sign that is contrary to theoretical expectations), then something must have gone wrong in the model.

17.5 EXAMPLES OF THE GENERAL LINEAR REGRESSION MODEL

17.5.1 Example 1(continued): Traction Coefficients of 25 Lubricating Oils

In Section 17.3 we modeled the relationship between the traction coefficients and the flow activation volume (FAV) of 25 lubricating oils. We wondered whether we could improve the model by including a quadratic term, $(FAV)^2$.

We now fit the quadratic model

$$Y = \beta_0 + \beta_1 FAV + \beta_2 (FAV)^2 + \text{noise}.$$

Here we list part of the output from a regression package:

Traction at 100 kg

$$\widehat{\text{Tract100}} = 8.6 + 1.47\,FAV - 0.00638\,(FAV)^2$$

Predictor	**Coef**	**StdDev**	***t*-ratio**	***p***
Constant	8.59	12.05	0.71	0.483
FAV	1.4734	0.3845	3.83	0.001
$(FAV)^2$	−0.00637	0.002887	−2.21	0.038

$$R^2 = 90.0\% \quad \text{and} \quad s_e = 4.053$$

Traction at 150 kg

$$\widehat{\text{Tract150}} = 12.5 + 1.43\,FAV - 0.00636\,(FAV)^2$$

Predictor	**Coef**	**StdDev**	***t*-ratio**	***p***
Constant	12.48	13.71	0.91	0.372
FAV	1.4264	0.4374	3.26	0.004
$(FAV)^2$	−0.006361	0.003284	−1.94	0.066

$$R^2 = 85.8\% \quad \text{and} \quad s_e = 4.611$$

The results indicate that the model was improved by adding $(FAV)^2$. For traction coefficients at 100 kg the probability value for $(FAV)^2$, 0.038, is smaller than 0.05. Also, for traction coefficients at 150 kg the probability value, 0.066, is close to 0.05. This indicates that the quadratic component in the model is beneficial. Also the R^2 improves by adding $(FAV)^2$ to the model: from 87.8 percent to 90.0 percent for 100 kg load; from 83.3 percent to 85.8 percent for 150 kg load.

17.5.2 Example 2(continued): Tensile Strength as a Function of Hardness and Density

In Section 17.3 we modeled the tensile strength of an aluminum die casting in terms of hardness, and in terms of density. We considered linear models with a single explanatory variable; in the first we regressed tensile strength on hardness; in the second we regressed tensile strength on density. In this section we include both explanatory variables in the model, and consider

$$\text{Strength} = \beta_0 + \beta_1\,\text{Hardness} + \beta_2\,\text{Density} + \text{noise}.$$

We obtain the following results:

$$\widehat{\text{Strength}} = -18.3 + 0.150\,\text{Hardness} + 14.8\,\text{Density}$$

Predictor	Coef	StdDev	*t*-ratio	*p*
Constant	−18.35	10.69	−1.72	0.092
Hardness	0.150	0.037	4.05	0.000
Density	14.835	4.527	3.28	0.002

$R^2 = 55.9\%$ $s_e = 2.689$

Both explanatory variables are needed in the model. The small probability value for the coefficient of hardness, 0.000, says that "hardness" explains tensile strength, even if one has already factored in "density" as an explanatory variable. The small probability value for the coefficient of density, 0.002, says that "density" helps explain tensile strength, even if one has already factored in "hardness." Hence both explanatory variables are needed; neither variable can be omitted. Also, $R^2 = 55.9$ percent for the model with both hardness and density is an improvement over the simpler models ($R^2 = 47.6$ for the regression on hardness; $R^2 = 43.3$ for the regression on density).

Shewhart's goal was to find substitute (and cheaper) measurements for tensile strength. Hardness and density can be used to approximate tensile strength, even though they only explain roughly more than half of the variation.

17.6 MODEL SELECTION PROCEDURES

When modeling a response variable Y, it is very common to start out with a long list of explanatory variables that could, conceivably, have an influence on the response. The problem is that you just don't know which of these variables are important. How can you sort out the active factors, that is, the explanatory variables that have an effect?

A straightforward approach is to run *all possible regressions*. Now this may amount to a lot of different regressions; if you have 10 explanatory variables, there are $2^{10} = 1{,}024$ different models. Just list them: There is the model with no explanatory variables which models the response in terms of a mean and added noise; the model with just X_1; the model with just X_2; ...; the model with just X_{10}; the model with X_1 and X_2; the model with X_1 and X_3; ...; and so on, until you reach the model which includes all ten explanatory variables. Carrying out all these regressions may seem a lot of hard work, but with today's computer technology this is easily carried out as most computer software packages include routines for doing this. The output from fitting all possible regressions is usually arranged in a table that lists for each model size (number of explanatory variables) the best two or three models. For example, it will list the best two models with a single explanatory variable; the best two models with two explanatory variables; and so on. How do we decide which of the models is best?

The coefficient of determination R^2 is usually taken as one criterion. More complicated models (that is, models with more and more explanatory regression variables and regression coefficients) will lead to smaller and smaller error sum of squares. For this reason one cannot look at the resulting table and try to locate the model that leads to the maximal R^2, because this will always be the model that includes all explanatory variables. The strategy is to look at this table and locate the model where the increases in the R^2 become marginal. For example, it may not be worth it to go from a model with three explanatory variables to one that includes four, if the associated increase in the R^2 is small. We illustrate this modeling strategy with the following example.

17.6.1 Example 3: Fuel Efficiency of Cars

J.D. Cryer and R.B. Miller (1992) list the fuel efficiencies and characteristics of 45 cars. The data is given in Table 17.4 (page 502). Here we analyze CityGPM = 100(1/CityMPG), where CityMPG is given in the first column. CityGPM reflects the gallons of fuel that are needed to drive 100 miles. We get this by taking the reciprocal of miles per gallon and multiplying this ratio by 100. We consider the following seven explanatory variables: weight; displacement; number of cylinders; horsepower; transmission (1 = auto; 0 = manual); number of transmission gears; and country of origin (1 = foreign; 0 = domestic). The summary information from fitting all possible regressions is given in Table 17.5 (page 503).

The best model with a single explanatory variables is the model with weight; the R^2 for this model is 90.9 percent. The second best among models with one explanatory variable is the model with displacement; however, its $R^2 = 64.8$ percent is considerably smaller. The best models with two explanatory variables are listed next. Adding transmission to weight increases the R^2 to 92.7 percent; adding gears to weight increases the R^2 by a slightly smaller amount ($R^2 = 92.5$ percent). Does an increase in R^2 of 1.8 percent justify the inclusion of an extra variable? We need to look at the estimates of the regression coefficients and their t-ratios, and check whether it is possible to omit one of these variables from the model.

The results of a regression on weight and transmission are given below; the t-ratios of the regression coefficients are given in parentheses below the estimates:

$$\widehat{\text{CityGPM}} = \underset{}{0.146} + \underset{(13.71)}{1.903}\ \text{Weight} + \underset{(3.20)}{0.529}\ \text{Trans.}$$

The t-ratio 3.20 indicates that the regression coefficient for transmission is significantly different from zero; it implies that transmission should be included in the model. Transmission is coded as 1 if the car has an automatic transmission, and it is 0 for a car with a manual transmission. The positive estimate of the regression coefficient implies that cars with automatic transmission need, on average, an additional 0.529 gallon to drive 100 miles.

The best model with three explanatory variables is the one with weight, cylinders, and transmission ($R^2 = 93.8$); the model with weight, displacement, and transmission is a close second ($R^2 = 93.5$). The increase in R^2 is 1.1 percent over the best model with two explanatory variables.

TABLE 17.4 Data on Eleven Variables and Forty-Five Cars

22	32	36	2.365	1.6	4	113	0	5	1	1	Acura Integra RS
22	33	38	2.430	1.6	4	108	0	5	1	1	Toyota Corolla FX16
29	42	51	1.895	1.3	4	60	0	4	1	1	Honda Civic 2dr
21	36	38	2.320	1.6	4	74	1	3	1	0	Chevrolet Nova
18	32	35	2.330	1.6	4	82	1	3	1	1	Mercury Tracer
20	34	36	2.255	1.5	4	68	1	3	1	1	Plymouth Colt
18	36	43	2.350	1.6	4	74	1	3	1	1	Pontiac Le Mans
28	41	47	1.635	1.3	4	58	0	4	1	1	Ford Festiva
24	36	38	2.070	1.6	4	82	0	4	1	1	Mazda 323
22	34	39	2.115	1.5	4	68	0	4	1	1	Mitsubishi Precis
23	35	39	1.840	1.1	4	52	0	4	1	1	Yugo GVS
27	43	49	1.970	1.5	4	78	0	4	1	1	Toyota Tercel
31	51	58	1.575	1.0	3	48	0	5	1	1	Chevrolet Sprint
24	37	41	2.185	1.5	4	68	0	4	1	1	Hyundai Excel
24	36	41	2.115	1.8	4	81	0	4	1	1	VW Fox
16	28	35	3.040	2.2	4	145	1	4	2	1	Mazda 626 4ws turbo
19	34	35	2.620	2.0	4	108	1	3	2	1	Audi 80
14	25	29	3.230	3.0	6	142	1	4	2	1	Mitsubishi Galant Sigma
18	29	35	2.745	2.0	4	102	1	4	2	1	Mitsubishi Galant
17	28	32	2.573	1.9	4	110	1	4	2	1	Peugeot 405 DL
17	27	32	2.802	2.3	4	100	1	3	2	0	Ford Tempo GLS
18	31	39	2.699	2.0	4	90	1	3	2	0	Chevrolet Corsica LT
21	36	43	2.695	2.2	4	110	0	5	2	0	Ford Probe
18	31	43	2.885	2.5	4	100	0	5	2	0	Dodge Daytona
13	23	28	3.310	5.0	8	225	1	4	2	0	Ford Mustang LX
13	23	32	3.430	5.0	8	170	1	4	2	0	Chevy Camaro RS
18	29	34	2.670	2.2	4	97	1	3	2	0	Plymouth Sundance
19	35	44	2.925	2.0	4	115	1	4	2	1	Toyota Camry LE
16	28	36	2.735	2.5	4	98	1	3	2	0	Pontiac Grand AM LE
15	29	37	3.155	3.0	6	140	1	4	3	0	Ford Taurus
16	30	36	2.995	3.0	6	150	1	4	3	0	Eagle Premier
15	27	34	3.150	3.0	6	136	1	3	3	0	Dodge Dynasty
16	29	33	2.950	2.8	6	125	1	3	3	0	Buick Century
15	26	33	3.295	3.8	6	140	1	4	3	0	Mercury Cougar
16	28	34	2.915	2.5	4	100	1	3	3	0	Chrysler Le Baron coupe
16	29	37	3.220	2.8	6	125	1	4	3	0	Buick Regal coupe
16	26	31	2.900	2.2	4	146	1	3	3	0	Chrysler New Yorker turbo
15	27	33	3.205	2.5	4	153	1	4	4	1	Toyota Camry wagon
16	26	30	2.930	2.2	4	103	1	3	4	0	Eagle Medallion wagon
14	25	31	3.320	3.0	6	157	1	4	4	1	Nissan Maxima wagon
16	26	31	3.080	2.3	4	114	1	4	4	1	Volvo 240 wagon

(*continues*)

TABLE 17.4 (*continued*)

13	24	28	3.625	3.0	6	136	1	3	5	0	Plymouth Grand Voyager
12	23	28	3.665	3.0	6	145	1	4	5	0	Ford Aerostar
13	22	27	3.625	2.4	4	106	1	4	5	1	Nissan GXE van
14	23	27	3.415	2.4	4	107	1	4	5	1	Mitsubishi van

Col. 1: MPG(miles per gallon for city driving); Col. 2: MPG(trip); Col. 3: MPG(expressway); Col. 4: weight (in 1,000 pounds); Col. 5: displacement (in cubic liters); Col. 6: number of cylinders; Col. 7: horsepower; Col. 8: transmission (1 = auto; 0 = manual); Col. 9: number of transmission gears; Col. 10: size (1 = small; 2 = compact; 3 = medium; 4 = wagon; 5 = minivan); Col. 11: origin (1 = foreign; 0 = domestic).
SOURCE: Cryer, J.D. and Miller, R.B., *Statistics for Business*, 2nd Ed. Belmont, CA: Duxbury Press, 1992, p. 669.

TABLE 17.5 Output from Fitting All Possible Regressions

Vars.	R^2	R^2_{adj}	C_p	s_e	Weight	Displ.	Cyl.	HP	Trans.	Gears	Origin
1	90.9	90.7	19.0	0.38806	X						
1	64.8	64.0	189.9	0.76156		X					
2	92.7	92.3	9.2	0.35200	X				X		
2	92.5	92.2	10.1	0.35546	X					X	
3	93.8	93.3	3.8	0.32797	X		X		X		
3	93.5	93.1	5.4	0.33437	X	X			X		
4	94.0	93.4	4.1	0.32504	X	X				X	X
4	94.0	93.4	4.5	0.32678	X		X			X	X
5	94.2	93.5	5.0	0.32423	X		X		X	X	X
5	94.2	93.4	5.2	0.32509	X	X			X	X	X
6	94.3	93.4	6.2	0.32520	X	X	X		X	X	X
6	94.2	93.3	7.0	0.32843	X		X	X	X	X	X
7	94.4	93.3	8.0	0.32864	X	X	X	X	X	X	X

The regression results for the model with the three explanatory variables,

$$\widehat{\text{CityGPM}} = \underset{}{0.015} + \underset{(11.15)}{1.689\ \text{Weight}} + \underset{(3.67)}{0.567\ \text{Trans}} + \underset{(2.72)}{0.150\ \text{Cyl}},$$

show that all three t-ratios are larger than 2. We cannot simplify the model by omitting one of these three variables. There is some evidence that all three explanatory variables may be needed.

Table 17.5 shows that the increases in R^2 become smaller and smaller as more variables are entered. In summary, it appears that a model with just weight alone explains most of the variability in CityGPM. You can improve the predictive ability of the model somewhat if you add a variable for transmission and one for the number of cylinders.

The usual output from fitting all possible regressions includes two other measures of goodness-of-fit. One is the *adjusted* R^2. For a model with p explanatory variables, and thus $p + 1$ regression coefficients that need to be estimated, this coefficient is defined as

$$R^2_{\text{adj}} = 1 - \frac{SSE/(n-p-1)}{SSTO/(n-1)}.$$

It is very similar to the R^2, except that it adds a penalty for each estimated coefficient. The adjusted R^2 is always slightly smaller than R^2. The R^2 increases as you add more components to the model as by adding more coefficients and flexibility you are bound to decrease the error sum of squares. However, the adjusted R^2 may actually decrease if you add variables that are not really needed in the model. The adjusted R^2 in our example reaches its maximum with anywhere between three and five explanatory variables.

Another useful measure is the C_p *statistic*. It is common output in most regression packages. While we don't show you how to calculate this statistic, we would like you to understand its interpretation and its usefulness. Note that the C_p statistic in regression has no connection with the C_p capability index that was studied in Chapter 13.

If a regression model with k explanatory variables, and thus $k+1$ regression coefficients, is adequate, then its C_p statistic should be approximately $(k + 1)$. If the model is not yet adequate, then the C_p statistic is larger than $(k + 1)$. We are looking for the simplest model with a good C_p statistic, that is, a C_p statistic which is close to the number of the estimated regression coefficients in the model. In our example, a model with two explanatory variables is still not very satisfactory. The best C_p statistic is 9.2, which is considerably larger than a "good" value of $2+1 = 3$. The model with three explanatory variables (weight, cylinders, transmission), however, is quite adequate, as its C_p statistic of 3.8 is roughly $3+1 = 4$, a number that we would expect for a good model.

In summary, the model with weight, number of cylinders, and a variable for transmission does a good job explaining the variability in CityGPM.

17.7 FURTHER TOPICS IN REGRESSION

17.7.1 Multicollinearity

We speak of multicollinearity if the explanatory variables are highly correlated among themselves. This implies that the explanatory variables contain very similar information.

Multicollinearity makes regression model selection difficult. For example, assume that you want to explain the fuel efficiency of a car by its weight in pounds (X_1) and its weight in kg (X_2). Here X_1 and X_2 are perfectly related, as $X_1 = (2.2)X_2$. Forcing both X_1 and X_2 into the model and estimating the coefficients in $Y = \beta_0 + \beta_1 X_1 + \beta_2 X_2 + \text{noise}$, causes problems. The regression method has difficulties coming up with unique estimates for β_1 and β_2. Because of the relationship between X_1 and X_2 we can write $Y = \beta_0 + \beta_1 X_1 + \beta_2 X_2 + \text{noise} = \beta_0 + [(2.2)\beta_1 + \beta_2]X_2 + \text{noise}$. While it is easy to estimate the linear combination $\beta^* = (2.2)\beta_1 + \beta_2$, there are an infinite number of ways of representing that number β^* through the two coefficients β_1 and β_2.

Since in multicollinear situations the regression coefficients cannot be estimated reliably, the standard errors of these estimates are very large. Consequently, the t-ratios will be small, leading to the erroneous conclusion that these explanatory variables are not needed in modeling the response. However, one must guard against omitting from the model both multicollinear explanatory variables X_1 and X_2. Recall that the regression coefficients (and their t-ratios) are partial effects. The small t-ratio for X_1 says that X_1 (the weight in pounds) is not needed, if X_2 (the weight in kg) is already in the model. This is not surprising, as weight is already included. Similarly, the small t-ratio for X_2 says that X_2 (weight in kg) is not needed, if X_1 (weight in pounds) is already in the model; this makes sense. However, you shouldn't make the mistake of omitting both variables from the model, as weight clearly matters. Thus, you need to consider either X_1 or X_2, but certainly not both.

Here we discussed a very extreme case. However, you can think of many other realistic situations. Consider the explanatory variables in the fuel efficiency example in Section 17.6. Different car characteristics are closely related; for example, engine displacement and horse power change together as you can't have a small engine with large horsepower. Or, consider indicators of the economy in a regression on economic variables; most of them are closely related and they tend to move in the same direction.

The key to circumventing multicollinearity is to avoid models that include redundant explanatory variables. Simplify the model in the first place.

17.7.2 Automatic Variable Selection Procedures

Several automatic procedures are available to select the most appropriate regression models. *Stepwise regression* is one such procedure. It starts with the simplest model (that is, the model with just one explanatory variable) and adds explanatory variables if they help explain the variability in the response. If no more explanatory variables can be added and if the model cannot be simplified by dropping variables from the model, then the procedure stops.

Automatic procedures are helpful, but one shouldn't trust such methods blindly. We prefer to look at the output from fitting all possible regressions.

17.7.3 Transformations

Transformations of the response and also of the explanatory variables are very useful as they often help simplify thc model. We already saw one example, where the reciprocal transformation, GPM = 100(1/MPG), turned out to be helpful. We recommend that you try various transformations, such as the logarithmic transformation, the reciprocal transformation, and power transformations (such as the square root or the square) of both the response as well as the explanatory variables.

17.7.4 Indicator Variables for Categorical Explanatory Variables

One of your explanatory variables may be a qualitative (that is, categorical) variable. Size of the car is a good example. In Example 3 and Table 17.4, Size = 1 for small cars; 2 for compact cars; 3 for medium cars, 4 for wagons; and 5 for minivans. In such a situation one creates *indicator variables*. Since there are five possibilities for size, we create five indicator variables: IND_1 through IND_5. IND_3, for example, is set to 1 if the car is of medium size, and it is set to 0 otherwise; see the illustration given below.

Size	IND_1	IND_2	IND_3	IND_4	IND_5
1	1	0	0	0	0
2	0	1	0	0	0
3	0	0	1	0	0
4	0	0	0	1	0
5	0	0	0	0	1

After you have created these five indicator variables for each car, then you put four of them (always one less than the number of possibilities of the categorical variable) into the model. It doesn't really matter which one you leave out. The one you leave out becomes the standard against which the effects of the others are measured. For example, you may get a fitted regression equation such as

$$\widehat{\text{GPM}} = 0.6 + (1.9)\text{Weight} - (0.5)\text{IND}_1 - (0.3)\text{IND}_2 - (0.2)\text{IND}_3 - (0.05)\text{IND}_4.$$

Here size = 5 (minivan) is the standard. After having factored in the effect of weight, small cars (size = 1) need 0.5 gallon less fuel to drive 100 miles than a minivan. Compact cars (size = 2) need 0.3 gallon less than a minivan, and so on.

17.7.5 Model Checking

You must check whether the fitted model provides an adequate description of the data. Residual plots, where one plots the residuals against the fitted values, should always be carried out. For adequate models the residuals should contain no information, and there should be no patterns in a scatter plot of residuals against fitted values. Furthermore, residuals should be plotted against the explanatory variables in the model, as well as any other explanatory variables one may consider useful. Patterns in these plots are an indication that there is information in the residuals that has not been incorporated into the model. The model can be improved by adding these omitted variables to the model.

17.8 RESPONSE SURFACE METHODS

Often experimenters wish to find the conditions under which a process attains its optimal results. The process response, Y, is related to a set of predictor (explanatory) variables $X_1, X_2, \ldots, X_k$. For example, the response may be the yield of a certain chemical reaction, and the predictors the temperature and pressure of the reaction, and the type of catalyst. Or, the response may be the seal strength of a certain plastic wrap, and the predictors the sealing temperature and the amount of a polyethylene additive. Or, the response may be the growth of an organism, and the predictors the proportion of glucose, the concentration of yeast extract, and the time allowed for organism growth. In certain situations the relationship between the response and the predictor variables is known from underlying engineering, chemical, and physical theory. However, in the vast majority of cases the relationship is unknown and an empirical model must be constructed that relates the response to the predictor variables. The exploration and the optimization of response surfaces is known as *response surface analysis*.

Response surface analysis involves the following three components:

1. Data Collection: The relevant data must be obtained through experiments where one studies the response for changing levels of the predictor variables. This is where experimental design comes into play. In Chapter 15 we discussed two-level factorial experiments, and some of the examples in Chapter 16 illustrated orthogonal array designs with predictor variables at more than two levels. Here we discuss the *central composite design*, which is especially useful for response surface analysis. Let us illustrate a central composite design in the case of two predictor variables ($k = 2$). One starts with the standard two-level factorial design, which, in terms of coded units, calls for the four runs at $(-1, -1)$, $(1, -1)$, $(-1, 1)$, and $(1, 1)$; these are the four corners of the square in Table 15.2. One adds to this design one (or more) "center points"; that is, one runs an experiment at (0,0). Furthermore, one adds "star points"; that is, one runs four experiments at $(-w, 0)$ and $(w, 0)$, and at $(0, -w)$ and $(0, w)$, where w is a number that usually is slightly larger than 1. The combination of the 2^2 factorial experiment and the star and center points requires a total of nine runs. Graphically, the design points of a central composite design are the corners of a square, a center point, and star points that lie on the coordinate lines that go through the origin. Note that each predictor variable is being studied at five levels.

How would a central composite design look for the case of three predictor variables ($k = 3$)? There the design consists of the eight corners of the cube (the 2^3 factorial design), the center point, and the six star points that lie on the coordinate lines that go through the origin—a total of 15 design points.

2. Model Fitting: The next step is to fit empirical models to the data. This is where regression comes into the picture. The simplest empirical model is the one where all predictors enter the model linearly:

$$Y = \beta_0 + \beta_1 X_1 + \beta_2 X_2 + \cdots + \beta_k X_k + \text{noise}.$$

This is called a *first-order model.* For $k = 1$ factors, the response is modeled through a straight line; for $k = 2$ factors, the response is approximated by a plane; for $k = 3$ factors by a hyperplane, and so on.

In first-order models the response will increase without bounds by making the predictor variables smaller or larger; there is no finite optimum for a straight line or for a plane. If you want to characterize response surfaces that have optima, then you need to allow for more complicated models. *Second-order models* contain squares and cross-products of predictor variables. For example, for $k = 1$ the second-order model is the quadratic model

$$Y = \beta_0 + \beta_1 X_1 + \beta_{11}(X_1)^2 + \text{noise}.$$

For $k = 2$, the second-order model is given by

$$Y = \beta_0 + \beta_1 X_1 + \beta_2 X_2 + \beta_{11}(X_1)^2 + \beta_{22}(X_2)^2 + \beta_{12}(X_1 X_2) + \text{noise}.$$

Regression methods can be used to fit these models. However, note that you cannot fit a second-order model to data from a two-level factorial experiment. With just two levels on each predictor variable, there is not enough information to determine the curvature effects (that is, the second-order terms). With data from two-level factorial designs you can only fit first-order models. For second-order model fitting you need at least three levels for each predictor variable; this is where the central composite designs come into play.

3. Exploration of the Fitted Response Surface: The third element in response surface analysis has to do with optimization techniques. After fitting the model one wants to learn about the nature of the fitted response surface. One wants to know the location of the optimum; one wants to know whether the optimum is a maximum, a minimum, or a saddle point; and one wants to know the direction in which the response surface increases the fastest or the slowest. This information is useful as it indicates the sensitivity of the response to changes from the optimal conditions.

With two predictor variables it is quite easy to plot the fitted response surface; such plots are always highly recommended. However, plots of the response surface are difficult in higher dimensions when three or more predictor variables are involved. In such cases it is helpful to have numerical techniques available that help us interpret the fitted response surface.

Our introduction to response surface methods was very brief. If you want to know more about this important area of statistics, you should read one of the many books on this topic. Particularly good and complete treatments are given in the books by R.H. Myers and D.C. Montgomery (1995) and G.E.P. Box and N.R. Draper (1986). For a simple introduction, you may want to read Section 9.6 of the book *Applied Statistics for Engineers and Physical Scientists*, by R.V. Hogg and J. Ledolter (1992).

17.9 EXERCISES

17.1 Consider the following four pairs of data:

$$\begin{array}{ll} x_1 = 1 & y_1 = 5 \\ x_2 = 2 & y_2 = 9 \\ x_3 = 3 & y_3 = 16 \\ x_4 = 4 & y_4 = 23 \end{array}$$

Calculate (by hand or by computer) the least squares estimates of the coefficients in the linear regression model $Y = \beta_0 + \beta_1 X +$ noise. Calculate the fitted values and the residuals, and plot the results. Obtain and interpret the coefficient of determination R^2.

17.2 Consider the data on Trip mileage in column 2 of Table 17.4. Transform the response variable and consider gallons per hundred miles, GPM = 100(1/MPG). Using your regression software, obtain the least squares estimates in the simple linear regression model of GPM on Weight. Calculate the fitted values and the residuals. Calculate *SSTO*, *SSE* and *SSR* and obtain R^2. Estimate the average GPM for cars that weigh 2,500 pounds and obtain a 95 percent confidence interval (you may be able to use your regression software for the calculations; however, use the equations in Section 17.2 if your software does not have a function for estimating the mean response). Repeat this for cars that weigh 6,000 pounds. What are the dangers with this last estimate?

17.3 Consider the data in Exercise 17.2.

(a) Repeat the analysis, but also add $(\text{Weight})^2$ to the model. Do you need to include it?

(b) Repeat the analysis for City GPM and Expressway GPM. Do you get different conclusions?

(c) Analyze the untransformed response MPG (miles per gallon). Construct the appropriate models. Would you prefer models for GPM over models for MPG? Why?

17.4 Consider the data on steam consumption (Y), temperature (X_1), and operating days (X_2). The data that follows is taken from Draper and Smith (1981, p. 9).

(a) Obtain the regression coefficients in the regression of Y on X_1. Calculate and interpret R^2.

(b) Obtain the regression coefficients in the regression of Y on X_2. Calculate and interpret R^2.

(c) Obtain the regression coefficients in the regression of Y on X_1 and X_2. Calculate and interpret R^2.

Y Pounds of steam used per month	X_1 Average atmospheric temperature in degrees Fahrenheit	X_2 Number of operating days per month
10.98	35.2	20
11.13	29.7	20
12.51	30.8	23
8.40	58.8	20
9.27	61.4	21
8.73	71.3	22
6.36	74.4	11
8.50	76.7	23
7.82	70.7	21
9.14	57.5	20
8.24	46.4	20
12.19	28.9	21
11.88	28.1	21
9.57	39.1	19
10.94	46.8	23
9.58	48.5	20
10.09	59.3	22
8.11	70.0	22
6.83	70.0	11
8.88	74.5	23
7.68	72.1	20
8.47	58.1	21
8.86	44.6	20
10.36	33.4	20
11.08	28.6	22

17.5 Consider the data on oxygenation rate (Y), velocity (X_1), and depth (X_2) of selected rivers. Construct all pairwise scatter plots. Obtain the least squares estimates and the coefficient of determination R^2 in the regression of log Y on X_1, and of log Y on X_2. Regress log Y on both X_1 and X_2, calculate R^2, and compare the results with the two models that contain only one explanatory variable. What reasons can you give for transforming the response variable and for using log Y instead of Y?

Mean velocity X_1 in ft/sec	Mean depth X_2 in ft	Mean oxygenation rate Y in ppm/day
3.69	5.09	1.44
3.07	3.27	2.27
2.10	4.42	0.98
2.68	6.14	0.50
2.78	5.66	0.74
2.64	7.17	1.13
2.92	11.41	0.28
2.47	2.12	3.36
3.44	2.93	2.79
4.65	4.54	1.57
2.94	9.50	0.46
2.51	6.29	0.39

17.6 Consider any other regression situation for which you can get data. Build the appropriate model(s). Discuss applications of regression modeling for product and process improvement.

17.7 Consider the simple linear regression model in Section 17.2.

(a) Show, algebraically, that the sum of the residuals must be zero.

(b) Show, algebraically, that the coefficient of determination R^2 in the simple linear regression model is the same as the square of the correlation coefficient between Y and X. That is, $R^2 = (r)^2$.

17.8 Expanded Polystyrene (EPS), commonly known as styrofoam, is pre-expanded by adding water, allowed to dry, and then formed in a molding machine. The amount of water content at the time of forming affects the run time and thus the cost of producing EPS. Data on water content and run time are given below.

X Water content	Y Run time
1.1	11.7
2.6	10.2
3.6	9.8
3.0	8.4
5.1	7.6
6.2	5.7
8.0	5.2
8.2	4.6
10.0	3.4
10.5	2.6
11.1	1.6
13.0	0.7

Construct a scatter plot of run time against water content. Estimate the linear regression model and calculate the coefficient of determination R^2. Check your model by plotting the residuals against the fitted values and the residuals against values of the explanatory variable, water content.

17.9 Consider the following regression model:

$$\text{Salary (in \$1000)} = 30 + (3)X + (5)Z + (0.7)(XZ)$$

where X is the number of years of experience, and Z is an indicator variable that is 1 if you have obtained an MBA degree and 0 otherwise; XZ is the product between years of experience and the indicator variable Z.

(a) What is the salary of an employee with an MBA and 10 years of experience?

(b) Determine the effect of an extra year of experience on the salary of an employee with an MBA. Graph the fitted regression lines for employees with an MBA, and for employees without an MBA. Show the two lines on the same graph.

17.10 Our company is having difficulties understanding why some salespeople achieve higher new orders than others on a recently introduced product. Historical data on a new product was reviewed. The sales volume over the last twelve months for twenty sales representatives is listed below. Additional information on each sales person and on the regional district that he or she covers is given.

Sales person	X_1	X_2	X_3	X_4	X_5	X_6	Y
1	6	1416	7	105	34	976	734,900
2	9	1955	4	88	18	1460	3,069,000
3	7	1279	8	86	35	1960	1,498,700
4	5	1224	5	76	24	795	687,700
5	6	1659	4	110	19	1963	2,532,600
6	9	1733	4	115	17	1143	2,324,900
7	10	2052	5	90	21	1684	3,137,000
8	6	1194	4	121	19	1590	2,013,200
9	7	2073	9	111	38	970	690,100
10	8	1962	6	122	25	1042	1,342,200
11	8	1632	6	77	25	912	1,104,200
12	5	1116	8	122	38	647	309,300
13	7	1929	5	120	22	849	1,120,100
14	6	1702	6	115	28	1460	1,194,000
15	7	967	3	88	16	1428	2,533,200
16	9	1520	7	102	31	1525	1,765,300
17	7	772	9	106	40	765	572,000
18	5	1172	9	90	39	588	330,800
19	7	2084	7	124	33	1319	1,160,000
20	7	1022	8	103	37	1299	1,048,500

Average daily sales calls (X_1); Average monthly expenses (X_2); Number of distributors (X_3); Territory size in square miles (X_4); Number of retail outlets (X_5); Population density per square mile (X_6); Annual sales volume in dollars (Y).

Analyze and interpret the data. Make appropriate scatter plots and investigate regression models that relate sales volume to the explanatory variables that are listed. Find out which variables have an effect on the response.

17.11 Write a brief report discussing the importance of regression for quality and quality improvement. What problems can you attack with regression analysis? Consult a manufacturing company in your immediate vicinity and ask them about their applications of regression modeling.

17.10 REFERENCES

Box, G. E. P., and N. R. Draper. *Empirical Model Building and Response Surfaces.* New York: Wiley, 1986.

Cryer, J. D., and R. B. Miller. *Statistics for Business*, 2nd Ed. Belmont, CA: Duxbury Press, 1992.

Draper, N., and H. Smith. *Applied Regression Analysis*, 2nd Ed. New York: Wiley, 1981.

Hogg, R. V., and J. Ledolter. *Applied Statistics for Engineers and Physical Scientists.* New York: Macmillan,1992.

Koyotani, T., H. Yoshitake, T. Ito, and Y. Tamai. "Correlation Between Flow Properties and Traction of Lubricating Oils," *Transactions of the American Society of Lubricating Engineers*, Vol. 2, 1986, pp. 102–106.

Myers, R. H., and D. C. Montgomery. *Response Surface Methodology: Process and Product Optimization Using Designed Experiments.* New York: Wiley, 1995.

Real Life Statistics: Regression Analysis and Quality Control in Manufacturing. Films for the Humanities and Sciences, Box 2053, Princeton, NJ 08543-2053.

Shewhart, W. A., *Economic Control of Quality of Manufactured Product.* New York: Van Nostrand, 1931.

PROJECTS FOR SECTION 5

PROJECT 16

This project is based on the article by Ashenfelter, Ashmore, and Lalonde, in *Chance Magazine*, 1995.

Traditionally the quality of the Bordeaux vintage is first evaluated by experts in March of the following year. However, it turns out that these first ratings are rather unreliable because the four-old-month old wine is a rather foul mixture of fermenting grape juice, and little like the magnificent stuff it can become years later. Wouldn't it be wonderful to be able to rate the quality (and hence predict the price) of the most-recent Bordeaux vintage immediately, as compared to having to wait for several months before the vintage can be evaluated? A statistical approach that predicts the price of the vintage as a function of its age, rainfall, and temperature allows us to do exactly that.

Consider the following data on rain during the harvest season (rain in August and September, in total millimeters), average temperature during the growing season (April through September, in degrees Centigrade), the age of the vintage, and the average price for the Bordeaux vintage relative to the year 1961. Data for the years 1952 through 1980 is listed below. The prices for the 1954 and 1956 vintages are missing. Relative prices for these two vintages could not be established because these were poor vintages and very little wine is now sold from these two years.

Vintage year	Summer temp.	Harvest rain	Age of vintage	Relative price
1952	17.12	160	31	0.368
1953	16.73	80	30	0.635
1954	15.38	180	29	*
1955	17.15	130	28	0.446
1956	15.65	140	27	*
1957	16.13	110	26	0.221
1958	16.42	187	25	0.180
1959	17.48	187	24	0.658
1960	16.42	290	23	0.139
1961	17.33	38	22	1.000
1962	16.30	52	21	0.331
1963	15.72	155	20	0.168

(*continues*)

(*continued*)

Vintage year	Summer temp.	Harvest rain	Age of vintage	Relative price
1964	17.27	96	19	0.306
1965	15.37	267	18	0.106
1966	16.53	86	17	0.473
1967	16.23	118	16	0.191
1968	16.20	292	15	0.105
1969	16.55	244	14	0.117
1970	16.67	89	13	0.404
1971	16.77	112	12	0.272
1972	14.98	158	11	0.101
1973	17.07	123	10	0.156
1974	16.30	184	9	0.111
1975	16.95	171	8	0.301
1976	17.65	247	7	0.253
1977	15.58	87	6	0.107
1978	15.82	51	5	0.270
1979	16.17	122	4	0.214
1980	16.00	74	3	0.136

Construct a regression model that explains the price of the vintage as a function of its age, rainfall, and temperature. Interpret the data through appropriate scatter plots (such as plots of price against the various explanatory variables), summary statistics, and the output from the regression analysis. How successful is the regression approach? Can you use it to predict the price of the new vintage?

Hint: It may be beneficial to transform the response, price, into logarithm (price).

PROJECT 17

Most people claim that gender has an important effect on salary. Investigate this claim, using the salary data that is available for professors at your educational institution. If you are a student at a public university, you should have no problems obtaining information on salary; salaries are public. If you are a student at a private university (where salaries are kept secret), you may want to use data for a public institution in your state. (This project extends the analysis of the data collected for Exercise 7.11 in Chapter 7.)

Questions

1. Collect information on salary. If you are a student at a large university, we recommend that you obtain the salaries for the College of Business. This will keep your project at a manageable level. Stratify the salary data according to gender. Analyze the information and state your preliminary findings.

2. Construct an Ishikawa cause-and-effect diagram for "salary." Discuss the factors that—in your opinion—affect salary. Do you think that the salary comparison in question 1 represents a valid and fair assessment of a possible salary discrimination on the basis of gender?

3. Develop measures for the factors that you have identified in question 2. These factors are potential causes, but their effects must still be confirmed by subsequent analysis.

   Experience may have an effect. Discuss how you would measure this variable.

   Hint: You may define experience in terms of the number of years since obtaining a Ph.D. Or you may define it by the "rank" of the professor (assistant, associate, or full professor), or possibly both.

   Excellence in research may have an effect, especially at large research institutions. Discuss how you would measure "research performance."

   Hint: Research excellence may be quite difficult to measure; you could obtain and evaluate professors' resumes. The Dean's office or the Departmental Offices should give you access to the resumes. You may also want to try the Web site of your school.

   Excellence in teaching may have an effect. Develop measures of teaching excellence.

   Hint: Teaching performance may be even harder to measure; you may want to start by looking for teaching awards on resumes, by asking fellow students to rate instructors, etc.

   The salary may also depend on *administrative duties*. Keep track of whether the professor is also a Dean or a departmental officer.

4. Discuss the difficulties that arise in the measurement of these factors.

5. With the information in hand, construct a multivariate regression model that helps explain the salary in terms of gender and the explanatory variables that you identified in question 2 and measured in question 3. How many of the variables that you identified as potential causes are really necessary for explaining the differences in salary? Did the estimated regression coefficients for the explanatory variables have the anticipated, "correct" signs? Do the estimation results make sense? What is the interpretation of the regression coefficient for gender? Does it help you answer the question whether your institution engages in salary discrimination with respect to gender?

   Notes: Gender is a binary variable, and can be coded as 0 or 1.

Rank (for instance, assistant, associate, full professor) is a categorical variable with three possible outcomes. You may want to transform this information into indicator variables. You will need two indicator variables: The first one, say IND1, is set 1 for associate professors and 0 otherwise. The second, IND2, is set 1 for full professors, and 0 otherwise. This convention makes assistant professors the standard for the comparisons; the regression coefficient for IND1 expresses the difference in salary between associate and assistant professors; the coefficient for IND2 expresses the difference between the salaries for full and assistant professors.

In large and departmentalized Colleges of Business you may want to keep track of the department in which each professor teaches. Professors in accounting and finance departments are usually paid higher salaries than professors in the human resources department. You may want to use additional indicator variables to characterize this information.

6. What other data, besides the current salary, could be used to address this issue? For example, would the information on the last yearly (percentage) raises be helpful?
7. Write a report that summarizes your analysis and your findings. What is your conclusion? What are the shortcomings of your analysis?

PROJECT 18

Write a report that summarizes the importance of statistics and statistical thinking to industry and business. What are some of the contributions that a person well-trained in statistics can make to quality and quality improvement?

Here we ask you to summarize the message that we tried to convey in this book. This project relates to all sections of the book, not just the last one.

Research the literature, drawing on books and articles in the quality area. For example, you may want to study the paper "The Role of Statistical Thinking in Management," by Lynne B. Hare, Roger W. Hoerl, John D. Hromi, and Ronald D. Snee in *Quality Progress*, February 1995, pp. 53–60, and the paper "Using Statisticians to Help Transform Industry in America," by Brian L. Joiner in *Quality Progress*, May 1986, pp. 46–50. You also may want to consult the book by Brian L. Joiner, *Fourth Generation Management*, published by McGraw-Hill, 1994, especially Part 3: Managing in a Variable World.

PROJECT 19

Contact one or more companies in your immediate area. Ask the plant manager or the staff in the quality assurance department about the problem-solving tools that they use as part of their daily work. Which of the statistical tools do they use?

What is their experience with these tools? Which of the tools do they view as the most important ones? What training in these techniques do their employees get? What statistical software do they use?

Do they use tools that are *not* mentioned in this book? If so, which ones? Describe these tools in your own words.

References for Projects for Section 5

Ashenfelter, Orley, D. Ashmore, and R. Lalonde. "Bordeaux Wine Vintage Quality and the Weather," *Chance Magazine*, Vol. 8, 1995, No. 4, pp. 7–14; see also *Barron's*, December 30, 1996, pp. 17–19.

Hare, L. B., R. W. Hoerl, J. D. Hromi, and R. D. Snee. "The Role of Statistical Thinking in Management," *Quality Progress*, Vol. 28, February 1995, pp. 53–60.

Joiner, B. L. "Using Statisticians to Transform Industry in America," *Quality Progress*, Vol. 19, May 1986, pp. 46–50.

Joiner, B. L. *Fourth Generation Management*, New York: McGraw-Hill, 1994.

INDEX

D